UNFINISHED BUSINESS

The adoption of the EU Takeover Directive (TOD) in 2004 was marked by significant challenges, with negotiations spanning over a decade. This book provides comprehensive analysis, practical insights and forward-looking policy recommendations. It discusses contentious issues such as the mandatory bid rule, acting in concert and takeover defences. It also looks at developments such as sustainability in takeovers, multiple voting rights and new ways to structure ownership changes. It offers a clear and engaging understanding of the TOD's historical evolution, its transposition, the current institutional design of takeover authorities, conflict of law issues and the enforcement of takeover law across the EU. And it looks at the TOD's practical impact as well as its future developments. With contributions from leading experts, international comparisons and case studies, it is an authoritative guide to takeover law in Europe and beyond.

Susan Emmenegger is full professor of law and the director of the Institute of Banking Law at Bern University. She served as vice president of the Swiss Takeover Board and as a member of the board of directors of the Swiss Financial Supervisory Authority (FINMA). She is a member of the European Company Law Experts Group (ECLE).

Martin Winner is full professor of law at WU Vienna University of Economics and Business and currently the WU's vice-rector for human resources and digital infrastructure. He served as chairman of the Austrian Takeover Commission and is a member of the European Company Law Experts Group (ECLE).

Andrés Recalde Castells is full professor of business and corporate law at the Autonomous University of Madrid. He is co-editor of the *Revista de Derecho de Sociedades* and a member of the managing board of the *European Company and Financial Law Review*. He is a member of the European Company Law Experts Group (ECLE).

Rolf Skog is the Director General of the Swedish Takeover Panel. He is adjunct professor of company law at the University of Stockholm. He is senior adviser to the Swedish Ministry of Justice in the field of company law and a member of the European Company Law Experts Group (ECLE).

CAMBRIDGE UNIVERSITY PRESS

International Corporate Law and Financial Market Regulation

Corporate law and financial market regulation have major implications for how the modern economy is organized and regulated and for how risk is managed and distributed – domestically, regionally and internationally. This Series seeks to inform and lead the vibrant scholarly and policy debate in this highly dynamic area by publishing cutting-edge, timely and critical examinations of the most pressing and important questions in the field.

Series Editors

Unfinished Business

TWO DECADES WITH THE EU TAKEOVER DIRECTIVE

Edited by

SUSAN EMMENEGGER
University of Bern

MARTIN WINNER
University of Vienna

ANDRÉS RECALDE CASTELLS
Autonomous University of Madrid

ROLF SKOG
University of Stockholm

CAMBRIDGE
UNIVERSITY PRESS

CAMBRIDGE
UNIVERSITY PRESS

Shaftesbury Road, Cambridge CB2 8EA, United Kingdom

One Liberty Plaza, 20th Floor, New York, NY 10006, USA

477 Williamstown Road, Port Melbourne, VIC 3207, Australia

314–321, 3rd Floor, Plot 3, Splendor Forum, Jasola District Centre, New Delhi – 110025, India

103 Penang Road, #05–06/07, Visioncrest Commercial, Singapore 238467

Cambridge University Press is part of Cambridge University Press & Assessment, a department of the University of Cambridge.

We share the University's mission to contribute to society through the pursuit of education, learning and research at the highest international levels of excellence.

www.cambridge.org
Information on this title: www.cambridge.org/9781009654425

DOI: 10.1017/9781009654432

When citing this work, please include a reference to the DOI 10.1017/9781009654432

First published 2026

Cover image: Stock exchange / Olga Yastremska / Alamy Stock Photo

A catalogue record for this publication is available from the British Library

A Cataloging-in-Publication data record for this book is available from the Library of Congress

ISBN 978-1-009-65442-5 Hardback

Contents

Notes on Contributors

Peter Agstner is Professor for Business and Insolvency Law at the Free University of Bozen-Bolzano (Faculty of Economics and Management).

Anna Christie is Departmental Lecturer in Law and Finance, Faculty of Law, University of Oxford, and Director of Studies in Law at Newnham College, University of Cambridge.

Paul Davies is Professor Emeritus, University of Oxford, and Senior Research Fellow, Commercial Law Centre, Harris Manchester College, Oxford.

Rui Dias is Professor of Law, University of Coimbra, and Integrated Researcher, UCILeR (University of Coimbra Institute for Legal Research).

Blanaid Clarke is McCann FitzGerald Chair of Corporate Law, Trinity College Dublin, and an executive in the Irish Takeover Panel.

Susan Emmenegger is Professor for Private and Banking Law at the University of Bern.

Luca Enriques is Professor of Corporate Law, Faculty of Law, University of Oxford, and Fellow Member, ECGI.

Guido Ferrarini is Emeritus Professor of Business Law, University of Genoa, founder of the Genoa Centre for Law and Finance, and an academic member at EUSFil, Jean Monnet Centre of Excellence for European Sustainable Finance and Law.

Philipp Fidler is Assistant Professor of Business Law at WU Vienna University of Economics and Business.

Javier García de Enterría is Professor of Commercial and Corporate Law at CUNEF (Madrid) and consultant (and former partner) of Clifford Chance.

Matteo Gargantini is Assistant Professor of Business Law at the University of Genoa.

Matteo Gatti is Professor of Law, Rutgers Law School, and Research Member, ECGI.

Jesper Lau Hansen is Professor of Law, University of Copenhagen.

Klaus J. Hopt is Emeritus Professor of Law, Max Planck Institute for Comparative and International Private Law, and member of the German National Academy of Sciences Leopoldina.

Susanne Kalss is Professor of Commercial and Company Law at WU Vienna University of Economics and Business.

Erik Lidman is Professor of Company Law at the Universities of Stockholm and Gothenburg, and director of the Swedish Corporate Governance Institute.

Adam Opalski is Professor of Civil Law and Commercial Law, and Chair of Private International and Commercial Law, at the Faculty of Law and Administration, University of Warsaw.

Jennifer Payne is Professor of Corporate Finance Law and Warden, Merton College, Oxford.

Alain Pietrancosta is Professor of Law, Sorbonne Law School, University of Paris.

Dörte Poelzig is Professor of Private, Commercial and Company Law at the University of Hamburg.

Andrés Recalde Castells is Full Professor of Business Law at the Autonomous University of Madrid.

Markus Roth is Professor of Civil Law, Labour Law, German and European Commercial and Business Law, Institute for Business, Commercial and Labour Law, University of Marburg.

Edmund Schuster is Associate Professor of Law, London School of Economics.

Michele Siri is Professor of Corporate Law and Financial Markets Regulation, University of Genoa, Director of the Genoa Centre for Law and Finance, and Director of EUSFil, Jean Monnet Centre of Excellence for European Sustainable Finance and Law.

Erik Sjöman is the Special Counsel to the Panel Executive of the Swedish Takeover Panel (the Securities Council) and a member of the Panel, and a capital markets and public M&A partner at the law firm Vinge.

Therese Strand is Associate Professor, Center of Corporate Governance, Copenhagen Business School.

Rolf Skog is Director General of the Swedish Takeover Panel (the Securities Council), Adjunct Professor, Stockholm University, and Research Member of ECGI.

Martin Winner is Professor for Business Law at WU Vienna University of Economics and Business.

Introduction

Susan Emmenegger, Martin Winner, Andrés Recalde Castells and Rolf Skog

The EU Takeover Directive (TOD) has significantly shaped the landscape of mergers and acquisitions within the EU. The process of reaching an agreement on its text was exceptionally challenging, spanning over a decade. The ultimate version is an incomplete harmonization effort, leaving numerous areas and options for the Member States. Its 20th anniversary gives the occasion to take a closer look at how the TOD has been implemented by different Member States, shedding light on how the Directive has influenced corporate behaviour, market dynamics and the overall European economy.

Part I of this book delves into the origins of the Directive, recalling the key disputes and providing insights into the compromises and trade-offs which were reached in order to come to an agreement. It also addresses the challenges arising from the incorporation of the Directive into the domestic legal frameworks of the Member States, highlighting disparities which continue to exist. The differences include the institutional design of the takeover authorities, with a 'great divide' between the countries who follow the UK model of an independent takeover panel and those who delegate takeover matters to the financial supervisor. The question is to what extent this divergence impacts the flexibility, predictability and speed of takeover proceedings. Another foundational issue addresses the enforcement of takeover law and the implications of the private and public law avenues for protecting minority shareholders' rights. This Part concludes with a central concern of all EU legislation: the cross-border constellation and the ensuing intersection between matters relating to the takeover bid procedure and matters relating to company law, each potentially subject to the laws of different Member States.

Part II focuses on the central piece of takeover regulation – the mandatory bid rule (MBR). Initially, the idea that a change in control of a company should trigger an exit right of the minority shareholders was groundbreaking. Chapter 6 details the development of the MBR. It explains how the acceptance and adoption of the MBR by several Member States for reasons unrelated to minority shareholder protection, and the simultaneous weakening of the MBR in the drafts of the Directive, paved the way for its inclusion in the final version of the Directive. Nevertheless, the MBR has remained a constant source of debate. Member States have the authority to define exemptions from the MBR, provided that the General Principles of the Directive are respected. The result is that the relationship between the exemptions and the protection of minority shareholders is unclear, to say the least. The limited harmonization also results in uncertainty around the concept of acting in concert, which was initially designed as an anti-circumvention rule but now risks undermining shareholder collaboration in some Member States. The complexity of the MBR is further compounded by the economic, social and governance (ESG) objectives of corporate governance. There is a contention that the prevailing law-and-economics approach to the MBR, which holds that controlling shareholders are inherently detrimental, may need reassessment in light of the new ESG and corporate purpose environment.

A key objective of the TOD was to facilitate takeovers across Europe. However, change of control issues never had an easy stand. Part III explores the various strategies employed to resist takeovers. It chronicles the European Commission's inability to secure an unequivocal prohibition on post-defensive measures taken by boards without shareholder consent. Considering the possibilities of circumvention anchored in national jurisdictions, the impact of this failure is, however, limited. This argument is reinforced by the argument that the law and practice in the European market for corporate control have changed profoundly since the introduction of the TOD. Various factors, ranging from market forces to broader changes in corporate governance as well as changes in the political and macroeconomic landscape, have contributed to the gradual erosion of the initial notion that takeovers should be encouraged while defensive measures should be minimized. Indeed, considerations regarding ecological, social and governance issues are among the defining elements of modern corporate governance. In the takeover context, ESG offers additional defences grounded in the idea that a responsible corporation should always consider the sustainability implications of a takeover.

Part IV is devoted to the emerging trends and new developments in the realm of takeovers. It explores schemes of arrangements as an alternative and increasingly prevalent method for facilitating recommended bids in the UK. It is argued that the distinctions regarding minority protection are justifiable, asserting that existing legal safeguards and oversight mechanisms effectively protect the rights of dissenting and minority shareholders. Chapters in this section of the book highlight the changing ownership landscape of corporate Europe and discuss the implication of increasing institutional ownership and asset manager concentration, the role of activist hedge funds, the influence of foreign investors on corporate control, and the rising prevalence of private equity-driven deals. Another noteworthy development is the diminishing resistance toward multiple-voting rights. While integral to corporate law in the Nordic countries, they faced significant opposition in countries like

Germany. The tide appears to be turning; this raises new questions in the takeover context, especially regarding the share premium, and the impact of multiple-voting structures on the MBR. Concluding with an assessment of the suitability for harmonization of market-related European legislation, it is contended that while securities law is suitable for harmonization, the same does not hold true for company law. For takeover law, this means that the TOD should be stripped of all provisions that concern the internal process of decision-making, including the internal process of minority protection.

This book project originated in a meeting of the European Company Law Experts (ECLE, https://europeancompanylawexperts.wordpress.com) in the summer of 2022 in Cologne. We thank the Fritz Thyssen Foundation for its support over many years and for its hosting of the Cologne meeting. The ECLE held another meeting in Paris in July 2023 to further prepare the conference. We thank the Cabinet Ginestié Magellan Paley-Vincent for hosting us. In October 2023, we held a workshop in Stockholm, where the contributors presented their preliminary findings. We thank the law firm Vinge for hosting us and the Swedish Corporate Governance Institute for sponsoring the meeting. The contributions of this book were presented at a conference in November 2024 in Vienna. We thank the Vienna University of Economics and Business, the University of Bern and the Austrian Takeover Board for sponsoring the conference.

PART I

Foundation

1

The Genesis of the Takeover Directive

Blanaid Clarke and Rolf Skog

1.1 INTRODUCTION

One of the defining characteristics of a market economy is that corporate earnings prospects are crucial to the allocation of equity capital. Equity finds its way to industries and companies with the best prospects. But earnings prospects also create an incentive for players in the economy to seek out information about companies and to realise the economic value of this knowledge by influencing company operations.

In terms of the decision as to how the company's resources are best used, only the shareholders who control the company are guaranteed the opportunity to put their views and objectives into action and to profit by the value of the information they have gathered. Control, therefore, has an economic value, and the role of the stock market is to transfer resources to the person who values them the most (i.e. to facilitate a change in control). Such a change can be carried out through a series of open market purchases, through negotiated block transactions or through an offer to the shareholders to tender their shares – a takeover bid. Hence, takeovers are simply a species of corporate control transactions.

In a takeover bid, the bidder can come into contact, at low cost and in a short time, with shareholders, even in companies with very large and widespread shareholder bases. Thus, it is not surprising that takeover techniques originated in countries where such ownership structures are common, primarily the UK and the US, where takeovers first gained acceptance as a way of gaining control of listed companies in the 1950s.

Takeover regulation in Europe was introduced first in the UK. The first version of the UK Takeover Code was introduced in 1968, following public and political concern in the wake of a number of controversial takeovers and calls for the

The authors would like to thank Manne Airaksinen, Ilkka Harju, Noel Hinton, Miceal Ryan and Karel Van Hulle for their comments on an earlier draft of this chapter.

introduction of clearly formulated rules.[1] The imposition of hard law by a state regulator was avoided by the market's players in the City agreeing to introduce such rules and to establish a self-regulatory body – the Panel on Takeovers and Mergers – to update, implement and oversee compliance with these rules.

1.2 THE PROPOSALS FOR A TAKEOVER DIRECTIVE

The UK rules on takeovers were unique in Europe for some time. In most other European countries, takeover bids were still so rare that the introduction of special regulations was not considered to be necessary.[2] However, in the early 1970s, the European Commission, anticipating that takeovers were likely to become more prevalent, explored the need for harmonised takeover legislation. This reflected a concern that, although abuses and unfair practices occurred in connection with takeover bids, a considerable difference in standards existed between Member States, some of which had national legislation, codes or professional rules, whereas others had no regulation of any kind.

1.2.1 *The Pennington Report 1974*

The Commission appointed company law professor Robert Pennington, a UK company law expert, to draw up a draft directive for takeover bids. He opined at the outset that, because of the need to protect private interests during takeovers, legislation was needed to lay down 'precise substantive rules and prescrib[e] a fairly detailed procedure'. The emphasis of the draft, which was presented in 1974, was on restraining abuses and malpractices and protecting 'private interests', specifically those of 'shareholders and bondholders'.[3] It was strongly influenced by the UK Takeover Code and similarly based on the principle of equality of treatment of all shareholders in a target company. The draft contained rules dictating the proceedings before the publication of the offer document; the obligation to make a general offer; the offer document and publicity; the period for acceptance and the conclusion of a general bid; the conduct of the parties to a general bid; and civil and penal liabilities.

Although the Pennington draft was discussed with Member States' representatives, there was limited interest and, after a number of years, the entire project was put to one side.[4]

1 D. Kershaw, *Principles of Takeover Regulation*, pp. 88–101 (Oxford: Oxford University Press, 2016).

2 E. Berglöf and M. Burkart, 'European Takeover Regulation' (2003) 18 *Economic Policy* 171.

3 R. R. Pennington, *Report on Takeover and Other Bids* (1974) COM Doc XI/56/74.

4 R. Skog, 'Does Sweden Need a Mandatory Bid Rule? A Critical Analysis' (1997), *SUERF Studies*, No. 2.

1.2.2 *The Commission's 1989 Proposal*

During the latter part of the 1980s, European stock markets became more active and the number of takeover offers increased dramatically.[5] Markets also saw a move from the traditional takeover negotiated between the acquirer and the target company's management to a takeover offer made directly to shareholders. This offer was often preceded by little or no prior negotiations with management or it occurred after negotiations had proved unsuccessful. At this time, there was also an increase in cross-border corporate takeovers, with foreign firms often vying for control of companies in other countries through public takeover bids.[6] These changes gave rise to renewed debate on the conditions for company takeovers in Europe. In a common market where companies were entitled to freedom of establishment in any Member State and where capital supposedly flowed freely across national borders, it was clear that significant differences emerged amongst Member States' perspectives on takeovers. Some Member States, such as the UK, favoured allowing free markets to take their course, whereas others had in place complex institutional and legal obstacles capable of impeding the acquisition of corporate control.[7]

In 1985, the Commission published a white paper on the completion of the internal market in which it identified the need for a directive to harmonise Member States' rules on takeover bids and it promised to present a proposal in 1987.[8] That year, the Commission circulated for discussion a preliminary draft proposal for a Directive on Takeover and Other General Bids. The proposal's Explanatory Memorandum noted that, although the frequency of takeovers varied greatly from one Member State to another, 'their importance is growing with the gradual liberalization of capital markets'.[9] It was envisaged that the directive would not set out an exhaustive set of rules but would rather provide a minimum level of protection for target shareholders.

In takeover regulation, as in many other areas of regulation, industry events can have an immediate and significant impact on political receptiveness to reform. One such event was the launching of a bid in January 1988 by the Italian businessman Carlo de Benedetti for a controlling shareholding in the giant Belgian holding company Société Générale de Belgique. This started what became one of Europe's most controversial takeover fights of the decade.[10] Société Générale de Belgique was described not only as one of the 'most significant companies' in the

5 R. Skog, 'The Takeover Directive – An Endless Saga?' (2002) 13 *European Business Law Review* 301, 302.

6 Ibid.

7 Ibid.

8 COM White Paper COM (85) 310 final.

9 Preliminary Draft, Proposal for a Council Directive on Takeover and Other General Bids, xv/63/87,5.

10 M. Ventoruzzo, 'Europe's Thirteenth Directive and U.S. Takeover Regulation: Regulatory Means and Political Economic Ends' (2006) 41 *Texas International Law Journal* 171, 203.

Belgian economy, having assets valued at nearly one-third of the total Belgian economy, but as a 'source of national pride'.[11] Although ultimately the bid was blocked by an alliance of investors led by La Compagnie financière de Suez of France which acquired a 51 per cent majority,[12] the battle for the company described as 'la vieille dame' galvanised the Commission's plans for a directive.[13] Pressed by the European Parliament, the Commission in January 1989 presented a complete proposal for a Thirteenth Directive on company law concerning takeover and other general bids.[14]

Although at this stage there was still no agreement that a European directive was necessary, the 1989 proposal kicked off an intense debate on the form any such directive would take. A number of Member States believed that a directive should take the form of a limited set of basic principles upon which national rules could be based, allowing Member States discretion as to the details. Moreover, there was sharp criticism of individual provisions in the proposed directive.

One of the Member States most highly critical of the proposal was the UK, which feared it would have to abandon its self-regulation in favour of legislation. The UK was also highly critical of certain details of the proposal. The British criticism was especially difficult for the Commission, given that the UK Takeover Code had served as the model for the takeover regulations that by then were gradually beginning to take shape across Continental Europe.[15] It had also been carefully scrutinised by the Commission when formulating the proposed directive.

In January 1990, a substantially amended proposal was approved by the Parliament.[16] In September 1990, the Commission issued an amended proposal, reflecting a number of amendments proposed by the Parliament, Member States and the Economic and Social Committee.[17]

In June 1991, the negotiations were suspended and, by the end of the year, the Commission announced it would prepare yet another draft to respond to criticism raised and to reflect the principle of subsidiarity introduced by the Maastricht Treaty.[18] It was clear too that a significant number of Member States, including Germany and the UK, saw the benefit in a framework directive which would allow them to retain many of their existing regulations and traditions.[19] By contrast, right

11 B. White, 'Conflicts in the Regulation of Hostile Business Takeovers in the United States and the European Union' (2003) 9 *Ilus GENTIUM* 162, 180.

12 P. Montgomery, 'The End of the Battle in Belgium', *New York Times* (25 June 1988).

13 Skog, 'Does Sweden Need a Mandatory Bid Rule?'

14 [1989] OJ C64/8; COM (88) 823 final; Bull EC Supp 3/89.

15 Skog, 'The Takeover Directive – An Endless Saga?' 303.

16 [1990] OJ C 38/41.

17 [1990] OJ C 240/7; COM(90) 416 final. See V. Edwards, 'The Directive on Takeover Bids – Not Worth the Paper It's Written On?' (2004) 1 *European Company and Financial Law Review* 416, 428.

18 Skog, 'The Takeover Directive – An Endless Saga?' 303.

19 Edwards, 'The Directive on Takeover Bids'.

up until the time the directive was passed, a small number of Member States, including Italy, maintained their preference for a greater level of harmonisation at EU level.

1.2.3 *The Commission's 1997 Proposal*

In February 1996, the long-heralded new proposal was published[20] and it too was amended in late 1997, taking into account comments made at the first reading in Parliament.[21] This latter proposal differed in several respects from the 1990 version. Firstly, it was shorter and less detailed, involving a proposal for a 'framework directive', containing few detailed provisions but five general principles Member States would have to follow in their national takeover rules. A number of provisions in the 1990 proposal had been replaced by a general requirement that Member States adopt rules in these areas, but without being overly prescriptive as to their material content.

A second distinction was that Member States could choose to implement the Directive either in the traditional manner by enacting a law or by government decree, but also through self-regulation. Article 1 thus referred to 'mechanisms or arrangements established by organizations officially authorized to regulate the markets' as well as regulations and the recitals referring to supervision by 'self-regulatory bodies'. Similarly, Article 4.1 provided that the national competent authorities appointed by Member States to supervise bids could include 'associations or private bodies'. This change was designed by the Commission to reduce UK opposition to the directive by facilitating the continued role of the UK Takeover Panel as competent authority.[22]

Based on the 1997 proposal, intense negotiations started within the Council to reach a 'common position'. Representatives from national governments and takeover or securities regulators discussed each provision in the proposal and in many cases disparate views emerged. Often participants advocated for a position consistent with their own existing rules or legal systems to ensure fit and perhaps to avoid unnecessary disruption. Often too, shared experiences allowed the drafters to identify and provide for textual amendments to create a more effective proposal and to reflect different national contexts. A Council Working Party considered many amended

20 [1996] OJ C 162/5; COM (95) 655.

21 COM (97) 565 final.

22 See B. Clarke, 'Takeover Regulation: Through the Regulatory Looking Glass' (2007), *Comparative Research in Law & Political Economy. Research Paper* No. 18/2007, available at https://ssrn.com/abstract=1002675. The UK government had expressly acknowledged the advantages of the UK Takeover Panel's system of regulation, including: flexibility, speed and certainty in decision making; principles-based regulation; involvement of City stakeholders in rule development; and a consensual approach to regulation amongst those involved in the markets (DTI, *Company Law Implementation of the European Directive on Takeover Bids, A Consultative Document* (2005), 2.11).

proposals in 1998[23] and 1999, culminating in a revised joint compromise proposal of the Commission and the presidency in May 1999 and an amended proposal before Council in June 1999. When the settlement arrived at the ministerial level for ratification, however, Spain announced that it opposed the directive and the text noted that the Spanish delegation was keeping at that stage a general political reservation on the proposal. To no one's surprise, Spain's problem had less to do with public takeover bids than with its recurring claim to recover the sovereignty of Gibraltar.[24] This gave rise to concerns amongst some Member States that, as the UK had been relatively lukewarm in respect of the introduction of a directive, it might be slow to reach out to resolve the political dispute. Indeed, it took a year of bilateral discussions between Spain and the UK and pressure from other Member States for a common position to finally be agreed upon by all Member States on 19 June 2000, under the German presidency of the Council.[25] Although the Commission was not legally required to do so, it accepted this common position on 26 July 2000.

1.3 THE COUNCIL'S 2000 COMMON POSITION

The proposed directive negotiated by the Council bore a strong resemblance to the Commission's 1997 proposal, but with Member States' interventions and demands for clarification having been taken into account, the text became a little more comprehensive and detailed.

1.3.1 *The Scope of the Directive*

Article 1 provided that the coordination measures prescribed by the Directive should apply to Member States'

> laws, regulations, administrative provisions, codes of practice or other arrangements of the Member States, including arrangements established by organisations officially authorised to regulate the markets ... relating to takeover bids for the securities of a company governed by the law of a Member State, where such securities are admitted to trading on a regulated market within the meaning of Article 1(13) of Council Directive 93/22/EEC.

This linguistically challenged provision, which remains largely unchanged, meant that the Directive would apply to takeover rules taking the form of both hard law

23 'In October 1998, Member States failed to agree on the proposal during a three-day meeting of which one senior delegate was reported as saying "The word shambles would be gracing it with a clarity of purpose that it didn't have."' *Financial Times*, 9 October 1998 (cited in Edwards, 'The Directive on Takeover Bids', 428).

24 The question arose in the context of designating and communicating with a Gibraltar competent authority. Eventually, an agreement was reached between Spain and the UK, and it was understood that contact with any future authority in Gibraltar could be via a Post Office Box system.

25 Common Position (EC) No 1/2001 [2001] OJ C 23/1.

(i.e. legislation and government regulations) and soft law (i.e. self-regulatory codes, such as the UK Takeover Code). This was of utmost importance not only to the UK but also for Sweden which has a self-regulatory system very similar to that of the UK system.

As the Directive applies to takeover bids for companies with shares traded on regulated markets, its application is not dependent on the nationality of the bidder or whether it is an individual or a legal entity.

1.3.2 *General Principles*

Obviously inspired by the UK Takeover Code, Article 3 included six General Principles:

(a) all holders of shares of the target company of the same class shall be given equal treatment;
(b) the shareholders of the target company shall be given sufficient time and information to reach a properly informed decision on the bid;
(c) the board of the target company shall act in the interests of the entire company and not deny shareholders the opportunity to decide on the merits of the bid;
(d) false markets shall not be created in such a way that the prices of the company's securities rise or fall in an artificial manner;
(e) a takeover bid may be announced only after the offeror has ensured it has the resources to fulfil the bid; and
(f) a takeover bid may not hinder the target company from conducting its affairs for longer than reasonable.

As Member States would be obliged to respect these principles in their national takeover regulation, they would become important to the interpretation of more detailed provisions not only in the Directive, but also in the national rules implementing the Directive. Although deliberately broad, only Principle (c) was considered controversial by Member States. After lengthy debates over the extent to which a broader stakeholder approach should be included in the Directive as opposed to a shareholder primacy approach, the reference to acting in the 'interests of the company' in Principle (c) was agreed. It was understood that this would allow Member States to adopt either a broad or narrow interpretation of the term, depending on their chosen national approach. This degree of flexibility was confirmed in the European Court of Justice's subsequent decision that the General Principles must be viewed as 'guiding principles' for the implementation of the Directive by the Member States and not as independent General Principles of Community law.[26]

[26] *Audiolux SA e.a v Groupe Bruxelles Lambert SA (GBL) and Others and Bertelsmann AG and Others* Case C-101/08, 51. See B. Clarke, 'EU Takeover Regulation as a Means of Safeguarding

1.3.3 *Supervisory Authority and Applicable Regulation*

Much time was spent debating Article 4, dealing with supervisory authority and jurisdictional issues. If the target company was listed only in the Member State where it had its registered office, the authority competent for supervising the bid would be that of that Member State and the rules applicable would be the rules of that Member State as well. Where the shares of the target company were listed both in its home Member State and in another Member State or only in another Member State, the decision as to the competent supervisory authority and the applicable law was clearly more complicated. This turned out to be one of the most difficult problems to solve in the negotiations. It was agreed finally that if the shares were listed in more than one Member State, the authority competent for supervising the bid would be that of the Member State where the shares were first listed. If the shares were listed only in another Member State, then the competent authority would be that of that Member State. In both cases, there is a split when it comes to applicable rules and jurisdiction is shared. Matters relating to the consideration and 'matters related to the bid procedure', including information on the offeror's decision to make a bid, the offer document and the disclosure of the bid would be dealt with in accordance with the rules of the Member State of the competent authority. By contrast, for matters relating to information to be provided to the target's employees and in 'matters related to company law', including the mandatory bid and defensive measures by the target's board, the applicable rules and the competent authority would be those of the Member State in which the target company had its registered office. Concerns were voiced at the time that distinguishing between matters related to 'bid procedure' and 'company law' might not always be straightforward and the Directive itself provided no mechanism to manage a dispute between parties or supervisory authorities in this regard.

1.3.4 *Mandatory Bids*

The 'mandatory bid' rule is a key provision in the UK Takeover Code which obliges a person who acquires shares representing 30 per cent of the voting rights in a company to make a bid for the remaining shares. A mandatory bid provision was also included in the 1989 proposed directive, but it encountered stiff opposition from several Member States. The concern was that, while mandatory bids might perhaps be the right kind of minority protection in Member States where companies typically have diversified ownership, it might not be appropriate in those where ownership is more concentrated.[27]

the Interests of Employees: Re-opening Pandora's Box' in H. Siekmann, A. Cahn, T. Florstedt, K. Lagenbucher, J. Redenius-Hovermann, T. Troger, and U. Segna (eds.), *Festschrift for Theodor Baums* (Baden: Mohr Siebeck, 2017).

[27] Skog, 'The Takeover Directive – An Endless Saga?', 307.

Over time, however, opposition to this part of the proposed directive gradually subsided as a growing number of Member States added their own rules on mandatory bids to their takeover regulation and as the proposed mandatory bid provision was refined. The 1989 proposal had required a bid to be made when a person aimed to acquire securities which, when added to their existing holdings, would give a percentage of the voting rights in a company 'which may not be fixed at more than 33 1/3 %'. Article 5 in the Common Position clarified that mandatory bids would only be required if control was obtained, and it allowed Member States to determine the percentage of voting rights which conferred 'control'. In response to concerns that the mandatory bid provision would be triggered in inappropriate circumstances, Article 5(2) stated clearly that, if control was obtained through a voluntary bid to all shareholders, there would be no obligation to make a second bid. Similarly, Recital 6 clarified that the obligation to make a bid would not apply to those controlling holdings already in existence at the time the Directive was introduced.

Article 5 did not mandate the price that has to be offered for securities in a mandatory bid, only that it be 'equitable'. Benefitting from the UK's experience of such bids, it did, however, contain a new provision, agreed by a majority of Member States in 1999, to the effect that a mandatory cash alternative would be included.

1.3.5 *Frustrating Actions by the Target Company*

The most controversial aspect of takeovers and takeover regulation is the discretion afforded to the board of the target company to take actions to frustrate a takeover bid, thus denying shareholders an opportunity to consider the offer. A takeover has consequences for the board and management of the target company. Once completed, changes in the board and management frequently ensue, particularly in the event of a hostile bid. The likelihood of this occurring gives rise to a potential conflict of interest and creates a risk that the board or management may take certain actions to impede takeover bids they do not support.

To eliminate the risk of such frustrating or defensive actions, the UK Takeover Code provides that, if a bid has been made or the board of the target company has reason to assume that a bona fide bid is imminent, the board may not take any measures intended to undermine or frustrate the bid or its acceptance without the approval of the general meeting given after the offer is made. The proposed directive adopted the same principle.

1.4 THE EUROPEAN PARLIAMENT'S VIEWPOINT

The Council's Common Position was submitted to Parliament for a second reading, and in December 2000, Parliament approved the Common Position with eighteen amendments to the proposed directive.[28]

[28] [2000] OJ C 232/168.

One of the most important changes required by Parliament was that the board of the target company be given extensive opportunity to frustrate unwanted takeover bids. This position was made forcefully by the rapporteur of the Parliament, the German Conservative MEP Klaus-Heiner Lehne.

At the time of the negotiations, relatively few large German corporations were listed, and amongst those that were, ownership structures were highly concentrated. Takeover bids were rare and seen by many as 'a foreign, undesirable element in German business', particularly in the event of hostile bids by foreign bidders for German companies.[29] One such controversial bid was that by the UK telecommunications company, Vodafone AirTouche, for Germany's Mannesmann in the autumn of 1999. The fact that the Vodafone bid eventually succeeded only served to bolster the opinion that corporate boards should be given considerable freedom to defend their companies against hostile takeovers.

It was against this background that a number of large German companies became intensely involved in Parliament's response to the proposed takeover directive, and it was said that 'the rapporteur, in practice, became a spokesman for VW, BASF and other large German companies' who were keen to avoid the risk that they too would become the subject of a hostile bid and end up in foreign hands.[30] These companies viewed the Council's proposal to give shareholders the ultimate decision-making right on defensive actions as a 'crazy idea'.

1.5 THE CONCILIATION PROCESS

As early as January 2001, the Council, under the Swedish presidency, clearly stated that the amendments proposed by Parliament could not be accepted without modifications.[31] This triggered the process of 'conciliation' between the Council and Parliament provided for in the Treaty to arrive at a compromise. Through this process, which commenced informally in March 2001 and formally on 10 April 2001, an agreement was gradually reached point by point on the proposed directive. This involved Parliament dropping some of its demands, others being met by relatively simple means, and others requiring substantial concessions by the Council, following intense internal deliberations.[32]

Finding common ground on the issue of defensive actions proved particularly challenging. As noted, the common position stated that such actions could only be taken with the approval of the general meeting after a bid had been made public. By contrast, the Parliament's conciliation delegation, controlled by the rapporteur, argued that the general meeting should be permitted to authorise the board in

[29] Skog, 'The Takeover Directive – An Endless Saga?', 308.
[30] Ibid.
[31] Ibid.
[32] Ibid.

advance of any bid being made to take such defensive actions. It has been reported that the Council's opposition on this issue 'raised the ire of the German business community' which intensified its lobbying efforts and attempted to create a rift in the Council.[33] At a meeting on 23 April, representatives of Volkswagen, BASF and other companies, together with labour union representatives, issued their demand for changes to the proposed directive directly to the German Chancellor Gerhard Schröder.[34] Two days later, Germany's deputy representative to the EU notified the Swedish presidency that Germany no longer backed the common position, and its future support rested on shareholder approval for frustrating actions being eliminated from the relevant provision, Article 9, or on the entire article being removed from the directive.[35] This was a highly unusual turnaround given the involvement of the German presidency in January–June 1999 in reaching the compromise and it provoked an immediate response from other Member States on the Council. The secretary to the UK Takeover Panel opined that the change proposed would 'depriv[e] the directive of any real purpose',[36] and not only the Member States that so vociferously pushed for shareholders' sovereignty but also those that traditionally took a more relaxed stance toward defensive actions took exception to the German approach. It was felt that Germany was 'overstepping the rules by rejecting the Council's common position after a year of highly sensitive negotiations and it was de facto taking sides with Parliament'.[37] As the Council held to its convictions, Germany became isolated in the Council. The Parliament's conciliation delegation also maintained its position and used the conflict to push even harder in conciliation negotiations to allow boards to take frustrating actions with the support of prior authorisation.

In accordance with the Treaty, the conciliation process was required to conclude by 6 June and failure to reach an agreement by that time would lead to the rejection of the proposed directive. Although negotiations in May did not lead to a breakthrough, a final conciliation session was scheduled for the evening of 5 June in Luxembourg. Whilst at the outset agreement seemed unlikely, with Parliament accusing the Council of an unwillingness to compromise, a few hours into 6 June and assisted greatly by the active mediation of the Commission officials, agreement was reached.[38] A division emerged in the parliamentary delegation with the rapporteur, Mr Lehne, being in the minority.

[33] Ibid.

[34] Klaus Hopt suggests that it is likely that Chancellor Schröder, hailed as 'the automobile chancellor', had previously been made aware of this contentious issue by Volkswagen's chief executive Ferdinand Piech with whom he had developed very close ties whilst he was a member of Volkswagen's supervisory board (K. Hopt, 'Takeover Regulation in Europe – The Battle for the 13th Directive on Takeovers', (2002) 15 *Australian Journal of Corporate Law* 1, 10).

[35] Skog, 'The Takeover Directive – An Endless Saga?', 309.

[36] Edwards, 'The Directive on Takeover Bids – Not Worth the Paper It's Written On?', 426.

[37] Skog, 'The Takeover Directive – An Endless Saga?', 309.

[38] Ibid.

Whilst in reaching this agreement the Council made several concessions to Parliament on various points, Article 9 remained unamended. The board of a target company would not therefore be permitted to take any defensive actions without the express approval of the shareholders after a bid had been presented. However, Member States would be allowed to postpone the application of Article 9 for one year after the Directive's implementation deadline. Other compromises included extending the implementation period from three years to four; additional safeguards for employees in the target company in the form of informational rights; and an undertaking by Frits Bolkestein, the Internal Market Commissioner, to establish an expert group to review three key areas of contention in Parliament: (1) the definition of the 'equitable price' for shareholders in the event of a mandatory bid; (2) the right of the majority of shareholders to acquire the shares of minority shareholders after a successful bid; and (3) the equal treatment of shareholders in Member States. It was agreed that the expert group would submit a report in March 2002 and the Commission would respond with a proposal to address the suggestions made in this report.

The conciliation process was thereby complete, and a joint text approved by the Conciliation Committee was published on 19 June. All that remained then was for Parliament in plenary to vote (by a simple majority) on the matter – 'something most observers, based on compromises on other directives, expected to be little more than a formality'.[39]

1.6 PARLIAMENTARY VOTE

The proposed takeover directive was important to corporate ownership and influence, with major and immediate financial implications. The German business community was therefore unwilling to give up the fight and made use of the period before the vote on 4 July to lobby elected officials.[40] Skog explained that:

> Convincing a majority of the MEPs to reject the results of more than ten years of work and abandon the conciliation agreement was no simple matter, however. Saying no to the directive would most certainly cast a shadow over Parliament for a long time to come. The strategy therefore was to create displeasure also with other aspects of the proposed directive than the regulation of frustrating actions.[41]

Supporters of the vote too sought to persuade parliamentarians to support their cause and both sides engaged in concerted efforts to vote 'correctly'. The day before the vote, the party groups met. It became evident that differences in opinion, or what has

[39] Ibid.
[40] Ibid.
[41] Ibid., 309–310.

been described as 'a clash of capitalisms'[42] between the 'liberal market economies'[43] such as the UK and the 'coordinated market economies'[44] such as Germany,[45] split both the conservative and socialist camps, and the vote would therefore be 'free'.[46]

When the vote was taken, the president of the Parliament, Madame Fontaine, read the results: 273 votes in favour, 273 against and 22 abstentions. A further fifty-eight had missed the vote. After some initial confusion about the exact meaning of a 'yes' and 'no' vote,[47] it became clear that, by the smallest possible margin, the proposed Directive had not received the simple majority it needed. Parliament had rejected the conciliation compromise and the proposed directive. There was some discussion as to whether Madame Fontaine, who had not voted, should have exercised her vote to sustain the conciliation procedure. Her response was that her actions were 'in line with those of all the presidents before me, who always used the sensible rule of only voting in extremely exceptional circumstances, and not on problems that have divided Parliament to this extent'.[48] Concerns with the text were aired by parliamentarians and even many of those who supported the proposal acknowledged that 'this directive will not win any prizes'.[49] One parliamentarian explained the vote on the basis that 'nervousness led to a retreat into protectionism, which shattered the fragile agreement that had been reached in conciliation. The German MEPs found that many Netherlands, Spanish and Italian colleagues gradually came to support their strategy of rejection.'[50] This view was supported by media reports that Italy feared their companies would be taken over by French state-owned companies and especially Electricité de France, and the Italian European Affairs Minister was quoted as stating: 'The Italian government changed its position in reaction to the aggression of EDF.'[51] Other reports suggested that 'German MEPs, in essence on a government whip, voted against, and that a group of

[42] H. Callaghan and M. Höpner, 'European Integration and the Clash of Capitalisms: Political Cleavages of Takeover Liberalization' (2005) 3 *Comparative European Politics* 307.

[43] P. Hall and D. Soskice (eds.), *Varieties of Capitalism. The Institutional Foundations of Comparative Advantage* (Oxford: Oxford University Press, 2001).

[44] Ibid.

[45] G. Jackson and H. Miyajima, 'Varieties of Capitalism, Varieties of Markets: Mergers and Acquisitions in Japan, Germany, France, the UK and the USA' (2007), *RIETI Discussion Paper* Series 07-E-054, available at https://ssrn.com/abstract = 1012210.

[46] Skog, 'The Takeover Directive – An Endless Saga?', 310. Despite this concession, it is noteworthy that the Liberal Democrat Group voted as one.

[47] Even after the initial vote, confusion reigned as, due to a technical slip-up, the official record initially stated 273 for, and 272 against (European Parliament, *Verbatim report of proceedings*, 4 July 2001, available at www.europarl.europa.eu/doceo/document/CRE-5-2001-07-04_EN .html.)

[48] Ibid.

[49] Maaten, Manders, Mulder, Plooij-van Gorsel, Sanders-ten Holte and Wiebenga. European Parliament, *Verbatim report of proceedings* (4 July 2001).

[50] Bourlanges, European Parliament, *Verbatim report of proceedings* (4 July 2001).

[51] D. DeRosa 'Europe steps backwards by axing takeover rules'(8 July 2001), Bloomberg, available at www.taipeitimes.com/News/biz/archives/2001/07/08/0000093267.

Spanish MEPs switched sides after being offered support for increased fishing subsidies.'[52] The Commission itself explained the defeat as motivated by three main political considerations:

> (1) rejection of the principle whereby, in order to take defensive measures in the face of a bid, the board of the offeree company must first obtain the approval of shareholders once the bid has been made, and this until such time as a level playing field is created for European companies facing a takeover bid; (2) regret that the protection which the directive would afford employees of companies involved in a takeover bid was insufficient; (3) the failure of the proposal to achieve a level playing field with the United States.[53]

Commissioner Bolkestein described the outcome as the frustration of 'Europe's broader interests ... by certain narrow interests'.[54]

1.7 RESTARTING THE PROCEDURE

The rebuff by Parliament was an obvious blow to the Commission, and only on one prior occasion had Parliament rejected a conciliation agreement.[55] The effect of Parliament's decision was to return the issue of a European takeover directive to the Commission. Despite what must have been a difficult task for the Commission in generating enthusiasm for re-initiating the legislative process, it had little choice. As was noted, whilst the practical importance of the takeover directive may have been debatable, its symbolic value was huge and both the Council and the Commission had emphasised the vital role the directive played in efforts to realise the vision of an internal market.[56] The directive, which formed part of the Financial Services Action Plan,[57] had been identified by the Council at a special meeting in Lisbon as a priority for the integration of European financial markets. Thus, in July 2001, Commissioner Bolkestein announced his intention of presenting a new draft directive.

1.7.1 *The High Level Group of Company Law Experts*

In September 2001, Commissioner Bolkestein made good on this promise and established a High Level Group of seven company law experts, chaired by Dutch law professor Jaap Winter to advise the Commission on the next draft. The

[52] Edwards, 'The Directive on Takeover Bids – Not Worth the Paper It's Written On?', 427.

[53] Explanatory Memorandum OJ C 45 E/1.

[54] Press Release, European Commission, 'Commission Regrets Rejection of Takeovers Directive by the European Parliament' (4 July 2001).

[55] The conciliation agreement on the proposal for a Directive on the legal protection of biotechnological inventions, COM (1988) 496 in 1995. See R. Skog, 'The Takeover Directive, the "Breakthrough" Rule and the Swedish System of Dual Class Common Stock' (2004) 15 *European Business Law Review* 1439, 1441.

[56] Skog, 'The Takeover Directive – An Endless Saga?', 310.

[57] COM(1999) 232 final, 11 May 1999.

establishment of such a group to consider company law harmonisation in this context had been flagged by the Commission in advance of the final vote in July. In January 2002, the High Level Group presented its report to the Commission.[58] It proposed that European company law should aim to create a level playing field for takeover bids and should be guided by two principles.

The first principle was that the ultimate decision on a takeover bid must be taken by the shareholders. The board of the target company should express its views and advise the shareholders, but it should not be entitled to decide on the fate of the bid. No defensive measures should be taken without the approval of the general meeting and this approval could not be given in advance. This was a welcome message to most Member States, but not to Germany which in January 2002 had introduced takeover legislation permitting the general meeting to give an authorisation to the board to take defensive measures in the case of a future bid. The German law went even further than this, allowing the management to take defensive measures with the approval of the supervisory board.[59]

The second principle was that there ought to be proportionality between the ultimate economic risk and control, at least in the context of takeovers. For this purpose, the High Level Group proposed a 'breakthrough' rule which would come into effect once a bidder had made a bid for all the shares of a listed company and reached a certain threshold of ownership of the 'risk-bearing' capital as a result of the bid.[60] The threshold should be fixed by the Member States, thereby allowing them to take into account the relevant majority requirements in their company laws. It should not, however, be set at a percentage higher than 75 per cent. A bidder acquiring the relevant percentage of risk-bearing capital would be allowed to exercise a corresponding share of voting rights at a general meeting of shareholders. In other words, the rule would 'break through' or neutralise provisions in the articles of association on, for example, voting caps or multiple-voting shares.

The High Level Group also addressed the concerns expressed in Parliament that the introduction of a prohibition on frustrating action in Article 9 would create an unlevel playing field between the EU and the United States.[61] It acknowledged that boards of American companies generally do have a broad discretion to introduce defensive devices under the business judgment rule and that many individual states have enacted laws specifically permitting the board to consider other interests than shareholders' interests. However, it took the view that the American approach would be less beneficial to the development of efficient integrated capital markets in

58 *Report of the High Level Group of Company Law Experts on issues related to takeover bids* (Brussels, 2002).

59 T. Baums, 'The Regulation of Takeovers under German Law', (2004) 15 *European Business Law Review* 1453, 1457.

60 The proposed rule was inspired by rules in Italian but also French and German law (*Report of the High Level Group of Company Law Experts on issues related to takeover bids*, 30.

61 Baums, 'The Regulation of Takeovers under German Law', 1458.

Europe.[62] It also opined that the proposed prohibition 'would not give American companies an unfair advantage when trying to exploit the European internal market by taking over European companies, as compared with the conditions which apply to European companies exploiting the American market by taking over American companies'.[63] However, it concluded that, if political concerns persisted, the benefit of the application of Article 9 could be restricted to listed European bidders bidding for other listed European companies 'to the extent this would not violate international agreements and could practically be enforced'.[64]

1.7.2 *The European Court of Justice Decisions on Golden Shares*

On 4 June 2002, three decisions were rendered by the European Court of Justice (ECJ) in relation to actions initiated by the European Commission against Portugal, France and Belgium in respect of their golden share regimes.[65] These shares were held by the three Member States to give their governments greater control over acquisitions and transfers of shares in certain of their prized domestic companies or sectors. The ECJ found that both Portugal and France had violated the freedom of movement of capital under the EC Treaty. Klaus Hopt, a member of the High Level Group, noted that these decisions were consistent with the group's report and its recommendation that the breakthrough rule apply to golden shares. The decisions thus helped 'in doing away with cross-frontier barriers by national laws and restrictive state rights'.[66]

Hopt also observed that, following the ECJ's decisions, Commissioner Bolkestein announced that he would present the next draft of the Directive in July 2002, but that Chancellor Schröder intervened with the president of the Commission, Romano Prodi, to ensure the process would not interfere with the upcoming German elections and as a result the new draft was postponed until October 2002.

1.8 THE 2002 DIRECTIVE PROPOSAL

Having considered the arguments, the Commission on 2 October 2002 adopted and submitted a new Directive Proposal.[67] This text was drafted by Karel Van Hulle,

62 Clarke, 'Takeover Regulation – Through the Regulatory Looking Glass', 22–23.

63 *Report of the High Level Group of Company Law Experts on issues related to takeover bids*, 42.

64 Ibid., 8.

65 *COM v Portugal* C-367/98; *COM v French Republic* C-483/99 and *COM v Belgium* C-503/99. At this time, the Commission planned to initiate an action against Germany in respect of its Volkswagen statute which gave the Federal government and the Land of Niedersachsen a veto against a majority acquisition while holding only 20 per cent of the shares. The action was not launched, however, until 2005 and only in 2007 did the European Court of Justice rule that the provisions violated the Treaty's free movement of capital guarantees (Case C-112/2005).

66 Hopt, 'Takeover Regulation in Europe – The Battle for the 13th Directive on Takeovers', 14.

67 Proposal for a directive of the European Parliament and of the Council on takeover bids, 2 October 2002, COM (2002) 534, [2003] OJ C45/1.

head of the Company Law unit, with contributions from the High Level Group.[68] It sought to accommodate the concerns expressed by Germany whilst retaining the support of the other Member States. Unusually, the College of Commissioners held a formal vote on the adoption of the proposal and one French Commissioner (Pascal Lamy, Trade) and both German Commissioners (Günther Verheugen, Enlargement, and Michael Schreyer, Budget) voted against it, while the Belgian Commissioner (Philippe Busquin, Research) abstained.[69] The proposal appeared to take account of the objections to abolishing dual voting rights and the German Commissioners were reported to be particularly concerned by the proposal's failure to tackle the problem of multiple-voting rights, discussed further in Section 1.8.1.[70]

The proposal was similar in many ways to the proposal agreed in June 2001, pursuing the same objectives, retaining the same scope and including many of the same provisions. It retained, for example, the prohibition in Article 9 on frustrating actions by the target unless it has the prior authorisation of the general meeting of shareholders for the purpose. It did, however, contain several important differences, including: a definition of 'equitable price' in the event of a mandatory bid; a new article on employee information and consultation in response to concerns voiced by certain members of Parliament regarding protection of employees of the target and the bidder; a sell-out right; a procedure for revision of the provisions; a three-year transitional period for complying with Article 9; and greater disclosure in companies' annual reports of the defensive structures and mechanisms that could hinder the acquisition and exercise of control over the company by an offeror.

1.8.1 *The Breakthrough Rule and Multiple-Voting Rights*

One of the most contentious changes, however, related to the breakthrough rule. Based on the High Level Group's report, but without adhering to it in detail, the Commission introduced in Article 11 a 'mini breakthrough rule', with a view to increasing the number of takeovers in the EU by eliminating those corporate governance arrangements which might otherwise impede takeovers.[71] Its effect would be, for example, to allow a bidder who, following a takeover bid had obtained a specific percentage of the votes in a target company, to call a general meeting of the target company to appoint a new board without being hindered by voting caps in the company's articles of association that might otherwise limit the number of votes each shareholder could cast at that meeting. Provided that the offeror had obtained

[68] K. Van Hulle, *Aktuelle Entwicklungen im europäischen Gesellschaftsrecht in Europäisches Wirtschafts und Steuerrecht* (2000) pp. 521–526 and K. Van Hulle, 'Does the EU have a role to play in company law?' in M. Neville and K. Engsig Sørensen (eds.), *The Regulation of Companies. A Tribute to Krüger Andersen*, 29–36 (Copenhagen: Forlaget Thomson, 2003).

[69] Edwards, 'The Directive on Takeover Bids – Not Worth the Paper It's Written On?', 428.

[70] Ibid.

[71] *Report of the High Level Group of Company Law Experts on issues related to takeover bids*, 29.

sufficient votes in the target company to amend the articles of association, such restrictive provisions would 'cease to have effect' at the first general meeting after the bid had completed. The idea behind the Commission's proposed rule was to 'break through' pre-bid defences that would work to isolate a company and entrench management in a takeover situation.

In this draft, Article 11 did not include securities carrying double- or multiple-voting rights. This reflected a fierce debate that had taken place on this subject amongst Member States. In the Nordic countries, multiple-vote shares had always been permitted and were frequently used by listed companies. Sweden, Finland and Denmark argued in this context that there was no empirical data suggesting that multiple-vote share structures prevented takeovers.[72] This was acknowledged by the Commission and it also accepted that the suppression of such rights, especially without compensation, would in some legal systems give rise to constitutional problems and possibly necessitate constitutional amendments.[73] Ireland was one of the Member States that harboured such a concern in light of constitutionally protected property rights and it entered scrutiny reservations on compatibility with the property rights enshrined in the European Convention on Human Rights.[74] The likely complexities involved in giving effect to the breakthrough rule were also raised, along with the need to clarify how compensation would be calculated and by whom it would be paid.

Germany argued that Article 9 on post-bid defensive measures should be made less restrictive, to accommodate the German model, which allowed authorisation of defensive measures against future takeover bids. It also proposed that the breakthrough rule in Article 11 should be expanded to include multiple-vote share structures. This attitude to including multiple-voting rights was shared by many other Member States, including the UK, Austria and the Netherlands. Similar signals were given by the rapporteur, Klaus-Heiner Lehne, in late 2002. He opined that the ownership problem could be resolved by a system of compensation and that a level playing field for takeovers could not exist while multiple-vote share structures were permitted in some Member States but not in others.[75]

1.8.2 *The Level Playing Field*

The issue of the lack of a level playing field between the EU and the United States continued to be a focal point of discussion in 2002. The Commission questioned whether there was strong evidence that EU companies were at a disadvantage. It also

72 See Skog, 'The Takeover Directive, the "Breakthrough" Rule and the Swedish System of Dual Class Common Stock'.

73 COM (2002) 534, [2003] OJ C45/1.

74 Council Legal Services was subsequently able to provide comfort on this point.

75 Edwards, 'The Directive on Takeover Bids – Not Worth the Paper It's Written On?', 428.

queried whether, even if this were proven to be the case, the directive would be the appropriate place to address such reciprocity issues.

1.9 THE 2003 NEGOTIATIONS AND PROPOSAL

After listening to Germany and other Member States, Greece, which took over the presidency of the Council from Denmark at the start of 2003, concluded that the Commission's proposal would not gain the support of a large enough majority in the Council and would not be accepted by Parliament.[76]

In February 2003, the situation changed abruptly, however, and it was reported that the UK had 'struck an informal deal' with Germany in the latter's campaign to include multiple-voting rights in the prohibited defensive measures.[77] It was claimed that the UK had withdrawn its support for the Commission's proposal and aligned with Germany, in return for Germany agreeing to oppose a proposed directive giving more rights to temporary agency workers.[78]

1.9.1 *The March 2003 Proposal*

A compromise proposal was tabled by the Greek presidency in February 2003 with a view to building consensus around the outstanding issues, including the correct balance to strike between Articles 9 and 11. It included amendments which had been suggested by the Danish presidency as well as a small number of new amendments. Following discussions in the Working Party, on 4 March 2003, the presidency presented a revised Directive Proposal but also circulated a non-paper, setting out a possible compromise for Articles 9 and 11, which it reserved the right to put forward at a later stage. The non-paper expanded Article 11 to include multiple-voting rights; specified in a recital that compensation would be left to Member States; introduced a fallback clause stating that the breakthrough rule would apply in any event where the bidder held at least 75 per cent of the securities; and exempted newly listed companies for the first five years after listing on an EU regulated market.

Three days later, the presidency published a revised compromise proposal in which Article 9 was unchanged but Article 11 was amended to take account of the original compromise proposal. The latter, as envisaged by the High Level Group's proposal, had been extended to include dual-class common shares.[79] A definition of

[76] Skog, 'The Takeover Directive, the "Breakthrough" Rule and the Swedish System of Dual Class Common Stock'.

[77] F. Guerrera and B. Jennen, 'Germany and UK in Joint Bid to Toughen EU Takeover Rules', *Financial Times*, 3 February 2003.

[78] Edwards, 'The Directive on Takeover Bids – Not Worth the Paper It's Written On?', 428.

[79] Article 11(3) was amended to include the sentence 'Multiple voting securities shall carry one vote only at the general meeting which decides on any defensive measures in accordance with Article 9.'

'multiple voting securities' as 'securities included in a *distinct and separate class* and carrying more than one vote' was introduced in Article 2, with the effect that the particular French system of loyalty shares, where voting rights are tied to seniority rather than classes of shares, would no longer be affected by the Directive. Hence, the French opposition disappeared. The rapporteur, Klaus-Heiner Lehne, opined that Member States could 'offset the inclusion of multiple voting rights by appropriate compensation for the additional value'[80] and the recitals specified that the matter of compensation would be left to Member States.

The Nordic Member States, which had previously signalled their support in principle for the Commission's proposal, strongly opposed the extension of the 'breakthrough' rule to cover multiple-vote shares.[81] In sum, they argued that the right of companies to issue dual-class shares is an important part of their right to determine their own financial structure and that the extended 'breakthrough' rule would: create considerable uncertainty as to the value of an investment in high-vote shares, thus limiting the financing opportunities available to companies; be detrimental to the corporate governance system, promoting rather than restraining management entrenchment; and encroach on the property rights of the owners of high-vote shares and give rise to complicated questions of compensation. Finally, it was argued that there was no evidence of takeover activity being adversely affected by the existence of multiple classes of shares carrying different voting rights.

Other changes included in this proposal related to the consideration to be offered in a mandatory bid. An amendment to Article 5 defined the equitable price to be paid by reference not only to the price paid by the offeror or a concert party for the same securities in the previous six to twelve months but also during the bid itself. It also provided that Member States could allow a cash consideration as an alternative in all cases. Changes were also introduced to the triggers in Articles 14 and 15 for squeeze-out and sell-out rights.

1.9.2 *The April and May 2003 Proposals*

Discussions continued and in early April 2003 a revised presidency compromise proposal was tabled. This included a new requirement to disclose in the offer document the compensation offered for the rights which might be removed as a result of the breakthrough rule and details on the method to be used in determining such compensation and how it should be paid. Given that there was still intense debate in the Working Party on how both these particulars would operate in practice, this was an important but complex matter which Member States would have to resolve in due course. A new provision was added to Article 5 providing that,

80 Committee on Legal Affairs and the Internal Market, 11 March 2003.

81 See Skog, 'The Takeover Directive, the "Breakthrough" Rule and the Swedish System of Dual Class Common Stock', 1444.

if the offeror or a concert party acquired securities during the bid at a higher price than the one already offered, this would be considered to be the equitable price and a revised offer would be required. This draft was followed by a further proposal by the Greek presidency in early May.

Despite this apparent progress, discussions remained deadlocked.[82] The three outstanding issues identified at this time were: (1) the relationship between Articles 9 and 11, including compensation payable under the breakthrough rule; (2) the need to amend the general derogation clause in Article 4(5); and (3) the level playing field with the United States. In relation to the latter, Germany had suggested removing from the scope of the Directive takeover bids made by offerors established outside the EU or by their EU subsidiaries. Other jurisdictions, including the UK and Austria, supported this idea.

By May, in a change of position, Germany, rather than seeking the inclusion of multiple-voting rights among prohibited measures, proposed the removal of Article 9. Although reported to have the support of the United Kingdom, the Netherlands and (in return for the removal of the proposed restrictions on multiple-voting rights) the Nordic countries, Germany did not have the support needed to override the Commission's opposition to its proposal.[83]

The month of May might also be described as a turning point in the Directive. On 15 May, the Portuguese delegation suggested in Coreper a very complicated compromise to take account of the differences in company law in the Member States while simultaneously offering a harmonised solution. It proposed introducing provisions allowing opting in and opting out of Articles 9 and 11. Member States would be permitted to require the application of Articles 9 and 11, but if they decided not to do so, companies would be allowed either: to apply Articles 9 and 11; or not to apply Articles 9 and 11. Though perhaps a pragmatic suggestion in the sense of overcoming intransigence among the Member States, this controversial proposal set in train discussions that would eventually lead to a degree of optionality which undermined one of the key aims of the Directive.

In June, the Portuguese delegation, at the request of the Greek presidency, Member States and the Commission, provided a more detailed version of the optionality plan. Describing it as a 'market-oriented solution', it was presented as a possible benchmark for defensive measures. It allowed Member States options with respect to their own national laws; allowed companies choices within the framework provided by the Directive and applicable national laws; and ensured transparency of choices and regimes. On the issue of the level playing field, the proposal was described as acknowledging the concerns of companies about their vulnerability

[82] J. Christensen, 'The New Draft Takeover Directive – A Breakthrough for Levelling the Playing Field in Europe?', in M. Neville and K. Engsig Sørensen (eds.), *The Regulation of Companies*, 214 (Copenhagen: Karnov Group, 2003).

[83] Edwards, 'The Directive on Takeover Bids – Not Worth the Paper It's Written On?', 416.

to preserve their existing defensive measures, whilst creating an incentive to those who wished to be open to the prospect of a takeover where they operated in a fair environment to progressively abolish defensive devices. In order to provide such an incentive, the proposal also included a reciprocity provision under which Member States could disapply bans on defensive actions without shareholder approval where the bidder came from a jurisdiction such as the United States where poison pills were permitted. Despite encouragement from the Commission, the Portuguese proposal was not tabled by the Greek presidency on the basis that it would defeat the whole purpose of the Directive. Instead of providing for a level playing field and greater integration of the EU capital markets, it would lead to even greater disparity and opacity. This proposal was the subject of intense discussions in Coreper in the following months, with a view to simplifying the options and dealing with practicalities such as the ability of companies opting in to opt back out and the application to subsidiaries of companies from the aforementioned jurisdictions.

1.9.3 *The November 2003 Proposals*

On 21 November, the Italian presidency presented a further compromise proposal to the Council, reflecting many of the amendments agreed at Coreper. It contained parliamentary scrutiny reservations by several Member States, including the UK, and also general reservations by other Member States, including Sweden. The article on optionality arrangements was simplified. It allowed Member States to reserve the right not to require companies to apply Articles 9 and/or 11, but where Member States availed themselves of this option, they were required to give companies a reversible option, to be taken at a shareholders' meeting, to apply the articles. The reciprocity provision was reformulated too to make it clearer that Member States in their national law may exempt companies which apply Articles 9 and/or 11 from applying them if they become subject to an offer launched by a company, or a subsidiary of a company, which does not apply the same articles as they do. At the last minute, Sweden managed to insert a 'review clause', requiring the Commission to examine the Directive five years after the deadline for implementation, and if necessary, propose revisions.

A piece in the influential Lex Column in the *Financial Times* three days later was scathing about the proposed directive. It commenced: 'A fruit ripened as slowly as the European Union's planned takeover directive ought to taste unusually sweet. Alas, 14 years of deliberations have produced a sour, shriveled thing, replete with the rancid overtones of political horse-trading.'[84] The German government was criticised for being 'consistently wrong' and the UK government for 'pawn[ing] its residual integrity by trading its vote on this grubby compromise for German backing over the rights of temporary workers'. There were reports too, the same week, that

[84] *Financial Times* (24 November 2003).

the United States was stepping up contacts with all EU governments to complain that making it harder for US companies to pursue hostile bids in Europe would create the perception of 'Fortress Europe'.[85]

Despite this reception, the proposal with its compromise text was adopted by the Council on 26 November 2003 with unanimous agreement, pending the European Parliament's first reading opinion and with the abstention of Spain on a general approach. France reportedly supported Germany, even though it fully intended to apply the provisions in Articles 9 and 11 and hence had no interest in their being made optional, in return for German assistance in negotiations on the common agricultural policy.[86] The Commission stated that it was not in a position to support the text.[87]

The following day, the parliamentary committee responsible adopted the rapporteur Klaus-Heiner Lehne's report amending the proposal under first reading and accepting the Council's view as to the need for optionality.[88] On 16 December 2003, Parliament adopted a resolution drafted by Klaus-Heiner Lehne, accepting agreement on the compromise agreements. While the resolution was adopted by 321 votes to 219, there seemed to be little cause for celebration. Parliament's own summary noted that 'members generally agreed that the directive as now amended represented little progress towards a genuine level playing field on takeovers in the EU, but most also supported the rapporteur's position that "half a loaf is better than none" and that it was time to "put an end to this never-ending story"'.[89] This view was not shared by everyone. In a speech in January 2004, Commissioner Bolkestein, referring expressly to the Directive, stated: 'Deals between Member States to neutralize the impact of reforms render all our efforts useless. This is a self-defeating strategy which may preserve some short term political interests, but only at the longer term's expense.'[90] The Council, confirming its approval of the amendments proposed by the European Parliament, adopted the Directive on 30 March 2004, and on 21 April the Directive was signed by the presidents of Parliament and Council, just over 15 years after the publication of the first proposal.

1.10 CONCLUSION

A total of thirty years passed between the publication of the Pennington Report and the adoption of the Directive. During this time, there were periods of intense debate and progress and periods of apathy and inaction. In the final five to six years, the

85 D. Dombey, 'US warns of wider trade rift with EU', *Financial Times* (24 November 2003).
86 Edwards, 'The Directive on Takeover Bids – Not Worth the Paper It's Written On?', 416.
87 C/03/337 15141/03 (Presse 337) 26/27 November 2003.
88 Legislative Observatory 'Company law: takeover bids' 2002/0240(COD) – 27 November 2003.
89 Legislative Observatory 'Company law: takeover bids' 2002/0240(COD) – 16 December 2003.
90 Address at ELDR Seminar 'Reviving European Growth', European Parliament (8 January 2004).

negotiations, lobbying, political manoeuvring and consensus building became more intense. Ideological debates became intertwined with economic debates and practice with theory.

The fact that agreement was finally reached might be seen as a positive outcome – notwithstanding, perhaps, the reservations identified above. Around the table at the Council Working Party meetings, which the authors were privileged to attend, discussions stretched from very detailed practical issues, such as the possibility of organising an extraordinary general meeting in an appropriately sized venue at short notice to approve defensive actions, to high-level debates. The latter included theoretical discussions as to whether the Directive constituted a 'company law' directive and whether the 'interests of the company' included the interests of employees. A number of other corporate law academics, including Professor Peter Doralt, then Head of the Austrian Takeover Commission, enriched these debates with their insights and perspectives. It should, however, be acknowledged that many participants considered that the balance on occasion was not always correct and that excessive time was spent earlier in the Directive's life cycle on academic discussions rather than in negotiating the Commission's proposals. Of course, many of the participants in these meetings, whether at or beside the table, were senior staff at the national takeover regulators, including the UK Takeover Panel, and these individuals brought a depth of experience and expertise which contributed greatly to the final text of the Directive. Finally, the key role played by the Commission's representatives in reaching a consensus deserves recognition. Particularly in the final stages following the introduction of the Portuguese compromise, Commission officials played an increasingly important role. Karel Van Hulle, for example, was invited by the Italian presidency in Coreper to participate directly in the negotiations with the deputy representatives. This very unusual step reflected both the complexity of the issues to be agreed and the determination of the relevant parties to bring matters to a conclusion in as efficient a manner as possible.

Much time was spent during the drafting process on provisions which were anticipated to be likely to lead to problems in implementation. These included discussions on how differences of interpretation of 'matters relating to company law' and 'matters relating to the bid procedure' might cause problems for the operation of shared jurisdiction transactions (Article 4); the practical workings of the breakthrough rule and the calculation of the appropriate compensation which might arise (Article 11); and how the optionality arrangements might apply to US bidders (Article 12). In retrospect, these issues have not given rise to problems in interpreting or implementing the Directive. One provision which has worked better than expected is the requirement to establish a contact committee to facilitate harmonised application of the Directive 'through regular meetings dealing with practical problems arising in connection with its application' (Article 18). ESMA's Takeover Bids Network, subsequently renamed the 'Shareholder Transactions Working Group', became an excellent forum for representatives from the national competent authorities to meet once or twice a year to exchange supervisory experiences and discuss developments in the application of the Directive. This network has provided transparency and useful guidance on how Member States assess shareholder cooperation and acting in concert. Bringing together supervisors from different jurisdictions in this way leads to real cooperation and idea exchanges which increase the likelihood of harmonisation and greater ease in coordinating cross-border takeovers.

The complexity of the matters involved in this Directive, the political differences it exposed, and the disparate considerations to be included suggest that there would be little appetite amongst Member States to reopen the Directive. It is submitted that arriving at a consensus in the current divisive political climate would be likely to be even more problematic.

2

Basic Issues Surrounding the TOD's Transposition

Markus Roth, Klaus J. Hopt and Adam Opalski

2.1 INTRODUCTION

The Takeover Directive (TOD) of 2004[1] applies to listed companies having both their headquarters and listing in the European Union[2] and coordinates the law of the Member States relating to takeover bids for securities of companies. Initially titled the 13th Company Law Directive, the first proposals for the Takeover Directive date back to the 1980s, when a takeover wave emerged first in the US[3] and then Member States began to implement mostly voluntary takeover codes based on self-regulation and the European example of the UK Takeover Code.[4] The European Commission presented its first proposal for a Directive[5] in 1989,[6] a second proposal in 1996,[7] and the third proposal based on recommendations of the Winter group[8] in

[1] Parliament and Council Directive 2004/25/EC On Takeover Bids, 2004 O.J. (L142).

[2] Art. 1(1) TOD.

[3] Concerning Section 203 Delaware General Corporation Act Practicing Law Institute, see The New Delaware Takeover Statute, 1988; as early as the 1960s, the Williams Act 1968 provided for full disclosure of corporate equity ownership of securities under the Securities Exchange Act of 1934.

[4] The City Code on Takeovers and Mergers was first drawn up in 1969; P. Davies, *The Regulation of Takeovers and Mergers* (London: Sweet & Maxwell, 1976), p. 37; see also A. Johnston, *The City Take-Over Code* (Oxford: Oxford University Press, 1980).

[5] See Commission Recommendation 77/534/EEC concerning a European code of conduct relating to transactions in transferable securities, 1977, supplementary principle 17 (equal treatment of shareholders after a change of control).

[6] Commission, 'Proposal for a Thirteenth Council Directive on Company Law concerning takeover and other general bids', COM(88) 823 final (3 March 1989); see K. J. Hopt and E. Wymeersch (eds.), *European Takeovers* (London: Butterworths, 1992); N. Basaldua, 'Towards the Harmonization of ES-Member States' Regulations on Takeover Bids: The Proposal for a Thirteenth Council Directive on Company Law' (1989) 9 *Northwestern Journal of International Law and Business* 487.

[7] Commission, 'Proposal for a 13th European Parliament and Council Directive, 96/C 162/05, on company law concerning takeover bids', COM (95) 635 final (7 February 1996).

[8] Report of the High Level Group of Company Law Experts, on Issues Related to Takeover Bids, Brussels, 10 January 2002.

2002.[9] In the 1990s, Member States began to enact mandatory legislation on takeovers and kept doing so in the early 2000s,[10] when the takeover of Mannesmann by Vodafone changed the German attitude towards regulating takeovers and influenced the formulation of the Takeover Directive at European level.[11]

Both the Directive and later the Member States – in their national transpositions – had to adapt to the variety of capital markets, corporate governance regimes and differing degrees of stakeholder/shareholder orientation in the European Community of the early 2000s.[12] The Directive is to be seen in the context of the 1999 Financial Services Action Plan[13] and the Report of the High Level Group of Company Law Experts (chairman Jaap Winter) of 2001; and later the 2003 EU Company Law Action Plan referred to integrated financial markets and improved shareholder rights while remaining sensitive to social and environmental performance in view of long-term sustainable growth.[14] Due to its conception as a Framework Directive, Member States had the discretion to balance stakeholder interests and to frame an adequate national regime for the takeover market.

Core elements of the Takeover Directive deal with capital markets, company law and corporate governance issues.[15] The mandatory bid rule and the requirements for bids (information, supervision) are building blocks of the European capital market and to be attributed to securities law. Especially corporate governance issues were controversial during the discussions on the Directive;[16] the authority to make the decision to accept or to frustrate a bid is fundamental to company law in each

9 Commission, 'Proposal for a Directive of the European Parliament and of the Council on takeover bids', 2003 C 45 E/01 (2 October 2002).

10 See T. Baums and G. Thoma (eds.), *Takeover Laws in Europe*, loose-leaf, second delivery (Cologne: RWS, 2003); for the German Takeover Act, see also M. Peltzer and E. Voight (eds.), *Wertpapiererwerbs- und Übernahmegesetz*, German Securities Acquisition and Takeover Act, German–English Text (Cologne: Otto Schmidt, 2002).

11 B. Clarke and R. Skog, in this book, Chapter 1.

12 Generally, Gelter EU Company Law Harmonization between Convergence and Varieties of Capitalism, in H. Wells (ed.), *Research Handbook on the History of Corporate and Company Law* (Cheltenham: Elgar Publishing, 2018); see also ECGI Law Working Paper 355/2017; stressing market forces, M. Ventoruzzo, 'Europe's Thirteenth Directive and U.S. Takeover Regulation: Regulatory Means and Political and Economic Ends' (2006) 41 *Texas International Law Journal* 171, 220.

13 Commission, Implementing the Framework for Financial Markets: Action Plan, Brussels, COM (1999) 232 final, 1999.

14 Commission, Modernising Company Law and Enhancing Corporate Governance in the European Union – A Plan to Move Forward, Brussels, COM (2003) 284 final, 2003, p. 3; concerning squeeze-out and sell-out rights, p. 21.

15 S. Grundmann, 'The Structure of European Company Law: From Crisis to Boom' (2004) 5 *European Business Organization Law Review* 601, 633, describing organizational law as for the first time being closely linked to capital market law.

16 See, inter alia, C. Kirchner and R. Painter, 'European Takeover Law – Towards a European Modified Business Judgement Rule for Takeover Law' (2000) 1 *European Business Organization Law Review* 353 as compared to P. Mülbert and M. Birke, 'In Defense of Passivity – the Proper Role of a Target's Management in Response to a Hostile Tender Offer' (2000) 1 *European Business Organization Law Review* 445.

Member State and is subject to ongoing discussions in the Member States. Such authority might be granted either only to the shareholders[17] or also or solely to the board by allowing takeover defences. The final form of the Takeover Directive that was adopted abstained from providing a uniform rule and preserved the discretion of the Member States by restricting itself to minimum harmonization, and even this only in parts of the Directive. In its transposition, Member States may choose to go beyond minimum harmonization, an approach often referred to as gold-plating.

The goal of the Takeover Directive is Community-wide clarity and transparency in respect of the legal issues to be settled in the event of takeover bids.[18] The Directive aims at minority shareholder protection when control of the company is acquired,[19] which is to be achieved through a mandatory bid at a fair price and sell-out rights.[20] The mandatory bid rule as well as squeeze-out and sell-out rights are mandatory minimum standards. This does not include the vibrantly discussed board neutrality rule, which is not mandatory in the United States, but which is very much so in the UK.[21] The board neutrality rule and extending employee participation beyond other European legislative Acts are subject to full Member State discretion as mandatory provisions in national legislation. For Member State transposition of the Directive, besides traditional law principles and economic consequences, also the wider implications of the implementation of a takeover regime are to be reflected. The core issue for Member States in transposing the Directive is to balance the interests of the different stakeholders.

Several basic issues concerning the transposition of the Takeover Directive will be discussed in this contribution. First of all, Member States have to decide on the legal structure for the transposition and supervision of takeover bids (see Section 2.2). Member States have to choose the adequate legal instrument for the transposition. This might be inclusion into an existing Securities Act or a separate Takeover Act. Concerning the mandatory bid (see Section 2.3), there is no choice for Member States in principle, but Member States have to define a control mechanism which triggers the mandatory bid and, very important for the capital market, the pricing of the mandatory bid. Under the current version of the TOD, it is left to the Member States to design the mandatory bid and to implement a general framework for voluntary and mandatory bids (see Section 2.4). The TOD is applicable only to

17 Report of the High Level Group of Company Law Experts on Issues Related to Takeover Bids in the European Union, 2002, p. 20: principle of shareholder decision-making.

18 Recital 4 TOD. On the regulatory and agency problems of control transactions, see P. Davies, K. J. Hopt and W. G. Ringe, 'Control Transactions', in R. Kraakman et al. (ed.), *The Anatomy of Corporate Law*, 3rd ed. (Oxford: Oxford University Press 2017), ch. 8.

19 Recital 9, sentence 1 TOD.

20 On the economic theory behind mandatory bids, K. J. Hopt, 'European Takeover Reform of 2012/2013 – Time to Re-examine the Mandatory Bid' (2014) 15 *European Business Organization Law Review* 143 at 148 et seq., 167 et seq.

21 K. J. Hopt, 'Takeover Defenses in Europe: A Comparative, Theoretical and Policy Analysis' (2014) 20 *Columbia Journal of European Law* 249 at 254 et seq., 258 et seq.; on the economic theory behind the board neutrality rule,ibid. at 261 et seq., 263 et seq.; K. J. Hopt, *Europäisches Übernahmerecht* (Tübingen: Mohr Siebeck, 2013), p. 69 et seq., 73 et seq.

mandatory bids; Member States have to frame the general information given by the bidder and the time allowance for a bid.[22] Despite being a building block for the European capital market, uniform rules are mostly lacking. This is also true for worker participation (information and consultation of worker representatives)[23] at the target company. The Directive foresees a choice for Member States as to how and in parts whether to implement core corporate governance principles, such as the board neutrality rule and the breakthrough rule (see Section 2.5), and it foresees squeeze-out and sell-out rights (see Section 2.6).

2.2 GENERAL ASPECTS OF TRANSPOSING THE TOD INTO NATIONAL LAW

2.2.1 *Transposition and Scope of the TOD (Arts. 1, 2)*

2.2.1.1 Transposition of the Takeover Directive (Art. 21 TOD: Until 2006)

The transposition of the Takeover Directive was subject to an external study[24] by the European Commission.[25] The Takeover Bids Directive Assessment Report ('Assessment Report') was published in 2011 and comprised a total of then twenty-two Member States,[26] which accounted for 99 per cent of the market capitalization of EU-listed companies.[27] The Assessment Report focused on five main EU jurisdictions[28] – in alphabetical order, France, Germany, Italy, Spain and the United Kingdom; the Report is the central reference for this chapter. Despite Brexit, this entry will not be restricted to the four biggest Member States (France,[29] Germany,[30]

[22] Recital 14 TOD.

[23] Recital 23 TOD.

[24] The Takeover Bids Directive Assessment Report, 2011, undertaken by Marcuss Partners and the Centre for European Policy Studies (CEPS) for the European Commission (MARKT/2010/10/F). On the Assessment Report, Hopt, *Europäisches Übernahmerecht*, p. 16 et seq.

[25] Art 20 TOD. Revision of the Directive five years after the transposition date is prescribed in Art. 21 TOD.

[26] The United Kingdom later left the European Union.

[27] Assessment Report, 2011, p. 3.

[28] Ibid., p. 24 (scope and definitions).

[29] On the initial transposition, see I. Urbain-Parleani, 'The Implementation of the Thirteenth Directive 2004/25, Country Report on France', in T. Baums and A. Cahn (eds.), *Die Umsetzung der Übernahmerichtlinie in Europa* (Berlin: De Gruyter, 2006), p. 3.

[30] D. A. Verse, 'Selected Issues in German Takeover Law. Mandatory Bids, Minimum Pricing Rules', in H. Fleischer, H. Kanda, K. S. Kim and P. Mülbert (eds.), *German and East Asian Perspectives on Corporate and Capital Market Law: Investors versus Companies* (Tübingen: Mohr Siebeck, 2019), p. 143. Takeover Directive Transposition Act 8 July 2006, Federal Gazette 2006 I 1426; on the discussion, see C. H. Seibt and K. J. Heiser, 'Analyse der EU-Übernahmerichtlinie und Hinweise für eine Reform des deutschen Übernahmerechts' (2005), *Zeitschrift für Unternehmens- und Gesellschaftsrecht* 200; for legal texts, see T. Stohlmeier (ed.), *German Public Takeover Law*, 3rd ed. (The Hague: Wolters Kluwer, Law & Business, 2015).

Italy,[31] Spain[32]) but will also address the United Kingdom[33] as the role model for TOD as well as certain selected Member States such as Austria and Poland[34] and some Nordic countries (Sweden).[35] But at the same time it should be realized that Brexit has considerably changed the importance of the City Code on Takeovers and Mergers as a source of regulation and as a model for regulatory practice.[36]

As is usual, some Member States transposed the Directive with some delay and not within the time frame.[37] While Art. 21 TOD foresaw that Member States were to bring into force the laws, regulations and administrative provisions necessary to comply with TOD no later than 20 May 2006, six Member States transposed the Directive in 2007[38] and a further two in 2008.[39] However, when the Takeover Bids Directive Assessment Report was published in 2011, all Member States included in the Report[40] had transposed the Takeover Directive.[41] Since Art. 20 TOD foresaw the examination of the Takeover Directive five years after transposition (2006), this article may build on the published Assessment Report from 2011 as well as on other comparative studies and national reports.

With initial takeover rules and by transposing material law provisions of the Takeover Directive, Member States were framing the market and the supervisory

[31] On the discussion, see G. Ferrarini, 'Implementing the European Takeover Directive in Italy: Requirements and Options', in Baums and Cahn (eds.), *Die Umsetzung der Übernahmerichtlinie in Europa*, p. 101.

[32] N. Alcalde and I. Pérez-Soba, 'Has the EU Takeover Directive Improved Minority Shareholder Protection? The Spanish Evidence' (2016) 17 *European Business Organization Law Review* 261.

[33] D. Kershaw, *Principles of Takeover Regulation* (New York: Oxford University Press, 2016).

[34] T. Regucki, 'Polish Takeover Regulation' (2024) 25 *European Business Organization* 385.

[35] For specific country reports from a practitioner's perspective, see P. Van Houghten (ed.) *The European Takeover Directive and Its Implementation* (New York: Oxford University Press, 2009); S. Maul, D. Muffat-Jeadet and J. Simon (eds.), *Takeover Bids in Europe* (Freiburg: Memento, 2008); D. Van Gerven (ed.), *Common Legal Framework for Takeover Bids in Europe*, Volumes I and II (Cambridge: Cambridge University Press, 2008 and 2010). On the discussion in Sweden, see R. Skog, 'The Takeover Committee's Proposal for the Implementation of the EC Takeover Directive in Swedish Law', in Baums and Cahn (eds.), *Die Umsetzung der Übernahmerichtlinie in Europa*, p. 53; on the implementation, see the translation of Canter, Swedish Takeover Rules, 2007.

[36] On the City Code on Takeovers and Mergers as the source of regulation by the 2004 Takeover Directive, see Hopt, 'European Takeover Reform of 2012/2013 – Time to Re-examine the Mandatory Bid', at 153 et seq.

[37] See Commission Staff Working Document, 'Report on the implementation of the Directive on Takeover Bids', SEC (2007) 268 (21 February 2007).

[38] Assessment Report, 2011, p. 25: Belgium, Cyprus, Italy, Netherlands, Slovakia and Spain.

[39] Ibid.: Czech Republic

[40] Ibid., p. 24 (scope and definitions); p. 25 (transposition dates): Austria (2006), Belgium (2007), Cyprus (2007), Czech Republic (2008), Denmark (2006), Estonia (2008), France, Germany, Greece, Hungary, Ireland (all 2006), Italy (2007), Luxembourg (2006), Netherlands (2007), Poland (2005, complete transposition 2022), Portugal (2006), Romania (2005), Slovakia, Spain (both 2007), Sweden, UK (both 2006).

[41] Ibid., p. 25; on the countries comprised; p. 24, including twenty-two countries of the then European Union; not covered were Latvia, Lithuania, Bulgaria, Slovenia, Malta; Croatia was not yet an EU member (joined in 2013); the UK later left the European Union.

bodies. Some Member States transposed the Directive in various legislative Acts.[42] The Assessment Report stated in 2011 that transposition of the Directive was complete,[43] but it did not examine in detail whether the transposition was in line with and covered every respect of the Directive. Only the Finnish Code was questioned as an adequate transposition due to its non-binding nature,[44] although Art. 1 TOD explicitly mentions Codes of Best Practices. Due to the often vague language of the Directive, the Assessment Report assumes some gaps,[45] especially concerning takeover bids affecting more than one (Member) state. The Commission reflected on the external study and considered reforms,[46] but did not immediately propose changes to the Directive.[47]

The Takeover Directive, which was first discussed as the 13th Company Law Directive,[48] covers company law but also securities law (material securities law and supervisory law) and labour law (worker participation). In transforming the Takeover Directive, Member States adjusted or introduced at national level a special Takeover Act (as in Austria, Germany, Ireland and Sweden) or a Takeover Code (United Kingdom and Sweden); adopted the takeover rules in the general securities law (France, Italy, Netherlands, Poland and Spain); or adopted national company law (Czech Republic, Netherlands).[49] In the UK and in Sweden, the Takeover Code, as the classical piece of self-regulation, maintained its central position.[50] In most Member States, in addition to central pieces of legislation (e.g. a takeover Act or general securities law), administrative Acts were also adopted by ministries, supervisory agencies or private supervisory bodies.

2.2.1.2 Scope of the Directive (Art. 1)

According to Art. 1 TOD,[51] the Directive applies to takeover bids for securities of companies which are admitted to trading on a regulated market in one or more

42 Providing examples from the French and Italian takeover regulation, Assessment Report, 2011, p. 58; for worker participation in Germany see Section 2.4.3.

43 Assessment Report, 2011, p. 25, 58.

44 Ibid., p. 58.

45 Ibid., p. 92.

46 Commission, Report, 'Application of Directive 2004/25/EC on takeover bids', COM (2012) 347 final (28 June 2012).

47 Proposal by Hopt, 'European Takeover Reform of 2012/2013 – Time to Re-examine the Mandatory Bid'.

48 Transposition also in company law in the Netherlands, R. van het Kaar and J. Cremers, 'Implementation of the Takeover Bids Directive in the Netherlands', in J. Cremers and S. Vitols (eds.), *Takeovers With or Without Worker Voice* (Brussels: ETUI, 2016), p. 181, 182, and in Belgium.

49 In Estonia, also the board neutrality rule is transposed in securities law, A. Nirgi and S. Papp, 'Estonia' in Van Gerven (ed.), *Common Legal Framework for Takeover Bids in Europe*, Vol. I, p. 145, 159.

50 However, the Takeover Panel became a state body; see Section 2.5.5.

51 Article by Article Commentary of the Takeover Directive by S. Maul and L. Furtwengler in P. Kindler and J. Lieder, *European Corporate Law* (Baden-Baden: Nomos, 2021).

Member States for companies which are governed by the laws of a Member State. Both the headquarters and the listing have to be in the European Union; the Assessment Report portrays this as one of the few gaps in the Directive.[52] Since the focus of the Takeover Directive is on the European Union, not the national market, transposition focusing on the national market may result in further gaps for cross-country listings. Also, other Member States are to be covered by national transpositions; therefore, difficulties arise when Member States transpose the Directive by referring to a special corporate governance regime such as the German two-tier board system, which has a supervisory board and a management board for defence measures.[53]

Although the focus of the Takeover Directive is on the capital market and most Member States transposed the Directive in the general securities law, it might be appropriate to extend the scope of national transpositions also to EU companies having non-EU listings. This is relevant not only for listings in the US.[54] The Assessment Report referred to Swiss companies and questioned whether such companies listed in France that are said to have incorporated a mandatory takeover bid rule in their articles of association provide full protection due to enforcement issues for company's shareholders.[55] On the other hand, since securities listed in the European Union are covered, Member States which focus on their securities market irrespective of the origin of the listed companies have an incentive also to include non-EU companies listed in the Member State.

2.2.2 *Initial Takeover Act versus Adoption of Existing Rules*

2.2.2.1 Pre-existing Takeover Regulation in Most Member States

Most Member States – notably the bigger Member States (France, Germany,[56] Italy, Poland,[57] Spain and initially the UK) but also other Member States like Austria,[58]

[52] Assessment Report, 2011, p. 92.

[53] Sections 1, 33 German Takeover Act. The European Commission usually confines itself to ensuring that the rules apply to the two-tier system as well, without really taking into account its specificities. On convergence of the systems and remaining path dependencies, K. J. Hopt, 'Der Aufsichtsrat' (2019) *Zeitschrift für Unternehmens- und Gesellschaftsrecht* 507.

[54] For German companies, Linde and BionTech should be named in this respect.

[55] Assessment Report, 2011, p. 92.

[56] See J. Adolff, B. Meister, C. Randell and K.-D. Stephan (eds.), *Public Company Takeovers in Germany* (Munich: C.H. Beck, 2002); G. Apfelbacher, G. Barthelmess, T. Buhl and C. Dryander (eds.), *German Takeover Law* (Munich: C.H. Beck, 2002); J. Payne (ed.) *Takeovers in German and English Law* (Oxford: Hart, 2002).

[57] Regucki, 'Polish Takeover Regulation', 390–392.

[58] S. Kalss, 'The Austrian Law in Public Offers and Takeovers (2000) 1 *European Business Organization Law Review* 479.

Ireland[59] and Sweden[60] – had already regulated takeovers before the Takeover Directive was adopted.[61] The core concept of the Directive, the mandatory bid rule, was enacted in all larger Member States (with the exemption of the Netherlands; see Section 2.3.1) while differences in takeover-defence regulations remained untouched by the Directive and subject to almost free Member State regulation. The Takeover Directive mirrors the variation of pre-existing takeover regulation in Member States with its own variations and exemptions. A comparative survey was undertaken before the Austrian Takeover Act was introduced in 1998;[62] alongside the takeover regimes of European Countries accessible in English,[63] there were in addition practitioner's guides which gave an easily accessible overview on the takeover law landscape in the European Union.[64]

2.2.2.2 Adaptations and Newly Introduced Takeover Regimes

Since most Member States introduced takeover rules during the discussions on the Takeover Directive, the vast majority simply had to revise existing legal regimes. From the Member States covered by the Assessment Report, only three (Cyprus, Luxembourg, Greece) had no takeover regulation before transposing the Directive.[65] The centerpiece of the Takeover Directive binding the Member States, the mandatory bid rule (Art. 5 TOD), had been enacted in most Member States, but was not seldom modified by enacting the Takeover Directive.[66] However, there had been no mandatory bid rule in the Netherlands.[67] Towards the board neutrality rule, there were different approaches before the adoption of the TOD in Member States. During the initial transposition of the Takeover Directive, most states adhered to their previous approach, but later, with France and Italy, important Member States changed the rules for the boards of target companies (see Section 2.5).

59 B. Clarke, *Takeover and Mergers Law in Ireland* (Dublin: Round Hall, Sweet & Maxwell, 1999).
60 Skog, 'The Takeover Committee's Proposal for the Implementation of the EC Takeover Directive in Swedish Law', p. 53, 54–55: NBK takeover rules and statements of the Swedish Securities Council (self-regulation).
61 All countries other than Poland are covered in Baums and Thoma (eds.), *Takeover Laws in Europe*.
62 P. Doralt, C. Nowotny and M. Schauer (eds.), *Takeover-Recht* (Vienna: WUV Service Fachverlag, 1997).
63 English translations (2003): Baums and Thoma (eds.), *Takeover Laws in Europe* (Austria, Belgium, Denmark, France, Germany, Greece, Finland, Ireland, Italy, Luxembourg, Netherlands, Portugal, Spain, Sweden, United Kingdom and also Switzerland).
64 'A Practitioner's Guide to Takeovers and Mergers in the European Union, City & Financial Publishing', 3rd ed. (London: City & Financial Publishing, 2001).
65 Assessment Report, 2011, p. 25, 62.
66 Ibid., p. 64–66, 121–163.
67 Ibid., p. 66.

In some countries, there was a gradual transposition[68] of the Takeover Directive.[69] Nevertheless, according to the Assessment Report, all national transformation was compliant with the Directive, with some concerns expressed on Finland's partially non-binding[70] rules on takeovers.[71] Another Member State with incomplete initial transposition was Poland.[72] The two-threshold system of the mandatory bid adopted under Polish law was clearly incompatible with the Directive (see Section 2.3.1). Moreover, the initial silence of the Polish legislature on board neutrality could not be regarded as a full and proper implementation of the Directive.[73] The opt-in model for board neutrality was formally introduced in Poland in 2009 (but could not play any role as the option was linked to the second threshold of 66 per cent of votes when control was already acquired by the bidder). Full implementation of the Directive occurred in Poland only in 2022.[74]

2.2.2.3 Gold-Plating versus Minimum Standards

In the context of the Takeover Directive, and in light of more ambitious proposals on the harmonization of the European takeover law,[75] most scholars – at least when the Directive was adopted – called for gold-plating the European minimum harmonization. In the Assessment Report, Art. 3(2)(b) TOD, which explicitly allows for more intensive national regulation, is referred to as permitting such gold-plating.[76] This can be contrasted with the growing emphasis on over-regulation generally. In other contexts, such as the European Structural and Investment Funds, which provide a total investment of 731 billion Euros fostering socio-economic convergence, territorial cohesion, social Europe and a smooth green and digital transformation, gold-plating is associated with extra requirements and administrative burden.[77] Due to the concept of a Framework Directive, Member States have considerable discretion in transposing

[68] Ibid., p. 58.

[69] On the impact of the Directive on national law, see also the country reports in J. Grant, *European Takeover: The Art of Acquisition* (London: Euromoney Books, 2005).

[70] Assessment Report, 2011, p. 58, 91 (addressing the Helsinki Takeover Code in more detail) and 93 (revision of the Finnish system announced); see Securities Markets Act, 14 December 2012.

[71] On Finland, see V. Kajala, 'Takeover Rules at the Intersection of Company Law and Securities Law', in *Festschrift in honour of Rolf Skog* (Stockholm: Norstedts Juridik, 2021), p. 687, and the Helsinki Takeover Code 2022.

[72] Regucki, 'Polish Takeover Regulation', 394–396. Referring to circumvention, Assessment Report, 2011, p. 91.

[73] See the earlier contribution of M. Bobrzynski, K. Oplustil and M. Spyra, in Maul, Muffat-Jeadet and Simon (eds.), *Takeover Bids in Europe*, no. 2750, in no. 2751 referring to a draft law.

[74] Regucki, 'Polish Takeover Regulation', 409–410 (critical of the 50 per cent threshold; see Section 2.3.2.1).

[75] V. Edwards, 'The Directive on Takeover Bids – Not Worth the Paper It's Written On?' (2004) 1 *European Company and Financial Law Review* 416.

[76] Assessment Report, 2011, p. 96 names dual thresholds, content of the offer document and rights of employees as examples.

[77] 4th Meeting of the High Level Expert Group on Monitoring Simplification for Beneficiaries of ESI Funds, 16 November 2016, Interim Report on Gold-Plating.

the Directive. Member States using their discretion have to balance interests and find practical solutions for companies, their stakeholders and financial markets. Gold-plating might aim to prevent circumventing the principles of the Takeover Directive by similar actions to gain or foster control of a company.

Since the UK permits schemes of arrangement also for restructuring the member structure and thereby gaining control of a company, the UK Takeover Code also contains a section on schemes of arrangement.[78] In Sweden, the Takeover Code applies also to mergers.[79] Furthermore, some Member States introduced a mandatory bid rule not only in terms of acquiring, but also as regards fostering control. Various Member States introduced not only a threshold for acquiring control but also additional circumstances triggering the obligation to publish a public offer. Some Member States introduced two thresholds (for example, 30 and 50 per cent); others refer to the acquisition of a certain percentage of voting shares. Concerning company law, the board neutrality rules in the UK are applied also during a scheme of arrangement,[80] and in Sweden they apply during a merger. Germany gold-plated in respect of worker participation,[81] going beyond mere information pursuant to Art. 15 TOD and general German board-level codetermination.

2.2.3 *Definitions and General Principles (Arts. 2, 3 TOD)*

2.2.3.1 Limited Number of Definitions

The Takeover Directive contains a small number of definitions, including the bid, a takeover bid, offeree company, persons acting in concert, securities, parties to a bid, and multiple-voting securities (Art. 2(1) TOD); as regards acting in concert, Art. 2(2) TOD refers also to Directive 2001/34/EC (later revised by the Transparency Directive). Member States may not deviate from the definitions in the Takeover Directive but may extend their scope. The German Takeover Act defines bids according to the definition of the Directive (voluntary and mandatory) but also in general for the acquisition of securities. The acting in concert definition lacks clarity[82] and is furthermore not coherent in the TOD and in the Transparency Directive, relevant in situations potentially resulting in the duty to issue a mandatory bid. With the definition on multiple voting, the Takeover Directive deviates from the 'one share, one vote' rule.[83]

78 In detail see Jennifer Payne, in this book, Chapter 13.

79 G. Nyström, R. Ohlsson, E. Sjöman and R. Skog, *The Swedish Takeover Code: An annotated commentary* (New York: Informa Law from Routledge, 2017).

80 See Payne, in this book, Chapter 13.

81 On works councils, see Section 106 (3) No. 9a and Section 109a Works Councils Act.

82 Assessment Report, 2011, p. 62.

83 On dual-class shares in Sweden and takeovers, R. Skog, 'The European Union's Proposed Takeover Directive: the "Breakthrough" Rule and the Swedish System of Dual Class Common Stock' (2004) *Scandinavian Studies in Law* 293; altering the European approach concerning

2.2.3.2 General Principles in Art. 3 TOD

Member States have to decide whether and how to transpose the general principles mentioned in Art. 3 TOD,[84] which might be classified as company law and securities law principles, with only some referring to the specifics of a takeover bid. According to Art. 3(2) TOD, Member States are to ensure compliance with these principles. They must ensure that the minimum requirements set out in the Directive are observed, and they may lay down additional conditions and provisions more stringent than the TOD for the regulation of bids. When the general principles of Art. 3(1) are respected, Member States may derogate in order to take account of circumstances determined at national level.

General principles attributable to company law are the principles of equal treatment[85] and acting in the interest of the company as a whole. The board of an offeree company must act in the interests of the company as a whole;[86] this includes the protection of other stakeholders.[87] General principles attributable to securities law on the whole concern not creating a false market[88] and having sufficient resources for the proposed action. The offeror is permitted to announce a bid only after ensuring that he or she can fulfil the bid in cash or other types of consideration.[89] That means that national legislatures might require a guarantee to be provided by the offeror.[90]

In addition, there are two principles for the specific situation of a takeover. There should be sufficient time for a properly informed decision on the bid, and the board of the offeree company should be hindered only as long as necessary. Sufficient time and notice provided to the holders of the securities of an offeree company should enable them to reach a properly informed decision on the bid.[91]

dual-class shares recently, the final compromise concerning a Directive on multiple-vote share structures, 14 February 2024, Interinstitutional File 2022/0406(COD).

84 For an international comparison, see Assessment Report, 2011, p. 107–108. There are no such principles in the German Takeover Act.

85 Art. 3(1)(a) TOD; for general company law, see ECJ Case C-101/08, *Audiolux SA e.a. v. Groupe Bruxelles Lambert SA and others* [2009], along with the note by F. M. Mucciarelli, 'Equal Treatment of Shareholders and European Union Law' (2010) *European Company and Financial Law Review* 158; in Germany, see the general rule in the Stock Corporation Act (Section 53a, equal treatment of shareholders); in Poland, the similar general rule was enacted in the Code of Commercial Companies (Art. 20).

86 Art. 3(1)(a) TOD; in Germany, there is no specific rule but one finds a common understanding in company law.

87 Art. 3(1)(c); Assessment Report, 2011, p. 104–106.

88 Art. 3(1)(d) TOD.

89 Art. 3(1)(e) TOD.

90 Assessment Report, 2011, p. 100; bank guarantee, French law; in Germany, as regards cash, Section 13(1)2 Takeover Act.

91 Art. 3(1)(b) TOD.

The offeree company must not be hindered in its affairs for longer than is reasonable by a bid for its securities.[92] There is a cross-reference to Art. 7 TOD (time allowed for acceptance); Art. 7(1) mentions this principle and, if implemented, allows extensions of the ten-week period as the longest period mentioned for normal circumstances.

2.2.4 *General Considerations for Member States in Transposing the Takeover Directive*

In transposing or adapting national takeover regulations, Member States set national legal conditions for a takeover market within the framework of the Takeover Directive. The main legal provisions have different implications concerning the facilitation of takeovers. While in terms of its overall effects the mandatory bid rule is making takeover bids more costly and is therefore negative for the takeover market, board neutrality and the breakthrough rule tend to facilitate takeover bids. Member States and the European Union itself have an interest in ensuring that adequate takeover markets are in place for transforming established businesses and to allow innovators to achieve scale at a fast pace. In framing national takeover markets, it is necessary to take account of other jurisdictions, such as the US, due to global competition and the relevance of takeover for resilient and sustainable national economies.

In transposing the Directive and adapting national takeover law to more recent legal developments, Member States also have to balance the interests of employees and other stakeholders.[93] Member States differ in their approach towards employee participation in corporate boards and the powers of works councils. Various corporate governance regimes are in place.[94] Taking national interest into account led some Member States to a less takeover-friendly regulation after the initial transposition of the Directive. Especially Member States which incorporated the mandatory bid rule but not the board neutrality rule tend to have a hostile takeover environment and have to reflect on other means to enhance the consolidation of established businesses and accelerate the growth of innovators.[95]

92 Art. 3(1)(f) TOD.

93 Generally, Gelter EU Company Law Harmonization between Convergence and Varieties of Capitalism, in H. Wells (ed.), *Research Handbook on the History of Corporate and Company Law* (Cheltenham: Elgar Publishing, 2018); see also ECGI Law Working Paper 355/2017.

94 Critical of harmonization, J. L. Hansen, 'The Directive on Takeover Bids: Unwanted Harmonisation of Corporate Law', in Birkmose et al. (eds.), *The European Financial Market in Transition* (Alphen aan den Rijn: Kluwer Law International, 2012), p. 29.

95 On such choices, see also M. Gatti, 'Optionality Arrangements and Reciprocity in the European Takeover Directive' (2005) *European Business Organization Law Review* 553.

2.2.5 *Supervisory Authority (Art. 4 TOD)*

The Takeover Directive concedes more freedom concerning supervisory authorities than in the field of substantive law.[96] Member States are to designate the authority or authorities competent to supervise bids for the purposes of the rules which they make or introduce pursuant to this Directive, Art. 4(1)1 TOD. The authorities thus designated must, according to Art. 4(1)2 TOD, be either public authorities, associations or private bodies recognized by national law or public authorities expressly empowered for that purpose by national law. Until now, all Member States designated authorities based in the respective Member States[97] and not joint or European authorities as is done for banking supervision. This is a second-best approach, given the aim of the Takeover Directive to contribute to a European capital market. The Takeover Directive indeed allows for a common or even a European supervisory authority, something which has not yet been erected and is therefore until now only a theoretical possibility and not a real option for Member States.[98] ESMA already has a limited role, having harmonized to some degree national practices concerning acting in concert, based on the cooperation provision in Art. 4(4) TOD.[99]

Currently, most Member States rely on a public body such as a supervisory authority, whether a separate body,[100] the general financial supervisory authority[101] or even the central bank. A private body exists in two of the most active European capital markets, in Sweden and in the UK. In the UK, as well as in Ireland, there is a Takeover Panel. The Irish Takeover Panel is regulated in the Takeover Panel Act[102] and issues takeover rules.[103] The Irish Takeover Panel is a public company, but private associations nominate directors.[104] In Austria, the Takeover Commission is a public body, but it is equipped with nominees of private institutions. In Sweden, supervisory authority was given in principle to the financial supervisory authority (Finansinspectionen), a public body, but according to the Act on Public Takeover

96 M. Winner, 'Übernahmerecht – Die europäische Perspektive', in R. Veil, H. C. Grigoleit and M. Habersack (eds.), *Öffentliche Unternehmensübernahmen* (Tübingen: Mohr Siebeck, 2022), p. 135, 145.

97 In the UK, the Takeover Panel is a state body resulting from the transposition of the Takeover Directive, Kershaw, *Principles of Takeover Regulation*, 3.02, p. 66; A. Johnston, 'Takeover Regulation: Historical and Theoretical Perspectives on the City Code' (2007) 66 *Cambridge Law Review* 422, 447.

98 N. Moloney, *EU Securities and Financial Markets Regulation*, 4th ed. (Oxford: Oxford University Press, 2024), p. 56–57.

99 Proposal to strengthen the role of ESMA in the takeover context: Hopt, 'European Takeover Reform of 2012/2013 – Time to Re-examine the Mandatory Bid', 161.

100 Kalss, 'The Austrian Law in Public Offers and Takeovers, 506.

101 Germany: Section 4 German Takeover Act; Poland: Section 77a–77c of the Act on Public Offering.

102 Irish Takeover Panel Act, 1997.

103 Irish Takeover Panel Act 1997, Takeover Rules 2022 ("Takeover Rules").

104 Section 6 Irish Takeover Panel Act.

Offers on the Stock Market, Finansinspectionen[105] has delegated certain duties to the Swedish Securities Council,[106] a private body. Such split authority between Finansinspectionen and the Swedish Securities Council is presumably efficient, given the activity on the Swedish financial and takeover market. Generally, Member States have to assign supervisors sufficient powers.[107] Since the enactment of the Takeover Directive, the role of the supervisory agencies and the relevance, also time-wise, of the various regulatory procedures have gained much more importance than before. Enforcement has become a major concern.[108]

2.2.6 *Reform Issues Not or Not Fully Taken Up by the Takeover Directive*

Numerous reforms mentioned by the Commission or put forward in the discussion have not yet been taken up:[109] (1) extensions to the mandatory bid (definition of the controlling majority, calculation of the minimum price, more clarity on the exceptions); (2) further mandatory offers for acquisitions of between 30 and 50 per cent (low-balling, creeping in); (3) acting in concert; (4) simplification of share exchanges; (5) more harmonization of board neutrality and the breakthrough rule; (6) recognition of deal protection agreements; (7) harmonization of takeover squeeze-outs; (8) greater transparency of voting/share ownership (in particular for cash-settled swaps/contracts for difference and similar financial instruments) and harmonization of the sanctions for violations of the law (in particular the loss of voting rights and high fines); and (9) introduction of a 'put up or shut up' rule along the lines of the reform of the UK City Code on Takeovers and Mergers of 19 September 2011.

Other reform requests from practice have concerned, for instance, the scope of application of the Directive (registered office/administrative headquarters), the supervisory body and the applicable law (Art. 4), the disclosure of information in the context of due diligence as extended to the bidder and to co-bidding bidders and, more generally, unresolved questions about the relationship between the Takeover Directive and the Market Abuse Directive, at least as regards disclosure of inducement fees, exclusion of directors with conflicts of interest in the opinion of the board pursuant to Art. 9, ambiguities in cross-border takeovers as to the relationship between the Takeover Directive and the Prospectus Directive; and, finally, issues relating to the law of corporate groups.

[105] Finansinspectionen's Regulatory Code; Finansinspectionen's regulations regarding operations on market places, FFFS 2007:17, chapter 14.

[106] See R. Skog and E. Sjöman, 'The Swedish Securities Council: A Takeover Panel, and More' (2014) *European Company and Financial Law Review* 1; chapter 7, Section 10 Swedish Takeovers Act (FFFS 2006:451).

[107] Assessment Report, 2011, p. 92.

[108] On takeover and securities law enforcement, P. Davies, K. J. Hopt and W. G. Ringe, *Control Transactions* (Oxford: Oxford University Press, 2017), chapter 9.2; P. Agstner, 'EU Takeover Regulation: Some "Hot" Research Topics' (2024) *SSRN*.

[109] See Hopt, *Europäisches Übernahmerecht*, p. 24 et seq., with further references.

2.3 MANDATORY BID TRIGGERED BY ACQUIRING CONTROL

2.3.1 *The Concept of the Mandatory Bid Rule*

The mandatory bid rule is supposed to protect minority shareholders, in conjunction with the fair pricing of mandatory bids.[110] Most EU countries had a pre-existing mandatory bid rule,[111] while the mandatory bid rule was introduced by transposing the Directive in Cyprus, Luxembourg and the Netherlands.[112] The mandatory bid rule is not a European peculiarity, despite the fact that federal US securities law does not impose such an obligation on shareholders of listed companies. There are similar provisions in some US states[113] and also in the other countries[114] dealt with in the Assessment Report,[115] notably China,[116] India,[117] Japan[118] and Switzerland.[119]

Some Member States implemented a mandatory bid rule only shortly before the Takeover Directive was adopted. Among them were Sweden[120] and Germany, which in 2002 first introduced its binding Securities and Acquisition and Takeover Act (Takeover Act).[121] By contrast, the Netherlands and Luxembourg, two Member States with vibrant capital markets, introduced the mandatory bid rule for the first time when transposing the Takeover Directive.[122] The mandatory bid rule was altered by transposition of the Directive, inter alia, in the Czech Republic and Poland.[123] In recent years, critique of the concept behind the mandatory bid rule has

110 Recital 9 TOD. Cf. Hopt, 'European Takeover Reform of 2012/2013 – Time to Re-examine the Mandatory Bid', 166 et seq.; on the economic theory of the mandatory bid with its pros and the cons, Hopt, *Europäisches Übernahmerecht*, p. 33 et seq.

111 Assessment Report, 2011, p. 64–66: nineteen of twenty-two countries included in the study (among them Germany) previously had such a rule. See the earlier Commission Recommendation (77/534) of 25 July 1977, based on the Pennington Report, Report on Takeovers and other Bids, doc. XI/56/74-E.

112 Assessment Report, 2011, p. 64, 66; on p. 27 and 67, also Germany is named (falsely).

113 N. Andronikos, 'A US lawyer's perspective on the EU Takeover Directive', in Van Gerven (ed.), *Common Legal Framework for Takeover Bids in Europe*, Vol. I, p. 61, 2.46, 57.

114 For Asian perspectives, see U. Varottil and W. Y. Wan (eds.), *Comparative Takeover Regulation, Global and Asian Perspectives* (Cambridge: Cambridge University Press, 2018).

115 Assessment Report, 2011, p. 163–166.

116 See W. Cai, 'The Mandatory Bid Rule in China' (2011) 12 *European Business Organization Law Review* 653.

117 Security and Exchange Board of India (SEBI), 'Substantial Acquisition of Shares and Takeovers Regulations 2011', LAD-NRO/GN/2011-12/24/30181 (last amended on 6 March 2017).

118 See J. Lee, 'The Current Barriers to Corporate Takeovers in Japan: Do the UK Takeover Code and the EU Takeover Directive Offer a Solution?' (2017) 18 *European Business Organization Law Review* 761.

119 Art. 135 Financial Market Infrastructure Act.

120 Critical of its introduction in Sweden, R. Skog, *Does Sweden Need a Mandatory Bid Rule? A Critical Analysis* (Stockholm: Juristförlaget, 1995).

121 See Verse, 'Selected Issues in German Takeover Law. Mandatory Bids, Minimum Pricing Rules', 147–152.

122 Assessment Report, 2011, p. 66.

123 Ibid., p. 27, 64, 66; also later in 2022, see Regucki, 'Polish Takeover Regulation', 392–394.

been growing,[124] and it is stressed that the Takeover Directive did not create a level playing field in European capital markets.[125]

2.3.2 *Acquiring Control by a Single Bidder (Art. 5(1, 3) TOD)*

2.3.2.1 The Concept of Control in Art. 5(1) and Art. 5(3) TOD

Generally, there is discretion for Member States as to how to transpose the mandatory bid rule and in defining when control is acquired. According to Art. 5(1)1 TOD, a mandatory bid is required when control is acquired. According to Art. 5(3) TOD, the percentage of voting rights which confers control for the purpose of Art. 5(1) and the method of its calculation are to be determined by rules of the Member State in which the company has its registered office. Despite initial concerns,[126] harmonization was reached without prescribing a uniform threshold in the Takeover Directive since nearly all Member States introduced a threshold in the small range of 30% up to one-third. Without naming a specific threshold, in Estonia a concept of actual control is implemented, while the only apparent outlier is Poland, which introduced in 2022 a 50% threshold.[127]

A significant number of Member States implemented a threshold of one-third or of 33%, most Member States implementing a 30% threshold.[128] According to the Assessment Report, of the twenty-two surveyed countries, twelve Member States (Austria, Belgium, Cyrus, Czech Republic, Finland, France, Germany, Ireland, Italy, the Netherlands, Sweden and the United Kingdom) introduced a threshold of 30%, while initially seven countries (Greece, Hungary, Luxembourg, Portugal, Romania, Slovakia and initially Poland) introduced a threshold of 33% or of a third (33⅓ per cent).[129] Three surveyed countries introduced a more complex threshold, by referring to actual control (Estonia)[130] or by a mixed approach featuring both a threshold (Spain: 30%; Denmark: one-third of the voting rights) and the exercise of a

[124] M. Habersack, 'Non-frustration Rule and Mandatory Bid Rule – Cornerstones of European Takeover Law?' (2018) *European Company and Financial Law Review* 1; J. L. Hansen, 'The Mandatory Bid Rule: Still Unnecessary, Unjustifiable and Inefficient After All These Years', in *Festschrift in honour of Rolf Skog* (Stockholm: Norstedts Juridik, 2021), p. 509. On the UK, Kershaw, *Principles of Takeover Regulation* (seen 33), 8.43 (p. 255); see also the earlier contribution of L. Enriques, 'The Mandatory Bid Rule in the Takeover Directive: Harmonization Without Foundation?' (2004) *European Company and Financial Law Review* 440.

[125] M. Winner, 'Does the European Union Have a Mandatory Bid Rule?', in *Festschrift in honour of Rolf Skog* (Stockholm: Norstedts Juridik, 2021), p. 1179, 1195.

[126] Edwards, 'The Directive on Takeover Bids – Not Worth the Paper It's Written On?', 439.

[127] Regucki, 'Polish Takeover Regulation', 405–409.

[128] Assessment Report, 2011, p. 39

[129] Ibid., p. 38–39.

[130] A. Nirgi and S. Papp, 'Estonia', in Van Gerven (ed.), *Common Legal Framework for Takeover Bids in Europe*, Vol. I, p. 145, 150, 6.15.

controlling influence over the company. Since voting (and not necessarily also attendance) in general meetings rose, voting rights of 30%, 33% or 33⅓% do not necessarily constitute a majority in the general meeting.

Some Member States implemented a second threshold of 50% or more. Finland implemented thresholds of 30% and 50%, Portugal of 33⅓% and 50%. Poland initially introduced thresholds of 33% and 66% (however, only exceeding 66% of the votes triggered the obligation of the bidder to offer the acquisition of all remaining shares in the company; exceeding 33% obliged the bidder to acquire merely up to 66% of shares). This model was clearly incompatible with the Directive and was replaced in 2022; now a single threshold of 50% applies.[131] Another solution was adopted in Estonia, where actual control is required.[132] In Hungary, besides the generally used threshold of 33%, a lower threshold of 25% applies, if no other shareholder in the target company holds at least 10% of the voting rights.[133] Thresholds lower than 30% are implemented in some US states[134] and internationally in Australia, Canada and India. Member States generally foresee the same threshold for all companies, but in Italy, there is a different threshold for SMEs, subject also to the articles of association of the SMEs.[135]

2.3.2.2 Corporate Governance of the Bidder

Unlike the Company Law Directive for mergers,[136] the Takeover Directive contains no rules concerning the authority of the board or the general meeting to issue a bid. Therefore, the corporate governance regime and general principles of company law in the Member States apply as long as no special provisions are in place. The general rule sees power vested in the board in the one-tier system or in the management board in the two-tier system, subject to the consent of the supervisory board. In the UK, a substantial transaction representing 25 per cent of the gross assets, market value, profits or gross capital requires a resolution of the general meeting.[137] In Germany, the Holzmüller rules were not applicable in the Bayer/Monsanto case, which for its part resulted in heavy losses for shareholders of the offeree company Bayer, who were not involved in the decision but would likely have rejected the acquisition.[138]

131 Regucki, 'Polish Takeover Regulation', 405–409.
132 Assessment Report, 2011, p. 38–39.
133 Section 68(1)(a) Hungarian Capital Markets Act, J. de Servigny and Z. Fekete, 'Hungary', in Van Gerven (ed.), *Common Legal Framework for Takeover Bids in Europe*, Vol. I, p. 214.
134 15 Pennsylvania Consolidated Statutes §§ 2543(a), 2544 (right to receive payment).
135 Art. 106 I–*ter* Consolidated Law on Finance.
136 Art. 93 Company Law Directive.
137 FCA Listing Rules 10; on the effects, M. Becht, A. Polo and S. Rossi, 'Does Mandatory Shareholder Voting Prevent Bad Acquisitions?' (2016) 29 *The Review of Financial Studies* 3035.
138 With proposals concerning the German Stock Corporation Act and the German Corporate Governance Code, K.-D. Stephan and C. Strenger, 'Die Zuständigkeit der Hauptversammlung

2.3.3 *Acquisition of Control by Acting in Concert (Art. 5(1) TOD)*

Control must not be acquired by a single person. Acting in concert (Art. 5(1) TOD) is one of the hot spots not only in takeover law but also in securities law, as a result of the Transparency Directive.[139] The concepts in the Takeover Directive and in the Transparency Directive differ. The Takeover Directive defines acting in concert as aiming to acquire control of the company (Art. 2(1)(d) TOD), and the acting-in-concert provisions aim to prevent circumventing the mandatory bid requirement through the collective action of persons who do not by themselves exert control, holding less than 30 per cent. By contrast, the Transparency Directive's Article 10(a) focuses on an agreement which obliges a concerted exercise of voting rights. The Commission mentioned in the Revision of the Directive acting in concert as the first topic for reform[140] and called for a clarification of the concept of acting in concert at EU level. Later, ESMA issued a statement on acting in concert.[141]

According to the Assessment Report, the UK and Italy, as primary jurisdictions, followed the definition in the TOD, while France, Germany and Spain, also as primary jurisdictions, added the concept of the Transparency Directive.[142] Among the other jurisdictions covered, eight Member States were identified as operating under the definition of the Takeover Directive,[143] six Member States operated under the approach of adding the concept of the Transparency Directive,[144] while three were labelled as intermediates.[145] Acting in concert is dealt with in detail in another contribution[146] and was subject to court decisions, inter alia, in Germany[147] and Austria.[148]

bei Strukturveränderungen – ein anlassbedingter Vorschlag' (2017) *Die Aktiengesellschaft* 346, and J. Redenius-Hövermann and C. Strenger, 'Zur Akzeptanz des Deutschen Corporate Governance Kodex in DAX-40' (2023) *Zeitschrift für Wirtschaftsrecht* 2121, 2128.

139 See J. García de Enterría and M. Gargantini, in this book, Chapter 8.

140 Commission, Report, 'Application of Directive 2004/25/EC on takeover bids', COM (2012) 347 final (28 Jun 2012), no. 23.

141 ESMA Public Statement, Information on shareholder cooperation and acting in concert under the Takeover Bids Directive, 20 June 2014, last update 8 January 2019, ESMA 2014/677-REV; see also J. García de Enterría, 'Reflecting on concerted action in relation to mandatory takeover bids: Shareholder agreements and the concerted exercise of voting rights', available at https://ssrn.com/abstract=4343791; D.W. Puchniak and U. Varottil, 'Rethinking Acting in Concert: Activist ESG Stewardship is Shareholder Democracy', ECGI Law Working Paper No 731/2023.

142 Assessment Report, 2011, p. 134.

143 Austria, Cyprus, Denmark, Hungary, Ireland, Luxembourg, Netherlands and Slovakia.

144 Belgium, Finland, Poland, Portugal, Romania and Sweden.

145 Czech Republic, Estonia and Greece.

146 García de Enterría and Gargantini, in this book, Chapter 8.

147 BGH, 13.12.2022 – II ZR 14/21, BGHZ 235, 295 (Postbank); report from V. Sander, 'Aktuelle Rechtsprechung des II. Zivilsenats des BGH zum Kapitalmarktrecht' (2024) *Wertpapier-Mitteilungen* 141, 142–145.

148 ECJ, Case C-605/18 (Adler Real Estate).

2.3.4 *Increase of Shareholdings and a Second Threshold*

Various Member States introduced rules requiring a (second) mandatory bid[149] if the offeree company acquires 'more' shares; according to the Assessment Report, this is to deal with low price bids used to acquire control.[150] This might be the acquisition of a single share as in the United Kingdom, or of 0.05% (Ireland), 2% (Austria, France), 3% (Greece) or 5% of voting rights (Italy),[151] and formerly 5% and 10% of voting rights (Poland, until 2017 when the rule was repealed).[152] Various Member States introduced a second threshold triggering a further mandatory bid.[153]

2.3.5 *Pricing of Mandatory Bids (Art. 5(4, 5) TOD)*

Article 5 headlines the notion of an equitable price in its title and mentions it in Art. 5(1). The general principle[154] of owing an equitable price is subject to more concrete provisions in Art. 5(4 and 5) TOD. The bidder has to offer the highest price paid for the same security by the offeree or by persons acting in concert.[155] Whether the offeror has to offer cash or a cash alternative[156] is subject also to some discretion of the Member States. Cash is to be offered when at least 5 per cent of the voting rights were acquired by cash.[157] Member States may provide that a cash consideration must be offered, at least as an alternative, in all cases,[158] and may prescribe further instruments intended to protect the interests of the holders of securities.[159]

Member States have to set a reference period of not more than twelve but at least six months for the highest price paid by the offeror before the bid.[160] According to the Assessment Report, most (former) Member States specify a twelve-month period (inter alia, Austria, Belgium, France, Ireland, Italy, Spain, United Kingdom), but some specify a six-month period (Finland, Germany, Greece, Portugal).[161] Member

[149] See Section 2.3.2.1; Hopt, 'European Takeover Reform of 2012/2013 – Time to Re-examine the Mandatory Bid', 177.

[150] Assessment Report, 2011, p. 355

[151] Ibid., p. 127, 130.

[152] Regucki, 'Polish Takeover Regulation', 391, 415–416.

[153] Assessment Report, 2011, p. 129: Finland, Poland (until 2022), Portugal.

[154] Not mentioned in Art. 3 TOD; see Section 2.2.3.2.

[155] Art. 5(4) TOD. On the attribution of a part (80 per cent in Brazil) of the control premium to common shareholders, J. C. Coffee, Jr., 'Racing Towards the Top?: The Impact of Cross-Listing and Stock Market Competition on International Corporate Governance' (2002) 102 *Columbia Law Journal* 1757, 1809.

[156] Art. 5(5) TOD.

[157] Art. 5(5)(3) TOD.

[158] Art. 5(5)(4) TOD.

[159] Art. 5(6) TOD.

[160] Art. 5(4)(1)(1) TOD. Reform proposal by J. W. Fedderke and M. Ventoruzzo, 'The Biases of an "Unbiased" Optional Takeovers Regime: The Mandatory Bid Threshold as a Reverse Drawbridge', ECGI Law Working Paper 304/2016, p. 30.

[161] Assessment Report, 2011, p. 157.

States may also introduce additional criteria for determining the 'equitable price' (Art. 5(4)(2)(3) TOD)[162] and allow for an adjustment of the price by the supervisory authority.[163]

2.3.6 *Exemptions and Derogations*

2.3.6.1 Acquiring Control Following a Voluntary Bid (Art. 5(2) TOD)

The Takeover Directive sets standards for the pricing and the processing of takeover bids. However, the TOD is applicable only for mandatory bids, and if a voluntary bid resulted in the acquisition of control, under Art. 5(2) TOD, the offeror has no obligation to issue a mandatory bid.[164] Therefore, Member States have an incentive to set uniform rules for mandatory and voluntary takeover bids concerning not only their submission and processing, but also as regards the pricing of the bid. Such voluntary takeover bids must comply with six general principles.[165]

2.3.6.2 Other Exemptions and Derogations

Member States may grant their supervisory authorities the power to waive national rules.[166] Therefore, there might be exemptions determined by supervisory authorities.[167] Furthermore, and also subject to a ruling of the European Court of Justice,[168] supervisory authorities can adjust prices.[169] Such a derogation might also be laid down in the national rules.[170] Member States have laid down so-called whitewash procedures for exemptions decided by shareholders.[171] The Assessment Report also identifies technical exemptions,[172] the protection of creditors[173] and

162 Ibid., p. 157–159.
163 Ibid., p. 159–162.
164 In Germany, Section 35(3) Takeover Act.
165 D. Van Gerven, 'Rules of Community Law Applicable to Takeover Bids', in Van Gerven (ed.), *Common Legal Framework for Takeover Bids in Europe*, Vol. I, p. 16, 1.20; this requirement is not waived.
166 Art. 4(5)(2)(ii) TOD. See for the initial transposition, Commission Staff Working Document, 'Report on the Implementation of the Directive on Takeover Bids', SEC (2007) 268 (21 February 2007), p. 15–16.
167 Assessment Report, 2011, p. 140; in Germany, Section 37 Takeover Act.
168 See ECJ Case C-206/16, *Marco Tronchetti Provera SpA and Others v. Commissione Nazionale per le Società e la Borsa*, opinion of the advocate general, no. 22; second case concerning TOD, Directive 2004/25/EC.
169 Art. 5(4)(3) TOD, Edwards, 'The Directive on Takeover Bids – Not Worth the Paper It's Written On?', 433.
170 Art. 4(5)(2)(i) TOD. See Commission Staff Working Document, 'Report on the Implementation of the Directive on Takeover Bids', SEC (2007) 268 (21 February 2007), p. 15–16.
171 Assessment Report, 2011, p. 140.
172 Ibid., p. 141.
173 Ibid., p. 147–148.

specific situations[174] when a real change of control has taken place.[175] Other exemptions protect the offeror or controlling shareholder if there is no real change of control.[176] In the Report on the application of the Directive, the Commission mentioned acting in concert and the mandatory bid rule as topics for reform;[177] in their second and third reform proposal, the Commission discussed derogations and exemptions from the mandatory bid rule.[178]

2.4 SUBMISSION AND PROCESSING OF A BID

2.4.1 *General Information on Bids (Arts. 6, 8, 10 TOD)*

While in the US there is a federal SEC rule on tender offers,[179] there are not yet any harmonized transparency provisions in the European Union. Nevertheless, transparency was increased by the transposition of the disclosure regime of the Takeover Directive.[180] According to Art. 6(1) TOD, the decision to make a bid is to be made public without delay; according to Art. 6(2) TOD, there has to be an offer document; the information that is to be contained in the offer document is subject to Art. 6(3) TOD; and rules on the application of Art. 6(3) TOD are subject to Art. 6(4) TOD. According to Art. 8(1) TOD, Member States are to ensure that the bid is made public. The offer document has to be in the form of a prospectus in accordance with the Prospectus Directive.[181]

In Germany, general information requirements apply not only to mandatory bids pursuant to Art. 5 TOD but also to voluntary bids.[182] A bid is defined as a voluntary or mandatory bid for securities;[183] special rules exist for bids having the objective of acquiring control of the offeree company.[184] According to the definition in Art. 2(1)(a) TOD, a 'takeover bid or bid shall mean a public offer [...] made to the holders of the securities of a company [...] which follows or has as its objective the acquisition of control of the offeree company in accordance with national law'. Therefore, only mandatory bids are included in the Directive.

[174] Ibid., p. 148–152.
[175] Ibid., p. 144–147.
[176] Ibid., p. 142–144.
[177] Commission, Report, 'Application of Directive 2004/25/EC on takeover bids', COM (2012) 347 final (28 June 2012), no. 23, 24. For acting in concert, see Section 2.3.3.
[178] See R. Skog and E. Sjöman, 'No Rule, Just Exemptions?' (2014) *European Company and Financial Law Review* 393.
[179] Regulation 14E.
[180] Commission Staff Working Document, 'Report on the implementation of the Directive on Takeover Bids', SEC (2007) 268 (21 February 2007), p. 10.
[181] Van Gerven, 'Rules of Community Law Applicable to Takeover Bids', 23, 1.35.
[182] Section 10 German Takeover Act.
[183] Section 2(1) German Takeover Act.
[184] Sections 29–39 German Takeover Act.

2.4.2 *Time Allowance for Acceptance and Notice by the Offeree's Board (Arts. 7, 9(5) TOD)*

The time allowed for the acceptance of the bid should be regulated,[185] according to Art. 7(1) TOD for a period of not less than two and not more than 10 weeks, roughly in line with the international time frame.[186] For specific cases, there might be deviating rules in national law (Art. 7(2) TOD). During the period determined by the time allowance, the board neutrality rule applies, thus hindering the board of the target company from frustrating the bid.[187] The board of the offeree company is required to make public a document setting out its opinion of the bid.[188]

2.4.3 *Worker Participation (Art. 14 TOD) and Stakeholder Interests*

Protecting employees[189] is not mandatory according to the Directive, which names as a general principle the interest of the company as a whole but does not define specific consequences for boards and shareholders in the takeover context. The specific provision in Article 14 on worker participation is drafted as enabling legislation, simply mentioning several Directives[190] and leaving improvements to the Member States. In terms of relevant Member State legislation, works councils vested with consultation rights[191] are to be mentioned since no specific codetermination was introduced at board level in the takeover context. Germany, in transposing the Directive, strengthened the works council of the offeror company[192] and also later introduced provisions concerning the works council of the target company.[193] Beyond the disclosure of information, consultation and even co-decision rights are also possible.

Some Member States introduced stakeholder-oriented reforms while transposing the Takeover Directive.[194] Several Member States explicitly mention the interests of the employees that are to be taken into account by the boards in the takeover context. In the US, thirty states have adopted constituency statutes that, at least in the context of a change of control transactions, allow (and in some cases require) the board to

185 Recital 14 TOD.
186 Assessment Report, 2011, p. 111.
187 Art. 9(2) TOD; for the transposition, see Section 2.5.
188 Art. 9(5) TOD.
189 Assessment Report, 2011, p. 61, noting that the Directive recognized the need to protect employees.
190 94/45/EU, 98/59/EC, 2001/86/EC, 2002/14/EC.
191 Assessment Report, 2011, p. 102.
192 Section 10(5) Takeover Act, new sentence.
193 Section 106(3) No. 9a and Section 109a Works Councils Act.
194 Assessment Report, 2011, p. 28.

consider the effects on the target's employees and other stakeholders.[195] The study conducted for the Commission portrayed employee protection outside the EU as extremely weak,[196] with employee representatives in the EU being nevertheless critical concerning the level of employee protection in the EU, as mentioned not only in the Assessment Report but also in the Report of the Commission.[197]

2.5 DEFENCE MEASURES OF THE OFFEREE (TARGET) COMPANY

2.5.1 *Board Neutrality Rule (Art. 9 TOD)*

2.5.1.1 Concept and Implementation of Art. 9 TOD

In balancing the interests of different stakeholders, defence measures adopted by the target company are crucial and highly controversial both in economics and in political discussions, with the UK and the US being the widely observed models for and against the board neutrality rule and other defence measures.[198] The Takeover Directive favours unhindered decisions being made by the shareholders of the target company in line with the UK model and therefore imposes in Art. 9(2 and 3) TOD the board neutrality rule. With Austria, Cyprus, Czech Republic, Estonia, France,[199] Greece, Ireland, Italy,[200] Portugal, Romania, Slovakia, Spain, Sweden and the UK, the majority of countries included in the Assessment Report have at least initially incorporated the board neutrality rule in their national takeover regime.[201] In most of these countries,[202] there was a pre-existing board neutrality rule; only three survey countries newly introduced a board neutrality rule when transposing the Directive (Cyprus, Finland and Greece).[203] Besides these countries, Belgium also applies the board neutrality rule.[204] Corporate governance systems in most Member States which introduced the board neutrality rule share two features – a one-tier board and the absence of codetermination at board level.

With a codetermined supervisory board, Austria does not fit into the current scheme in terms of both features, while Finland applies some codetermination. Nevertheless,

195 Andronikos, 'A US lawyer's perspective on the EU Takeover Directive', 66, 2.70 (Pennsylvania and others).
196 Assessment Report, 2011, p. 101.
197 Commission Report, 'Application of Directive 2004/25/EC on takeover bids', COM (2012) 347 final (28 June 2012), no. 27; for employee representatives, Assessment Report, 2011, p. 356.
198 On the market for corporate control and external corporate governance, Hopt, 'Takeover Defenses in Europe: A Comparative, Theoretical and Policy Analysis', at 261 et seq.
199 On the current legal regime, see Section 2.5.2.
200 On company opt-out, see Section 2.5.1.2.
201 Assessment Report, 2011, p. 42, 191. For later developments in France and Italy, see Section 2.5.2 and 2.5.1.2.
202 Assessment Report, 2011, p. 191.
203 Ibid., p. 42.
204 Now Art. 7:152 Belgium Companies and Associations Code, initially Art. 557 Companies Code.

the Austrian example fits into path dependency and was in line with the then existing German legal doctrine. When Austria introduced its Takeover Act in 1998, Germany also followed the board neutrality rule.[205] The voluntary Takeover Code by the German Exchange Experts Commission (Börsensachverständigenkommission) built on the UK City Code[206] and foresaw that the board of the target company may not take any measures that run counter to the interest of the holders of the securities in taking advantage of the tender offer.[207] The notes accompanying the governmental draft of the initial Austrian Takeover Act therefore referred not only to the proposal for a 13th Directive and the City Code, but also to the then existing German Takeover Code.[208] The proposed Austrian board neutrality rule was also in line with the (at the time) new Swiss Exchange Act[209] and stated that the interests of the employees, the creditors and the public are also to be taken into account by the organs of the offeree company.[210] Since Austrian companies typically had controlling shareholders, academia supposed that management generally would not try to prohibit a takeover bid.[211]

2.5.1.2 Opting Out of the Board Neutrality Rule on the Basis of Member State Takeover Regulation

Not explicitly mentioned in the Directive is opting out of the board neutrality rule on the basis of Member State takeover regulation. A company opt-out as a result of passivity was introduced in Italy.[212] In Italy, it is up to the general meeting to decide

205 Referring to the board neutrality rule as a 'Stillhaltepflicht' and as the majority view in academia, T. Baums, 'Notwendigkeit und Grundzüge einer gesetzlichen Übernahmeregelung', in R. von Rosen and W. G. Seifert (eds.), *Die Übernahme börsennotierter Unternehmen* (Frankfurt am Main: Deutsches Aktieninstitut, 1999), p. 165, 175; referring to it as 'allgemein anerkannt' (universally accepted), Hirte and Schander, 'Die Organpflichten bei Unternehmensübernahme', in R. Rosen and Seifert (eds.), *Die Übernahme börsennotierter Unternehmen*, p. 341, 348.

206 S. Schuster and C. Zschocke (eds.,) *Übernahmerecht Takeover Law* (Frankfurt am Main: Knapp-Verlag, 1996), p. 23; for the text, see also 'Der neue Übernahmekodex der Börsensachverständigenkommission' (1995) *Zeitschrift für Wirtschaftsrecht* 1464.

207 Art. 19 Takeover Code, naming as such measures (among others) resolutions with respect to the issuance of new securities, a substantial change in the assets or liabilities of the target company, and the conclusion of agreements outside the scope of ordinary business activity. Takeover Code of the Exchange Expert Commission at the Federal Ministry of Finance of 14 July 1995, printed in Schuster and Zschocke (eds.), *Übernahmerecht Takeover Law*, p. 75, 95, 97.

208 For Belgium, see P. Doralt, C. Nowotny and M. Schauer (eds.), *Takeover-Recht* (Vienna: WUV Service Fachverlag, 1997), with comparative reports, p. 207, 257; for the German report, see Thomas Mayer, Der Übernahmekodex der Börsensachverständigenkommission beim (deutschen) Bundesministerium für Finanzen, p. 27.

209 Art. 29 BEHG (Bundesgesetz über die Börsen und den Effektenhandel); see A. Tuczka in Doralt, Nowotny and Schauer (eds.), *Takeover-Recht*, p. 125.

210 Art. 12 Austrian Takeover Act; see for the notes accompanying the governmental draft, Doralt, Nowotny and Schauer (eds.), *Takeover-Recht*, p. 207, 257.

211 P. Doralt in Doralt, Nowotny and Schauer (eds.), *Takeover-Recht*, p. 1, 10.

212 Assessment Report, 2011, p. 28 footnote 18, p. 59, with the history of Italian takeover regulation.

on board neutrality and (if preferred) to waive the board neutrality rule, which is the general principle in Italy. Such a solution has widespread and growing support in academia and is described as a default board neutrality rule for companies.[213] Such a rule is endorsed by US[214] and European scholars from Germany,[215] the UK[216] and Belgium.[217]

2.5.2 *Defence Measures Allowed by Member States (Art. 12 TOD)*

2.5.2.1 Allowance of Defence Measures by Member States

A significant proportion of Member States opted out of the board neutrality rule (Art. 12(1) TOD) by not introducing it in their jurisdiction. Recital 21 of the Takeover Directive acknowledged existing differences in Member States' company law mechanisms and structures. This refers to different company law traditions. According to the Assessment Report, there is no board neutrality rule in Belgium,[218] Denmark, Germany, Hungary, Luxembourg, Netherlands, Poland[219] or (later) also in France.[220] In Germany, the Netherlands, Denmark, Luxembourg, Hungary and France, the rejection of the board neutrality rule as a general concept correlates to board-level employee representation. The majority of countries which did not introduce the board neutrality rule as a general concept (Germany, Netherlands, Denmark, Luxembourg, Hungary) foresee board-level codetermination of at least a third of the board members.[221] Other Member States relaxed the neutrality, too, in transposing the Directive.[222]

Currently, Austria is the only Member State with a dual board structure and mandatory codetermination at board level, having opted for the board neutrality rule. France introduced a codetermination system after transposing the Takeover

[213] Generally promoting choices for companies, G. Hertig and J. A. McCahery, 'Company and Takeover Law Reforms in Europe: Misguided Harmonization Efforts or Regulatory Competition?' (2003) 4 *European Business Organization Law Review* 179, 204.

[214] L. Enriques, R. J. Gilson and A. M. Pacces, 'The Case for an Unbiased Takeover Law (with an Application to the European Union)' (2014) 4 *Harvard Business Law Review* 85, 122.

[215] Habersack, 'Non-frustration Rule and Mandatory Bid Rule – Cornerstones of European Takeover Law?', (2018), 28; Hopt, *Europäisches Übernahmerecht*, p. 103–105.

[216] P. Davies, E.-P. Schuster and E. van de Walle de Ghelcke, 'The Takeover Directive as a Protectionist Tool?', in U. Bernitz and W.-G. Ringe (eds.), *Company Law and Economic Protectionism* (Oxford: Oxford University Press, 2010), p. 105.

[217] E. Wymeersch, 'A New Look at the Debate about the Takeover Directive', *Festschrift in honour of Peter Hommelhoff* (Cologne: Dr. Otto Schmidt Verlag, 2012), p. 1375, 1396.

[218] On Belgium, see Section 2.5.1.1.

[219] Assessment Report, 2011, p. 193.

[220] Loi Florange, 3 LOI n° 2014-384 du 29 mars 2014 visant à reconquérir l'économie réelle, modification of Art. L233–32 Code de Commerce.

[221] A. Conchon, Board-level employee representation rights in Europe: Facts and trends (Brussels: ETUI, 2011).

[222] Assessment Report, 2011, p. 191.

Directive and subsequently switched from a mandatory board neutrality rule to reciprocity and in the end rejected the board neutrality rule.[223] Highlighting employee interests, the Assessment Report cited the concept of team production,[224] stating that shareholders should be disincentivized from 'unduly extracting team production value'. Also the European Commission in its Report stressed that employee representatives are not satisfied with the application of the Takeover Directive.[225]

Abstaining from introducing the board neutrality rule correlates with a restricted authority of the general meeting and its exclusion from running the affairs of the company. When Germany switched from its traditional concept of the general meeting as the supreme body of the company by introducing the Stock Corporation Act 1937, there had also been some comparative research beforehand.[226] Owing especially to a monograph authored by Zahn on business leadership,[227] the current German doctrine of excluding the general meeting from managing the company[228] might be seen as an adoption of traditional US stock corporation law principles;[229] Zahn referred to Ballantine on Corporations, identifying the board and not the general meeting as the supreme body of the corporation.[230] Similarly, Dutch company law gives board discretion more weight and, similar to the majority view in Germany, does not accept even advisory resolutions of the general meeting.[231]

Additionally, the allowance of defence measures can be discussed as a protectionist tool;[232] but also in the US, there is no board neutrality rule. In France, the Loi

[223] Highlighting the French reform as an instance of the 'grip of nationalism', M. Pargendler, 'The Grip of Nationalism on Corporate Law' (2020) 95 *Indiana Law Journal* 533, 543.

[224] Assessment Report, 2011, p. 32.

[225] Commission Report, 'Application of Directive 2004/25/EC on takeover bids', COM (2012) 347 final (28 June 2012), no. 20.

[226] Generally, but not covering this aspect, W. Hallstein, *Die Aktienrechte der Gegenwart* (Berlin: F. Vahlen, 1931).

[227] J. Zahn, *Wirtschaftsführertum und Vertragsethik im neuen Aktienrecht* (Berlin: De Gruyter, 1934). Later HSBC-Trinkhaus manager Zahn was invited by the then CEO of Munich Re, who presided over the Academy for German Law's section on stock corporations, which was asked to present its findings in the preparations of the Stock Corporation Act 1937.

[228] Now Section 119(2) German Stock Corporation Act.

[229] On the Stock Corporation Reform in the 1930s, see W. Schubert et al. (eds.), 'Protocols of the Committees of the Academy for German Law 1933–1945' (Akademie für Deutsches Recht, Protokolle der Ausschüsse), Volume 1, Stock Corporation Law (Ausschuss für Aktienrecht) (Berlin: De Gruyter, 1986), p. xlvii.

[230] Zahn, *Wirtschaftsführertum und Vertragsethik im neuen Aktienrecht*, p. 90,footnote 3, referring to H. Ballantine, *On Corporations* (Chicago, IL: Callaghan, 1927), p. 319.

[231] S. Cools, 'Climate Proposals: ESG Shareholder Activism Sidestepping Board Authority', in T. Kuntz (ed.), *Research Handbook on Environmental, Social and Corporate Governance* (Cheltenham: Edward Elgar, 2024), p. 138.

[232] Bernitz and Ringe (eds.), *Company Law and Economic Protectionism*; Hopt, 'Takeover Defenses in Europe: A Comparative, Theoretical and Policy Analysis', at 254 et seq.; Hopt, *Europäisches Übernahmerecht*, p. 69 et seq.

Florange swept away the board neutrality rule to protect French companies from hostile takeovers.[233] In Germany, the Takeover Act 2001 is seen as a reaction on the cross-border takeover of Mannesmann by Vodafone.[234] The German government's reaction was to change its view on the issue of board neutrality.[235] This was a protectionist reflex, but it was also inspired by the facts of the Mannesmann takeover, being an international takeover – first hostile and later friendly – in which the board of the target company created value for its shareholders by prompting the offeror to increase the offer through its actions and defence measures.[236]

2.5.2.2 Option for Companies to Opt In

In Germany, even without the provision in the Takeover Act, it is highly unlikely that the power to implement a board neutrality rule could be attributed to the general meeting. The same is true for the Netherlands. Contrary to the current understanding of the powers of management and the general meeting in Germany and in the Netherlands, the High Level Company Law Experts Group, featuring a Dutch chairman and a German expert, called for shareholder decision-making as the general principle.[237] In the stricter sense, decisions by the shareholders are secured by a mandatory board neutrality rule; however, it has been maintained that the authority of the shareholders to implement the board neutrality rule also constitutes a shareholder decision, even if (regularly) the board neutrality rule is not implemented in practice. But this neglects the fact that an opting-out rule, which has been recommended in legal literature, is much more favourable to the shareholders than an opt-in rule which is difficult to achieve.[238]

At a minimum, options for companies to opt in as regards the board neutrality rule or the breakthrough rule are to be implemented into national law and,

[233] M. Rohwoldt and D. Starke, 'The Role of Governments in Hostile Takeovers – Evidence from regulation, anti-takeover provision and government interventions' (2016) 47 *International Review of Law and Economics* 1; M. Lutter, W. Bayer and J. Schmidt, *Europäisches Unternehmens- und Kapitalmarktrecht*, 6th ed. (Berlin: De Gruyter, 2018), no. 28.124.

[234] P. Mülbert, 'Entwicklung des Übernahmerechts. Betrachtung aus der Perspektive der Wisenschaft', in Veil, Grigoleit and Habersack (eds.), *Öffentliche Unternehmensübernahmen*, p. 3; M. Habersack, 'Verhinderungsverbot und Pflichtangebotsregel – Eckpfeiler des europäischen Übernahmerechts?' (2017) 181 *Zeitschrift für das gesamte Handels- und Wirtschaftsrecht* 603, 605.

[235] W. Underhill and A. Austmann, 'Defence Tactics', in J. Payne (ed.), *Takeovers in English and German Law* (Oxford: Hart, 2002), 87, 96; critical of the traditional approach, C. Kirchner and R. Painter, 'European Takeover Law – Towards a European Modified Business Judgement Rule for Takeover Law' (2000) 1 *European Business Organization Law Review* 353.

[236] The granting of appreciation awards to the CEO was later the subject of a criminal trial; M. Roth, 'Outside Director Liability: German Stock Corporation Law in Transatlantic Perspective' (2008) 8 *Journal of Corporate Law Studies* 337, 343.

[237] Report of the High Level Group of Company Law Experts on Issues Related to Takeover Bids, Brussels, 10 January 2002, p. 20.

[238] See Section 2.5.1.

according to Art. 11(2) TOD, are subject to a decision of the general meeting. Hence there was a new rule in the German Takeover Act as a result of the transposition.[239] The duty of neutrality is optional also for Danish companies; it is up to the general meeting to decide on the board neutrality rule.[240] In the Netherlands, the opt-in by the company has to be laid down in the articles of association.[241] In Poland, the legislature was initially silent on board neutrality, which could not be regarded as a full and proper implementation of the Directive.[242] In the end, the option for companies to opt in – in favour of neutrality – in the articles of association was introduced. Though the rule plays no practical role, Polish legal commentators have attempted to derive a duty to abstain from measures frustrating the bid from the general duty of loyalty owed by board members and the duty to abstain from decision-making in a conflict-of-interest situation.

2.5.2.3 Authority and Discretion for Defence Measures

As for the corporate governance of the bidder,[243] the Takeover Directive is silent on the authority and discretion for defensive measures. The powers and duties of directors are subject to common or specific provisions in Member State law. Director duties in takeover situations are subject to general principles of company law, namely the duty of loyalty and the duty of care. In the US, a modified business judgment rule is applied to defences in takeover situations.[244]

2.5.3 *Breakthrough Rules on Certain Defence Measures (Art. 11 TOD)*

The breakthrough rule (Art. 11 TOD)[245] aims to limit pre-bid defences by neutralizing such rules.[246] In its substantive provisions, there are restrictions on transferring securities[247] and restrictions on voting rights. Restrictions on voting rights[248] can be enacted in the articles of association, they can be contractual agreements or they can be multiple-vote securities. The 'one share, one vote' principle is thus a default for companies if the breakthrough rule is enacted by the Member State.[249] Member

239 Section 33a German Takeover Act.
240 J. S. Christensen in Maul, Muffat-Jeadet and Simon (eds.), *Takeover Bids in Europe*, no. 1140.
241 S. F. G. Rammeloo inibid., no. 2531.
242 M. Bobrzynski, K. Oplustil and M. Spyra inibid., no. 2750.
243 See Section 2.3.2.2.
244 On the European discussion of US principles, see Kirchner and Painter, 'European Takeover Law – Towards a European Modified Business Judgement Rule for Takeover Law', 364–372, 382–400.
245 With material provisions in Art. 11(2–4) TOD.
246 Art. 11(4) TOD deals with an offeror holding 75 per cent of the voting rights following a bid; Art. 11(5) foresees equitable compensation when rights are removed.
247 Art. 11(2) TOD.
248 Mentioned in Art. 11(3) TOD.
249 Enriques, Gilson and Pacces, 'The Case for an Unbiased Takeover Law (with an Application to the European Union)', 119.

States may opt out of the breakthrough rule,[250] which all Member States except Estonia[251] did.[252] The breakthrough rule was partially transposed in Italy and France.[253] Consequently, the provision for a breakthrough rule was not evaluated as successful in the Assessment Report.[254]

2.6 FURTHER COMPANY LAW PROVISIONS IN THE TOD AND THEIR RELEVANCE FOR TAKEOVERS

2.6.1 *Squeeze-Out (Art. 15 TOD)*

According to Art. 15(2)1 TOD, Member States are to ensure that an offeror is able to require all the holders of the remaining securities to sell these securities to him at a fair price.[255] However, Art. 15(2)2 reduces the scope of that right dramatically in that it explicitly prescribes that such a right is to be introduced by the Member States in only one of the following two situations: the offeror holds securities representing 90 per cent of the capital carrying voting rights or 90 per cent of the voting rights in the offeree company at the moment of the bid or following the acceptance of the bid.[256] As far as this 'acceptance test' is concerned, Member States may not impose a higher threshold. Additionally, Art. 15(2)2(a) TOD contains an 'ownership test' and foresees a squeeze-out where the offeror holds securities amounting to not less than 90 per cent of the voting rights. This threshold can be raised to 95 per cent.[257]

The wording of the squeeze-out provision lacks clarity; Art. 15(2)2 might be understood in the sense that Member States are permitted to provide a squeeze-out takeover. Such clarity is needed for properly balancing the facilitation of business opportunities and protecting outside shareholders. US bidders are generally not bound by a board neutrality rule and companies may conduct freeze-out mergers with a simple majority. Hinting at US freeze-out mergers and calling for a transatlantic level playing field, German lawyers recommend a squeeze-out at the fair price paid for the bid if the bidder reaches 75 per cent of the shares,[258] with this standard being based on the threshold for inter-company contracts under German

[250] Art. 12 TOD. For France, I. Urbain-Parleani, 'The Implementation of the Thirteenth Directive 2004/25, Country Report on France', in Baums and Cahn (eds.), *Die Umsetzung der Übernahmerichtlinie in Europa*, p. 3, 10–11.

[251] Assessment Report, 2011, p. 195; no case reported.

[252] Member States which allow an opt-in also allow reciprocity; Assessment Report, 2011, p. 196.

[253] Assessment Report, 2011, p. 195.

[254] Ibid., p. 355.

[255] Tables for squeeze-out and sell-out are found in the Assessment Report, 2011, p. 230–236; see also C. van der Elst and L. van den Steen, 'Balancing the Interests of Minority and Majority Shareholders: A Comparative Analysis of Squeeze-out and Sell-out Rights' (2009) *European Company and Financial Law Review* 391.

[256] Art. 15(2)(2)(b) TOD.

[257] Art. 15(2)(3) TOD.

[258] See Section 2.6.3.

Konzernrecht. For a genuinely level playing field in transatlantic capital markets and so as not to overshoot the requirements of the German Konzernrecht, a simple majority may be sufficient and adequate. By allowing a freeze-out merger with a simple majority in Weinberger v. UOP,[259] US company law facilitates the integration of acquired companies. If European innovators are to find an equal playing field also in the European Union, post-bid integration has to be de-bureaucratized dramatically, but it might rest to some degree on the authority of the Member States.

In transposing the Takeover Directive, Ireland removed the provision that allowed a squeeze-out with an 80 per cent majority also in the takeover context. This provision applies now only if a company is not subject to the Takeover Directive.[260] Specific provisions for squeeze-out in a takeover situation were newly introduced in Cyprus, Czech Republic, Germany, Greece, Luxembourg, Slovakia and Spain to transpose the Takeover Directive.[261] In line with the TOD's general rule,[262] most Member States introduced a 90 per cent threshold for both sell-out and squeeze-out.[263] Some Member States (Belgium, France, Germany, Italy, Luxembourg, Netherlands, Poland and Slovakia) introduced a 95 per cent requirement for at least some squeeze-outs.[264] Art. 15 TOD does not hinder Member States from implementing several squeeze-out rules in national law. Frequently, there are also squeeze-out provisions so as to allow consolidation of membership outside of the takeover context. In Germany, three squeeze-out regimes exist: in the Stock Corporation Act, the Merger Act and the Takeover Act. Squeeze-out in Germany was pre-existing in general stock corporation law, then introduced into the Takeover Act in transposing the TOD and later implemented also in the Merger Act. The situation is similar in Poland, with three squeeze-out regimes: for private joint stock companies, for groups of companies in the Code of Commercial Companies and for takeovers in the Act on Public Offerings.

Squeeze-out rights independent from takeover bids[265] are also frequently enacted by Member States for listed companies in other situations, for non-listed companies and for other forms of business associations. Germany enacted its first squeeze-out rule with the German Takeover Act in 2001 in the German Stock Corporation Act,[266] and it introduced squeeze-out and sell-out rights in the takeover situation when transposing the Takeover Directive in 2006. In Austria, there is a separate Squeeze-out Act[267] for stock corporations and close corporations; squeeze-outs are

[259] 457 A.2d 701 (Del. 1983); see also Section 2.4.3.
[260] M. Green and K. Ryan, 'Ireland', in Van Gerven (ed.), *Common Legal Framework for Takeover Bids in Europe*, Vol. I, p. 250, no. 10.67.
[261] Assessment Report, 2011, p. 64–66.
[262] Art. 15(2)(2) TOD.
[263] Assessment Report, 2011, p. 221
[264] Ibid.
[265] Ibid., p. 225–226.
[266] Sections 327a–327f German Stock Corporation Act.
[267] Member of a Company Exclusion Act (Gesellschafter-Ausschlussgesetz).

not regulated in the Austrian Takeover Act.[268] In Germany, there is a threshold of 95% in the Takeover Act, but one of 90% in the Merger Act (UmwG). In the Czech Republic, there is a threshold of 90% in the Commercial Code.[269] In Poland, the Code of Commercial Companies law prescribes a general threshold of 90% (the articles of association can lower it up to 75% for a squeeze-out in a subsidiary belonging to a group of companies) and one of 95% for public companies (inside and outside the takeover context).

2.6.2 *Sell-Out (Art. 16 TOD)*

The introduction of a sell-out right was new, at least in the takeover situation, in Belgium, Cyprus, Czech Republic, Estonia, Germany, Greece, Luxembourg, Netherlands, Slovakia and Spain;[270] or, for example, in Germany it was a novelty as such in company law, since no sell-out rights had been included in the German Stock Corporation Act. The sell-out right is laid down in the German Takeover Act; also, in the Czech Republic, sell-out is included in the Takeover Act and not in the Commercial Code like squeeze-out.[271] The sell-out right is a protection mechanism for the members (shareholders) and securities holders of the offeree company. In most Member States, it is a specific feature in takeover situations and is seldom provided for outside of takeover situations.[272] In Poland, the sell-out right applies both inside and outside the takeover context and was introduced prior to the transposition of the Directive.[273] The Code of Commercial Companies grants a sell-out right to shareholders of private joint stock companies as well as to shareholders of subsidiaries which belong to a group of companies.

2.6.3 *Other Post-Takeover Issues: Incorporating Elements of a Freeze-Out Merger?*

The playing field for bidders, shareholders, boards and capital market participants is not restricted to the subject matter of the Takeover Directive; rather, it also bears upon other fields of law which interact with explicit takeover regulation. Such interaction may also be decisive for the efficiency of national takeover regimes. The early critique of the European mandatory bid rule as too costly for (hostile) bidders[274] maintains that post-bid rights of the bidder have to be taken into account

[268] See F. Khol and T. Berghammer, 'Austria', in Van Gerven (ed.), *Common Legal Framework for Takeover Bids in Europe*, Vol. I, p. 91.
[269] P. Kasik and V. Pihera, 'Czech Republik', inibid., p. 143, 5.39.
[270] Assessment Report, 2011, p. 64–66.
[271] Kasik and Pihera, 'Czech Republik', p. 143, 5.40.
[272] Assessment Report, 2011, p. 226.
[273] Section 83 of the Act on Public Offering.
[274] L. Enriques, 'The Mandatory Bid Rule in the Takeover Directive: Harmonization Without Foundation?', 440.

and might be necessary to provide adequate positions to bidders, shareholders and boards. A recent proposal for the reform of both the German Takeover Act and the Takeover Directive highlights interdependencies and the need for benefits following the duty of bidders to issue a mandatory bid.

A leading German practitioner[275] recommends changing Section 39a of the German Takeover Act (the German takeover squeeze-out) and in parallel the TOD so as to allow the bidder to acquire all outstanding shares after acquiring 75 per cent of the shares at the fair price according to the TOD.[276] That would allow a one-step post-bid approach for such takeovers. Until now – and based on German Konzernrecht and the corporate governance system – after a successful takeover, a bidder which has acquired at least 75 per cent of the shares enters into an inter-company agreement (control agreement combined with a profit and loss absorption agreement), which is typically followed by a delisting of the target company and a squeeze-out of the remaining outside shareholders if one of the thresholds (at least 90 per cent) is reached. A better approach might be to have this occur in one step.

Facilitating a post-bid squeeze-out of up to 24.99 per cent of the shares would create more favourable circumstances for bidders. However, taking the argument of a transatlantic level playing field seriously, one has to admit that even such a rule falls short of Weinberger v. UOP.[277] Furthermore, it also sets higher hurdles than German Konzernrecht for an inter-company agreement. Such agreements have to be decided by the general meeting with a majority of three-quarters, but not of the share capital, only of the capital represented at the general meeting. Hence, allowing a squeeze-out with a simple majority of the share capital might be a more adequate means of counterbalancing the mandatory bid and the restrictions of defence measures. Such an approach would allow faster consolidation of acquired companies and therefore set better conditions for European stock corporations, allowing them to obtain leading positions in future technical disruptions and transformations.[278]

2.7 CONCLUSION AND OUTLOOK

In transposing the Takeover Directive, Member States – within the framework of the Takeover Directive – had to balance the interests of the different stakeholders and to entrust a body with supervision of the takeover process. Surprisingly, Member States transposed the mandatory bid rule with little variation in the definition of control,

275 C. H. Seibt, 'Deutschland braucht eine Reform des Übernahmerechts' (2023) *Neue Zeitschrift für Gesellschaftsrecht* 1197.

276 See also C.A. Krebs, 'Freeze-Out Transactions in Germany and the U.S.: A Comparative Analysis' (2012) 13 *German Law Journal* 941, 978.

277 457 A.2d 701 (Del. 1983).

278 Citing digitalization and the green transposition, see also Seibt, 'Deutschland braucht eine Reform des Übernahmerechts'.

with thresholds varying narrowly in nearly all Member States, between 30 per cent and a third. Also concerning the supervisory authority and concerning squeeze-out and sell-out rights, the transposition of the Directive had a harmonizing effect. Therefore, the occasionally encountered opinion that the Takeover Directive was a clear failure is plainly incorrect. However, as a result of Member State discretion in transposing the Directive, the overall picture is mixed and harmonization is far from complete. Vested interests and lobbying were simply too strong. Member States vary not only in their legislative approach concerning the offeree's defence measures, but also in respect of derogations and deviations from the mandatory bid rule.

In order to balance the interests of different stakeholders, the defence measures of the target company are of crucial importance. History shows different and evolving approaches to the board neutrality rule, which was the topic subject to the most heated debate before an agreement on the Takeover Directive could be reached. While in the late 1990s the board neutrality rule was dominant on the continent, Germany, France and Italy – the largest economies – altered their takeover regimes and now favour a more flexible approach – in France and Italy even after the initial transposition of the Takeover Directive. A growing number of Member States later changed their initial transposition of the Takeover Directive's breakthrough rule. But more flexibility should not be confused with a plea for non-binding takeover law; in principle, meaningful takeover law at the European level should be mandatory.[279]

Overall, in transposing the Takeover Directive, a one-stop approach is not suitable and ongoing monitoring is needed to provide an effective national takeover regime. In assessing the current legal regime, there might be a case for rebalancing the facilitation of business opportunities and the protection of outside shareholders, at least at the level of Member State laws. US companies can conduct freeze-out mergers with a simple majority. If European innovators are to find an equal playing field in the European Union, post-bid integration has to be de-bureaucratized considerably. The Framework Directive gives discretion to the Member States and allows ongoing adaptations to current developments, yet it may also be subject to a revision initially postponed in the 2010s.

In a future reform of the Takeover Directive, the focus should remain not solely on the legal and regulatory problems discussed so far, such as the mandatory bid and the board neutrality rule; instead it should also be realized and taken into account that the markets for corporate control have changed dramatically since the 2010s, certainly in Germany but also throughout the continent.[280] Today, shareholder activism, ETFs and passive funds that are incapable of tendering the shares of the

[279] Hopt, 'European Takeover Reform of 2012/2013 – Time to Re-examine the Mandatory Bid', at 162 et seq., with a discussion on the economic objections and rejecting the theory of complete autonomy for company statutes and general meetings of shareholders.

[280] Seibt, 10 Theses on German Takeover Practice, lecture given at the Max Planck Institute for Comparative and International Private Law in Hamburg in March 2024.

target company during the offer period have a significant impact. Mandatory takeover bids have become rare; usually voluntary takeover bids take place in which the bidder and the board of the target company agree on modalities later presented to the shareholders. This increasingly leads to a serious danger of conflicts of interest and insider dealing. Most economically important takeover transactions are P2P transactions aimed at taking the target company private. The consequence is a further reduction of listings with problems for the stock exchanges. Private equity plays an ever-increasing role in the transactions. The takeovers take much longer than formerly, up to 12 months, due to various regulatory agencies and proceedings involved. Addressing these problems might lead to a rather different regulatory landscape both in Europe and in the Member States as well as in the United Kingdom.[281]

[281] See also Davies, Hopt and Ringe, *Control Transactions*, ch. 8.5, in particular concerning the different regulatory environments, political economy considerations and regulatory uncertainty.

3

The Institutional Design of Takeover Law

Susan Emmenegger and Martin Winner

3.1 INTRODUCTION

The European Takeover Directive of 2004[1] (TOD) established important principles such as the mandatory bid rule and, at least to some extent, the prohibition of defensive measures by the management board. It did not attempt to harmonize the institutional side of takeover law. This large organizational discretion is owed to the UK Takeover Panel on Mergers and Acquisitions, which was a model for the EU proposals for a TOD.[2] Established in 1968, the UK panel was a self-regulatory body operating on a non-statutory basis and disposing of an internal review process, with judicial courts exercising judicial restraint when reviewing takeover decisions.[3]

From the beginning, the EU proposals were careful to include the UK organizational regime in the Directive.[4] According to Article 4(1) of the TOD as in force today, the competent authorities in takeover matters may be 'public authorities,

The authors would like to thank Guntis Cerbulis (Letonia), Ville Kajala (Finland), Rolf Skog (Sweden), Kjell Vidjeland (Norway) and Blanaid Clarke (Ireland). Any mistakes or misrepresentations are the responsibility of the authors.

[1] Directive 2004/25/EC of the European Parliament and of the Council of 21 April 2004 on takeover bids, OJ 1985 No. L 142/12.

[2] R. Skog, 'The Takeover Directive – An Endless Saga?' (2002) *European Business Law Review* 301, 302. See also E. Armson, 'Lessons for the Australian Takeovers Panel from the United Kingdom' (2014) *Australian Journal of Corporate Law* 6, 27.

[3] For an overview of the history of the UK Takeover Panel, see D. Kershaw, *Principles of Takeover Regulation* (Oxford: Oxford University Press, 2016), mn. 3.05–3.89; A. Johnston, 'Takeover Regulation: Historical and Theoretical Perspectives on the City Code' (2007) 66 *Cambridge Law Journal* 422. See also the Datafin decision, which is the foundational decision for judicial review in takeover matters – and where the court noted that the Takeover Panel performed its function 'without visible means of legal support'; *R v. Panel on Take-overs and Mergers, Ex parte Datafin Plc* [1987] QB 815, 824.

[4] For a discussion on how the proposals catered to (mostly) UK concerns, see T. Papadopoulos, *EU Law and the Harmonization of Takeovers* (Alphen aan den Rijn: Wolters Kluwer, 2010), p. 140 et seq.; V. Edwards, 'The Directive on Takeover Bids – Not Worth the Paper It's Written On?' (2004) 2 *European Company and Financial Law Review* 416, 421 et seq.; B. Pettet, 'Private

associations or private bodies recognized by national law or by public authorities expressly empowered for that purpose by national law'. In addition, Preamble 7 of the TOD confirms that 'self-regulatory bodies should be able to exercise supervision'. Finally, Art. 4(6) TOD states that Member States are autonomous in the designation of the authorities dealing with disputes and that the Directive does not affect the power which courts may have in a Member State to decline to hear legal proceedings. This confirms the UK practice of judicial restraint when courts review takeover decisions.[5] Court proceedings must, however, be compatible with the Charter of Fundamental Rights of the European Union.[6]

All in all, the TOD went to great lengths to make room for the establishment of a panel structure. However, the predominant institutional arrangement is that takeover authorities form an integral part of the financial supervisory authority. This is surprising, given that the panel model was commonly seen as offering a greater level of flexibility, predictability and speed.[7] This chapter argues that this general assumption needs closer examination. Across Europe, takeover panels and takeover supervisory authorities exist in great variety. While the panel structure tends to promote flexibility and predictability, these attributes are not inherently tied to the institutional identity of the takeover authority. The same could potentially be said about speed. However, this analysis focuses solely on flexibility and predictability.

3.2 MAPPING THE INSTITUTIONAL DESIGN ACROSS JURISDICTIONS

When mapping the European[8] takeover regulation, two main forms of organizing the takeover authorities emerge: the integration into the relevant financial supervisor or the establishment of a separate takeover panel. There are no established prerequisites to allow a body to be called a takeover panel. Generally, the expectation would be that it is a regulatory body that is distinct from the overall administration, possesses a significant degree of independence and is predominantly composed of financial market participants. Beyond these general features, there are significant differences between the European takeover panels, as we will see in the following.

versus Public Regulation in the Field of Takeovers' (2000) *European Business Law Review* 381, 384 et seq.

5 This, in turn, mirrors the 1987 Datafin decision, *R v. Panel on Takeover and Mergers, Ex Parte Datafin Plc* [1987] 1 QB 815.

6 Case C-546/18, *Adler Real Estate et al.* [2021] ECLI:EU:C:2021:711, paragraph 40–42.1.

7 D. Awrey, B. Clarke and S. Griffith, 'Resolving the Crisis in U.S. Merger Regulation: A Transatlantic Alternative to the Perpetual Litigation Machine' (2018) 35 *Yale Journal on Regulation* 1, 4. In a similar vein (discussing the change from a court system to a panel system in Australia): E. Armson, 'Flexibility in Decision-Making: An Assessment of the Australian Takeovers Panel' (2017) *University of New South Wales Law Journal* 460.

8 This includes the EU and the EEA, as well as the UK and Switzerland.

According to the list of competent authorities in takeover matters published by ESMA,[9] out of the twenty-seven Member States and the three EEA countries, only Austria and Ireland list a panel as the competent authority in takeover matters. For all other countries, the designated competent authority is the financial supervisor. The list requires some adjustments. In Sweden, the panel-like Securities Council exercises substantial authority in takeover matters. Furthermore, Finland has a takeover panel, although one with only non-binding authority. Outside the EU and EEA, the UK and Switzerland both have a panel structure.

In sum, out of thirty-two European countries (twenty-seven members, three EEA countries, the UK and Switzerland), only six have a panel structure to begin with: the UK, Ireland, Austria, Sweden, Switzerland and Finland. The remaining countries do not have a panel structure at all. Instead, takeover matters are solely in the hands of the financial supervisory authority. These countries include France, Germany, Italy and Spain. We will refer to countries that use their financial supervisors as takeover regulators as operating under a 'supervisory authority regime', while those with a panel structure will be described as following a 'panel regime'.

3.2.1 *Standard Design: Supervisory Authority Regimes*

Among the countries with a supervisory authority regime in takeover matters are France and Germany, both of which also have important stock exchanges (Euronext Paris and Deutsche Börse Frankfurt). In Germany, the regulation of public takeovers shifted from self-regulation to statutory regulation in 2001, when the Bundesamt für Finanzwesen (BaFin) assumed the function as the relevant takeover authority.[10] This contrasts with France, where public supervision was installed as early as 1967 with the establishment of the Commission des opérations de bourses (COB). COB was merged into the Autorité des marchés financiers (AMF) in 2003.[11]

9 See ESMA, List of competent authorities designated for the purposes of Directive 2004/25/EC on takeover bids (Takeover bids Directive), last updated 02/04/2025, available at www.esma.europa.eu/sites/default/files/takeover_bids_directive.pdf (accessed 13 July 2025). The following countries have listed the financial supervisor as competent authority: Belgium, Bulgaria, Czech Republic, Denmark, Germany, Estonia, Greece, Spain, France, Croatia, Italy, Cyprus, Latvia, Lithuania, Luxembourg, Hungary, Malta, Netherlands, Poland, Portugal, Romania, Slovenia, Slovakia, Finland, Sweden, Iceland, Liechtenstein. In some countries, the financial supervisor is the central bank (Czech Republic, Latvia, Lithuania, Hungary, Slovakia and – more recently – Iceland [2020] and Norway [2025]).

10 See § 4(1) cl. 1 Securities Acquisition and Takeover Act (4110-7) of 20 December 2001 (WpÜG). In the former self-regulatory regime in force until the end of 2001, the Takeover Code was developed by the German Stock Exchange Expert Commission and the designated competent body was the Takeover Commission. See K. Hopt, 'Europäisches und deutsches Übernahmerecht' (1997) 161 *Zeitschrift für das gesamte Handelsrecht* 368, 393 et seq.

11 For an overview of the new institutional regime of financial supervision in France see Autorité des marchés financiers (AMF), Rapport annuel AMF 2003 – Préambule, p. 5 et seq.

The financial supervisor is also the competent authority for takeover matters in other countries with financial markets of notable size, namely Spain and Italy. In Spain, takeover matters were initially the responsibility of the competition authority until jurisdiction fell to the newly created Comisión Nacional del Mercado de Valores (CNMV) in the course of the legislative reform in 1988.[12] In Italy, the Commissione Nazionale per le Società e la Borsa (CONSOB) serves as the regulatory authority responsible for overseeing matters related to public takeovers.[13] Instituted in 1974, it was appointed to supervise listed companies in 1985.

3.2.2 *Exceptional Design: Panel Regimes*

As mentioned above, six European countries feature a panel regime:[14] the UK, Ireland, Sweden, Austria, Switzerland and Finland.

The UK Takeover Panel on Mergers and Acquisitions is the archetype of all panel-based systems. When it was established in 1968, it was the first of its kind, and it remains the point of reference for other panel regimes. Today, the Takeover Panel is on a statutory footing. Initially, the UK Takeover Panel also regulated takeovers in connection with companies residing in Ireland whose shares were listed either on the London or UK stock exchanges. This changed with the enactment of the Irish Takeover Panel Act 1997 and the establishment of the Irish Takeover Panel.[15]

Austria's Takeover Commission was established under the Takeover Act of 1999, and thus before the finalization of the TOD. Although formally part of the Vienna Stock Exchange, the Takeover Commission is an independent body.[16] Switzerland is another panel country. Before its formal establishment under the Takeover Act of

[12] For a general description see www.cnmv.es/portal/quees/funciones/funciones.aspx?lang = en (accessed 13 July 2024). For its competences see Art. 18 of the Securities Markets and Investment Services Act [Ley 6/2023 de 17 de marzo, de los Mercados de Valores y de los Servicios de Inversión LMVSI), BOE núm. 66, de 18/03/2023] (hereinafter referred to as LMVSI).

[13] Art. 79-duodecies (4) and Art. 101-*ter* (1) Legislative Decree No. 58 of 24 February 1998, Consolidated Law on Financial Intermediation pursuant to Arts 8 and 21 of Law No. 52 of February 1996 [Decreto Legislativo 24 febbraio 1998,n. 58, Testo unico delle disposizioni in materia di intermediazione finanziaria, ai sensi degli articoli 8 e 21 della lege 6 febbraio 1996, n. 52] (hereinafter referred to as Testo Unico della Finanza, TUF).

[14] There are no established prerequisites to allow a body to be called a Takeover Panel. Generally, the expectation would be that it is a regulatory body that is distinct from the overall administration, possesses a significant degree of independence and is predominantly composed of financial market participants.

[15] Available at www.irishstatutebook.ie/eli/1997/act/5/enacted/en/html (accessed 14 July 2024). For a brief account of the history of the Irish Takeover Panel, see Irish Takeover Panel, *Annual Report* 1998, p. 7, available at https://irishtakeoverpanel.ie/wp-content/uploads/2024/05/ITP-Annual-Report-1998.pdf (accessed 14 July 2025). Unlike the UK, Ireland decided to put the panel on a statutory basis from the beginning.

[16] For an overview, see M. Winner, 'Die österreichische Übernahmekommission. Bemerkungen zu Organisation, Verfahren und Rechtsschutz', in H. U. Vogt, H. Fleischer and S. Kalss (eds.), *Protagonisten im Gesellschaftsrecht* (Tübingen: Mohr Siebeck, 2020), p. 147 et seq.

1995, the Swiss Takeover Commission had a self-regulatory predecessor which was set up by the Swiss stock exchanges.[17]

The Irish Takeover Panel and the Austrian Takeover Commission were established by a law, whereas in the UK and in Switzerland the panel structure began as a self-regulatory regime on a non-statutory basis. This is also true for Sweden, which initially established a self-regulatory panel system in 1986.[18] Today, the Takeovers Act of 2006[19] designates the Swedish Financial Supervisory Authority (SFSA) as the competent authority to supervise takeover bids, while granting the SFSA the power to delegate certain functions to self-regulatory bodies such as the Securities Council.[20] However, important parts of takeover regulation remain in the self-regulatory Takeover Code. As a result, the Securities Council exercises statutory functions deriving from the Takeovers Act and self-regulatory functions deriving from the Takeover Code.[21] This puts Sweden in the camp of panel-based countries.

Although Finland has chosen a mixed approach in the institutional design of its takeover regime similar to that of Sweden, the practical outcome is quite different.[22] The financial supervisor (Finnish Financial Supervisory Authority, FIN-FSA) is the competent supervisory authority[23] and the Securities Markets Act is the main regulatory source for takeover bids.[24] The Finnish Securities Market Association

[17] The Commission for Regulatory Questions (Kommission für Regulierungsfragen) was established by the Swiss Takeover Codex, a self-regulatory agreement between the (then several) stock exchanges. For an overview, see S. Emmenegger and A. Bigler, 'Shaping Takeover Law: Die personelle Zusammensetzung der UEK und ihrer Vorgängerorganisation', in R. Trigo Trindade, R. Bahar and G. Neri-Castacane (eds.), *Vers les sommets du droit, Liber amicorum pour Henry Peter* (Geneva/Zurich: Schulthess, 2019), p. 177 et seq.; S. Emmenegger, 'Die schweizerische Übernahmekommission – Schlüsselfigur bei der Gestaltung des Übernahmerechts', in H. U. Vogt, H. Fleischer and S. Kalss (eds.), *Protagonisten im Gesellschaftsrecht*, p. 127 et seq.

[18] R. Skog, 'The Proposal for a 13th Company Law Directive on Takeovers: The Swedish Perspective' (1996) 11 *European Financial Services Law*, 305 et seq.; R. Skog and E. Sjöman, 'The Swedish Securities Council: A Takeover Panel, and More' (2014) *European Company and Financial Law Review* 3, 5.

[19] Law on public takeover bids on the stock market [Lag om offentliga uppköpserbjudanen på aktienmarknaden], issued on 24 May 2006, SFS 2006:451.

[20] Chapter 7 § 1 Swedish Takeovers Act.

[21] For an overview, see Skog and Sjöman, 'The Swedish Securities Council', 1; Skog, 'The Proposal for a 13th Company Law', 305 et seq.

[22] For an overview, see V. Kajala, 'Takeover Rules at the Intersection of Company Law and Securities Law', in R. Gilson, M. Isaaksson, E. Lidman, J. Munck and E. Sjöman (eds.), *Festskrift til Rolf Skog* (Stockholm: Nordstedts Juridik, 2021), p. 687 et seq.; J. Mähönen, 'Finland: Corporate Governance: Nordic tradition with American spices', in A. Fleckner and K. Hopt (eds.), *Comparative Corporate Governance: Functional and International Analysis* (Cambridge: Cambridge University Press, 2013), p. 394 et seq., 424 et seq.

[23] See ESMA, List of competent authorities designated for the purposes of Directive 20004/25/EC on takeover bids (Takeover bids Directive), last updated 02/04/2025, available at www.esma.europa.eu/sites/default/files/takeover_bids_directive.pdf (accessed 13 July 2025).

[24] Kajala, 'Takeover Rules', p. 688.

administers the Helsinki Takeover Code and appoints the Takeover Board.[25] The Code contains recommendations on good practices in takeover proceedings on a comply or explain basis, whereas the Takeover Board's main task is to monitor compliance with the Code.[26] But the binding authority for legal issues is left in the hands of the financial supervisor.

3.2.3 *Particular Case: Norway (until 2025)*

Norway kept the regulatory regime that was in place since the 1990s for three and a half decades. The Securities and Trading Act designated the 'regulated market on which the shares are quoted' as the competent takeover supervisory authority.[27] The Oslo Stock Exchange was the only regulated market in Norway and thus the competent authority.[28] As of 1 April 2025, the Norwegian financial supervisory authority has taken over the function as the competent authority in takeover matters.[29]

3.3 DOES THE INSTITUTIONAL DESIGN HAVE AN IMPACT ON THE FLEXIBILITY OF TAKEOVER LAW?

Flexibility is an undisputed goal in takeover regulation. Recital 6 of the TOD emphasizes that 'in order to be effective, takeover regulation should be flexible and capable of dealing with new circumstances as they arise and should, accordingly, provide for the possibility of exceptions and derogations'.[30] The common perception is that panels are better equipped to achieve this goal than financial supervisors.[31] This perception deserves a closer analysis.

The starting point is the flexibility associated with the mother of all panels – namely, the UK Takeover Panel. According to Kershaw, the flexibility of the UK

[25] On the Securities Market Association, the Takeover Code and the Takeover Board see www.cgfinland.fi/en/ (accessed 27 July 2024).

[26] See Kajala, 'Takeover Rules', p. 688, 690; Mähönen, 'Finland: Corporate Governance', p. 436. See also the tab 'About us, self-regulation' on the website of the Finnish Securities Market Association, available at www.cgfinland.fi/en/ (accessed 27 July 2024).

[27] Section 6-4 of the Securities Trading Act.

[28] Historically, the Oslo Exchange also had the function of monitoring compliance with prospectus and reporting regulations.

[29] https://www.finanstilsynet.no/en/topics/takeover-bids/ (accessed 20 September 2025).

[30] See also B. Muston, 'Coping with Change: A View from the UK Takeover Panel', in J. Muston and R. Skog (eds.), *The Securities Council 25 Years – An Anthology* (Stockholm: Capital Markets Board, 2011), p. 69 et seq., available at www.aktiemarknadsnamnden.se/UserFiles/AMN25ar_kap06_utanKOM_kap06-165x242%20(2).pdf (accessed 13 July 2024).

[31] Awrey, Clarke and Griffith, 'Resolving the Crisis', 4. In a similar vein (discussing the change from a court system to a panel system in Australia): Armson, 'Flexibility in Decision-Making', 460.

system stems from the fact that the panel not only creates but also interprets the takeover rules – it is the 'rulemaker and final arbiter of meaning'.[32] A core factor to achieve flexibility is therefore the supervisory authority's power to make rules in a timely manner and at its own discretion, without having to go through an extensive multi-stage legislative process. The other is the broad discretion in the determination of the meaning of the rules: the panel can interpret the rules according to their 'spirit',[33] to which the panel has unparalleled insights since it designed the rules in the first place. The TOD emphasizes another factor which contributes to flexibility – namely, the possibility of granting derogations and exceptions. Other factors mentioned in connection with flexibility are the informal procedures and the fact that the UK panel is staffed by market participants.[34] This refers to the question of 'who' is making and/or applying the rules. One could call this a 'background-driven' flexibility. Very similar factors were mentioned as motors for flexibility in the Australian reform process which replaced the role of the courts with a panel system for resolving takeover disputes in 1999.[35]

How do these factors play out in the context of the institutional design of takeover regulation in Europe? In other words, does the choice in the institutional design per se favour or inhibit flexibility?

3.3.1 *Flexibility through Rulemaking*

The 'flexibility through rulemaking' factor refers to the power of the takeover authority to adapt the applicable takeover law in a timely manner and at its own discretion, without having to go through an extensive multi-stage legislative process. This, in turn, enables takeover authorities to adapt the applicable takeover rules to the ever-changing takeover landscape, resulting in takeover rules with a strong market proximity.

The UK Takeover Panel was the reference point for flexibility through rulemaking when the TOD was developed, and it remains the authority with the most extensive rulemaking power even today. Taking the UK Takeover Panel as a benchmark, one can assess whether the panel-based countries generally assign a greater rulemaking power to their panels than the countries where the takeover authority is exercised by the financial supervisor.

[32] Kershaw, *Principles of Takeover Regulation*, mn. 3.81.

[33] For this aspect see J. Armour and D. Skeel Jr., 'Who Writes the Rules for Hostile Takeovers and Why? The Peculiar Divergence of US and UK Takeover Regulation' (2007) 95 *Georgetown Law Journal* 1727, 1729; Muston, 'Coping with Change', p. 72.

[34] Armour and Skeel Jr., 'Who Writes the Rules', 1729.

[35] On the Corporate Law Economic Reform Program Act 1999 (CLERP Reform) which entered into force on 13 March 2000, see Armson, 'Flexibility in Decision-Making', 460 et seq., and 461 et. seq. for the flexibility factors.

3.3.1.1 Panel-Based Countries

The UK implemented the TOD via the Companies Act of 2006.[36] The Act put takeover law on a statutory footing and transformed the Takeover Panel into a state body. However, the statutory framework was designed to uphold the identity of the panel as a self-regulatory entity to the greatest extent possible: it was to be 'a state body in name only'.[37] Essentially, this was achieved by creating a mirror image of the TOD in the form of Schedule 1C of the Companies Act. The panel was then tasked with giving effect to the provisions of the Schedule by making rules.[38] These rules are set out in the Takeover Code (formerly the City Code on Takeovers and Mergers).[39] The TOD is only a Framework Directive and Member States were called upon to enact more specific implementing legislation, which contains many core policy decisions not predetermined by European law. In the UK, the 'implementing legislation' was delegated to the Takeover Panel, more precisely to its Code Committee.[40] Therefore, core issues such as the control threshold are defined by the Takeover Panel via the Takeover Code.[41] As a further backstop, the Companies Act entrusts the panel with a generic rulemaking power in takeover matters.[42]

By implementing the TOD, the UK formally entrenched the basic framework and the general provisions of takeover regulation in law.[43] But the rulemaking power has essentially remained in the hands of the Takeover Panel.

The Irish Takeover Panel was modelled after its 'big sister' – that is, the UK panel. The Irish panel issues the Takeover Rules[44] as well as the Substantial Acquisition

[36] The relevant provisions are set forth in Part 28, Chapters 1–3 and in Schedule 1C of the Companies Act 2006.

[37] Kershaw, *Principles of Takeover Regulation*, mn. 4.03.

[38] The rulemaking delegation is set forth in Companies Act 2006, § 943(1). The exceptions regard the squeeze-out and the sell-out provisions, which are included in Chapter 3 (§ 979–991) of the Companies Act 2006.

[39] Available at www.thetakeoverpanel.org.uk/the-code (accessed 13 July 2024).

[40] Takeover Code, Introduction, Section 4(b); D. Awrey and B. Clarke, 'A Transatlantic Perspective on Shareholder Litigation in Public Takeovers', in S. Griffith, J. Erickson. D.H. Webber and V. Winship (eds.), *Research Handbook on Representative Shareholder Litigation* (Cheltenham/Northampton: Edward Elgar, 2018) p. 12; Kershaw, *Principles of Takeover Regulation*, mn. 4.23.

[41] See Rule 9.1. Takeover Code (30%).

[42] Companies Act 2006, § 943(2). Kershaw, *Principles of Takeover Regulation*, mn. 4.18 notes that '[t]o ensure no stone was left unturned in providing the authorized Panel with the same rulemaking power that it had prior to its statutory authorization, the Act provides in effect that anything it did before it can continue to do'. Not within the legislative competence of the UK Takeover panel are the rules concerning the right to squeeze- and sell-out. These matters are instead regulated within the UK Companies Act, see § 979 et seq. (squeeze-out) and § 983 et seq. (sell-out).

[43] Armson, 'Lessons for the Australian Takeovers Panel', 29.

[44] Takeover Panel Act § 5(1)(b), referring to the rules under § 8. The Takeover Rules 2022 are available at https://irishtakeoverpanel.ie/rules/takeover-rules/ (accessed 13 July 2024).

Rules,[45] a comprehensive set of regulations that further develop the statutory framework. These rules apply to all takeover transactions in Ireland and provide the panel with an extensive discretionary scope regarding takeover regulation. However, several matters (such as sanctions and directions given by the panel) are regulated in detail within the Irish Takeover Panel Act.[46] Also, core issues such as the control threshold are set out in the Irish Takeover Panel Act and not in the Rules issued by the Irish Takeover Panel.[47]

Switzerland, another 'UK follower',[48] provides for a rulemaking function for the Takeover Board as well. The Financial Markets Infrastructure Act (FMIA) of 2015 contains a few articles on takeover law.[49] Most of them are succinct and contain key guidelines. Regulation is largely delegated to the Takeover Commission.[50] The Commission primarily regulates via the Takeover Ordinance (TOO).[51] The ordinance addresses important aspects regarding takeovers, such as the contents of the prospectus, the admissible conditions, the applicable rules of fairness, and the specifications on acting in concert.[52] In contrast to the UK, core issues such as the applicable threshold for control are set out in the law.[53] Also, the TOO and its rules are subject to approval by the Swiss Financial Market Authority (FINMA).[54] Therefore, the Swiss regime does not provide its panel with the same extent of rulemaking power as the UK or even the Irish system.

In Austria, the Takeover Act 1999[55] authorized the Takeover Commission to issue ordinances on crucial issues, such as the threshold for the mandatory bid and the definition of parties acting in concert. However, this power was revoked in

45 The Substantial Acquisition Rules 2022 are available at https://irishtakeoverpanel.ie/rules/substantial-acquisition-rules (accessed 13 July 2024).

46 With regard to sanctions, see Art. 10 of the Takeover Panel Act for Ireland and Companies Act (2006), § 952 for the UK. With regard to directions, see Art. 9(3) of the Takeover Panel Act for Ireland and Companies Act (2006), § 946 for the UK.

47 See Art. 1 and 8(3) of the Irish Takeover Panel Act, 1997, the former defining what constitutes relevant 'control' over a company. According to Art. 1(1) of the Takeover Panel Act, 'control' requires 'not less than 30 per cent of the voting rights', stating that other percentages may be prescribed. Considering the extensive general rulemaking power of the panel which derives from Art. 8 of the Takeover Panel Act, it can be assumed that the panel could hypothetically provide for a higher threshold with regard to mandatory bids.

48 Emmenegger, 'Die Schweizerische Übernahmekommission', p. 129.

49 Art. 125-141 FMIA [Finanzmarktinfrastrukturgesetz, FinfraG] of 19 June 2015, SR 958.1. Only ten articles relate to material takeover regulation (e.g. obligations of the bidder and of the target company, examination of the offer, right of withdrawal, competing offers, mandatory bid rule and exemptions, squeeze-out).

50 A large delegation is included in Art. 131 FMIA. Other provisions of the FMIA contain additional delegations.

51 English translations available on the website of the Takeover Commission: www.takeover.ch/legaltexts (accessed 13 July 2024).

52 See Art. 131 FMIA.

53 Art. 135(1) FMIA (33⅓%).

54 See Art. 126(2) FMIA.

55 Takeover Law [Übernahmegesetz] of 14 August 1998, Federal Law Journal I 1998/127.

2006 because of a decision by the Austrian Constitutional Court, which held that independent authorities cannot issue ordinances because the corresponding competence is only available to those administrative authorities that are integrated into the normal administrative structure.[56] This forced the legislator to abandon its original concept. The 2006 amendment[57] repealed the authorizations to issue ordinances and integrated the corresponding provisions – particularly the threshold for the mandatory offer – directly into the text of the law. Hence, the Austrian Takeover Commission has no regulatory powers, but is only able to further develop takeover law by interpreting the applicable legal bases.[58]

The Swedish Securities Council formally lacks a rulemaking power, since the rules are issued by a separate self-regulatory body pertaining to the equity market. The implementation of the TOD by the Takeovers Act in 2006[59] resulted in a split of the takeover regime. The Takeovers Act contains the fundamental rules on takeover bids, such as the mandatory bid rule and the board neutrality rule,[60] which the Securities Council adjudicates (but does not regulate). Other rules remain in the Takeover Rules[61] which are issued by the Swedish Stock Market Self-Regulation Committee.[62] The Securities Council participates in the regular overhauls of the Takeover Code.[63] In any case, the Takeover Code itself pertains to non-binding self-regulation.

The Finnish Takeover Panel, in its role as a body that issues recommendations regarding the interpretation of the self-regulatory Helsinki Takeover Code, lacks rulemaking power altogether. The Securities Market Act delegates rulemaking in takeover matters to the Ministry of Finance and to the Financial Supervisor.[64]

56 Austrian VfGH 6.10.2006, G 151/05 ua, V 115/05 ua, VfSlg 17.961.

57 Übernahmerechts-Änderungsgesetz (ÜbRÄG) 2006, Federal Law Journal I 2006/75.

58 See M. Winner, 'Das österreichische Übernahmerecht – ein Rechtstransplantat aus dem Vereinigten Königreich', in R. Cierpial-Magnor, A. Wudarski and M. Winner (eds.), *Ziele, Wege und Methoden des Rechtstransfers: Erfolge und Misserfolge der Rechtstransplantate* (Vienna: Linde, 2024) p. 293, 308.

59 Law on Public Takeover Bids on the Stock Market [Lag om offentliga uppköpserbjudanen på aktienmarknaden], issued on 24 May 2006, SFS 2006:451.

60 Skog and Sjöman, 'The Swedish Securities Council', 5, 6.

61 Takeover rules for Nasdaq Stockholm and Nordic Growth Market NGM, available at www.aktiemarknadsnamnden.se/UserFiles/EnglishDocuments/TO_rules_2021_Reglerade_marknader.pdf (accessed 13 July 2024).

62 See www.regelkommitten.se (accessed 25 April 2025); Skog and Sjörman, 'The Swedish Securities Council', 6. The Swedish Securities Market Act of 2007 formally designates the Swedish stock exchanges as competent for the administration of the Takeovers Code,ibid., note 13.

63 Ibid.

64 Delegation to the Ministry of Finance: Chapter 11 Section 30 Securities Markets Act (offer documents). Delegation to the Financial Supervisor: Chapter 11 Section 31 Securities Markets Act (matters relating to acting in concert and exemptions). There seems to be only one FINS-FSA regulation on takeovers; see FIN-FSA, Regulations and Guidelines 9/2013, Takeover bid and the obligation to launch a bid, available at www.finanssivalvonta.fi/globalassets/en/regulation/fin-fsa-regulations-and-guidelines/2013/09_2013/9_2013.m1_en.pdf (accessed 27 July 2024).

To round out the picture, the Oslo Stock Exchange, which was the competent authority in takeover matters until 2025, exercised purely supervisory functions and had no role in rulemaking.

In sum, the panel design may favour the rulemaking power of the takeover authority but does not guarantee it. In fact, the broad powers of the UK Takeover Panel remain a singular phenomenon. Out of the five remaining panel countries, only Ireland provides for a genuine rulemaking power of the takeover panel. In Switzerland, the panel's rulemaking is subject to approval by the financial supervisor. In Austria and Sweden, the panel has no rulemaking power at all. This is also true for Finland which is at the far end of the range of panel-structure countries.

3.3.1.2 Countries with a Supervisory System

Continuing with the countries that served as examples in mapping the institutional design of takeover regulation (and which feature substantial capital markets), we can proceed with an examination of the takeover authorities in France, Germany, Italy and Spain.

In France, the primary legislative decree, the Code monétaire et financier, contains the general legislative framework on takeovers which consists of only seven (albeit lengthy) articles.[65] It is supplemented by a number of provisions in the Code de Commerce, notably regarding defensive measures, notification duties related to thresholds, and the definition of acting in concert.[66] Both codes provide for extensive rulemaking delegation to the AMF to enact the detailed regulations. The roughly 110 articles of the relevant General Regulations[67] contain general principles and rules on conditions, on procedures for public offers, and on competing offers and improved offers, as well as conditions and procedures for mandatory public offers (including exemptions from the mandatory bid rule[68]). They also address questions concerning squeeze-out and sell-out rights.[69] Overall, the AMF's rulemaking power is extensive, although less so than that of the UK Takeover Panel which, in fact, fulfils the role of the implementing legislator under the TOD.

In Italy, the Testo Unica della Finanza (TUF),[70] as the main legislative Act regarding takeover matters, contains the general legislative framework in fourteen

[65] L.433-1 – L.433.4 Code monétaire et financier.

[66] L.233-6 – L.233.15 Code de Commerce (notification and acting in concert); L.233.32 – L233.40 (defensive measures).

[67] Règlement général de l'AMF, Titre III – Offres publiques d'aquisition (Art. 231-1–238-5), available at www.amf-france.org/en/eli/fr/aai/amf/rg/20230730/notes (accessed 13 July 2024).

[68] Art. 234-9 Règlement général de l'AMF.

[69] Art. 236-1 –236-7 Règlement général de l'AMF.

[70] Legislative Decree No. 58 of 24 February 1998, Consolidated Law on Financial Intermediation pursuant to articles 8 and 21 of Law No. 52 of February 1996 (as of February 2024) [Decreto Legislativo 24 febbraio 1998,n. 58, Testo unico delle disposizioni in materia di intermediazione

provisions, eight of which are dedicated to the mandatory bid rule.[71] The Act is supplemented by the Issuers' Regulation (IR),[72] a set of secondary rules issued by CONSOB. Within the confines of the TUF, CONSOB is completely independent in its rulemaking authority. Compared to the AMF, CONSOB has a similar degree of rulemaking power covering similar matters.[73] Unlike the AMF, however, CONSOB is not authorized to issue rules on deadlines, the equitable price or the type of consideration in the context of mandatory bids.[74]

The Spanish CNMV possesses only very limited rulemaking power. Takeover bids are primarily regulated in the Securities Markets and Investment Services Act (LMVSI)[75] as well as the Royal Decree 1066/2007 of 27 July 2007 which contains more detailed rules regarding the general principles set out in the LMVSI.[76] The CNMV is only authorized to make rules concerning the contents and publication modalities of announcements and offer documents as well as about specific matters relating to guarantees, the rights to squeeze- and sell-out, and the optional regulatory matters provided for in Art. 13 TOD.[77] It exercises these rulemaking powers by the issuance of circulars to provide detailed instructions and interpretations of the legal bases.[78]

Very limited regulatory power lies with the German BaFin.[79] Its only rulemaking power relates to the content and form of the communication of a foreign target

finanziaria, ai sensi degli articoli 8 e 21 della lege 6 febbraio 1996,n. 52] (hereinafter referred to as Testo Unico della Finanza, TUF), available at www.consob.it/web/consob-and-its-activities/laws-and-regulations (main page) (accessed 26 July 2024).

71 TUF Chapter II, Public Offers to buy or exchange financial instruments, Art. 101*bis* – Art. 112.

72 CONSOB Regulation No. 11971 of 14 May 1999 (as of 29 February 2024), Part II, Title II: Takeover Bids or Exchange Tender Offers, available at www.consob.it/web/consob-and-its-activities/laws-and-regulations (main page) (accessed 26 July 2024).

73 Rulemaking powers are delegated with regard to the following matters: the categories of securities and derivatives that should count towards the threshold for mandatory bids (see § 105(3), (3-*bis*) TUF); certain calculation modalities for the threshold in the context of mandatory bids (see § 106(3), (3-*bis*) TUF); exceptions to the obligation (see § 107 TUF); the contents and publication terms of announcements, offer documents and target company responses (see § 102, 103 TUF and § 37 et seq. IR); certain transparency rules (see § 41 IR); acceptance periods for tender offers (see § 40 IR); publication terms and the rules to determine the equivalence of company statutes in the context of defensive measures (§ 104-*ter*(3), 104-*ter*(4) TUF); specific modalities in the context of the rights to squeeze- and sell-out (§ 108(4), (5), (7), 111(2) TUF, implemented in § 50 et seq. IR); optional regulatory matters as provided for in Art. 13 TOD (implemented in § 43 et seq., IR).

74 See § 106(II), (II-*bis*) TUF.

75 Art. 108 – 117 Ley 6/2023 de 17 de marzo, de los Mercados de Valores y de los Servicios de Inversión LMV), BOE núm. 66, de 18/03/2023 (LMV).

76 Available at www.boe.es/buscar/act.php?id = BOE-A-2007-14483 (accessed 13 July 2024).

77 § 15(2), 16(5), 17(1), 18(4) and (5), 43 and 48(11) of the 1066/2007 Royal Decree on public takeovers.

78 See, for example, Circular 8/2008 of 10 December 2008.

79 See, for example, U. Ehricke, '§ 4', in M. Beurskens/U. Ehricke/J. Ekkenga, *Kommentar WpÜG*, 2nd ed. (Munich: Beck, 2021), mn. 9.

company regarding their choice of the competent supervisory authority.[80] Other ordinances in the field of takeovers are issued by the Ministry of Finance.[81]

3.3.1.3 Conclusion

We find that there is no clear correlation between the institutional designs chosen by the countries examined and the extent of rulemaking power delegated to the respective takeover authorities. In other words, it cannot be concluded that panels are generally equipped with more rulemaking power than supervisory authorities or vice versa.

3.3.2 *Flexibility through Exemption Powers*

Once the regulations are in place, the flexibility of an authority is reflected by the discretionary powers it is granted by national legislation regarding the application of the rules. Hence, even a takeover authority without rulemaking power can have a certain degree of flexibility, provided it has a high degree of discretion in the application of the rules. Article 4.5, paragraph 2, of the TOD stipulates that Member States have the discretion within their national legal frameworks to establish specific exemptions or derogations from the TOD's rules. The legislators implement this assignment in different ways, with the takeover authorities being granted varying degrees of discretion.

Overall, it is appropriate to distinguish whether the national law of a (non-) Member State grants the takeover authority a *general competence to grant exemptions* from takeover regulation or whether the takeover authority is restricted to *granting exemptions for specific provisions*. Most of the states refrained from the former and only implemented the latter, solely granting their takeover authorities the power to grant exemptions from specific rules.[82] As a proxy, we will take one of the core issues of takeover law – namely, exemptions from the mandatory bid rule – knowing quite well that, in practice, many other areas of exemption – for example, those from the minimum price in a mandatory bid – are of similar importance. In the following, we will deal exclusively with these two aspects of exemptions. We will not look at another important, albeit hard-to-determine factor – namely, the level of specificity of the rules: the supervisory authority has considerably more leeway if the rules on takeovers are more principled in nature and contain less specific regulation. However, investigating this issue would probably entail an in-

[80] Verordnung zur Übertragung von Befugnissen zum Erlass von Rechtsverordnungen auf die Bundesanstalt für Finanzdienstleistungsaufsicht of 13 December 2002, §1(2) and WpÜG §1(5).

[81] Especially the WpÜG-Angebotsverordnung (WpÜG-AngV), dealing with core issues such as exceptions from the mandatory bid and pricing.

[82] For example, certain exemptions from the obligation to publish profit forecasts and other financial statements (see Rule 28 of the Irish Takeover Rules).

depth analysis of the different sets of rules, which goes beyond the scope of this contribution.

3.3.2.1 General Power to Grant Exemptions

A general power to grant exemptions is found within the national law of most panel countries – namely, the UK, Ireland, Sweden and Switzerland.

According to the UK Takeover Code, the Takeover Panel is entrusted with a judicial function: it may give (binding) rulings on the interpretation, application or effect of the takeover rules.[83] This includes the power to derogate or grant a waiver to a party from the application of a rule, if circumstances appear where the panel considers that the particular rule would operate unduly harshly or in an unnecessarily restrictive, burdensome or otherwise inappropriate manner.[84] Of course, any exceptions granted must 'respect' the general principles of the Takeover Code, which transpose Art. 3(1) TOD,[85] and must not violate any superior law, but nevertheless this provision is very extensive and grants the UK Takeover Panel a particularly broad discretion in the application of the Takeover Code, which simultaneously allows the panel to be highly flexible in the application of the rules.[86]

Similarly, the Irish Takeover Act stipulates a general competence of the Irish Takeover Panel to 'grant derogations from, or waive, any rules under this section in relation to a particular matter where, in the opinion of the Panel, having regard to the exceptional circumstances of the matter, but taking into consideration the scheduled principles, it is appropriate to do so'.[87] The scope of the rule appears to be more or less identical to the respective provision in the UK. Although the Irish provision does not specify the circumstances for granting an exemption in detail, they are most likely to be the same (overly harsh, restrictive, burdensome or otherwise inappropriate operation of the rule). The provision expressively states that the respective general principles of the Code must always be taken into consideration.

In the same vein, the Swiss Takeover Commission has a general competence to grant exemptions if they are justified by overriding interests. Formally, this power is restricted to exemptions from its own regulations – namely, the Takeover Ordinance.[88] However, court rulings have confirmed that the Takeover Commission may also grant

[83] Companies Act 2006, § 945. Regarding the generally binding nature of rulings, see Introduction 6(b) of the Takeover Code.

[84] See Introduction 2(c) of the Takeover Code.

[85] Exceptionally, the panel may grant a waiver notwithstanding that, in doing so, one or more of the General Principles might not be respected, especially in rescue operations.

[86] See Marccus Partners, *The Takeover Bids Directive Assessment Report*, p. 106, available at https://op.europa.eu/en/publication-detail/-/publication/65701b75-7583-4b0d-a551-33051d8e27c1 (accessed 13 July 2025).

[87] See Section 8(7) Irish Takeover Panel Act 1997.

[88] Art. 4 of the Takeover Ordinance, available at www.takeover.ch/legaltexts (accessed 13 July 2024).

exemptions from statutory provisions if they are substantiated by prevailing interests of the parties concerned and are in line with the legislative objectives of Swiss takeover law.[89] As a result, the general competence to grant exemptions of the Swiss Takeover Panel is, in its scope, comparable to the competences of the UK and Irish panels.

In Sweden, the exemption power of the Securities Council is not general in its form, but nevertheless extensive in its content. Exemption powers exist for mandatory bids and defensive measures, and thus for the two core areas where exemptions are materially relevant,[90] as well as for all of the requirements in the Takeover Rules. Some tasks are, however, not assigned to the Securities Council and therefore remain outside of its exemption power. For instance, the monitoring of takeover bids (approval of offer documents) is performed by the Swedish Financial Supervisory Authority (SFSA).[91] In sum, the exemption power of the Swedish Securities Council is extensive, but – for lack of a general exemption power in all takeover matters – not as extensive as in the UK, Ireland and Switzerland.

Given the general tendency among panel countries to provide their supervisors with broad discretion as to the application of takeover rules, it is noteworthy that Austria does not provide the ATC with a general competence to grant exemptions.[92] However, one has to consider that a certain rule may not be applied by way of purposive interpretation: if the aim of the legislation, as determined, inter alia, by the general principles according to Art. 3(2) TOD, is not achieved by the application of a specific rule, it may be disapplied (the so-called teleological reduction); this, in theory, does not depend upon a formal waiver by the ATC, although, in practice, parties will clarify the situation with the authority beforehand. The exact circumstances under which the ATC may make use of this rule are not clarified and instances of its application are rare[93] and typically not subject to formal rulings.

[89] See D. Gericke and K. Wiedmer, *Kommentar Übernahmeverordnung (UEV)*, 2nd ed. (Zurich: Schulthess, 2020) Art. 4 mn. 5. In the academic discourse this practice is criticized from the perspective of certain constitutional principles, as Art. 4(1) TOO is not a sufficient statutory framework. As examples, see the following decisions of the Swiss Takeover Commission (available at www.takeover.ch, Search): TOB 0547/01 in the matter of International Minerals Corporation of 23 September 2013 (cons. 4, margin o. 15); TOB 0609/01 in the matter of SHL Telemedicine Ltd of 14 July 2015 (cons. 3.2, margin o. 12), TOB 0443/01 in the matter of Mach Hitech AG in liquidation of 16 June 2010 (cons. 2., margin o. 4).

[90] Chapter 7 § 5 Swedish Takeovers Act. The exemption power is conferred to the Financial Supervisor which is granted the power to delegate certain functions to self-regulatory bodies such as the Securities Council (Chapter 7 § 1 Swedish Takeovers Act). See also I.2 of the Takeover Rules for Nasdaq Stockholm and Nordic Growth Market NGM (granting the Securities Council exemption powers from the self-regulatory Takeover Rules).

[91] 2a Chapter §5 Act on Trading Financial Instruments).

[92] Winner, 'Das österreichische Übernahmerecht', p. 308. (The Austrian legislator would have seen this as a violation of certain constitutional principles.)

[93] See, however, recently the decision GZ 2022/3/2-11, available at www.takeover.at/uploads/u/pxe/A2_Entscheidungen/Stellungnahmen/Stellungnahme_S_IMMO_-_23.05.2022_-_GZ_2022-3-2.pdf (accessed 13 July 2024), where such a reduction was discussed for two separate legal norms and applied to one of them.

Lastly, it follows from the role of the Finnish Takeover Panel as an authority which solely issues recommendations that it cannot grant exemptions from any binding takeover rules. Instead, this power is given to the Finnish financial supervisor: the Securities Market Act provides the Finnish Financial Supervisory Authority with the competence to grant – for 'a special reason'[94] – a permission to derogate from any obligation provided in chapter 11 of the Securities Market Act, which regulates takeover bids and the obligation to launch a bid.[95] There is an (ongoing) discussion about transferring the power of exemption to the Finnish Takeover Panel.[96]

Finland remains an exception. If one looks at countries with the general financial supervisor as regulator for takeovers, the picture is quite the opposite: few of them provide their supervisor with a general power to derogate from takeover rules. For Germany, commentators assume that the BaFin cannot derogate from specific rules unless these rules foresee such a waiver; however, as explained for Austria, in exceptional circumstances a specific rule may not be applicable.[97] Neither does the French AMF have a power to derogate from the applicable laws or its own General Regulations in a particular case. Similarly, the Spanish CNMV does not have the general power to waive the application of specific rules, although it has some discretionary powers when dealing with exceptions to the mandatory bid.[98] Under Italian law, CONSOB has the power to identify takeover bids involving financial products other than securities where the general takeover rules may not apply.[99] However, such a derogation cannot result in a case-specific waiver, but must happen by regulation for generally defined cases; hence, in Italy, the power to grant exemptions is restricted in scope and is delimited by its own rulemaking power.

In summary, it can be stated that the institutional design of takeover authorities does not necessarily influence their flexibility. But the tendency is clear: panel countries tend to provide greater flexibility than most of the countries with a traditional supervisory structure.

3.3.2.2 Limited Power to Grant Exemptions from the Mandatory Offer

All countries covered in this article have provisions that allow their respective takeover authority to grant exceptions from certain provisions in individual cases.[100] Most of these provisions concern the obligation to make a mandatory offer, of which

94 See Part IV, Chapter 11, Section 26 Securities Market Act.

95 Ibid.

96 Mähönen, 'Finland: Corporate Governance', p. 436.

97 Ehricke, '§ 4', mn. 10.

98 See Section 3.3.2.2.

99 See Art. 101-bis (3-bis) TUF.

100 For an overview of the situation in around 2015, see M. Winner, 'Ausnahmen von der Angebotspflicht in Europa – ein Überblick', in W. Blocher, M. Gelter and M. Pucher (eds.), *Festschrift für Christian Nowotny* (Vienna: Manz, 2015) p. 685.

we will give a brief overview. But even here, we see considerable differences both in the scope of the exemptions and the discretion given to the takeover authorities.

This is perfectly clear for those countries which grant their authorities a general power to waive the application of certain rules, such as the UK. The Takeover Code contains specific notes on exemptions to the mandatory bid,[101] which give an indication of how the panel will exercise its discretion when waiving the bid obligation, indicated by wordings such as 'the Panel will not normally require an offer if [. . .]'.[102] As a result, the UK (and Irish) approach provides the panel with a broad discretion. Similarly, according to Chapter 7 Section 5, the Swedish Securities Council may grant an ad hoc exemption from the provisions on mandatory bids 'if there are special reasons'; as there are no statutory exemptions, the Council's decisions on ad hoc exemptions are numerous.[103]

The situation in Switzerland is comparable: for some cases, the law itself provides an exemption from the bid obligation.[104] In addition, it contains a list of cases where the Takeover Commission 'may' grant an exemption.[105] Lastly, the Takeover Ordinance[106] contains a general exemption clause which – as we mentioned above[107] – is interpreted broadly to target not only the provisions of the Ordinance but also the statutory provisions.

Again, Austria is an outlier within the panel countries as the exceptions from the mandatory bid are enumerated by law.[108] In principle, the Takeover Commission cannot introduce additional exceptions, unless by analogy to existing cases,[109] which it has done in several instances.[110] However, this provides much less flexibility than a general power to waive the application of the mandatory bid rule. Apart from the Austrian example, however, countries with a panel structure provide their supervisors with considerable discretion in applying the mandatory bid.

Lastly, Finland's Takeover Panel obviously lacks any power to introduce exceptions to the mandatory bid rule. Finland's panel has a different role

[101] See Takeover Code, Notes on Dispensations from Rule 9.

[102] Similarly, Irish Takeover Code, Notes on Possible Waivers of and Derogations from Rule 9.

[103] See R. Skog and E. Sjöman, 'No Rule, Just Exemptions? Mandatory Bids in Sweden and the EU' (2014) 3 *European Company and Financial Law Review* 393.

[104] See Art. 136(2) FMIA: Voting rights acquired by donation, succession, partition of an estate, matrimonial property law, execution proceedings.

[105] See Art. 136(1) FMIA: e.g. transfers within a group, temporary passing of the threshold, recovery measures.

[106] See Art. 41(1) and (2) Takeover Ordinance (TOO).

[107] See Section 3.3.2.1.

[108] See Art. 24 et seq. Austrian Takeover Act.

[109] See also the explanatory memorandum to the 2006 amendment of the Takeover Act, ErlRV 1334 BlgNR XXII. GP, p. 17.

[110] For example, decisions GZ 2009/1/2-42, available at www.takeover.at/uploads/u/pxe/A2_Entscheidungen/Stellungnahmen/GZ_2009-3-2-42_Strabag_SE_-_27.4.2009.pdf (accessed 13 July 2024); GZ 2002/3/3-63, available at www.takeover.at/uploads/u/pxe/A2_Entscheidungen/Bescheide/GZ_2002-3-3-63_Anonym__-_6.8.2002.pdf (accessed 13 July 2024).

altogether – which underlines the fact that the existence of a panel does not automatically include an institutional design that is aligned with the UK model.

If one looks at non-panel countries, the situation is much more diverse. Starting with Germany, cases for a waiver of the mandatory bid are enumerated in an ordinance issued by the Ministry of Finance.[111] However, most of these cases[112] leave discretion to BaFin. Additionally, the enumeration is not exclusive and BaFin can grant additional exemptions based on several rather broad criteria contained in the law.[113] In contrast, the conditions under which the AMF may grant an exemption from the bid obligation are set by the regulator itself in its General Regulations.[114] It has discretionary power to refuse to grant an exemption. Additionally, the AMF has given itself the right to grant an ad hoc waiver, although this is not expressly foreseen in the legal bases.[115] Hence, in both countries, the regulators have considerable discretion.

The Italian and Spanish regulators have less leeway. Under Italian law, CONSOB does not have the general power to waive the application of the mandatory bid rule but can only grant exemptions in specific cases, which are enumerated in Art. 106 TUF. These cases are further specified in an ordinance, the IR, which is issued by the regulator.[116] However, Art. 106(6) TUF states that CONSOB may establish that a takeover bid shall not be considered mandatory in cases mentioned in this rule, even if they are not expressly covered by the detailed rules of the regulation. Hence, the regulator has some discretion, but cannot exceed the limits posed by the TUF. Similarly, the Spanish CNMV is bound by the cases set out in Art. 8 RD 1066/2007, which contain exceptions which operate by law and do not depend upon a waiver by the authority. However, some of these cases use wording which leaves a wide margin for interpretation.

Summing up, the discretion in waiving the mandatory bid rule is considerable for almost all countries with a panel structure, except for Austria. Among those countries with non-panel supervisors, it is not possible to discern a clear trend.

[111] See Art. 9 WpÜG-AngV.

[112] In certain constellations, BaFin is obliged to exempt the bidder from the obligation to make an offer if certain conditions are met (§ 20 and § 36 WpÜG). In others, BaFin is not obliged to do so, even if the requirements of the relevant provision are met, § 24, § 26(2), and § 37 WpÜG.

[113] See A. Meyer, '§ 37' in L. Angerer, T. O. Brandi and R. Süßmann, *Wertpapiererwerbs- und Übernahmegesetz*, 4th ed. (Munich: CH Beck, 2023), mn. 1, 29. For the criteria, see Art. 37(1) WpÜG.

[114] See Art. L 433-3 I. Code monétaire et financier and Art. 234-4, 234-7 to 234-10 (especially, Art. 234-9) General Regulations.

[115] See Paris Court of Appeal, 2 April 2008, Sacyr v. Eiffage, CA Paris No. 07/11675; Marccus Partners, *The Takeover Bids Directive Assessment Report*, p. 140; R. Skog/E. Sjöman, *Derogations from the mandatory bid rule*, European Corporate Governance Institute Law Working Paper No. 760/2024, pt. 2.1, available at www.ecgi.global/sites/default/files/working_papers/documents/derogationsfromthemandatorybidrule.pdf (accessed 13 July 2024).

[116] See Art. 49 IR.

3.3.3 *Flexibility through Diversity of the Decision-Makers*

It is not only important to what extent the takeover authority can make rules and what flexibility it has in the application of rules but also to look at *who* makes and applies the rules, as it is assumed that a takeover authority staffed by market participants with a broad range of backgrounds (e.g. law, business, financial markets, economics and accounting) possesses greater flexibility than a rather homogeneously composed board of decision-makers.[117] Although there are no empirical studies on this, the assumption is intuitively plausible: the combination of decision-makers with different backgrounds automatically leads to a more diverse approach, which in turn enables the authority to undertake a more differentiated evaluation of the different interests involved, and thus ensures a higher quality of the decisions made. The question to be asked here is whether the decision-makers within panels come from more diverse backgrounds than the personnel within takeover authorities.

If we look at the panels, we can see that the UK Takeover Panel consists of up to thirty-five members split into five different committees.[118] The current list of thirty panel members[119] shows the broad involvement of practitioners in the Panel's work. Additionally, different business or trade associations (e.g. The Association of British Insurers, The Investment Association, the Pensions and Lifetime Savings Association) have the right to appoint up to ten members, who automatically become part of the hearings committee responsible for the review of rulings by the Panel's executive.[120] Furthermore, the Takeover Code specifies the composition of the Code Committee, which carries out the rulemaking functions of the panel: 'The Code Committee is drawn from a spread of shareholder, corporate, practitioner and other interests within the Panel's regulated community.'[121] The Panel Executive, that is the body carrying out the day-to-day business, giving guidance and issuing rulings, is composed of a mixture of seasoned employees and officers on secondment from the City's institutions, among the latter the Panel's Director General.[122] A diverse range of members from different sectors with different professional backgrounds is therefore already foreseen by the Takeover Code itself. As a result, the UK Takeover Panel enjoys a particularly wide range of personal backgrounds among its members.

[117] See Armson, 'Flexibility in Decision-Making', 461 et seq.

[118] The hearings committee, the code committee, the finance audit and risk committee, the nomination committee and the remuneration committee.

[119] Available at www.thetakeoverpanel.org.uk/structure/panel-membership (accessed 13 July 2024).

[120] See Introduction 4(a) Takeover Code. See also Kershaw, *Principles of Takeover Regulation*, mn. 4.20 et seq.

[121] See Introduction 4(b) Takeover Code.

[122] Available at www.thetakeoverpanel.org.uk/structure/executive (accessed 13 July 2024). See also Kershaw, *Principles of Takeover Regulation*, mn. 4.29.

A comparable arrangement regarding the composition can be found in the Swiss Takeover Panel. It must be composed of expert representatives of securities firms and listed companies as well as investors.[123] With this affiliation requirement, the Swiss legislator has made it clear that a certain degree of interdependence between the Takeover Panel and the industry it monitors is a deliberate objective. Hence, the Swiss Takeover Board also distinguishes itself by the broad composition of its panel members.[124]

Similar regulations regarding the composition of members can be found in the other panel countries – Ireland,[125] Sweden[126] and Austria.[127] Overall, all the examined panel countries seem to aim at a broad composition of members.

For the non-panel countries, things look quite different. There does not seem to be a statutory basis or declaration of intent regarding the inclusion of market participants within the decision-makers for BaFin[128] (Germany), CONSOB (Italy) or CNMV (Spain). According to its information, the French AMF, as a non-panel and purely governmental authority, is committed to a broad composition of decision-makers,[129] even though there does not seem to be any legal obligation in this respect. The board of the AMF comprises sixteen members drawn from the Council of State, the Court of Cassation, the Court of Auditors, the French national bank and the Accounting Standards Authority as well as professional members, who are appointed by the Minister of Finance after consulting representative organizations. The board of the AMF therefore consists of people from the government as well as market participants.

Overall, the decision-makers within the takeover panels generally seem to include market participants, while this is rather unusual with the general supervisors. This is not surprising: by creating a separate panel, a certain externalization of this

[123] See Art. 126(1) Swiss FMIA.

[124] The current composition of the Swiss Takover Panel is available at www.takeover.ch/takeover board/members (accessed 13 July 2024).

[125] Art. 6 Takeover Panel Act; Awrey and Clarke, 'A Transatlantic Perspective', p. 415, 427.

[126] Skog and Sjöman, 'The Swedish Securities Council', 7. The members of the Securities Council are appointed by the Swedish Association of Best Practices in the Securities Market for two years. The Council consists of about thirty members, mostly business executives, lawyers, bankers and representatives of various investor categories. The Secretariat consists of the Director General and one other officer. They prepare the cases and respond to consultations but have no mandate to give formal rulings.

[127] Art. 28 Takeover Act. However, the members of the Takeover Commission's panels are appointed by the Minister of Justice and typically are members of academia, judges and representatives of trade and labour associations, but not practitioners in takeover law; see also Winner, 'Das österreichische Übernahmerecht', p. 306.

[128] Although since 2021 BaFin has had a foreign national with experience in non-EU financial markets as president; see www.bafin.de/EN/DieBaFin/Leitung/Praesident/praesident_node_en .html (accessed 13 July 2024).

[129] See the notes on the website of the AMF, available at www.amf-france.org/en/amf/our-organisa tion/amf-board (accessed 13 July 2024).

governmental task takes place. The tasks and competences of the panel members are limited to takeover matters, allowing members to be selected solely with the aim of ensuring the most proficient board to handle the supervision (and sometimes regulation) of public takeovers, whereas senior staff within the financial supervisory authority are generally subject to further requirements. In other words, the panel as a structure offers greater flexibility in terms of staffing, making it easier to include active market participants.

Summing up, the panel countries are better at integrating market participants into their decision-making boards, which allows for greater flexibility in decision-making and, ideally, a better quality of decisions. The institutional design of a takeover authority, therefore, influences its flexibility with regard to its decision-makers.

3.3.4 *Conclusion*

Our findings indicate that flexibility through rulemaking is not inherently tied to a panel structure. For instance, prominent panels like the Swedish Securities Council and the Austrian Takeover Commission lack rulemaking power. Finland's Takeover Commission is even more modest: it issues non-binding statements on compliance with the non-binding Helsinki Takeover Code. Conversely, the French AMF and Italian CONSOB have extensive powers to enact general implementing regulations.

In terms of general exemption authority, panel regimes typically have such powers, whereas supervisory regimes often do not, though this is not a strict rule. Austria's Takeover Commission lacks formal exemption powers, while only Finland's financial supervisory authority can derogate from legal provisions in takeover matters – Finland being the country whose takeover panel has very little power. For exemptions from the mandatory bid rule, supervisory regimes such as those in France, Italy and Germany exhibit notable discretion, whereas Austria is more restricted.

Regarding background-driven flexibility, panel countries generally demonstrate significant diversity, involving market participants in their boards and commissions. This contrasts with supervisory countries, except France, where external members are included in the authority.

In conclusion, flexibility through diversity is the only clear-cut case in comparative flexibility analysis. Exceptions exist on both sides for rulemaking and decision-making flexibility.

3.4 DOES THE INSTITUTIONAL DESIGN HAVE AN IMPACT ON THE PREDICTABILITY OF THE TAKEOVER PROCESS?

Considering the economic resources which are at stake in a takeover bid, the predictability of the takeover process is of paramount importance for the parties involved. Predictability includes several elements.[130] One element is the transparency regarding the takeover process – that is, who needs to do what and when. Usually, this does not cause major issues. Another element is the *transparency* regarding the decisions of the authority. Are parties to a takeover confronted with a black box, or can they gain a reasonable understanding of the considerations which the authority may have regarding the application of takeover rules in certain situations? One way to measure transparency is to look at whether the decisions of the authority are published, either integrally or via practice statements. Another element of predictability concerns the possibility of approaching the takeover authority for *guidance* to clarify certain questions before launching the bid, or to clarify the authority's position on a possible exemption from the mandatory bid rule. Still another element of predictability is to what extent decisions by the regulator are final or whether they can be *challenged* in the courts. We will look at each of these aspects in turn, in view of possible trends regarding panel regimes and supervisory authority regimes.

3.4.1 *Predictability through Decisional Transparency*

A central element regarding the predictability of a takeover regime is the transparency in the application of takeover rules by the authority.[131] Transparency is primarily determined by the amount and depth of information provided to the public and to the affected stakeholders. The publication of such information can happen in various formats. A high degree of transparency exists if the decisions of the takeover authority itself are publicly accessible. Otherwise, a certain degree of transparency can still be ensured if the activities of the takeover authority are in some way publicly documented (e.g. in the form of an annual report). Additionally, the competent takeover authorities can outline their practice using circulars, FAQs and the like.

In takeover matters, the level of regulatory and supervisory transparency varies greatly between the different authorities of the respective countries. Certainly, multiple factors contribute to this variation. The question is whether one can reasonably assert that the organizational structure of these authorities and the level of transparency correlate significantly. We will analyse in the following the

130 For another perspective see E. Armson, 'Certainty in Decision-Making: An Assessment of the Australian Takeovers Panel' (2016) 38 *Sydney Law Review* 369 (distinguishing between the element of consistency and that of finality).

131 See, for example, the definition of transparency in the glossary of the WTO ('*Degree to which trade policies and practices, and the process by which they are established, are open and predictable*', available at www.wto.org/english/thewto_e/glossary_e/transparency_e.htm (accessed 13 July 2024); see also J. Barth, A. Prabha and C. Wihlborg, 'Transparency of Financial Regulation', in J. Forssbæck and L, Oxelheim (eds.), *The Oxford Handbook of Economic and Institutional Transparency* (Oxford: Oxford University Press, 2014), p. 258.

transparency of the decisions by the authorities themselves; we do not look at transparency of judicial decisions following challenges to decisions by the takeover authorities.

3.4.1.1 Panel Countries: Best in Class

It appears that it is precisely the few countries using a panel regime (Austria, Ireland, Sweden, UK, Switzerland, Finland) that provide a substantial level of transparency regarding the practice of their takeover authorities. The same was true for Norway, whose institutional identity was initially closer to a panel regime than to a (classic) financial supervisory regime.

A leading example in accessibility of the decisions and all other relevant considerations of the takeover authority is the Austrian Takeover Commission. It has a particularly well-structured website[132] on which both past and current takeover bids,[133] the corresponding decisions[134] of the Takeover Commission and information about the current composition of the authority[135] are easily accessible.

Following a similar structure, the websites of the Swiss Takeover Board, the Swedish Securities Council and the Finnish Takeover Panel also provide access to the decisions[136] and other related information (circulars) as well as the composition of the authority.[137] Norway also provided easy access to its decisions:[138] all rulings were published,[139] and the Stock Exchange also published an annual collection which included all circulars issued in the course of the year, excerpts

[132] See the website of the Austrian Takeover Commission, available at www.takeover.at/ (accessed 13 July 2024).

[133] See the tab 'Übernahmeangebote' on the website of the Austrian Takeover Commission, available at www.takeover.at/uebernahmeangebote/ (accessed 13 July 2024).

[134] See the tab 'Entscheidungen' on the website of the Austrian Takeover Commission, available at www.takeover.at/entscheidungen/ (accessed 13 July 2024).

[135] See the tab 'Die Übernahmekommission' on the website of the Austrian Takeover Commission, available at www.takeover.at/die-uebernahmekommission/ (accessed 13 July 2024).

[136] See the tab 'Transactions, All' on the website of the Swiss Takeover Commission, available at www.takeover.ch/transactions/all (accessed 13 July 2024); see the list of decisions of the Swedish Securities Council available at (only in Swedish) www.aktiemarknadsnamnden.se/uttalanden/uttalanden-sorterade-efter-publiceringsd__3614 (accessed 13 July 2024); see the list of decisions of the Finnish Takeover Panel, available at www.cgfinland.fi/en/takeover-code/, (accessed 27 July 2024).

[137] See the tab 'Members' on the website of the Swiss Takeover Board, available at www.takeover.ch/takeoverboard/members> (accessed 13 July 2024); see the tab 'members' on the website of the Swedish Securites Council, available at www.aktiemarknadsnamnden.se/about-the-swedish-securities-council/members-of-the-swedish-securities-counci__3672 (accessed 13 July 2024); see the tab 'about us, members' of the Finnish Takeover Panel, available at www.cgfinland.fi/en/takeover-code/ (accessed 27 July 2024).

[138] See the website of the Oslo Stock Exchange, available at www.euronext.com/nb/markets/oslo (accessed 13 July 2024).

[139] Available at www.euronext.com/nb/markets/oslo (accessed 13 July 2024, under the heading 'Decisions made by Euronext Oslo Børs').

from the Stock Exchange decisions, letters and other statements which were thought to be of interest to the takeover community because they illustrated interpretations and practices.[140] The newly competent Norwegian financial supervisory authority has announced that it will regularly publish decisions, clarifications, practices and other relevant information related to takeover bids. It remains to be seen whether the previous level of transparency is maintained.[141]

As to the mother of all takeover panels, the UK Panel publishes its decisions on the panel website. However, one must remember that the Panel Executive usually responds to queries and complaints by phone;[142] accordingly, published Panel Executive decisions are rare. But all other relevant information, including the rulings of the Hearing Committee, the practice statements,[143] the panel bulletins,[144] and even the condolences on the death of the queen, are consolidated and published as 'Panel Statements'.[145] Not unexpectedly, the Irish Takeover Panel follows the UK model.[146]

3.4.1.2 Middle Ground

Since financial supervisory authorities have a large portfolio of responsibilities, information on the specific topic of takeover bids will necessarily be more difficult to find than in a country with a panel structure. It is always several 'clicks' away, and navigation often proves challenging. Therefore, countries with a supervisory structure do not make the 'best in class' list.

The French AMF does list the offer documents and its decisions on takeover bids in an accessible and structured manner – but one first has to find the relevant database.[147] Also, important legal documents, such as the relevant laws and regulations, are placed under different headings. Spain's CNMV also publishes a wide

[140] Available at www.euronext.com/nb/markets/ (accessed 13 July 2024, under the heading 'Circulars, decisions and statements').

[141] https://www.finanstilsynet.no/en/topics/takeover-bids/ (acessed 20 September 2025)

[142] Awrey, Clarke and Griffith, 'Resolving the Crisis', 33.

[143] Practice Statements provide informal guidance as to how the executive usually interprets and applies particular provisions of the Code in certain circumstances; see UK Takeover Code, Introduction 6 (a). See also Kershaw, *Principles of Takeover Regulation*, mn. 4.32.

[144] 'Panel Bulletins are published by the Panel Executive from time to time to remind practitioners and market participants of the operation of specific provisions of the Takeover Code in the light of issues of which the Executive becomes aware.' See www.thetakeoverpanel.org.uk/communications/panel-bulletins (accessed 13 July 2024).

[145] Available at www.thetakeoverpanel.org.uk/communications/panel-statements (accessed 13 July 2024).

[146] See the 'Announcements' on the website, available at https://irishtakeoverpanel.ie/announcements/page/2/ (accessed 13 July 2024). There are no entries related to the Panel Executive because – in contrast to the UK – the Irish Panel Executive does not issue (formal) rulings. See Awrey/Clarke/Griffith, 'Resolving the Crisis', 36.

[147] On www.amf-france.org/fr use the search function. There you find the link 'BDIF (base des décisions et informations financières)' which leads you to selected topics, among them the topic 'takeover bid' or 'thresholds, shareholder agreements, waivers and examinations'. Searching the menu for relevant key words is useless.

range of documents, including tender offers and the supporting documentation, as well as the (standard form) authorization by CNMV that the offer document can be published.[148] Other decisions by CNMV are referred to in the supporting documentation of the parties. However, one does not find a list of CNMV's decisions and its holdings in a specific matter or on a topical list. Italy's CONSOB publishes offer documents and the decisions (including those on offer obligations) on its website, although at different locations – the steps to get there definitely do not qualify as 'easily accessible'.[149] Germany's BaFin limits itself to the publication of the decisions concerning the exemption from the obligation to submit a mandatory offer.[150] However, the website is (very) difficult to navigate and information is not found easily.

In sum, neither France, Spain, Italy or Germany – all countries with important takeover markets – offer a comprehensive information 'package' on takeover matters.

Instead of publishing their decisions, some Member States' regulators use other formats to share information about their practices. The Belgian Financial Services and Markets Authority (FSMA) publishes 'Communications' and 'Opinions'.[151] Moreover, the FSMA offers a short FAQ section that addresses specific questions which may arise for involved parties.[152] The Slovakian National Bank provides a guideline to answer the most pressing questions regarding the submission of a mandatory offer.[153] The Greek Financial Authority (Hellenic Capital Market Commission, HCMC) provides several 'Clarifications'.[154] The Slovenian

[148] See www.cnmv.es (accessed 27 July 2024). The takeover documentation is listed under 'Prospectuses', 'Takeover bids', where one has to enter a date (not a search name) to find a takeover transaction.

[149] See www.consob.it (accessed 27 July 2024). The offer documents are listed under 'Consob and its Activities', 'Prospectuses and Takeover Bids Documents'. The decisions can be found in the 'Bolletino' and 'Delibere' which are listed under the Italian tab of 'Pubblicazioni'. The 'Bolletino' is not listed in the English version.

[150] The list of the decisions is available at www.bafin.de/SharedDocs/Veroeffentlichungen/DE/Liste/WPUeG/li_befreiung_wpueg_36_37.html;jsessionid = 725A.internet002 (accessed 13 July 2024). The BaFin also publishes circulars and other information for specific issues; see Merkblatt – Auslegung des § 35 Abs. 3 WpÜG durch die BaFin; available at www.bafin.de/SharedDocs/Veroeffentlichungen/DE/Merkblatt/WA/mb_070712_35wpueg.html (accessed 13 July 2024).

[151] See, e.g. FSMA, Communication FSMA 2019/13 'Communication on the procedures for the submission and processing of dossiers relating to public offers', available at www.fsma.be/sites/default/files/media/files/2024-12/fsma_2019_13_en.pdf (accessed 13 July 2025). See also, e.g. FSMA, Opinion on the standstill period provided for in the Royal Decree on Takeover Bids of 14 May 2019, available at www.fsma.be/en/opinion/fsma-opinion-standstill-period-provided-royal-decree-takeover-bids (accessed 13 July 2024).

[152] Available at www.fsma.be/en/takeover-bids (accessed 13 July 2024).

[153] Available at https://nbs.sk/dohlad-nad-financnym-trhom/dohlad/trh-cennych-papierov/ponuky-na-prevzatie-a-uplatnenie-prava-vykupu-a-prava-na-odkupenie/ (accessed 13 July 2024).

[154] However, these clarifications are exclusively accessible in Greek, and not all of them are available for download. See www.hcmc.gr/en_US/web/portal/relinfo7 (accessed 13 July 2024).

Securities Market Agency (ATVP) has published guidelines regarding the regulation of takeovers and the role of the ATVP.[155]

While these alternative sources of information enhance predictability and thus transparency regarding authority decisions, they cannot replace the publication of the decisions themselves. When examining some of the aforementioned examples, it is evident that they lack the depth of content to provide precise information about the practice of the authority in charge. They answer specific questions selected by the competent authority but do not allow for a comprehensive overview of the regulatory practice.

3.4.1.3 Special Cases

If one starts with the 'best in class' and continues with the 'middle ground', the term which comes next would be 'laggards'. But this would hardly be fair. While it is true that for some countries hardly any information seems to be available, there may be good reasons for this. The countries in question are Denmark, Iceland, Estonia, Latvia, Poland, Slovakia and Hungary – all Member States with a small to virtually non-existent takeover market (between zero and three public takeovers a year). The authorities of some of the aforementioned countries were contacted by the authors. The feedback received confirmed the assumption that the competent authorities of these countries do not publish their decisions in takeover matters.[156]

3.4.1.4 Conclusion

In conclusion, the level of regulatory transparency in takeover regulation varies significantly among the different countries observed, with panel regimes generally achieving a higher level of transparency than countries using a supervisory authority structure. Within the latter, some countries do provide some information using alternative formats (e.g. FAQs and Opinions). However, these sources do not allow affected stakeholders to thoroughly inform themselves about the authority's practice.

Two reasons may explain this discrepancy. The first one has to do with organizational independence, and the second one has to do with stakeholder involvement. First, today the accessibility of information is determined by the website of the authority. Panels operate their own websites. They are not part of the huge and cumbersome IT infrastructure of the financial supervisor, which, to make matters worse, may be part of the general IT infrastructure of the government. The design and content of the panel website can largely be determined independently, and

155 Available at www.a-tvp.si/storage/app/media/Documents/ENG/PRESS/Zlozenka-ZPRe_1G_angleska_FINAL.doc (accessed 13 July 2024).

156 This does not preclude that copies or extracts of the decisions could be made available upon individual request.

changes can be implemented rapidly. Second, the panel members are – to a large degree – market participants. The design and content of the panel websites are bound to reflect the expectations of its members and their respective stakeholder group. In sum: panels[157] are agile and customer-oriented, and this creates a good environment for transparency.

One might argue that public availability of the decisions and other relevant information is only a partial and incomplete indicator for transparency, since takeover law is a highly specialized field; therefore, the essential indicator for transparency is that the decisions are available for the specialists – lawyers, analysts, institutional investors, investment bankers and the like. This is an issue we cannot analyse in depth here. However, one should consider that an important stakeholder group are the shareholders of both the offeror and the target company. Easily accessible information, especially on ongoing bids, is highly important for them.

3.4.2 *Predictability through Guidance by the Authority*

Another factor which impacts the predictability of the takeover proceeding is whether the takeover authority can be approached for a preliminary view on certain legal questions involving the takeover. From the perspective of the parties involved in a takeover, the supervisory authority should not only assess facts, but also options for action. In other words, in addition to taking decisions ex post, the supervisory authority should also provide guidance on hypothetical facts or mere plans. In this case, it enters into regulatory conversation[158] with the parties.

3.4.2.1 Panel Countries

A particular feature of the panel countries is that the panels are usually given a formal guidance function by the applicable takeover rules. The introduction to the UK Takeover Code states that the Panel Executive may be approached for general guidance on the interpretation or effect of the Code and how it is usually applied in practice, as well as for guidance in relation to a specific issue on a 'no names' basis.[159] It also clarifies that the guidance – as opposed to a formal ruling – is not binding.[160] Hence, the Panel offers non-binding real-time ('24/7') advice to parties in takeover transactions. As a corollary, parties must consult with the Panel's executive if they are in any doubt whatsoever as to whether a proposed course of conduct is in

[157] Similar reasons can explain the transparency of the former Norwegian set-up: the Oslo Stock Exchange is a private enterprise which has an intrinsic interest in attracting activities in the takeover market.

[158] See J. Black, 'Regulatory Conversations' (2002) 29 *Journal of Law and Society* 163.

[159] See Introduction 6(a) of the Takeover Code.

[160] UK Takeover Code, Introduction 6(a). Kershaw, *Principles of Takeover Regulation*, mn. 4.30.

accordance with the General Principles or the rules; legal outside advice is not considered to be an appropriate alternative.[161]

Since Ireland has followed the UK Takeover Code for many years, it is not surprising to find the guidance principle in the Irish Takeover Panel Act as well. The introductory notes state that the Panel Executive is available for consultation and to give guidance before and during takeover transactions.[162] Its guidance function is extensive in practice.[163]

Under Austrian law, one of the central tasks of the Takeover Commission is to issue opinions, provide advice, and – less important in practice – amicably settle differences of opinion regarding the application of takeover rules.[164] The so-called opinion[165] is an instrument whereby the parties or their legal advisers receive legally non-binding information on the authority's opinion on a specific issue. In doing so, the authority does not assess the facts independently, but takes them for granted (apart from a plausibility check). The advantage of this instrument is that it allows the parties to submit hypothetical facts for assessment – for example, on the basis of an MoU (instead of a signed contract). On the other hand, this real-time supervision makes enforcement easier, which can be matched to the fact that penalty notices and enforcement ex post are of comparatively little significance in Austrian takeover practice.[166]

In Switzerland, the issuance of an opinion on the interpretation and the application of takeover law is also explicitly mentioned, albeit indirectly in the sense that the relevant regulation states that the Takeover Commission may levy a fee for answering information requests.[167] In addition, the Secretariat of the Takeover Commission may provide information on the interpretation of the takeover provisions.[168] This information does not bind the Commission;[169] however, if difficult or important matters arise, the Secretariat will refer the issue to the Commission.

The Swedish Securities Council, as the body inter alia responsible for issuing rulings regarding the interpretation of the Takeover Rules[170] and the Takeovers Act,[171] is also available for informal consultation on the interpretation of

[161] UK Takeover Code, Introduction 6(b).

[162] Irish Takeover Panel Act, Introduction to the Takeover Rules 5b (T7).

[163] Awrey and Clarke, 'A Transatlantic Perspective', p. 424 et seq. See also the description of the panel on the Irish Takeover Website, stating that the panel is available for consultation and to give guidance before and during takeover transactions, available at https://irishtakeoverpanel.ie/about/the-panel/ (accessed 13 July 2024).

[164] See § 29(1) Austrian Takeover Act.

[165] 'Stellungnahme' in the German original.

[166] For the importance of the advisory opinions see also Winner, 'Die österreichische Übernahmekommission', p. 155 et seq.

[167] Art. 118(1) Financial Market Infrastructure Ordinance.

[168] Art. 55(4) Takeover Ordinance.

[169] Art. 55(5) Takeover Ordinance.

[170] See Takeover Rules I.2.

[171] See Chapter 7, Section 4 Takeovers Act.

the rules,[172] although consultation with the authorities is not explicitly mentioned in the Takeovers Act or the Takeover Rules. Such advice by the Council's Secretariat,[173] which cannot give formal rulings, is not made public and is not binding, though in practice is important guidance in areas where the Council's practice is firm.

In Finland, the Takeover Board has a formalized procedure, easily accessible on the website,[174] to request a 'recommended decision' on the procedure to be followed in a takeover bid.[175] The application for such a recommended decision can be discussed with the Takeover Board beforehand (albeit for a separate fee).[176] However, the FIN-FSA is not bound by the issued opinions of the Takeover Board, even though it will only deviate from the opinion with significant reason. The interpretation and application of the applicable legislation lies solely within the authority of the FIN-FSA.[177] The Takeover Board thus performs exclusively advisory functions.

In Norway, former the competent authority in takeover matters (until 2025), the Norway Stock Exchange, was a private actor, but relied on public law for its supervisory functions. In practice, it offered guidance on any questions posed.[178]

3.4.2.2 Supervisory Authority Countries

It appears that for none of the countries with a supervisory authority structure the advisory or guidance function is formally embedded in the applicable legal framework for takeovers. The Italian CONSOB highlights the guidance function in its promotional materials,[179] but it is not mentioned in the statutes and regulations. There is also no mention of the guidance function in the French and Spanish

[172] See Skog and Sjöman, 'The Swedish Securities Council', 13 et seq.; G. Nyström, R. Ohlsson. E. Sjöman and R. Skog, *The Swedish Takeover Code. An Annotated Commentary* (Informa Law from Routledge: New York, 2016), p. 4.

[173] See Skog and Sjöman, 'The Swedish Securities Council', 7.

[174] See the tab 'Takeover Code' on the website of the Securities Markets Association, available at www.cgfinland.fi/en/ (accessed 27 July 2024).

[175] Mähönen, 'Finland: Corporate Governance', p. 436.

[176] See the website of the Finnish Securities Market Association, Tab 'Takeover Code', available at www.cgfinland.fi/en/ (accessed 27 July 2024). See also Helsinki Takeover Code 2022, p. 8, available on the same website, Tab 'Helsinki Takeover Code'; Rules of Procedure of the Finnish Takeover Board § 3(c) [in Finnish only], available on the same website, Tab 'About US', 'Takeover Board'.

[177] See Helsinki Takeover Code 2022, p. 8, available at www.cgfinland.fi/en/, Tab 'Takeover Code' (accessed 27 July 2025). See also Chapter 1, Section 6 of the Securities Market Act (746/2012) of 14 December 2012.

[178] Information by Kjell Vidjeland, Head Legal, Oslo Stock Exchange, on 4 September 2023.

[179] The materials state that '[CONSOB] answers questions interpreting the laws and regulations' in order to 'provide […] guidelines for the application of regulations and make […] the behaviour of operators homogeneous, thus contributing to better protection of investors.' See CONSOB, *Supervisory authority for the investor's protection*, p. 22 et seq., available at www.consob.it/documents/1912911/2374158/Brochure_La_CONSOB_EN.pdf/25783fb7-bdf8-fef4-6f96-171d272c961b (accessed 13 July 2024).

regulations. This can be taken as an indication that in these countries the advisory function is not equally important in comparison to (panel) countries that mention it explicitly.

The lack of such rules does not mean that authorities in the supervisory authority regimes cannot be approached for guidance. Generally, in financial supervision, there are informal contacts and discussions before any formal request by a supervised entity is submitted. Furthermore, the administrative procedural law of some countries may include a general obligation of the authorities to give preliminary guidance regarding a certain legal situation, if requested by a party. By way of example, the German Act on Administrative Procedure states that 'where necessary, [the authority] shall provide information on the rights and obligations of the parties involved in the administrative procedure'.[180]

However, these general rights to receive information on one's legal situation are not qualitatively comparable to the guidance function of a specialized takeover panel. The difference is that the takeover authorities of panel countries are formally entrusted with a consultative (guidance) function, which is central to their role.

3.4.2.3 Conclusion

Panel countries are likely to have a guidance function anchored in their respective legal frameworks, whereas supervisory authority countries do not. Hence, panels tend to intervene earlier and in 'real time'. This is intended to ensure that legal violations do not occur in the first place – and not just by sanctioning misconduct. This concept of guidance rather than repression is a central issue in the self-image of most takeover panels and thus in their culture. Firstly, it avoids at least some of the costs associated with correcting matters that have gone astray. Secondly, experience shows that it is easier for an authority to enforce its interpretation of the law if a transaction is still in the structuring phase than if the parties (and their advisors) have already committed to a different legal opinion. Under the guidance concept, sanctions would appear to be less important, since they would not be used as frequently, ceteris paribus. However, one has to consider that those subject to the law are well aware of the possibility of sanctions and are perhaps therefore willing to cooperate with the supervisory authority in earlier phases. On the other hand, this close cooperation with the legal representatives of the applicants leads to the risk of regulatory capture – that is, the risk that the authority (unintentionally) unduly promotes the interests of its counterparts in these consultation processes.[181]

While most traditional supervisors fulfil some guidance functions as well, it is probably not to an equal extent part of their DNA. We do not believe that these authorities limit themselves to reviewing the facts of a case that has already been

[180] § 25 (1) Verwaltungsverfahrensgesetz.

[181] On this see also Winner, 'Die österreichische Übernahmekommission', p. 156 et seq.

realized and react to legal violations by imposing sanctions. However, it is noteworthy that, as far as we could ascertain, the guidance function is not formally embedded in the relevant legislation and, hence, probably not equally central to the role of the authorities as in the panel countries.

3.4.3 *Predictability through Finality (Challenging the Regulator's Rulings)*

The judicial review of a decision taken by the takeover regulator will invariably delay the takeover process and can therefore be used for strategic purposes. Predictability in takeover matters is enhanced when there is little or no possibility of using litigation to change the regulator's rulings. In such cases, the takeover authority's decision holds, allowing market participants to confidently assume that the takeover process will proceed as expected.

There are several ways to minimize tactical litigation and thereby enhance predictability. One is to establish an internal review process which is characterized by a substantial degree of informality. The other is to keep the classic judicial hierarchy, but to limit the scope of the judicial review. The third is to allow judicial review, but to enforce the decision of the regulator even though judicial proceedings are pending – that is, not recognizing the suspensive effect of the complaint.

The question is whether countries with a panel regime are better suited to address challenges to the rulings of their takeover authority in a timely and final manner than countries with a supervisory regime.

3.4.3.1 The Charter of Fundamental Rights of the European Union

One could assume that the Member States of the European Union have discretion in deciding whether to permit appeals against rulings by the regulator. After all, Art. 4(6) TOD provides that

> [t]his Directive shall not affect the power of the Member States to designate judicial or other authorities responsible for dealing with disputes [...] or the power of Member States to regulate whether and under which circumstances parties to a bid are entitled to bring administrative or judicial proceedings. In particular, this Directive shall not affect the power which courts may have in a Member State to decline to hear legal proceedings and to decide whether or not such proceedings affect the outcome of a bid.

Clearly, this had in mind the situation in the then member the UK,[182] where judicial review of the Panel's rulings is largely unavailable.[183]

[182] See P. Davies, S. Worthington and C. Hare, *Gower: Principles of Modern Company Law*, 11th ed. (London: Sweet & Maxwell, 2021) mn. 28-003 et seq.; see also J. Mukwiri, 'The Myth of Tactical Litigation in UK Takeovers' (2008) *Journal of Corporate Law Studies* 373, 377 et seq.

[183] See Section 3.4.3.2.

However, the discretion of the Member States, especially the ones who have chosen a panel structure, has seen some limitation set by the European Court of Justice. In the case of *Adler Real Estate*[184] the Court has held that parties to proceedings in takeover law must have the right to an effective remedy against decisions by the supervisor before a court or a tribunal (as defined in Article 47 of the Charter of Fundamental Rights of the European Union). Inter alia, a tribunal must be independent and impartial – although not necessarily a court in the traditional understanding. Impartiality also asks for separating the role of the prosecutor/investigator from the body taking the ultimate decision; hence, if the investigating body makes a ruling, an appeal to a tribunal on both questions of law and of fact must be possible. As a result, Member States today cannot make full use of the wide discretion provided by Art. 4(6) TOD.

In particular, the *Adler* judgment casts doubt on a strategy used in some Member States – namely, limiting the grounds for appeals. For instance, the Austrian legislator initially weighted the need for quick and binding decisions far higher than the possibility of seeking legal protection and provided an extremely limited possibility of seeking legal redress against decisions of the Takeover Commission: its decisions could only be appealed to the Constitutional Court if an unconstitutional law or an unlawful ordinance had been applied or if the fundamental rights of a person subject to the law had been violated. In other words, a 'merely' unlawful decision could not be challenged. This changed first in that a 'leapfrog' appeal directly to the Austrian Supreme Court was introduced in 2013, which was, however, limited to questions of law.[185] Due to *Adler*, in 2022[186] the possibility of appealing questions of fact was introduced; additionally, parties may appeal against decisions by the Takeover Commission to the Higher Regional Court in Vienna, a court with panels specializing in commercial issues. Subsequently, parties may appeal on questions of law to the Austrian Supreme Court. There are no special timelines for judicial decisions in Austria, and practice under the new rules is still missing.

3.4.3.2 Internal Review and Judicial Restraint

Looking first at the UK, rulings during ongoing proceedings are made by the executive. Such rulings can be challenged in an internal review procedure before the hearings committee, another body of the Takeover Panel.[187] Very few of these requests for review are successful.[188] Any party to a proceeding before the hearings

[184] Case C-546/18 *Adler Real Estate et al.*, [2021] ECLI:EU:C:2021:711.

[185] In practice, this did not cause significant delays in the takeover proceedings, also because the Supreme Court ruled extremely swiftly in the few proceedings that reached it; see, e.g. Austrian Supreme Court v. 13 March 2014, 6 Ob 37/14f.

[186] See Art. 30a Takeover Act as amended by Act of 27 July 2022, Federal Law Journal I 2022/124. For the development see Winner, 'Das österreichische Übernahmerecht', p. 309 et seq.

[187] For details see Appendix 9: Hearings Committee Rules of Procedure to the Takeover Code.

[188] See Kershaw, *Principles of Takeover Regulation*, mn. 4.27.

committee can appeal to the Takeover Appeal Board, which is an independent body separate from the panel.[189] Very few appeals are made, and even fewer are successful.[190] Typically, review and appeal take only a few days each.[191] This system ensures that decisions on appeals are taken by takeover specialists.

In addition, legal recourse to the ordinary courts against decisions of the Takeover Panel is largely cut off. The leading 1987 *Datafin* decision[192] asserted the court's power to review panel decisions but limited the nature of such review. First, the judgment clearly states that the applicant must comply with the panel's rulings even if she seeks judicial review; any application for permission to apply for judicial review does not suspend the ruling's effects for the duration of the court proceedings.[193] Second, the court in *Datafin* narrowly limited the nature of its review: judicial review is only available if standards of fairness and natural justice[194] are not complied with – for example, if an interpretation of the Takeover Code is so far removed from the ordinary meaning of the words as to mislead an ordinary market participant.[195] This exacting standard will hardly be met unless 'the panel goes off the rails'.[196] In substance, the court implicitly seems to defer to the superior experience of the panel in the takeover field.[197] Third, the courts generally refuse to intervene in ongoing bids; in Sir John Donaldson's words in *Datafin*, 'the relationship between the panel and the court [is] to be historic rather than contemporaneous'.[198] Therefore, any court order may relieve individuals of disciplinary sanctions or contain a declaratory judgment for the panel's future action, but will not quash the ruling in question. All this does not encourage parties to the takeover proceedings to initiate a review process, which therefore seldom happens.[199]

3.4.3.3 Judicial Review Limited in Scope

Even among the panel-based regimes, the UK is clearly an outlier. This is probably not due to the Charter of Fundamental Rights, as there are good arguments that the

[189] See its website, available at www.thetakeoverappealboard.org.uk (accessed 13 July 2024).
[190] Kershaw, *Principles of Takeover Regulation*, mn. 4.38.
[191] Ibid., mn. 4.28 and 4.38.
[192] *R v. Panel on Takeovers and Mergers, ex parte Datafin Plc* [1987] 1 QB 815.
[193] *R v. Panel on Takeovers and Mergers, ex parte Datafin Plc* [1987] 1 QB 815, 840. For a more recent decision where the court confirmed the restrictive approach under the 2006 Company Act, see P. Davies, 'Enforcing the Takeover Panel's Decisions: Panel v. King [2018] CSIH 30', *Oxford Law Blogs*, 25 June 2018, available at https://blogs.law.ox.ac.uk/business-law-blog/blog/2018/06/enforcing-takeover-panels-decisions-panel-v-king-2018-csih-30 (accessed 13 July 2024).
[194] See also Lord Woolf in *R. v. Panel on Takeovers and Mergers, ex parte Guiness Plc* [1990] 1 QB 146, 193 et seq.
[195] *R v. Panel on Takeovers and Mergers, ex parte Datafin Plc* [1987] 1 QB 815, 841 et seq.
[196] *R v. Panel on Takeovers and Mergers, ex parte Datafin Plc* [1987] 1 QB 815, 827.
[197] This is especially apparent in the later Guinness judgment; *R. v. Panel on Takeovers and Mergers, ex parte Guinness Plc* [1990] 1 QB 146, 200.
[198] *R v. Panel on Takeovers and Mergers, ex parte Datafin Plc* [1987] 1 QB 815, 842.
[199] J. Mukwiri, 'The Myth of Tactical Litigation, 382.

UK process would be in line with its requirements, especially due to the separate Takeover Appeal Board.[200] In any case, another way to enhance the finality of the the regulator's rulings is to limit the scope of the remedies. Ireland chose that approach.[201]

Judicial review of rulings by the Irish Takeover Panel[202] is possible and explicitly foreseen in the relevant legislation.[203] However, the application for leave to apply for judicial review will only be granted if the court is satisfied that there are substantial grounds for contending that the rule, derogation, waiver, ruling or direction is invalid or ought to be quashed,[204] which is a higher standard than in judicial review generally.[205] Judicial review is primarily concerned with the decision-making process rather than with the substance of the decision – for example, in the case of alleged breaches of natural justice and fair procedures. But in judicial review proceedings, the ruling will be tested for 'reasonableness' as well – that is, whether the panel abused its jurisdiction. As a relief, the High Court can quash panel decisions (certiorari); however – and crucially – it cannot invalidate a transaction that has been carried out.[206]

3.4.3.4 Appeal Proceedings

Most countries permit appeals against the decisions by the regulator without special limitations as to the scope of this appeal. The example of Austria has already been mentioned.

In Switzerland, the decisions of the Takeover Commission are reviewed by the financial supervisor (FINMA). The review follows an accelerated schedule[207] and FINMA is a specialized authority, but otherwise the general rules of administrative procedure (including the procedural rights of the parties) apply. FINMA decisions can be reviewed by the Federal Administrative Court.[208] Sweden has taken a similar

[200] See, again, Case C-546/18 *Adler Real Estate et al.*, [2021] ECLI:EU:C:2021:711.

[201] As did Austria until 2022; see, Section 3.4.3.1.

[202] Which is the body which takes decisions, while the executive only gives guidance; see Irish Takeover Code T7 et seq.

[203] See Art. 13 Irish Takeover Panel Act, 1997.

[204] Art. 13(3) Irish Takeover Panel Act, 1997.

[205] In general, an arguable case is sufficient for judicial review, see The Law Reform Commission, Consultation Paper on Judicial Review Procedure (LRC CP 20 – 2003), p. 52, available at www.lawreform.ie/_fileupload/consultation%20papers/cpJudicialReviewProcedure.pdf (accessed 13 July 2024).

[206] Art. 15 Irish Takeover Panel Act, 1997.

[207] According to the Financial Infrastructure Law, the appeal has to be lodged with FINMA within five trading days (Art. 140 I FinMIA). Also, the general statutory provisions on legal holidays do not apply in takeover proceedings (Art. 139 IV FinMIA).

[208] Art. 141 Financial Markets Infrastructure Act. Note that the appeal has to be lodged on an accelerated schedule (10 days) and that the statutory provisions on legal holidays are not applicable (Art. 141 FinMIA). There will be changes made to Art. 141 FinMIA, but the general framework remains unchanged.

approach. Decisions by the Securities Council can be appealed to the SFSA,[209] while decisions by the SFSA in turn can be appealed in administrative courts.[210] The same was true for Norway. The decisions of the Oslo Stock Exchange were reviewed by the Stock Exchange Appeals Committee and therefore a specialized body, whereas a further appeal was formerly heard by the regular courts.[211]

Turning to countries whose regulator for takeovers is the general supervisor for financial markets, it is not surprising that they apply the general system of remedies for actions taken by that supervisor to takeover matters as well. Hence, in France,[212] Germany,[213] Italy[214] and Spain,[215] decisions by the regulator can be appealed to the courts. As in all countries, this wide possibility of appeal brings the danger of a loss of specialization in the appeals stage of the proceedings, especially if general administrative courts decide upon takeover issues. Germany[216] and Austria[217] address this problem by giving jurisdiction to a civil court specializing in commercial law issues instead of the general administrative courts.

Of course, in all countries there is some need to limit the possibility of appealing decisions by the takeover regulator. We cannot go into detail as to the variety of measures by which this can be achieved but would like to mention two important aspects:

[209] Chapter 8, Section 1 Takeovers Act.

[210] Chapter 8, Section 3 Takeovers Act.

[211] On the Appeals Committee in general (competence, composition, case handling) see Chapter 12 (II) Securities Trading Regulations. On the appeals function: Section 12-3(1) Securities Trading Regulations. See also the website of Oslo Stock Exchange, Tabs 'Regulatory Responsibilities', available at www.euronext.com/en/markets/oslo, (accessed 27 July 2024) Norway does not have a separate administrative tribunal. All judicial review is conducted by the ordinary courts of law.

[212] Art. L621–30 Code monétaire et financier. The competent Cour d'Appel de Paris has to render a decision within five months. The five-month period was introduced in 2014 with the goal of increasing the competitiveness of the French takeover market. See also E. Coumoul and A. Renard 'Vers une remise en cause de la sécurité juridique des offres publiques d`acquisition?' (2016–2017), *Revue Sorbonne*, Master 2 OFIS 2. The revision was part of the so-called Loi Florange.

[213] §§ 48 et seq. Wertpapierübernahmegesetz (WpÜG).

[214] Art. 133 subs l) Code of Administrative Procedure [Codice del processo amministrativo]. The relevant court is the Administrative Court of Rome (Tribunale ammnistrative per il Lazio) which has exclusive jurisdiction over decisions of independent authorities such as CONSOB. The decision of the Admnistrative Court can be appealed to the Council of State (Consiglio di Stato). The only exception is when CONSOB issues a sanctioning provision; these decisions are reviewed by the civil court of appeal of the domicile of the natural person (or of the registered office of the company), whereas the appeal is heard by the Supreme Civil Court (Corte di Cassazione). For a takeover proceeding, see e.g. Case C-206/16 *Marco Trochetti Provera Spa et al. v. Commissione Nationale per le Società e la Borsa (Consob)*, ECLI:EU:C:2017:572.

[215] Art. 23 Ley de los Mercados de Valores y de los Servicios de Inversión (LMVSI).

[216] § 48(4) WpÜG: Higher Regional Court in Frankfurt.

[217] § 30a(1) Austrian Takeover Act: Higher Regional Court in Vienna (which has chambers specializing in commercial issues).

First, in many countries appeals can only be brought by those who were parties to the proceedings in front of the supervisory authority. If, additionally, a legal system provides only for a narrow circle of parties, tactical litigation with regard to decisions by the regulator are a remote possibility. Such a limited standing is provided for by the German legislation: the BaFin operates solely in the public interest.[218] Therefore, only the addressees of its acts can appeal its decisions,[219] which means that, for example, only the new controlling shareholder can appeal a decision on an exemption from the mandatory bid requirement, not the target company or its shareholders. Clearly, this limits the possibilities of tactical litigation and helps speed up proceedings.[220] The situation in Austria is similar,[221] although shareholders can initiate proceedings on whether a mandatory bid has to be made or on the legality of the bid ex post.[222] The Swedish position is a bit broader, as it has to be decided on a case-by-case basis whether parties other than the applicant can appeal the Securities Council's decisions.[223]

Second, in many countries, appeals against the takeover authority's decisions do not have suspensive effect. Hence, a decision by the authority can be provisionally enforced even though the appeal is still pending. Quite clearly, this means that, in ongoing takeovers, where time is of the essence, the supervisory decisions have great authority; appealing is of little practical importance to the applicants or other parties (unless, of course, the appeal procedure is extraordinarily swift). The situation may be different for decisions that are less time-sensitive, such as decisions on whether the obligation to launch a bid has been met or on the pricing of a bid that has been settled. Rules excluding a stay in the procedure either by law or because of a decision by the supervisory authority can be found, for example, in Germany,[224] Austria,[225] Sweden,[226] France[227] and Switzerland.[228]

[218] See § 4(2) Wertpapierübernahmegesetz (WpÜG).

[219] See D. Döhmel, '§ 4', in D. Assman, T. Pötzsch and U. Schneider, WpÜG Kommentar, 3rd ed. (Cologne: ottoschmidt, 2020), mn. 27.

[220] See Döhmel, '§ 4', mn. 29.

[221] See the decision GZ 20043/13-175 (available at www.takeover.at/uploads/u/pxe/A2_Entscheidungen/Bescheide/GZ_2004-3-13-175_Anonym_-_14.1.2005.pdf (accessed 13 July 2024).

[222] See § 34 Takeover Act.

[223] See Nyström, Ohlsson, Sjöman and Skog, The Swedish Takeover Code, p. 82 et seq.

[224] § 49 WpÜG enumerates a few cases where the application for review has suspensive effect (all cases of revocation of BaFin decisions favouring the bidder); as a general rule, such application does not have suspensive effect. However, according to § 50(3) WpÜG, the court may grant suspensive effect upon application, especially if the immediate enforceability would cause undue hardship.

[225] § 30a(1) last sentence Austrian Takeover Act: exclusion of suspensive effect by the Takeover Commission if the early execution of the contested decision is urgently required due to imminent danger.

[226] Chapter 8, Section 2 Swedish Takeovers Act: Securities Council may decide that an order shall enter into force immediately.

[227] L631–32 Code monétaire et financier.

[228] Art. 141 II Financial Markets Infrastructure Act.

3.4.3.5 Conclusion

Appeals against decisions by the takeover regulator are possible in all countries. The UK largely avoids judicial intervention through an internal appeals mechanism within the Takeover Panel. But the choice of a panel structure does not automatically lead to this outcome. All other countries – panel countries and countries with a more traditional supervisory setting alike – provide for a review of the supervisor's rulings by the courts, although the precise scope varies. Hence, the choice of institutional setting does not determine the approach to court intervention, although a separate appeals procedure is easier to achieve in a panel country.

3.4.4 *Summary*

We have chosen three factors to assess the predictability of the takeover process. First, whether decisions of the takeover authority are easily accessible to the public, be it the market participants or the retail investor. Second, whether and to what extent market participants can get comfort at an early stage of the takeover process because the role of the takeover authority is not limited to an ex post monitoring function, and instead includes an ex ante guidance function. Third, whether and to what extent the structure of the review and appeal process favours the finality of the original decision of the takeover authority. The core question was whether countries with a panel regime offer a greater degree of predictability than the countries where takeover matters are in the hands of the financial supervisor.

We find that, from an overall point of view, countries with panel regimes tend to achieve a higher level of transparency compared to those using a supervisory authority structure. Panel countries also tend to have a more deeply ingrained guidance function within their legal frameworks, allowing for earlier and more proactive intervention. Regarding the finality of the decisions taken by the takeover authority, the presence of a panel structure does not universally lead to reduced court involvement.

Overall, the choice between a panel regime and a supervisory authority structure impacts regulatory transparency and the formalization of guidance functions, but does not significantly influence the mechanisms for challenging regulatory decisions.

3.5 CONCLUSION

Despite the Takeover Directive (TOD) extensively accommodating the establishment of a panel structure, such a structure remains an exception – even more so since Brexit. The predominant institutional arrangement in Europe is for takeover authorities to be integrated into financial supervisory authorities. This is unexpected, considering that panel-based regimes are generally perceived as offering greater flexibility, predictability and speed. This chapter has examined the first two attributes: flexibility and predictability. It finds that there is no inherent and unalterable connection between these attributes and the institutional identity of the takeover authority.

Regarding flexibility, we examined three factors: rulemaking power, derogation/exemption power, and diversity of the decision-makers. Authorities who can create and change the rules themselves infuse a great amount of flexibility into takeover law. The same is true if the authority can, if warranted by specific circumstance, abstain from applying a rule. Finally, flexibility is also enhanced if the authority's composition includes market participants, as they will favour a need-based regulatory framework.

We find that, while panel regimes show a higher degree of background-driven diversity, the impact of the institutional design of takeover authorities in connection with rulemaking powers and exemption powers is not solely determined by whether the authority operates under a panel regime or as part of a financial supervisory structure. By way of example, the French AMF and the Italian CONSOB have robust rulemaking powers, whereas the Austrian Takeover Commission and the Swedish Securities Council lack those powers. Finland has a Takeover Board whose powers are extremely modest, yet its financial supervisory authority can issue exemptions from the application of takeover law.

Regarding predictability, we again examined three factors: accessibility of the takeover decisions, ex ante guidance by the authority, and the degree of finality of the original decision by the takeover authority.

We find that countries with panel regimes generally achieve higher transparency and have a more deeply ingrained guidance function within their legal frameworks, thus enhancing predictability for stakeholders. In contrast, the mechanisms for challenging regulatory decisions are not tied to the institutional identity of the takeover authority. Thus, the presence of a panel structure does not automatically reduce the extent of a possible court involvement and enhance the finality of the decision by the takeover authority.

In summary, the institutional design impacts regulatory flexibility and predictability in distinct ways. Panel regimes typically provide greater transparency and proactive guidance, contributing to predictability, whereas flexibility in takeover law is influenced by various factors beyond the mere presence of a panel structure. Exceptions exist on both sides, underscoring the complexity and variability inherent in the regulatory frameworks of different countries.

4

Enforcement of Takeover Law

Peter Agstner and Dörte Poelzig

4.1 INTRODUCTION

Enforcement of takeover law varies considerably between Member States in the EU. Traditionally, EU law creates obligations for private parties, such as the mandatory bid rule in the Takeover Directive (TOD), and leaves the enforcement of these obligations to the national law of the Member States. While some Member States have focused on public enforcement mechanisms, others have implemented private law to enforce the mandatory bid rule. However, the written law is only worth as much as it is actually enforced. Different enforcement systems in the Member States lead to inconsistent application of takeover law. Harmonised law on enforcement of takeover law is not only important for overcoming fragmentation and creating a single capital market; rather, a coordinated and efficient enforcement mechanism is crucial to ensure the attractiveness of capital markets to issuers and investors.[1] Since the study by La Porta/Lopez-de-Silanes/Shleifer at the latest, it has been known that laws mandating or facilitating private enforcement through liability rules benefit stock markets.[2]

This chapter consists of four main sections. Section 4.2 introduces the EU law on enforcement of minority shareholder rights. In Section 4.3, the advantages and disadvantages of private and public enforcement are presented, followed by an outline of various enforcement models in Italian and German law in Section 4.4. It will then be examined whether and to what extent European liability law in the TOD can and should be harmonised.

Italian regulation on academic evaluation requires some form of identification of each author's individual contribution to a joint law paper. Exclusively for this purpose, we mention that Section 4.4.1. was written with the prevalent contribution of Peter Agstner, and Section 4.4.2. with the prevalent contribution of Dörte Poelzig. The authors equally contributed to other sections.

1 R. Veil, M. Wiesner and M. Reichert, 'Disclosure and Enforcement under the EU Listing Act' (2022) 19 *European Company and Financial Law Review* 445, 503.

2 R. La Porta, F. Lopez-de-Silanes and A. Shleifer, 'What Works in Securities Laws?' (2006) 61 *The Journal of Finance* 1 et seq.

4.2 EU LAW ON ENFORCEMENT

Like many recent European legal acts, the Takeover Directive says little about enforcement matters. It mainly leaves it to the Member States. According to Art. 17 TOD, Member States shall determine the sanctions to be imposed for infringement of the national measures adopted pursuant to this Directive and shall take all necessary steps to ensure that they are put into effect. The sanctions thus provided for shall be effective, proportionate and dissuasive. Especially, the principle of effectiveness requires a minimum level of sanctions. In other words, the Directive only generically requires Member States to safeguard minority shareholders but does not say anything in relation to the concrete instruments or mechanisms available for this purpose.[3] Different factors seem to contribute to such legal uncertainty. First, the TOD does not affect the power of Member States to designate the (public or private) authority competent to supervise bids and to regulate whether and under which circumstances parties to a bid are entitled to bring administrative or judicial proceedings (Recital 8; Art. 4(1) and (6) TOD), neither does it indicate the kind of remedy concretely available (subjective public right and/or individual civil claim).[4] Second, at the supranational level traditionally, except for antitrust law matters[5] and in the recent past for the General Data Protection Regulation (GDPR) or Markets in Crypto-Assets Regulation (MiCAR), we observe a strong resistance by the European Court of Justice and the European Commission to impose on Member States an obligation to recognise civil law claims in favour of investors,[6] here probably

[3] Cf. H. Fleischer, '§ 1 WpÜG', in N. Paschos and H. Fleischer (eds.), *Handbuch Übernahmerecht nach dem WpÜG* (Munich: C.H. Beck, 2017), § 1 mn. 70; M. Ventoruzzo, 'Takeover Regulation as a Wolf in Sheep's Clothing: Taking U.K. Rules to Continental Europe' (2008) 11 *University of Pennsylvania Journal of Business Law* 135; very critical M. Winner, 'Does the European Union have a mandatory bid rule?', in R. J. Gilson, M. Isakson, E. Lidman, J. Munck and E. Sjöman (eds.), *Festskrift till Rolf Skog* (Stockholm: Norstedts Juridik AB, 2021), p. 1194 ('Rather, the European principle allows legislators – after paying lip-service to the protection of securities holders – to deviate from the core points of the MBR. I find it difficult to call this a success').

[4] Art. 17 of the TOD only states that 'the sanctions thus provided for shall be effective, proportionate and dissuasive'.

[5] Case C-453/99, *Courage Ltd v. Bernard Crehan* [2021] ECR I-6314: for a comment, G. Wagner, 'Prävention und Verhaltenssteuerung durch Privatrecht – Anmaßung oder legitime Aufgabe' (2006) 206 *Archiv für die civilistische Praxis* 352, 404 et seq.; D. Poelzig, *Normdurchsetzung durch Privatrecht* (Tübingen: Mohr Siebeck, 2012), p. 141 et seq.; followed in the case law by Case C-295/04 to C-298/04, *Vincenzo Manfredi v. Lloyd Adriatico Assicurazioni SpA, Antonio Cannito v. Fondiaria Sai SpA, Nicolò Tricarico and Pasqualina Murgolo v. Assitalia SpA* [2006] ECR I-6641. See also Antitrust Damages Directive 2014/104/EU, which states (Recital 3) that 'national courts thus have an equally essential part to play in applying the competition rules (private enforcement)'.

[6] For such a restrictive approach, heavily dependent upon the principles of equivalence and effectiveness of the national sanctionary apparatus, Case C-219/15, *Elisabeth Schmitt v. TÜV Rheinland LGA Products GmbH* [2017] ECLI:EU:C:2017:122; Case C-604/11, *Genil 48 SL and Comercial Hostelera de Grandes Vinos SL v. Bankinter SA and Banco Bilbao Vizcaya*

exacerbated by the fact that a general principle of equal treatment of minority shareholders upon a change of control does not apply.[7] All taken together, this might well explain the profoundly different paths taken by the judicial interpretation prevailing in some Member States.[8]

4.3 PUBLIC VERSUS PRIVATE ENFORCEMENT

The following analysis is focused on two paradigmatic experiences characterised by conflicting enforcement models made available to minority shareholders. On the one hand, the private enforcement instruments recognised by the dominant Italian case law; on the other hand, the public enforcement-centred approach adopted by the German regulator.[9] But before diving into details, a preliminary notation is essential to better frame and understand the mentioned juxtaposition. In fact, at the *statutory* level, the relevant legislation generally provides enforcement mechanisms of the duty to bid, the activation of which is mainly delegated to public supervisory authorities. Typically, such safeguards consist of the freezing of the voting rights attached to the shares held by the predator and in the application of administrative fines. All these sanctionary devices are meant to force the predator to comply with the mandatory bid requirements.[10] No private right of action is granted to minority

Argentaria SA [2013] ECLI:EU:C:2013:344, with reference to the MiFID I Directive 2004/39/EC). In the literature, P. Pohlmann, 'Rechtsschutz der Aktionäre der Zielgesellschaft im Wertpapiererwerbs- und Übernahmeverfahren' (2007) 36 *Zeitschrift für Unternehmens- und Gesellschaftsrecht* 1, 7 et seq.

7 Case C-101/08, *Audiolux SA e.a v. Groupe Bruxelles Lambert SA (GBL) and Bertelsmann AG* [2009] ECR I-09823: for a comment, F. M. Mucciarelli, 'Equal treatment of shareholders and European Union law' (2010) 7 *European Company and Financial Law Review* 158 et seq.; on this topic also P. L. Davies, 'The Notion of Equality in European Takeover Regulation', in J. Payne (ed.), *Takeovers in English and German Law* (London: Bloomsbury Publishing, 2002), p. 9 et seq.

8 For first indications, cf. P. Giudici, 'Private Law Enforcement in a Formalist Legal Environment: The Italian Sai-Fondiaria Case' (2008), available at: https://papers.ssrn.com/sol3/papers.cfm?abstract_id=1103985; R. Veil, 'Enforcement of Capital Markets Law in Europe – Observations from a Civil Law Country' (2010) 11 *European Business Organization Law Review* 409; T. Tridimas, 'Financial regulation and private law remedies: an EU law perspective', in O. O. Cherednychenko and M. Adenas (eds.), *Financial Regulation and Civil Liability in European Law* (Cheltenham/Northampton: Edward Elgar, 2020), p. 47 et seq.

9 For a slightly incorrect assessment, S. Balthasar, 'Die Preisregeln des deutschen Übernahmerechts', in R. Veil, H. C. Grigoleit and M. Habersack (eds.), *Öffentliche Unternehmensübernahmen* (Tübingen: Mohr Siebeck, 2022), p. 130–131, who asserts that in other Member States, unlike Germany, the issue of civil claims brought by the target's minority shareholders plays no substantial role in practice: such an assumption, as we will see, might be true in some respects, for example, for France and Spain, but certainly not for Italy. For comparative references, P. Agstner and D. Marchesini Mascheroni, 'Breach of the Mandatory Bid Rule' (2020) 17 *European Company and Financial Law Review* 726, 744 et seq.

10 For this argument, see explicitly the German Federal Supreme Court in the case BKN: BGH, 11 June 2013 – II ZR 80/12, (2013) *Zeitschrift für Wirtschaftsrecht*, 1565, mn. 22 ('the law contains

shareholders for the immediate protection of their interests.[11] The merits of public enforcement are the following: firstly, supervisory authorities are vested with all the powers necessary for the purpose of carrying out their duties, especially investigatory powers (see Art. 4(5) TOD); secondly, public authorities are able to impose targeted and balanced sanctions in individual cases.

However, public enforcement mechanisms, due to common incentive problems as well as the risks of regulatory capture, may have no teeth and thus prove ineffective in sanctioning violations or abuses.[12] Public authorities are not able to control the whole market and often do not learn about violations. In order to avoid under-enforcement, it may therefore be vital to complement and integrate the regulatory architecture with private enforcement devices available to minority shareholders for the protection of their interests.[13] Such a mixed law enforcement system would allow for a decrease in the enforcement costs due to the supportive intervention by minority shareholders and the correlated higher probability to detect, prosecute and sanction violations of the law. In fact, minority shareholders have superior knowledge and informational advantages due to 'closeness' to the infringement event (i.e. breach of

sufficient means of exerting pressure on the controlling party to force the latter to publish a mandatory bid').

11 See Cass. 10 February 2016, n. 2665, (2016) *Banca borsa e titoli di credito* II, 375, 377 (sanctions posed by law 'do not have any impact on the damages suffered by the minority shareholders').

12 Cf. G. S. Becker and G. J. Stigler, 'Law Enforcement, Malfeasance, and Compensation of Enforcers' (1974) 3 *The Journal of Legal Studies* 1 et seq.; on the phenomenon of regulatory capture, G. J. Stigler, 'The Theory of Economic Regulation' (1971) 2 *The Bell Journal of Economics and Management Science* 3 et seq.; R. A. Posner, 'Theories of Economic Regulation' (1974) 5 *The Bell Journal of Economics and Management Science* 335, 341 et seq.; in a broader perspective, arguing that a system of takeover regulation that provides parties with the ability to challenge regulatory decisions in courts is bound to cause delays and uncertainty in the takeover process, J. Mukwiri, 'Negative Implications of Greater Access to the Courts in the Takeover Process' (2023) 20 *European Company and Financial Law Review* 358, 369 et seq.

13 For an overview on the optimal enforcement structure, with sometimes different accents, cf. H. E. Jackson and M. Roe, 'Public and Private Enforcement of Securities Laws: Resource Based Evidence' (2009) 93 *Journal of Financial Economics* 207 et seq.; S. Shavell, 'The Optimal Structure of Law Enforcement' (1993) 36 *The Journal of Law & Economics* 255 et seq.; M. Polinsky and S. Shavell, 'The Economic Theory of Public Enforcement of Law' (2000) 38 *Journal of Economic Literature* 45 et seq.; J. C. Coffee Jr, 'Law and the Market: The Impact of Enforcement' (2007) 156 *University of Pennsylvania Law Review* 229 et seq.; Poelzig, 'Normdurchsetzung', p. 18 et seq., 375 et seq.; L. Klöhn, 'Private versus Public Enforcement of Laws – A Law & Economic Perspective', in R. Schulze (ed.), *Compensation of Private Losses. The Evolution of Torts in European Business Law* (Berlin: Springer, 2011), p. 34, 179 et seq.; R. Veil and A. Brüggemeier, 'Kapitalmarktrecht zwischen öffentlich-rechtlicher und privatrechtlicher Normdurchsetzung', in H. Fleischer, S. Kalss and H.-U. Vogt (eds.), *Enforcement im Gesellschafts- und Kapitalmarktrecht* (Tübingen: Mohr Siebeck, 2015), p. 277 et seq.; G. Wagner, 'Rechtsdurchsetzung im Kapitalmarktrecht: Public versus Private Enforcement', in M. Casper, L. Klöhn, W.-H. Roth and C. Schmies (eds.), *Festschrift für Johannes Köndgen* (Cologne: RWS, 2016), p. 649, 664 et seq.

the MBR).[14] Moreover, at least institutional investors have sufficient incentives to enforce their claims. And last but not least, while public authorities are limited by the principle of territoriality and are not in a position to take extraterritorial action against foreign companies, private claims can also be enforced across borders on the basis of international private law.

Clearly, there are drawbacks here as well, since only institutional investors are likely to take legal action, while other minority shareholders suffering only dispersed damages may be rationally apathetic.[15] This problem is accentuated by the fact that, at least in most continental European jurisdictions, the securities class action, if available, does not work efficiently, thus preventing a useful aggregation of individual claims.[16] Last but not least, for private parties it may be difficult to prove a breach of the duty to bid – for example, that the offeror holds securities giving him/her control of a company (see Art. 5(1) TOD) or that the offeror paid a higher price for the same securities before the bid (see Art. 5(4) TOD).

4.4 ENFORCEMENT MODELS

Let us now see the different trajectories followed by the two selected model samples – namely, the Italian and German enforcement systems of the duty to bid. This will allow, in a second step, to ascertain whether further harmonisation efforts are recommendable in order to contribute to an efficient capital market, also considering other regulatory measures taken at the Community level.[17]

4.4.1 *Mainly Private-Driven Enforcement Model: The Case of Italy*

The origins of the Italian mandatory bid rule go back well before the coming into force of the TOD, with a first embryonic regulation contained in the Law no. 149 of 1992 on public takeovers.[18] Today, the relevant Italian Consolidated Financial

[14] S. Shavell, 'Liability for Harm versus Regulation of Safety' (1984) 13 *The Journal of Legal Studies* 357, 359–360 ('private parties should generally enjoy an inherent advantage in knowledge'); Giudici, 'Private Law Enforcement', p. 26 ('minority shareholders are … the best private enforcers').

[15] Poelzig, 'Normdurchsetzung', p. 381 et seq.

[16] Ibid., p. 384 et seq.; in the Italian case law, see recently, Trib. Milan, 11.1.2023, (2023) *Le Società* 1262 et seq., where the first-instance judges excluded that a tendering shareholder could bring a class action to enforce the alleged collusion perpetrated by the bidder to obtain full control at an inadequate price. For the somehow different situation in the UK, see, also for empirical data, F. Restrepo, 'The Capital Market Effects of Introducing Private Rights of Action in Securities Regulation: Evidence from the United Kingdom' (2023) 66 *The Journal of Law & Economics* 183 et seq.

[17] Reference here goes in particular to 'adjacent' enforcement systems: for details, see Section 4.5.2.

[18] On this regulation, R. Weigmann, 'Le offerte pubbliche d'acquisto', in G. E. Colombo and G. B. Portale (eds.), *Trattato delle società per azioni*, 19 vols. (Turin: UTET, 1993), vol. 10**, p. 355

Service Act (CFSA), differentiating on the basis of the ownership structure and the size of the company, establishes as the threshold for the launch of a mandatory bid the holding of 25 or 30 per cent of the share capital or the voting rights[19] in the general meeting of the listed target company.[20] The CFSA sanctions the breach of the MBR by freezing the exercise of the overall voting rights held by the bidder and by imposing the compulsory sale of the shares exceeding the relevant threshold within twelve months (Art. 110). The supervisory authority CONSOB, alternatively to the requirement of a compulsory sale, may order the launch of a mandatory bid at the price established by the same authority (Art. 110(1-*bis*) CFSA);[21] at the same time, though, the public watchdog has not the power, otherwise exceeding the scope of application of the aforementioned provision, to simply impose a price adjustment in

et seq.; for historical references also C. Mosca, 'L'offerta pubblica di acquisto obbligatoria', in M. Cera and G. Presti (eds.), *Il Testo unico finanziario, Mercati ed emittenti*, 2 vols. (Bologna: Zanichelli, 2020), vol. 2, p. 1400 et seq.

19 In this regard, of relevance is the provision in Art. 127-*quinquies* CFSA, which allows the articles of association to provide for double voting rights in favour of long-term shareholders (i.e. holding uninterruptedly shares for at least 24 months). Now, with the entering into force of the so-called *Legge Capitali* of 5 March 2024, no. 21, this threshold has been raised for non-listed joint-stock companies to ten votes per share, with maintenance of these shares even after the initial public offering (Art. 13, modifying Art. 2351(4) Civil Code). In addition, the current wording of Art. 14(1)(b) of the mentioned law, by modifying Art. 127-*quinquies* CFSA, allows listed companies adopting the increased voting mechanism to provide in the articles of association (opt-in) that, in addition to the ordinary double voting right, such rights may be further increased to the extent of one vote per share for each period of 12 months of continuous share ownership, up to a maximum of 10 votes per share (so-called step-up mechanism); in such latter case, dissenting shareholders have a withdrawal right.

20 See Art. 106(1) CFSA. Actually, the relevant threshold may vary depending on the ownership structure and the size of the company. The current legislation, indeed, lays down a differentiated system of thresholds for listed companies, with the aim of simplifying entering into the capital market for all enterprises, including SMEs. Thus, in addition to the threshold of 30 per cent, Art. 106(1-*bis*) CFSA, with reference only to 'companies other than SMEs', introduced a new and alternative trigger event, i.e. mandatory takeover bid must be made even if the bidder comes to own by purchase a stake exceeding 25 per cent of the share capital *and* no other shareholder holds a larger holding. As for SMEs, the articles of incorporation may establish a threshold different from the ordinary one, but this contractual threshold must be between 25 and 40 per cent of the share capital (Art. 106 (1-*ter*)). For a comment, C. Mosca, 'L'offerta pubblica', p. 1406 et seq.; this regulatory approach received positive evaluation also by German scholars: D. A. Verse, 'Pflichtangebot – Status quo und Reform 20 Jahre nach Inkrafttreten des WpÜG', in R. Veil, H. C. Grigoleit and M. Habersack, *Öffentliche Unternehmensübernahmen* (Tübingen: Mohr Siebeck, 2022), p. 59, 70.

21 This provision was introduced in 2007 by the Legislative Decree 19 November 2007, no. 229. Generally, in the literature on CONSOB's power to adjust the takeover price, C. Mosca, 'L'offerta pubblica', p. 1426 et seq.; F. Cadorin, *OPA obbligatoria e prezzo 'equo'* (Milan: Giuffrè, 2024), p. 95 et seq. Even further goes the French case law, where in two prominent cases (*Hyparlo* and *Billon*, both pronounced in 2005 by the Paris Court of Appeal) the judge ordered (*injonction judiciaire*) in lieu of the public supervisory authority, AMF, the execution of a mandotory bid. For a comment, see A. Pietrancosta, 'L'exécution forcée d'une offre publique obligatoire: des injonctions judiciaires prononcées dans les affaires "Hyparlo" et "Billon"' (2010), available at: www.lexbase.fr (accessed 11 April 2024).

the case of the takeover bid having already been made by the predator.[22] Moreover, administrative and criminal fines are applied (respectively, Art. 192 and Art. 173). In contrast, no statutory reference is made to a shareholder's right to claim for damages.[23] Thus, no private enforcement of minority shareholders' rights in the case of violation of the duty to bid was in place, neither at the statutory level nor in the judicial application.

4.4.1.1 The 'Disruptive' Fondiaria-SAI Case: Factual Background

The restrictive approach to private enforcement of the duty to bid substantially changed, at least at the judicial level, with the 'disruptive' *Fondiaria-SAI* case, considered by many the most interesting dispute in the securities law area of the last decade.[24] The case's origins go back to 2001 when SAI, a large Italian insurance company, by acting in concert with Mediobanca, committed to buying a large stake in Fondiaria, another large Italian insurance company. Such a purchase by SAI would have triggered the mandatory takeover rules. In order to avoid this obligation, SAI and Mediobanca engaged five intermediaries (including JP Morgan and Commerzbank), which bought the stake on behalf of SAI in February 2002. The five intermediaries claimed to have acted independently, despite the large premium they were paying on the shares. The public watchdog CONSOB received many complaints but did not carry out an investigation. SAI's and Fondiaria's shareholders agreed to merge with resolutions of 19 September 2002 and, shortly afterwards, SAI bought from the white knights their stake in Fondiaria. Following this, the antitrust authority, and not the financial markets supervisory authority, opened proceedings against all the companies involved in order to assess the impact of the resulting concentration on the insurance market, hereby discovering the existence of secret agreements, which also involved SAI's controlling party, Premafin. In this scenario, CONSOB tried to take corrective actions and stated that SAI and Mediobanca had concerted the acquisition of Fondiaria and that the white knights were actually SAI's proxies. Given the infringement of the mandatory bid rules, CONSOB forced

[22] N. de Luca, 'OPA a prezzo incongruo e azioni risarcitorie di classe. Le azioni non sono beni di consumo, l'azionista non è consumatore, l'offerente non è professionista' (2023) *Le Società* 1266, 1272.

[23] Giudici, 'Private Law Enforcement', p. 27 ('The law is mute on whether or not minority shareholders are entitled to damages'). For an overview on the sanctionary apparatus provided by the CFSA, cf. F. M. Mucciarelli, 'Le offerte pubbliche d'acquisto e di scambio', in R. Costi (ed.), *Trattato di diritto commerciale* (Turin: G. Giapachelli Editore, 2014), p. 202 seq.; L. Enriques, 'Mercato del controllo societario e tutela degli investitori' (Bologna: Il Mulino, 2002), p. 211 et seq.; C. Mosca, 'L'offerta pubblica', p. 1462 et seq.

[24] Cf. Agstner and Marchesini Mascheroni, 'Breach of the Mandatory Bid Rule' (2020) 17 *European Company and Financial Law Review* 734 et seq.; P. Giudici, 'Il private enforcement in caso di elusione dell'obbligo di offerta pubblica di acquisto' (2013) *Le Società* 180 et seq.; C. Mosca, 'Acquisti di concerto, partecipazioni incrociate e responsabilità per inadempimento dell'obbligo di opa' (2007) 52 *Rivista delle società* 1290.

Mediobanca and Premafin to sell some of their shares in the new company FonSai. However, as a result of the above-mentioned merger and the legal impossibility of invalidating the operation,[25] Premafin had already achieved its final goal and remained in control of FonSai, as planned from the very outset of the transaction.

4.4.1.2 The Different and Varying Court Rulings with the Final Recognition of Private Enforcement Rights

These facts initiated a huge wave of judicial litigation among FonSai and Mediobanca on one side, and the harmed minority shareholders of Fondiaria on the other. The fundamental issue focused on whether the financial market regulation (i.e. the CFSA) excludes or limits the possibility for an individual investor to trigger separately private law remedies for the protection of her interests.[26] The line of reasoning embraced at first by the Italian courts, at least until the arrival of the case before the Supreme Court, was not very linear and sometimes even contradictory. In fact, while the first-instance Tribunal of Milan recognised a contractual right for minority shareholders to receive the mandatory takeover offer,[27] the Court of Appeal took the diametrically opposite view and charged the bidder with a pre-contractual tort liability.[28] In the Court of Appeal's opinion, in the absence of a duty to purchase, there is no obligation to pay damages. Thus, the freezing of voting rights and the duty to sell the exceeding shares are the only applicable sanctions in the event of a breach of the MBR.[29]

[25] Art. 2504-*quater* Civil code.

[26] For the relationship between civil/company law and capital market law, see in the ECJ's case law the Case C-174/12, *Alfred Hirmann v. Immofinanz* AG [2013] ECLI:EU:C:2013:856.

[27] Tribunal Milan, 26 May 2005 no. 6688, Giurisprudenza commerciale 2005, II, 753. In the first instance, judges shared the view that MBRs form a compulsory part of the company contract functional to assuring equality among shareholders. In their opinion, by signing the articles of incorporation everyone agrees to become entitled to rights as well as to be subject to obligations *ex lege*. One of these is the obligation to promote a takeover bid upon fulfilment of the conditions set forth in Art. 106 CFSA. However, minority shareholders could claim for redress only if the damage caused by the failure to bid persisted in spite of the activation of the public enforcement remedies. In contrast, if similar sanctions re-establish the *status quo ante*, nothing will be owed to the target shareholders. After this decision, the Milan Tribunal essentially confirmed its view in different subsequent rulings.

[28] Milan Court of Appeal, 15 January 2007 no. 54. In general, it is debated whether the pre-contractual liability is contractual or tort. Recently, the Italian Supreme Court, with reference to different factual backgrounds, has sometimes opted for the contractual nature of the *culpa in contrahendo*: cf. Supreme Court of Cassation, 20 December 2011, no. 27648; Supreme Court of Cassation, 12 July 2016, no. 14188, Europa e diritto privato 2017, 1129, with comment by Antonio Albanese; in other cases, on the contrary, the pre-contractual liability was qualified as liability in tort: Supreme Court of Cassation, 25 January 2012, no. 1051.

[29] With a ruling made a few months later (20 December 2007 no. 3425), confirmed also by decisions of 27 February 2012 no. 712 and of 12 April 2013 no. 1584, the mentioned Court of Appeal adopted an even stricter view (so-called *lex perfecta* theory), thus excluding both the

Only with the decisions delivered by the Supreme Court of Cassation starting from 2012 was a definitive solution to the long and controversial debate on the consequences of the breach of the mandatory takeover bid duty provided.[30] The Supreme Court rejected both approaches previously sustained by the Court of Appeal and agreed with the Tribunal's view by ascribing a contractual liability to the bidder. However, a different line of argumentation was followed in order to support this conclusion. Specifically, the Supreme Court granted minority shareholders an individual contractual right to receive the offer and highlighted that the liability arising for the debtor who does not exactly fulfil the duty imposed by *law* is contractual not only in the event of this obligation resulting from a contract, but even as a result of the incorrect performance of a pre-existing obligation. According to this approach – the so-called social contact theory, which goes back to fundamental studies of eminent German private law scholars[31] – a qualified or special relationship between the parties is already in existence before the occurrence of the breach. Because of the said proximity, the bidder owes a duty of protection to the minority shareholders, who are entitled to rely on conduct that is reasonable and in good faith demanded from the bidder. Since this relationship already exists before the violation of the obligation to offer occurs, it follows that the bidder's liability has a contractual character and the same applies to the compensation for damages.

4.4.2 *Mainly Public-Driven Enforcement Model: The Case of Germany*

In Germany, the relevant normative framework is constituted by the Wertpapiererwerbs- und Übernahmegesetz (WpÜG), the German Securities Acquisition and Takeover Act, which came into force in 2002 and was amended in 2006 to implement the TOD.[32] § 35(2) WpÜG provides that a mandatory takeover bid has to be made if the bidder acquires control over the target

contractual right to receive the bid and the pre-contractual shareholders' claim for breach of legitimate expectations relied on in the launch of the offer.

30 Supreme Court of Cassation, 10 August 2012, no. 14400; identical decisions were delivered by Supreme Court of Cassation, 10 August 2012, no. 14392; and by Supreme Court of Cassation, 10 August 2012, no. 14399; following, among others, Supreme Court of Cassation, 26 September 2013, no. 22099; Supreme Court of Cassation, 13 October 2015, no. 20560; Supreme Court of Cassation, 10 February 2016, no. 2665.

31 Cf., H. Stoll, 'Abschied von der Lehre von der positiven Vertragsverletzung' (1932) 136 *Archiv für die civilistische Praxis* 257, 287; H. Dölle, 'Außergesetzliche Schuldpflichten' (1943) 103 *Zeitschrift für die gesamte Staatswissenschaft* 72; K. Larenz, 'Culpa in contrahendo, Verkehrssicherungspflicht und "sozialer Kontakt"' (1954) 9 *Monatsschrift für deutsches Recht* 515. Today, with the reform of the German law of obligations of 2002, the mentioned principles have been codified in §§ 241(2) and 311(2-3) *Bürgerliches Gesetzbuch* (*BGB*). Similarly, Grant Gilmore (ed.), *The Death of Contract* (Columbus: Ohio State University Press, 1974), p. 88, pictures such quasi-contracts as 'a sort of no-man's land lying between contract and tort'.

32 For a general overview on the development of German takeover law, see e.g. H. Fleischer, '§ 1 WpÜG', in Paschos and Fleischer (eds.), *Handbuch Übernahmerecht nach dem WpÜG*, § 1 mn. 1 et seq.; H. Hirte and H. Gildehaus, 'Einleitung', in H. Hirte, C. Seibt, S. Mock and S.

company – that is, the direct or indirect holding by the bidder of at least 30 per cent of the voting rights in the target company according to § 29(2) WpÜG. Once this threshold is crossed, the bidder, within seven days at the latest, has to inform the market and must submit within the following four weeks to the Federal Financial Supervisory Authority (Bundesanstalt für Finanzdienstleistungsaufsicht or BaFin) the required offer document (§ 35 WpÜG).

4.4.2.1 Public Enforcement

In the event of violation of this obligation, various administrative sanctions apply. First, fines of up to 5 per cent of the company's revenues and up to ten million euros can be imposed (§ 60(4) WpÜG). Besides this, the BaFin can enforce the duty to publish a mandatory takeover bid by means of an order (§ 4(1) WpÜG). However, target shareholders have no subjective public right of action against the supervisory authority.[33] Paragraph 4(2) WpÜG expressly stipulates that the authority shall only act in the public interest and not on behalf of the individual investor.[34] Hence, they do not have the right to force the BaFin to take action.[35] Shareholder protection at the administrative level is excluded.

4.4.2.2 Private Enforcement

Therefore, it is decisive whether the target shareholders enjoy a private right of action in the event of a breach of the mandatory bid rule.[36] Besides the administrative sanctions, the WpÜG contains some private enforcement instruments: most importantly, pursuant to § 59 WpÜG, all rights deriving from the shares held by the predatory party are suspended, including pre-emptive rights and the right to dividend. Furthermore, the predator is obliged to pay interest (i.e. five percentage points

Schwarz (eds.), *Kölner Kommentar zum WpÜG* (Cologne: Carl Heymanns Verlag, 2022), 3rd ed., Einl. mn. 35 et seq.; for some empirical data, Verse, 'Pflichtangebot', p. 59, 61 et seq.

33 Oberlandesgericht (Higher Regional Court) Frankfurt a.M., 27 May 2003 - WpÜG 1/03, (2003) *Zeitschrift für Wirtschaftsrecht* 1297 (*ProSiebenSat.1 I*); Oberlandesgericht (Higher Regional Court) Frankfurt a.M., 09.10.2003 - WpÜG 3/03, (2003) *Zeitschrift für Wirtschaftsrecht* 2206 (*ProSiebenSat.1 II*); Oberlandesgericht (Higher Regional Court) Frankfurt a.M., 08.01.2018 - WpÜG 1/17; in the literature, A. Cahn, 'Verwaltungsbefugnisseder Bundesanstalt für Finanzdienstleistungsaufsicht im Übernahmerecht und Rechtsschutz Betroffener' (2003) 167 *Zeitschrift für das gesamte Handelsrecht und Wirtschaftsrecht* 265.

34 The ECJ has declared this to be in conformity with EU law ECJ, 12 October 2004, Case C-222/02, *Peter Paul, Cornelia Sonnen-Lütte, Christel Mörkens v. Bundesrepublik Deutschland* [2004] ECLI:EU:C:2004:606.

35 U. Noack and D. Zetzsche, '§ 4 WpÜG', in E. Schwark and D. Zimmer (eds.), *Kapitalmarktrechts-Kommentar*, 5th ed., (Munich: C.H. Beck, 2020), § 4 mn. 21.

36 Generally on this topic, cf. D. Horcher, 'Zivilrechtlicher Rechtsschutz im Übernahmeverfahren', in Veil, Grigoleit and Habersack (eds.), *Öffentliche Unternehmensübernahmen*, p. 265 et seq.; Nietsch, '§ 29 WpÜG', in Paschos and Fleischer (eds.), *Handbuch Übernahmerecht nach dem WpÜG*, § 29 mn. 6 et seq.

above basic interest rates on the mandatory bid price) to the offerees for the period of the violation of the duty to make a compulsory tender offer (§ 38 WpÜG).[37] However, there is no written individual private right of action for minority shareholders in the event of a violation of the mandatory bid rule. Therefore, reference has to be made to a line of judgments starting in 2013 with the *BKN* leading case,[38] followed soon afterwards by the *Postbank* decision[39] and ending – for the moment – with the two *Celesio* rulings of 2017 and 2021, respectively.[40] The type of breach of duty is decisive for the question of private claims.

4.4.2.2.1 FAILURE TO MAKE A MANDATORY OFFER (ART. 5(1) TOD). If the bidder violates his or her duty to make a mandatory bid, the shareholders of the target company have no right to claim. This was subject of the *BKN* case. In this case, the Federal Supreme Court (Bundesgerichtshof or BGH) was confronted with the following facts. The plaintiff was an offshore investment company with headquarters in the Turks and Caicos Islands, while the defendant was a US investment fund. The target company, BKN International AG, also had an office in Cologne, Germany. The plaintiff argued that the investment fund had crossed the 30 per cent threshold several times. Furthermore, it was asserted that the investor's wife, because of her holding in the target company, had acted in concert with the defendant. Hence, assuming a violation of the duty to bid, the plaintiff claimed the payment of 987,000 euros as consideration for the transfer of 300,000 shares held in the target company and, subordinately, the same amount as interest on capital.

Against this factual background, the Federal Supreme Court expressed the following principles. First, the shareholders of the target company have no right to counter-performance if the bidder violates his or her duty to make a mandatory bid. The right to interest payment requires equally that a tender offer has been launched, though on delay.[41] Second, it is stated that § 35 WpÜG does not represent a protective law (*Schutzgesetz*) in the sense meant by § 823(2) BGB, and therefore does not justify an ensuing tort liability of the bidder.[42] In the motivation of the

[37] In detail cf. J. Ekkenga and C. Schirrmacher, '§ 35 WpÜG', in M. Beurskens, U. Ehricke and J. Ekkenga (eds.), *Wertpapiererwerbs- und Übernahmegesetz* (Munich: C.H. Beck, 2021), 2nd ed., § 35 mn. 101 et seq.; M. Nietsch, '§ 29 WpÜG', in Paschos and Fleischer (eds.), *Handbuch Übernahmerecht nach dem WpÜG*, § 29 mn. 1 et seq.; Poelzig, 'Normdurchsetzung', p. 226 et seq.; M. Santelmann, '§ 59 WpÜG', in R. Steinmeyer (ed.), *WpÜG. Kommentar* (Berlin: Erich Schmidt Verlag, 2019), 4 ed., § 59 mn. 4 et seq.

[38] BGH, 11 June 2013 – II ZR 80/12, (2013) *Zeitschrift für Wirtschaftsrecht* 1565.

[39] BGH, 29 July 2014 – II ZR 353/12, (2014) *Zeitschrift für Wirtschaftsrecht* 1623; today again in the *Postbank* 'saga', BGH, 13.12.2022 – II ZR 14/21, *BGHZ* 235, 295 (on acting in concert matters).

[40] BGH, 7 November 2017 – II ZR 37/16, *BGHZ* 216, 347 (*Celesio I*); and BGH, 23.11.2021 – II ZR 312/19, *BGHZ* 232, 46 (*Celesio II*); see also BGH, 23 May 2023 - II ZR 219/21, (2023) Zeitschrift für Wirtschaftsrecht 1528 (*Stada*).

[41] For the inapplicability of § 38 WpÜG in the case of a tender offer not being launched at all, see already BGH, 18 September 2006 – II ZR 137/05, BGHZ 169, 98 (*WMF*).

[42] BGH, 11 June 2013 – II ZR 80/12, (2013) *Zeitschrift für Wirtschaftsrecht*, 1565, mn. 36.

judgment, the Federal Supreme judges particularly stressed that the WpÜG is primarily capital-market-law-centred.[43] The merely reflexive shareholder protection is proved by the fact that the supervisory authority performs its tasks *only* in the public interest (§ 4(2) WpÜG). Thus, the German Takeover Act is not primarily directed at the protection of the shareholder's interest but serves the efficient functioning of the securities market.[44]

4.4.2.2.2 BREACH OF THE MINIMUM PRICE RULE (ART. 5(4) TOD). In contrast, shareholders have a claim if the offeror has made an offer in accordance with Art. 5 (1) but has not offered a price that meets the minimum requirements under Art. 5(4) TOD. This point of view was shared in the later cases *Postbank*, *Celesio I* and *Celesio II*. Although concerning voluntary bids, the principles of law established in these decisions are applicable also to (incorrect) mandatory tender offers.[45] The *quaestio iuris* dealt with by the courts concerned, therefore, not the violation of the duty to bid, but the application of the minimum price rules in the case of a takeover bid having actually been made. Accordingly, shareholders who accepted the (voluntary) takeover bid have a right to claim for the minimum price on the basis of Art. 5 (4) TOD. This specified, in the *Postbank* dispute, the plaintiff Effecten-Spiegel-AG, which had accepted the (voluntary) takeover offer made by Deutsche Bank AG on the shares of Postbank AG at the price of 25 euros per share, sued Deutsche Bank for the payment of the difference between the offered price and the alleged higher amount due to the plaintiff (57 euros per share) on the basis of a mandatory takeover bid that should have been previously made because of an assumed change of control. The right to claim is based on the contract between the bidder and the shareholder which accepted the bid. Consequently, the Federal Supreme Court granted such entitlement only to the target shareholders which had tendered their shares to the bidder.[46] This opinion was finally confirmed in the two *Celesio* judgments.[47]

[43] BGH, 11 June 2013 – II ZR 80/12, (2013) *Zeitschrift für Wirtschaftsrecht*, 1565, mn. 19.

[44] BGH, 11 June 2013 – II ZR 80/12, (2013) *Zeitschrift für Wirtschaftsrecht*, 1565, mn. 20. In the literature, Poelzig, 'Normdurchsetzung', p. 233 ('Instrumente der Marktregulierung zum Schutz funktionsfähiger Kapitalmärkte'). Still, one might reply that if the shareholders are not protected ex ante, then they are less incentivised to invest in the company, thereby undermining the efficient functioning of the capital market.

[45] For this opinion Horcher, 'Zivilrechtlicher Rechtsschutz', p. 283; Nietsch, '§ 29 WpÜG', in Paschos and Fleischer (eds.), *Handbuch Übernahmerecht nach dem WpÜG*, § 29 mn. 22.

[46] BGH, 29 September 2014 – II ZR 353/12, *BGHZ* 202, 180, mn. 23.

[47] In the *Celesio* cases, concerning the voluntary takeover of Celesio AG by McKesson, the legal question was whether the price paid by the bidder for the purchase of convertible bonds from another shareholder is material for the purposes of the best price rule; the German Federal Supreme Court answered the question affirmatively, thus condemning McKesson to pay an additional sum of 7.45 euro to the plaintiff Magnetar, a US hedge fund. With the *Celesio II* ruling, the Supreme Court excluded a pre-contractual secondary obligation (*vorvertragliche Nebenpflicht*) by the bidder towards the target shareholders. For a comment, cf. M. Brellochs,

4.4.2.2.3 RELUCTANCE TO USE PRIVATE ENFORCEMENT. In conclusion, it can be said that, although the German takeover regulation provides for private enforcement instruments, above all the suspension of shareholders' rights, it denies the individual private right of actions of the duty to bid and limits the target shareholders' claims to the right to get adequate consideration for the shares tendered. According to this regulatory philosophy, public enforcement measures offer instead an adequate toolset to ensure the efficient functioning of the market for corporate control. Certainly, some scholarship expresses dissenting views,[48] but the outlined judicial practice seems settled.[49]

4.5 HARMONISATION OF THE PRIVATE ENFORCEMENT REGIME IN THE TOD

At this point, the central question becomes whether, in view of the different national law-in-action approaches outlined above, new EU legislation introducing a common rule of civil liability in the event of a breach of the MBR is advisable (or feasible) or not.[50]

4.5.1 *Civil Liability as an Enforcement Instrument*

Raising such an issue seems legitimate and sensible if one only considers that the TOD elevates the protection of minority shareholders to an explicit regulatory goal, whose fulfilment must therefore be assured in a satisfactory manner. However, the practical experience shows that this is not always the case. In fact, there might well

'Zur Angemessenheit der Gegenleistung im Übernahmerecht', (2018) 47 *Zeitschrift für Unternehmens- und Gesellschaftsrecht* 811 et seq.; T. Tröger, 'Keine private Durchsetzung der Preisregeln im Übernahmerecht' (2022) 51 *Zeitschrift für Unternehmens- und Gesellschaftsrecht* 433 et seq.

48 Cf. Ekkenga and Schirrmacher, '§ 35 WpÜG', in Beurskens, Ehricke and Ekkenga (eds.), *Wertpapiererwerbs- und Übernahmegesetz*, § 35 mn. 104–108; W. Meilicke and F. Meilicke, 'Die Postbank-Übernahme durch die Deutsche Bank – eine Gestaltung zur Vermeidung von Pflichtangeboten nach § 35 WpÜG?' (2010) *Zeitschrift für Wirtschaftsrecht* 558, 566; Balthasar, 'Die Preisregeln', p. 116, 128 et seq.; K. Hasselbach, '§ 35 WpÜG', in Hirte, Seibt, Mock and Schwarz (eds.), *Kölner Kommentar zum WpÜG*, § 35 mn. 294; C. Seibt, 'Rechtsschutz im Übernahmerecht' (2003) *Zeitschrift für Wirtschaftsrecht* 1873–1874; T. Tröger, 'Keine private Durchsetzung', 438, 444.

49 For a good overview, Horcher, 'Zivilrechtlicher Rechtsschutz', p. 285 et seq., 290. Interestingly, the Austrian scholars, traditionally strongly influenced by their German peers, unanimously recognise private minority shareholder protection in the case of a breach of the duty to make a mandatory takeover bid pursuant to § 22 *Übernahmegesetz* (*ÜbG*): cf. M. Winner, 'Gedanken zum Sanktionensystem im Übernahmerecht. Festheft für Peter Doralt zum 80. Geburtstag' (2019) *Der Gesellschafter* 121; C. Diregger, S. Kalss and M. Winner (eds.), *Das österreichische Übernahmerecht* (Vienna: Linde, 2007), 2 ed., § 158 mn. 337.

50 For such a question with reference to the MAR, V. D. Tountopoulos, 'Market Abuse and Private Enforcement', (2014) 11 *European Company and Financial Law Review* 332.

be a concrete risk of under-enforcement, as the *Fondiaria-SAI* case distinctly showed, with the violation of mandatory takeover bid rules thus remaining undetected. The same applies for German law, where in the *Postbank* case the breach of the mandatory bid rule initially remained undetected and was only uncovered by the later voluntary takeover bid.[51] Hence, private remedies may play an important deterrence role, thus delivering a significant, preventive incentive for lawful behaviour on the capital market.[52] Furthermore, the confidence-building function of private liability cannot be neglected, insofar as it ensures also in this field that investors can rely on being compensated for their losses in the case of violation of the duty to bid. Facilitating private enforcement through liability rules benefits stock markets.[53] From this perspective, a liability rule is not intended to serve individual protection alone, but rather must be seen as an additional instrument for the protection of the market as an institution.[54]

4.5.2 *Policy Indications from 'Adjacent' Enforcement Systems?*

Although this evidence clearly speaks in favour of harmonising private enforcement rules, at the EU level, as already mentioned, it is not necessary for Member States to grant a private right of action to minority shareholders for the immediate protection of their interests.[55] In order to better understand the logic and rationality of such a policy choice and subsequently assess the opportunity of revising the same, it seems useful to look at 'adjacent' enforcement regimes. In many legislative acts with a focus on capital markets, enforcement is exclusively based on public law instruments: for example, the Market Abuse Regulation (EU) No 2014/596 (MAR), like its predecessor,[56] by relying on specific and severe administrative and also criminal

[51] BGH 29 September 2014 – II ZR 353/12, *BGHZ* 202, 180 (*Postbank*).

[52] Giudici, 'Private Law Enforcement', p. 18 et seq.; D. Markworth, 'Marktmissbrauchsverordnung und effet utile' (2019) 183 *Zeitschrift für das gesamte Handelsrecht und Wirtschaftsrecht* 67; for an in-depth analysis of the regulatory function of private law, A. Hellgardt, *Regulierung und Privatrecht* (Tübingen: Mohr Siebeck, 2016), p. 47 et seq.; Poelzig, 'Normdurchsetzung', p. 361 et seq.; Veil and Brüggemeier, 'Kapitalmarktrecht zwischen öffentlich-rechtlicher und privatrechtlicher Normdurchsetzung', p. 278 ('Haftungsrecht soll auch präventiv wirken'); for a systematic overview, Wagner, 'Prävention und Verhaltenssteuerung durch Privatrecht – Anmaßung oder legitime Aufgabe', (2006) 206 *Archiv für die civilistische Praxis* 352.

[53] La Porta, Lopez-de-Silanes and Shleifer, 'What Works in Securities Laws?', (2006) 61 *The Journal of Finance* 1.

[54] For such reasoning, referred to the MAR but valid also for the present discussion, Markworth, 'Marktmissbrauchsverordnung und effet utile', 61.

[55] See Section 4.2.

[56] Market Abuse Directive 2003/6/EC (Art. 14); in the case law, Case C-174/12, *Alfred Hirmann v. Immofinanz* AG [2013] ECLI:EU:C:2013:856 mn. 40.

sanctions,[57] omits any reference to a private right of action against those responsible for market abuses. The same is true for the Securitisation Regulation (EU) No 2017/2402. Hence, both the availability and the degree of private enforcement fall entirely within the domain of national laws.[58] The restrictive approach is certainly not imposed by limitations resulting from the application of Art. 114(1) TFEU (principle of approximation of laws) or Art. 5(3) TEU (principle of subsidiarity).[59] Instead, it seems to correspond to a specific policy choice.[60]

In fact, in other legislative acts, such as Art. 11 of the Prospectus Regulation (EU) No 2017/1129 (PR) and, similarly, Art. 7 of the Transparency Directive (EU) No 2004/109 (TD),[61] it is stated in a quite laconic and programmatic way[62] that Member States shall ensure that their laws, regulations and administrative provisions on civil liability apply to the persons responsible for the infringement of the protected interests, thereby leaving the design of the civil liability regime (i.e. issues of causality, assessment of damages, etc.) to the individual Member States.[63] In this way, Member States, also in order to reflect their specific institutional settings, retain

57 Directive 2014/57/EU of 16 April 2014 on criminal sanctions for market abuse (CRIM MAD): for a comment, E. Basile, 'Criminal Sanctions', in M. Ventoruzzo and S. Mock, *Market Abuse Regulation* (Oxford: OUP, 2022), 2nd ed., p. 175 et seq.

58 Cf. D. Busch, 'The private law effect of the EU market abuse regulation' (2019) 14 *Capital Markets Law Journal* 296, recalling the *Immofinanz, Genil* and *Nationale-Nederlanden* cases; Markworth, 'Marktmissbrauchsverordnung und effet utile', 46 et seq., 49, 66; C. Thomale, 'Appendix to Art. 30 MAR – Private Enforcement', in S. Kalss, M. Oppitz, U. Torggler and M. Winner (eds.), *EU Market Abuse Regulation* (Cheltenham: Edward Elgar, 2021), p. 364 et seq., 367; Tountopoulos, 'Market Abuse and Private Enforcement', 305 et seq., 322 et seq.; very critical towards the absence of a harmonised framework of private liability Poelzig, 'Private enforcement', 801, 816, 846 seq. ('*funktionale Subjektivierung*'); R. Veil, 'Private Enforcement in European Capital Markets Law', in B. Gsell and T. M. J. Möllers (eds.), *Enforcing Consumer and Capital Markets Law* (Cambridge: Intersentia, 2020), p. 405, 421–422; for comparative references, J. W. Flume, 'Private Enforcement of the Market Abuse Regulation in European Law, Austria and Germany', in Ventoruzzo and Mock (eds.), *Market Abuse Regulation*, p. 75 et seq.

59 Generally on these principles, A. F. P. Brüggemeier (ed.), *Harmonisierungskonzepte im europäischen Kapitalmarktrecht* (Tübingen: Mohr Siebeck, 2018), p. 43 et seq.; T. Kahnert (ed.), *Rechtsetzung im Europäischen Gesellschaftsrecht* (Tübingen: Mohr Siebeck, 2012), p. 19 et seq.

60 Thomale, 'Appendix to Art. 30 MAR', p. 364–365.

61 Art. 7 was not amended by Directive 2013/50/EU of 22 October 2013.

62 M. Ventoruzzo, 'Like Moths to a Flame – International Securities Litigation after Morrison: Correcting the Supreme Court's Transactional Test' (2012) 52 *Virginia Journal of International Law* 405, 413 ('vague European rule').

63 Cf. P. Giudici, 'Private Enforcement of Transparency', in V. Tountopoulos and R. Veil (eds.), *Transparency of Stock Corporations in Europe* (London: Bloomsbury Publishing, 2019), p. 297, 298 et seq.; O. Mörsdorf, 'Private enforcement im sekundären Unionsprivatrecht: (k)eine klare Sache?' (2019) 83 *Rabels Zeitschrift für ausländisches und internationales Privatrecht* 797, 831 et seq.; Veil and Brüggemeier, 'Kapitalmarktrecht zwischen öffentlich-rechtlicher und privatrechtlicher Normdurchsetzung', p. 294; M. Wundenberg, 'Perspektiven der privaten Rechtsdurchsetzung im europäischen Kapitalmarktrecht' (2015) *Zeitschrift für Unternehmens- und Gesellschaftsrecht* 124 et seq., 160.

significant autonomy as to the 'how' – but no longer as to the 'whether' – to enforce civil liability by means of a private right of action. Because of this minimum degree of harmonisation, we still see a disparate implementation of civil law enforcement instruments in the Member States.[64]

However, younger legislative acts foresee an EU-law-based civil liability regime, such as in Art. 35a Rating Regulation (EU) No 462/2013, Art. 11 PRIIPS Regulation (EU) No 1286/2014 and, most recently, in the Markets in Crypto-Assets Regulation (EU) No 2023/1114 (Arts. 15, 26, 52 MiCAR). In these newer legislative packages, an EU standard for civil liability in financial market law has been emerging. The civil liability rules are inter alia open to other claims under national law, are of mandatory character and refer to national law for the scope of liability and statute of limitations. In these cases, Member States lack not only the autonomy to decide 'whether', but to a large extent also 'how', to implement civil liability for violations of the law.[65]

A look at 'adjacent' enforcement regimes reveals: while the European legislator was initially rather reluctant towards private enforcement of its own financial market regime,[66] there has been greater willingness to introduce specific and (more) detailed civil liability to enforce capital market regulations in more recent legislation. With reference to level 1 acts of European capital markets law, we witness not only an advanced harmonisation of public enforcement in MAR, PR and TD, but now also more harmonisation of private enforcement. In fact, while civil liability is either absent or relegated to a secondary role in older legal acts, in newer legal acts private enforcement plays an equal role. This constant policy approach reflects the fact that the EU legislator is free either to formulate the investor protection regulations it has enacted as subjective rights and thus subject them to a compulsory enforcement regime under private law or, alternatively, to regulate the enforcement standard itself conclusively, eventually with sole recourse to sanctions under public law.[67] Moreover, there is a strong tendency in EU law to mix public and private enforcement.

4.5.3 *Consequences for the TOD*

In the light of this development towards more private enforcement, it is worth considering whether a bidder's civil liability for the breach of the mandatory bid

[64] For this account and critical towards such enforcement architecture, Veil, Wiesner and Reichert, 'Disclosure and Enforcement', 503 et seq.; D. Busch, 'The influence of the EU prospectus rules on private law' (2021) 16 *Capital Markets Law Journal* 3 et seq.

[65] Critical towards the MiCAR enforcement regime, recently, P. Maume, 'The Regulation on Markets in Crypto-Assets (MiCAR): Landmark Codification, or First Step of Many, or Both?' (2023) *European Company and Financial Law Review* 243, 273 et seq. ('a missing puzzle piece').

[66] For this statement, Thomale, 'Appendix to Art. 30 MAR', 361–362.

[67] For this view, Mörsdorf, 'Private enforcement im sekundären Unionsprivatrecht', 832.

requirements should explicitly be introduced in the TOD. An argument in favour of civil liability is that otherwise there is a risk of under-enforcement. Public authorities are not able to completely monitor the whole market. In contrast, aggrieved minority shareholders often learn about violations much more quickly and directly. Especially, in cross-border cases, which are typical for capital markets, public authorities reach their limits. Due to the principle of territoriality they are not allowed to take investigative or sanctioning measures abroad. Private international law, on the other hand, offers a possibility of enforcing claims across borders. All in all, an effective enforcement system requires not only public law instruments but also a civil liability. A regulation at the EU level is needed because otherwise it is to be feared that different levels of enforcement – as we can well see from the comparison of Italian and German law – lead to uneven application of the TOD.[68]

If we decide to introduce civil liability in the TOD, the next policy step requires ascertaining whether an eventual harmonisation effort should be directed towards the design of a detailed liability basis under EU law – as in the younger legal acts, such as MiCAR, PRIIPS Regulation or Rating Regulation – or towards harmonising national law through a rather vague rule – as in the TD or PD. The first option (i.e. a detailed EU-law-based liability rule) would ensure a homogeneous level playing field with reduction of transaction costs of cross-border activities;[69] on the other hand, it might risk distorting the multi-layered sanctionary framework – ranging from administrative to criminal law, and sometimes involving private law – which at national level eventually proves to be already effective, proportionate and dissuasive (Art. 17 TOD), and thus ultimately compatible with the *effet utile* principle (Art. 4(3) TEU). This has particularly been stressed by the German courts that consider their enforcement system to be effective and sufficient.[70] Thus, a detailed EU-law-based liability rule, such as in the Rating Regulation, PRIIPS Regulation or MiCAR, should only be preferred if, at the same time, the law on public enforcement in

68 The legislative competence of the EU harmonising private enforcement for the purpose of building a Common Market can be envisaged in Art. 114 and Art. 115 TFUE: for this opinion, Wundenberg, 'Perspektiven', 149–150; Veil, Wiesner and Reichert, 'Disclosure and Enforcement', 457; referring also to Art. 50(2)(g) TFEU, T. Kahnert (ed.), *Rechtsetzung im Europäischen Gesellschaftsrecht: Harmonisierung, Wettbewerb, Modellgesetze* (Tübingen: Mohr Siebeck, 2012), p. 13 et seq.

69 For the debate on pros and cons of harmonisation versus regulatory competition, cf. in the vast literature W. Bratton, J. McCahery, S. Picciotto and C. Scott (eds.), *International Regulatory Competition and Coordination* (Oxford: Oxford University Press, 1996); L. Enriques and M. Gatti, 'The Uneasy Case for Top-down Corporate Law Harmonization in the European Union' (2006) 27 *University of Pennsylvania Journal of International Economic Law* 939; C. Gerner-Beuerle, 'United in Diversity: Maximum versus Minimum Harmonization in EU Securities Regulation' (2012) 7 *Capital Market Law Journal* 317 et seq.; H. Fleischer and K. U. Schmolke, 'The Reform of the Transparency Directive: Minimum or Full Harmonisation of Ownership Disclosure?' (2011) 12 *European Business Organization Law Review* 121, 134 seq.; Kahnert, 'Rechtsetzung im Europäischen Gesellschaftsrecht', p. 109 et seq.

70 BGH 29 September 2014 – II ZR 353/12, *BGHZ* 202, 180, mn. 21 (*Postbank*).

the TOD were also harmonised at the EU level.[71] This is the only way to ensure that over-enforcement and frictions between public and private enforcement are avoided. However, given the tortuous gestation of the TOD, a detailed rule on civil liability and a holistic harmonisation of public and private enforcement do not seem realistic at this point.[72]

Therefore, a (merely) programmatic rule of the kind provided for in the PR and the TD appears to be the preferable solution. Though not assuring absolute legal certainty, a programmatic rule still could be valued – *de lege ferenda* – as a significant step forward in harmonising a core MBR issue.[73]

4.6 CONCLUSIONS AND OUTLOOK

(1) Like many other EU capital markets directives adopted before the financial market crisis, the TOD is silent on private enforcement. In particular, it does not provide for a private right of action for minority shareholders in the event of a breach of the mandatory bid rule. The Directive only provides for public enforcement, such as administrative fines.

(2) The analysis of the Italian and German law has revealed that there is a significant lack of homogeneity in civil liability at the national level. Some Member States, such as Italy, provide for private enforcement by giving shareholders the right to claim damages for breach of the duty to bid. Others, such as Germany, rely mainly on public enforcement and are rather reluctant to provide for private rights of action for minority shareholders. However, an uneven level of (private) enforcement carries the risk that the harmonised rules on duties will be applied dissimilarly across the Member States.

71 For this view also Wundenberg, 'Perspektiven', 160.

72 For the same opinion also M. Winner, 'Übernahmerecht – Die Europäische Perspektive', in Veil, Grigoleit and Habersack (eds.), *Öffentliche Unternehmensübernahmen*, p. 139 ('ein einheitlicher Rechtsrahmen ohnehin nicht erreicht werden kann'); M. Winner, 'Does the European Union have a mandatory bid rule?', p. 1195; more generally on the full harmonisation *Lamfalussy* procedure in the capital market, T. M. J. Möllers, 'Vollharmonisierung im Kapitalmarkt', in B. Gsell and C. Herresthal (eds.), *Vollharmonisierung im Privatrecht* (Tübingen: Mohr Siebeck, 2009), p. 247 et seq. See also the more cautious approach of A. Recalde and M. Winner, 'Public Takeovers', in R. Veil (ed.), *Regulating EU Capital Markets Union* (Oxford: Oxford University Press, 2024), p. 444 et seq.

73 Generally favourable to further harmonisation of private enforcement at the EU level, Veil, Wiesner and Reichert, 'Disclosure and Enforcement', 452 et seq., 456 ('it is sensible to further harmonise private enforcement of European capital markets law instead of choosing regulatory competition as an alternative strategy'); Veil, 'Private Enforcement in European Capital Markets Law', p. 423; Busch, 'The influence of the EU prospectus', 30; in a long-run perspective, once supervisory law is fully harmonised, Wundenberg, 'Perspektiven', 152 et seq.

(3) Therefore, this chapter suggests that a rule on civil liability for a breach of the mandatory bid rule should be included in the Directive. Whereas supervisory authorities have the necessary investigative powers and the ability to impose targeted and proportionate sanctions in individual cases, public enforcement mechanisms may be ineffective due to incentive problems, the risk of regulatory capture, and the principle of territoriality. In contrast, minority shareholders may have informational advantages and sufficient incentives to enforce their claims. Finally, private claims can also be enforced across borders on the basis of international private law.

(4) From a policy perspective, when considering the remedies available to ensure a more uniform level playing field, which is ultimately the objective of the minimum harmonisation directive on cross-border takeover bids, it was decided to avoid solutions that could lead to the opening of a Pandora's box. Thus, further harmonisation efforts of the TOD, irrespective of their very difficult, if not unlikely, political feasibility, should in any case be carefully weighed on a case-by-case basis against the benchmark of the efficient functioning of the internal market for corporate control. Therefore, following the examples offered by adjacent regulations (i.e. the PR and TD), we recommend the introduction of a programmatic rule recognising a private right of action against the bidder for failure to launch a mandatory bid.

5

Conflict of Laws in Takeovers

Rui Dias

5.1 INTRODUCTION

In a global economy, more and more often we find situations where a takeover is not merely domestic. Cross-border takeovers, bearing connections to more than one legal order, raise legal issues that bridge takeover law and private international law. The latter is the legal discipline that deals with the international element of the legal relationship.

In this chapter, we start by generally providing a very brief, but necessary overview of the problem – namely, the cross-border situation – and the solutions that are given by private international law, or conflict of laws, through its typical methods – namely, the process of putting different legal materials into different 'drawers': for a given legal category a certain connecting factor is established as decisive in order to recognize jurisdiction to prescribe (and also, on a different level, to adjudicate and enforce)[1] the set of legal rules that address the problems to be solved within that legal category.

We then proceed with an analysis of how choice of law intersects with takeover law, in view of the growing cross-border fact constellations in European and global markets. Attention is given to the Takeover Directive,[2] which did not neglect the possibility of a cross-border takeover and dedicated some of its rules to the subject. But the existence of such rules, even if generally well drafted and commonly considered a successful feature of the Directive, inexorably leaves space for the typical choice-of-law characterization issues, at the frontiers between matters relating to the bid procedure, subject mainly to the law of the Member State on a regulated market of which the company's securities are admitted to trading, and matters

1 For a brief description of this triptychal notion of jurisdiction, S. Emmenegger, 'Extraterritorial Economic Sanctions and Their Foundation in International Law' (2016) 33 *Arizona Journal of International & Comparative Law* 631, 638–639.

2 We refer of course to Parliament and Council Directive 2004/25/EC On Takeover Bids, 2004 O.J. (L142).

relating to company law, subject to the law of the Member State in which the offeree company has its registered office (Article 4(2)(e) of the Directive).

In this context, we deal with this dichotomy of bid procedure versus company law, seeking to understand the reasons behind it. It is then fit to delve into questions particularly raised by cross-border takeovers, and try to find legal strategies to solve them. These include rules on information, given that this is essential both for the exercise of shareholders' rights (company law) and for the pricing of securities (capital markets law); rules on corporate governance, which cater not only to shareholders and members of corporate bodies, but also (more and more) to the community at large; and rules on defensive measures, typically at the heart of takeover regulation. On a related matter, more recent developments concerning corporate sustainability deserve to be tackled, so that we reflect on how they should be taken into consideration while we seek an answer to the question of whether current societal and ecological concerns should operate as a justification for allowing boards of companies to defend themselves against cross-border takeover bids.

5.2 CONFLICT-OF-LAWS ANALYSIS AND METHOD

For a given legal category, a certain connecting factor is established as decisive in order to determine the applicable law. That, in a nutshell, is how conflict-of-laws classical methodology operates. It is also a method we find in the Takeover Directive, mainly in Article 4(2)(e). For the legal category *matters relating to company law* (in brief[3]), the place of the registered office of the offeree company serves as the connecting factor. For the legal category *matters relating to the bid procedure*, we have an indirectly defined connecting factor: the applicable rules will be the ones in force in the Member State of the competent authority – which means that we must *first* apply the conflicts rule determining the competent authority (not, or not directly, the applicable law), and then the same result achieved for competence of the authority will equally extend to the law applicable.[4] If the authority were judicial, we would call this applying *forum law*, or *lex fori*. Mutatis mutandis (and conflict of laws does love Latinisms), we can call it *lex auctoritatis*.[5]

Technically, the legal category and the connecting factor(s) compose the conflicts rule. Discussion may arise both as to the appropriate delimitation of the scope of the legal category for which the applicable law (and the competent court or authority) is determined, and as to the choice of the most suitable connecting factor. Legal categories may thus raise *characterization* issues, and connecting factors *concretization* issues. That is: in given situations, we may struggle to determine

[3] The full extension of the legal category is transcribed in Section 5.3, when analysing Article 4 of the Takeover Directive.

[4] See again Art. 4 TOD and Section 5.3.

[5] See also e.g. C. Ryngaert, 'Cross-Border Takeover Regulation: A Transatlantic Perspective' (2007) *European Company and Financial Law Review* 434.

whether rule (or matter) *x* subsumes to legal category *L* or *M* (for an example in another area of the law: does *culpa in contrahendo* pertain to contract or tort?). Likewise, we may have difficulties determining where exactly connecting factor C is concretized; on this will hinge the application of one or the other law among those in connection with the case (e.g. it may be doubtful where the place of habitual residence or central administration of a person or entity lies).

But this is only the all-too-simplified description of the classical technique. Other problems may arise in the course of its mobilization. To name only two of the practically most acute ones, general or public interests may come to the foreground and somewhat distort the normal functioning of this technique, either (ex ante) by imposing *overriding mandatory provisions*, which, as the name makes clear, will override the normally applicable law,[6] or (ex post) by affecting the latter's application in terms of an *ordre public* (or *public policy*) control, again derogating the normally applicable law.[7]

Moreover, this classical technique is not alone in the conflicts' methodological toolbox – and ever less so. Independently of wider discussions on its theoretical underpinnings, orientations and goals,[8] recent decades have witnessed an enduring (if not growing in significance) pluralism, where on the side of the classical, so-called designation method, we also find so-called recognition and cognizance assuming important roles.[9]

This tripartite method,[10] in other words, adds to the conflicts rule (acting through choice-of-law designation), first, the idea of recognition, which has been widely developed under the umbrella of European fundamental freedoms.[11] By recognition we refer to the effects being granted in a State of recognition to a certain situation,

[6] For their definition by the law, see only Article 9(1) of the Rome I Regulation ((EC) No. 593/2008 of the European Parliament and of the Council of 17 June 2008 on the law applicable to contractual obligations).

[7] Using Rome I (n 6) once more as an example, see Article 21.

[8] See e.g. recently H. Muir Watt, *The Law's Ultimate Frontier: Towards an Ecological Jurisprudence – A Global Horizon in Private International Law* (Oxford: Hart Publishing, 2023).

[9] M.-P. Weller, 'La méthode tripartite du droit international privé: désignation, reconnaissance, considération' (2022) 427 *Recueil des Cours* 109, 123 et seq.

[10] Ibid.

[11] See H.-P. Mansel, 'Anerkennung als Grundprinzip des Europäischen Rechtsraums – Zur Herausbildung eines europäischen Anerkennungs-Kollisionsrechts: Anerkennung statt Verweisung als neues Strukturprinzip des Europäischen internationalen Privatrechts?' (2006) 70 *RabelsZ* 651, 651 et seq.; concerning financial services, M. Ortino, 'The Role and Functioning of Mutual Recognition in the European Market of Financial Services' (2007) 56 *ICLQ* 309, 309 et seq. *Recognition* also has a strong connection to the idea of *deference* or *substituted compliance* that has more recently been addressed: see H. Buxbaum, 'Capital Markets and Conflict of Laws: from Mutual Recognition to Substituted Compliance', in C. Benicke and S. Huber (eds.), *National, International, Transnational: Harmonischer Dreiklang im Recht – Festschrift für Herbert Kronke zum 70. Geburtstag am 24. Juli 2020* (Bielefeld: Gieseking, 2020), p. 31 et seq.; M. Lehmann, 'Extraterritoriality in financial law', in A. Parrish and C. Ryngaert (eds.), *Research Handbook on Extraterritoriality in International Law* (Cheltenham: Edward Elgar, 2023), p. 421–422.

effective in a State of origin, without demanding a previous verification of its conformity with the law that has been originally applied.[12] In the Takeover Directive, Article 6(2), second paragraph, is an example of such (mutual) recognition imposed on, or accepted by, all Member States.[13]

Then, a second and last addition to this tripartite method is to be found in cognizance or taking into consideration. This expression bundles several mechanisms, often regarded as adjustments to the conflicts method, such as the adaptation that seeks to overcome normative contradictions between two sets of equally designated national rules, when these are somehow incompatible, the substitution of applicable substantive rules in a way that permits taking into account the internationality of the situation when interpreting and applying them, or also the so-called *Datumtheorie*, under which one could refer to substantive rules not pertaining to the a priori designated law as 'data' to be taken into consideration in that process (and not as fully applicable rules).[14]

5.3 RULES ON CONFLICT OF LAWS IN THE TAKEOVER DIRECTIVE

The Takeover Directive is a legal instrument where we find echoes of the plurality in method described in the previous point.

European lawmakers did not neglect the possibility of a cross-border takeover and dedicated some of its rules to the choice-of-law features of the matter. For many, those rules represent one of the most positive aspects of the European harmonized rules.[15]

[12] P. Lagarde, 'La méthode de la reconnaissance: est-elle l'avenir du droit international privé?' (2015) 371 *Recueil des Cours* 9, 19 et seq.

[13] See Section 5.3.

[14] For an overview, see Weller, 'La méthode tripartite', p. 200 et seq.; referring to the *Datumtheorie* in the cross-border listing context as one possible approach that leads to taking into consideration regulatory rules of a foreign law, F. J. Garcimartín Alférez, 'Cross-Border Listed Companies' (2008) 328 *Recueil des Cours* 9, 88, fn. 163.

[15] See M. Siems, 'The Rules on Conflict of Laws in the European Takeover Directive' (2004) *European Company and Financial Law Review* 458, 458 (evaluating the Directive's normative solutions 'overall positively'); J. v. Hein, 'Zur Kodifikation des europäischen Übernahmekolli sionsrechts' (2005) *Zeitschrift für Unternehmens- und Gesellschaftsrecht* 528, 563 (the rules are no masterpiece of clarity and legal elegance, but are nevertheless a considerable improvement on the previous legal situation); M. Winner, 'Übernahmerecht – Die europäische Perspektive', in R. Veil, H. C. Grigoleit and M. Habersack (eds.), *Öffentliche Unternehmensübernahmen – Grundsatz- und Praxisfragen des Übernahmerechts 20 Jahre nach Mannesmann/Vodafone* (Tübingen: Mohr Siebeck, 2022), p. 142 (the rules represent real progress, even if complicated and to a certain extent arbitrary); A. Recalde Castells and M. Winner, 'Public Takeovers', in R. Veil (ed.), *Regulating EU Capital Markets Union – Volume I: Fundamentals of a European Code* (Oxford: Oxford University Press, 2024), B.2. (the Directive's approach is conceptually coherent and generally seems to work well, even though it may lead to complications in individual cases). Pointing out how they are complex, stained with legal uncertainties and only intelligible under the light of the compromise that characterized the process leading to their approval, K. J. Hopt, *Europäisches Übernahmerecht – Eine rechtsvergleichende, rechtsdogmatische und rechtspolitische Untersuchung* (Tübingen: Mohr Siebeck, 2013), p. 110.

Article 1(1) addresses the *scope* of the Directive and thereby ultimately determines the relationship between EU law and third countries' laws. According to Article 1(1), the Directive lays down measures to coordinate the laws of the Member States 'relating to takeover bids for the securities of companies governed by the laws of Member States, where all or some of those securities are admitted to trading on a regulated market [. . .]'.

A first condition is thus established, for the application of the European rules, of a minimum spatial contact with the EU, deriving from the issuing company being *governed by the laws of a Member State*. But what is a company 'governed by the laws of a Member State'? The Directive does not provide an answer. Sure, it would not be expected for a takeover law instrument of the EU to take a stand on the general issue of the law applicable to companies – namely, the *lex societatis*. But the question at stake here is a different one[16] – namely, the criterion on which the applicability of the Directive itself is dependent. Given the absence of European common rules for choice of *lex societatis*,[17] and by linking the Directive's applicability to the company being 'governed by the laws of a Member State', the EU legislator is ultimately referring to *national* legislation on conflict of laws, where divergent approaches are to be found.[18] A more unequivocal delimitation of the scope of application[19] of the Directive would result from a different approach, where the Directive's reach would depend solely, for example, on the place of trading (in one of the Member States) or, for example, on a direct reference to a connecting factor (place or law of incorporation; real or statutory seat; a combination of any of them), and not intermediated by what a Member State considers to be decisive for it to govern a company according to its own private international law.

The absence of such a clear indication is also regrettable in light of the evolutions taking place in the European approach to the conflict of laws vis-à-vis companies.

[16] J. Wouters, P. Van Hooghten and M. Bruyneel, 'The European Takeover Directive: A Commentary', in P. Van Hooghten (ed.), *The European Takeover Directive and its Implementation* (New York: Oxford University Press, 2009), p. 11.

[17] Notwithstanding proposals such as the one by the Deutscher Rat für Internationales Privatrecht: H. J. Sonnenberger and F. Bauer, 'Vorschlag der Spezialkommission für die Neugestaltung des Internationalen Gesellschaftsrecht auf europäischer/deutscher Ebene', in H. J. Sonnenberger (ed.), *Vorschläge und Berichte zur Reform des europäischen und deutschen internationalen Gesellschaftsrechts – Vorgelegt im Auftrag der zweiten Kommission des Deutschen Rates für Internationales Privatrecht, Spezialkommission Internationales Gesellschaftsrecht* (Tübingen: Mohr Siebeck, 2007), p. 3 et seq.; or the more recent European Group for Private International Law's proposal, presented and analysed in F. J. Garcimartín Alférez, 'GEDIP's Proposal on the Law Applicable to Companies' (2016) *Rivista di diritto internazionale privato e processuale* 949.

[18] For a comprehensive study, see C. Gerner-Beuerle, F. M. Mucciarelli, E. Schuster and M. Siems, 'Part 1: General Part', in C. Gerner-Beuerle, F. M. Mucciarelli, E. Schuster and M. Siems (eds.), *The Private International Law of Companies in Europe* (Munich/Oxford/Baden-Baden: Beck/Hart/Nomos, 2019), p. 1 et seq., with conclusions at 206–208.

[19] And not yet of the relevant connecting factor(s), to be determined by Article 4 of the Takeover Directive.

While there is as yet no general and uniform regulation on the applicable *lex societatis*, decisions of the Court of Justice, starting with *Centros*[20] and its progeny, have created a situation where the absence of uniform conflicts rules in no way signifies that national company law is immune to EU principles and rules. On the contrary, EU fundamental freedoms demand, if not a generally applicable connecting factor,[21] at least that companies regularly incorporated in one Member State see their legal capacity recognized in all other Member States;[22] that rules on central aspects such as minimum capital and director's liability should remain the ones of the State of incorporation;[23] and also that cross-border restructuring and conversions cannot be dealt with in a discriminatory manner vis-à-vis purely domestic operations of the same kind, and this independently of a genuine economic activity in the State of destination.[24]

Still according to Article 1(1) of the Takeover Directive, a further condition is that some or all of that company's securities – carrying voting rights[25] – are admitted to trading on a 'regulated market', as defined in another European Directive.[26] This

[20] Case-212/97, *Centros Ltd. v. Erhvervs- og Selskabsstyrelsen* [1999] ECR 1-1459.

[21] But see most recently Case C-276/22, *Edil Work 2 Srl et al. v. STE Sàrl et al.* [2024] ECLI:EU:C:2024:348, apparently determining in general terms that the application of the real seat theory amounts to a 'restriction on freedom of establishment' (no. 37), thus justifiable only if it does not go beyond what is necessary to attain the objective of protecting the interests of creditors, staff and minority shareholders (nos. 43, 39).

[22] Case C-208/00, *Überseering BV v. Nordic Construction Company Baumanagement GmbH (NCC)* [2002] ECR I-9919.

[23] Case C-167/01, *Kamer van Koophandel en Fabrieken voor Amsterdam v. Inspire Art Ltd* [2003] ECR I-10155.

[24] Case C-411/03, *SEVIC Systems AG* [2005] ECR I-10805; Case C-106/16, *Polbud – Wykonawstwo sp. z o.o.* [2017] ECLI:EU:C:2017:804; on the latter, J. Meeusen, '*Polbud*: new perspectives for corporate mobility in the internal market', in B. Hess, E. Jayme and H.-P. Mansel (eds.), *Europa als Rechts- und Lebensraum – Liber amicorum für Christian Kohler zum 75. Geburtstag am 18. Juni 2018* (Bielefeld: Gieseking, 2018), p. 313 et seq.; following the *Polbud* decision, see Parliament and Council Directive (EU) 2019/2121 as regards cross-border conversions, mergers and divisions.

[25] Only securities *carrying voting rights* are considered *securities* under the definition relevant for the Directive: see Article 2(1)(e). See e.g. P. O. Mülbert, 'Umsetzungsfragen der Übernahmerichtlinie – erheblicher Änderungsbedarf bei den heutigen Vorschriften des WpÜG' (2004) *Neue Zeitschrift für Gesellschaftsrecht*, 636; S. Maul and D. Muffat-Jeandet, 'The Directive on takeover bids', in S. Maul, D. Muffat-Jeandet and J. Simon (eds.), *Takeover Bids in Europe – The Takeover Directive and Its Implementation in the Member States* (Freiburg: Memento Verlag, 2008), no. 56 (p. 12); Wouters, Van Hooghten and Bruyneel, 'The European Takeover Directive: A Commentary', p. 10; M. Habersack and D. A. Verse, *Europäisches Gesellschaftsrecht – Einführung für Studium und Praxis*, 5th ed. (Munich: C. H. Beck, 2019), § 11 no. 10 (p. 460).

[26] That is, initially in Council Directive 93/22/EEC of 10 May 1993 on investment services in the securities field, now in MiFID II, according to which '"regulated market" means a multilateral system operated and/or managed by a market operator, which brings together or facilitates the bringing together of multiple third-party buying and selling interests in financial instruments – in the system and in accordance with its non-discretionary rules – in a way that results in a contract, in respect of the financial instruments admitted to trading under its rules and/or

also means that takeover regulation derived from the Directive – for example, its rule on the mandatory bid – is not necessarily applicable to target companies *not incorporated or seated in a Member State*, thus *not governed by one of such laws*, even if its (voting) securities are admitted to trading on a European regulated market – unless, of course, otherwise provided by national transposing law broadening the European rules' scope.[27] Assuming these criteria are met, offerors from third countries are not excluded by the legal definition of 'offeror', and so are also covered by the Directive's scope of application.[28]

Then, it is mainly Article 4 that deals with determining the *competent supervisory authority* and the *applicable law*.

Competent authority is that of the Member State in which the offeree company has its *registered office*, if that company's securities are admitted to trading on a regulated market in that same Member State (Art. 4(2)(a)).[29] To the *registered office* in the English version of the Directive we assimilate as its functional equivalent in other European jurisdictions the *statutory* seat – that is, the seat indicated in the

systems, and which is authorised and functions regularly and in accordance with Title III of this Directive' – see Article 4(1)(21) of Parliament and Council Directive 2014/65/EU of 15 May 2014 on markets in financial instruments and amending Directive 2002/92/EC and Directive 2011/61/EU (recast).

[27] See C. Clerc, F. Demarigny, D. Valiante and M. de Manuel Aramendía, *A Legal and Economic Assessment of European Takeover Regulation* (Brussels/Paris: Marccus Partners/Centre for European Policy Studies, 2012), p. 32, where the following illustration can be found: 'a majority of the mandatory public takeover bid rules applicable to Swiss or French public companies are inapplicable to a company with a registered office in Switzerland and shares admitted to trading on the French regulated market. Given that such a company is headquartered in Switzerland, a country that is neither a member of the EU nor the EEA, under the general regulations of the Autorité des marchés financiers (AMF), provisions relating to mandatory public takeover bids and squeeze-outs do not apply. Swiss regulations do not apply to such a company either, as its shares are not listed on a Swiss stock exchange.' *See* also E. Torralba Mendiola, 'OPAs transfronterizas', in J. Juste Mencía and A. Recalde Castells (eds.), *Derecho de OPAs – Estudio sistemático del régimen de las ofertas públicas de adquisición en el Derecho español* (Valencia: tirant lo blanch, 2010), p. 773.

[28] See Article 2(1)(c) of the Directive; S. Maul and L. Furtwengler, 'Directive 2004/25/EC of the European Parliament and of the Council of 21 April 2004 on takeover bids', in P. Kindler and J. Lieder, *European Corporate Law – Article-by-Article Commentary* (Baden-Baden/Munich: Nomos/C. H. Beck, 2021), annot. 8 to Art. 1 (p. 983). Pointing out, and criticizing, the absence of rules relating to trading or listing in a third country, E. Wymeersch, 'A New Look at the Debate about the Takeover Directive', in B. Erle, W. Goette, D. Kleindiek, G. Krieger, H.-J. Priester, C. Schubel, M. Schwab, C. Teichmann and C.-H. Witt (eds.), *Festschrift für Peter Hommelhoff zum 70. Geburtstag* (Cologne: Verlag Dr. Otto Schmidt, 2012), p. 1387.

[29] If there is no such coincidence between place of offeree company's registered office *and* place of trading, other solutions are provided for in Article 4(2)(b) and (c), either by granting competence to the authority of the place of trading (or, in case of multiple listings, to the authority of the place where the securities were *first* admitted to trading), or, concerning simultaneous multiple listings, by granting competence to the authority chosen by the offeree company itself, to be notified by the latter to the markets and respective authorities on the first day of trading. See infra, p. 130.

articles of association, thus relevant for commercial registration purposes.[30] To consider other alternative concretizations of the 'seat' notion would not fit with the harmonizing objectives of the Directive.[31]

If, however, *registered office* does not coincide with sole place where the securities are admitted to *trading*, difficulties arise and a 'complex rule'[32] enters into play.

First, this non-coincidence leads the legislator in Article 4(2)(b) and (c) to voice preference for one of those connecting factors to determine the competent authority, which is the *place of trading*. Consequently, Article 4(2)(b) grants competence to the authorities of the Member State of the place of trading in the first place (first sentence). In the second sentence of Article 4(2)(b), a dual or other multiple listing is dealt with through a *prior in tempore* rule: the competence to supervise the bid falls upon the authority of the market where securities were *first* admitted to trading. Because this criterion does not solve the problem of *simultaneous* multiple listings, Article 4(2)(c) grants the offeree company the power to *choose the competent authority*, and then notify the markets and the authorities involved (first sentence).[33] All these decisions are to be made public (Art. 4(2)(d)).

Second, the non-coincidence of registered office *and* place of trading, at the origin of the need for the rules we find in (b) and (c), also brings about the question of what subject matters shall be dealt with by the local law of the competent authority, which may not be that of the place where the offeree company has its registered office, and what other matters shall stay linked to the latter.

To solve this, Article 4(2)(e) then divides the relevant takeover-law subject matters into two realms.

The *lex fori* of that competent supervisory authority – essentially, the law of the place of trading – applies to questions comprised in the bid procedure (in full: 'matters relating to the consideration offered in the case of a bid, in particular the price, and matters relating to the bid procedure, in particular the information on the offeror's decision to make a bid, the contents of the offer document and the disclosure of the bid'). This coincidence (so-called *Gleichlauf*, or *forum-ius* correlation) on the criteria for both aspects (competent authority and applicable law) seeks

30 *See* Hein, 'Zur Kodifikation', p. 545–546; Siems, 'The Rules on Conflict of Laws', p. 470 (referring to it as 'registered seat'; but note that the Directive in English uses 'registered office' and not 'statutory seat' (see also Hein, 'Zur Kodifikation', p. 545, fn. 87)); Maul and Furtwengler, 'Directive 2004/25/EC', annot. 13 to Art. 4, (p. 993), fn. 4; Habersack and Verse, *Europäisches Gesellschaftsrecht*, § 11 no. 17 (p. 464).

31 On the discussion in Germany, see only Hein, 'Zur Kodifikation', p. 547–554.

32 Siems, 'The Rules on Conflict of Laws', p. 473.

33 In the case of the simultaneous multiple listing being *previous* to the Directive, its rules granted a four-week period for authorities to agree on which of them shall supervise, after which, in the case of no agreement, it would be for the offeree to choose (Article 4(2)(c), second and third sentences).

to avoid the perils of a national authority having to deal with the application of *foreign* law concerning that subject matter.[34]

Differently, company-law matters (i.e. 'matters relating to the information to be provided to the employees of the offeree company and in matters relating to company law, in particular the percentage of voting rights which confers control and any derogation from the obligation to launch a bid, as well as the conditions under which the board of the offeree company may undertake any action which might result in the frustration of the bid'[35]) are subject to the law of the company's *registered office*, irrespective of the place of trading. Unlike in bid procedure matters, there is hence the possibility of local authorities or adjudicators having to deal with foreign law applicable to company-law matters raised in the context of a takeover.

Yet another provision related to cross-border situations included in the Takeover Directive is Article 5(3), a conflicts rule on the *percentage of voting rights conferring control*[36] and on the *method of its calculation*. For such legal category, the *registered office* of the offeree company is elected as connecting factor. The European legislator chose to remain silent, at least partially,[37] on the pivotal issue of the definition of *control*,[38] and aligned such a question on the side of the matters where the law of the offeree company's registered office is better positioned to apply, rather than the law of the place of trading.

Also Article 6(2), second paragraph, pays attention to a possible connection with different legal orders – namely, when the offeree is admitted to trading on the

34 Preference for this *Gleichlauf* prevailed over the competing view in favour of a general applicability of the law of the offeree company: see Maul and Furtwengler, 'Directive 2004/25/EC', annot. 3 to Art. 4 (p. 990).

35 For Mülbert, 'Umsetzungsfragen der Übernahmerichtlinie', p. 638, matters covered by Articles 9(5) (obligations of the board of the offeree company to opine on the bid and communicate that opinion to employees), 11 (breakthrough), 12 (optional arrangements), 15 (right of squeeze-out) and 16 (right of sell-out) also line up as company-law matters in this respect. Analyzing the German law (WpÜG) in line with Article 4 of the Directive, M. Beurskens, '§ 1 WpÜG', in M. Beurskens, U. Ehricke and J. Ekkenga (eds.), *Wertpapiererwerbs- und Übernahmegesetz*, 2nd ed. (Munich: C. H. Beck, 2021) (see nos. 26–27) also mention, due to the reference to 'any derogation from the obligation to launch a bid', the inclusion of regulation on substantive conditions for a mandatory bid. The *obligation to launch a bid* is not literally included in Article 4(2)(e) second sentence; but there should be no doubt of its company-law nature. Plus, the short delimitation in such a rule might be understood as a consequence of Article 5(1) first sentence already laying out the essential substantial conditions for the duty to launch the bid. A further systematic argument for this characterization is: if the *exceptions* are regulated by company law, then the *conditions* for the *rule* should too, given that a decision on those exceptions should be made by the law that determines the rule.

36 This first part of the rule, delimitating the legal category, is repeated from Article 4(2)(e), as mentioned by Siems, 'The Rules on Conflict of Laws', p. 473 fn. 68.

37 This mitigation is appropriate considering that Article 5(1) already indicates some important features of what shall be considered as control, by expressly giving relevance to control that is indirect and/or obtained through persons acting in concert with a natural or legal person. See only Habersack and Verse, *Europäisches Gesellschaftsrecht*, § 11 no. 20 (p. 466).

38 See also ibid., no. 10 (p. 460–461), no. 20 (p. 466).

markets of multiple Member States. In such a case, the Directive imposes (mutual) recognition of the offer document previously approved by the competent supervisory authority also 'in any other Member State on the market of which the offeree company's securities are admitted to trading, without its being necessary to obtain the approval of the supervisory authorities of that Member State', subject to any translation required, therefore creating a kind of European passport for takeover offer documents. This is founded on the idea of *recognition* we have mentioned before,[39] and it is possible only on the basis of an underlying harmonization of laws that reassures each national legislator and authority against imposing extra burdens on cross-border takeovers.[40]

5.4 BID PROCEDURE VERSUS COMPANY LAW

It could be thought that the existence of a significant level of harmonization, even if far from a full harmonization, would diminish the practical importance of conflict-of-laws rules within the European Union. In fact, if conflicts are reduced to marginal issues, the consequences are positive for all involved, in terms of legal certainty derived from the existence of harmonized rules or standards. Still, there remain spaces where overlaps or inconsistencies between different laws may, and still do, arise. That is where the choice-of-law arsenal becomes useful.

In purely domestic cases, one does not have to care too much about the precise borderline between what pertains to the *bid procedure* as opposed to *company law*. But cross-border cases bring added importance to the inquiry, given the risk of having two different legal systems deal separately with each of these matters. To be sure, the simultaneous application of two (or more) laws is not in itself a problem. However, difficulties may arise when those two laws draw the borderline in different ways, bringing about situations of overlapping or vacuum.

The said dichotomy is often referred to as *capital markets law* vs *company law*; but to be faithful to the Directive's text, as seen above, we should keep aware of the exact terms of the division we find in Article 4(2)(e) – namely: *bid procedure* vs *company law*, with the latter being also alongside 'matters relating to the information to be provided to the employees of the offeree company'.[41]

39 See Section 5.2.

40 See Article 6(2); Maul and Muffat-Jeandet, 'The Directive on takeover bids', no. 143 (p. 31); Maul and Furtwengler, 'Directive 2004/25/EC', annot. 6 et seq., to Art. 6 (p. 1001); Wouters, Van Hooghten and Bruyneel, 'The European Takeover Directive: A Commentary', p. 34–35. Lining up 'minimum harmonization' of material laws, 'mutual recognition' and 'reciprocal co-operation' as the three pieces of the strategy adopted by the EU lawmakers, and speaking of a 'minimum harmonization + mutual recognition' mechanism of 'co-ordination' as exemplified by the EU, Garcimartín Alférez, 'Cross-Border Listed Companies', p. 82–83.

41 In fact, to be precise, Article 4(2)(e) identifies these three matters: the ones relating to the bid procedure, and relating to company law, both of which are subject to further characterization ('in particular [. . .]'); and the said employee-related matters, which appear on the *side* of

The line between capital markets law and company law is 'fuzzy at best'.[42] And takeover law is certainly one of the areas where this fuzziness reaches its peak.

In tightly encapsulated terms: among the traditional *core functions of company law*, we find the definition of the legal form of the enterprise, and the 'containment' of agency conflicts among constituencies (shareholders vs managers; shareholders vs shareholders; company/shareholders vs third parties).[43] To *contain* conflicts of interest is not to fully eliminate them, as they are inherent to the different positions of the said participants in the enterprise.

And as *core functions of capital markets law*, we generally identify both the promotion of market efficiency and the guarantee of investor protection.[44]

With this broad description in mind, many rules of national law, particularly in the context of takeovers, may overlappingly contribute to both functions. While this does not appear a novel problem for conflict of laws, the tightness of the overlap may increase the difficulty in answering which fundamental goals appear more vividly in the foreground, and consequently in subsuming certain provisions into one or the other legal category.

A layer of complexity is added by the realization that different models of takeover regulation may cater more strongly to certain regulatory goals: this would mean that rules addressing the same issues could tend to one or the other categorization depending on their different substantive answers. As Andrés Recalde Castells summarizes, an Anglo-Saxon model of takeover regulation tends to accentuate the capital markets' perspective, by paying attention to the problems emerging from massive acquisitions of shares, and to the modification of the original basis for investment; whereas a company-law perspective, especially one linked to group

company law, sharing with it the connecting factor, but not exactly included in company law as legal category.

42 J. C. Coffee Jr., 'The Future as History: The Prospects for Global Convergence in Corporate Governance and Its Implications' (1999) 93 *Northwestern University Law Review* 641, 669. Placing takeover law at the intersection between company law and capital markets law, among many others, see e.g. J. v. Hein, 'Grundfragen des europäischen Übernahmekollisionsrechts' (2001) 46 *Die Aktiengesellschaft* 213, 219; for very insightful, more general approaches to the interaction of the conflict of laws with capital markets and also with company law, including of course takeover regulation, H. Kronke, 'Capital Markets and Conflict of Laws' (2002) 286 *Recueil des Cours* 245; Garcimartín Alférez, 'Cross-Border Listed Companies', p. 9 et seq.

43 J. Armour, H. Hansmann, R. Kraakman and M. Pargendler, 'What Is Corporate Law?', in R. H. Kraakman et al. (eds.), *The Anatomy of Corporate Law – A Comparative and Functional Approach*, 3rd ed. (Oxford/New York: Oxford University Press, 2017), p. 22; G. Bachmann, H. Eidenmüller, A. Engert, H. Fleischer and W. Schön, *Regulating the Closed Corporation* (Berlin/Boston: Walter de Gruyter, 2014), p. 8 et seq.

44 On these two (market efficiency and investor protection) as general objectives of securities regulation, and also of takeover law, Recalde Castells and Winner, 'Public Takeovers', B.4. (which should 'serve as sufficient grounds for a market approach and for its [i.e. regulation of takeovers'] inclusion in a securities codification'); see already Garcimartín Alférez, 'Cross-Border Listed Companies', p. 72; more generally on regulatory goals, scope and concepts of takeover law, K. J. Hopt, 'Europäisches und deutsches Übernahmerecht' (1997) 161 *Zeitschrift für das gesamte Handelsrecht und Wirtschaftsrecht* 368, 374.

law, would mainly be interested in giving shareholders the possibility of exiting the company when a change of control occurs, due to the risk of oppression or abuse vis-à-vis the remaining shareholders.[45]

This dichotomy is also present when pondering the necessity of a fully fledged European takeover law, harmonizing takeover regulation beyond the minimal framework achieved twenty years ago, because a capital markets' perspective would be more prone to harmonization, or unification. As Martin Winner explains, national law allows local specificities to be taken into consideration, and so aspects such as the definition of control continue to benefit from national responses, at the level of which differences among Member States – for example, in regard to owning structures (dispersed vs concentrated) – can be taken into account. Yet under a capital markets' viewpoint, not only for potential acquirers of control, but also for other investors, it is good to have a unified legal framework, leading to diminished transaction costs.[46] In addition, this enhanced harmonization would facilitate the role of institutional investors in promoting good practices in corporate governance, as national differences weaken their impetus to intervene and cooperate.[47] This is, however, insufficient for an assessment favourable to legal reform, which is unrealistic in the current context of a certain re-nationalization within the EU and of prioritization of other subject matter – namely, under today's buzzword of sustainability.[48]

The analysis of where we stand in regard to further harmonization versus keeping the status quo, considering the reasons that lead many voices to discourage a *Vollharmonisierung* at the current stage, is not only relevant as a *de lege ferenda* discussion on the future of takeover law in general, but may also impact the

45 A. Recalde Castells, 'Régimen jurídico de las OPAs: concepto, función económica y princípios de la ordenación', in J. Juste Mencía and A. Recalde Castells (eds.), *Derecho de OPAs – Estudio sistemático del régimen de las ofertas públicas de adquisición en el Derecho español* (Valencia: tirant lo blanch, 2010), p. 46–47. In an opposite direction, there can be influences of takeover law over (general) company law. Peter Mülbert makes the interesting point that takeover law has always been characterized by a strong influence of law and economics arguments when dealing with its main questions, such as the mandatory bid rule, or board neutrality – more than what we see in general company law. From the perspective of legal science, this means that takeover law could pave the way for the acceptance of law-and-economics constructions in company law: P. O. Mülbert, 'Entwicklung des Übernahmerechts. Betrachtungen aus der Perspektive der Wissenschaft ', in R. Veil, H. C. Grigoleit and M. Habersack (eds.), *Öffentliche Unternehmensübernahmen – Grundsatz- und Praxisfragen des Übernahmerechts 20 Jahre nach Mannesmann/Vodafone* (Tübingen: Mohr Siebeck, 2022), p. 26.

46 Winner, 'Übernahmerecht – Die europäische Perspektive', p. 139–140.

47 European Commission, 'Application of Directive 2004/25/CE on takeover bids (Report from the Commission to the European Parliament, the Council, the European Economic and Social Committee and the Committee of the Regions)' (2012) https://eur-lex.europa.eu/LexUriServ/LexUriServ.do?uri = COM:2012:0347:FIN:EN:PDF (accessed 20 May 2024), p. 6 ('The existence of different definitions and interpretations on national level is a source of uncertainty for international investors who wish to cooperate with each other and might have a limiting effect on their willingness to engage actively with investee companies').

48 Winner, 'Übernahmerecht – Die europäische Perspektive', p. 141–142; already sceptical of there being real chances for legal reform, Hopt, *Europäisches Übernahmerecht*, p. 20–21.

approach to the conflicts side of the question *de lege lata*. In fact, one of the main arguments against further harmonization is the lack of internal coherence[49] of the Takeover Directive. As we know, this is to a great extent a result of the political compromise in 2004 that drew us into a patchwork of optional arrangements. Now, conflict of laws relies heavily in its functioning on the teleological foundations of substantive rules to be characterized: it is such a foundation that allows us to sort them into different categories. So, even if the most common assessment of Article 4(2)(e) is to consider it satisfactory,[50] the reality is that 'hard cases' may not find proper guidance in it, due to the absence of a more coherently justified division line.

Finally, it should be kept in mind that matters relating to the bid procedure are more clearly linked to a supervisory authority, which according to Article 4 is determined to be competent and will apply its own *lex auctoritatis*. To the contrary, no authority is specifically determined to be competent for company-law matters. This is understandable given the typically close connection of capital-market rules to an internal public policy of the marketplace, which often leads to its overriding character[51] or a public-law characterization,[52] in line with the general, market-wide interests they are protecting. It will lead, in turn, to the sensation of weaker enforcement of rules on company law, as if no authority were competent for company-law matters, except the courts.[53] This may influence, more or less consciously, the characterization of substantive rules as bid-procedure-related rather than company law, whenever the interpreter is pushing for their application in a given case.

5.5 EXAMPLES OF QUESTIONS RAISED BY CROSS-BORDER TAKEOVERS

5.5.1 *Rules on Information*

Information is key in both the company context and the capital market world. It is essential for the exercise of shareholders' rights (company law) as well as for the pricing of securities (capital-markets law). As a point of departure, there is the 'simple principle' proposed almost two decades ago by Garcimartín Alférez in his seminal writing on cross-border listed companies: 'the information relevant to the public in general is governed by the law of the market, while the information relevant to the shareholders as such is determined by the *lex societatis*'.[54] Or, as

[49] Recalde Castells and Winner, 'Public Takeovers', B.4.

[50] Seen 15.

[51] Kronke, 'Capital Markets and Conflict of Laws', p. 333.

[52] See Garcimartín Alférez, 'Cross-Border Listed Companies', p. 76.

[53] So Wymeersch, 'A New look at the Debate about the Takeover Directive', p. 1388; this does not mean, of course, that the supervisory authority is unable to enforce the foreign applicable company law, even if it may at times be more difficult to ascertain and apply than local law.

[54] Under the heading 'disclosure duties', Garcimartín Alférez, 'Cross-Border Listed Companies', p. 117.

suggested by Kronke in his influential text on the subject: there should be a 'functional characterization', so that the answer would hinge on whether the *purpose of disclosure* is an 'interest embodied in company law', or rather the 'protection of investors and markets'.[55]

Difficulties arise, nonetheless, when we try to dissect this approach through examples of information requirements, and attempt to insert them in only one of those two legal drawers. We could try to separate information relevant *to the shareholders* vs *to the general public*; but information as an element for the decision to (dis)invest is actually relevant for both. Often information requirements will be envisaged as a derivation of shared normative goals, which may exist here and elsewhere.[56] Plus, the growing body of information requirements that derive from EU law aimed at serving the interests of broader constituencies or stakeholders, other than merely the shareholders, and not necessarily dependent on a listing in a regulated market, helps blur the dividing line: it suffices to recall the growth of information demands linked to sustainability reporting,[57] as well as corporate due diligence over the supply chain under the soon-to-be CSDDD or CS3D (Corporate Sustainability Due Diligence Directive).[58]

In the face of an overlap, the more demanding rule tends to apply. There is typically no technical problem in doing that, as it amounts to 'simply' providing more information,[59] and so, contradictory indications in both laws are not to be expected. If there are such, a compatibilization of both applicable rules should be sought. The unilateral public-policy approach[60] that tends to be inherent in capital market rules favours a *vis atractiva* of the *lex mercatus* to the detriment of company law in case of an overlap, but this does not prejudice the necessary search for compatibilization of both laws whenever possible.

5.5.2 *Rules on Corporate Governance*

Corporate governance, as 'the company's operating system, a braided framework encompassing legal and non-legal elements',[61] has its rules cater not only to the

55 Kronke, 'Capital Markets and Conflict of Laws', p. 298–299.

56 On shareholder protection, in particular minority shareholder protection, as a shared normative goal between takeover law and company law, in particular group law, *see* J. M. Embid Irujo, 'OPAs, modificaciones estructurales y derecho de grupos', in J. Juste Mencía and A. Recalde Castells (eds.), *Derecho de OPAs – Estudio sistemático del régimen de las ofertas públicas de adquisición en el Derecho español* (Valencia: tirant lo blanch, 2010), p. 461 et seq.

57 Parliament and Council Directive (EU) 2022/2464, of 14 December 2022, 2022 O.J. (L322).

58 This legislative Act is not yet in force, but was approved by the European Parliament on 24 April 2024 and adopted by the Council of the EU on 24 May 2024.

59 Garcimartín Alférez, 'Cross-Border Listed Companies', p. 117.

60 Kronke, 'Capital Markets and Conflict of Laws', p. 333.

61 R. J. Gilson, 'From Corporate Law to Corporate Governance', in J. N. Gordon and W.-G. Ringe (eds.), *The Oxford Handbook of Corporate Law and Governance* (Oxford/New York: Oxford University Press, 2018), p. 6.

interests and needs of shareholders and members of corporate bodies, but also (more and more) to the community at large. They can be frequently placed on both sides of the spectrum. In many cases, substitution[62] between corporate law and capital-market law provides the answer, to the extent that rules similarly guaranteeing appropriate levels of disclosure[63] and shareholder/investor protection could be seen as 'fungible': by applying only one set of them, the regulatory goals are fulfilled, and this eliminates the need either to apply the other or to develop standards to fill an apparent gap. For a brief example, in a case where a company incorporated in Luxembourg, a subsidiary of a Chinese company, made a public offer for acquisition of shares in two companies listed in Portugal, one incorporated and seated in Spain, the other in Portugal, the latter asked for the supervisor's clarification on the applicable rules vis-à-vis access to information, participation in board meetings and voting, in respect to members of the board of the target that were linked to the bidder. The supervisor replied that, in the absence of specific provision of capital-markets law (or a regulation of the supervisory authority) on this issue, general rules of company law, namely on conflicts of interest, would apply.[64] Implicit in this position is the idea that capital-market rules of the *lex mercatus*, and regulations of the competent supervisory authority, can override the generally applicable company-law rules, which is an assertion of the *vis atractiva* of the former we have mentioned before.

The developments we are witnessing, on the side of company law, in the sense of a growing attention paid to broader constituencies[65] may, here also, somewhat blur the dividing lines with capital-markets law. The more company law incorporates environmental and human rights protection, or contribution to a net-zero transition, as part of its own regulatory goals, and not of adjacent areas of the law, the less clear will be the borderlines to those other areas – namely, the ones that cater to broader, societal interests. If, and to the extent to which, company law changes its fundamental features, this will also impact on its relationship with capital-markets law.

[62] Garcimartín Alférez, 'Cross-Border Listed Companies', p. 119.

[63] On disclosure through corporate governance codes, *see* generally G. Bachmann, 'Disclosure of Corporate Governance by Codes', in V. Tountopoulos and R. Veil (eds.), *Transparency of Stock Corporations in Europe – Rationales, Limitations and Perspectives* (Oxford/Portland, OR: Hart Publishing, 2019), p. 57 et seq.

[64] In a reply that was publicly available at www.cmvm.pt/pt/AreadoInvestidor/rec_oper/Operacoes/opaedp2018/Pages/requerimento-ctg_edp_24052018.aspx until a recent reorganization of the Portuguese supervisor's website.

[65] This is not necessarily, but possibly, linked with discussions on corporate purpose: for instance, see R. Nurgozhayeva and D. W. Puchniak, 'Corporate Purpose Beyond Borders: A Key to Saving Our Planet or Colonialism Repackaged?' (2024) 744/2023 *ECGI Working Paper Series in Law*, http://ssrn.com/abstract_id=4652012, referring to corporate purpose alterations as a result of director focus shifts along the shareholder–stakeholder continuum (p. 36).

5.5.3 *Rules on Defensive Measures*

As expressly stated in Article 4(2)(e), rules on defensive measures by the target board are typically construed as company-law matters. But this raises the issue of coherence with other corporate restructuring techniques, such as mergers;[66] and it may, too, pose the question of whether takeover-law-specific rules, such as the board neutrality rule, have advantages for being more visible than general corporate law, and are also enforceable with the help of specialist regulators,[67] or rather general company-law duties applicable to all defensive tactics contribute to minimize the effectiveness of pre-bid measures that escape the board neutrality rule and takeover law in general. Even if we agree that different forms of corporate restructuring should not introduce stark disparities in terms of shareholder protection, the effectiveness of takeover regulation on defensive tactics would discourage a withdrawal in favour of more general, but less effective, reliance on general company-law duties.

And, here again, the 'trend towards broadening the notion of company interest', decoupling it from those of the shareholders alone,[68] poses challenges to the characterization of the applicable rules.

In any case, differences in characterization may not be as sensitive here as in other matters, given that both for takeover law (through the Directive) and for general company law (through national law, but influenced by EU case law), the connecting factors tend to coincide.

5.6 FINAL THOUGHT: THE GROWING ROLE OF CORPORATE SUSTAINABILITY, ALSO FOR CONFLICT OF LAWS IN TAKEOVERS?

This brief analysis has been made under the aegis of the 'fuzziness' characterizing the divide between what the Takeover Directive calls *bid procedure* and *company law*. All the examples above make it clear that current developments concerning *corporate sustainability* may play a role, and further contribute to the fuzziness.

Curiously, that is a subject on which the Takeover Directive is seemingly silent. With interest for the shareholderism versus stakeholderism debate, it is worth mentioning that the only constituency besides shareholders to be mentioned in the Directive are the *employees* (Arts. 4(2)(e), 6(3)(i) and 9(5)); but see also the general principle of Article 3(1)(c), according to which 'the board of an offeree

[66] Describing, in light of a recent case, how a proposal to start discussions on a statutory merger did not trigger takeover regulation on competing bids, see V. Kajala, 'Takeover Rules at the Intersection of Company Law and Securities Law', in R. J. Gilson, M. Isaksson, E. Lidman, J. Munck and E. Sjöman (eds.), *Festskrift till Rolf Skog* (Stockholm: Norstedts Juridik, 2021), p. 697.

[67] In this sense, see P. Davies and A. Pietrancosta in Chapter 10 of this book.

[68] As Davies and Pietrancosta put it, while analyzing defensive measures in Chapter 10 of this book.

company must act in the interests of the company *as a whole*'). And yet, the context of the bid may very well be one where a conflict between shareholder financial gain and broader societal interest most clearly emerges.[69]

In takeovers, unlike in many other areas of the law, choice-of-law rules are intensely influenced by a substantive-law stance taken by the legal order; only then is the applicable law defined in conformity. This should be kept in mind when asking, as Jaap Winter does, whether current *societal and ecological concerns* should operate as a 'justification for allowing boards of companies to defend against takeover bids', while defending the argument that Member State permission for companies not to be subject to board neutrality could indirectly amount to a permission of boards to 'defend against takeover bids that favour the interests of other stakeholders and wider societal and ecological concerns'.[70]

However, by recognizing this power to the board, without a clearer orientation concerning the terms that frame the way how, and to what extent, the advancement of such societal and ecological concerns is legitimate and/or due, an unwanted, pernicious effect may be to contribute to insulate directors from liability, in such a way that neither financial gains nor societal and ecological interests are effectively favoured. Introducing these concerns without proper safeguards can play the role of a Trojan horse for excessive managerial discretion to the detriment of the company's interest, in both its narrower and wider reading. It is difficult to advance in this area without developing a better understanding of general company-law[71] duties of directors that accommodate those advances.

Conflict of laws, while not actively participating in this debate, remains at the receiving end of the developments to come, and will have to be called to articulate them whenever different laws interact in a cross-border situation, while remaining faithful to the search for coherence in the application of two or more laws to a given case.

69 J. Winter, 'Sustainable Corporate Governance and the Takeover Bids Directive', in R. J. Gilson, M. Isaksson, E. Lidman, J. Munck and E. Sjöman (eds.), *Festskrift till Rolf Skog* (Stockholm: Norstedts Juridik, 2021), p. 1205.

70 Ibid.

71 Or, alternatively, of specific company law for listed companies: see Recalde Castells and Winner, 'Public Takeovers', C.2.

PART II

Mandatory Bid Rule

6

Development and Impact of the Mandatory Bid Rule in Europe

Philipp Fidler and Martin Winner

6.1 INTRODUCTION

In the controversy surrounding the legislative proceedings concerning the Takeover Bids Directive (TOD), the European mandatory bid rule (MBR) was a key factor.[1] In this chapter, we will trace the history of the MBR and its development. We also aim to highlight the crucial issues that ultimately led to the MBR becoming a 'cornerstone of European Takeover Law'.[2] 'Cornerstone', however, is a relative term. Our core thesis is that the changing mood in the Member States was primarily responsible for the shift in opinion that created the potential for the introduction of the MBR at the European Union level in the first place. Furthermore, we will argue that the influence of the MBR on the capital markets of the Member States has so far been limited and that the TOD has failed to achieve its regulatory objective at any rate. The prolegomena of our article will be the origins of the MBR in the United Kingdom.

6.2 PROLEGOMENA: THE ORIGINS IN THE UNITED KINGDOM

From a comparative law perspective, the United Kingdom was the pioneer of the MBR. Consequently, the development of the MBR in the European Union has its roots in the United Kingdom. We will try to keep this part brief since the story of the MBR in the United Kingdom has been told by other authors already.

The most important legal source for the regulation of takeover bids in the United Kingdom is the Takeover Code, formerly referred to as the City Code on Takeovers

For valuable comments and support in writing this chapter, the authors thank Romana Cierpial-Magnor, Benedikt Fürst, Alain Pietrancosta and Rolf Skog.

[1] Parliament and Council Directive 2004/25/EC on Takeover Bids, 2004 O.J. (L142).

[2] According to M. Habersack, 'Non-frustration Rule and Mandatory Bid Rule – Cornerstones of European Takeover Law?' 15 *European Company and Financial Law Review* 1 (2018), although with a question mark at the end.

and Mergers.[3] The Takeover Code is made up of six principles ('General Principles'), further rules ('Rules') and explanations of these rules ('Notes on the Rules'). In addition to its considerable length (a file of 443 pages), the Takeover Code is characterised by two additional distinctive features.[4] First, neither the courts nor the general capital market supervisory authorities in the United Kingdom (e.g. Financial Conduct Authority, Financial Reporting Council) have the competence to enforce and administer the Takeover Code. Rather, as is well known, the responsibility lies with a special body of enforcement, the 'Panel on Takeovers and Mergers' (commonly referred to as the 'Takeover Panel'). It is controlled and managed by the financial community in the City of London, despite the fact that, formally speaking, it has had the status of a state supervisory authority since the TOD came into force.[5] Secondly, the Takeover Panel was able to effectively enforce the Takeover Code for a long time without having to impose regulatory sanctions on bidders or target companies. Rather, it made use of informal sanctions, such as 'cold shouldering', which historically worked in the relatively homogenous City of London. This fact testifies to the traditionally broad acceptance of both the Takeover Code and the Takeover Panel among the large majority of market participants.

In this regulatory environment, the MBR has always been one of the cornerstones of the Takeover Code.[6] The MBR was first introduced in 1972, four years after the initial publication of the Takeover Code. In its current version, Rule 9.1(a) of the Takeover Code requires any person that acquires shares representing at least 30 per cent of the voting rights of a company to make a mandatory offer to all shareholders.

The introduction of the MBR was the Takeover Panel's response to a bidding war for the target company, Venesta International.[7] In October 1971, Ozalid Company Limited initially announced a hostile takeover bid for the shareholders of Venesta International. However, the board of Venesta advised its shareholders to reject the offer. In the meantime, another shareholder, David Rowland, began buying Venesta shares on the stock exchange. In November, Nocros Limited went public with another competing offer for Venesta. Following this announcement,

3 https://code.thetakeoverpanel.org.uk/tp.

4 See D. Kershaw, *Principles of Takeover Regulation* (Oxford: Oxford University Press, 2016), mn. 3.01 and 3.02.

5 See Art. 4(1) TOD: 'Member States shall designate the authority or authorities competent to supervise bids for the purposes of the rules which they make or introduce pursuant to this Directive. The authorities thus designated shall be either public authorities, associations or private bodies recognized by national law or by public authorities expressly empowered for that purpose by national law.'

6 Kershaw, *Principles of Takeover Regulation*, mn. 3.88.

7 See J. Armour and D. Skeel, 'Who Writes the Rules for Hostile Takeovers, and Why? The Peculiar Divergence of US and UK Takeover Regulation' (2007) 95 *Geo. L.J.* 1727, 1763 et seq.; J. Pereira, 'An Ocean Apart: The Mandatory Takeover Rule in Brazil and in Europe' (2022) 10 *Emory Corp. Governance & Accountability Rev.* 67, 71 et seq.; H. Krause, *Das obligatorische Übernahmeangebot* (Baden-Baden: Nomos, 1996), 65 et seq.

David Rowland acquired further shares in the market. Whilst Rowland claimed that he was merely seeking to stabilise the value of his investment and fend off the takeover, his purchases via the market gave him a controlling stake in Venesta – without, however, having made a takeover bid to the other shareholders. The minority shareholders of Venesta therefore had no opportunity to sell their shares under the more favourable terms of Rowland's market purchases compared to the competing offers from Ozalid and Nocros. Although the Takeover Panel had investigated a possible breach of the 1968 version of the Takeover Code, it later held that the Takeover Code 'did not impose any obligation on an individual who has acquired control by a series of purchases in the market to endeavour to obtain the remaining shares'.[8]

In response to these transactions, the Takeover Panel added a new 'Rule 35' to the Takeover Code, 'requiring any person who purchases 40% or more of a company's shares to make a bid for the remaining shares'.[9] The Takeover Panel subsequently lowered the threshold from 40 to 30 per cent in 1974.[10] The threshold has not changed since then, not even as a result of the implementation of the TOD.[11] Although the choice of the threshold, first 40 per cent, then 30 per cent, is considered unavoidably arbitrary, it still reflects the idea that a bidder can de facto control the target company with far less than a majority of all voting rights.[12]

The functionality of the MBR has remained unchanged since the first version in 1972 and is based on two fundamental premises. First, all shareholders should be given an exit right on favourable terms in the event of a change of control through share purchases by the new controlling shareholder, and second, the bidder should (proportionally) share any control premium with all other shareholders.[13] These arguments are still used today to justify the European MBR in its current version.[14]

[8] See The Panel on Takeovers and Mergers, *The Consolidated Signal Company Limited/Venesta International Limited* (6 January 1972), 4, www.thetakeoverpanel.org.uk/wp-content/uploads/2008/12/1972-01.pdf.

[9] See The Panel on Takeovers and Mergers, *Report for the Year ended 31st March 1972* (1972), www.thetakeoverpanel.org.uk/wp-content/uploads/2008/11/report1972.pdf (at p. 7 stating that the addition of Rule 35 'brings within the scope of the Code any series of purchases (or other acquisitions) of shares, however gradual, which brings about a change of effective control').

[10] See A. Johnston, 'Takeover Regulation: Historical and Theoretical Perspectives on the City Code' (2007) 66 *Cambridge L.J.* 422, 455, also for a more comprehensive elaboration on the details of the amendments.

[11] J. Armour, J. Jacobs and C. Milhaupt, 'The Evolution of Hostile Takeover Regimes in Developed and Emerging Markets: An Analytical Framework' (2011) 52 *Harv. Int'l L.J.* 219, 237 et seq.; Kershaw, *Principles of Takeover Regulation*, mn. 8.05 ('no changes were required to implement the directive').

[12] Kershaw, *Principles of Takeover Regulation*, mn. 8.04

[13] Pereira, 'An Ocean Apart', 73.

[14] See M. Winner, 'Does the European Union have a Mandatory Bid Rule?', *Festschrift in Honour of Rolf Skog* (Stockholm: Norstedts Juridik, 2021), 1179, 1180.

6.3 THE EUROPEAN LEGISLATIVE HISTORY

The MBR was already included in the preliminary drafts of the TOD and was a central component of the initiatives at a European Union level.[15] The starting point is the 'Report on Takeover and other Bids' written by Robert Pennington on behalf of the European Commission.[16] The Pennington Report was published in 1974, coinciding with the UK's accession to the European Economic Community (EEC).[17] The (extensive) text of the report's Article 7 already contained a detailed obligation to 'compulsorily submit a mandatory offer' for all voting shares if, inter alia, a person was able to exercise at least 40 per cent of the voting rights of a target company. The minimum offer price was to be equivalent to the highest cash consideration paid within the twelve months prior to the bid.

All subsequent recommendations and drafts for the TOD also included provisions regarding the MBR. To be more precise, at least *in principle*, they did. Compare the following list of the most important cornerstones of the development at the EU level:

- The first proposal of the Commission for a TOD in **1989** in Article 4 (obligation to make a bid if a certain number of shares are to be acquired that are linked to a percentage of voting rights that may be held by the Member States set at a maximum of one-third of the total voting rights);[18]
- The amended proposal of the Commission for a TOD in **1990**, also in Article 4 (obligation to make an offer if, as a result of an acquisition, a person holds securities giving him/her at least a percentage of the voting rights which may be set at a maximum of one-third of the total voting rights);[19]
- The renewed proposal of the Commission for a TOD in **1996** in Article 10 (mandatory bid as a Member State option);[20]
- The – again – amended proposal of the Commission for a TOD in **1997** in Article 10 (mandatory bid as a Member State option, virtually unchanged in comparison to 1996);[21]

[15] D. Kleindiek, 'Funktion und Geltungsanspruch des Pflichtangebots nach dem WpÜG' (2002) *Zeitschrift für Unternehmens- und Gesellschaftsrecht* 546, 548.

[16] Commission Document XI/56/74-E, the text is reprinted in H. Fleischer and S. Kalss, *Das neue Wertpapiererwerbs- und Übernahmegesetz* (Munich: C. H. Beck, 2002), 831 et seq.

[17] Habersack, 'Non-frustration Rule and Mandatory Bid Rule', 2.

[18] Proposal of 19 January 1989 for a Thirteenth Council Directive on Company Law concerning takeover and other general bids, OJ No C 64/8, 14 March 1989.

[19] Amended Proposal of 17 September 1990 for a Thirteenth Council Directive on Company Law concerning takeover and other general bids, OJ No C 240/7, 26 September 1990.

[20] Proposal of 7 February 1996 for a 13th European Parliament and Council Directive on company law concerning takeover bids, OJ No C 162/5, 6 June 1996.

[21] Amended Proposal of 11 November for a 13th European Parliament and Council Directive on company law concerning takeover bids, OJ No C 378/10, 13 December 1997.

- The Common Position of the Council in 2000 and the joint text of the Council and the Parliament ('Compromise Proposal') in 2001 in Article 5 (mandatory bid if a certain threshold to be determined by the Member State is surpassed);[22]
- The proposal of the Commission presented – following the temporary failure of the enactment – for a TOD in 2002 in Article 5 (mandatory bid if a certain threshold to be determined by the Member State is surpassed with additional pricing rules);[23]
- And eventually the final version of the TOD in 2004 in Article 5 ('Protection of minority shareholders, the mandatory bid and the equitable price').

A closer analysis reveals that the legislative history of the MBR was somewhat erratic at the European level. Although all drafts and recommendations provided for a MBR in principle, the Commission's numerous drafts differed significantly from the early proposal in the Pennington Report. In terms of content, the Commission's proposals for the MBR did not reflect a European consensus, which was still notably missing at that time. Rather, the individual drafts differed fundamentally from one another in the wording and precise contents of the MBR. Not even the core question of whether the TOD should include a 'mandatory' bid at all could be answered consistently between 1989 and 2000. The Commission's drafts from 1989 and 1990, for example, contained an MBR with a full offer for all securities of the target company specifically to avoid purely speculative takeover bids.[24] These drafts also instructed the Member States to set the threshold that triggers the MBR at a maximum of 33⅓ per cent of the company's total voting rights. However, large and/or politically influential Member States such as Germany and the Netherlands strongly criticised the MBR. They claimed the rule would promote concentration, make takeovers much more expensive and thus prevent economically reasonable acquisitions of shares, and ultimately make it more difficult to restructure companies. Finally, at a more fundamental level, Member States denied the need for harmonisation at the European level in general.[25] At the time, and as a result of the

[22] Common Position (EC) No 1/2001, adopted by the Council on 19 June 2000 with a view to adopting a Directive on company law concerning takeover bid, OJ No C 23/1, 24 January 2001; Joint Text approved by the Conciliation Committee regarding the Directive of the European Parliament and of the Council on company law concerning takeover bids, Dossier 96/0085 (COD), PE-CONS 3629/01, 6 June 2001.

[23] Proposal of 2 October for a Directive of the European Parliament and of the Council on takeover bid, OC No C 45/E1, 25 February 2002.

[24] See M. Schlitt, '§ 35 WpÜG mn. 11', in W. Goette and M. Habersack (eds.), *Münchener Kommentar zum Aktiengesetz*, Vol. 6, 5th ed. (Munich: C. H. Beck, 2021); H.-C. Knoll, *Die Übernahme von Kapitalgesellschaften* (Baden-Baden: Nomos, 1992), 172.

[25] See T. Baums, 'Zur Harmonisierung des Rechts der Unternehmensübernahmen in der EG', in H.-W. Rengeling (ed.), *Europäisierung des Rechts* (Heymann, 1996), 91, 93; Krause, *Das obligatorische Übernahmeangebot*, 38; M. Lutter, W. Bayer and J. Schmidt, *Europäisches*

widespread criticism from the aforementioned Member States, the adoption of the directive was out of reach.

The 1996 and 1997 Commission's draft directives made substantial changes to the MBR. The drafts dispensed with fixed thresholds and in Article 3(2) delegated the competence to determine the percentage of voting rights which confers control and the method of its calculation to the Member States. According to Article 10(2) of the drafts, partial (mandatory) bids were also permissible, but had to reach a 'substantial part' of the outstanding shares, which according to the 1997 draft, meant 'no less than 70 % of the securities, except where duly justified authorisation has been given by the supervisory authority'. The most serious change, however, was that, according to Article 3(1), Member States could also choose whether to ensure the protection of minority shareholders in the event of a change of control through a mandatory bid in accordance with Article 10 or *alternatively* through 'other appropriate and at least equivalent means'. The Commission thus reduced its proposal to a mere 'framework directive', which it hoped would give more leeway to and thus be more popular amongst Member States.[26] Meanwhile, politically, the alternative to the MBR was, according to Klaus Hopt, a lazy compromise that aims 'to please everyone' and, in terms of content, was obviously referring to German group law which the Commission specifically wanted to recognise as equivalent to the UK's MBR under Rule 9 of the Takeover Code.[27] In essence, the Commission wanted to use this concession in Article 3 to ensure Germany's agreement on the TOD draft. However, at this time, Hopt noted that an international trend towards the embrace of the MBR as part of modern takeover law was already recognisable, at least outside the US. Indeed, shortly afterwards, Germany finally gave up on its resistance against the TOD (see Section 6.4.4). Under the German presidency of the Council, the request for (German) group law to be recognised as an equivalent means to the MBR was ultimately dropped in 1999, in particular, because Germany could no longer justify its special request against the other Member States. Furthermore, the equivalence of German group law was increasingly disputed in the German literature.[28]

Accordingly, the Common Position from 2000 onwards removed the 'equivalent clause' in the draft as an alternative to the MBR, with the exemption of a one-year

Unternehmens- und Kapitalmarktrecht, 6th ed. (Berlin: De Gruyter, 2017), mn. 28.31; H. Fleischer in Fleischer and Kalss, *Das neue Wertpapiererwerbs- und Übernahmegesetz*, 49.

[26] Fleischer in Fleischer and Kalss, *Das neue Wertpapiererwerbs- und Übernahmegesetz*, 50.

[27] K. Hopt, 'Europäisches und deutsches Übernahmerecht' (1997) 161 *Zeitschrift für das gesamte Handels und Wirtschaftsrecht*, 368, 384 et seq.

[28] H. Krause and T. Pötzsch, '§ 35 mn. 18', in H.-D. Assmann, T. Pötzsch and U. Schneider (eds.), *Kommentar zum Wertpapiererwerbs- und Übernahmegesetz*, 3rd ed. (Cologne: Otto Schmidt, 2020); U. Wackerbarth, 'Von golden shares und poison pills: Waffengleichheit bei internationalen Übernahmenangeboten' (2001) *Wertpapiermitteilungen*, 1741, 1745 et seq.; Kleindiek, 'Funktion und Geltungsanspruch des Pflichtangebots nach dem WpÜG', 556; Lutter, Bayer and Schmidt, 'Europäisches Unternehmens- und Kapitalmarktrecht', § 28 mn. 28.31.

transition period, and in Article 5(1) also abolished the option of partial bids. Instead, the draft demanded that the bid be addressed to all holders of securities for all of their holding. However, the draft continued to refrain from determining the percentage of voting rights which confers control of the company and left the task of setting the threshold to the Member States. In other words, the MBR was preserved, albeit in a considerably watered-down version. Moreover, the 'Compromise Proposal' from 2001 – which was intended to finally enact the TOD under the Swedish Council Presidency – did not change this core issue. The draft resolution was then defeated in a memorable vote in the European Parliament following a change of heart on the part of the German government which was brought about by intensive lobbying as a result of the experience of the Mannesmann/Vodafone takeover bid (see Section 6.4.4).[29]

However, the negative vote in the European Parliament only delayed the enactment of the TOD by a few years. The Commission was not ready to abandon the idea of a TOD after all. Based on the 'Winter Report',[30] the Commission submitted a new proposal in October 2002.[31] In principle, the design of the MBR was similar to the preliminary drafts. Until the final version of the TOD arrived, the MBR did not undergo fundamental change. In particular, one important part of the MBR survived all drafts and eventually found its way into the final version of the TOD: the percentage of voting rights which confers control and the method of its calculation should still be determined by the Member States (Art. 5(3) TOD).

In general, the development of the EU's MBR essentially involved weakening the rule's content. However, the area of pricing is one important exception. While the Pennington Report had contained precise rules on the minimum offer price, such rules were absent from later proposals,[32] apart from the general demand that the offer price be equitable. Only in its 2002 proposal – and because of earlier negotiations with the European Parliament[33] – did the Commission include a best price rule with a look-back period between six to twelve months prior to the bid, which is to be determined by the Member States.[34] At its core, this rule has made it into

[29] For reflections on the vote see H. Krause, 'Das deutsche Übernahmegesetz vor dem Hintergrund der EU-Richtlinie' (2002) *Zeitschrift für Unternehmens- und Gesellschaftsrecht* 500, 507; R. Skog, 'The Takeover Directive – An Endless Saga?' (2002) *European Business Law Review* 301, 308 et seq.

[30] J. Winter et al., 'Report of the High Level Group of Company Law Experts on Issues Related to Takeover Bids in the European Union', reprinted in G. Ferrarini (ed.), *Reforming Company and Takeover Law in Europe* (Oxford: Oxford University Press, 2004), Annex 2.

[31] See V. Edwards, 'The Directive on Takeover Bids – Not Worth the Paper It's Written on?' (2004) 1 *European Company and Financial Law Review* 416, 427 et seq.

[32] Apart from the automatic revision of the bid in case of purchases by the bidder above the offer price during the offer period; see Art. 16 of the 1989 and 1990 proposals.

[33] See B. Clarke and R. Skog, 'The Genesis of the Takeover Directive', Chapter 1 of this book.

[34] And only the final version again included a revision of the bid in case of purchases by the bidder above the offer price during the offer period.

Article 5(4) of the TOD as it has entered into force and is one of the few examples of meaningful regulation in the Directive.[35]

6.4 THE LEVEL OF MEMBER STATES

EU harmonisation efforts have often had an anticipatory effect on national legislation in the Member States.[36] At the same time as the work on the TOD, many Member States enacted or substantially improved takeover legislation themselves and autonomously adopted an MBR rule into their national legal systems. However, this resulted in a reciprocal dynamic, as the development at Member State level had a knock-on effect on European legislation; the introduction of a European MBR became easier once a considerable number of Member States had already introduced such a rule.

The motives behind introducing the MBR, moreover, have varied greatly between Member States. That is, both influential lobby groups that wanted to assert their interests and spectacular takeovers that exerted pressure on the Member States' governments served to play a role in that process.

In the following, we briefly trace the reasons for enacting an MBR in some selected Member States, in chronological order.

6.4.1 *France*

France was one of the first continental European countries to introduce an MBR by Law no. 89-531 of 2 August 1989 concerning 'the security and transparency of the financial markets'. The new regulations were triggered by several hostile takeover bids in the preceding years, which had been among the largest in French business history.[37] At the time, responsibility for regulating takeover bids lay with two authorities, the 'Commission des Opérations de Bourse' (COB) and the 'Conseil des Bourses des Valeurs' (CBV). This dual supervisory structure characterised the former French takeover law. The structure was only ended by Law no. 2003-706 of 1 August 2003, which merged the authorities and transferred the supervision of takeovers to the 'Autorité des marchés financiers' (AMF).[38] Before that, the French legislator left the detailed content of the MBR to the CBV, including the threshold of voting rights which confer control to the bidder. The threshold was defined in the 'General Regulations' as the acquisition of one-third of the voting rights or capital shares of the target company (Title V of the General Regulation of the CBV).[39]

[35] See Winner, 'Does the European Union have a Mandatory Bid Rule?', 1179, 1190 et seq.

[36] See Krause, 'Das obligatorische Übernahmeangebot', 39 et seq.

[37] A. Marquardt, 'Tender Offers in France: The New Rules' (1990) 9 *Int'l Fin. L. Rev.* 35, 35.

[38] See N. Barouk, *Der angemessene Preis im deutschen und französischen Übernahmerecht* (Berlin: Duncker & Humblot 2008), 19.

[39] Marquardt, 'Tender Offers in France: The New Rules' 38; Barouk, 'Der angemessene Preis im deutschen und französischen Übernahmerecht', 118.

Initially, a person who crosses this threshold was required to file a takeover bid enabling him/her to hold at least two-thirds of the total number of shares conferring voting rights. This rule was greatly criticised, however, and the option of launching a partial bid ultimately disappeared in 1992.

Apparently, the introduction of the MBR was politically less controversial than in other European countries and was geared towards protecting minority shareholders. As a justification for the MBR, the COB referred to a 'breach of the investment contract' ('rupture du contrat d'investissement').[40] Accordingly, the shareholders had made their investment decisions under the impression of certain individuals leading the company and following a predefined corporate policy. In the takeover, control is conferred on a new acquirer, thereby exerting a profound influence on the shareholders' investment decision. The focus of the reasoning was therefore purely on the protection of minority shareholders who were to be given the right to tender their shares to the acquirer because of the change of control.

6.4.2 *Austria*

The Austrian Takeover Act (ÜbG) came into force on 1 January 1999, several years before the TOD was enacted. At the time the law was drafted, the Commission's 1996 proposal had already become available as a template for the Austrian legislator. In December 1996, the then Federal Minister of Justice, Nikolaus Michalek, had set up a small working group to draft an Austrian position on the recently issued Commission proposal.[41] The reduction of the proposal to a mere 'framework directive' was taken in Austria as an opportunity to transpose the European requirements into national law in advance so that there would be no immediate need for adaptation once the TOD had been enacted – which was apparently assumed to be taking place fairly soon.[42]

However, the situation evolved rapidly and work on a new 'law on public takeover bids' commenced just one month later. This was due to the takeover of the Creditanstalt-Bankverein (CA), one of the largest Austrian banks at the time which

[40] Barouk, 'Der angemessene Preis im deutschen und französischen Übernahmerecht', 119 with reference to Rapport annuel COB 1988, 89: 'Chaque année, la commission rend compte dans son rapport des possibilités de retrait offerts aux actionnaires dans des cas de changement de contrôle non couverts par la réglementation relative à la négociation des blocs de contrôle ou, du fait d'opérations de restructuration, les droits des actionnaires ont pu être modifiés de manière importante. En effet, toute modification importante du pacte social peut affecter la clause du contrat d'investissement par lequel l'actionnaire a adhéré à la société.'

[41] P. Doralt, 'Preface' in P. Doralt, Ch. Nowotny and M. Schauer (eds.), *Takeover-Recht* (Vienna: Service Fachverlag, 1997).

[42] See P. Doralt, 'Überlegungen zur Gestaltung der Vorschriften über das Recht des öffentlichen Übernahmeangebotes in Österreich', *Festschrift in honour of Bruno Kropff* (Düsseldorf: IDW, 1997), 53, 56.

was traditionally close to the Conservative Party (ÖVP) who were governing in a coalition with the Social Democrats (SPÖ) at that time. In the course of the privatisation of CA, a state holding of 69.45 per cent of the shares was sold to Bank Austria just before Christmas 1996 and after Bank Austria won a bidding contest with many other companies. Bank Austria was Austria's largest bank at the time and had close ties to the SPÖ. The takeover of a 'conservative' bank by a 'socialist' bank then sparked a government crisis and the coalition between the SPÖ and ÖVP arrived at a breaking point; even a change of coalition partners before the halfway point of the legislative period was on the cards.[43] In the end, the coalition remained intact. In an informal committee meeting in January 1997, the governing parties reached an agreement on 'how to proceed with privatisations in future' and on a 'capital market reform', the latter including the plan to enact a takeover law.[44] This political wish was reaffirmed in a resolution of the Austrian Parliament on 14 January 1997. According to the political declarations of intent, the protection of minority shareholders was to be the primary regulatory objective.[45] However, the contents of the new Takeover Law were not further specified. Initially, it was not even clear whether an MBR was to be introduced or whether other means of protecting minority shareholders were preferable.

The legislative proposal was based on a draft prepared by a scholar – namely, Peter Doralt – with the support of one co-author.[46] The Ministry of Justice sent the draft for review in 1997. During the review process, the MBR, as proposed in the draft, received a great deal of attention for the very first time. However, before the first proposal was on the table, hardly any discussion took place about the pros and cons of such a rule. The Austrian draft must be understood against the background of the Commission proposals from 1996/97. Hence, introducing an MBR was in no way lacking alternatives. However, the drafters did not want to secure the protection of minority shareholders via 'other equivalent means', since Austrian company law did not (and does not) contain rules on group law according to the German model. Although the drafters and the Ministry were aware of the economic criticism, they nevertheless suggested introducing an MBR, reasoning that such a rule is 'in the interest of the capital market' and 'makes participation in Austrian stock corporations more attractive for institutional investors (e.g. domestic and foreign investment and pension funds) as well as for retail investors'.[47] Moreover, the MBR according to Rule 9.1 Takeover Code had a major influence on the Austrian legislator,[48] as

43 K. Grubelnik, *Die Rote Krake. Eine Bank erobert Österreich* (Vienna: Molden, 1998), 15 and 17.
44 Ibid., 23.
45 Explanatory Remarks to the Government Bill 1276 BlgNR 20. GP at p. 18.
46 Ibid. at p. 22.
47 Ibid. at p. 21.
48 See Doralt, *Festschrift in honour of Bruno Kropff*, 53, 62, 66 and 69; for preliminary work see E. Stern, 'Übernahmeangebote im englischen Recht' (1992) *Österreichisches Bankarchiv* 1065 and 1993, 27.

evidenced not only by the closely related content, but also by the fact that the explanatory remarks to § 22 ÜbG 1999 expressly refer to Rule 9.1 and 9.2 of the Takeover Code.[49] The Austrian MBR is thus an impressive example of the influence of the UK regime on continental Europe even before the TOD came into force.[50]

Immediately upon publication of the draft, considerable resistance to the MBR arose. In essence, this was due to the (still today) highly concentrated ownership structures of listed companies in Austria. The obvious prediction was that a change of control would primarily occur through block trading over the counter. Listed companies in Austria were often controlled by influential families (e.g. by family foundations), syndicates, or well-known Austrian 'industrialists'. These types of shareholders soon realised that full equal treatment by way of a mandatory bid based on the UK model – that is, with a best price rule and a look-back period of twelve months – would force the selling blockholder to share 'his' or 'her' control premium with the minority shareholders. This form of 'equal treatment' gave rise to defensive reactions to the legislative proposal: 'The majority shareholders are defending their sole power of disposal over the control premium (the block premium).'[51]

The resistance did not ultimately bring down the legislative proposal but nevertheless led to some watering down of the initially stringent rules. The legislator accommodated the core shareholders by allowing a discount of 15 per cent to the highest price paid by the offeror within the look-back period (see section 26(1) ÜbG 1999), following the (then) Swiss model. The only reason given was to 'significantly reduce the burden on the current majority shareholders'.[52] Additionally, to make the MBR more attractive to controlling shareholders, the legislator predicted that they would also benefit from the MBR, seeing as it would facilitate the sale of their shares on the stock exchange and would also lower the cost of capital for the company. Finally, the 15 per cent discount became inadmissible when the TOD came into force and was thus removed upon transposition of the directive into the Austrian Takeover Law in 2006 (see section 26 ÜbG 2006). During this reform, the legislator for the first time introduced a fixed percentage of voting rights which confers control of a company and subsequently sets a mandatory bid in motion. The threshold was set at 30 per cent and has remained there since. The previous Takeover Act from

[49] Explanatory Remarks to the Government Bill 1276 BlgNR 20. GP at p. 41.

[50] See M. Ventoruzzo, 'Takeover Regulation as a Wolf in Sheep's Clothing: Taking UK Rules to Continental Europe' (2008) 11 *J. Bus. L.* 135, 146, stating that Austria 'adapted the "British style" mandatory bid already prior to the XIII. Directive'. In detail M. Winner, 'Das österreichische Übernahmerecht – ein Rechtstransplantat aus dem Vereinigten Königreich', in R. Cierpial-Magnor et al. (eds.), *Erfolge und Misserfolge des Rechtstransfers* (Vienna: Nomos & Facultas, 2024), 293, 297 et seq.

[51] Doralt, 'Festschrift in honour of Bruno Kropff', 53 and 63.

[52] Explanatory Remarks to the Government Bill 1276 BlgNR 20. GP at p. 21 and 46, admitting that '[the discount] takes into account the financial interests of the potentially willing sellers, i.e. the core shareholders frequently found in Austrian stock corporations, at the expense of the other shareholders'.

1999 had followed a 'material concept' of control, leaving the precise definition of 'control' in the regulatory hands of the Austrian Takeover Commission. The concept was heavily criticised by lobby groups during the legislative process and was also partly subject to constitutional concerns.[53]

We can thus conclude that the MBR was introduced not because of any legislative plan going beyond 'protecting minority shareholders', but because a government crisis precipitated the need to do *something* or, probably, the need to be *seen* doing something. The scholar who asked to prepare a first draft happened to be convinced of the justification of the MBR himself and, in turn, managed to convince the Ministry of Justice on this issue. Once the draft was published, it became impossible for pressure groups to prevent its subsequent adoption altogether.

6.4.3 *Sweden*

Swedish developments also paint a revealing picture of the pressure that political and economic forces can exert on legislation, sometimes emanating from powerful business families. A contribution by Rolf Skog from shortly before the turn of the millennium offers some preliminary insight into the Swedish perspective.[54] At that time, Skog, who was responsible for the Swedish takeover rules as well as the Swedish negotiations of the TOD, was sceptical as to whether the TOD would be adopted by the Council of Ministers, but perceived the chances to be much higher if the MBR in the proposal were abolished, as this step would significantly reduce resistance from Germany and the Netherlands.[55] He himself rejected the introduction of an MBR, in line with argumentation in contemporary economic literature.[56]

Having said this, the public debate on the introduction of an MBR in Sweden dates to the 1980s.[57] This period was characterised by increased takeover activity on the Swedish capital market, which attracted considerable media attention. In the 1980s, Social Democratic policymakers spoke out in favour of introducing an MBR. The Standing Committee on Laws of the Swedish Parliament subsequently sent a draft for a reform of capital-market law, including the introduction of a new MBR, to several state institutions and interest groups. However, the proposal met with fierce opposition, particularly from Swedish industry and employers. Both argued that the MBR would make potential block transactions more expensive and thus have a disruptive effect on the constant reshaping of listed companies. As a result of this

53 Explanatory Remarks to the Government Bill 1334 BlgNR 22. GP at p. 2.

54 R. Skog, *Does Sweden Need a Mandatory Bid Rule? A Critical Analysis*, SUERF Studies, No. 2 (1997), 1.

55 Following Skog, *Does Sweden Need a Mandatory Bid Rule?*, 1, 21.

56 See C. Bergström, P. Högfedt and J. Molin, 'The Optimality of the Mandatory Bid Rule', 13 *J. L. Econ. & Org.* 433 (1997).

57 Skog, *Does Sweden Need a Mandatory Bid Rule?*, 1, 36.

criticism, the Standing Committee withdrew its reform proposal. Moreover, despite the MBR getting placed on the political agenda once again over the next few years – this time by members of the Liberal Party – the categorical rejection of the MBR remained unwavering.

However, influential Swedish business families, among others, were soon to discover takeover law as an instrument for asserting their own interests. This was due to the realisation that the MBR on capital markets with a concentrated ownership structure and active block trading actually makes it easier for controlling shareholders to fend off unwanted bidders.[58]

When considering controlling shareholders in Sweden, mention of the Wallenberg family cannot be avoided. This family symbolises the Swedish corporate governance model in a paradigmatic way – concentrated shareholder structures supported by cross-ownership and a system of dual-class shares.[59] At the turn of the millennium, the Wallenberg family controlled fourteen large listed companies with a market value of SEK 922 billion, corresponding to 42 per cent of the market capitalisation on the Stockholm Stock Exchange.[60] The Wallenbergs actively supported the Industry and Commerce Stock Exchange Committee's introduction of the MBR from 1 July 1999, as a part of the Swedish self-regulatory system.[61]

The political influence of the Wallenbergs was perhaps even more perceptible in the negotiations on the TOD after the failed vote in the European Parliament, especially in connection with the breakthrough rule in Article 11, which was mandatory in first drafts. The rule is directed against selected takeover obstacles, such as transfer restrictions, special rights for shareholders under the articles of association, or even multiple-voting rights. The bidder is not bound by such instruments at the first general meeting after the end of the offer if it holds at least 75 per cent of the voting shares. Obviously, a mandatory breakthrough rule would have had the potential to overturn the Swedish corporate governance model in many companies, not just those controlled by the Wallenberg family, and would have made them far more susceptible to hostile takeovers.[62] As a result, the Wallenbergs attacked the Commission's plans with considerable vigour and, not

58 Ventoruzzo, 11 *J. Bus. L.* 135, 140 (2008).

59 See K. Jonnergård and U. Larsson-Olaison, *Doxa of Shareholders and Owners: On the Threshold of Financialization, Accounting, Economics, and Law: A Convivium* (Berlin: De Gruyter, 2018), 1, 4; M. Henrekson and U. Jakobsson, 'The Swedish Corporate Control Model: Convergence, Persistence or Decline?', 20 *Corporate Governance: An International Review* 212, 216 (2012), stating that 'the Wallenberg family has long been the leading exponent of the Swedish corporate control model'.

60 J. Agnblad, E. Berglöf, P. Högfeldt and H. Svancar, 'Ownership and Control in Sweden: Strong Owners, Weak Minorities, and Social Control', in F. Barca and M. Becht (eds.), *The Control of Corporate Europe* (Oxford: Oxford University Press, 2002), 228, 244.

61 Ibid., 241.

62 See R. Skog, 'The European Union's Proposed Takeover Directive, the "Breakthrough" Rule and the Swedish System of Dual Class Common Stock', 15 *European Business Law Review* 1439 (2006).

holding back, publicly announced that the breakthrough rule violated 'human rights and the constitution'.[63] The Social Democratic government backed the Wallenbergs' demand and declared the protection of multiple-voting shares to be of 'national interest'.[64] Majority shareholders in Sweden should still be able to negotiate a control premium with the bidder during a takeover situation.

The intensive lobbying by the Wallenberg family and other parts of the Swedish establishment paid off.[65] Under the Italian Council presidency and the rapporteur Klaus-Heiner Lehne, a compromise was reached in the winter of 2003 which downgraded the breakthrough rule under Article 11 to an option for the member states (Art. 12). The compromise was included unchanged in the final version of the TOD. In fact, not only Sweden, but almost all Member States were to opt out of the breakthrough rule.[66]

6.4.4 *Germany*

The development in Germany was particularly influential for the European legislative history of the MBR. It has therefore already been briefly mentioned and will be analysed in more detail here.

After the Commission published the first drafts for a '13th EC Directive on Takeover Bids' in 1989/90, the predominant tenor in Germany was that the TOD should not be adopted,[67] or, insofar as the enactment was considered unavoidable, only with generous options for the Member States in order to avoid causing a conflict with national group law (sections 291 et seq., 311 et seq. of the German Stock Corporation Act).[68] According to Klaus Hopt, the MBR was the main cause of

[63] W. Magnuson, 21 *Pace Int'l L. Rev.* 205, 232 (2009), with reference to C. Brown-Humes and F. Guerrera, 'Wallenberg Attacks EU Over Takeover Proposals', *Financial Times* (London), 31 January 2002, 10.

[64] P. Högfeldt, 'The History and Politics of Corporate Ownership in Sweden', in R. Morck (ed.), *A History of Corporate Governance around the World: Family Business Groups to Professional Managers* (Chicago, IL: University of Chicago Press, 2005), 517, 565 (including fn. 30); S. Nachemson-Ekwall, 21 *J. Manag. Gov.* 27, 35 (2017).

[65] A. Nilsen, *The EU Takeover Directive and the Competitiveness of European Industry*, OCGG Economic Analysis No. 1 (2004), 1, 4 (www.files.ethz.ch/isn/110044/Analysis-1_EU_Takeover_Directive.pdf).

[66] See K. Hopt, *Europäisches Übernahmerecht* (Tübingen: Mohr Siebeck, 2013), 95 with further references.

[67] See B. Grunewald, 'Was bringt der Vorschlag einer 13. EG-Richtlinie über Übernahmeangebote für das deutsche Recht?' (1989) *Zeitschrift für Wirtschafts- und Bankrecht (WM)* 1233; H.-J. Mertens, 'Förderung von, Schutz vor, Zwang zu Übernahmeangeboten?' (1990) *Die Aktiengesellschaft* 252; for an (implicitly) positive economic assessment see J. Reul, *Die Pflicht zur Gleichbehandlung der Aktionäre bei privaten Kontrolltransaktionen* (Tübingen: Mohr Siebeck, 1991), 127 et seq., 250 (result): 'duty to treat shareholders equally in control acquisitions has proven to be efficient in economic analyses'.

[68] See P. Hommelhoff and D. Kleindiek, 'Takeover-Richtlinie und europäisches Konzernrecht' (1990) *Die Aktiengesellschaft* 106; T. Baums, 'Übernahmeregeln in der Europäischen Gemeinschaft' (1989) *Zeitschrift für Wirtschaftsrecht* 1376.

concern in the discussion at that time.[69] Of course, German scholars realised that the MBR is an important means of protection law against the formation of a group under a capital market; as a matter of fact, German literature had long been considering preventive mechanisms at the 'Archimedean point' of group formation.[70] From a German perspective, however, the MBR was 'a piece of group law without an overall concept that does not fit into the legal environment of group law',[71] even acting as a 'Trojan horse', which bursts 'the citadel of the law of affiliated companies'.[72] The critics also raised political concerns,[73] in the end also preventing the adoption of the Commission's proposal for the TOD at the European level.

However, this rejection proved not to be sustainable. Within a few years after the initial discussion, an Expert Committee of the German Stock Exchange drafted the 'Übernahmekodex' (i.e. Takeover Code) and presented it to the public without any legal obligation and without much prior discussion, at least at a scholarly level.[74] Market participants were supposed to consider the 'Übernahmekodex' starting from 1 October 1995. The Expert Committee's aim was to make Germany's financial market more attractive by introducing new and modern rules for takeover bids.[75] The role model was, once again, the UK Takeover Code. The 'Übernahmekodex' relied on self-regulation by market participants through voluntary contractual commitments to a takeover commission, which could not be a state authority but had to derive its legal power from the Stock Exchange Expert Committee.[76] Article 16 of the 'Übernahmekodex' contained an MBR, which stipulated that only the acquisition of more than 50 per cent of the shares in the target company would trigger the obligation to make an offer. The introduction of 'mandatory takeover bids' and their content were immediately criticised; the threshold of 50 per cent was considered too high, the exemptions were regarded as inconsistent and, in general, the only reason for introducing an MBR was seen in the fact that it was 'regarded internationally as the standard for takeover bid regulations and as a sign of the reputability of such

69 K. Hopt, 'Übernahmeangebote im europäischen Recht', *Festschrift in honour of Fritz Rittner* (Munich: C. H. Beck, 1991), 187, 199 et seq.

70 Baums, 'Übernahmeregeln in der Europäischen Gemeinschaft' 1376, 1379 et seq.; in general see H. Wiedemann, *Die Unternehmensgruppe im Privatrecht* (Tübingen: Mohr Siebeck, 1988), 50 et seq., 66 et seq.

71 K. Hopt, 'Harmonisierung im europäischen Gesellschaftsrecht' (1992) *Zeitschrift für Unternehmens- und Gesellschaftsrecht* 265, 282.

72 P. Hommelhoff, 'Konzerneingangs-Schutz durch Takeover-Recht?', *Festschrift in honour of Johannes Semler* (Berlin: De Gruyter, 1993), 455, 467.

73 See *Stellungnahme des Bundestages*, BT-Drucks. 11/6612 and 12/1465 and *Stellungnahme des Bundesrates*, BR-Drucks. 136/89; cited after Fleischer and Kalss, *Das neue Wertpapiererwerbs- und Übernahmegesetz*, 49 including fn. 227.

74 See H. Kallmeyer, 'Der Übernahmekodex der Börsensachverständigenkommission' (1996) *Die Aktiengesellschaft* 169.

75 Hopt, 'Harmonisierung im europäischen Gesellschaftsrecht', 394; Fleischer and Kalss, *Das neue Wertpapiererwerbs- und Übernahmegesetz*, 49 with fn. 44.

76 G. Thoma, 'Der neue Übernahmekodex der Börsensachverständigenkommission' (1996) *Zeitschrift für Wirtschaftsrecht* 1725, 1725.

regulations'.[77] Irrespective of this criticism, the 'Übernahmekodex' was also unable to achieve its goal. According to common opinion, the practical experience with the 'Übernahmekodex' was good, but acceptance of the regulations among market participants fell significantly short of expectations. By 30 April 1997, only 259 of the 678 listed companies had submitted to the 'Übernahmekodex'.[78] As a result, the Stock Exchange Expert Committee abandoned the model of self-regulation in February 1999 and instead publicly recommended a statutory takeover law.

In spring 2000, work on a draft law to regulate takeover bids commenced. The German government set up a commission of experts who agreed on ten key points for a future takeover law, which were then recommended to the German Bundestag as the basis for future legislation. These key points included the regulation of mandatory offers.[79] Both the ensuing draft bill and the government bill for a law to regulate public offers for the acquisition of securities and company takeovers[80] notably contained an MBR. In stark contrast to the situation a decade earlier, by this time only a few market participants or scholars were still openly criticising the concept of mandatory bids.[81] There were no major changes between the first discussion draft and the final version of the MBR, to be found in section 35 WpÜG, which has not undergone substantial changes until today.

The German legislator was not subject to any EU law requirements when drafting the MBR, because, at that time, the European Parliament had already rejected the adoption of the TOD (on 4 July 2001). Consequently, the government draft no longer had to follow the requirements of the Council's Common Position from 2000. Nevertheless, Germany voluntarily decided to introduce the MBR.

This was due to two main reasons. First, Germany had already given up its resistance to the MBR at the European level after taking over the presidency of the Council at the beginning of 1999. The Common Position, the academic view that German group law was not equivalent to the MBR, but that the two instruments instead complemented each other, had already prevailed.[82] If the 'equivalence

[77] H.-D. Assmann, 'Verhaltensregeln für freiwillige öffentliche Übernahmeangebote' (1995) *Die Aktiengesellschaft* 563, 570; Thoma, 'Der neue Übernahmekodex der Börsensachverständigenkommission', 1726; see also H. Kallmeyer, 'Die Mängel des Übernahmekodex der Börsensachverständigenkommission' (1997) 161 *Zeitschrift für das gesamte Handelsrecht* 435, 436 et seq.

[78] Hopt, 'Harmonisierung im europäischen Gesellschaftsrecht', 395; for further figures see Fleischer and Kalss, *Das neue Wertpapiererwerbs- und Übernahmegesetz*, 10.

[79] T. Pötzsch and A. Möller, 'Das künftige Übernahmerecht' (2000) *Zeitschrift für Wirtschafts- und Bankrecht (WM)-Sonderbeil.* 2, 13.

[80] T. Pötzsch and A. Möller, 'Das neue Übernahmerecht – Der Regierungsentwurf vom 11. Juli 2001' (2001) *Zeitschrift für Wirtschaftsrecht* 1256.

[81] For one of the remaining critics see H. Altmeppen, 'Neutralitätspflicht und Pflichtangebot nach dem neuen Übernahmerecht' (2001) *Zeitschrift für Wirtschaftsrecht* 1073, 1080 et seq.

[82] H.-W. Neye, 'Der gemeinsame Standpunkt des Rates zur 13. Richtlinie – ein entscheidender Schritt auf dem Weg zu einem europäischen Übernahmerecht' (2000) *Die Aktiengesellschaft* 289, 293; Fleischer and Kalss, *Das neue Wertpapiererwerbs- und Übernahmegesetz*, 28.

regulation clause' had remained in place instead, the TOD might have interfered with German group law – a concern that was present throughout the German literature.[83]

Second, shortly before the turn of the millennium, the policy focus in Germany shifted away from the MBR and towards the non-frustration rule, given the recent fallout from the hostile takeover of Mannesmann by Vodafone. Major German industry players (especially Volkswagen and BASF), which from then on saw themselves as potential takeover targets for foreign investors,[84] lobbied massively against a strict non-frustration rule, as provided for in the Common Position of the Council.[85] Industrial companies wanted greater freedom for the board of directors to decide on defensive measures against hostile takeovers. Meanwhile, the European Parliament, under the German rapporteur Klaus-Heiner Lehne, subsequently voted in favour of the Common Position only with an amendment that softened the strict non-frustration rule. Back then, Lehne was a lawyer in Düsseldorf, the headquarters of Mannesmann, and was almost certainly influenced by Vodafone's hostile takeover bid.[86] In a remarkable turnaround that has been described by US authors 'as a demonstration of the power of politics',[87] the German government changed its position and asked their MEP to vote against the adoption of the TOD, 'a break with custom once a common position has been agreed'.[88] As mentioned, the subsequent vote in the European Parliament failed and the enactment of the TOD was prevented for the time being.

6.5 SYNTHESIS

The MBR has undergone a lengthy and complex legislative process. While the Commission still had precise ideas about the design of the MBR in the early days of their intention to further legislation on takeover bids, the rule's content became less and less specific over time. Resistance in the Member States had to be overcome, and the Commission was prepared to pay the price – initially by concessions to German group law, and after Germany had given up its resistance, by delegating key aspects of the MBR to the Member States, above all determining the threshold of voting rights which confer control on the bidder and thus setting the trigger mechanism for the mandatory bid.

[83] Habersack, 'Non-frustration Rule and Mandatory Bid Rule', 29.

[84] Krause, 'Das deutsche Übernahmegesetz vor dem Hintergrund der EU-Richtlinie', 505 et seq.

[85] Edwards, 'The Directive on Takeover Bids – Not Worth the Paper It's Written on?', 425 et seq.

[86] W. Magnuson, 'Takeover Regulation in the United States and Europe: An Institutional Approach' (2009), 21 *Pace Int'l L. Rev.* 205, 231; K. Hopt, 'Auf dem Weg zum deutschen Übernahmegesetz', *Festschrift in honour of Hans-Georg Koppensteiner* (Vienna: LexisNexis, 2001), 61, 64.

[87] Magnuson, 'Takeover Regulation in the United States and Europe: An Institutional Approach', 230.

[88] Edwards, 'The Directive on Takeover Bids – Not Worth the Paper It's Written on?', 426.

Furthermore, the focus of the legislator had already shifted shortly before the adoption of the TOD. While at earlier stages, the MBR was in the limelight, after the turn of the millennium, both the content of the non-frustration rule and the bidder's possibilities to assert itself against preventive defensive measures (e.g. multiple-voting shares) at the (first) general meeting of the target company (break-through rule) proved paramount. In the TOD as enacted, both provisions are only optional for the Member States (Art. 12(1) and (2)). This optionality is supplemented by the 'reciprocity rule' (Art. 12(3)), which was only included in the negotiations in 2003 under the Portuguese presidency of the Council.[89] The TOD thus offers the Member States a very flexible model for organising takeover law according to their (national) wishes. It is completely in line with this approach that many key aspects of the MBR were also thus placed in the hands of the Member States accordingly.

On the whole, the attitude of the Member States towards the MBR was not always based on a considered judgement of the rule's merits. At least the introduction of the MBR in France can be traced back to the wish of the supervisory authorities at the time to compensate for the 'breach of the investment treaty'. In the other three countries included in this chapter, however, the changing outlook in the late 1990s and early 2000s was not merely a result of diverging objective assessments of the MBR's advantages. In Austria, policymakers only became more interested in take-over law when the governing parties came under pressure to remedy the existing lacuna in the law, following a spectacular takeover in the financial sector. The resistance of large shareholders prevented the full realisation of the principle of equal treatment and instead led (for the time being) to the introduction of a discount of 15 per cent in comparison to the price which the bidder had to pay in order to obtain the controlling block of shares. In Germany, the potential conflict with group law was the dominant topic of discussion for a long time. This conflict had to be resolved first, and only thereafter could the path be opened up for the introduction of the MBR. This was facilitated by the hostile takeover of Mannesmann by Vodafone, which drew the attention of large industrial companies and, subsequently, also led the German government to abandon the strict non-frustration rule. Influential stakeholders in Sweden had a similarly strong influence on national legislation. In the 1990s, the Wallenberg family discovered the MBR as a way to better defend their controlling stakes in listed companies against hostile takeover attempts from abroad. As a result, contrary to initial reservations, the family dropped its opposition to the MBR.

Briefly summarised, the political tug-of-war over the MBR, including attempts to hijack the legislation, commonly known as regulatory capture, has left its mark. Ultimately, however, the change of opinion in the Member States also facilitated the introduction of the MBR at the European level. While the TOD's MBR became

89 See M. Gatti, 'Optionality Arrangements and Reciprocity in the European Takeover Directive' (2003), *European Business and Organization Law Review* 553, 557, 572 et seq.

more open to Member State-specific solutions over time, reservations in Member States against the rule evaporated over time. Both developments taken together enabled the European legislator to pass its version of the MBR.

6.6 THE IMPACT ON CAPITAL MARKETS

When the TOD finally entered into force, mainly thanks to the many political compromises the Commission was willing to make, it was not met with unfettered enthusiasm. Some policymakers and scholars even stated that the directive '[has] fallen victim to horse-trading and unholy alliances'[90] or that it only has the character of 'housekeeping rules'.[91]

The MBR was not spared this criticism either. The academic literature recognised that Article 5 – together with the provisions on squeeze-outs and the sell-out right (Arts. 15 and 16) – could have a fundamental influence on the market for corporate control in Europe. However, according to its critics, the MBR does not create a level playing field in the Member States because it only regulates a fraction of the regulatory issues and delegates the rest to the Member States, resulting in twenty-five different MBRs.[92] Moreover, it was claimed that the MBR has highly dubious effects on shareholder wealth and the company's cost of capital, and lastly, although the MBR could perhaps strengthen the efficiency and integration of European capital markets, it would have to be coupled with the mandatory – not voluntary – option for shareholders to authorise defensive measures against takeover bids.

This assessment is largely in line with the findings of an earlier article by one of the co-authors.[93] As a result, the MBR under the TOD failed to establish a level playing field, mainly because there was no political agreement between the Member States. The regulatory approach of the TOD allowed them to introduce additional safeguards, which may make sense for fitting the provision into the respective local environment, but to a large extent misses the original objective of the TOD. Indeed, the European legislator was also unsuccessful in harmonising the MBR. In particular, the triggering event lacks substantial provisions with binding requirements for the Member States – for example, with regard to the threshold for voting rights that activate the MBR and exemptions therefrom. Finally, the provisions on acting in concert only have a minimal effect. In fact, there are many

90 Statement by Frits Bolkestein, Internal Market Commissioner; cited in Magnuson, 'Takeover Regulation in the United States and Europe: An Institutional Approach', 233.

91 L. Enriques, 'The Mandatory Bid Rule in the Takeover Directive: Harmonization Without Foundation?' (2004), 1 *European Company and Financial Law Review* 440, 441.

92 Ibid., 456; see also Edwards, 'The Directive on Takeover Bids – Not Worth the Paper It's Written on?', 434, stating that the 'harmonising effect of Article 5 may prove minimal given its failure to define a uniform threshold for control; certainly, the prospect of varying thresholds across the Union is at odds with the avowed aim of creating a level playing field'.

93 Winner, 'Does the European Union have a Mandatory Bid Rule?', 1179, 1193 et seq. (results and outlook).

different approaches in the European Union as to how the MBR has been shaped legislatively.

Consequently, the MBR in the TOD had only a minimal impact on the capital markets in Europe. The larger jurisdictions already had an MBR in place prior to the adoption of the TOD, except for Germany, where the WpÜG only came into force in 2002. However, for smaller Member States without a long tradition of takeover law and/or strong capital markets, the assessment may be different and the MBR may have had a greater influence. One interesting example is Poland, whose takeover law has undergone various reforms over the last thirty years. The implementation of the TOD provided the impetus for a major reform of takeover law following Poland's accession to the EU.[94] However, the combination of two control thresholds (33 and 66 per cent respectively) that followed the reform was predominantly viewed negatively by the academic community, and was considered to be an inadequate implementation of Article 5 of the TOD; it has been changed only very recently.[95]

6.7 CONCLUSIONS

- The MBR has had an eventful legislative history, characterised by political compromises, the active influencing of legislative procedures (regulatory capture) and ongoing controversies about the economic rationale behind the MBR.
- Although the changing mood at Member State-level enabled the introduction of the MBR and ultimately the adoption of the TOD, the Commission had to pay dearly for this: Art. 5 TOD reflects a minimum compromise that leaves many regulatory issues of the MBR open and delegates decisions to the Member States. The TOD has not created a level playing field for market participants and has therefore failed to fulfil a key regulatory objective, also in the area of the MBR.
- The MBR did not have a major impact on the European market for corporate control. Most of the larger jurisdictions in Europe already had an MBR in place when the TOD finally came into force. The impact on smaller Member States which do not have a long tradition in takeover law might justify a more nuanced view.

[94] See T. Regucki, 'Polish Takeover Regulation: The Recent Chapter in the Long Story of Flawed Rules, Legislative Hesitation and Policy Mistakes' (2024), 25 *EBOR* 385, 392 et seq. (Pt 4.1: Regulatory Background and Typology of Takeover Bids in the Act on Public Offering).

[95] See the recent amendments to Art. 72 Act on Public Offering, Conditions Governing the Introduction of Financial Instruments to Organised Trading and Public Companies by Art. 11 Act of 22 April 2022, *Journal of Laws* 2022, item 872, in force from 26 September 2023.

7

Derogations from the Mandatory Bid Rule

Rolf Skog and Erik Sjöman

7.1 INTRODUCTION

The primary mechanism provided by the EU Takeover Bids Directive[1] intended to ensure that minority shareholders' interests are protected on a change of control is the mandatory bid rule.[2] This rule provides that when, as a result of an acquisition of securities, a person (alone or with parties acting in concert) reaches the threshold for control set at national level, at the earliest opportunity that person must make a bid to all other holders of the securities for all their holdings at an equitable price.

The Directive states that Member States may provide derogations from their national rules in this area, provided that the general principles of the Directive are respected.[3]

Recital 6 of the Directive reads:

> (6) In order to be effective, takeover regulation should be flexible and capable of dealing with new circumstances as they arise and should accordingly provide for the possibility of exceptions and derogations. However, in applying any rules or exceptions laid down or in granting any derogations, supervisory authorities should respect certain general principles.

Article 4(5), second paragraph, of the Directive reads:

> Provided that the general principles laid down in Article 3(1) are respected, Member States may provide in the rules that they make or introduce pursuant to this Directive for derogations from those rules:
>
> (i) by including such derogations in their national rules, in order to take account of circumstances determined at national level;
> and/or

[1] Parliament and Council Directive 2004/25/EC On Takeover Bids, 2004 O.J. (L142/12) (the Directive).

[2] Article 5 of the Directive and Recital 9 of the preamble.

[3] Article 4(5) of the Directive.

(ii) by granting their supervisory authorities, where they are competent, powers to waive such national rules, to take account of the circumstances referred to in (i) or in other specific circumstances, in which case a reasoned decision must be required.

The general principles of the Directive include the principle that if a person acquires control of a company, the other holders of the securities must be protected.[4] As set out in Article 4(5), derogations from the mandatory bid rule may be provided either by including them directly in the national legislation or by granting the national supervisory authorities powers to waive the national rules (ad hoc or in casu dispensations or exemptions).

All Member States have made or allowed for derogations from the mandatory bid rule. In this chapter, we use the term 'derogation' or 'exemption' as the broader notions, covering both statutory derogations and derogations by way of dispensation in an individual case.

We do not address in this chapter whether the mandatory bid rule is at all an efficient tool to achieve the overall goals of European takeover regulation.[5] Rather, we accept, for the purposes of this chapter, the mandatory bid rule and its intended purposes as is. Nor do we address the implementation generally of the mandatory bid rule in the Member States but focus entirely on derogations.

7.2 THE MANDATORY BID RULE AND THE SCOPE FOR DEROGATIONS

7.2.1 *The 2012 External Study*

As part of the mandatory five-year review of the application of the Directive in accordance with Article 20 of the Directive, an external study was carried out on behalf of the Commission (the External Study).[6]

The External Study included an extensive review of the application of the mandatory bid rule, including the possibility to derogate from it. The External Study showed that all Member States, as permitted by the Directive, allowed

4 Article 3(1)(a) of the Directive.

5 See, for example, J. L. Hansen, 'The Mandatory Bid Rule: Still Unnecessary, Unjustifiable and Inefficient After All These Years', and M. Winner, 'Does the European Union have a mandatory bid rule?' Both papers are published in *Festschrift in Honour of Rolf Skog* (Stockholm: Norstedts Juridik, 2021). See also R. Skog, 'Does Sweden Need a Mandatory Bid Rule?' (1995); L. Enriques, 'The Mandatory Bid Rule in the Takeover Directive: Harmonization Without Foundation?' (2004) *European Company and Financial Law Review* 440; E. Schuster, 'The Mandatory Bid Rule: Efficient, after All?' (2013) *Modern Law Review* 529; and P. Agstner and D. M. Mascheroni, 'Breach of the Mandatory Bid Rule: Minority Shareholders' Protection in the Public vs. Private Enforcement Debate' (2020) *European Company and Financial Law Review* 726.

6 Marccus Partners, in cooperation with the Centre for European Policy Studies, 'Study on the application of Directive 2004/25/EC on takeover bids' (June 2012).

derogations from the mandatory bid rule, but that the Member States had chosen quite different approaches in this regard.

The External Study distinguishes between Member States which rely entirely or primarily on statutory derogations and those with a system primarily based on ad hoc (or in casu) derogations, where the supervisory authority or similar body (such as a Takeover Panel) tries applications for dispensation in each individual case. The latter category includes, among others, Ireland and the Nordics. The German supervisory authority can also grant exemptions from the mandatory bid rule 'if, having regard to the interests of the applicant and the holders of shares in the target company, this appears justified in view of the manner of attainment, the objectives being pursued with the attainment of control, a drop below the control threshold subsequent to the attainment of control, the shareholder structure of the target company, or the actual possibility of exercising control'.[7] In France, the regulations do not give the supervisory authority an express right to discretionarily grant exemptions, but the authority has given itself this right anyway. A relatively common feature is that, in certain situations, a derogation is permissible provided that the shareholders of the listed company in question approve that a mandatory bid need not be made. This is commonly referred to as a whitewash procedure.

The External Study thoroughly reviewed the basis for granting mandatory bid derogations either by law or in the practices of the relevant supervisory authority.

Several different categories of derogations can be identified.

(1) The first category may be referred to as *technical exemptions*. This includes exemptions due to the characteristics of the individual listed company – for example, if the listed company is an open-ended investment company. The Directive states that Member States in these cases do not need to apply the mandatory bid rule, and in many Member States this is reflected in the wording of the mandatory bid rule itself. In some Member States, however, such as the Netherlands and Hungary, explicit exemptions are stipulated by law.

The technical exemption category also covers cases where an investor exceeds the mandatory bid threshold and, in doing so, becomes such a large shareholder in the target company that a compulsory acquisition procedure (squeeze-out) can be initiated. In several Member States, such as Austria and Sweden, the mandatory bid rule does not apply in such situations.

In the same vein, this category includes the case where an investor which has exceeded the mandatory bid threshold and become a controlling owner in a company enters into an agreement with the controlled company whereby the latter submits to the controlling

[7] 37 Wertpapiererwerbs- und Übernahmegesetz vom 20. Dezember 2001 (BGBl. I S. 3822).

company's management. Such a *Beherrschungsvertrag* can be entered into in Germany and the Czech Republic, which, in such cases, also constitutes exemptions from the mandatory bid rule, provided that the controlling company effects a buyout of the minority shareholders.

(2) A significantly larger and, in practical terms, more important sub-group is *exemptions granted (for lack of a better word) to 'protect' the controlling shareholder or offeror*.

This includes transactions which have *not resulted in a real change of control* even though the mandatory bid threshold has formally been exceeded – for example, when the transaction is carried out among parties that are members of the same group of companies. Exemptions of this type are available in Germany, France, Italy, the Netherlands, Sweden and a number of other Member States.

A related situation that falls within this category is where someone has exceeded the threshold but *there is an even larger shareholder in the company*. In certain Member States the exemption is worded as simply as that, while in others it is more complicated. In Germany, for example, no mandatory bid is required if a shareholder has exceeded the threshold but, against the backdrop of the level of participation at the last three general meetings, cannot be expected to obtain a majority of the votes at the next general meeting because there is another, larger shareholder.

The category also includes instances where the mandatory bid threshold has been *exceeded by mistake or without the intent of taking control of the company*, in certain cases provided that the holding only marginally exceeds the threshold, typically by no more than a couple of percentage points. Among Member States with such exemptions are Ireland, Germany, France, Italy and the Netherlands. These Member States invariably require that the holding is reduced below the threshold within a specific period of time. In certain Member States, such as Germany, this must be done without delay; others provide a specific time limit: one month in the Netherlands, within half a year in France and within one year in Italy, to name a few.

There are also a number of situations where an exemption is granted to a shareholder potentially facing a mandatory bid even though exceeding the threshold has, in fact, resulted in a change of control. This includes cases where the threshold has been exceeded through a *voluntary bid* to acquire all the shares. Although the Directive clearly states that a mandatory bid obligation does not apply in this case,[8] the transposition of this provision varies by Member State. Certain Member

[8] See Article 5(2) of the Directive.

States, such as the Netherlands, Belgium, Portugal and Sweden, do not require more than what is stated in the Directive – that is, an offer to acquire all the shares in the company. In other Member States, such as Germany, Spain and Greece, the exemption requires a certain minimum price in the voluntary offering. Another qualification may be that, for the exemption to apply, the voluntary offering may only be implemented if the bidder obtains at least half of the votes of all outstanding shares in the company.

Moreover, there are cases where the mandatory bid threshold is exceeded *without the shareholder in question actively acquiring any shares* – for example, if the company reduced its total number of shares through a redemption and thereby pushed the shareholder beyond the mandatory bid threshold. Exemptions are permitted in such cases in Ireland, Germany, France, Italy and Sweden, among others.

This group of exemptions also includes *indirect shifts in controlling ownership*. Several Member States have rules for cases where someone takes control of a listed company by acquiring shares in a holding company, where a substantive test is performed, and the mandatory bid rule does not apply if the shares in the listed company represent only a certain small percentage of the net assets of the holding company (in Germany not more than 20 per cent). Other Member States that apply the substantive test include France, Belgium and Austria.

A fairly obvious group of exemptions related to shareholders who potentially face a mandatory bid are cases in which shares have been acquired by gift, inheritance, marriage, divorce and so on. Such exemptions are available in most Member States. In Spain, to take one example, exemptions are made for acquisitions without consideration *causa mortis* and *inter vivos*, the latter only on the condition that the buyer has not acquired shares in the company during the most recent twelve-month period and has not entered into a cooperation agreement with the seller.

(3) A third category is *exemptions related to creditors*. This typically involves exemptions from a mandatory bid in cases where the shares in question have been acquired as a result of the realization of a pledge or similar. In certain Member States, such as Germany and Denmark, this exemption is unconditional. In others, such as Belgium, the shares in question must be disposed of within a specific time and may not be voted at the general meeting before this is done.

(4) A fourth and final category is *exemptions related to stakeholders other than creditors*. The External Study states that the purpose of such an exemption is to maintain an acceptable balance between the interests

of shareholders and other stakeholders in light of the company's long-term interests.

One example comprises cases where control is obtained in order to rescue a company in financial distress. Exemptions of this type are granted in most Member States by law or in practice. In certain Member States, the exemption is fairly straightforward. In Ireland, the only condition is that the shares are subscribed in a share issue necessary for the company's survival. In other Member States, such as Italy, it is considerably more complex.

This category also includes exemptions in situations where an investor has exceeded the threshold for a mandatory bid as the result of a company's business decision or other corporate action that ultimately is likely to benefit its shareholders. A typical example is exemptions related to new share issues. In Ireland, Denmark, Sweden and Finland, for example, exemptions are granted if a shareholder subscribes for its pro rata share of a rights offering and exceeds the threshold due to low take-up by others. Exemptions are also granted in several Member States in connection with directed share issues, but this generally requires a whitewash procedure. In Cyprus, for example, exemptions are granted provided that the decision to disapply shareholder pre-emption rights has been made by the shareholders, that the decision is supported by a simple majority of the votes excluding shares represented by the shareholder(s) targeted by the directed issue, and that the shareholders have been duly informed prior to the general meeting. Exemptions are also available in several Member States if the threshold is exceeded due to a merger, demerger or similar arrangement to reorganize the company.

There are also Member States where mandatory bid exemptions are provided by law to defend against hostile takeovers. In the Netherlands and Belgium, a company may, in certain circumstances, separate the voting rights of the shares from their economic rights and place the voting right component in a protective foundation to defend management against a hostile takeover. Not surprisingly, a transaction can be exempted from a mandatory bid in cases where such a foundation's holding exceeds the threshold.

Lastly, this category of exemptions includes acquisitions of controlling holdings within the framework of privatizations of formerly publicly owned enterprises. In Greece, for example, the takeover rules contain an exemption from mandatory bids for just such an acquisition.

In total, the External Study cited as many as thirty-six reasons for mandatory bid derogations, whether statutory or ad hoc.

7.2.2 *The 2012 Commission Review Report*

Also in 2012, the European Commission published its report on the application of the Directive.[9] Broadly, the Commission concluded, based on the External Study, that the regime created by the Directive was working satisfactorily and that no structural compliance issues had emerged. Consequently, the Commission's report concluded that the Directive should not be amended – for example, by making its optional articles mandatory.

The conclusion that the mandatory bid rule was 'effective' is by no means the same as declaring it 'economically efficient' but probably merely reflects the finding that the rule was generally observed in national law. The External Study rather recognized the mandatory bid rule as an anti-takeover measure, which implied an 'intrinsic contradiction' between the rule and the intended purpose of the Directive – namely, to facilitate takeovers as an instrument of industrial reorganization and development.[10] This contradiction could perhaps be explained as part of an ambition to strike a balance between furthering takeovers and protecting minority shareholders, provided of course that one accepts the premise that such protection is indeed needed beyond merely safeguarding fair play when takeover bids are actually made.

Nevertheless, the report identified a number of areas where the rules of the Directive could merit clarification in order to improve legal certainty and the effective exercise of the rights of shareholders. One of these areas was the protection of minority shareholders in the case of a change of control.

The Commission noted that, within the range of different national derogations to the mandatory bid rule, it is not always clear how the protection of minority shareholders is ensured on a change of control. As set out in Article 4(5) of the Directive, Member States that provide for derogations must respect the general principles of the Directive, one of which is the above-mentioned principle that, if a person acquires control of a listed company, the other holders of securities must be protected.

The Commission noted in this regard that the Directive does not regulate how Member States are to ensure that the general principles are respected and said that it intended to carry out further investigation on how minority shareholders are protected when a national derogation to the mandatory bid rule applies. More information, the Commission continued, was needed on the scope of application of national derogations to the mandatory bid rule, on the extent to which national

[9] 'Report from the Commission to the European Parliament, the Council, the European Economic and Social Committee and the Committee of the Regions, Application of Directive 2004/25/EC on takeover bids', COM (2012) 347 final. See also Commission Staff Working Document, 'Report on the Implementation of the Directive on Takeover Bids', SEC (2007) 268 (21 February 2007).

[10] External Study, p. 18.

derogations limited the protection of minority shareholders in change of control situations and, where relevant, what alternative mechanisms existed in national law to protect minority shareholders on a change of control. The Commission said that, if the protection of minority shareholders proved to be inadequate, the Commission would take necessary steps (for example, through infringement procedures) to restore the effective application of the relevant general principle of the Directive.

Accordingly, in 2013, the Commission collected information on the topic from the Member States to better understand the state of play in the Member States. This collection of information confirmed the findings in the External Study but did not lead to any further measures being taken or proposed by the Commission. Apparently, the Commission found that there was not sufficient cause for taking any further action after all. An updated inquiry by us with colleagues across the Member States in 2023 shows that the situation identified already in 2012–2013 is still true in most if not all regards.

In its 2012 report, the Commission also referenced the findings of the External Study when it comes to the mandatory bid exemption included directly in the Directive for situations where control has been acquired following a voluntary bid for all shares of the company.[11] It was noted that this had sometimes created a possibility for offerors to circumvent the mandatory bid rule by acquiring a stake close to the mandatory bid threshold and then launching a voluntary bid for a low price (so-called *creep in*). As a consequence, the offeror would cross the mandatory bid threshold without giving minority shareholders a fair chance to exit the company and share in the control premium. The Commission noted that this was clearly not in line with the objective of the Directive to protect minority shareholders on a change of control, although it did not appear to breach the letter of the Directive. Examples in national legislation, such as additional mandatory bid thresholds or minimum acceptance conditions to takeover bids, showed, the Commission stated, that there are possibilities to prevent the use of this technique. The Commission stated that it would take the appropriate steps to discourage the use of this technique across the EU, such as through bilateral discussions with the relevant Member States or Commission recommendations. We are not aware of any such bilateral discussions and to our knowledge no recommendations have been issued.

7.3 DEROGATIONS AND THE PROTECTION OF MINORITY SHAREHOLDERS

The proviso in Article 4(5) of the Directive makes reference to *all* general principles set out in Article 3(1). However, only Principle (a), regarding the protection of minority shareholders on a change of control, is relevant in practice when it comes to a derogation from the mandatory bid rule.

[11] See Article 5(2) of the Directive.

The mandatory bid rule itself is intended to protect the minority shareholders on a change of control by affording them an exit right and a share in the control premium. Per definition, if an exemption from the mandatory bid rule is granted, the shareholders will *not* be afforded this protection.

What, then, does the reference in Article 4(5) to the minority protection principle in Article 3(1) mean in the case of a derogation from the mandatory bid rule?[12]

Arguably, when it comes to exemptions from the mandatory bid rule, the reference to the principles does not appear to add much at all, which may explain why several Member States have not explicitly incorporated the reference to the principles in their statutory mandatory bid exemption regimes. Surely, however, the reference cannot be assumed to mean nothing.

We believe that it is helpful to analyse the minority protection requirement in light of the various types of derogation used.

(a) An apparently uncontroversial example is when the mandatory bid rule is formally triggered despite there being *no real change of control*. In such a situation, there is no valid reason for upholding the mandatory bid rule regardless of any other minority protections. In these cases, the derogation – which typically comes in the form of an ad hoc dispensation – rather serves as a safety valve to take care of situations which should not have been caught by the mandatory bid rule in the first place.

(b) From the point of view of affording specific minority protection in connection with a specific derogation, situations where the derogation is available subject to compliance with a *whitewash procedure* are straightforward. In these cases, the whitewash procedure itself offers minority protection through shareholder scrutiny and approval by a majority of the minority. The whitewash approach is typically used for situations where it might otherwise have been more difficult to identify how minority protection would be safeguarded. A typical example is where a dispensation is granted for a corporate acquisition by the listed company, with a sufficient number of new shares being issued as consideration to lead to control by the seller. Another example is dispensations enabling an underwriter of a rights offering to honour its obligations even if this leads to control.

    Another example of a typical case of derogation where the context of the derogation includes immediate alternative minority protection, is when the acquirer immediately upon obtaining control goes on to

[12] Article 4(5) of the Directive allows for derogations from *other* provisions of the Directive too. The specific question here, however, is what the reference to the general principles means in the context of derogating from the mandatory bid rule.

pursue an adequately protective compulsory acquisition procedure (squeeze-out; cf. Article 15 of the Directive).

(c) In many other situations, the question of minority protection is rather a matter of generally testing whether the reasons for an exemption, typically or in an individual case, *outweigh* the reasons for a mandatory bid.[13]

This is relevant, for example, upon receipt of a gift or inheritance of a controlling stake, in creditor-related derogatory situations, in cases of financial distress or otherwise when the derogation is deemed necessary to achieve an outcome which is more beneficial to the collective of shareholders than in foreseeable alternative scenarios. The latter can, for example, be the case if a derogation is granted to allow a significant directed share issue needed to rescue the listed company from imminent bankruptcy, a scenario which would clearly be more damaging to the interests of all shareholders than a shift in control without a mandatory bid.

Commonly, in these situations, the derogations require a decision from the supervisory authority or similar body involving the exercise of some degree of discretion on its part. This allows for the interests of minority shareholders to be appropriately taken into account in the specific situation at hand. All Member States seem to take the view that their national supervisory authorities, when granting a dispensation from the mandatory bid rule, must always comply with the general principle of minority protection, despite this not always being explicitly set out in statute.[14,15]

In these instances, it may be relevant to take into account the general corporate law minority protection regime that applies in the listed company in question. Such a regime may include, for example, corporate law provisions designed to prevent resolutions which provide a shareholder with an undue advantage to the detriment of the company or other shareholders. It may also include rules requiring certain

[13] Clearly, this is true also in the whitewash examples, though without the specific protection afforded by the whitewash procedure itself.

[14] In our home Member State (Sweden), for example, the typical examples of grounds for ad hoc dispensations, and the need to take into account the intended purpose of the mandatory bid rule when trying applications, are set out in the preparatory works pertaining to the mandatory bid rule. In practice, this means that, even if a particular application for dispensation relates to a situation where dispensation is typically granted, the Swedish Takeover Panel (the Securities Council) cannot grant a dispensation in the specific case unless deemed appropriate in light of the interests of the minority shareholders.

[15] Also, decisions granting dispensations from the mandatory bid rule are typically appealable, cf. Recital 8 of the Directive.

resolutions to be passed by a qualified majority vote of the shareholders, special rules on related-party transactions and so on.[16]

As a general rule, derogations are often rightly seen as a necessary tool to provide the flexibility needed to ensure the smooth functioning of the market and avoiding unfair or disproportionate consequences of the mandatory bid rule. It may sometimes simply, and completely legitimately, be a matter of concluding in an individual case that the reasons for upholding the mandatory bid rule, in light of the purpose of the rule, do not outweigh the reasons for a dispensation – that is, the minority holders are better off, or at least not relevantly worse off, if a dispensation is granted.[17]

Here the difficulty rather lies in the concrete application of derogatory powers in a potentially widely diverging set of circumstances. When and to what extent, more precisely, should the interests of other stakeholders prevail over the interests of minority shareholders otherwise protected by the mandatory bid rule? It has been discussed whether a solution would be for the Commission to draw up an exhaustive list of acceptable derogations. Clearly, however, this is not a workable solution. In practice, the situations that arise are diverse and cannot be adequately covered by detailed rules, and any such detailed rules should in any event be left for the Member States to decide in light of the specificities of their own governance models.[18]

In countries with active stock markets, it has proven appropriate or even necessary, for the purposes discussed above, to grant the supervisory authority or similar body discretion to decide on ad hoc dispensations.

[16] One might ask how situations where a mandatory bid has been triggered by mistake, or only technically or temporarily, fit into this line of reasoning? Here, requiring the shareholder to sell down within a specified period of time is typically a relevant tool.

[17] Cf. the European Court of Justice's judgment of 15 October 2009 in case C-101/08, *Audiolux SA e.a v Groupe Bruxelles Lambert SA (GBL) and Others and Bertelsmann AG and Others* [2009] ECR I-9823, paragraph 58: 'The establishing of an obligation on dominant shareholders and the fixing of the conditions triggering such an obligation would require a decision as to whether, in the specific situation in which a shareholder acquires or strengthens his control of a company, the minority shareholders need special protection which must be ensured by the imposition of an obligation on the dominant shareholder. Such a decision would presuppose both the weighing of the interests of the minority shareholders and those of the dominant shareholder and of the not inconsiderable consequences for corporate takeovers, and would require specific expression, in accordance with the principle of legal certainty, so that those concerned could ascertain unequivocally what their rights and obligations were and take steps accordingly (see, as regards the requirements for the principle of legal certainty, Case C-345/06, *Heinrich* [2009] ECR I-0000, paragraph 44).'

[18] See, for example, European Company Law Experts (ECLE), 'Response to the European Commission's Report on the Application of the Takeover Bids Directive', *University of Cambridge Faculty of Law Research Paper* No. 5/2014 and *Oxford Legal Studies Research Paper* No. 55/2014.

> This is desirable to provide optimal flexibility ensuring the smooth functioning of the market by avoiding unfair or disproportionate consequences of the mandatory bid rule in individual cases. This is also desirable particularly in light of the interest of the parties concerned to be able to get an expedient and authoritative decision on what applies. Courts will generally not be able to provide this at sufficiently short notice. The discretion of the supervisory authority cannot of course be exercised arbitrarily but must always properly take into account the minority protective purpose of the mandatory bid rule. Predictability and transparency are key aspects, and a transparent teleological application of the power to grant derogations is necessary to enable an evaluation of whether the derogatory practices are in line with the Directive.[19]

This analysis shows that, despite the multiplicity of derogations of various sorts, it is not a problem per se that there are a lot of derogations and that these vary amongst the Member States. On the contrary, correctly applied, the derogations are legitimate and rather confirm that the Directive was right in allowing the Member States to derogate, statutorily or ad hoc, from the mandatory bid rule. Accordingly, the fact that the Commission's collection of additional information back in 2013 did not lead to any measures being taken is no surprise. Rather, on balance, the current regime seems to be sensible and should not be materially altered.

The fact that rules and practices on derogations from the mandatory bid rule vary significantly among the Member States could be viewed of course as a failure from the point of view of the interest of harmonization. However, in this field of the law, arguably, harmonization is not an independent value, whereas flexibility and adaptability at Member State level furthers the overall objectives of the Directives, provided that the flexibility and discretion is exercised loyally with the purpose of the Directive.[20]

7.4 THE NATURE OF THE DEROGATION – IS THE SHAREHOLDER FREE TO INCREASE ITS HOLDING FURTHER?

One aspect which was not explored in detail in the 2012 External Study is the *nature* of the derogation – namely, what does it *mean* to have been granted an exemption or

[19] ECLE (see n 18) has highlighted a few suggestions on how to safeguard predictability and transparency when supervisory authorities exercise discretion, including ensuring that decisions are published, adequately reasoned and effectively challengeable. In fact, unqualified statutory derogations, without the possibility of *in casu* review by the supervisory authority on the basis of an application for dispensation, perhaps leaves the *most* room for doubt on how minority protection is ensured in each individual case.

[20] The fact that some Member States may not be entirely enthusiastic about the merits of the mandatory bid rule (cf.n 5) of course is *not*, as such, a valid reason for a liberal dispensation regime.

to rely on a statutory derogation? Is the shareholder free to increase its holdings further or does the mandatory bid rule strike again on further acquisitions or when reaching some second threshold of holdings? And if the shareholder reaches, say, 40 per cent in an exempt transaction, what applies if the shareholder then reduces the holding to, say, 35 per cent? Is the shareholder then entitled to increase again, back to 40 per cent, without a new exemption?

Again, all Member States have made or allowed for derogations from the mandatory bid rule to ensure the proper functioning of the market. But what, exactly, is the meaning of an exemption from the rule?

In our home Member State, Sweden, the substance of an exemption is merely that the shareholder may, due to the specific circumstances meriting the exemption, carry out *the particular exempt transaction* (i.e. the transaction leading to the 40 per cent holding in the example above) without having to make a bid for all shares. But, unless otherwise set out in the decision to grant the dispensation, the shareholder cannot acquire more shares outside the scope of that particular transaction. If the shareholder acquires one single share on top of the 40 per cent, the mandatory bid is triggered and a bid for all the remaining shares must be made.[21] This tight link to the exempt transaction even means that further acquisitions trigger a mandatory bid even if the shareholder has reduced its holding in the meantime.

The above is true as a principal rule in Sweden, but it does not always apply. For example, if a mandatory bid exemption is granted for a shareholder who inherits a controlling stake, and the deceased was free of any mandatory bid obligations (for example, because the deceased held the controlling stake already before the introduction of the statutory mandatory bid rule in 2006), the new shareholder will also be free to subsequently increase the shareholding. If you like, the new shareholder inherits not only the shares, it also 'inherits' the freedom from mandatory bid obligations upon any subsequent increase of the holding. This, however, is dependent on the terms of the specific ad hoc dispensation. Absent a provision in the dispensation to this effect, the principal rule described above will apply. In practice, the Swedish Takeover Panel will typically explicitly state *either/or*, for the sake of clarity.

In this regard, too, the rules and practices of the Member States vary. Some Member States have a similar principal rule as Sweden, depending on the type of derogatory situation. This is true, for example, for France and similarly Germany. Also, in some Member States the same would apply provided that the exempt transaction brings the shareholder's holdings to above 50 per cent. This is true, for

[21] In line with this, if the shareholder chooses to sell shares so that the shareholding then amounts to, say, 37 per cent, the mandatory bid rule is triggered upon the acquisition of one additional share – that is, the shareholder is not afforded the right to move freely up and down as long as 40 per cent is not passed.

example, in Ireland and Portugal. Conversely, in other Member States, such as Germany, Spain and Finland, the principal rule would be that the shareholder is indeed free to increase its shareholding beyond where it ends up following the specific transaction triggering the mandatory bid rule.

It is apparent already from the above very brief overview that this is another aspect where the Member States have taken quite different views. Sometimes it is relatively clear cut: either the exempt shareholder is free to increase its holding further, or it is not. Sometimes, however, this depends on the circumstances, notably sometimes on the particular basis for the exemption.

This is an aspect which is not specifically regulated by the Directive. Arguably, defining the specific meaning of a dispensation should be addressed in light of the reference in Article 4(5) to the general principles in Article 3(1).

The shareholder should only be allowed to increase further if the other shareholders are still adequately protected, or if there is at least no significant disadvantages for minority holders that outweigh the reasons for allowing the controlling shareholder to do so. In fact, linking the dispensation to the specific exempt transaction may be seen as a tool to satisfy the interest of minority protection when derogating from the mandatory bid rule, and, conversely, when a derogation does entitle the shareholder to increase its holding further, the requirement of Article 4(5) for alternative minority protection may be stricter.

The line of reasoning described above, however, is not necessarily shared by everyone. One different view, which is valid enough to be considered, is that if a derogation is available or granted for a transaction whereby someone acquires control over a listed company, then that should be it in terms of satisfying the purpose of the mandatory bid rule. The shareholder, one could argue, was entitled to take control without having to make a mandatory bid because sufficient cause to merit a mandatory bid did not exist. Why, then, should the shareholder be obliged to make such a bid at some *later* point in time, when the shareholder is *already* in control and the other shareholders (and the market generally) have already adjusted to the fact that there is a new controlling shareholder and no exit right or share in any control premium?

The question of the nature of the derogation in the context of further acquisitions is somewhat linked to the *creep-up* problem discussed in the External Study and the 2012 Commission report (see Section 7.2.2). Clearly, if a shareholder reaches, say, 40 per cent on the basis of an exemption granted, but under the general mandatory bid regime is in any event obliged to make a bid upon each acquisition of a further share between 30 and 50 per cent, then no further inquiry into the exact meaning of the exemption is needed. Conversely, in Member States without a creep-up regime (such as Sweden) the question of the nature of being exempt becomes more apparently important and reveals an additional dimension of complexity, and lack of convergence among the Member States, of the mandatory bid derogation regime.

7.5 TOO MANY DEROGATIONS?

It would appear that the Member States have chosen, for a wide variety of situations, to make use of the possibility offered by the Directive to statutorily derogate from the mandatory bid rule or to allow the supervisory authority or similar body to grant ad hoc dispensations. It has even been said that, in the context of the mandatory offer bid rule, 'the exception is the rule'.[22]

As noted already in the 2012 External Study, the mandatory bid rule in fact operates as an anti-takeover device.[23] Clearly, if an investor might be commercially interested in acquiring a controlling stake in a listed company but is unwilling or unable to finance an acquisition of *all* shares in the company, the investor simply will not put itself in a situation where a mandatory offer is triggered.[24] Clearly, also, an investor will not apply for a dispensation from the mandatory bid rule unless, under the practices of the supervisory authority or similar body, it is relatively clear that such a dispensation will be granted.[25]

Further, importantly, the fact that there may be many situations where a dispensation is typically merited, the number of actually granted dispensations will of course be large if these situations also occur frequently in practice. This is likely to be the case where the ownership structure of the market in question is fairly concentrated (as in Sweden) and the control threshold determined at national level is low in light of such concentration (30 per cent in Sweden, compared to 40 per cent when the mandatory bid rule was introduced in Swedish law well before the implementation of the Directive).

Is, then, the prevalence of a large number of granted dispensations from the mandatory bid rule an indication of a derogatory regime that is too liberal? Sometimes it is indeed argued that the fact that so many derogations are granted and so few mandatory bids are made is an indication of something being wrong with the mandatory bid derogatory regime. We argue that this is not the case. The above offers a few explanations. Indeed, national derogations from the mandatory bid rule affect the *effectiveness* of the rule, in that the rule applies in fewer instances than would otherwise have been the case. But this is by no means problematic if the instances where the mandatory bid rule is disapplied are such that, properly taking into account the interests of the minority shareholders, upholding the rule is not

[22] See ECLE (see n 18), p. 7, and R. Skog and E. Sjöman, 'No Rule, Just Exemptions? Mandatory Bids in Sweden and the EU' (2014) *European Company and Financial Law Review* 393.

[23] External Study, p. 18: 'Legal and economic analysis shows the intrinsic contradiction between the mandatory bid rule, which acts as an anti-takeover device, and the board neutrality rule, breakthrough and squeeze-out rules, the purposes of which are to facilitate bids.'

[24] This is the key reason for why it can be debated whether, ultimately, the mandatory bid rule is at all in the best interests of the shareholders and the overall objectives of the Directive; cf.n 5.

[25] And if the investor *is* willing and able to acquire the entire target company, the investor will typically choose to make a *voluntary* bid, thereby avoiding the restrictions associated with a mandatory bid.

merited.[26] We have so far not found any indications of significant deficiencies on an overall level in this regard, although, of course, the current state of play has by no means created harmonization across the Member States.

7.6 CONCLUDING REMARKS

The Member States have made use of their mandatory bid derogative powers in very different ways. Some derogations are ad hoc: they may be granted by supervisory authorities or approved by the shareholders pursuant to a so-called whitewash procedure. Other derogations are statutorily defined. The derogations can be categorized in different ways. Each category has its own rationale. Many derogations are entirely unproblematic. The best example is probably when a mandatory bid is indeed formally triggered but there is, in fact, no real change of control and hence no reason whatsoever to uphold a device intended to protect shareholders on a control shift.

The typical purpose of other derogations is to balance diverging interests, and not to uphold the mandatory bid rule in a situation where it is deemed to be in the best interest of the collective of shareholders to let a transaction take place without prompting a mandatory bid. These situations are not conceptually problematic either but require more careful attention because a weighing of pros and cons is needed in order to properly take into account the interests of the shareholders. This sometimes merits requiring the exempt transaction to be approved by the shareholders in a majority-of-the-minority resolution (a so-called whitewash procedure). In other cases, such as in rescue operations in an imminently bankrupt company, the reasons militating in favour of a dispensation from the mandatory bid rule may be sufficiently strong to merit a dispensation on the basis merely of the ordinary ex post minority protection afforded by general corporate law. According to the view taken in some Member States, this may particularly be the case if the derogation applies exclusively to the exempt transaction and does not entitle the shareholder to subsequently increase its holding further without triggering a mandatory bid.

Sometimes it is argued that the fact that so many derogations are granted and so few mandatory bids are made is an indication of something being wrong with the derogatory regime. Indeed, national derogations from the mandatory bid rule affect the effectiveness of the rule. But this is not problematic if the instances where the mandatory bid rule is disapplied are such that, properly taking into account the interests of the minority shareholders, they do not merit upholding the rule. We have not found any indications of significant deficiencies on an overall level

[26] On the contrary, it is problematic if national rules do *not* provide for derogations in such situations. One example is where a shareholder formally passes the control threshold but there is another shareholder with a larger, controlling, holding. Not all Member States provide for an exemption in this situation, which is clearly over-restrictive and therefore counter-productive in light of the overall objectives of the Directive.

in this regard. On the contrary, it would be more problematic in light of the overall purposes of the Directive if derogations were *not* offered for such situations.

Of course, the current state of play has not created convergence across the Member States. This, however, should come as no surprise. The mandatory bid rule as such is a minimum harmonization provision. It leaves it to the Member States to set the control threshold(s), to define more precisely what the equitable price is, and to define which parties are to be deemed to be acting in concert for purposes of the rule. It also leaves it to the Member States to define derogations from the rule, and to allow ad hoc dispensations by the supervisory authority or similar body, provided that the principle of minority protection on a change of control is duly taken into account in one way or another. It further leaves it to the Member States to define what the substantive meaning of a derogation is. Again, though, none of this is a bad thing as long as the Member States use the flexibility afforded by the Directive in a loyal way, duly taking into account the overall purpose of the Directive and the purpose of the mandatory bid rule, and apply the rules so as to make sense in the context of local corporate governance models, the structure of the local stock markets, and local protections afforded by general corporate law.

The appetite among the Member States for amendments to the Directive is likely to be very limited, to say the least. When it comes to the regime for derogations from the mandatory bid rule (provided that one accepts the premises for the existence of the mandatory bid rule in the first place), we do not see any pressing regulatory concerns that would argue in favour of trying to improve this appetite.

8

Acting in Concert

Javier García de Enterría and Matteo Gargantini

8.1 THE GENERAL MEANING OF CONCERTED ACTION IN TAKEOVER BIDS

Acting in concert or concerted action amongst several parties is one of the most elusive, imprecise and vague notions in relation to takeover bids, yet at the same time one of the most relevant. In general terms, concerted action plays an instrumental and accessory role, in the sense of preventing the offeror or the target company from using third parties to indirectly perform any action which takeover law prohibits or associates with specific legal consequences. The figure is embedded in takeover bid policy as a whole and affects practically all the duties and obligations binding both the offeror and the target company, which generally are extended to cover any other person collaborating or acting in concert with them.[1]

In the context of the Takeover Bids Directive, for example, the notion of 'parties to the bid' includes the offeror, the offeree company, their respective directors, the offeree company's shareholders, but also all other 'persons acting in concert with such parties' (Art. 2(1)(f)); the equitable price at which mandatory takeover bids must be made is defined as the highest price paid in a period, of a length ranging between six and twelve months, prior to the acquisition of control by the offeror or

This paper is part of a series marking the 20th anniversary of the Takeover Bids Directive and put together by the European Company Law Experts (ECLE) Group (https://europeancompany lawexperts.wordpress.com) with a view to publishing a book collection. The Italian regulation on academic evaluation requires some form of identification of each author's individual contribution to a joint paper. Exclusively for this purpose, we mention that Sections 8.2.3, 8.3.5 and 8.5 were written with the prevalent contribution of Matteo Gargantini, while the two authors equally contributed to the other sections.

[1] In relation to the general meaning of concerted action in takeover bids, see J. García de Enterría, 'Algunas cuestiones del proceso de OPAs sobre Abertis: de conciertos para la modificación de las OPAs y mejoras de la contraprestación en las OPAs de canje' (2019) 24 *Revista de Derecho del Mercado de Valores* 6 (also in J. García de Enterría, *Anuncios preliminares, concertación del voto y ofertas de canje. Estudios sobre OPAs (III)*, (Pamplona: Aranzadi, 2024), p. 149 et seq.).

by the 'persons acting in concert with him/her' (Art. 5(4)); the obligation to increase the bid price in the case of acquisition of shares at a higher price is linked to the acquisitions which may be made by the offeror 'or any person acting in concert with him/her' (Art. 5(5)); the obligation to offer a cash consideration at least as an alternative applies where the offeror or 'persons acting in concert with him/her' have acquired prior to the bid securities carrying 5 per cent or more of the voting rights of the offeree company (Art. 5(5)III); and the offeror must give information in the prospectus about his/her existing holdings in the offeree company, but also about those of the 'persons acting in concert with him/her' (Art. 6(3)(g)).

However, where concerted action is most relevant is in relation to mandatory takeover bids, where the concept's open-ended and elusive nature coexists with the severe impact of its associated effects. The Takeover Bids Directive imposes the obligation to launch the takeover bid where a person, 'as a result of his/her own acquisition *or the acquisition by persons acting in concert with him/her*', holds securities which, 'added to any existing holdings of those securities of *persons acting in concert with him/her*', give him/her a specified percentage of voting rights that confers 'control of the company' (Art. 5(1)).

For all these purposes, persons acting in concert are defined by the Takeover Bids Directive as the 'natural or legal persons who cooperate with the offeror or the offeree company on the basis of an agreement, either express or tacit, either oral or written, aimed either at acquiring control of the offeree company or at frustrating the successful outcome of a bid' (Art. 2(1)(d)). The concept's relevance is evidenced by the UK Takeover Code, from which the mandatory takeover system historically originates, and which had a decisive influence on the content of the Takeover Bids Directive. It states that 'the majority of questions which arise' in the context of the mandatory bid 'relate to persons acting in concert' (Notes on Rule 9.1).

In the European context, the uncertainty that generally accompanies the notion of concerted action itself is aggravated by the existence of different regulatory models for mandatory takeover bids. In some countries, the obligation to launch a takeover bid requires an acquisition of shares (or similar securities) above the relevant threshold, by two or more persons acting in concert. But in other countries the obligation may also be triggered without any acquisition of shares, when several shareholders who have acquired their shares independently (i.e. not in concert) subsequently reach an agreement to exercise their voting rights in a concerted manner. In this way, the intrinsic difficulties that per se characterise the definition and regulatory consequences of concerted action, due to its diffuse and open nature, are exacerbated by the different meaning of the concept in each of these regulatory models. The uncertainty and ambiguity of the concept of concerted action, and the serious doubts that arise with respect to certain forms of shareholder cooperation or collaboration, are particularly problematic at a time when effective shareholder engagement in corporate management has become a relevant legal policy objective.

These shortcomings have been evidenced in many EU countries. This is a result of the scant harmonisation achieved by the Takeover Bids Directive and the consequent persistence of ingrained differences between Member States as to the concept's meaning and scope. But in our opinion, the heart of the matter clearly goes beyond the instrumental and ancillary aspects of a technical definition of concerted action. It is more a matter of the rationale and definition of mandatory takeover bids, which is the real issue behind the debate and controversy that surrounds concerted action in many European countries. This is why it is necessary to start by briefly clarifying some preliminary notions in relation to the mandatory bid system which, despite being common knowledge, are essential to accurately deal with the meaning and notion of acting in concert.

8.2 THE CONCERTED ACQUISITION OF A CONTROLLING INTEREST

8.2.1 *Historical Background*

It is common knowledge that mandatory takeover bids, as a legal procedure imposed when control is acquired over a listed company, are historically derived from the UK Takeover Code (formerly known as the City Code on Takeovers and Mergers). The Code was implemented in the 1970s, when other European countries had practically no awareness of takeover bids as an institution and therefore lacked any regulatory experience in the matter.[2] In essence, following successive attempts and reforms, the Code imposed the obligation to launch a takeover bid on anyone directly or indirectly acquiring shares that conferred more than 30 per cent of the target company's voting rights.

From the very start, the obligation to launch a takeover bid has always been linked to the offeror's *purchase* or *acquisition* of shares (or, more recently, of an 'interest in shares', so as to cover derivatives and other contracts or instruments providing the offeror with a long economic exposure over the shares). This way, Rule 9 of the Code still today requires that a takeover bid be launched over 100 per cent of the capital stock 'if any person *acquires* an interest in shares which (taken together with shares in which the person or any person acting in concert with that person has an interest) carry 30% or more of the voting rights of a company'. As for the term 'acting in concert', this refers to 'persons who, pursuant to an agreement or understanding (whether formal or informal), co-operate to obtain [. . .] control [. . .] over a company [. . .]',[3] whose shares need to be aggregated for threshold calculations.

[2] For background facts and the formation of the mandatory takeover bid system in the United Kingdom, please refer to J. García de Enterría, *La OPA obligatoria* (Madrid: Cívitas, 1996), p. 31 et seq., with further references.

[3] This definition is completed with a series of presumptions where concert is presumed unless otherwise proven – e.g. a company and its other group members, a company and its directors, a management company and funds and companies under its discretionary management, a

The fact that a takeover bid is only triggered if two or more persons acting in concert *acquire* an interest exceeding 30 per cent of the voting rights (but not when the threshold is exceeded by a mere concerted voting agreement amongst shareholders) is something explained in the Code itself, in its Note on Rule 9.1 on 'Coming together to act in concert':

> When a person has acquired an interest in shares without the knowledge of other persons with whom that person subsequently *comes together to co-operate as a group to obtain [. . .] control of a company*, and the shares in which they are interested at the time of coming together carry 30% or more of the voting rights in that company, *the Panel* [in charge of applying the Code] *will not normally require an offer to be made*

under this Rule.[4] In relation to 'Collective shareholder action', another Note on this same rule further clarifies that 'the Panel will normally presume shareholders [. . .] to have come into concert once an agreement or understanding is reached between them in respect of a board control-seeking proposal with the result that *subsequent acquisitions* of interests in shares by any member of the group could give rise to an offer obligation'.[5]

Since its inception, this UK mandatory bid system has drawn from the principle of equal shareholder treatment and, more specifically, from the need to protect the interests of minority shareholders in change of control situations, in two different perspectives: (i) guaranteeing that minority shareholders are entitled to sell their shares in the same financial conditions as the relevant or controlling shareholders, in order to avoid the latter exclusively benefiting from the potential control premium; and (ii) recognising the right of all shareholders to sell their shares and thus exit the company, in the event of a change or acquisition of control by a third party, anticipating any foreseeable ensuing changes in the company's management and policies.[6]

person and his/her next of kin, etc. The Takeover Panel has recently reviewed these presumptions based on its experience: see *Public Consultation Paper* on *Presumptions of the Definition of 'Acting in Concert' and Related Matters*, 26 May 2022.

4 This issue was also highlighted by the Panel in its *Practice Statement* No. 26 (2009) on *Shareholder Activism*: the 'coming together' between various shareholders 'will not normally, of itself, result in a possible requirement to make a mandatory offer. A requirement to make a mandatory offer would only arise if a member of the concert party were to acquire additional interests in shares carrying voting rights' (section 4.3).

5 The Panel has also developed this idea in the aforementioned (n 4) *Practice Statement* No. 26 (2009): 'even if a "board control-seeking" resolution were to be proposed by activist shareholders, no mandatory offer would be required if, at the time that any such agreement or understanding is reached, steps are taken to prevent the acquisition of interests in shares in the relevant company by the activist shareholders' (section 1.6). Belgian law, which also links mandatory takeover bids only to share acquisitions, expressly foresees an obligation to launch a takeover bid by shareholders who have previously reached a concert agreement if any one of them acquires shares during the three years following formalisation of the concert; see P.A. Foriers, S. Hirsch and V. Marquette, *Les offres publiques d´acquisition. 10 ans d´application de la réglementation* (Brussels: Larcier Intersentia, 2018), p. 120.

6 For further details, see García de Enterría, *La OPA obligatoria* (n 2), p. 41 et seq.

8.2.2 *The Model of the Takeover Bids Directive*

The mandatory takeover bid model initially established in the United Kingdom not only progressively spread to other European countries. It also (and more significantly) influenced the European harmonisation on the matter, which culminated with the Takeover Bids Directive.[7] The Directive assumes an apodictic need to 'protect the interests of holders of the securities' in listed companies that 'are the subject of [...] changes of control' (Recital 2). Consequently, it imposes an obligation to launch a takeover bid if

> a natural or legal person, as a result of his/her own *acquisition* or the *acquisition by persons acting in concert* with him/her, holds securities of a company [...] which, added to any existing holdings of those securities of his/hers and the holdings of those securities of persons acting in concert with him/her, directly or indirectly give him/her a specified percentage of voting rights in that company, giving him/her control of that company [...], as a means of protecting the minority shareholders of that company. (Art. 5(1))

The protection of minority shareholders, in the event of a change of control in a company, is thus pursued (in the terms of Recital 9) 'by obliging the person who has *acquired control* of a company to make an offer to all the holders of that company's securities for all of their holdings at an equitable price in accordance with a common definition'.

In the same way as the original UK model, the obligation to launch a takeover bid is linked under the Takeover Bids Directive to obtaining control of a company, by two or more persons acting in concert, 'as a result [...] of acquisitions' of relevant securities. It is not triggered by the signing of a voting agreement above the relevant threshold by shareholders who have acquired their shares independently or not in concert.[8] The Takeover Bids Directive itself provides a definition of such persons

7 The influence deployed by the UK system over the Takeover Bids Directive has been universally recognised. Evidence of this (amongst many other circumstances) is the fact that the first draft of the Takeover Bids Directive was entrusted by the European Commission to R. Pennington, a British professor, one year after the United Kingdom adhered to the EEC. See García de Enterría, *La OPA obligatoria* (n 2), p. 35 et seq., with further references.

8 The fact that the Takeover Bids Directive makes mandatory takeover bids dependent on the *acquisition* of shares and equivalent securities, but not on mere concerted action or syndication agreements, has been extensivley highlighted by legal scholars, including M. Winner, 'Active Shareholders and European Takeover Regulation' (2014) *European Company and Financial Law Review* 369 (the Takeover Bids Directive 'only covers mandatory takeover bids as a result of an acquisition of shares'); D. Pérez Millán, 'Pactos parasociales, actuación en concierto y OPA obligatoria' (2009) 52 *Cuadernos de Derecho y Comercio* 99; C. Paredes Galego, J. Pereda Espeso and J. Redonet Sánchez del Campo, 'Ofertas públicas de adquisición de valores (I)', in R. Sebastián and M. Jordano (eds.), *Manual de fusiones y adquisiciones de empresas* (Madrid: La Ley, 2024, 4th ed.), p. 585. But cf. R. Veil, 'Foundations', in R. Veil (ed.), *European Capital Markets Law* (Oxford: Hart, 2022, 3rd ed.), p. 674, who considers that the Takeover Bids Directive 'contains no rule on how an offeree gains control over the target company'.

acting in concert, under this framework or context, covering (for our purposes) 'natural or legal persons who cooperate with the offeror [...] on the basis of an agreement, either express or tacit, either oral or written, aimed [...] at *acquiring control* of the offeree company' (Art. 2(1)(d)). This notion is clearly derived from the UK Takeover Code and is also reproduced – augmented or nuanced to a greater or lesser degree – in most European legal systems. For instance, this is the case with the Spanish Royal Decree 1066/2007 on Takeover Bids (Art. 5(1)(b)), that reproduces the Takeover Bids Directive's definition, or the Italian *Testo unico delle disposizioni in materia di intermediazione finanziaria*, that expands the definition to cover also 'invalid or ineffective' agreements (Art. 101-II.4). Hence, under this model, just as in the design of the Takeover Bids Directive, concerted action is exclusively conceived for mandatory takeover bids resulting from an *acquisition* of shares.[9] In other words, in these systems, if there is no acquisition, there can be no duty to launch a takeover by persons acting in concert.

8.2.3 *The Role of Concerted Action in the Context of the Acquisition of Shares*

In legal systems – like the Takeover Bids Directive – that link the takeover obligation to *acquiring* a controlling interest, concerted action is not an autonomous condition for the mandatory bid rule to apply. It is not a self-standing or substantive category triggering the obligation to launch a takeover bid, as it also requires above all an *acquisition* of shares (or equivalent instruments) by two or more shareholders over and above the threshold. It merely seeks to avoid the takeover obligation being shirked by easily fragmenting or piecing up the purchased shares amongst various parties who, albeit formally independent, are actually following a prior agreement or understanding with the common purpose of jointly availing themselves of their voting rights in order to take control of the company. But concert alone is insufficient to trigger a takeover bid: a controlling interest must be *acquired*, albeit not by a single shareholder acting individually, but through various shareholders acting in a joint and coordinated manner.

This implies that concerted action is basically conceived in these cases as a rule to fight fraud or circumvention,[10] to prevent a potential breach of the mandatory bid obligation when a controlling interest is acquired by various parties and not just one.

Clearly, it is possible that several shareholders acquiring shares in concert do so openly, publicly acknowledging the existence of a prior agreement or understanding

9 This is also highlighted, among others, by R. Ghetti, 'Acting in Concert in EU Company Law: How Safe Harbours can Reduce Interference with the Exercise of Shareholder Rights' (2014) *European Company and Financial Law Review* 608, and A. F. Muñoz Pérez, *El concierto como presupuesto de la OPA obligatoria*, (Madrid: La Ley, 2007), p. 39.

10 See Ghetti (n 9), p. 609, who refers to 'circumventing cooperation' given that concerted action seeks to avoid imperative rules; for further details, see also J. García de Enterría, *Limitación del voto, actuación concertada y ofertas condicionales. Estudios sobre OPAs (II)* (Madrid: Cívitas, 2002), p. 71 et seq.

and jointly seeking to ensure common control of the target company by aggregating their respective voting rights. In fact, one of the pieces of information that must generally be included in the offer document is the identity of any person acting in concert with the offeror and a description of the agreements or relations underlying such concerted action (see Art. 6(3)(g) and (m) of the Takeover Bids Directive). Such concerted action could, for instance, occur in the case of investor groups or consortiums coordinating their acquisitions in a regular and transparent manner.

But as evidenced by market practice, always in the context of the acquisition of shares, the most controversial situations of concerted action are those where such action is hidden or concealed by the concerted parties, who deny the existence of any mutual understanding or agreement among them and who pretend to carry out their respective acquisitions in an independent way. In these cases, the issue in dispute generally revolves around the legal interpretation of 'concert' or the evidence needed when there is no formalisation of an agreement, even though the parties tend to align in their conduct. The risk is that the concerted shareholders mutually assign or distribute the purchased shares among themselves in order to jointly reach a controlling interest in a veiled manner, concealing or covering up their agreement, with the intention of taking control of the target company, eluding the cumbersome and expensive obligation to launch a takeover bid. This explains why concert operates as a mere instrumental rule in these cases, without defining, modulating or extending the triggering event of the mandatory takeover bid. On the contrary, the notion of concert merely reinforces or consolidates this trigger, which continues to be the acquisition of a controlling stake, in order to ensure that the takeover bid obligation is not circumvented by fragmenting the acquisition among different concerted parties.

This anti-avoidance purpose is actually what explains the broad scope which, in these cases, defines concerted action. According to the Takeover Bids Directive's definition, concert not only includes express contracts and agreements, but also any other kind of arrangement or covenant, albeit tacit, informal or verbal, as long as the intent is to obtain control of the target company. Since concerted acquisitions are usually executed to avoid the obligation to launch a mandatory takeover bid, it is obvious that the concerted parties will hardly have any incentive to sign a genuine contract, let alone define their intent as a true syndication agreement. What is usually and foreseeably the case – as evidenced by market practice – is for such an action to rest on tacit agreements and understandings between the concerted parties, without any formalisation or articulation in writing among them, in order to hide the reason for their action and logically to remove any sign or trace that the market and the supervisory authorities could use to ascertain the existence of concerted action.[11] In the renowned words of the British Panel, concerted action may consist of

[11] According to Ghetti (n 9), p. 598, 'concert agreements are typically concealed and hard to prove, and identifying precisely when shareholders are cooperating to circumvent a legal

'a nod or a wink'.[12] Any formal, informal or tacit agreement or statement of will, handshake, understanding, or a mere exchange of information or intent,[13] or a 'nod or a wink,' may constitute concerted action, as long as all or some of the parties acquire shares further to such agreement or understanding, not for their own strategic or business reasons, but with the shared purpose of jointly achieving control of the company by pooling their respective voting rights.

In order to clarify the notion of acting in concert and to specify its content, most legal systems supplement the general definition with different presumptions, based on certain connections among natural or legal persons or on other circumstances where the legislator presupposes or assumes that concerted action exists. A clear example is the UK's Takeover Code which clarifies and supplements the general definition of '*acting in concert*' with a long list of cases where a plurality of persons is presumed to act in concert, 'unless otherwise proven' (a company and other group entities, a company and its directors, a management company and the funds or companies under its discretionary management, etc.).[14] The same thing happens under Italian law, which envisages conclusive presumptions of persons acting in concert (the parties to a shareholder agreement,[15] a person or company and other companies under its control, etc.), as well as cases where concert is presumed with a rebuttable presumption (a person and his/her next of kin, a person and his/her advisors, as long as these have acquired relevant shares). At the same time, Italian law also provides for other forms of 'cooperation amongst various parties that does not, per se, constitute concerted action' (the grouping of various shareholders to

obligation may not be easy. This difficulty brought the EU legislature to word the definition of acting in concert in the broadest possible way, using a catch-all approach.'

[12] UK Takeover Panel, *Statement* of 4 July 1989.

[13] See Winner (n 8), p. 367 for precedents where a mere exchange of information was considered to constitute concerted action, when two or more shareholders mutually inform each other of how they will take over a company in order to reciprocally obtain mutual support.

[14] UK Takeover Code, Definition of 'acting in concert'. As also pointed out by the Takeover Panel (in the *Public Consultation Paper* on 'Presumptions of the Definition of "Acting in Concert" and Related Matters', 26 May 2022, in relation to a recent process followed to review some of these presumptions), 'the definition of "acting in concert" sets out nine categories of persons who, without prejudice to the general application of the definition, are deemed to have such a degree of common interest with one another that they should be presumed to be acting in concert in relation to any Code company [. . .]. If the presumptions did not exist, the Panel would have to establish in every relevant situation whether, on the balance of probabilities and by reference to the available evidence, any particular person who has dealt in the shares of a Code company was actually acting in concert with (i) an offeror or the offeree company or (ii) another shareholder (as appropriate). This would be unworkable in practice. Accordingly, in relation to the categories of persons specified in the presumptions, who are regarded as having a significant degree of common interest with one another, the burden of proof is reversed, such that the persons will be considered to be acting in concert with one another unless the presumption is rebutted' (pp. 7 and 9).

[15] These shareholder agreements are a subset of the agreements referred to by the general definition of acting in concert (A. Tucci, '"Acquisto di concerto" e "azione di concerto"' (2010) *Rivista di diritto commerciale* 915, 928).

exercise minority rights, resolutions to appoint a minority of directors, cooperation to pass certain corporate resolutions, etc.).[16] The Spanish Royal Decree on Takeover Bids also presumes concert in similar cases, such as with voting rights held by companies belonging to the same group and to its management bodies, which are attributed to the same person 'unless otherwise proven' (Art. 5(1)(b)).[17]

These remarkable efforts to provide legal clarity cannot, of course, remove all the uncertainties surrounding the elusive nature of acting in concert. It may be uncertain, for instance, whether the presumptions above are effective only individually or can apply jointly, so that, for instance, a company is a concerted party with a close relative of its director, or a member of a shareholder agreement is a concerted party with a close relative of another member. In the UK, a reasonable interpretation of the Takeover Code seems to be that, as a matter of principle, the first pair of persons (a company and a close relative of its director) falls within the presumption, while the second (a member of a shareholder agreement and a close relative of another member) does not.[18] In Italy, both cases are regarded as a concert with an irrebuttable presumption, instead.[19]

On top of this, it is often difficult to determine to what extent the concert plays a role beyond the determination of the aggregate shareholding triggering the mandatory bid. A typical question is whether concerted parties other than the one that made the critical purchase are bound by the duty to launch a bid. In the UK, the duty is, in principle, upon the principal member alone of the group acting in concert, whether this made the purchase or not, and will only in exceptional circumstances involve other concerted parties.[20] A similar rule applies under Spanish law, where the obligation to launch a takeover bid falls on the shareholder with the highest percentage of voting rights.[21] But an opposite rule applies in Italy,

16 Art. 101-*bis*, section 4-*bis*, *Testo Unico della Finanza*, and Art. 44-*quater*, sections 1 and 2, CONSOB *Regolamento emittenti*. On this concept, see A. Sacco Ginevri, 'Sustainable governance and regulation of banks and public companies: A study of the concept "acting in concert"' (2017) *Corporate Governance and Sustainability Review*, 46.

17 As upheld by the CNMV itself, in *Preguntas y respuestas sobre ofertas públicas de adquisición (opas)*, updated in February 2022, the rule 'establishes a *iuris tantum* legal presumption of concerted action'; furthermore, albeit without constituting a presumption, 'the CNMV will usually consider the fact that the relevant shareholders of an entity holding an interest also own shares in the same listed company as a relevant indication of concerted action, when calculating voting rights' (section 5).

18 Under the Takeover Code definition of acting in concert, a company is presumed to be a concerted party with a close relative of its director (UK Takeover Code, Definition of 'acting in concert', No 4). At the same time, the persons listed in the presumptions are 'presumed to be persons acting in concert with other persons *in the same category*' (emphasis added).

19 Art. 109, section 3, *Testo Unico della Finanza*. The ensuing extension of acting in concert can become so broad that this kind of link was significantly labelled as 'concerto grosso': P. Ferro-Luzzi, 'Il "concerto grosso"; variazioni sul tema dell'o.p.a.' (2002) *Giurisprudenza commerciale* 655.

20 UK Takeover Code, Note on Rule 9.2 (Prime responsibility).

21 Art. 3.3 of the Spanish Royal Decree on Takeover Bids.

where all concerted parties are jointly and severally liable for the duty to launch a bid and are therefore exposed to serious consequences for their counterparties' conduct.[22]

Another problem arises when the notion of concert determines not only whether the control threshold is crossed, but also who, once that threshold is crossed, is bound to launch a bid. In this regard, a recurrent question is whether the duty to launch a bid involves persons that do not hold shares in the company, but nonetheless fall within the scope of concerted parties according to a presumption, whether rebuttable or not. In the UK, the Takeover Panel will normally answer in the negative, but may consider concerted parties who do not hold shares as bound by the duty to launch a bid in the exceptional circumstances mentioned above.[23] In Italy, concerted parties that do not hold shares are never subject to such duty in case of 'concerto grosso' and, according to some case law, the same applies to any kind of concerted action, although this latter interpretation is debated.[24] To be sure, regardless of the legal duty to launch a bid, those who did not actively contribute to the crossing of the threshold will normally have a claim against their active fellows in the concert, but the subjection to the duty can certainly increase legal risk.

In any case, the blurred lines of informal or tacit agreements that often characterise concert explains why concerted action is inevitably an open-ended and undefined category, the application of which inextricably depends on the specific and unique characteristics of each case. Although the notion is often criticised for this imprecision, its legal function certainly rules out any possibility of further regulatory detail. The broad range of situations that may arise in practice, and the very fact that concerted parties usually strive (as a means to avoid takeover bid laws) to cover up and conceal the true reason for their conduct and to generate a semblance of independent and separate action, explains why concert must necessarily be defined in broad and flexible terms, without consideration to specific formalities, in order to focus on the shared purpose to cooperate when acquiring the shares with the aim of jointly taking control of the target company.[25]

[22] Art. 109, section 1, *Testo Unico della Finanza*; G. Guizzi and A. Tucci, 'Acquisto di concerto', in M. Stella Richter Jr (ed.), *Le offerte pubbliche di acquisto* (Turin: Giappichelli, 2011), 266.

[23] UK Takeover Code, Note on Rule 9.2 (Prime responsibility).

[24] Art. 109, section 3, *Testo Unico della Finanza*; Milan Tribunal (ord.), Salini v. Igli, 11 July 2012, (2013) *Rivista di Diritto Societario* 96, with a comment by S. Legnani.

[25] As affirmed by the Takeover Appeal Board in decision 2017/1, which upheld that concerted acquisitions had been carried out amongst various shareholders to control the Scottish Rangers International Football Club PLC; 'there are a number of ways in which persons may act in concert. An exhaustive definition would be difficult. As explained by the Panel in its Statement in the case of *Guinness plc/The Distillery Company* [. . .], the nature of "acting in concert" called for a wide definition to cover, for example, tacit understandings or "nods or winks" between persons co-operating to purchase shares in a company in order to obtain control of it' (section 103(1)). For a list of the main cases of concerted action investigated by the Panel, see D. Kershaw, *Principles of Takeover Regulation* (Oxford: Oxford University Press, 2016), p. 241.

The informal nature that generally characterises agreements between concerted parties, along with the usual absence of direct evidence, explains the difficulties that supervisory authorities usually face in proving concerted action in the case of concomitant acquisitions by multiple investors.[26] And it also explains why supervisory authorities must generally proceed on the basis of mere signs or presumptions, if the share purchases and the shareholders' conduct have no other plausible and rational explanation than the fulfilment of a prior agreement or understanding.[27] The facts or signs that are particularly relevant include – as also evidenced in practice – those *subsequent to* combined acquisitions of shares by various shareholders, if these latter's conduct with respect to the company – typically by promoting and backing up 'board control-seeking proposals' – suggest that such acquisitions had to be necessarily and logically carried out in concert.

The notion of concert defined by the Takeover Bids Directive, which is applicable to cases of acquisition of shares by several persons acting under the common purpose of jointly acquiring control of the company, is also relevant in relation to the other obligations and duties that may bind the offeror or the offeree company within the takeover bid procedure. Such duties generally apply to all persons acting in concert (equitable price, best price rule, obligation to offer a cash consideration in case of previous acquisitions, etc.). In all these cases, logically, the need to prevent the bidder or the offeree company from trying to evade the legal consequences associated with certain acts or actions that they may carry out in the context of the takeover bid by using other persons requires that the broad and all-encompassing concept of acting in concert must also be taken into account, in the sense of including any type of agreement, even if tacit or informal.

[26] See Veil, 'Mandatory Bid', in Veil (ed.) (n 8), p. 693.

[27] The UK Takeover Appeal Board, in the cited Rangers decision, affirmed that 'Direct evidence of what has passed between those alleged to have acted in concert is rare. The existence and nature of an understanding between persons and whether their actions were concerted or co-incidental are often matters calling for the use of common sense and relevant experience in making reasonable inferences from all the surrounding circumstances in evidence in the case' (section 103). Also revealing, in France, is the judgment passed by the Court of Appeals of Paris on 2 April 2008, in Sacyr/Eiffage, which upheld AMF's decision demanding that Sacyr's offer over the French company Eiffage include a consideration in cash, due to acquiring more than 5 per cent in the target company during the twelve previous months in concert with another six shareholders. Although it was not possible to prove that an agreement existed, the Court presumed that existing signs (including that all were Spanish companies, bound by personal or commercial relations, which lacked any previous foreign investment and which had simultaneously acquired a significant amount of stock given their financial position) indicated that this was not just parallel conduct, but 'an organised and collective initiative that sought a common objective: to come together' in order to prevail at a general meeting that was scheduled and where certain board members would be appointed. In Spain, see CNMV Resolution of 24 October 2001, which ordered the closing of a sanctioning procedure brought against the companies Electrabel and TXU for possible concerted action in the acquisition of shares in Hidroeléctrica del Cantábrico. This resolution and its background facts are discussed in García de Enterría, *Limitación del voto* (n 10), p. 67 et seq.

8.3 CONCERTED VOTING AS AN ADDITIONAL CASE OF MANDATORY TAKEOVER BIDS

8.3.1 *Configuration and Meaning*

In contrast with the UK's and the Takeover Bids Directive's model of mandatory bids, which requires the *acquisition* of a controlling interest by persons acting in concert, in other legal systems the takeover bid is also triggered by a mere *agreement or syndication of voting rights* amongst shareholders who, as a whole, exceed the relevant threshold. In these cases, the obligation to launch a takeover bid is triggered by such concert alone and without requiring any further transaction involving the target company's shares, even if the shareholders have acquired their interests independently (not in concert) before they entered the agreement. The formation of a controlling interest through mere concerted voting is considered equivalent to the acquisition of shares for mandatory takeover bid purposes, by assuming that both scenarios constitute alternative means or procedures that would be functionally equivalent to acquiring control of a company. Controlling positions, which are *proprietary* in share acquisitions, have a *contractual* nature in the case of a mere voting agreement.[28]

The French model is a clear representation of this system. Under the *Règlement Général* of the *Autorité des Marchés Financiers* (AMF), a takeover bid must be launched 'if a legal or natural person, acting alone or in concert in the terms of article L.233-10 of the Commercial Code, directly or indirectly becomes the owner of more than 30% of a company's stock or voting rights'. According to this provision of the French Commercial Code, concerted action will be presumed if 'persons have reached an agreement with a view to acquiring, assigning or *exercising voting rights, in order to follow a common policy with respect to the company or to obtain the latter's control*'. Thus, the notion of concerted action is expanded to cover, in addition to agreements to acquire shares in a coordinated manner, as in the model of takeover bids due to an acquisition, those situations where the parties jointly exercise voting rights, in order to obtain control or to implement a common policy in the company's management or operation. Although this definition of concerted action is generally applicable and covers various matters related to listed companies, its greatest impact (and most severe consequences) is in fact apparent in the obligation to launch a takeover bid.[29] A similar definition of 'legal entities acting in concert' is included in Austrian law, where concert includes 'natural or legal

[28] In this regard, see J. García de Enterría, 'Commentary to Article 5', in J. García de Enterría and J. Zurita (eds.), *La regulación de las OPAs. Comentario sistemático del RD 1066/2007, de 27 de julio* (Madrid: Cívitas, 2009), p. 170 et seq.

[29] A general reference is made to this notion of concerted action in French law in A. Viandier, *OPA, OPE et autres offres publiques* (Paris: Francis Lefebvre, 2014, 5th ed.), p. 287 et seq.; C. Goyet, 'Action de concert' (2021) *LaBaseLextenso*, available at www.labase-lextenso.fr; F. Martin Laprade, 'Action de concert' (2021) *JurisClasseur Sociétés*, 2135.

persons who cooperate with the offeror on the basis of an agreement in order to acquire or exert control over the offeree company, *in particular by means of coordination of the voting rights*' (Paragraph 1(6) of the Federal Law on takeover bids or *Bundesgesetz betreffend Übernahmeangebote*). Germany follows a similar approach, as we shall see.

Obviously, in this model, concerted action goes way beyond a mere instrumental rule to allocate or assign newly acquired votes to the concerted parties as a whole, exclusively aimed at preventing any potential circumvention of the obligation to launch a takeover bid by various parties who break up or allocate amongst themselves the acquisition of a controlling interest. Rather, concerted action plays here a material or substantive role, by constituting *per se* an individual and self-sufficient trigger of the obligation to launch a takeover bid, other than takeover bids following an acquisition.

The consequence is that there are two coexisting regulatory models in the European Union: (i) one model imposing the mandatory bid only when the relevant threshold is exceeded through the acquisition of shares (or equivalent securities or instruments) by persons acting in concert (this is the case in Belgium, Italy[30] or Norway, just like the United Kingdom outside the Union), and (ii) another model also triggering the mandatory bid when several shareholders, which on aggregate hold a controlling interest, reach a concert agreement for exercising their voting rights, even if they acquire their respective stakes in an independent (not concerted) manner (this is the case in Austria, France, Germany, Netherlands, Sweden or Spain). As pointed out by ESMA in its Public Statement on *Information on shareholder cooperation and acting in concert under the Takeover Bids Directive* (the 'ESMA Public Statement'),[31]

> in some Member States, when shareholders come together to act in concert in relation to a particular company in circumstances where, independently, they have already acquired securities in that company which, in total, carry the specified percentage of voting rights that confers 'control' under national takeover rules, they will be required to make a bid to all other shareholders (a 'mandatory bid'). In other words, the mandatory bid obligation will be triggered even though no further securities have been acquired.
>
> In other Member States, no mandatory bid obligation will arise initially when the shareholders come together to act in concert in such circumstances. Such an obligation may, however, be triggered if any one of the shareholders regarded as persons acting in concert subsequently acquires further securities carrying voting rights in the company.

[30] However, see n 40 and accompanying text on the Italian system, whereby acquisitions of shares predating the concert will still trigger the mandatory bid rule when they took place in the year before a shareholder agreement is entered into, as this may be considered a presumption that the acquisitions themselves may have been concerted.

[31] Date 20 June 2014, but updated on 8 January 2019 (ESMA/2014/677-REV).

8.3.2 *Ground and Justification*

The fact that some European countries have imposed this regulatory model is a voluntary legal policy decision, which is not imposed by the Takeover Bids Directive. As the previous section has shown, the Directive envisages an obligation to launch a takeover bid by someone who 'following his own *acquisition*' or an acquisition '*carried out by persons with whom he is acting in concert*', is able to reach a percentage of voting rights that grant him/her control over the target company (Art. 5(1)). However, the Takeover Bids Directive has notoriously a limited mandatory content, as it often formulates a broad set of general rules and principles, which are in some cases voluntary or subject to reciprocity principles. This is due to its configuration as a *de minimis* Directive, open to other additional measures that may be adopted by Member States.[32] Overall, this indicates that Member States are entitled to extend the scope of the mandatory takeover bid to other types of situation. The Takeover Bids Directive expressly allows Member States to establish 'additional conditions and provisions more stringent than those of this Directive for the regulation of bids' (Art. 3(2)(b)). This explains why Member States, which are required by the Takeover Bids Directive to impose a takeover bid obligation when a controlling interest is *acquired*, are also entitled to extend it to other additional situations, such as mere *concerted or syndicated voting* (or the appointment of directors, as also envisaged in Spanish law).

In any case, as evidenced by the Takeover Bids Directive itself, the obligation to launch a takeover bid over the entire capital of the target company due to shareholders merely concerting their voting rights is not self-evident from the perspective of any of the legal grounds traditionally inspiring the mandatory bid system, whether this relates to the transfer of control or the creation of a control position in a company whose control was contestable.[33] Let us briefly see why.

[32] See Recital 26 of the Takeover Bids Directive, stating that it only establishes 'a framework consisting of certain common principles and a limited number of general requirements which Member states are to implement through more detailed rules in accordance with their national systems and their cultural contexts'. In fact, the European Commission itself pointed out that the Takeover Bids Directive 'has not led to major changes in the legal framework of the Member States [. . .], because similar rules already existed or were in the making at national level prior to the adoption of the Directive' (European Commission, *Report from the Commission to the European Parliament, the Council, the European Economic and Social Committee and the Committee of the Regions, Application of Directive 2004/25/EC on takeover bids*, COM(2012) 347 final (28 June 2012), p. 3). This was also highlighted in the 2012 *Takeover Bids Directive Assessment Report* (p. 18), ordered by the European Commission, which pointed out three factors explaining the limited practical impact on the law of the Takeover Bids Directive: 'in a number of countries, the Directive prescribed rules that had been in existence for a long time [. . .]; in other countries, changes were introduced in view of the future adoption of the Directive [. . .]; in several cases, the most important changes were introduced in reaction to sensitive bids or the economic situation, without there being a direct link with the Directive [. . .].'

[33] The merits of the mandatory bid rule in the case of the creation of control positions where there were none before are debated. See e.g. E. Wymeersch, 'A new look at the debate about

In the most traditional perspective, the essential and basic purpose of the mandatory bid rule is to guarantee that all shareholders – particularly minority shareholders – receive the same price and enjoy the same terms of sale in the event of an acquisition or change of control, avoiding the control premium payable by the acquirer exclusively ending up with the shareholder(s) that transfer control.[34] But all of this clearly falls outside mere concerted voting, which does not require any share acquisition and where there is therefore no risk or possibility of different economic treatment between majority or relevant shareholders and minority shareholders. In fact, the equality principle which underlies mandatory takeover bids is twisted in these cases, by demanding that the concerted shareholders submit an offer to the others in order to purchase their shares at a price they themselves have neither received nor paid. If a controlling interest is *acquired*, a takeover bid obligation ensures that all shareholders are able to sell their shares at the same price. But this is not the case of takeover bids due to *concerted action*, where the right to transfer shares in advantageous terms is limited to the minority shareholders, which is certainly not a consequence of the equal treatment principle.

Another oft-mentioned rationale for the mandatory bid rule lies with its ability to remove incentives to engage in value-decreasing control changes. As long as the premium paid by the new controlling shareholder to acquire control reflects the discounted value of the benefits of control he/she expects to gain in the future, the mandatory bid would work as a powerful tool to sterilise inefficient control changes. In fact, offering that price to all minority shareholders gives these latter the option to either retain the shares, the value of which can be expected to decrease if the expected private benefits of control will likely result in a substantive expropriation, or take advantage of the premium. In the scenario where all shareholders accept the offer, there will be no minorities left to expropriate.[35] Hence, the rationale of the mandatory bid rule has been identified in its ability to reduce the incentives to ex-post expropriation (for instance, through related-party transactions) by taking away, ex ante, incentives to engage in value-decreasing control changes.[36] To be sure, whether this freezing effect on inefficient control changes justifies the mandatory bid rule is debatable, if only because the rule has the same impact on value-

the takeover directive', in B. Erle et al. (eds.), *Festschrift für Peter Hommelhoff zum 70. Geburtstag* (Cologne: O. Schmidt Verlag, 2012), 1375; G. Psaroudakis, 'The Mandatory Bid and Company Law in Europe' (2010) *European Company and Financial Law Review* 550.

34 Critically L. Enriques, 'The Mandatory Bid Rule in the Takeover Directive: Harmonization Without Foundation?' (2004) *European Company and Financial Law Review* 440, 452 et seq.; J. L. Hansen, 'The Mandatory Bid Rule: Unnecessary, Unjustifiable and Inefficient' (2018), *Nordic & European Company Law LSN Research Paper Series*, p. 6 et seq., available at www.ssrn.com.

35 P. Davies, K. Hopt and W. G. Ringe, 'Control Transactions', in R Kraakman et al. (eds.), *The Anatomy of Corporate Law: A Comparative and Functional Approach* (Oxford: Oxford University Press, 2017), p. 228, 234.

36 See e.g. L. Enriques, 'EU Takeover Law: The Case for a Neutral Approach' (2011) *European Business Law Review* 623, 627.

increasing transactions, thus making the market for corporate control less efficient in this regard.[37] However, for the limited purposes of our analysis, what matters is that concerted voting takeover bids do not rest on any previous payment of a control premium, for the obvious reason that they do not involve any transfer of shares in the first place. While the law can look for a substitute, such as the average market price over a certain period of time preceding the voting agreement, the mandatory bid price cannot in any event reflect the bidder's assessment of the benefits he/she is expecting from gaining control. Hence, we can discard this incentive-based explanation as a credible rationale for mandating takeover bids on the sole ground of concerted voting.

A third rationale for the mandatory bid rule against which one can test concerted voting takeover bids is the consideration of mandatory bids as a functional instrument available to minority shareholders in order to exit or divest from the company in the event of formation of a contractual controlling position that may affect the company's composition or structure, something not contemplated when the shares were purchased. However, this reasoning is extremely weak as a general explanation of the mandatory bid rule, particularly given the extraordinary and disproportionate legal consequence the law attaches to it, and it becomes even more shaky when associated with mere concert. The shareholders of a listed company are able to get rid of their stock at any time, in the event of disagreement or mere suspicions about possible changes in the company's management. This right is not only consubstantial to structurally open listed companies, but it is also associated with regular and generalised investor conduct (investors tend to 'vote with their feet' rather than actively exercising their shareholder rights).

Even if control is acquired (and not obtained through mere concert), this unusual exit right granted to minority shareholders indicates an unjustified prevention or suspicion (contrary to basic economic logic) towards any policy or management changes that new relevant or majority shareholders may generate, in contrast to changes implemented by incumbent shareholders or directors which, logically, do not activate any specific protection other than those envisaged in general corporate law. In addition, in the event of mere concert or syndication, the controlling positions are usually more fragile and unstable than strictly proprietary positions (given their exposure to changes occurring over time in the relations between the concerted parties), and generally compromise the company's 'contestability' to a lesser extent, as they do not affect the number of shares available to other investors on the market.[38]

[37] L. A. Bebchuk, 'Efficient and Inefficient Sales of Corporate Control' (1994) *Quarterly Journal of Economics* 957, 972; M. Burkart and F. Panunzi, 'Takeovers', in X. Freixas, P. Hartmann and C. Mayer (eds.), *Handbook of European Financial Markets and Institutions* (Oxford: Oxford University Press, 2008), p. 282 et seq.

[38] In general, subsequent critical considerations on the grounds of takeover obligations due to concerted action are available in García de Enterría, 'Commentary to article 5' (n 28), p. 171 et

From this perspective, the general doubts and mistrust raised by the mandatory takeover bid model – not only due to its questionable material grounds but also to its undesirable economic consequences, which inhibit and increase the cost of circulation of controlling stakes in listed companies[39] – increase and exponentially multiply when the mandatory bid is imposed due to mere concerted or syndicated voting. Aside from the model's intrinsic defects, this specific mandatory bid is also inconsistent with the majority principle that actually underlies all capital stock companies and the shareholders' unconditional right to exercise and dispose of their voting rights as they see fit, with no further limitations than the corporate interest and the prohibition of abusive conduct.

8.3.3 *Practical Rationale of Takeover Bids due to Concerted Voting*

Ultimately, the most convincing explanation for concerted voting mandatory bids (which to a large extent seems to have influenced the decision of many countries, like Spain) is that this expansion of the mandatory bid rule counterbalances and somehow redeems the huge difficulties usually encountered by supervisory

seq.; A. Robles Martín-Laborda, *Sindicación de acciones y mercado de control societario* (Pamplona: Aranzadi, 2006), p. 117 et seq. (concerted action is not lasting or stable and that in these cases there is no controlling premium or an incoming new shareholder); Pérez Millán, 'Pactos parasociales' (n 8), p. 109 (the duty to launch a takeover bid is even more unjustifiable in these cases, given that there is no controlling premium or an incoming new shareholder, and the fact that controlling positions are not definitive and unchallengeable); Paredes Galego, Pereda Espeso and Redonet Sánchez del Campo, 'Ofertas públicas de adquisición' (n 8), p. 584 (contractual controlling positions are weaker and not lasting, as they are subject to the ups and downs of shareholder relations).

39 Although the mandatory takeover bid model has been questioned for a long time (see García de Enterría, *La OPA obligatoria* (n 2), p. 135 et seq., with further references), some authoritative European scholars have recently also pronounced themselves against this system, particularly because the Takeover Bids Directive imposes it without granting Member States opt-out rights such as those contemplated in relation to the non-frustration rule binding directors or the neutralisation of anti-takeover bid measures. See, inter alia, L. Enriques, R. J. Gilson and A. M. Pacces, 'The Case for an Unbiased Takeover Law (with an Application to the European Union)' (2014) *Harvard Business Law Review* 117 et seq.; A. Gurrea Martínez, 'New Agency Problems, New Legal Rules: Rethinking Takeover Regulation in the US and Europe', April 2016 (reviewed in February 2022), available at www.ssrn.com, p. 23 et seq.; M. Habersack, 'The Non-Frustration Rule and the Mandatory Bid Rule – Cornerstone of European Takeover Law?' (2017) *LSE Working Papers* No 9/2017, p. 8 et seq. In any case, the possibility of the European Union contemplating in the near future a reform or amendment of the Takeover Bids Directive seems implausible and unrealistic given, inter alia, the shaky equilibrium reached for its approval and the foreseeable reluctance of the European Commission and many Member States to revisit the matter. As affirmed by Hansen, 'The Mandatory Bid Rule: Unnecessary, Unjustifiable and Inefficient' (n 34), p. 1, 'the Takeover Directive [...] is a Pandora's box nobody wants to open and renegotiate [...] Arguing against the [mandatory takeover bid] rule [...] is the modern legal equivalent of tilting at windmills, except that the rule is not an imaginary evil but represents some very real problems that are characteristic of what is wrong with EU law today.'

authorities in pursuing and proving the existence of concerted action in share acquisitions. The obligation to launch a takeover bid due to mere concerted action would thus perform an essentially ancillary or subsidiary function. Namely, it reinforces the practical effectiveness of the basic model of takeover bids linked to an acquisition, by at least avoiding that shareholders who jointly acquire shares in a coordinated manner can subsequently execute or formalise a genuine agreement in order to syndicate or concert their voting rights, with no further legal consequences. One could argue, indeed, that the mandatory bid system, even if it is considered inefficient and counterproductive, should be designed and enforced in a way that prevents circumvention and preserves its function.

This ancillary function is, for example, evidenced by the Italian law which always requires an acquisition of shares in order to trigger the obligation to launch a takeover bid; this obligation is therefore excluded for concerted voting agreements, but only if the shareholders in concert have not acquired shares in the target company in the previous twelve months. This rule therefore works as an irrebuttable presumption that a concert already existed before the formalisation of the agreement, and is clearly meant to avoid circumvention of the mandatory bid rule.[40]

In this sense, even if some legal systems equate shareholder agreements to share acquisitions for mandatory bid purposes, the practical consequence of their approach (and probably the one actually sought by the legislator) is basically to discourage concerted voting agreements above the takeover bid threshold, with the intention of redirecting all takeover transactions towards the traditional and 'orthodox' route of share acquisitions. It is not really a case of expanding or extending mandatory takeover bids to non-acquisitions, but rather of preventing shareholders from resorting to concerted or syndicated voting agreements that the law (further to its vast and far-reaching interpretation of mandatory takeover bids) perceives as contradictory or incompatible with the institutional purposes of 'traditional' mandatory bids.

The foregoing is inferred from the scarce incentives that shareholders who wish to obtain control of a company generally have, when deciding amongst the existing various alternatives in systems that rely on concerted voting mandatory bids, to

40 In fact, Italian law ties mandatory takeover bids to 'an acquisition or increase in voting rights' above the relevant threshold (which varies depending on the size of the company and, for smaller companies, on charter provisions: Art. 106.1 *Testo Unico della Finanza*) and expressly indicates that no takeover bid will be mandated if the joint holding of a controlling interest by various shareholders is 'a consequence of signing a [shareholders'] agreement, unless the signatories came to jointly hold an interest in shares above the relevant thresholds during the twelve months preceding the agreement' (Art. 109.2 *Testo Unico*). On this regime, see M. Gargantini, 'Coordinamento (extra-)assembleare dei soci e azione di concerto nella s.p.a. quotata', in M. Campobasso et al. (eds.), *Organizzazione, finanziamento e crisi dell'impresa. Scritti in onore di Pietro Abbadessa* (Turin: UTET, 2014), p. 2097; F. M. Mucciarelli, *Le offerte pubbliche d'acquisto e di scambio* (Turin: Giappichelli, 2014), p. 198 (both arguing that the legal presumption is that share acquisitions were made in anticipation of a subsequent voting agreement).

trigger a mandatory takeover bid precisely by signing a syndicated voting agreement. In these cases, what is reasonable and expected, practically speaking, is for the shareholders, rather than coming together and launching a mandatory takeover bid, to previously launch a voluntary bid in order to acquire and consolidate their controlling position, before formalising or applying any voting rights agreement. From a logical and strategic point of view, what is clearly more appropriate is not to formalise or materialise a voting concert until control of the company has been legitimately acquired and the extent and degree of that controlling interest are known.

This circumstance seems to be firmly endorsed by the market experience of some relevant markets. In France, despite the broad notion of concert, it seems no mandatory takeover bid has been launched due to a mere pooling of various shareholders.[41] And the same is true for the Spanish market, where in over fifteen years, no mandatory takeover bid has resulted from a shareholder or concerted action agreement.[42]

8.3.4 *The Relevant Concept of Concerted Voting*

As seen, the unusual laxity of the Takeover Bids Directive and its few harmonisation effects have resulted in two coexisting regulatory models in the European Union: those that require a mandatory bid only in the case of an acquisition of shares (or equivalent instruments) by persons acting in concert, and those that additionally trigger the mandatory bid when the relevant threshold is passed by two or more shareholders who agree to exercise their voting rights in a concerted manner.[43]

As takeover bids due to concerted voting are not envisaged in the Takeover Bids Directive, the latter does not indicate what types or content of syndication agreements would trigger the mandatory bid. Its definition of 'persons acting in concert' (Art. 2(1)(d)) is conceived (as indicated) for share *acquisitions*, as an accessory and instrumental rule aimed to prevent the circumvention of the mandatory takeover bid by breaking up the acquisition of a controlling interest amongst several parties. This is why countries considering pure syndication agreements as trigger for mandatory bids, such as France, Germany or Spain, in the absence of any guide or indication from the Takeover Bids Directive, have usually availed themselves, to a greater or lesser extent, of the definition of concerted voting agreements contained in Directive 2004/109/EC, of 15 December, on the harmonisation of transparency

[41] See Martin Laprade, 'Action de concert' (n 29), p. 214.

[42] Since 2007 and until the end of 2022, when the current takeover regulations were enacted, there have been fifteen mandatory bids (of a total of eighty-two takeover bids, including delisting offers), but none of them involved concerted voting.

[43] In relation with this contradiction of models, see Winner (n 8), p. 369 et seq.

requirements in relation to information about issuers whose securities are admitted to trading on a regulated market (the 'Transparency Directive'). The Transparency Directive does not use the notion of 'persons acting in concert', but it extends the duties of notification applied to the acquisition of significant interests or 'major holdings' in listed companies to 'voting rights held by a third party with whom that person or entity has concluded an agreement, which obliges them to adopt, by concerted exercise of the voting rights they hold, a lasting common policy towards the management of the issuer in question' (Art. 10(a)).[44]

Based on the notion afforded by the Transparency Directive, it is inferred that the object of these agreements or covenants is not to acquire shares (as in the case of acquisition takeover bids), but to jointly exercise the voting rights held by the concerted shareholders. Such agreements should also be binding in the sense of requiring the shareholders to vote in a coordinated manner, which excludes mere conversations or negotiations preceding one or more meetings, or information exchanged on intended votes, in the absence of any commitment or obligation and if the shareholders keep their liberty to exercise their voting rights. These agreements should also be related to matters affecting the company's management. This vague and unspecified legal concept will generally require that the agreements affect the composition or control of the management body. And such agreements must have a lasting nature, which means that one-off or short-term agreements, which may refer to a single general meeting or specific corporate resolutions, are not relevant as a trigger of the mandatory bid rule.[45] As highlighted by the Judgment of 9 September 2021 of the European Court of Justice, which reproduces the opinion of the Advocate General, this provision of the Transparency Directive 'requires a

[44] The trend in countries imposing a takeover bid due to concerted action to apply the definition afforded by the Transparency Directive was already highlighted by the *Takeover Bids Directive Assessment Report* of 2012 (p. 133), by the European Commission in its 2012 *Report* (n 31), p. 7), in the *Response to the European Commission's Report on the Application of the Takeover Bids Directive* provided by European Company Law Experts, November 2013, p. 4, and has also been pointed out by ESMA in its *Public Statement on Information on shareholder cooperation*, (n 30) p. 16, and by legal scholars (Ghetti, 'Acting in concert' (n 9), p. 614). The Transparency Directive's definition is also relevant for other acquisition regimes, such as the notification and evaluation of 'qualifying holdings' in credit institutions: see Directive 2013/36/EU, of the European Parliament and of the Council, of 26 June 2013, on access to the activity of credit institutions and the prudential supervision of credit institutions and investment firms, which applies this regime to 'any natural or legal person or such persons acting in concert (the "proposed acquirer"), who have taken a decision either to acquire, directly or indirectly, a qualifying holding in a credit institution [...]' (Art. 22.1) and requires voting rights to be taken into account, referred to (inter alia) by Article 10 of the Transparency Directive (Art. 27); the same regime is contained in Directive 2009/138/EC, of the European Parliament and of the Council, of 25 November 2009, on the taking up and pursuit of the business of Insurance and Reinsurance (Arts. 57 and 63), and Directive 2014/65/EU, of the European Parliament and of the Council, of 15 May 2014, on markets in financial instruments (Art. 11), for investment firms.

[45] See Ghetti, 'Acting in concert' (n 9), p. 603.

high degree of commitment over a certain period of time, which cannot be fleeting or intermittent, and which must be uniform and addressed to the management of the company concerned'.[46]

Given that the legal consequences of concerted action in relation with mandatory takeover bids (the obligation to launch a bid over the entire share capital) are infinitely more serious and onerous than those related to transparency duties (which merely require that a significant interest be notified to the market), it can be assumed that the features of concerted action agreements required by the Transparency Directive should in principle apply as *de minimis* or as a common denominator for takeover bids, thereby limiting mandatory offers to qualified syndication agreements which, based on content and duration, are able to constitute contractual controlling positions which are comparable to proprietary ones. Otherwise, the burdensome and disproportionate obligation to launch a takeover bid over the entire share capital would result from a circumstance that, by contrast, would not need to be notified or disclosed as a significant holding due to the absence of authentic informative value for investors.

However, in the absence of harmonisation under the Takeover Bids Directive, domestic laws differ as to which concerted voting agreements are relevant for takeover bids, and do not always follow the literal wording of the Transparency Directive. Logically, there are some common components, such as that the agreement shall cover the exercise of voting rights and seek to implement a common policy within the company. Furthermore, despite the varied meaning that concerted action has in takeover bids following an acquisition compared to takeover bids due to concerted action, it is also frequent for national laws, when defining relevant concerted action agreements, to combine or integrate components of the Takeover Bids Directive and of the Transparency Directive, or to establish a single notion of concerted action, covering all share acquisitions and mere concert. As an example, France follows a particularly broad definition of concerted action that covers any agreement for share acquisitions and for the exercise of voting rights, if the aim is to 'apply a common company policy' (Art. L.233-10 of the French Commercial Code). In practice, agreements triggering the mandatory bid rule may be both express and tacit, irrespective of form, and may also be temporary, provided that they have binding effects on the shareholders.[47] In German law, where takeover bids are also

[46] Case C-546/18, *Adler Real Estate and Others* [2021] ECLI:EU:C:2021:711. The judgment deals with the legality of certain sanctions ordered by the Austrian Committee of Public Offers against the acquirers of a controlling interest in concert without launching a takeover bid, and examines issues related to the procedural guarantees required in sanctioning proceedings brought by reason of such breach.

[47] On different concerted action cases in French law, a general view is provided by Viandier, *OPA, OPE* (n 29) p. 270 et seq.; Goyet, 'Action de concert' (n 29), p. 15 et seq.; Martin Laprade, 'Action de concert' (n 29), para. 210 et seq. As pointed out, the AMF and the French courts tend to interpret the notion of 'common policy' very broadly and, as a consequence, any common objective of interest for shareholders could end up constituting concerted action (including

activated by a mere concerted exercise of voting rights, the offeror is presumed to hold the votes of any third party with whom it 'coordinates its conduct' in relation to the target company, 'further to an agreement or otherwise', if the offeror and the third party 'execute an agreement on how to exercise their voting rights or to otherwise cooperate to achieve a lasting and material change' in the company's management (Section 34(2) of the German Securities Transfers Act (WpHG) and Art. 30.2 of the Act on the Acquisition of Securities and Public Offers (WpÜG)).[48] And in Spanish law, until recently the mandatory bid by concerted action was only triggered where a genuine shareholders' agreement was signed, which offered the clear advantage of legal certainty. However, Law 6/2023 on Securities Markets and Investment Services has expressly extended the obligation to the entering of agreements 'of another nature', but without providing any additional indication as to the type of agreements that would be covered.

The problem, therefore, is that, despite the different meanings of concerted action in systems based on mandatory bid due to an acquisition and in systems based on mandatory bid due to mere voting agreements, many national regimes have ended up using a single broad and all-encompassing notion of concert, that includes all kinds of tacit and informal agreements (the Takeover Panel's 'nods or winks'). This fact does not raise any question in relation to takeover bids due to an acquisition, since in these cases the concert must by definition include – as we have seen – all kinds of agreements and understandings between the acquirers of the shares, without consideration of their nature or legal effectiveness, in line with the definition provided by the Takeover Bids Directive. But the same does not hold true for concerted voting because, in this case, expanding the mandatory bid rule beyond

many cases of shareholder activism and involvement in the company's management): K. Sergakis, *The Law of Capital Markets in the EU: Disclosure and Enforcement* (London: Hart, 2018), p. 141.

48 See C. Hoppe and M. Michel, 'Acting in concert in the version of the Risk Reduction Act' (2010) *BaFinQuarterly* Q2/10, p. 9 et seq., who point out that the requirement of cooperation 'in any way', introduced in 2008 in response to a restrictive judgment delivered by the German Supreme Court on 18 September 2006, seeks to cover shareholder cooperation unrelated to the general meeting, therefore including an influence on the board of directors or the supervisory council outside voting. On the concept of concerted action and its application, see BaFin, *Attribution of voting rights under section 34 of the WpHG*, available at www.bafin.de, and also BaFin's *Issuer Guidelines*, Module B, 19 June 2019 (but updated on 30 June 2022), p. 27, available at www.bafin.de. This open-endedness of the notion of concert has given rise to extensive case law, derived from both shareholders suing allegedly concerted parties who eluded a takeover bid (see, for example, judgments passed by the Higher Regional Court of Cologne on 16 December 2020, which dismissed the idea of a standstill agreement constituting concerted action, or the judgment delivered by the Higher Regional Court of Düsseldorf on 3 September 2018), and the challenging of corporate resolutions by shareholders deprived of their voting rights, due to allegedly acting in concert with other shareholders (judgment of 12 June 2019 delivered by the Higher Regional Court of Stuttgart). As also highlighted by Sergakis (n 47), p. 142, the fact that concerted action in Germany goes beyond formal agreements and eventually covers any other type of cooperation ultimately generates a more uncertain regulatory framework than the one in France.

qualified, formal, stable and binding agreements on the exercise of voting rights that affect the control or management of the company – in line with the notion provided by the Transparency Directive – can lead to serious legal uncertainty. The problem with linking mandatory takeover bids with tacit and informal agreements is that, in the absence of contractual controlling positions, even the parties involved may not be in a condition to understand whether they are collectively acquiring control. If the broad and extensive notion of concert is also extended to concerted voting, the inevitable consequence is that serious legal uncertainties are generated, when various relevant shareholders (typically related to the company´s management or in any event holding a significant interest, as in the case of institutional investors) exercise their voting rights de facto in a uniform manner, or openly agree in a more or less public manner on their position regarding the company´s policies, shareholder meetings or specific resolutions. This voting alignment may even take place in a stable and continuous manner over time, without strictly binding the shareholders under any formal syndication agreement and, consequently, in the absence of any legal obligation to do so. This kind of shareholder consultation, collaboration or association when exercising their voting rights (the extreme example of which would constitute shareholder activism) is commonplace in many listed companies and is often consubstantial with the formation of ordinary majorities – and sometimes of blocking minorities, in the presence of a controlling shareholder – at general meetings. Majority votes are hardly ever formed spontaneously and randomly at a meeting, but are usually anticipated, even when the basic and primary consequence of such majorities is to back up the corporate management and the board's proposal, let alone when they lead to coordinated opposition along with a common policy. This explains why it is essential to adequately define what specific types of agreements constitute relevant concerted voting, in order to cover only those agreements that have an actual and material impact on the control situation of the company, in view of the rationale of the mandatory bid system, but also to afford the legal certainty that is required in this field for economic agents.

The issue of the possible extension of the broad definition of concert to voting agreements is much more than a mere technical discussion to generate debate amongst legal scholars and academics, as the practical consequences of such an interpretation, without any hyperbole or exaggeration, are colossal: it would suffice for two or more shareholders who, on aggregate, hold more than 30 per cent of the voting rights to reach any kind of covenant, agreement or understanding on how to vote at general meetings in matters affecting the company's management, including a tacit or informal agreement that does not generate any legal obligation or future binding effects (a mere 'nod or wink'), to trigger the disproportionate obligation to launch a takeover bid over 100 per cent of the share capital.

All in all, whether or not one believes that concerted voting takeover bids are an efficient tool, it is crucial not to overlook that the most convincing explanation for those bids lies in their ability to police the traditional mandatory bid rule by acquisition of control. In this regard, there is always a trade-off between making this anti-avoidance function more effective, on the one hand, and maintaining sound corporate governance, on the other. Expanding concerted voting takeover bids beyond formal agreements can certainly prevent some strategies aimed at circumventing (national rules implementing) Article 5 of the Takeover Bids Directive. At the same time, however, that policy choice can have a problematic impact on corporate governance. In particular, despite its intention to protect minorities, such a policy can freeze shareholder coordination in a way that protects incumbent controlling shareholders from being challenged by insurgent activist investors, as we shall see. Albeit less evident than the immediate positive impact of a mandatory bid on minority shareholders, this has certainly a negative effect on the very same shareholders – and the net effect of these two conflicting consequences is certainly hard to quantify.

8.3.5 *Other Concert Situations: Acquisition of Control by Concerted Persons and Changes in Pre-existing Concert Agreements*

As we have seen, the concept of concerted action plays a dual role in mandatory bid systems, depending on the cases to which the national legislator associates the corresponding obligation to make a bid. In systems that require an acquisition, it is openly conceived as a purely instrumental rule, designed to prevent the mandatory bid obligation from being circumvented by the simple expedient of splitting or fractioning the acquisition of the controlling interest among several persons. In systems imposing the takeover bid by mere concerted action in the exercise of voting rights, even though the most convincing rationale of this rule remains to avoid circumvention of the mandatory bid rule by concealing an initial mutual understanding, concert plays a material or substantive role, as it represents the fact or event that triggers per se the obligation to launch the bid.

However, concert may also be relevant in other hybrid or intermediate cases, in which an acquisition of shares coexists with a pre-existing concert agreement between several shareholders. This would be the case of a group of shareholders that are already linked through an agreement, when any of them proceeds to make acquisitions that raise the aggregate participation of all of them above the relevant threshold. In these cases, since the interests of the concerted shareholders are calculated jointly for these purposes, a takeover bid should be launched even though none of them individually exceeds the relevant threshold. The declared or implied purpose of the agreement may not relate to acquiring corporate control (or fending off other offers), but will still be relevant in determining the joint calculation of votes.

Another case, which is known, for instance, in the UK but is of a particular practical relevance in legal systems where shareholder agreements are common, such as the Italian one, occurs in relation to agreements having the alleged effect not so much of changing the corporate control as of maintaining control upon the seller of a stake in the company. This may relate to situations where a shareholder previously holding control sells part of his/her stake to a new shareholder, with whom he/she contextually enters into an agreement that makes the control situation more elusive to understand for an external observer. For instance, agreements of this kind may sometimes enable the seller to retain a substantive grasp on the corporate policy, but can also involve some significant rights being granted to the new shareholder. Such rights may include veto powers on certain matters or the appointment of some board members.

The scrutiny of such cases against their ability to trigger the mandatory bid rule often leads to complex assessments that inevitably involve a high level of discretion. These assessments become all the more difficult in the absence of a formalised agreement. For instance, the UK Takeover Panel will try to ascertain whether a control change occurred and, in doing so, will consider elements such as whether the vendor is an insider, the amount of the transferred shares and the price paid to purchase them.[49] In Italy, CONSOB will ascertain whether the scope of the powers granted to the new shareholder is such that it materially weakens the incumbent's powers – an assessment that can prove uncertain even when the shareholder agreement is formalised in a document.[50]

Other difficult assessments are required for changes involving a group of concerted shareholders that enjoy joint control of the company, typically through an openly declared shareholder agreement. This can occur when a third party joins the control group, contributing its shares to it or acquiring the stake of one of the previous shareholders and replacing him/her within the agreement, but also when acquisitions take place between the shareholders themselves, when such changes substantially modify the qualitative composition and the distribution of power within the group.[51] Once again, supervisors and/or courts will need to resort to some level of discretion when ascertaining the need to require a bid. In the UK, for instance, the Takeover Panel will normally require a bid when shares are purchased from outside the group of concerted parties holding collectively more than 30 per cent (but less than 50 per cent) of voting rights. For intra-group transactions, the Panel will instead consider whether a single member of the group crosses the 30 per cent threshold and, in this case, if the leader of the group has changed due to the acquisition, the price paid for the transaction and the stability of the concert.

49 See Note 6 to Rule 9.1 of the UK Takeover Code, on the 'Vendor of part only of an interest in shares'.

50 See e.g. CONSOB, Communication n. DIS/99024712, 31 March 1999; Communication n. DCL/DEM/85385, 16 November 2000; Communication n. DEM/11016918, 4 March 2011; for an analysis Gargantini (n 40), p. 2117 et seq.

51 See Note 4 to Rule 9.1 of the UK Takeover Code, on 'Acquisition of interests in shares by members of a group acting in concert'.

8.4 TAKEOVER BIDS DUE TO CONCERTED VOTING, SHAREHOLDER COOPERATION AND SHAREHOLDER ACTIVISM

8.4.1 *The Problems Created by the Different Meanings of Concerted Action in Europe*

The vagueness and legal ambiguity inherent to concerted action, along with the different notions used in European national laws, have generated great legal uncertainty in Europe as regards regular shareholder cooperation and other forms of collaboration touching upon or nearing the field of concerted action in the proximity of control thresholds, which could trigger the exorbitant obligation to launch a takeover bid for 100 per cent of the share capital. It is worth noting that this uncertainty is obviously higher in systems where shareholder (express or implied) agreements suffice to trigger the mandatory bid rule, but is well known in other countries, too. In this regard, the main difference is that, in systems where mandatory bids are made subject to an acquisition of relevant securities, investors that are part of an occasional coalition can protect themselves from the risk of being subject to purchasing all the outstanding capital by avoiding any purchase during the time the coordination lasts – this restriction to the trading strategies investors can adopt is however not without cost, as we shall see.

These uncertainties affect the natural process of formation and consolidation of majorities within the general shareholders' meeting, something that is consubstantial with rules governing the approval of corporate resolutions and the governance of companies. As a consequence, concerns derived from the lack of specification and haziness of the notion of concert immediately arose amongst large international investors after the Takeover Bids Directive was passed and implemented in European national laws. Investors, which operate in many different markets, were not only forced to handle and cover various types of concert in their investment policies in the different countries where they invest, but also faced the unacceptable risk of certain regular forms of cooperation or activism in a company's corporate governance – particularly if the management body is affected – constituting concerted action and thus triggering an obligation to launch a takeover bid in the case of the control threshold being crossed.[52] As affirmed, the effectiveness and

[52] A recent example is provided by W. G. Ringe, 'Investor-led Sustainability in Corporate Governance', *ECGI Law Working Paper* No. 615/2021, November 2021, who highlights the growing relevance of collaboration between institutional investors and hedge funds in ESG initiatives, through 'coalitions', platforms and networks, and how these are constrained by concerted action rules in many European jurisdictions (p. 35). On the chilling effect of acting in concert under the Takeover Bids Directive for shareholder cooperation see T. Papadopoulos, 'The European Union Directive on Takeover Bids: Directive 2004/25/EC' (2008) *International and Comparative Corporate Law Journal* 13, 37 et seq.

instrumental nature of concerted action in various European countries has ended up becoming a 'conundrum' for investors.[53]

The European Commission had already shown full awareness of the problem ever since its initial assessment of the Takeover Bids Directive (first in its Report on the application of the Takeover Bids Directive[54] and later in its Action Plan on European company law and corporate governance[55]). In particular, the Commission suggested that the problem be resolved by further clarifying the notion of concerted action in Europe, so as not to compromise shareholder cooperation and involvement in company's management. Specifically, the Action Plan (section 3.4) states that 'shareholders need to know when they can exchange information and cooperate with one another without running the risk that their actions may trigger unexpected legal consequences'. This is why the European Commission, in an attempt to address and reduce this risk, entrusted ESMA with drawing up guidelines and suggestions on the type of shareholder cooperation that would be totally regular and undisputed and other forms of cooperation which, instead, could constitute concert for takeover bid purposes.[56]

ESMA completed the task with its aforementioned Public Statement on *Information on shareholder cooperation and acting in concert under the Takeover Bid Directive*,[57] which basically collates and sets out the various national practices in relation to concerted action and offers investors certain guidelines, in the form of a safe harbour, on forms of shareholder cooperation that would not be regarded as triggering a mandatory bid. To that end, ESMA drew up a 'white list' of activities which, per se and absent additional circumstances that may lead to concluding otherwise, would not amount to concerted action if jointly undertaken by several shareholders. These activities include discussions on matters to be submitted to the board of directors, the delineation of policies or actions proposed to the board, the request to call a general meeting or an agenda supplement, or a decision to jointly vote on certain resolutions presented to the general meeting, albeit restricted in all cases to matters other than the appointment of directors (such as directors'

[53] Sergakis (n 47), p. 140.

[54] European Commission (n 31), indicating that the 'concept of concerted action' is the first thing that needs to be clarified 'in order to improve legal certainty for the parties concerned and the effective exercise of (minority) shareholder rights' (p. 10, 11).

[55] *Action Plan: European company law and corporate governance – a modern legal framework for more engaged shareholders and sustainable companies*, 12 December 2012.

[56] For a more detailed explanation of these background facts, see Winner (n 8), p. 374 et seq.

[57] Dated 20 June 2014, albeit updated on 8 January 2019. The reason for ESMA approving a 'public statement', which lacks any mandatory content and just gathers 'information' provided by the different national authorities, instead of including technical rules, guidelines or recommendations as is often the case in other fields, is related to ESMA's limited regulatory competence in relation to the Takeover Bids Directive; this Directive is excluded from the remit of ESMA's powers, pursuant to Regulation (EU) n° 1095/2010 (Art. 1.2), which generically authorises ESMA to 'also take appropriate action in the context of take-over bids', amongst other matters (Art. 1.3). See Winner (n 8), p. 378 et seq., and Ghetti (n 9), p. 630 et seq.

remuneration, a capital increase or reduction, distribution of dividends, annual accounts). The white list expressly excludes any form of shareholder cooperation related to the appointment of members of the management body, as this matter is 'particularly sensitive when applying the mandatory takeover bid rule', including for a lack of common understanding among national authorities.[58] Even so, ESMA's Statement still addresses certain matters pertaining to concerted voting to appoint or dismiss one or more directors, whilst also highlighting some factors usually taken into account by national authorities when assessing potential concert, such as any relationship between the shareholders and candidate directors, the number of directors appointed or dismissed, or any possible changes that could arise in the balance of power on the board.[59] Unfortunately, the Statement could not but acknowledge at all times that many different criteria are applied by the authorities in this field.[60]

It is therefore not surprising that ESMA's Public Statement seems to have had scant utility in practice, albeit providing useful guidance on certain matters. In its stocktaking exercise, the Statement indicates the extension that the notion of concerted action has reached in many European countries, and therefore the particularly broad scope of application of the mandatory bid system itself. What reduces the added value of the white list is that it refers to a list of corporate actions that are often commonplace in Member States and which are mostly far from being able to have any significant impact on a company's control (although they can play a role in countries – like Italy – where a coalition of shareholders is deemed as acting in concert even when it merely provides for regular consultations among its members[61]). But even with this limited objective scope, ESMA is careful to point out that even such 'permitted' activities may in fact be unacceptable in certain situations, requiring an inevitable examination based on the specific circumstances of the case (that can always indicate a greater degree of concert), and recommends

58 See also, arguing for a strict interpretation of acting in concert that does not encroach upon the shareholders' right to jointly propose director nominees for election at the general meeting, A. Taleska, 'Shareholder Proponents as Control Acquirers: A British, German and Italian Perspective on the Regulation of Collective Shareholder Activism via Takeover Rules' (2018) *European Business Organization Law Review* 797.

59 See e.g. C. Mosca, 'Attivismo degli azionisti, voto di lista e "azione di concerto"' (2013) *Rivista delle società* 118, 148 et seq.

60 A similar 'white list' is included in the *Joint Guidelines on the prudential assessment of acquisitions and increases of qualifying holdings in the financial sector*, 20 December 2016 (but updated on 31 March 2023), jointly passed by EIOPA, EBA and ESMA (para. 4.9), that also recommend that supervisors 'should not apply the regime relating to the notification and prudential assessment of acquisitions of, or increases in, qualifying holdings in such a way as to inhibit cooperation between shareholders aimed at exercising good corporate governance' (para. 4.7); a similar recommendation is included in the *Guide on qualifying holding procedures* of the European Central Bank, March 2023, p. 12; on the notion of acting in concert in the financial sector, see. A. N. Kostyuk and A. Sacco Ginevri, '"Acting in Concert" in the banking and financial sectors' (2016) *Law and Economics Yearly Review*, 257 et seq.

61 See Art. 101-*bis*.4-*bis*.a) and 122.5.a) *Testo Unico della Finanza*.

that the supervisory authorities be consulted if in doubt.[62] In this regard, the reiteration of the phrase 'in and of itself' throughout the list and its accompanying documents shows that the Public Statement provides (in and of itself, one might say) limited legal certainty, as the definition of the boundaries of concerted action remains national.

The limited practical effects of these guidelines have been recognised by ESMA itself, which has advocated the need to review its Public Statement in order to generate greater certainty for investors in concerted action matters, specifically appraising whether the white list activities should also include active investor collaboration related to ESG risks.[63] Following up on this assessment, ESMA has recently announced its intention to update the white list, at the request of the European Commission, 'to ensure that acting in concert rules do not create an obstacle to collective engagement by investors around common sustainability goals'.[64] The very fact that ESMA feels obliged to specify that collaboration between investors on sustainability issues does not constitute concerted action for the purposes of the mandatory bid system, if anything, reveals the clear distortion and deformation to which the concept has been subject.

On a positive note, ESMA's Public Statement has at least served to evidence the serious problems surrounding the boundaries of concerted action in many countries and the pressing need (of which all national supervisors are apparently aware) to avoid extensive interpretations that could end up compromising and hindering regular shareholder activism and cooperation amongst large institutional investors in corporate governance matters, while retaining the role of acting in concert as a tool to prevent circumvention of the mandatory bid rule.

In any case, the fact that the European national authorities have been forced to clarify that certain regular and unsubstantial corporate actions included in the white list do not per se constitute concerted action, does confirm that a badly designed mandatory takeover bid system may end up hindering not only effective operation of the market for corporate control but also the basics and principles of the majority rule prevailing in companies, to the detriment of effective shareholder cooperation or engagement in corporate management matters.

62 Likewise, indicating the limited effects of ESMA's statement, see Winner (n 8), p. 387 et seq.

63 *Report. Undue short-term pressure on corporations*, 18 December 2019, p. 68 et seq.

64 2024 *Annual Work Programme*, 28 September 2023 (ESMA22–50751485-1368). Of great interest in this regard are BaFin's note on 'Collaborative engagement and the attribution of voting rights: When can things get tricky?' of 30 May 2023 (which analyses different examples of collaboration between investors in ESG matters and their possible consideration as acting in concert). See also W. Puchniak and U. Varotttil, 'Rethinking Acting in Concert: Activist ESG Stewardship is Shareholder Democracy' (2023) *ECGI Law Working Paper* n°731/2023 (who analyse the risk that the 'activist stewardship' embraced by many institutional investors may trigger the acting in concert rules, and who propose to redesign such rules to distinguish between ESG activism battles and takeover contests).

In this regard, investors (particularly institutional investors and collective asset managers) are subject to somewhat contradictory regulatory policies. On the one hand, EU law considers the mandatory bid rule (and the definition of concerted action that supports it) as a tool to protect minority shareholders, and therefore views concerted practices with some suspicion. On the other hand, the same EU law also supports the exercise of shareholder rights and shareholder engagement within listed companies as a good governance tool – the Shareholder Rights Directive[65] gives clear indications in this regard. As shareholders can use their rights more effectively when they reach critical thresholds, coordinated action plays a positive role in this regard. Remarkably, this positive role acts for the benefit of all investors and can therefore be regarded as a protective measure. Lastly, the G20/OECD *Principles of Corporate Governance* (2023) state that 'shareholders, including institutional shareholders, should be allowed to consult with each other on issues concerning their basic shareholder rights as defined in the Principles, subject to exceptions to prevent abuse' (§ II.D);[66] and the same Principles recommend policymakers to issue 'guidance on forms of co-ordination and agreements that do or do not constitute such acting in concert' in the context of takeover and other rules, in order to distinguish forms of cooperation and coordination between investors aimed at improving the corporate governance of the company from those that, on the contrary, seek 'to obtain control over a company, with a view to bypass takeover or disclosure regulations' (§ II.D).

8.4.2 *The Basic Issue: The Different Models of Mandatory Takeover Bids and the Confusion about the Relevant Notion of Concert*

The previous analysis shows that, in a broader perspective that also looks at market practices, investor uncertainty derived from different concerted action notions coexisting in Europe goes way beyond a mere technical difference as to the definition of the concept, or the way in which Member States have transposed the Takeover Bids Directive.[67] Rather, it has more to do with the existence of

[65] Directive 2007/36/EC of the European Parliament and of the Council of 11 July 2007 on the exercise of certain rights of shareholders in listed companies, amended by Directive (EU) 2017/828 of the European Parliament and of the Council of 17 May 2017 amending Directive 2007/36/EC as regards the encouragement of long-term shareholder engagement. On the risk of contradiction between the Shareholder Rights Direcitve and acting in concert in the Takeover Bids Directive, see M. Maugeri, 'Azione di concerto ed engagement degli investitori istituzionali' (2023) *Rivista delle società* 1128, 1131 et seq.

[66] G20/OECD, *Principles of Corporate Governance* (Paris: OECD Publishing, 2023).

[67] See, for example, Ghetti (n 9), p. 612 et seq., who points out that Member States have incorporated the idea of concerted action envisaged in the Takeover Bids Directive in materially different terms, or Veil (n 8), who considers that the differences among Member States regarding acting in concert are 'mainly due to the fact that neither the Transparency Directive nor the Takeover Directive gives a precise definition of the concept, only minimum requirements regarding implementation' (p. 692) and who recommends 'to develop a uniform definition of this concept and ensure a uniform application across the EU' (p. 696).

different mandatory takeover bid models and, specifically, the fact that many countries expanded the scope of Article 5 of the Takeover Bids Directive by extending the mandatory bid to situations of mere concerted voting, other than an acquisition of shares, and also applying in this context a broad and expansive notion of acting in concert. This has resulted in a polysemic and vague definition of concerted action, as the same legal concept is used to cover different regulatory strategies dealing with control changes. Concert is conceived as a mere rule to calculate or assign votes in the legal systems that impose the mandatory bid in the case of acquisition, where it operates as a merely instrumental notion aimed at preventing avoidance of the obligation to launch a takeover bid. But in the systems that impose the bid in the event of concerted voting, the anti-avoidance origin of the concept has been pushed to the point of making it an autonomous and self-sufficient notion, which by itself triggers the takeover bid obligation. Beyond a mere difference of opinion as to the meaning or definition of concerted action, this is in our view what actually lies behind its undefined boundaries and uncertainty.

In takeover bids due to an acquisition, the regulatory purpose of concerted action demands a flexible and all-encompassing definition in order to cover any potential situation where various parties work together to acquire shares and obtain control of the target company eluding the takeover bid obligation. This is why, in these cases, concerted action must include (as inferred from the definition of the Takeover Bids Directive) all sorts of tacit or verbal agreements, irrespective of form and binding effects, thereby covering gentlemen's agreements, 'handshakes' or, in the eloquent words of the UK Takeover Panel, 'nods or winks', as long as the parties act under a common purpose to jointly take control of the company. But in these cases, the inevitable requirement of the mandatory bid continues to be the *acquisition* of a controlling interest, which is why concerted action becomes particularly relevant if the parties acquiring the shares wish to elude the obligation to launch a takeover bid (as, otherwise, there would be no issue). As a result, the hypothetical risk of ordinary forms of shareholder cooperation and coordination in corporate governance or company management matters constituting concerted action for takeover bid purposes is reduced[68]. Concerted voting may be relevant in these cases to ascertain the potential existence of concerted action in the acquisition of shares, particularly in two different situations: if it indicates that share acquisitions by the concerted parties had to be inevitably a consequence of a prior agreement or

[68] Also pointed out by Winner (n 8), p. 369: 'for institutional investors coordinating their vote before a general meeting, there is less cause for concern. If they act in concert to cooperate and as long as no shares are acquired as a result of such cooperation, they cannot be forced to launch a takeover bid', and Ghetti (n 9), p. 610 et seq., who believes there is a higher risk of general concerted action discouraging activism (or monitoring cooperation, rather than circumventing cooperation) in countries where a takeover bid is imposed due to mere concert.

understanding seeking to acquire control of the company,[69] and if the concerted parties subsequently acquire shares to increase their joint interest above the relevant threshold. But, even so, the unambiguous and unequivocal meaning of mandatory takeover bids and its structural association with *acquiring* a controlling interest (objective conduct that is easy to ascertain) comparatively reduces the risk of regular shareholder coordination or voting agreements being mistaken or considered as concerted action.[70] To be sure, this is cold comfort if one considers that a relevant number of investors, such as ETFs or index mutual funds, have a passive management strategy that may force them to buy in some circumstances. For this kind of shareholders, the difference between mandatory bid rules based on acquisitions and on mere concert may not be as large as it appears at first sight.

In any event, systems that extend mandatory bids to the coordinated action of several shareholders who jointly exercise their voting rights, in a more or less public and open manner, increase for all shareholders the level of uncertainty surrounding the interferences between concerted action and regular shareholder cooperation or collaboration.[71] The breadth and legal vagueness of the usual components of concerted action as delineated at national level, covering mere voting agreements that pursue a common policy in corporate management matters, and the fact that this legal concept clearly overlaps with the ordinary process of formation and changes of majorities within the companies, imply that practically any type of cooperation on relevant corporate matters amongst shareholders who jointly own an interest exceeding the relevant threshold can fall within its field of action, especially when the requirement of a lasting common policy is interpreted as

[69] In fact, in takeover bids following an acquisition, it is commonplace for supervisory authorities, faced with the difficulty of proving that concerted action has been agreed upon, to rely on evidence arising from the conduct of 'suspect' shareholders after the shares were acquired, in the sense that the fact of promoting initiatives to obtain control of the company may indicate that their previous acquisitions were concerted. This was what the Spanish CNMV claimed in a notorious precedent (sanctioning procedure brought against TXU and Electrabel in 2001 due to an alleged concerted acquisition of shares in Hidroeléctrica del Cantábrico), given that the different actions followed by both companies as shareholders seemed to confirm the absence of any type of prior agreement or understanding; on the matter, see García de Enterría, *Limitación del voto* (n 10), p. 91.

[70] Although the risk cannot be totally ruled out in takeover bids following an acquisition, as indicated by the UK Takeover Panel publishing *Practice Statement* n°26 in 2009 on 'Shareholder Activism', in order to address the concerns of some management companies and institutional investors, fearing that collective action could qualify as concerted action; the Panel basically pointed out that mandatory takeovers would only apply if shareholders were to jointly present a 'board control-seeking resolution' and, consequently, were to acquire shares to raise their joint interest to more than 30 per cent; instead, as seen, a mere 'coming together to act in concert' will not usually trigger a mandatory bid if none of the concerted parties subsequently acquires shares.

[71] Arguing in favour of a strict definition of acting in concert so as not to hamper shareholder coordination (but leaving companies flexibility to broaden the definition) see Enriques (n 36), p. 635.

broadly as to include shareholders' conduct that does not directly and openly seek to take control.[72]

This ambiguity is also exacerbated by the blurredness and lack of precision of the institutional purposes underlying mandatory bids due to mere concerted voting, as a way out for minority shareholders in the event of a change in majorities or corporate policies. This determines that the mandatory bid ends up having a very broad practical scope that includes situations qualitatively unrelated to the traditional grounds of the mandatory bid system. The experience of the French, German or Spanish legal systems regarding the definition of relevant concerted action agreements in takeover bids is a case in point. In these countries, the definition of concerted action has generally expanded over time, in response to certain court decisions or controversial cases.[73] Their experience shows that, once the mandatory takeover bid due to concerted action is enshrined in the system, the legislator may be fatally induced to progressively expand the perimeter of the relevant agreements, in order to close the system and avoid any circumvention through conduct or action different from that envisaged but with similar practical effects. We have explained above that this focus on the risk of avoidance often leads to the costs of implementing the strategies addressing it being overlooked.

The significant differences amongst European legal systems in takeover bids due to concerted voting, besides indicating the varying grounds of mandatory takeover bids, may be partly explained by the structural features of each country's securities market and, in particular, by the greater or lesser degree of concentration and stability of their listed company shareholding structure. In countries where ownership is more concentrated, concerted voting could be expected to bear greater weight as a way of obtaining and consolidating control, as opposed to share acquisitions, thus triggering the legislator's interest in addressing this type of concert.[74] Takeover bids are also connected to essential corporate law principles and have an impact on economic and even cultural issues that are particularly sensitive in some Member States. This became apparent during the vicissitudes and difficulties that arose during the approval process of the Takeover Bids Directive and is also corroborated by the latter's scant imperative content.[75] Consequently, even if one

[72] See Puchniak and Varottil (n 64), p. 5, who consider that the limitations that institutional investors face to escalate matters with companies specifically on ESG issues 'is an affront to shareholder democracy'.

[73] Also pointed out by Ghetti (n 9), p. 366.

[74] See the Report issued by European Company Law Experts (n 44), p. 5 ('the prevalence of dispersed ownership or ownership concentration and of shareholders agreements differs from one member state to another, creating different control situations in each member state'); Winner (n 8), p. 389 ('the fact that [takeover bid] triggers differ may reflect underlying differences in market structure, which influence and affect how Member States interpreted the function of mandatory takeover bids').

[75] On the matter, see J. García de Enterría, 'El deber de pasividad de los administradores de la sociedad afectada por una OPA' (2008) *Revista de Derecho del Mercado de Valores*, 92 et seq., with subsequent references, pointing out the economic and cultural factors (the 'collision of

were to enthusiastically encourage an amendment or reform of the Takeover Bids Directive to unify – not so much the concerted action notion, but rather – the mandatory bid system and the conditions that trigger it, it is very unlikely that this would become a reality in the short to medium term.[76] Also, similar provisions on paper may correspond to different approaches in reality (and vice versa), depending on the supervisory style of the competent authority.

However, the fact remains that the concept of acting in concert, which historically emerged as an anti-circumvention rule for mandatory bids in relation to situations exclusively involving the acquisition of control of listed companies, has been subject to a persistent process of expansion in many national legal systems, to the point of jeopardising ordinary situations of cooperation and collaboration among shareholders that do not affect the control and management of the company. In the absence of European harmonisation, one can only rely on the restraint and reasonableness of national legislators and supervisory authorities in defining and applying this concept.

8.5 CONCLUSION

This chapter has explored the concept and implications of acting in concert in the light of the Takeover Bids Directive and its national implementing measures. The regulation of concerted action is one of the building blocks of the European approach towards takeover bids and plays a crucial role in the mandatory bid regime. The original role of acting in concert lies in its anti-elusive function, as a rule aimed to aggregate the shareholdings held by different persons that act in a coordinated manner in order to prevent such persons from circumventing the duty to launch a bid when they jointly acquire shares (or assimilated instruments) above the relevant control threshold. However, this anti-elusive function has been implemented in different ways at national level, which confirms the limited ability of the Takeover Bids Directive to harmonise takeover law in Europe. The overall picture emerging from the analysis reveals that Member States have followed different approaches on the crucial matter of shareholder coordination. In this regard, although every country has followed its own path, EU jurisdictions can basically be divided into two groups. The first group – following the example of the UK, where the mandatory bid system originated – has maintained the Takeover Bids Directive approach, which links the mandatory bid rule to holding shares and acquiring control as the result of an acquisition. In these countries, shareholder agreements or other forms of coordination are not sufficient, on their own, to trigger the mandatory bid rule, as an

capitalist systems') that conditioned the drafting and outcome achieved by the Takeover Bids Directive.

[76] Also highlighted by Winner (n 8), p. 388, indicating that the possibility of total harmonisation of the Takeover Bids Directive, to unify national systems in concerted action matters, does not seem to be currently realistic.

acquisition by at least one of the concerted parties is needed. The second group of countries has instead expanded the role of acting in concert beyond this Directive requirement. Here, a bid is required regardless of an acquisition of shares, as long as a group of shareholders coalesce to adopt a common (lasting) policy with regard to the listed company. The most convincing explanation for this kind of expansion is the willingness to further restrict the room for circumventing the mandatory bid requirement – typically by formalising, after an acquisition of shares, a pre-existing agreement.

The analysis has shown that national laws implementing the Takeover Bids Directive fall short of providing sufficient legal certainty for investors. This applies to all Member States, but linking the mandatory bid rule to concerted action alone, even in the absence of an acquisition, exacerbates such uncertainty. The problem stems to a large extent from the decision of many States to extend the notion of concerted action of the Takeover Bids Directive, which is exclusively designed for share acquisitions and is characterised by its wide scope, to cases of mere concerted voting, where a more formal and lasting agreement should be required. The meritorious attempts by ESMA to provide clarity on this matter cannot of course compensate for national variations. All in all, the patchwork-like scenario that characterises the Union seems to have the effect of limiting investor protection by making shareholder coordination more difficult unless this involves a relatively small amount of the outstanding capital – a paradoxical effect if one considers the original purpose of the mandatory bid rule. On top of this, cross-border investments are made more difficult, as investors have to become familiar with as many regulatory frameworks as there are European countries they invest in.

9

Conceptual Issues of Equal Treatment and the Mandatory Bid Rule

Edmund Schuster

9.1 INTRODUCTION

This chapter revisits the age-old debate of the merits and demerits of the mandatory bid rule. Section 9.2 starts by discussing the theoretical foundations of the rule, and summarises the consensus about the rule's effects. Section 9.3 proceeds by examining private contracting practices related to the mandatory bid rule, as well as its second-order effects. Given the significant uncertainties about the rule's costs, calls for its optionality ultimately seem justified. Realistically, however, the Takeover Directive (TOD) is unlikely to be amended to embrace optionality. The chapter then argues that developments over the past two decades mean that Member States have more significant choice about the application of the rule than they did when the TOD was enacted, potentially leading to meaningful levels of experimentation with the mandatory bid rule in the EU. Section 9.4 concludes.

9.2 THEORETICAL FOUNDATIONS OF THE MANDATORY BID RULE

9.2.1 *Origins of the Mandatory Bid Rule*

The mandatory bid rule, contained in Article 5 of the TOD, has its origins in UK takeover regulation, where it was added to the City Code in 1972.[1] At the European level, the rule was already included in the earliest Commission proposals for the TOD,[2] as recommended in the initial Pennington report.[3] The later abandoned

[1] See The Takeover Panel, 'Announcement by the City Working Party', No 1972/2 (18 January 1972) (available at www.thetakeoverpanel.org.uk/wp-content/uploads/2008/12/1972-02.pdf). On the history of the mandatory bid rule, see D. Kershaw, *Principles of Takeover Regulation* (Oxford: Oxford University Press 2016), at 8.01–8.04.

[2] Proposal for a Thirteenth Council Directive on Company Law concerning takeover and other general bids, COM (88) 823 final (16 February 1989).

[3] See 'Report on Takeovers and other Bids', COM Doc XI/56/74. On the history of the TOD, see e.g. R. Skog, 'The Takeover Directive – An Endless Saga?' (2002) 13 *European Business and*

plan for a Ninth Company Law Directive harmonising group law also contained a rule that can be regarded as functionally equivalent to the mandatory bid rule.[4]

As is well documented,[5] much of the European political discussion surrounding the TOD concerned hostile takeovers and the role of target boards to defend against such takeovers – a topic covered elsewhere in this book.[6] While important, the debate about takeover defences and the board neutrality rule is of course largely (though not entirely)[7] irrelevant in companies with controlling shareholders, and such companies still dominate the corporate landscape in the EU – particularly so after Brexit.[8]

From this perspective, the mandatory bid rule is arguably the most consequential rule for continental European deals,[9] and the impact the rule would have on the takeover markets in EU Member States with more concentrated ownership was predicted long before the TOD came into force.[10]

Takeovers of controlled companies typically begin with a negotiation between the potential acquirer and the blockholder (or controlling concert group) of the target, and control will often be transferred via a private sale of the controlling share block.[11]

Organisation Law Review 301; K. J. Hopt, 'Takeover Regulation in Europe: The Battle for the 13th Directive on Takeovers' (2002) 15 *Australian Journal of Corporate Law* 1; V. Edwards, 'The Directive on Takeover Bids – Not Worth the Paper It's Written On?' (2004) 1 *European Company and Financial Law Review* 416.

4 See K. Bohlhoff and J. Budde, 'Company Groups – The EEC Proposal for a Ninth Directive in the Light of the Legal Situation in the Federal Republic of Germany' (1984) 6 *Journal of Comparative Business & Capital Market Law* 163, 188 (Annex, Article 15).

5 See e.g. Edwards, 'The Directive on Takeover Bids – Not Worth the Paper It's Written On?'; Skog,n 3.

6 See Chapters 10, 11 and 12.

7 Only in the rarest of circumstances will a target board deploy takeover defences against the wishes of a de facto controller. Takeover defences still matter where they can be used to entrench an insecure (<50%) blockholder, however; see the discussion in P. L. Davies, E. Schuster and E. Van de Walle de Ghelcke, 'The Takeover Directive as a Protectionist Tool?' in: U. Bernitz and W.-G. Ringe (eds.), *Company Law and Economic Protectionism* (Oxford, Oxford University Press 2010) 105. In these situations, the rules on mandatory bids and takeover defence regulation do interact, as the mandatory bid rule may prevent the blockholder from selling shares at a price exceeding her reservation price, rendering the availability of takeover defences more valuable to the blockholder.

8 See e.g. M. Faccio and L. H. P. Lang, 'The Ultimate Ownership of Western European Corporations' (2002) 65 *Journal of Financial Economics* 365.

9 See e.g. P. O. Mülbert and A. Sajnovits, 'Lowballing under the EU Takeover Bid Directive: Strategies, Concerns, and Gold-Plating Remedies' (2024) *European Corporate Governance Institute – Law Working Paper* No. 778/2024, available at https://ssrn.com/abstract=4877825, at 6. It is worth emphasising, however, that many continental European jurisdictions had adopted mandatory bids before the TOD; see K. J. Hopt, 'European Takeover Reform of 2012/2013 – Time to Re-examine the Mandatory Bid' (2014) 15 *European Business Organization Law Review* 143, 166.

10 See P. L. Davies, 'The Notion of Equality in Corporate Takeovers' in: J. Payne (ed.), *Takeovers in English and German Law* (Oxford: Hart, 2002), p. 9, 14.

11 See e.g. the discussion in E. Schuster, 'The Mandatory Bid Rule: Efficient, After All?' (2013) 76 *Modern Law Review* 529.

It is in this setting that the mandatory bid rule, a 'dramatic example of [a] unilateral exit right',[12] has its most obvious effect, as it forces any person[13] who through the acquisition of shares[14] obtains control over a listed[15] company to make an offer to buy out all remaining shareholders of the target.[16]

The acquirer has to extend an offer to all shareholders of the target, and such an offer must be made at an 'equitable price'.[17] Two obvious questions immediately emerge. First, the definition of control is clearly crucial, since acquiring control is the main trigger for the obligation. Second, the significance of an obligation to offer the acquisition of shares to minority shareholders clearly depends on the terms of the offer – primarily the (minimum) consideration to be offered, and the form of the consideration.[18]

The definition of what should count as an equitable price was long controversial, and it was one of the issues on which the Commission sought the advice of the High Level Group.[19] Its suggestion was to apply the 'highest price paid' rule, rather than attempting to assess the 'intrinsic value' of the target company's shares – a difficult and uncertain process.[20] Following this suggestion, the TOD requires the bidder to pay a price at least equal to the highest price she paid for shares of the target company during a reference period of between six and twelve months preceding the acquisition of control.

In practice, the rule means that the bidder has to offer the same (per-share) consideration to outside shareholders that the former controller receives. In particular, any control premium will equally be shared by all shareholders, rather than just benefitting the blockholder.[21] The mandatory bid rule is thus a very strong 'equal treatment' rule. An important limitation of this equal treatment right in the TOD, however, is that it is restricted to equal treatment within the same class of shares.[22]

[12] Davies,n 10, at 22.

[13] Legal or natural, see Art. 5 and the definitions in Art. 2(1)(c) and (d).

[14] I.e. *voting* securities, Art. 2(1)(e).

[15] I.e. trading on a regulated market, see Art. 1(1).

[16] See Art. 5(1).

[17] Art. 5(1) TOD.

[18] See Davies,n 10, 12–13; see also L. Enriques, 'Mandatory Bid Rule in the Takeover Directive: Harmonization without Foundation' (2004) 1 *European Company and Financial Law Review* 440, 448.

[19] See European Commission, 'Company law: Commission creates High Level Group of Experts', IP/01/1237 (4 September 2001).

[20] J. W. Winter, J. S. Christensen, J. M. Garrido Garcia, K. J. Hopt, J. Rickford, G. Rossi and J. Simon, 'Report of the High Level Group of Company Law Experts on Issues Related to Takeover Bids in the European Union' (Brussels, 2002).

[21] In addition to the highest price paid rule, several Member States (e.g. Austria, Belgium, Germany, Greece, Portugal, Romania and Spain) require bidders to also offer at least the average stock market price during a period (often between three and six months) before the bid; see Marccus Partners, 'The Takeover Bids Directive Assessment Report' (2011), 67.

[22] See also Section 9.3.5.

The TOD does not define what control means for the purposes of the mandatory bid rule.[23] Instead, Article 5(2) leaves this decision to the home Member State.[24] Although this would in theory create significant scope for diversity, Member States in fact follow the same approach and define control at or around 30 per cent of the company's voting rights,[25] a threshold first introduced in the UK in 1974.[26]

9.2.2 *Takeovers of Controlled Companies: Conflicts between Blockholders and Outside Shareholders*

The mandatory bid rule is usually understood as primarily a minority shareholder protection device, aimed at addressing problems that arise in takeovers of companies dominated by significant blockholders.[27] Though there are other possible rationales for the rule,[28] it is this minority shareholder protection function that the TOD explicitly cites as justification for the rule.[29]

What, then, are the main conflicts between blockholders and outside shareholders in takeovers of controlled companies? A blockholder can usually decide the outcome of a proposed takeover single-handedly, which introduces an inherent risk that the controller's decision to sell her stake could impose costs on other shareholders of the target. This harm to outside shareholders is mainly related to private benefits of control – that is, the observation that a controlling blockholder

[23] As we have seen above, it does rely on the control concept from accounting regulation for the purposes of the reciprocity rule. This concept (appropriately) does not apply to the mandatory bid rule, however.

[24] I.e. the state of incorporation; see Art. 5(3) TOD.

[25] See Marccus Partners,n 21, at 129, showing that Member States have generally opted for either 30 or 33 per cent thresholds.

[26] When the mandatory bid rule was introduced in 1972, the threshold was initially set at 40 per cent. It was lowered to 30 per cent two years later, and has remained unchanged since; see J. Armour and D. A. Skeel, 'Who Writes the Rules for Hostile Takeovers, and Why? – The Peculiar Divergence of US and UK Takeover Regulation' (2007) 95 *Georgetown Law Journal* 1727.

[27] See e.g. Kershaw,n 1, at 8.29; Enriques,n 18; J. L. Hansen, 'The Mandatory Bid Rule: Unnecessary, Unjustifiable and Inefficient' (2018) *Nordic & European Company Law Working Paper* No. 18-01 (available at https://ssrn.com/abstract=3112100).

[28] For a discussion see Enriques,n 18, at 447 et seq., and Davies,n 10.

[29] See Art. 5(1). That protecting minority shareholders was the main focus of the TOD's adoption of the mandatory bid rule is also highlighted by the fact that an early draft of the TOD contained a carve-out from the requirement for Member States to adopt the mandatory bid rule where they adopted 'other appropriate and at least equivalent' minority shareholder protection rules – an option generally understood as a referring to German-type group law. On this, see Art. 3(1) of the Proposal for a 13th European Parliament and Council Directive on company law concerning takeover bids, COM (95) 655 final (7 February 1996), available at http://aei.pitt.edu/10077/1/10077.pdf and the discussion in M. Habersack, 'Non-frustration Rule and Mandatory Bid Rule – Cornerstones of European Takeover Law?' (2018) 15 *European Company and Financial Law Review* 1, at 29; see also K. J. Hopt, 'Europäisches und deutsches Übernahmerecht' (1997) 161 *Zeitschrift für das Gesamte Handels- und Wirtschaftsrecht* 368, 384 et seq.

(usually) benefits *disproportionally*[30] more from her shareholding than other (i.e. minority) shareholders.[31] This is because the ability to control a company has a separate value that goes beyond the dividend rights attached equally[32] to all shares.

There are different sources for the separate value of corporate control,[33] but they are ultimately all based on the fact that a controlling blockholder can unilaterally make decisions about how the company is run,[34] and will – subject to constraints from general company law – rationally do so in ways that best reflect the controller's interests, even where the benefits produced by the corporation will not result in overall higher profits (and hence, eventually, dividends).[35]

Two distinct risks arise from this situation. First, the blockholder may oppose a change of control (by not selling the controlling block), even though such a sale would create value overall – that is, a takeover could be social, but not privately optimal. Imagine, for instance, a shareholder with ambitions to run for public office controlling a large media company. Selling her controlling interest, she would not only give up future dividend payments, but perhaps also lower her chances of being elected.[36] Because this cost is borne privately by the controller, she may oppose what is a lucrative offer to all other shareholders.[37] This reluctance to sell will affect both

[30] I.e. on a per-share basis. In other words, a 60 per cent blockholder will derive *more than ten times* the value from its shareholding than a 6 per cent shareholder does.

[31] See e.g. L. A. Bebchuk and M. Kahan, 'A Framework for Analyzing Legal Policy Towards Proxy Contests' (1990) 78 *California Law Review* 1071, 1090; R. La Porta et al., 'Investor Protection and Corporate Governance' (2000) 58 *Journal of Financial Economics* 3, 4; S. J. Grossman and O. D. Hart, 'One Share-One Vote and the Market for Corporate Control' (1988) 20 *Journal of Financial Economics* 175, 177; O. Ehrhardt and E. Nowak, *Private Benefits and Minority Shareholder Expropriation (or What Exactly are Private Benefits of Control?)* (EFA 2003 Conference Paper 809, 2003), available at ssrn.com/abstract=423506.

[32] Whether or not dividends are shared equally depends, of course, on the company's constitution, subject to constraints under applicable corporate law. However, disproportionality between risk-bearing capital and control exacerbates, but does not fundamentally alter, the problem. Schuster,n 11.

[33] For an overview and examples see Schuster,n 11, 540–546.

[34] I.e. use her position as shareholder (and potentially as director) to influence corporate decision-making in privately optimal ways.

[35] For a discussion of private benefits, see e.g. Ehrhardt and Nowak,n 31; L. Enriques 'The Mandatory Bid Rule in the Proposed EC Takeover Directive: Harmonization as Rent-Seeking?' in: G. Ferrarini, K. J. Hopt, J. Winter and E. Wymeersch (eds.), *Reforming Company and Takeover Law in Europe* (Oxford: Oxford University Press, 2004), p. 767; S. Johnson, R. La Porta, F. Lopez-de-Silanes and A. Shleifer, 'Tunneling' (2000) 90 *American Economic Review* 22; Schuster,n 11, 541 et seq.

[36] For a more rigorous treatment of this problem, see Schuster,n 11, 541 et seq., and the literature cited there.

[37] Taxation can have a similar 'distortive' effect, where selling a controlling block of shares entails a taxable realisation of profits; see e.g. A. Weber, 'An empirical analysis of the 2000 corporate tax reform in Germany: Effects on ownership and control in listed companies' (2009) 29 *International Review of Law and Economics* 57; M. Becht and E. Boehmer, 'Voting control in German corporations' (2003) 23 *International Review of Law and Economics* 1.

value-increasing and value-destroying transactions.[38] The problem here is that a potentially value-*creating* transaction does not take place due to the blockholder's presence.

Second, the reverse problem may also arise. A blockholder may *want* to sell control over the target company to a particular acquirer, but to an acquirer who is likely to run the company in a way harmful to minority shareholders.[39] Here, the risk lies in the possibility of value destruction to the benefit of the selling blockholder and at the expense of the outside shareholders.

Both these problems will to some extent be addressed outside takeover regulation. Private benefits may stem from conduct that is, or should be, illegal under general company law, group law, creditor protection rules or other parts of the legal framework.[40] Consequently, the magnitude of the two problems outlined above at least partly depends on country-specific factors, including the quality of legal rules and their enforcement.[41] Nevertheless, enforcement is never perfect, and perhaps more importantly, unquestionably legitimate practices, such as the realisation of synergies, lead to the very same problem as the extraction of illegal private benefits of control.[42]

How can takeover regulation contribute to the solution of the two problems? As far as the first problem (the blockholder's *un*willingness to sell) is concerned, no easy direct solution exists. The TOD's attempt to address a subset of the problem through the breakthrough rule – namely, the situation where the unwilling blockholder uses control-enhancing mechanisms, rather than a large holding of the company's risk-bearing capital, to exercise control – has ultimately been unsuccessful as it plays no role in practice due to its optionality.[43]

The availability of corporate restructuring techniques can somewhat limit the costs associated with this first problem,[44] but this is likely to only mitigate extreme

[38] Where the premium offered by the bidder for 100 per cent of the shares is lower than the private benefits of control the controller would have to give up, the blockholder's unwillingness to sell to the bidder is socially optimal, even though it results in minority shareholders foregoing a valuable exit opportunity.

[39] I.e. to a 'looter'; see e.g. Enriques,n 18, at 449; Schuster,n 11, at 550 et seq.

[40] See also J. C. Coates IV, 'Mergers, Acquisitions and Restructuring: Types, Regulation, and Patterns of Practice' in: M. Wright et al. (eds.), *The Oxford Handbook on Corporate Law and Governance* (Oxford: Oxford University Press, 2014, 2nd ed.).

[41] See e.g. the study by Dyck and Zingales (A. Dyck and L. Zingales, 'Private Benefits of Control: An International Comparison' (2004) 59 *Journal of Finance* 537).

[42] See in detail Schuster,n 11, 543–546.

[43] See R. Skog, 'The Takeover Directive, the 'Breakthrough' Rule and the Swedish System of Dual Class Common Stock' (2004), 15 *European Business Law Review* 1439.

[44] The argument is fairly complex, and a detailed analysis goes beyond the scope of this chapter. The basic idea is that the current blockholder may attempt to buy out the minority shareholders or otherwise (e.g. through an upstream merger) achieve a 100 per cent shareholding in the target. As long as she can do so at or near the current stand-alone value of the target's shares, she may subsequently be able to reach an agreement with the value-enhancing acquirer. Many practical problems arise, however, including some created or exacerbated by takeover

cases. One could attempt to force large shareholders to sell their block to a value-increasing acquirer, if the reluctance to sell is based on the enjoyment of private benefits. Unsurprisingly, however, legislators are very reluctant to do so. Apart from constitutional law concerns, these include the difficulties of detecting many forms of private benefits,[45] and the problems of reliably identifying transactions that – absent the controller's unwillingness to sell – would create value. There are indirect ways of mitigating the problem. The legal system may discourage concentrated ownership altogether – for example, through rules of corporate and tax law. In part this can be achieved by limiting the scope for blockholders to extract private benefits, a strategy which tackles the problem both directly (by realigning the positions of minority and majority shareholders) and indirectly – if controlling a company offers fewer benefits, small, diversified investments may become relatively more attractive for blockholders.

How does the mandatory bid rule fit into this description of the problem? In short, the mandatory bid rule addresses the second problem (value-destroying transactions brought about by the blockholder's decision to sell), but does so at the cost of significantly exacerbating the first problem (*un*willingness to sell).

The mechanism used to achieve this is shareholder choice and a formal equality requirement: upon a control change, shareholders can decide whether they want to stay invested in the company or rather exit at the same price as the previous blockholder. This right obviously protects shareholders from being exposed to 'looters', at least where the looting is predictable, as they can simply exit the company instead. As a result, the mandatory bid rule prevents value-destroying bids that would otherwise be privately optimal,[46] because any control change that destroys value will be rendered unprofitable by the prospect of buying out all shareholders at a price acceptable to the current controller. As the likely outcome of a value-destroying control change is that the new controller will own 100 per cent of the company, it will internalise the negative effects of the transaction – naturally, stripping assets of a wholly owned subsidiary is not profitable, at least as long as other corporate constituencies are effectively protected.

The mandatory bid rule is remarkable in that it protects shareholders from a mere *abstract risk* of future expropriation of private benefits of control, rather than an acquirer's observed behaviour.[47]

regulation, such as top-up obligations under national law. For a formal analysis see L. A. Bebchuk, 'Efficient and Inefficient Sales of Corporate Control' (1994) 109 *Quarterly Journal of Economics* 957, 966.

45 See e.g. Johnson et al.,n 35; A. Dyck and L. Zingales, 'Private Benefits of Control: An International Comparison' (2004) 59 *Journal of Finance* 537.

46 I.e. for the current blockholder and the bidder.

47 On this, see Davies,n 10, at 25; see also Kershaw,n 1, at 8.30.

9.2.3 *Economic (In-)Efficiency of the Mandatory Bid Rule*

Despite the mandatory bid rule's ability to screen out value-destroying transactions, most corporate law scholars, particularly those following a law and economics approach, view the mandatory bid rule rather critically.[48] They do so mainly for three, largely undisputed reasons. First, by requiring an offer to all shareholders at the same price, the mandatory bid rule prevents some otherwise profitable and value-increasing transactions. The rule thus has a 'chilling effect' on takeovers, reducing the number of profitable control transfers and thus reducing economic efficiency. Second, cash-constrained bidders may not be able to finance the acquisition of all outstanding shares of the target, particularly where cash compensation is required. Third, minority shareholder protection should be addressed through direct rules that constrain the blockholder from harming his co-shareholders, rather than in the 'roundabout way' the mandatory bid rule takes.[49]

The first criticism is perhaps most important. Where a controller derives private benefits from her shareholding, she will not sell unless she is fully compensated for losing these benefits, together with the anticipated value of the company's future dividends. The mandatory bid rule, however, forces the acquirer to pay the same price to *all* shareholders. Since the current controller will still require full compensation of both the shared (i.e. dividend) value and any private benefits, this means that minority shareholders will receive 'compensation' for something they never had – the controller's private benefits.[50] Takeovers are thus made more expensive in the sense that the bidder will only succeed in taking over the target, if she can create enough value, through synergies, better management or otherwise, to be able to offer all shareholders the same high price the current blockholder demands.

This may not always be the case, meaning that the mandatory bid rule 'immobilises' controlling blocks, chilling the market for corporate control. The rule has thus been described as an 'anti-takeover rule'.[51] Even if corporate control could better be allocated to another shareholder, the mandatory bid rule will sometimes make it

48 From the vast literature on the topic, see e.g. F. H. Easterbrook and D. R. Fischel, 'Corporate Control Transactions' (1982) 91 *Yale Law Journal* 698; L. Enriques, 'The Mandatory Bid Rule in the Proposed EC Takeover Directive: Harmonization as Rent-Seeking?' in G. Ferrarini, K. J. Hopt, J. Winter and E. Wymeersch (eds.) *Reforming Company and Takeover Law in Europe* (Oxford: Oxford University Press, 2004) 767; Enriques,n 18; Hansen,n 27; L. A. Bebchuk, 'Efficient and Inefficient Sales of Corporate Control' (1994) 109 *Quarterly Journal of Economics* 957; M. Kahan, 'Sales of Corporate Control' (1993) 9 *Journal of Law, Economics, & Organization* 368. But see e.g. Hopt,n 9, for the opposite view. See also the review of the literature in Schuster,n 11.

49 See e.g. Easterbrook and Fischel,n 48; Bebchuk,n 48; Enriques,n 48, 785; C. Bergström. P. Hogfeldt, J. R. Macey and P. Samuelsson, 'The Regulation of Corporate Acquisitions: A Law and Economics Analysis of European Proposals for Reform' (1995) *Columbia Business Law Review* 495, 518.

50 See Hansen,n 27; Schuster, n 11, at 553.

51 E.g. Hansen,n 27, 4; Enriques,n 18.

impossible for the involved parties to reach a mutually acceptable bargain.[52] Moreover, it may be questioned whether the equal treatment of the seller of a majority stake on the one hand, and of a minority shareholder on the other is indeed necessary for fairness reasons, or whether equality of treatment between shareholders can indeed be seen as desirable in itself.[53]

The second criticism is also connected to the mandatory bid rule making takeovers more expensive, albeit in a different way. The argument is simply that a mandatory bid obligation results in a higher aggregate investment by the bidder than if he were to buy only, say, 51 per cent of the target's shares. The argument depends on the efficiency of financial markets and the availability of credit. Where markets work imperfectly, the bidder may indeed be unable to raise the necessary funds for the acquisition.[54]

The third criticism is that the mandatory bid rule protects shareholders from abusive exercise of power by the controlling shareholder, but it does so by giving them an exit right before any wrongdoing could possibly have taken place (i.e. at the time control is established).[55] Easterbrook and Fischel compare this to the 'preventive detention of people who never have robbed banks, but have acquisitive personalities'.[56] Instead of letting shareholders leave due to *potential* and *future* misconduct by the acquirer, the argument goes, law should rather focus on direct regulation of the minority–majority conflict and ensure that minority shareholders are protected as such.[57] This argument had also been used by Germany in the early negotiations on the TOD to object to the mandatory bid rule,[58] and early drafts of the Directive did indeed contain a provision that allowed Member States to apply 'other and at least equivalent means in order to protect the minority shareholders' of the target – in fact a derogation for effective group law rules.[59]

The economic arguments against the mandatory bid rule in controlled companies can thus be summarised as follows: while the rule does prevent value-destroying control transfers, it also blocks many value-increasing transactions, making it likely that the rule is overall value destructive. It is, then, uncertain whether the rule provides meaningful protection of minority shareholders *at all*, because the cost of reduced takeover activity is partly borne by them. It thus appears

52 See, in more detail, Enriques,n 18, and Schuster,n 11, and the literature cited there.

53 See Davies,n 10, at 13; Professor Davies also points out that a higher (per-share) value of a controlling shareholding has been acknowledged by UK case law; see *Short* v *Treasury Commissioners* [1948] A C 534, HL. See also Enriques,n 18.

54 See Bebchuk,n 48, who shows that absent market failures, this problem can be overcome by the bidder, and that it cannot render an otherwise profitable transaction unprofitable.

55 Davies,n 10, at 25; see also Kershaw,n 1, at 8.30.

56 Easterbrook and Fischel,n 48, 719.

57 See e.g.ibid.; N. Jennings, 'Mandatory Bids Revisited' (2005) 5 *Journal of Corporate Law Studies* 37, 38; Enriques,n 18; Hansen,n 27.

58 See e.g. R. Skog, *Does Sweden Need a Mandatory Bid Rule?* (Amsterdam: SUERF, 1997).

59 See Habersack,n 29; Hopt,n 29; G. Psaroudakis, 'The Mandatory Bid and Company Law in Europe' (2010) 7 *European Company and Financial Law Review* 550; Bohlhoff and Budde,n 4.

possible, and perhaps likely, that minority shareholders may suffer greater losses from prevented value-increasing bids under a mandatory bid rule than they avoid from the screening out of unfavourable transactions.

The situation is different in companies with widely dispersed ownership structures, as the absence of private benefits on the part of selling shareholders means that the most important criticism of the rule does not apply. Consequently, the costs of the mandatory bid rule are likely much lower, as the rule mainly affects the structuring options of the bidder, rather than directly affecting the bidder's ability to gain control.[60] For instance, the rule pre-empts certain coercive bid tactics and thus protects undistorted shareholder choice in takeovers of companies with dispersed shareholding.[61] However, these effects could likely be replicated by direct regulation of the bid process.

Notwithstanding the relatively broad consensus on the mandatory bid rule's inefficiencies among law and economics scholars, most developed countries have adopted a version of the rule, with the US being the notorious and important exception.[62] There are currently no signs suggesting any serious challenge to the rule in the European Union, the UK or indeed most other jurisdictions.

9.3 RE-ASSESSING THE MANDATORY BID RULE

9.3.1 *The Mandatory Bid Rule: Lessons from Private Markets?*

Given the opposition to the mandatory bid rule among law and economics scholars discussed above, it is tempting to view the rule as a somewhat typical, inflexible, mandatory legal rule that may well serve some political purpose,[63] but ultimately merely imposes efficiency costs on control transactions – inefficiencies that more tailored solutions emerging from private contracting could easily avoid. From this perspective, the obligation of Member States to impose a mandatory bid rule prevents experimentation and horizontal learning, and it is the mandatory (rather than default) nature of the rule that imposes these costs.[64]

What is interesting, however, is that the contractual equivalent of the mandatory bid rule – tag-along rights[65] – has long been used in private company governance, particularly in situations where growing, controlled companies seek to raise funds

60 For a detailed analysis, see Davies,n 10.

61 See ibid.

62 For a summary of the typical position under US state corporate law, see e.g. Schuster,n 11, 535 et seq.

63 The rule may be politically desirable *because* it reduces takeover activity.

64 Enriques et al., n 63; see also Kershaw,n 1, at 8.43.

65 See I. S. Lacave and N. B. Gutiérrez, 'Specific Investments, Opportunism and Corporate Contracts: A Theory of Tag-along and Drag-along Clauses' (2010) 11 *European Business Organization Law Review* 423, 449.

from outside financial investors, such as venture capital or private equity funds.[66] Tag-along rights ensure that minority shareholders can participate in the sale of shares on the same terms as the majority or controlling shareholder, allowing them to share in any exit premium. These rights come in two main varieties: they either require any acquirer to extend the offer made to the blockholder to all other shareholders (with the blockholder prohibited from selling shares unless the acquirer complies with this obligation); or they require a pro-rata acquisition from all shareholders for any sub-100 per cent acquisition.[67] This closely mirrors the two main variants of the 'sharing rule' in public takeovers: the classic mandatory bid rule and what is sometimes referred to as an equal opportunity rule, mandating the acquisition of control via a general pro-rata offer.[68] Tag-along rights are thus largely equivalent to the mandatory bid rule in their operation, and where outside investors cannot force a sale of the business, the effects on blockholders mirror those of the mandatory bid rule.

Tag-along rights are a near ubiquitous feature of venture capital transactions, and are often also used in joint ventures and other closely held companies. This raises the question why a supposedly inefficient and highly costly rule is voluntarily replicated in transactions between sophisticated, well-advised players. Based on the above summary of the economic assessment of the mandatory bid rule, and given tag-along rights' resemblance to the rule, one would naturally expect that, when given the choice, market participants would usually avoid the costly arrangement.

One possible explanation is the increased visibility of private benefits of control in private companies, with venture capital and private equity investors often benefitting from board representation and special information rights in the investee company. The resulting reduction in opportunities of blockholders (often the founders) to extract meaningful levels of classic[69] private benefits of control, and the typical absence of synergies between the investee company and the blockholder may simply render tag-along rights in private companies cheaper than the mandatory bid rule in listed corporations.

Another possible explanation is that contractual tag-along rights operate differently in private companies than the mandatory bid rule does in public companies. For instance, it has been suggested that tag-along rights protect firm-specific investments by minority shareholders in closely held companies, a function the

66 See S. Witney, *Corporate Governance and Responsible Investment in Private Equity* (Cambridge: Cambridge University Press, 2021); S. Zambelli, 'Private Equity Governance and Financing Decisions', in: D. Cumming (ed.) *Oxford Handbook of Private Equity* (Oxford: Oxford University Press, 2012), p. 156–196. See also S. Gomtsian, 'Private Ordering of Exit in Limited Liability Companies: Theory and Evidence from Business Organization Contracts' (2016) 53 *American Business Law Journal* 677.

67 See e.g. Gomtsian,n 66.

68 See e.g. Schuster,n 11, discussing how both rules are economically equivalent in most settings.

69 I.e. value extraction, e.g. via related party transactions and other forms of 'tunnelling'; see e.g. Johnson et al., n 35.

mandatory bid rule does not play in listed firms.[70] While certainly true in some private companies, it is submitted that this cannot be a full explanation. The dramatic increase in large private firms ('unicorns') over the last two decades[71] saw private companies raise vast amounts of capital from primarily financial investors unlikely to make significant firm-specific investments in the investee companies.

9.3.2 *Second-Order Effects of the Mandatory Bid Rule?*

The prevalence of tag-along rights in private companies does not necessarily mean that investors value equality *as such*, even if it comes at an efficiency cost. It may, however, suggest that sharing rules can have beneficial secondary effects that are easily overlooked when analysing only the control transfer as such, rather than the ex ante incentives created by the tag-along rights and the mandatory bid rule.

As discussed above and in more detail elsewhere,[72] the mandatory bid rule directly affects private sales of control by effectively preventing transactions in which an acquirer's valuation does not exceed the total value of the firm by a specific multiple[73] of the private benefits of control enjoyed by the current blockholder. The typical analysis of the mandatory bid rule's efficiency effectively assumes an independently set level of private benefit extraction.[74]

Both voluntarily adopted tag-along rights and the mandatory bid rule are only triggered when control is actually sold, but they also affect the ex ante incentives of blockholders before any transfer takes place. This is because – unless one assumes infinite investment horizons – a sharing requirement subtly changes the calculus of private benefit extraction, by imposing an additional cost on controllers: the immobilisation of their controlling share. If this is correct, both the mandatory bid rule and contractual tag-along rights may disincentivise some types of rent-seeking behaviour by blockholders ex ante,[75] at least where the ability of extracting private benefits is a function of strategic decisions made by the blockholder about the company's business scope and strategy.[76] This mechanism may not only explain

70 On this point, see, in detail, Lacave and Gutiérrez,n 66.

71 See e.g. K. C. Brown and K. W. Wiles, 'The Growing Blessing of Unicorns: The Changing Nature of the Market for Privately Funded Companies' (2020) 32 *Journal of Applied Corporate Finance* 52. See also Morningstar Indexes, 'Unicorns and the Growth of Private Markets' (24 June 2024), available at: https://indexes.morningstar.com/insights/analysis/blt81d5614b4c2ccd2b/unicorns-and-the-growth-of-private-markets, for a description of the growth of private markets.

72 See Schuster,n 11, for a formal statement of the transfer condition.

73 The multiple is essentially the inverse of the blockholder's stake in the company, i.e. two for a 50 per cent shareholder and three for a controller holding a third of the shares. Schuster,n 11, at 553.

74 Schuster,n 11, at 553.

75 See on this, in the context of tag-along rights, Lacave and Gutiérrez,n 66.

76 See also the discussion in Enriques,n 18, 449 (fn 17).

the prevalence of the sharing rule in private contracting contexts;[77] it may also be a channel that reduces the overall costs of the mandatory bid rule.

If this is correct, the mandatory bid rule can also be viewed as an (admittedly imperfect and crude) second-best instrument replicating value-increasing voluntary arrangements between outside investors and blockholders limiting future private benefit extraction.[78] Admittedly, however, this benefit would equally exist under an optional version of the rule.[79]

As discussed elsewhere, the mandatory bid rule also ensures that the highest value bidder succeeds in control contests – a feature the market rule lacks.[80] The recent battle for control over Paramount[81] illustrates the possible costs and uncertainties associated with blockholders unilaterally picking the winners in control contests, especially where they benefit from multiple-voting rights.[82]

9.3.3 *Costly – But Just* How *Costly?*

It is indisputable that the mandatory bid rule imposes some efficiency costs on the market for corporate control, and it does seem plausible that these costs outweigh at least the direct efficiency benefits of the rule in most circumstances.[83] Reliably estimating the costs of the mandatory bid rule is, however, extremely difficult. First, the fact that the mandatory bid rule primarily imposes costs via largely unobservable *transactions that do not take place*, means that any estimate is necessarily largely guesswork. Second, levels of private benefit extraction by blockholders likely vary significantly across jurisdictions,[84] industries and firms, and can likewise not easily be observed.

77 As explained by Lacave and Gutiérrez,n 66.

78 The crudeness of the rule may be justified in both private and public M&A contexts by the impracticability of drafting more targeted, complete contracts or creating credible bonding signals on private benefit extraction.

79 See Enriques,n 18, 449 (fn 17), who rightly points out that any such argument may favour adoption of the rule, but not its mandatory character, given blockholder incentives at IPO.

80 Schuster,n 11.

81 See e.g. C. Hughes, 'How Investors Can Prevent Another Paramount Fiasco', *Bloomberg Opinion* (17 May 2024).

82 Interestingly, the unequal treatment of outside shareholders and controller in the Paramount transaction has led to an outcry among Paramount shareholders (see Hughes,n 81), suggesting that, even in the US, some expectation of shared takeover premia exists despite the absence of a mandatory bid rule. The Paramount/Skydance transaction also showcases that a combination of powerful takeover defences and stringent directors' duties can, to some extent, operate as a functional substitute for the mandatory bid rule.

83 I.e. its ability to screen out value-destructive deals; see text ton 48. See specifically on estimates of relative costs and benefits Bebchuk,n 48, at 974 et seq.; Schuster,n 11, at 553 et seq.

84 See A. Dyck and L. Zingales, 'Private Benefits of Control: An International Comparison' (2004) 59 *Journal of Finance* 537.

It is also unclear how to quantify the costs and benefits of second-order effects of the rule, including its impact on ownership structures.[85] As a result, discussing the rule's efficiency or lack thereof always remains somewhat unsatisfactory, with theoretical arguments about the relative performance of the market[86] and the mandatory bid rule abounding, but a lack of empirical evidence as to the absolute costs involved. Given typical takeover premia, the rule's chilling effect can conceivably be significant, or indeed negligible, especially for larger issuers.[87]

9.3.4 *An Optional Mandatory Bid Rule?*

In the absence of clear evidence regarding the rule's cost, it seems logical to advocate for optionality,[88] ideally at company level.[89] Where this choice is made at the IPO stage, it is unlikely that such a move would hurt investors. It seems entirely possible that entrenched investor expectations would still lead to widespread application of the rule, given the uncertainties about the rule's cost, but it is hard to formulate a convincing argument against ab initio company-level choice, other than perhaps to invoke a combination of fairness and investor irrationality.

However, as Professor Hansen puts it, '[a]rguing against the rule is the modern legal equivalent of tilting at windmills',[90] given the unwillingness of European policymakers to revisit the rule. It does indeed seem highly unlikely that the mandatory bid rule will be removed, or made a company-level choice, in the foreseeable future.

9.3.5 *De Facto Optionality at Member-State Level?*

Arguably, however, developments over the past two decades have at least somewhat increased the extent of de facto optionality of the mandatory rule *at the Member-State level.*

First, the TOD only requires Member States to implement the mandatory bid rule for companies admitted to trading on a regulated market.[91] At the time the TOD was being negotiated, so-called alternative trading systems played a rather

85 See D. Kershaw and E. Schuster, 'The Purposive Transformation of Corporate Law' (2021) 69 *American Journal of Comparative Law* 478.

86 I.e. the US approach, which is simply the absence of a mandatory bid rule.

87 See text ton 91.

88 Optionality (at the company level) has convincingly been advocated by L. Enriques, R. J. Gilson and A. M. Pacces, 'The Case for an Unbiased Takeover Law (with an Application to the European Union)' (2014) 4 *Harvard Business Law Review* 85; see also L. Enriques and M. Gatti, 'Creeping Acquisitions in Europe: Enabling Companies to Be Better Safe than Sorry' (2015) 15 *Journal of Corporate Law Studies* 55; and Kershaw,n 1, at 8.43–8.45. For a related argument regarding takeover defences, see Kershaw and Schuster,n 81.

89 See Enriques, Gilson and Pacces,n 88.

90 Hansen,n 27.

91 See Art 1(1) TOD.

minor role in European markets, meaning the TOD almost necessarily covered the vast majority of publicly traded EU companies. The landscape has changed significantly since then, due to the rise of new and popular trading venues and segments outside of the regulated markets.[92]

What does that mean for the mandatory bid rule and its costs? It is worth noting that the efficiency cost of the mandatory bid rule likely decreases rapidly with the size of the issuer, at least where the blockholder is not a strategic investor.[93] The rise of non-regulated markets, and their usual focus on smaller companies therefore provides some room for Member States to create de facto optionality around the mandatory bid rule by simply not extending their implementation of the mandatory bid rule to markets outside the TOD's scope.[94]

Second, the acceptance and prevalence of dual-class share structures has risen markedly over the past two decades.[95] As of 2024, several of the world's most valuable listed companies have dual-class share structures, partly due to the rise in the value of tech stocks and the popularity of dual-class share structures entrenching founder control among tech entrepreneurs.

The EU Parliament has recently adopted the proposal for a Multiple Voting Rights Directive.[96] Germany has abolished its traditional insistence on the 'one share, one vote' principle for public companies,[97] and in the UK,[98] rules about the listing of dual-class shares have been relaxed, first in 2021,[99] and more completely liberalised in 2024.[100]

As discussed above, the version of the mandatory bid rule contained in the TOD only requires equal treatment *within* the same class of shares (and only for voting

92 See e.g. B. Penn and N. Pascal, 'Multilateral Trading Facilities (MTFs) and Organized Trading Facilities (OTFs)', in: M. Blair, G. Walker and S. Willey (eds.), *Financial Markets and Exchanges Law* (Oxford: Oxford University Press) 249, at 7.07 et seq.

93 I.e. because non-synergistic private benefit extraction cannot plausibly scale with the size of the issuer.

94 See also Kershaw,n 1, at 8.46 regarding the application of the UK Takeover Code to AIM-traded companies.

95 See e.g. J. R. Ritter, 'Initial Public Offerings: Dual Class Structure of IPOs through 2023', available at https://site.warrington.ufl.edu/ritter/files/IPOs-Dual-Class.pdf (11 April 2024), reporting that dual-class IPOs in the US have more than doubled in the past 20 years when compared to the period 1990–2004.

96 Proposal for a Directive of the European Parliament and of the Council on multiple-vote share structures in companies that seek the admission to trading of their shares on an SME growth market, COM (2022) 761.

97 See *Zukunftsfinanzierungsgesetz*; BGBl. I Nr. 354 (Germany).

98 Obviously, the UK is in any event no longer bound by the TOD.

99 See e.g. the detailed discussion by Cheffins and Reddy (B. R. Cheffins and B. V. Reddy, 'Will Listing Rule Reform Deliver Strong Public Markets for the UK?' (2023) 86 *Modern Law Review* 176).

100 See FCA, 'Primary Markets Effectiveness Review: Feedback to CP23/31 and final UK Listing Rules' (11 July 2024), available at www.fca.org.uk/publications/policy-statements/ps24-6-primary-markets-effectiveness-review-feedback-cp23-31-final-uk-listing-rules.

securities). While it is true that several Member States[101] have gold-plated their implementation of the TOD by requiring equivalent or comparable offers across all classes,[102] the TOD does not in fact prevent unequal treatment of shareholders of different classes, provided that all holders of voting securities receive an offer. When combined with the increasing acceptance of dual-class structures, this would in theory also provide some room for Member States to offer significant additional flexibility regarding the mandatory bid rule, even if the TOD remains unchanged, as one should expect.

9.4 CONCLUSION AND OUTLOOK

The mandatory bid rule arguably represents the most significant harmonised rule in the TOD. The rule enshrines an equality principle not found elsewhere in European corporate laws. A legal transplant from the UK, a jurisdiction in which blockholdings are far less common than in continental Europe, the rule is generally viewed as a costly method of protecting minority shareholders. While there is broad consensus on the origins of the rule's costs and benefits, there is no reliable way of quantifying the precise economic cost of the rule. It is commonly assumed that the mandatory bid rule achieves a type of 'equality' that is not valued or demanded by investors, and that it does so at the expense of a vibrant takeover market.

None of the arguments advanced in this chapter suggest that the mandatory bid rule is efficient, after all. Instead, the much more modest claim is that the costs associated with the rule could conceivably be lower than is commonly assumed, and perhaps even trivial for larger issuers, if it is accepted that the rule has some beneficial second-order effects.

The ubiquity of mandatory bid-like contractual arrangements in the booming private markets may also indicate that the rule could conceivably have survived the past decades not solely for political reasons, such as its symbolic value or its anti-takeover properties, but because the rule's effect on deals is not ultimately as dramatic as feared, particularly for larger companies. In other words, the rule may prevent sufficiently few (or sufficiently small) transactions, such that the pressure to abolish or reform it has never reached a critical level, at least outside of academia.

In addition, market and legal developments over the past two decades mean that Member States have somewhat more leeway for experimentation and variation in the rule's application than they did when the Directive was enacted in 2004. It is thus at least conceivable that we may yet see a level of de facto optionality, even if the TOD remains unchanged.

101 See Marccus Partners,n 21, at 98–99.

102 See also for the UK, Rules 9 and 14.1 of the UK Takeover Code.

PART III

Resisting Takeovers

10

The Defensive Measures Provisions of the Takeover Directive

From Ambition to Resignation to Distrust

Paul Davies and Alain Pietrancosta

10.1 THE FAILURE OF THE BAN ON DEFENSIVE MEASURES AT EU LEVEL

When the Commission in 2007 came to review the implementation of the Takeover Directive,[1] which had finally been adopted in 2004, it was upbeat about the economic benefits to be gained from a free market in corporate control. Its first sentence stated: 'The long-awaited Takeover Bids Directive – the result of more than 20 years of work – was intended to be one of the main pillars of the economic reform boosting Europe's competitiveness.' It endorsed both the disciplinary benefits of the threat of takeovers (keeping management up to the mark) and the scale-enhancing value of actual takeovers. A free market in corporate control would promote both the creation of the single European market and the competitiveness of European companies in the wider global markets. In highly positive introductory paragraphs, it put the argument as follows:

The Commission's proposal was based on the assumption that takeovers offer a number of benefits for companies, investors and ultimately for the European economy as a whole. Takeovers may be efficient drivers of value creation. They facilitate corporate restructuring and consolidation and provide a means for companies to achieve an optimal scale, a precondition for competing effectively on an integrated European market as well as on the global market. They help in disseminating good management practices and technology, and thus improve the quality of management and corporate performance. Furthermore, takeovers discipline management and stimulate competition. Such transactions are also beneficial for investors, allowing them to obtain a better return on their investments.

The aim of the Commission's proposal was to help exploit such benefits at European level and to promote integration of European capital markets by creating

[1] Commission Staff Working Document, 'Report on the implementation of the Directive on Takeover Bids', SEC (2007) 268 (21 February 2007).

favourable conditions for the emergence of a European market for corporate control: efficient takeover mechanisms, a common regulatory framework and strong rights for shareholders, including minority shareholders.[2]

Although a footnote[3] acknowledged that these benefits could not be claimed for every single takeover, the balance of advantage was presented as being overwhelmingly in favour of the market for corporate control, for 'in the long run, takeover facilitation is in the best interests of all stakeholders and the company'. In so doing, the Commission largely adopted the arguments developed by the High Level Group of Company Law Experts, which it had asked to produce a report to shed light on issues related to pan-European rules for takeover bids and subsequently on key priorities for modernising company law in the European Union.[4]

Turning to the implementation of this vision as far as company law was concerned, what was needed was 'the removal of some of the main company-related obstacles permitted under national company law', and the 'key' provisions[5] of the Directive to achieve this were the board neutrality rule (BNR) and the breakthrough rule (BTR). The former would prevent the management from using its powers to discourage the bidder from putting its offer to the shareholders or the shareholders from considering it on its merits unless the shareholders themselves agreed to these steps; the latter would prevent the distortion of shareholder voting in relation to takeovers through departures from the 'one share, one vote' (OSOV) principle. In other words, the Directive aimed at creating a level playing field for takeover bids guided by the two overarching principles of shareholder decision-making and of proportionality between risk-bearing capital and control.[6] On the one hand, Article 9 of the Directive, setting out the 'obligations of the board of the offeree company', provides that, during the takeover bid period, 'the board of the offeree company shall obtain the prior authorisation of the general meeting of shareholders given for this purpose before taking any action, other than seeking alternative bids, which may result in the frustration of the bid and in particular before issuing any shares which may result in a lasting impediment to the offeror's acquiring control of the offeree company'. On the other hand, Article 11 makes bylaw and contractual restrictions on the transfer of securities and departures from OSOV unenforceable against a bidder

2 Ibid., 1.1.

3 Ibid., fn 2.

4 'Report of the High Level Group of Company Law Experts on Issues Related to Takeover Bids', Brussels, 10 January 2002, ch 1.1: 'In the light of available economic evidence the Group holds the view that the availability of a mechanism for takeover bids is basically beneficial. Takeovers are a means to create wealth by exploiting synergies and to discipline the management of listed companies with dispersed ownership, which in the long term is in the best interests of all stakeholders, and society at large.'

5 Commission Staff Working Document, 'Report on the implementation of the Directive on Takeover Bids', 1.1.

6 Report of the High Level Group of Company Law Experts on Issues Related to Takeover Bids (n 4).

seeking acceptances from the target's shareholders or facing a resolution in the target's shareholder meeting to permit target management to take defensive action, and automatically dismantles these defences, as well as those concerning the appointment or dismissal of members of the board of directors or management board, when the bidder comes to hold after a successful bid the number of securities that would enable it to amend the target company's articles of association if OSOV applied.

One notable feature of the rationale articulated in the Commission's 2007 review is its movement beyond the traditional goals of harmonisation of national laws and the protection of shareholders (though those elements are clearly there) to embrace the broader goals of enhancing the efficiency of European industry. The many draft versions of the Directive and, indeed, the Directive itself referred only to the traditional rationales,[7] as was perhaps appropriate for a Directive proposed under Art. 44(2)(g) EC (now Art. 50(2)(g) TFEU). However, from an early stage, there was some positive reference to the economic benefits of takeovers. Thus, the Explanatory Memorandum to the Commission's proposal of 1995, which eventually led to the adopted Directive, stated that 'takeovers may be viewed in a positive light in so far as they contribute to the expansion and reconstruction of European companies, which is indispensable in order to meet international competition'.[8] By the time the Takeover Directive was adopted, however, the broader rationale had become predominant in the Commission's eyes, so that the Directive was indeed regarded as one of the 'the main pillars of the economic reform boosting Europe's competitiveness'.

Jonathan Rickford, a member of the Commission's High Level Group of Company Law Experts,[9] writing in a personal capacity in 2004,[10] attributed this shift in the hierarchy of rationales underlying the Directive to the decisions taken at the European Council meeting in Lisbon in early 2000. In the Presidency's Conclusions of that meeting, making 'rapid progress on the long-standing proposals on takeover bids' was identified as one of four steps to be taken to 'accelerate completion of the internal market for financial services'.[11] In Rickford's analysis,

7 Parliament and Council Directive 2004/25/EC On Takeover Bids, 2004 O.J. (L142), Preamble (1) (hereafter 'Takeover Directive'); and generally N. Moloney, *EC Securities Regulation* (Oxford: Oxford University Press, 1st ed. 2002), p. 819.

8 'Proposal for a 13th European Parliament and Council Directive on Company Law Concerning Takeover Bids', COM/95/0655 final (7 February 1996), Explanatory Memorandum, para 6.

9 See its 'Report on a Modern Regulatory Framework for Company Law in Europe', Brussels, 4 November 2002.

10 J. Rickford, 'The Emerging European Takeover Law from a British Perspective' (2004) *European Business Law Review* 1379. The quotations below are from p. 1380.

11 Lisbon European Council 23 and 24 March 2000, 'Presidency Conclusions', para 21 (available at www.europarl.europa.eu/summits/lis1_en.htm). See also Report of the High Level Group of Company Law Experts on Issues Related to Takeover Bids (n 4): 'An important goal of the European Union is to create an integrated capital market in the Union by 2005. The regulation of takeover bids is a key element of such an integrated market.'

'Restructuring EU industry, flexible redeployment of resources within the Union and the openness of financial markets and reduction of the costs of capital demanded regulation of the market in corporate control' so as to make takeover transactions 'free from interference by self-interested company management and by Member State governments animated by a desire to maintain local national control of corporate resources'.[12] Given this expansion of rationale, it is not surprising that the Directive, which began life in 1995[13] as a proposal for a 13th Directive in the company law harmonisation series, had lost that affiliation when a revised version of it was proposed by the Commission in 2002.[14]

In contrast to the ambitious description of the Directive's aims, the implementation Working Document was downbeat about the Directive's actual achievements in relation to its 'key' provisions. The lack of a political majority on the issue of reducing the defensive capacity of companies targeted by a hostile bid was one of the main stumbling blocks preventing the European Parliament from adopting the European Commission's ambitious proposal in July 2001. Such was the Commission's disappointment with the ultimate proposal of the Council that it almost gave up the whole text, with the European Commissioner for the Internal Market declaring that the proposal, stripped of its imperative content on anti-takeover defences, was no longer worth the paper it was written on. Agreement among the Member States could be reached only on the basis of a last-minute compromise, first proposed by Portugal and then taken up by the Italian presidency, watering down the board neutrality and breakthrough rules. Through a complex system of so-called optional arrangements (Art. 12), Member States were permitted not to require companies incorporated in their jurisdictions to comply with these provisions, although States were required to give companies the power to opt into these provisions by a shareholder vote, where the Member State had not made them mandatory.[15] Moreover, a Member State could choose to make available to an opting-in company a further option – namely, to relieve the company from the operation of the BNR and BTR if the bidder (inevitably from another State) was not subject to the relevant provision (or its equivalent) – the so-called reciprocity exception.[16]

10.2 THE DIRECTIVE'S IMMEDIATE IMPACT

The upshot of the above developments in the EU's legislative process was, as the Working Document put it, that 'the ultimate impact of the Directive therefore

[12] Rickford (n 10).

[13] See n 8.

[14] 'Proposal for a Directive of the European Parliament and of the Council on Takeover Bids', COM (2002) 534 final (2 October 2002).

[15] Takeover Directive, Art. 12.

[16] Art. 12.3. In fact, Member States interpreted this permission more broadly. See text attached to n 22 and n 23.

depends largely on the modalities of its implementation in the Member States and on the extent to which they will use the exemption provided for in the Directive'.[17] So, what did the Member States actually do?

According to the data collected by Davies, Schuster and Von der Walle,[18] sixteen of the twenty-seven Member States surveyed (which included the UK at that time) had an unqualified[19] BNR before the Directive was adopted, some adopting it during the long period during which the Directive was under negotiation.[20] Only one of these Member States (Hungary) took advantage of the Directive's final outcome to remove entirely a previously unqualified BNR. Of the remaining fifteen, nine Member States had an unqualified BNR in place both before and after the adoption of the Directive – that is, they did not make use of the freedom given by the Directive to downgrade their commitment to target management passivity. These were: Austria, Bulgaria, the Czech Republic, Estonia, Ireland, Lithuania, Slovakia, Sweden and the United Kingdom.

However, the six states which downgraded their BNR to some degree were almost counterbalanced by five Member States (Cyprus, Finland, Latvia, Malta and Romania) which introduced an unqualified BNR after the adoption of the Directive.[21] This does not look like a major reduction, overall, in the defensive orientation of the Member States. On paper, the Directive could even appear as a move in a bidder-friendly direction since all Member States were now required to offer their companies the possibility of opting into the BNR. Practically, however, such opting back in by companies is unheard of, since the option was designed in such a way as to place the burden of action on those proposing to opt back in (i.e. in most cases against the wishes of the incumbent management).

However, the position looks less good from the Commission's point of view when one considers the uptake by Member States of the newly legitimised reciprocity exception. This exception was aimed particularly at out-of-state bidders (but not necessarily from outside the EU) and was thus likely to undermine the integrationist objectives of the Commission's initial proposals. The Commission's view was that the reciprocity exception 'may hold back the emergence of an active takeover market, as opposed to the original objective of the Directive'.[22] Five Member

[17] See n 1, 1.1.

[18] P. Davies, E. Schuster and E. van de Walle de Ghelcke, 'The Takeover Directive as a Protectionist Tool?' *ECGI Law Working Paper* 141/2010, Table 2.

[19] That is, one without the reciprocity exception.

[20] Ironically, the impact of the Directive might have been greater had the Commission dropped its proposal rather than accepted the optional arrangements and the reciprocity exception, proposed at the end of the legislative process in order to secure the necessary level of Member State agreement. The States with newly introduced BNRs might have stuck with them and those with long-standing BNRs might not have introduced the reciprocity exception because its legality was still in doubt.

[21] No Member State seems to have moved from no BNR to a BNR subject to the reciprocity exception.

[22] See n 1, 2.1.3.

States, including two major economies, moved from an unqualified BNR beforehand to one incorporating a reciprocity exception afterwards: France, Greece, Portugal, Slovenia and Spain. At least for out-of-state bidders this was a potentially significant change for the worse. Moreover, most Member States which made use of the so-called reciprocity exception did not confine it to situations where companies chose to opt back into the BNR but made it available also in cases where the BNR was mandatory. This was the case, notably, in France, where concerns were voiced as to the validity of this decision on the grounds either that national law contravened the provisions of Article 12 of the Directive, or because the broader interpretation of the availability of the reciprocity exception contravened the provisions of the Treaty on the free movement of capital in Europe. However, France was not alone in adopting this interpretation of the Directive.[23]

In fact, in those Member States which showed interest in it, the dominant interpretation was the French one, so that the reciprocity exception was interpreted as being generally available to Member States. Some people thought this provision, as broadly interpreted, would encourage countries (both within and without the EU) to adopt the board neutrality and breakthrough rules, in order to make it easier for their companies to make foreign acquisitions, but there is no evidence that the reciprocity option had this impact.

Furthermore, the central failing of the Directive from the Commission's point of view was its failure to secure a BNR across the EU. Thus, five states did not have a BNR before the Directive was adopted and remained in that position afterwards. These were Belgium, Denmark, Germany, Luxembourg and Poland – a significant group of countries, including the EU's largest economy. As to the BTR, this turned out to be a complete failure. No Member State appears to have adopted it entirely, even those, such as the UK, which remained committed to an unqualified BNR. This is surprising, since the presence of an unqualified BNR would seem to provide potential target companies with strong incentives to put in place pre-bid defences.[24]

The mix of options available to Member States and national companies, outlined above, appears as an unprecedented way of conceiving European law applicable to companies, a sign of the defeat of top-down harmonisation, leaving the last hope of harmonisation to the goodwill of Member States and/or companies, navigating the constraints of market forces. Retrospectively, the EC's proposed ban on defensive measures appears paradoxically limited and overly optimistic. Limited in scope,

[23] See not. A. Maréchal and A. Pietrancosta, 'Transposition de la directive OPA: des incertitudes entourant le recours à la "clause de réciprocité"' (2005) *Lexbase Hebdo* n° 189, 10 November 2005 and (2005) *Bull. Joly Bourse*, 797 § 203; see also J. Winter, 'EU Company Law at the Cross-Roads' in G. Ferrarini, K. J. Hopt, J. Winter and E. Wymeersch (eds.), *Reforming Company Law and Takeover Law in Europe* (Oxford: Oxford University Press, 2004), p. 17 et seq.; P. Werdmuller, 'Compatibility of the EU Takeover Bid Directive Reciprocity Rule with EU Free Movement Rules' (2006) *Business Law Review* 64. Other states which adopted the same approach were Greece, Portugal, Slovakia and Slovenia.

[24] We discuss the BTR in more detail in Section 10.4.2.

because only the defences activated during the takeover period were strongly controlled, leaving out of reach the very many and varied defences operating ex ante, in a dissuasive mode. Overly optimistic, because of underestimation of national resistance, linked to the variety of national rights, cultures and ethos.[25] A dramatic example of this type of resistance was the successful opposition in 2001 of German MEPs, essentially organised by the German government, to the then version of the Takeover Directive on the grounds that it contained a mandatory BNR. The result of the European Parliament vote was a breach of convention, because the text on which the Parliament was voting had been agreed in the conciliation procedure between Council and Parliament representatives – that is, at the very end of the Union's legislative process – and the convention was that the Parliament as a whole supported the compromise agreed by its representatives.[26] The underlying reason for this sudden change of position on the part of Germany was the hostile bid for the German company Mannesmann launched by the British bidder Vodafone in 1999 and successfully completed in the following year and fears that more hostile bids would succeed, despite the dominance of controlling shareholders in large German companies.

10.3 THE LONGER TERM

Potentially as important as the immediate transposition failings, the Directive failed to secure a guarantee that controls over defensive measures, as they existed once Member States had implemented the Directive, would not be weakened in the future. On the contrary, the options to introduce the reciprocity exception or remove the BNR entirely were not, according to the Directive, time-limited choices which Member States had to make within a specific period after the Directive was adopted by the EU. Those options continued to be available to Member States into the indefinite future. France made use of them so as to move in stages from its pre-Directive position of having an unqualified BNR, through the introduction of the reciprocity exception, to abandonment of the BNR. At the end of the day, therefore, the two largest economies in the EU, Germany and France, ended up with no BNR, even of a qualified type.

In France, as a result of the initial transposition law no. 2006-387 of 31 March 2006, the choice was made to apply the provisions of Article 9 of the Directive on a mandatory basis, but with an exception for reciprocity.[27] To give substance to this reciprocity exception, the French legislator decided to authorise

[25] See J. Mukwiri, 'The End of History for the Board Neutrality Rule in the EU' (2020) 21 *European Business Organization Law Review* 253.

[26] This episode is described in Vanessa Edwards, 'The Directive on Takeover Bids: Not Worth the Paper it's Written on?' (2004) 1 *European Company and Financial Law Review* 426–427.

[27] See A. Pietrancosta, 'Loi n° 2006-387 du 31 mars 2006 relative aux offres publiques d'acquisition: des "options" françaises' (2006) *RTDF*, n° 1, June 2006, p. 5.

expressly the issue of share warrants ('bons de souscription d'actions' or 'BSA') by the board of directors or the management board. Such board action was conditional on a delegation of authority from an extraordinary general meeting of shareholders, acting, however, under the more lenient conditions of quorum and majority of an ordinary general meeting, given within the eighteen months preceding the filing of the offer. These so-called offer warrants, dilutive warrants, patriotic warrants or Breton warrants were inspired by the famous 'shareholder rights plans', colloquially known as 'poison pills', developed and widely used across the Atlantic. Essentially, by threatening a considerable dilution of its financial and voting stake, which would result from the exercise of share warrants at a knock-down price, the aim is to force the bidder to negotiate the terms of its takeover bid with the management of the target company. The French defence differs significantly from the American model, in particular because of its legislative, rather than judicial, origin; because of the ex ante decision power given to the shareholders' meeting rather than exclusively to the board of directors; and because of its active principle, which is not based on the immediate issue of stock options to shareholders as dividends nor on discrimination against the would-be bidder.

The real break, however, came with Law 2014-384 of 29 March 2014, known as the 'Florange' Act.[28] Reversing the initial decision to transpose Article 9 of the Directive, it abolished the special limit on the defensive powers of directors, arising out of the need for them to obtain the prior authorisation of the general meeting of shareholders before taking any action likely to frustrate the bid. Introduced by a simple parliamentary amendment, which also dispensed with the need for any impact analysis, this reform, which took France further away from the European standard, was driven by the desire of its promoters to protect French companies, notably strategic ones, from foreign appetites. Such companies were seen as 'particularly vulnerable to unsolicited takeovers such as hostile or creeping takeovers' because of their 'fragmented capital and low stock market valuation'. More generally, the promoters of this reversal displayed a certain mistrust towards the benefits of the takeover mechanism itself, which would favour shareholders' short-termism and be 'harmful to employment and the development of our industry'.[29] They clearly defended an orientation towards another path, more proactive and engaged, more interventionist and overtly 'patriotic', that the recent financial crisis had helped fuel.[30] Parliamentary work insisted indeed on the need to fight against French

[28] See A. Pietrancosta, 'The latest reform of French takeover law: the "Florange" act of March 29, 2014' (2014) *RTDF*, n° 3, p. 42.

[29] Rapport n° 1283 de la Commission des affaires économiques sur la proposition de loi visant à redonner des perspectives à l'économie réelle et à l'emploi industriel (n° 1037) par C. Valter, 17 July 2013, p. 24.

[30] See e.g. Investir dans l'avenir, Une politique globale de compétitivité pour la France, rapport de MM. L. Schweitzer and O. Ferrand, Fondation Terra Nova, July 2012; Rapport d'information n° 737 de MM. J.-M. Clément et P. Houillon, déposé en conclusion des travaux de la mission d'information sur la transparence de la gouvernance des grandes entreprises, February

deindustrialisation, caused by the prominence of finance over the real economy; to end the 'diktat of financial performance', which forces managers 'to focus on today's dividends rather than tomorrow's investments, jobs and exports'. This political orientation reflected the promoters' simplistic state of mind and limited knowledge of the field, where the complexity of the matter should, on the contrary, lead to a more politically agnostic approach.[31] In addition, this revised policy legitimised a series of additional restrictive provisions, of which probably the most important was the setting of a default rule of double voting rights for all shares listed on a regulated market, that are fully paid and registered in the name of the same shareholder for at least two years without discontinuity (tenure voting rights).

However, if the board of directors – or, in a two-tier board system, the management board, after authorisation of the supervisory board – of a target company is therefore relieved of the specific obligation not to take decisions aimed at frustrating the offer without prior shareholder approval, this defensive power is not without its limits. First, its use is limited where the law confers exclusive authority on the general meeting of shareholders. It follows, primarily, that the target board of directors may not, on its own, take the initiative of modifying the articles of association. In addition to the exclusive authority provided by law, the general meeting of shareholders may find itself empowered by way of soft law, especially when it comes to fundamental changes in the company. The most important example results from the AFEP-MEDEF French corporate governance code that, following an invitation of the French securities regulator,[32] recommends consultation of the shareholders' meeting before a disposal is contemplated, in one or more transactions, concerning at least half of the company's assets (Art. 6(4)).

The second general limitation comes from the requirement that the use of defensive measures does not hurt the corporation's interests. Since defensive measures may be designed to make the target company less attractive to the bidder, this explicit reminder of the necessary compliance with the interests of the company is quite understandable, even if such compliance is mandated for all corporate decisions. In a takeover context, this reservation was in fact imposed by the Directive, which establishes as a guiding principle the obligation for 'the board of the offeree

2013; L. Gallois, Pacte pour la compétitivité de l'industrie française, *Rapport au Premier ministre*, 5 November 2012; J.-L. Beffa, *La France doit agir* (Seuil, 2013).

31 See e.g. J. M. Fried, 'The Uneasy Case for Favoring Long-term Shareholders' (2015) 124 *Yale L J* 1346; L. Bebchuk, A. Brav and W. Jiang, 'The Long-Term Effects of Hedge Fund Activism' (2015) 115 *Columbia Law Review* 1085; F. Brochet, G. Serafeim and M. Loumioti, 'Short-Termism: Don't Blame Investors' (2012) 90 *Harvard Business Review* no. 6, June 2012; W. Kim, 'Value of Shareholder Activism: Evidence from the Switchers' (2009) 15 *Journal of Corporate Finance* 505; A. Allegret-Pilot, 'Should long-term shareholders be favored?' (2014) *Université Paris 1, Mémoire Master2 Droit financier*, June 2014. On takeover law specifically: L. Enriques, R. J. Gilson and A. M. Pacces, 'The Case for an Unbiased Takeover Law (with an Application to the European Union)' (2014) 4 *Harvard Business Law Review* 85.

32 AMF, Position-recommandation DOC-2015-05, 15 June 2015.

company' to 'act in the interests of the company as a whole'.[33] The 'PACTE law' of 22 May 2019 confirmed this general requirement, which is now enshrined at the heart of company law, in Article 1833 of the French Civil Code, which states that: 'The company is managed in its corporate interest, taking into consideration the social and environmental stakes linked to its business.' The only problem – and it is a major one – is the lack of legal certainty concerning the substantive content of the company interest concept,[34] aggravated by the PACTE Act.

In addition to these limitations laid down in French corporate law, one should take into consideration limitations provided for in French securities regulation. There comes immediately to mind the general principle referred to in Article 231-3 of the AMF General Regulation, according to which: 'To allow an offer to be conducted in an orderly fashion in the best interests of investors and the market, the parties concerned shall respect the principles of free interplay of offers and counter-offers, equal treatment and information for all holders of the securities of the persons concerned by the offer, market transparency and integrity, and fairness of transactions and competition.' The AMF decided not to repeal this principle despite the Florange Act, as it views it as the implementation of Article 3.1.c of the TOD, providing that 'the board of an offeree company must act in the interests of the company as a whole and must not deny the holders of securities the opportunity to decide on the merits of the bid'. It is not the least interesting aspect of Veolia's takeover bid for Suez that it tested the possibility of invoking these principles to limit the defensive capabilities of a target company.[35] In a public statement issued on 2 April 2021, the AMF rejected the argument that these principles had to be set aside to give full effect to the reversal operated by the Florange Act.[36] It reiterated the authority of these principles and took the view that they were undermined by the combination of defences put in place by the target company, based on the creation of an irrevocable Dutch foundation originally intended to protect certain essential assets, and plans to sell assets to a prospective rival bidder. The AMF's statement led the parties involved to come together and put an end to their legal dispute, so that no judicial response was provided to the question of the articulation between the defensive capacity of the target companies' directors and compliance with the general principles of takeover bids. Nor did this settlement allow us to measure the effectiveness of friendly agreements between companies ('accords d'amicalité'),

[33] Dir. OPA, art. 3.1 c). V. A. Pietrancosta and J.-F. Prat, 'Offres publiques et droit des sociétés' in G. Canivet, D. Martin, N. Molfessis (eds.) *Les offres publiques d'achat* (LexisNexis, Litec, 2009), n° 318.

[34] See n 33 and the discussion in Section 10.4.1.1.

[35] See A. Pietrancosta, 'Droit des OPA – Affaire Veolia c/ Suez: de la contestation des principes généraux du droit des OPA comme limites aux moyens défensifs des sociétés cibles' (2021) *Revue de Droit bancaire et financier* n° 5, Sept. 2021, dossier 25.

[36] *Suez-Veolia: Communication de l'AMF*, 2 April 2021; see also, *Précisions sur le rôle de l'Autorité des marchés financiers dans le cadre de l'offre publique initiée par Veolia sur Suez*, AMF, 18 May 2022.

whereby one of them undertakes in advance not to initiate a takeover bid without the agreement of the target's board of directors. In the Veolia/Suez case, Suez obtained an initial summary judgment prohibiting Veolia from making a bid,[37] but this judicial decision was revoked a few days later for lack of territorial jurisdiction.[38] On the substance, what Suez considered to be a genuine friendly agreement was analysed by Veolia as a mere declaration of intent, and as such, subject to change according to circumstances. In another famous litigious takeover case, Scor and Covea put an end to their dispute by means of a settlement agreement, of 10 June 2021, containing a standstill agreement that forbade Covea to increase its participation in the share capital of Scor and to launch a takeover on Scor's shares. It is currently difficult to measure the practical effectiveness of such a defence, which depends on whether the AMF, as an administrative authority, is able or obliged to prevent a takeover bid prohibited by a private law contract from being initiated.

Both before and after the Florange Act, hostile takeover bids remain relatively infrequent on the Paris stock exchange, although they are not non-existent and give rise to high-profile stock market and legal battles.[39] Between 2010 and 2021, seven transactions have been identified in France, including three between 2015 and 2021. The Florange Act has not led to a proliferation of ex ante defences, however, but has undoubtedly increased the threat of post-bid reactive measures,[40] as the Veolia/Suez case has shown.

Despite the removal of the legislative BNR, French companies are free to reintroduce it in their articles of association, but few have done so. When this procedure is used, the reintroduction is carried out on an ad hoc basis in the context of general meeting resolutions relating to delegations of power or authority, stipulating that all or some delegations may not be used during the takeover bid period. There has therefore been no increase in the number of authorisations and financial delegations granted by the general meeting to the administrative and management bodies that can be used during a takeover bid. The 'bons Breton' have not been very successful. The situation is different where double voting rights are concerned, with many companies electing to revert to a one share, one vote system through the

37 Trib. com. Nanterre, Ord. réf., 8 févr. 2021 RG n° 202100163.

38 Trib. com. Nanterre, Ord. réf., 23 févr. 2021, RG n° 2021R00167.

39 See not. Nestlé/Perrier in 1992; Auchan/Docks de France in 1996; Promodès/Casino-Rallye, Artémis-AGF-Ifil/Worms et Cie Agnelli-Allianz/AGF in 1997; BNP/Paribas-Société générale et TotalFina/Elf Aquitaine in 1999; Sanofi-Synthelabo/Aventis in 2004; Mittal/Arcelor in 2006; Eiffage/Sacyr in 2007; H. Partners Distribution/Du Pareil au Même, Groupe Open/Sylis ou Gemalto sur Wavecom in 2008; SiegCo/Valtech in 2009; AS Online Beteiligungs GmbH/ SeLoger.com ou Jacquet Metals/IMS in 2010; Gecina/Foncière de Paris in 2016; Vivendi/ Gameloft in 2019; Veolia/Suez in 2021.

40 See O. De Vilmorin and A. Berdou, 'Des offres publiques d'acquisition "made in France"? Retour sur la loi n° 2014-384 du 29 mars 2014 visant à reconquérir l'économie réelle' (2014) *Dr. sociétés*, étude n° 10, spéc. n° 13; J. Deege, 'Défenses anti-OPA' (2020) *Dict. Joly Bourse*, n° 046.

articles of association, where a major shareholder (often the French state), which benefits from double voting rights, has not prevented this. The fact remains that double voting rights have increased steadily since 2007 for large listed companies, rising from 58.5 to 73.5 per cent in 2020, although more often than not offset by the introduction of a voting rights cap, which has also risen within the CAC 40 from 16.5 per cent in 2007 to 21.5 per cent in 2020. For non-controlled companies, which are said to represent about two-thirds of the listed companies included in the SBF 120 index, the real defences lie elsewhere. While some defences are losing ground, such as multi-listing of shares, aimed at complicating the law applicable to takeover bids, or transforming the company into a limited partnership with shares ('sociétés en commandite par actions'), which is under attack from outside shareholders, others are making progress, such as contractual change-of-control clauses, employee and 'reference' shareholding and, more recently, the possible instrumentalisation of the adoption of 'raison d'être' or the 'mission company' label.

Italy, also, shows the BNR rules being altered to cope with changing governmental views of the vulnerability of national companies. In Italy, however, the changes occurred during the relatively brief period between 2007 and 2010, after which they have remained stable. The initial choice in 2007 was to maintain pre-Directive BNR, but now with a reciprocity exception, which, following the French example, was viewed as an available choice even where the BNR was mandatory.[41] The credit crisis created concerns at the legislative level that Italian companies were vulnerable to opportunistic bids and the BNR was made optional on an opt-in basis (and the reciprocity option was continued).[42] Under the current law, introduced in 2010, the BNR remains optional but now on an opt-out basis. Thus, the default is that the BNR applies (with the reciprocity option) unless the shareholders decide otherwise. Putting the default this way around (and contrary to the arrangements contemplated in the Directive) makes it more likely the matter will come before the general meeting, given the presence in many Italian companies of management who are beholden to blockholders. In 2011 the Review of the Takeover Directive's implementation commissioned by the EU reported that nine companies had opted out of the default rule, including two substantial ones, Fiat SpA and Banca Carige SpA.[43]

10.4 DOES IT MATTER?

The above argument has been that the implementation of the provisions of the Directive on takeover defences did not achieve the objectives the Commission had

[41] Article 104 Consolidated Financial Services Act No. 58 of 1998 (CFSA) (2007 version).

[42] Articles 104(1), 104*bis* and 104*ter* CFSA (2008 version).

[43] Marccus Partners and the Centre for European Policy Studies, 'The Takeover Bids Directive: Assessment Report', 2011, p. 190. (The report is available at op.europa.eu/en/publication-detail/-/publication/67501b75–7583-4b0d-a551–33051d8e27c1.)

for them and subsequent developments at Member-State level have moved national laws further away from those objectives. Despite this limited impact of its key provisions – and the statement (even threat) in the implementation review that 'the Commission will analyse the reasons why Member States are so reluctant to endorse the fundamental rules of the Directive' and that 'in the light of this evaluation, the revision of the Directive scheduled for 2011 may, if necessary, be brought forward'[44] – the Commission apparently decided not to grasp this nettle again. When the (non-accelerated) Review of the Directive was published in 2011, it concluded that 'the debates that led to the optionality of Articles 9 and 11 of the Directive have not faded away. There is no clear consensus on how to move on the optionality and reciprocity issues and, generally speaking, there seems to be little appetite to change these rules.'[45] And, since then, the Commission has been content to leave the options in place.[46] In Brussels, disappointment thus made way to resignation.

Is the resulting situation a matter for concern from the point of view of the objectives of the Commission? There are two types of argument which can be advanced as to why the BNR is not an important provision, though these two types operate in very different ways. The first set of arguments suggests the BNR is unimportant because other mechanisms exist which perform the same function. This first set of arguments contains two sub-arguments, which are not mutually exclusive. One sub-argument refers to legal rules which, it is suggested, perform the same function as the BNR, even if the particular jurisdiction contains no BNR. The second sub-argument bases itself on the shareholder structure in a jurisdiction, arguing that concentrated shareholder structures can act functionally as a BNR.

The second set of arguments suggests that, even in the presence of a BNR, defensive measures are available to target management which the BNR does not catch. This argument also comes in two forms, one referring to the availability of pre-bid defences (so that the BTR is relevant here), the other to restrictions on takeovers which States may impose.

Thus, the first set of arguments proposes that the BNR is *unnecessary*: States which have a BNR do not need it and those which do not need not put one in place. The second set of arguments proposes that the BNR is *ineffective*: States which introduced a BNR have not in fact adopted a rule which significantly constrains target management and those which have not would be wasting legislative time and effort in introducing one. Figure 10.1 sets out the arguments in graphical form.

We consider each set of arguments in turn. In both cases, we argue that it is difficult to accept that the substitute mechanisms operate effectively over all EU

44 Working Document (n 1) *Conclusion*.

45 See n 42, 'Key Takeaways', para 4.

46 Commission, 'Application of Directive 2004/25/EC on Takeover Bids', COM (2012) 347 final (16 June 2012), para 26.

Suggested Triviality of the Takeover Directive's Rules on Defences	
Substitutes for the BNR	**Substitutes for ex post defenses**
• General corporate law	• Pre-bid defences
• Concentrated shareholding	• State action

FIGURE 10.1 Structure of arguments against the BNR

Member States, and will continue to do so, but also that in many Member States the defensive measures are currently a matter of limited policy salience.

10.4.1 *Substitutes for the BNR*

10.4.1.1 General Corporate Law

The first sub-argument that the BNR is unnecessary turns on an analysis of national corporate law systems which purports to find rules in those systems which do the job of a BNR, whether or not that system contains an explicit BNR.[47] Necessarily, these are rules whose content is different from a BNR – otherwise they could simply be relabelled – but whose operation, either alone or in conjunction with other rules of the national system, require post-bid shareholder approval of defensive measures. Although authors taking this line are correct to point out the importance of analysing the national law constraints on target management in the absence of a BNR, as we have indicated above in relation to France after the *Loi Florange*,[48] and that it is erroneous to suppose that target management can take whatever defensive action they like in the absence of a BNR, the strong argument that the BNR adds nothing to national corporate law is impossible to sustain across the EU.

The triviality proposition can be challenged on a number of grounds. Even assuming general corporate law does cover, in one way or another, the same substantive ground as the BNR, the latter may be more effective, for two reasons. The first relates to the *visibility* of the BNR as compared to rules derived from general corporate law. The BNR is a simple rule (a prohibition), which is both general (covering all post-bid defences) and specific (confined to takeovers), whose

[47] An important example of this style of analysis is C. Gerner-Beuerle, D. Kershaw and M. Solinas, 'Is the Board Neutrality Rule Trivial? Amnesia about corporate law in European takeover regulation' (2011) 22 *European Business Law Review* 559.

[48] See text attached to nn 31–37.

relevance to and impact on takeover defences is easy to discern.[49] It is likely, therefore, to have a bigger impact on the decisions of target management and the advice given to boards by their lawyers than national corporate law rules. Relevant national rules are likely to cover only certain defences (for example, rules requiring shareholder consent for share issues) or, if general, not focused on defensive tactics in the round. For example, the answer to the question of what fiduciary duties permit target management to engage in by way of defensive measures may be far from clear. It has been argued that the BNR is trivial in the UK because the fiduciary duty of directors not to act for an 'improper' purpose does the same job. However, there is only one decision,[50] at a low level, in which this doctrine was applied to defensive measures before the general law was overtaken by the BNR embodied in the UK Takeover Code. To be sure, the court held the defensive measure (issuance of new shares) to be void in that case, but this was an example of a non-coercive bid where there was a strong suggestion of managerial entrenchment. How a future court would have applied the improper purposes doctrine where the bid was coercive and/or the directors acted to promote a stakeholder value is anybody's guess.[51]

In Germany, which has not adopted the BNR and which does not insist on shareholder primacy and where a number of defensive measures explicitly require at least ex ante shareholder approval, the argument that the BNR is unnecessary across the board raises an unsettled issue about the scope of a controversial doctrine of German company law. The *Holzmüller*[52] decision of Germany's highest civil court raises the issue whether shareholder consent is needed in general for defensive measures in Germany, so that the directors cannot take defensive measures unilaterally. Although the German Stock Corporation Act appears to confine shareholder consent to the specific situations identified in that Act,[53] the *Holzmüller* decision creates the risk that any managerial decision of sufficient magnitude will be subject

49 See K. J. Hopt, 'Takeover Defenses in Europe: A Comparative, Theoretical and Policy Analysis' (2014) 20 *Columbia Journal of European Law* 249. At the margin there may be debates about what the BNR covers but these are not core problems. Neither the UK nor Sweden, with strong BNR, regards the rule as requiring target management to open the books to due diligence investigation by the bidder. In Spain, after some debate, for the target to initiate litigation was held not to fall within the rule, whereas the contrary has been held in the UK (though vigorous participation in regulatory proceedings is acceptable under the UK rules).

50 *Hogg v Cramphorn* [1967] Ch 254.

51 For an expanded version of this critique, see P. Davies 'Control Shifts via Share Acquisition Contracts with Shareholders', in J. Gordon and W.-G. Ringe (eds.), *The Oxford Handbook of Corporate Law and Governance* (Oxford: Oxford University Press, 2018) at 557–558. That there is some flexibility in the proper purposes doctrine is demonstrated by the later decision in *Gaiman v National Association of Mental Health* [1971] Ch 317 – charitable company permitted to use a provision in its articles of association to require the resignation from membership of Scientologists, who were feared by the incumbent directors to be seeking control.

52 (1982) BGHZ 83, 122.

53 Especially § 119 AktG.

to shareholder approval, even if there is no express legislative requirement to this end. However, *Holzmüller* itself was a decision about a corporate restructuring and its application to takeover defences is uncertain. The fact that the German Takeover Law[54] legitimises supervisory board approval for takeover defences proposed by management might be taken to indicate to the courts that it is not appropriate to add a requirement for shareholder approval to the statutory scheme through judicial development.

The uncertainty of the law is especially strong in those jurisdictions which do not straightforwardly identify the interests of the company with those of the shareholders. The problem is exacerbated by the trend towards broadening the notion of company interest through references to corporate purpose, social and environmental considerations, or the introduction, as in France, of new concepts such as 'raison d'être' or '*société à mission*'.[55] In France, the recent Veolia/Suez takeover case illustrated the difference that can exist between a blunt system of board neutrality and a defensive system only subject to the general limits of managers' powers.[56] The necessary consideration of social and environmental issues, and a fortiori of a raison d'être or a *mission*, as part of the decision-making process, substantially increases the defensive room for manoeuvre of the target company's directors/managers and considerably raises the burden of proof of possible mismanagement for those supporting the bid.

The second reason relates to the *enforcement* of the rules. Breaches of corporate law rules are typically adjudicated by the courts which proceed slowly, especially if appeals are possible, and sometimes conclude long after the circumstances giving rise to the bid have passed. Even if the courts seek to mitigate this problem by developing interlocutory remedies, this may not fully solve the problem of the strategic use of litigation to delay progress on an offer.[57] A bidder may not wish to revive its bid even after the legal position has been clarified in its favour, because the commercial situation has changed against it in the meantime. For example, a shareholder friendly to the target management may have increased its stake in the company substantially. By contrast, Article 4 of the Directive contemplates that the BNR should be enforced by a specialist regulator and one capable of acting quickly,

[54] §33(1).

[55] See A. Pietrancosta, 'Codification in Company Law of General CSR Requirements: Pioneering Recent French Reforms and EU Perspectives' (2022) *European Corporate Governance Institute – Law Working Paper* No. 639/2022, available at SSRN: https://ssrn.com/abstract=4083398 or http://dx.doi.org/10.2139/ssrn.4083398.

[56] See text attached ton 34.

[57] One way of tackling this problem would be to set a maximum time limit for the courts to rule in a takeover context. In France, this method was adopted by Act No. 2014-1662 of 30 December 2014 regarding appeals brought against takeover bid approval decisions, issued by the Autorité des marchés financiers, in order to combat the drift and instrumentalisation of stock market litigation, particularly harmful to the attractiveness of the Paris financial centre (C. mon. fin., art. L. 621–630).

often in real time, and gives Member States a wide freedom to constrain appeals from the takeover regulator to the courts.[58] This means that enforcement of the BNR is likely to be more effective than enforcement of general corporate law, even if the latter covers the same ground as the former.

Moreover, quite apart from these procedural advantages of the BNR, it is far from clear that, across the EU, general corporate laws always contain rules functionally equivalent to the BNR, so that the presence or absence of a BNR is a significant characteristic of a national corporate law system. In fact, it is clear that some jurisdictions give target management significant leeway to reject an unwelcome bid. This opens up the possibility that companies from other jurisdictions seeking strong takeover defences will reincorporate, through one mechanism or another, in the Member State offering this possibility. A ban on post-bid defensive measures across all Member States, it might be argued, is a precondition for a fully effective BNR in any one State.

The law of the Netherlands, an important jurisdiction for re-incorporations from other EU countries, as we see below, has been characterised as follows in relation to defensive measures:

> When faced with any approach or takeover proposal (whether recommended or hostile), the members of the managing board and the supervisory board have to consider the interests of all stakeholders (including all the company's shareholders (including minority shareholders), employees, customers, creditors and banks), and not only the interests of shareholders. The boards should act in accordance with the requirements of reasonableness and fairness towards all stakeholders involved in the target company . . . a Dutch target company that wants to oppose a takeover may choose to use certain defensive measures to reduce the likelihood of a hostile offer being made or being successful . . . Dutch case law suggests that the use of ad hoc defensive measures in the event of a hostile takeover is permitted, provided that the defensive measure is proportional, reasonable and temporary.[59]

In addition, Dutch law has accepted two effective and widespread forms of private ordering which create strong takeover defences. Both are linked to the establishment of a foundation (*Stichting*) whose board – the sole decision-making body of the foundation – is nominally independent of the target company's board but, it is to be anticipated, is well disposed towards the incumbent management. There are two core uses of the foundation. One is to separate the legal ownership of the shares from

58 Art. 4.5 of the Takeover Directive suggests that real-time operation by the regulator is required. The provisions on appeals were designed in particular to protect the modus operandi of the UK Takeover Panel.

59 Bonellierede, Bredin Prat, De Brauw, Hengeler Mueller, Slaughter and May, Uría Menéndez, *Guide to Public Takeovers in Europe*, 2016, p. 396, 398 (available at https://dzta7c9ve7na4.cloudfront.net/wp-content/uploads/sites/2/2016/06/27150210/Guide-to-Public-Takeovers-in-Europe-2016.pdf). To the same effect, C. de Brauw and O. Valk, 'Netherlands', in A. de Araoz (ed.), *European Takeovers: The Art of Acquisition*, 3rd ed., 2022, 234–235.

the economic interest in them by the use of depository receipts, the legal ownership (including voting rights on a hostile bid) being with the foundation and the economic interest with the investors. The second is to give the foundation, in case of the threat of a hostile bid or the arrival of activist shareholders, the right to call for issuance of a class of preference shares by the company.[60] The issue is without a premium and at a low nominal value, but extensive voting rights are attached to the shares, so as to swamp the voting position which the potential acquirer has assembled or might acquire.

Since in both cases the issuance of shares is involved, the consent of the general meeting is required for the issuance. This may seem to insert the shareholders into the decision-making on defensive measures, in line with the Directive's policy. However, it is doubtful whether ex ante shareholder approval operates as strongly to protect shareholder interests as approval given in the face of a bid. For the depository receipts, shareholder approval needs to happen only once, when the shares are issued, and could be given via a clause in the articles inserted before the company came to the market via an IPO. The depository receipts can be publicly traded. For this to happen, voting rights need to be given to the holders of the receipts, but an exception to this requirement exists for hostile bids, where the foundation recovers the voting rights. For the warrants over the preference shares, normally issued only when a threat emerges, the consent of the shareholders is also required, but the shareholders are permitted to delegate the right to issue the shares to the board for periods of five years at a time, as with the French BSA. Again, the initial delegation decision can be given before the company comes to the market, so that the company has an initial protected period of five years – and more if the shareholders agree.[61] It is normally enough to deter the bidder that the call right has been granted to the foundation – that is, the foundation does not usually need to exercise it. More than half the companies listed in the Netherlands have preference share mechanisms in place.[62]

The main protection for the shareholders is the power of the courts (notably the Enterprise Chamber) to review the board's decisions according to the fiduciary standards described above. As indicated, these standards are favourable from a

60 For an analysis of the preference share mechanism, see L. Chazen and P. Werdmuller, 'The Dutch Poison Pill: How is it Different from an American Rights Plan?' (available at corpgov.law.harvard.edu/2015/12/01/the-dutch-poison-pill-how-is-it-different-from-an-american-rights-plan/); and for both devices, Houthoff, *The Dutch 'Stichting' an Effective and Flexible Tool In Global Structuring*, 2020 (available at www.houthoff.com/-/media/houthoff/publications/pdevries/houthoff-whitepaper—stichting.pdf). The preference share mechanism is a post-bid defence (even if put in place pre-bid) as, it is arguable, is the depositary receipt since the receipt-holder's right to vote is removed only once a hostile bid emerges.

61 Within a group, it may be possible to erect an effective defence based on a foundation at a sub-group level, the requisite shareholder approval being given by the parent company.

62 H. Koster, 'Mergers and acquisitions in the Netherlands: Do listed companies need better defences?' (2021) 32 *International Company and Commercial Law Review* 166.

defensive perspective and there is some doubt about the scope of the Enterprise Chamber's review powers.[63]

We conclude that the Commission was correct to proceed on the basis that, if post-bid shareholder consent for defensive measures is the desired policy objective, incorporating a BNR into EU law would have advanced that policy to a significant extent. This would clearly be the case where national law endorses effective defensive measures, as in the Netherlands. But even where this is not so, leaving the issue to general corporate laws is a second-best policy, because general corporate laws are likely to be less impactful than the BNR and because their substantive coverage cannot be relied on to be comprehensive.

10.4.1.2 The Argument from Shareholder Composition

Although the triviality argument, based on the view that general corporate law already prohibits effective defensive measures without shareholder consent, is difficult to accept across the board, it is still possible to argue that an unqualified BNR is of limited interest across the EU because the composition of the shareholder body means that no bid can succeed without shareholder consent irrespective of the presence of a BNR. This is most obviously so where a company has a de jure controlling shareholder or shareholder group. Moreover, in such a case the disciplinary function of replacing ineffective management can be as effectively discharged by the controlling shareholder as by an outside bidder, while a controlling shareholder can probably bargain effectively with the offeror in a scale-enhancing takeover without any help from specific takeover laws. In jurisdictions where controlling shareholders predominate, therefore, the presence or precise configuration of the BNR may be a matter of little importance. The OECD reports that, as of the end of 2022, in seven EU Member States (Lithuania, Estonia, Italy, Austria, Portugal, Poland and Belgium) at least 40% of listed companies had a single shareholder holding 50% or more of the equity[64] and the percentage where the top three shareholders held 50% or more was, of course, much higher (exceeding 60% in all these cases except Belgium).[65] Germany, France, Hungary and Slovenia were all

[63] For an example of the Chamber's intervention, see the LVMH and Gucci case, analysed by M. Schoordijk, 'Netherlands: Company law – judicial enquiry' (1999) 10(8) ICCLR N59.

[64] See OECD *Corporate Governance Factbook 2023*, Figure 1.6. Strictly, from our point of view, the most relevant statistic is the percentage of voting rights held by the largest vote-holder. The table may underestimate the position of controllers in jurisdictions where departures from the one share, one vote principle are common. For example, Sweden appears in the table as a more dispersed jurisdiction than the United States, but this may fail to take account of the widespread use of weighted voting shares in the former country.

[65] The top-three percentage is thought to indicate a situation where coordination of action among the largest shareholders comes at a low cost, so that they act as a unit in the face of a bid. The 'top three' number is, of course, a rough proxy. One can easily think of situations where the top three are at loggerheads with each other and, by contrast, where coordination is feasible among a greater number of large shareholders.

close to the 40% figure and in all four cases the percentage of companies where the top three shareholders held 50% of the equity was itself in excess of 50%. Spain and Greece both appear as countries where the percentage for the top three shareholders (holding 50% or more of the equity) was at or above 40% (with the figure for Greece being more than 70%), while Denmark and the Netherlands fall just below 40%. To put the matter the other way around, the only EU or former EU Member States in the OECD table which had largely dispersed shareholdings at the end of 2022 were Ireland, Finland and the UK (all with a 'top three' percentage of less than 20%).

It is important to be clear that the above statistics give an indication only of the typical level of concentration of shareholdings in a particular jurisdiction. Moreover, the picture is static: the table itself does not indicate whether the trend in all or some jurisdictions is towards or away from greater concentration.[66] In addition, the table does not demonstrate that even in highly concentrated jurisdictions there are no widely held companies. Even when control is de facto in the hands of a small group of shareholders, it may be possible for a bidder to prise one or more blockholders from the group and then make a public offer which gains sufficient acceptances to give the bidder legal control of the company. So, takeovers implemented against the wishes of the incumbent management may take place probably at some level in all EU jurisdictions. Such takeovers, even if rare, may have significant political consequences, as we saw above in relation to the takeover of Mannesmann by Vodafone[67] or raise difficult legal issues, as with Veolia's bid for Suez.[68] What can be said is that the prevalence of concentrated shareholdings across the EU reduces the salience of the BNR. If one looks at the takeover from an industrial policy point of view, as the Commission did in its review of the implementation of the Directive,[69] sidelining incumbent management in order to promote takeovers becomes a less plausible policy in the presence of controlling shareholders, because (controlling) shareholders will decide on the takeover, with or without the BNR. In terms of this industrial policy, pressing Member States to adopt a BNR is an unrewarding use by the Commission of its political capital or goodwill vis-à-vis the Member States when there are likely to be many alternative calls on that capital. 'Resignation' on the part of the Commission in relation to the BNR becomes a rational choice. Instead, the core question becomes what the incentives of controlling shareholders might be to accept takeover offers, in the presence of private benefits of control, both financial and non-financial.[70]

66 See W.-G. Ringe, 'Changing Law and Ownership Patterns in Germany: Corporate Governance and the Erosion of Deutschland AG' (2015) 63 *American Journal of Comparative Law* 493 for evidence of such change in Germany.
67 See text attached to n 25.
68 See n 35.
69 See n 1.
70 See Section 10.4.2.1.

10.4.2 *Substitutes for Post-bid Defensive Measures*

10.4.2.1 Pre-bid Defences

As we have seen above, the argument that a mandatory BNR would give potential target companies a strong incentive to put in place pre-bid measures was recognised only after the unexpected defeat of the Directive in the European Parliament in 2000. The High Level Group of Company Law Experts,[71] to which the matter was referred, took the problem seriously and produced a wide-ranging mechanism to deal with it – the Breakthrough Rule. Before proceeding further, it is worth noting two limitations on the BTR, even in the form proposed by the High Level Group. First, it addressed only (some types of) structural defences and left transactional ex ante defences out of the picture. Moreover, transactional defences are more difficult to challenge under national law than ex post ones. If the pre-bid measure is an aspect of a transaction which has a commercial rationale, it will be more difficult to show that the measure constitutes a breach of duty than with a post-bid measure, where the timing of the transaction may give rise to suspicions. For example, the pre-bid issue of 'poison debt' (debt which is repayable on a change of control of the borrowing company) can be presented as a protection for the lender (and, in addition, the issuance of debt, unlike shares, does not normally need shareholder approval). Or a joint venture arrangement (again not a transaction routinely requiring shareholder approval) may give the co-venturer a right to buy out the target company (or to be bought out by it) at a very attractive price if there is a change of control in the target. Of course, in the event, the other party, for commercial reasons, may decide not to exercise its contractual rights, but the prospect of exercise may be enough to deter the bidder or cause it to negotiate extensively with the incumbent management of the target.

Again, the target may hold onto, or acquire, a business which it believes will strengthen the competition arguments against the bidder, if it launches a bid. Or, where the target company sponsors a defined benefit pension scheme, which is in deficit, potential bidders may be put off by the risk of having to make substantial contributions to the scheme in the future. Knowing this, the target may be happy to continue to run the scheme at a deficit.[72]

All the above are transactional pre-bid defences. The opportunity to put one in place cannot be guaranteed to be available at any particular time, though, over time, such opportunities are likely to arise and management fearing a hostile bid is likely to take advantage of them as they present themselves or even seek to generate them. Nevertheless, incumbent management may feel more secure with a permanent,

[71] See n 4. See also J. Arlen and E. Talley, 'Unregulable Defenses and the Perils of Shareholder Choice' (2003) 152 *University of Pennsylvania Law Review* 577.

[72] 'New powers for UK pension watchdog hit dealmaking', *Financial Times*, 27 December 2021.

structural defensive arrangement in place, if only because it is likely to be less restrictive of management's business freedom. Here one can see the second limitation on the BTR, namely, that its coverage of ex ante structural defences was incomplete. In particular, it did not deal comprehensively with controlling shareholders. This may seem logical since we have noted above that a controlling position is an effective substitute for the BNR so that, to this extent, the aims of the Directive were aligned with controlling positions. However, the issue of controlling shareholders reveals a policy dilemma underlying the Directive. In essence, if the policy is simply to sideline the board in a takeover, a controlling shareholder is a substitute for a BNR, no matter how that controlling position is created. However, if the policy is the more ambitious one of making control contestable, a controlling position raises difficult questions. This is because the controller, benefitting from private benefits of control, both financial and non-financial, may be unwilling to sell that controlling position at a price which is feasible for an efficient bidder, at least where a mandatory bid rule is in place, while sale to a bidder which will 'loot' the company is hardly good policy.[73]

In any event, the EU legislator hardly has the political legitimacy to break up controlling positions, where the control is proportionate to the economic interests of the controller, but it could contemplate targeting controlling positions 'artificially' created through control-enhancing mechanisms (CEMs), which is what the BTR proposal in fact aimed to do. Thus, the BTR emerged as a constraint on CEMs but, as proposed by the High Level Group, only on certain CEMs and, as proposed by the Commission, its range was even narrower. The Commission, fearing Member States would not accept such a deep intrusion into their corporate laws and practices, produced only a watered-down version of the Group's proposals for the legislative process. Confirming the Commission's predictions, even this version pleased none of the Member States, which, when optionality was introduced, were able to give effect to their views by not adopting it. However, in some jurisdictions, limited examples of implementation of the breakthrough concept can be found. Spain has a targeted breakthrough rule which removes the cap on voting rights once the bidder has reached a 70 per cent threshold.[74] In France, the stock market authorities have long advocated the suspension of any cap in the articles on shareholders' voting at the first post-bid general meeting, in the event that the bidder holds a fraction of the capital or voting rights at least equal to that required to amend the articles of association and up to a limit of 75 per cent, and this was made a requirement with the transposition of the Directive in France.[75]

Nevertheless, these limited occurrences of the breakthrough idea did not remove the significance of the big question generated by the failure of the BTR at EU level.

[73] Davies,n 51, chapter 21.
[74] 115.2 Ley 3/2023, of 17 March, LMVSI.
[75] AMF General Regulation, Art. 231–254.

Was it rational to place emphasis on the adoption of a BNR if there were no special restrictions on the adoption of pre-bid defences? To some extent, the answer to the question of whether incumbent management is in a position to take effective pre-bid defensive measures is a reprise of the question in relation to post-bid measures. As with post-bid defensive measures in the absence of a BNR, the scope for action pre-bid depends partly on the applicable legal rules and partly on the market reaction on the part of investors to pre-bid measures and to the financing needs of companies more generally. A notable example of market pressures is the UK whose rules have contained a strong BNR for the last half-century but at the same time are permissive in respect of pre-bid defences.[76] One might have expected in this situation a proliferation of pre-bid defences to have developed in that jurisdiction. They are not non-existent, but the notable feature of the UK position is how few pre-bid defences are routinely adopted. This is generally explained by the reluctance of the institutional shareholders to hold shares in companies which have adopted pre-bid defences, at least defences of a structural character. This explanation is consistent with that given for the presence of the BNR in the Takeover Code – that is, the capacity of the institutional shareholders to bring their influence to bear on this non-legislative Code.[77]

As to legal mechanisms, they operate principally by enhancing the voting rights of one subset of shareholders or reducing the voting capacity of another set or by hindering the transfer of shares.[78] There are a number of related mechanisms by which this can be achieved. In general, they are mechanisms of private ordering.[79] Resort to them is often not strongly controlled by national law and the tendency since the Directive has been to relax such controls as exist. This is despite the fact that the standard law-and-economics analysis of CEMs is unfavourable to them, on the grounds that they increase the incentives of those whose control depends on CEMs to extract private benefits of control from the company, as compared with OSOV controllers, who have a larger economic stake in the company and thus derive a smaller benefit from benefit extraction.[80] However, contemporary policy

[76] Even the much-discussed UK ban on weighted voting shares issued by premium-listing companies was not introduced until 2014 and has been progressively relaxed subsequently.

[77] See P. Davies, 'Shareholders in the United Kingdom' in J. Hill and R. Thomas (eds.), *Research Handbook on Shareholder Power* (Oxford: Oxford University Press, 2015). The decline in the percentage of the UK market held by domestic institutions in recent years is likely to test in the future the robustness of this institutional shareholder orientation.

[78] See the text followingn 6.

[79] We have already touched on the mechanisms which Dutch law offers above. See text attached to nn 59–61.

[80] See L. Bebchuk, R. Kraakman and G. Triantis, 'Stock Pyramids, Cross-Ownership and Dual Class Equity: The Mechanisms and Agency Costs of Separating Control from Cash-Flow Rights', in R. Morck (ed.), *Concentrated Corporate Ownership*, (Chicago, IL: Chicago University Press, 2000) p. 445. We do not analyse cross-holdings in this chapter on the grounds that they are not much used in Europe (in contrast, for example, with Asia). See M. Faccio and L. Lang, 'The Ultimate Ownership of Western European Corporations' (2002) 65 *Journal of*

analysis is more favourable, emphasising the monitoring benefits of controlling shareholders and suggesting that controllers are less swayed by short-term considerations than dispersed shareholders.[81] We do not need to investigate this debate in depth: the important point is that the swing in policy emphasis reinforces Member States' reluctance to apply the BTR, even though this development thus undermines the aim of the Takeover Directive which was to facilitate transfers of corporate control.

A popular CEM is some form of dual-class share arrangement, whereby two or more classes of share with identical economic rights nevertheless have disparate voting rights (possibly including no votes at all) attached to them, either on all votes taken in the general meeting or on those likely to be of most interest to a hostile bidder – for example, a resolution to remove the current directors from the board.[82] In principle, the issuance of dual classes of shares is likely to require shareholder approval, as with any other share issuance. However, the need for independent shareholder consent for departures from OSOV in favour of the existing controllers can be avoided in various ways. Consent may be given before shares are offered to the public (when the future beneficiaries of the dual-class arrangement are likely to be in control of the company) or, post-IPO, while the existing management still has de facto control of the shareholder meeting, or the opportunity to do so may arise if the company needs funding which the market is unwilling to provide but the existing controllers will if their position is made secure through weighted voting.

A number of countries have restrictions or prohibitions on the issuance of dual-class shares. However, the trend is towards their relaxation in the light of the global competition among exchanges for listings, at least at the IPO stage. Thus, the European Commission is currently seeking to shield newly listed companies from the ordinary play of the market for corporate control, through the use of multiple-vote share structures (MVSSs).[83] The Directive 2024/2810 of 23 October 2024 on multiple-vote share structures in companies that seek admission to trading of their shares on a multilateral trading facility (MTF) requires Member States to make the

Financial Economics 365, 378: 'Cross-holdings are only marginally significant in Norway, Germany, and Austria (accounting for 2.27, 2.62 and 1.01 per cent of cases respectively) but are insignificant elsewhere.'

81 See the discussion of the debates surrounding the Loi Florange (text attached to nn 27–30).

82 A Commission-sponsored study from 2006 suggests MVS were popular at that time in Sweden, Finland, France and the Netherlands: ISS, Shearman and Sterling and ECGI, 'Report on the Proportionality Principle in the European Union' 2006, para 3.2.1 (available at ec.europa.eu/docsroom/documents/14881/attachments/2/translations/en/renditions/pdf). However, this study lumps together MVS and tenure voting arrangements (which we treat differently) and excludes non-voting equity shares from the MVS category, while we include them in MVS. In any event, as indicated immediately below, MVS have subsequently become more widely available and probably more widely used.

83 'Proposal for a directive of the European Parliament and of the Council on multiple-vote share structures in companies that seek the admission to trading of their shares on an SME growth market', COM (2022) 761 final (7 December 2022).

option of using MVSSs available to newly listed companies on MTFs, subject to conditions.[84] It appears, however, that, on markets not covered by the Directive, like regulated markets, Member States may continue with any existing more generous provisions. This legislative move may appear ironic considering the long-standing inclination of the Commission towards OSOV, which it even considered at one point imposing as a general requirement (not just in relation to takeovers) on all European companies listed in the EU, before changing its mind in the absence of a clear demonstration of the benefits of such generalised application.[85] It only underlines the potential contradictions existing between an open market for corporate control and an attractive stock market for entrepreneurs, unwilling to lose their control as the result of an IPO. Their ability to overcome this entrepreneurial dilemma has made MVSSs popular throughout the world. There are, however, possible regulatory ways of reconciling those imperatives, of which the most popular is a sunset provision, so that the departure from OSOV is temporary, though not necessarily short-lived.

Functionally similar to, but treated as analytically separate from, MVSSs are tenure voting arrangements (or loyalty shares) whose development in France we mentioned above.[86] However, their attractions are by no means limited to French companies.[87] Italian companies in particular sought access to more favourable tenure voting arrangements than were then available in their home jurisdiction by taking the additional pre-bid defensive measure of reincorporation in a jurisdiction providing them, in this case the Netherlands. Belcredi et al.[88] argue that the Italian reincorporators to the Netherlands (as opposed to those from other countries) are notable in being motivated by the easier availability of CEMs in that jurisdiction,

[84] OJEU L, 14 November 2024. See A. Pietrancosta, 'Multiple-vote share structures: the genesis of the "Listing Act" directive', European Company Case Law (ECCL), 2024/2, p. 147–164; 'Les sources réelles et formelles de la consécration européenne du vote multiple en bourse', in Mélanges Hervé Le Nabasque, tbp; ECLE, 'The European proposal to open up multiple-vote share structures to listing companies: a simplification in *trompe l'oeil*', OBLB, 5 September 2023.

[85] Commission Staff Working Document, 'Impact Assessment on the Proportionality between Capital and Control in Listed Companies', Brussels, SEC (2007) 1705 (12 December 2007). See Klaus J. Hopt and Susanne Kalss, 'Multiple-voting shares in Europe – A comparative law and economic analysis', ECGI – Law Working Paper No. 786/2024, available at SSRN: https://ssrn.com/abstract=4887591 or http://dx.doi.org/10.2139/ssrn.4887591; A. Pietrancosta, 'Propositions françaises et européennes pour ouvrir le vote multiple aux sociétés entrant en bourse' (2023), *Bull. Joly Soc.*, January 2023, n° BJS201q7.

[86] See text attached immediately followingn 31. Tenure voting shares were excluded from the Commission's Proposal for a Directive on multiple-vote structures and so may be freely adopted by Member States: see COM (2022) 761 final, Recital 5 and Art. 2(b).

[87] Spain and the Netherlands should be added to the countries allowing tenured voting and a number of others are considering introducing it.

[88] See M. Belcredi, L. Favarzani and A. Signori, 'An Analysis of Italian Companies Moving Abroad' (available at centridiricerca.unicatt.it/fin-gov-Cos%C3%AC%20non%20fan%20tutte%20final%20June%202023%20clean.pdf.

especially tenure voting arrangements. They also argue that the tenure voting arrangements adopted upon reincorporation operated principally for the benefit of the existing controlling shareholders either by strengthening existing control positions or by allowing the maintenance of control whilst reducing the size of the economic stake in the company. Since, as we noted in Section 10.4.1.1, the Netherlands also contains two effective post-bid defences, the possibility of the Netherlands becoming the destination of choice for companies seeking either pre-bid or post-bid defences must be high.[89]

Even without reincorporation, the adoption of tenure voting strengthens the position of existing controlling shareholders. Thus, Declercq et al.[90] argue that this was the main impact of the introduction of tenure voting in Belgium (rather than combatting short-termism or encouraging IPOs). Those Belgian companies that sought to take up the tenure voting arrangement when it became available were predominantly companies with existing controlling (or large) shareholders, whose votes in the general meeting were enough to secure its adoption. A similar development is reported in relation to the Italian rules on tenured voting – that is, a concentration of tenured voting in companies with controlling shareholders[91] – and in France. For France, this development has been assessed empirically as positive, on the grounds that tenure shares indicate enhanced blockholder monitoring and enable financially constrained blockholders to retain control while reducing their economic exposure to the company.[92] However the academic debate on the utility of tenured voting arrangements is ultimately decided, it is clear that public debate has shifted towards emphasising the benefits rather than the costs of moving away from OSOV.

A third mechanism for separate voting rights from economic interests is the 'pyramid'. This is separation created by corporate structure rather than by unequal allocation of voting rights and so does not require a formal departure from OSOV, though this is functionally what is achieved. In a simple form of pyramid structure, an investor holds a controlling interest, say, 50 per cent, in the top company and then creates one or more intermediate holding companies between the topco and

89 In this context it is important to note that the Netherlands is an incorporation theory state, so that a company seeking to reincorporate in that jurisdiction would not be required to move its headquarters there. The Commission-sponsored study also suggests that priority shares and depository receipts are much less available outside the Netherlands:n 82, 3.2.5–6.

90 S. Declercq, J. Delvoie, T. Monnens and T. Vos, 'Loyalty Voting Rights in Belgium: Nothing More than a Control Enhancing Mechanism?' (2023) 20 *ECFLR* 27. See also M. Becht, 'Loyalty Voting Structures: A Better Dual Class?', ECGI Law Working Paper 769/2024.

91 C. Mosca, 'Should Shareholders Be Rewarded for Loyalty? European Experiments on the Wedge between Tenured Voting and Takeover Law' (2019) 8 *MICH. BUS. & ENTREPRENEURIAL L. REV.* 245, 270–272 – albeit tempered by the need to avoid the mandatory bid obligation; E. Bajo, M. Barbi, M. Bigelli and E. Croci, 'Bolstering family control: Evidence from loyalty shares' (2020) 65 *Journal of Corporate Finance* 101755.

92 F. Belot, E. Ginglinger and L. Starks, 'Encouraging long-term shareholders: the effects of loyalty shares with double voting rights' (available at papers.ssrn.com/sol3/papers.cfm?abstract_id = 3475429).

the ultimate operating company (or companies). The intermediate subsidiaries are not wholly owned but have outside investors (in fact, their shares may be publicly traded), but so that the company immediately above holds a controlling interest in the intermediate company; and the ultimate intermediate company holds a controlling interest in the operating company. In this way, an investment in the topco can yield control of the operating company, even though the controller of the topco has only a small economic interest in the operating company. In a simple example, with 50 per cent shareholdings and three companies in the group, the controller of the topco will have control of the operating subsidiary, but with only a 12.5 per cent economic interest in it.

This form of separation of economic and control rights used to be common in Italy,[93] but Bianchi and Bianco noted in 2006 a decline in the incidence of pyramids and a growth in the proportion of listed companies held by coalitions of blockholders, bound together by formal or informal agreements.[94] Since then there appears to have been an increase in the proportion of Italian listed companies with tenured voting arrangements. CONSOB identified about seventy such companies (or about one-third of the total) at the end of 2024, compared with only six which had adopted dual-class shares.[95] The effect, presumably, is to increase the control position of coalitions and to reduce the incentives of a large blockholder to sell out, except to an offeror approved by the coalition as a whole.

It is difficult precisely to estimate the availability, and use, of pre-bid defensive measures in Europe. However, it is possible to conclude that they are reasonably freely available. As far as transactional defences are concerned – that is, instances where the defence is bundled into a commercial transaction the company has entered into – this is not surprising. A permanent pre-bid prohibition of equivalent breadth to the BNR would impose heavy costs on the efficient running of the company, through the need to seek frequent shareholder consent for transactions. The costs of such a rule would very likely exceed any benefits arising from controlling managerial entrenchment. So, defences which are offshoots of running the company's business are not tightly constrained. At a minimum, it is likely to be necessary, but very difficult, to show that the defence was the main purpose of the transaction before a breach of duty by the directors could be shown.

Structural defences, by contrast, are easier to prohibit without impinging extensively on managerial freedom of action, as is shown by the fact that some

93 A. Aganin and P. Volpin, 'The History of Corporate Ownership in Italy', in R. Morck (ed.), 2000, n 80, at 365, suggest that pyramids were the result of large financing needs of Italian companies and under-developed capital markets – a view consistent with the decline in pyramids (see following note) and with the subsequent growth of Italian and European capital markets. The Commission-sponsored study from 2006 suggests that pyramids were also well used at that time in Belgium and Sweden:n 82 3.2.4.

94 M. Bianchi and M. Bianco, 'Italian corporate governance in the last 15 years: From pyramids to coalitions?' (2006) *ECGI Finance Working Paper* 144/2006.

95 See www.consob.it/web/consob-and-its-activities/listed-companies/voto-maggiorato-e-plurimo.

jurisdictions do prohibit specific examples of pre-bid defences, such as MVSSs. However, it is a separate question whether it is good policy to impose such prohibitions and to decide how widely to impose them. The Commission Study suggested that European states have been quite restrained in imposing legal prohibitions on pre-bid defences. It looked at sixteen of the then Member States and concluded that, typically, between seven and ten CEMs were available in those states, with the Netherlands being an outlier at the top of the distribution (11) and Greece an outlier at the bottom (6).[96] Actual use of CEMs in particular jurisdictions is a separate question but the study found that some CEMs were widely used across jurisdictions, notably pyramid structures, multiple voting rights and shareholder agreements.[97] Although the pattern of use of CEMs may well have changed since 2006, the availability of some pre-bid defences has increased since then, notably MVSSs, as has probably the propensity of companies to put in place pre-bid defences.

10.4.2.2 State Action

The final mechanism which can act as a substitute for defensive measures is appeal to a third party (usually a public authority) which has the power to block the bid which is regarded with disfavour by the incumbent management. This step has long been possible in relation to the competition authorities or regulators concerned with the assessment of whether a particular acquirer is a fit and proper person to be allowed into the industry in question. Not even the fiercest BNR jurisdictions have prohibited engagement with such regulatory authorities.[98] However, in recent years the chances of state intervention, which blocks unwelcome bids, have increased with the adoption by an increasing number of States of foreign direct investment screening measures (though it should be noted that such screening may also end up blocking takeovers which incumbent management favours). This trend has been furthered by the COVID pandemic which was thought to have generated a high level of uncertainty about the 'true' value of shares in nationally important companies.[99] In 2019, the EU adopted a Regulation[100] which encourages (but does not require) Member States to introduce such a mechanism and the overwhelming majority of Member States have now adopted such mechanisms.

[96] Seen 82, Figure 3.1.

[97] Ibid., Figure 4.7.

[98] UK Takeover Panel, 'BAT Industries', Statement 1989/20.

[99] See L. Enriques, 'Pandemic Resistant Corporate Law' (2017) 17 *ECFR* 257 – though advocating the introduction of only temporary protections.

[100] Regulation (EU) 2019/452 establishing a framework for the screening of foreign direct investment in the Union. A later Regulation (EU) 2022/2560 on foreign subsidies distorting the internal market applies to acquisitions by subsidised foreign entities. The Commission has stronger powers under this Regulation which is, in effect, an expansion of its traditional competition jurisdiction.

For the same reason, the Regulation does not stipulate the design of the screening mechanism which Member States must adopt if they choose to do so. The Commission's powers are essentially powers to coordinate responses (from itself and other Member States towards the Member State applying the mechanism) if and when a national mechanism is applied to a particular offer. So, the mechanisms vary in design from one Member State to another. However, the Regulation makes it clear that the Commission expects the national screening rules to apply only where issues of national security or public order are raised (though these are imprecise terms). The risk for a Member State which strays beyond these areas is that its rules may be found to be in breach of the Treaty's provisions on free movement of capital.[101]

The upshot is that the competition and national security provisions have an episodic impact on takeover offers. It is probably not attractive for incumbent managers to rely on them rather than to seek to put in place defences which are under their own control. There may be some exceptional industries where the national security provisions operate more broadly – for example, defence, where the state is often the principal customer as well as a core financer, directly or indirectly, of the industry. Here, the fate of the company is probably in the hands of the state, no matter what the general takeover rules stipulate.

10.5 CONCLUSION

The Commission was clearly disappointed by its failure to secure the BNR as the uniform rule across the EU and, perhaps even more so, by the decision to leave the fate of the rule in the hands of the Member States. This disappointment was based on the assumption, first, that the BNR was an effective rule for disciplining slack or incompetent management, for redrawing the boundaries of the firm and for deepening the integration of the EU internal market. Second, it was assumed that no substitute legal mechanism for constraining defensive tactics existed at national level. Third, it was assumed that a body of shareholders existed to whom the putative bidder could appeal over the heads of the incumbent management.

In this chapter, we have argued that the second assumption was largely accurate: national law does not act as a perfect substitute for the BNR. Generally applicable corporate rules (for example, fiduciary duties) are much less precise than the BNR, whilst the transaction-specific rules leave gaps through which the target can squeeze, as well as often allowing ex ante shareholder authorisation of defences. In addition, the BNR is more effectively applied than general corporate law rules. Consequently, the optional nature of the BNR in the Directive as ultimately adopted and the decisions of many Member States to take advantage of that optionality inflicted a severe blow on the Commission's ambitions.

[101] Art. 65, TFEU.

The first assumption is more questionable, as the Commission came to realise during the legislative process. A BNR would have little disciplining effect if companies could take effective pre-bid defensive measures. Defensive measures embodied in pre-bid transactions were not controlled in the Directive and probably could not be. Pre-bid structural measures were partially addressed in the BTR but it suffered from the ultimate optionality compromise and, even more so, from the virtually uniform use by the Member States of the option to cast BTR into the darkness of irrelevance.

The third assumption was also questionable. Across the EU as a whole, controlling shareholdings were a common feature of the corporate landscape, and in those cases there was no real division between the board and shareholders over the sort of strategic issues hostile bids raise. However, the Directive simply left on one side the issue of how far private benefits of control interfered with the policy of making control contestable. Writing in the early 1990s, Professor Gilson argued for an 'ecological' approach to takeover regulation which would justify the Commission's stance. He drew a distinction between technical, legal barriers to takeovers and structural ones (here meaning controlling shareholders whose control was based on OSOV). The focus, he argued, should be on technical barriers, so that companies were exposed to technological changes. Once that was done, 'structural barriers … will shift when technological change warrants it.'[102] The BTR proposed by the High Level Group can be seen as having this aim, albeit only partially and unsuccessfully.

Equally crying out for explanation is the Commission's failure to seek to remedy the defects, as it saw them, in the Directive as eventually adopted. The Commission was prepared initially to return to the fray, but nothing significant in fact happened. We suggest that this is to be explained by a fundamental change in the Commission's political and economic analysis of its industrial policy after the Directive was adopted. The proposal for a Takeover Directive emerged during the great push for globalisation of business activities, in the last quarter of the last century and the first decade of this one. In a situation of strong inter-firm competition, both from within and without the EU, mechanisms for strengthening the competitiveness of EU companies were to be facilitated. Competitiveness was viewed as embracing not only technological and human resource capacity but also a functional and cost-reducing corporate law. The latter was then associated with shareholder primacy in corporate law, on the grounds that shareholders had the strongest incentives to maximise the operational efficiency of their companies.[103]

Shareholder primacy had its opponents even at the height of the globalisation trend. And these opponents had some important legal successes, such as the

[102] R. Gilson, 'The Political Ecology of Takeovers', in K. Hopt and E. Wymeersch (eds.) *European Takeovers* (London: Butterworths, 1992) at 68.

[103] P. Davies, *Introduction to Company Law*, (Oxford: Oxford University Press, 3rd ed., 2020), pp. 309–311.

enactment in multiple states of the US anti-takeover statutes which relieved boards of their fiduciary duties to the shareholders, in whole or in part, during takeovers, and the acceptance by the Delaware courts of the poison pill as a defensive technique (Delaware not having an anti-takeover statute). In the EU, the major success on the part of the opponents of shareholder primacy was the optionality of the defensive measures provisions in the Directive.

Since that time, as Enriques and Gatti argue in Chapter 11, the legislative steps at EU level have all been away from shareholder primacy and in favour of embedding existing control arrangements. The encouragement of dual-class shares and of merger controls on national security grounds have been especially relevant for management seeking to defend against or pre-empt a bid. More generally, the Commission's (controversial) focus recently has been on the problem of short-termism, where the role of takeovers is ambiguous.[104] Why has this occurred? After all, the arguments against the BNR, such as the desirability of furthering shareholder commitment to the incumbent management's 'idiosyncratic vision', safeguarding local communities and their social capital, and retaining within the EU the skills and technology needed for a successful modern economy are not new and were deployed during the long legislative process leading up the adoption of the Directive. It seems likely that more fundamental changes this century have led to Commission scepticism about shareholder primacy and the role of takeovers in promoting it. One might mention the great financial crisis at the end of the first decade of this century, which undermined faith in markets; the re-emergence of geopolitical tensions which have made reliance on foreign suppliers appear more risky; the rise of climate change up the policy agenda, reduction of global warming often being seen as requiring companies to take action which will reduce their profits and so be opposed by investors – despite the uncertain counterbalance applied by ESG investing; and the emergence of new and more insistent methods for shareholders to apply pressure on corporate management – such as activist hedge funds – which have increased suspicion of shareholder primacy, while at the same time providing a substitute in part for the hostile takeover.

In short, although the defensive measures provisions of the Takeover Directive may appear as unfinished business when measured against the Commission's original goals, they are likely to constitute finished business de jure when viewed in the current policy context.

[104] See European Commission, *Study on Directors' Duties and Sustainable Corporate Governance, Final Report* at 3.1.1.1: 'the use of M&A as an indicator of long-termism is questionable, as the literature suggests that certain acquisitions boost short-term performance at the expense of long-run value and are a sign of hyperactivity and too much attention to financial market issues by boards'. Although the Report does not formally represent the views of the Commission, one is aware that a report which the Commission has initiated and funded will not contain anything which the Commission actively disagrees with.

11

Death by a Thousand Cuts

The Hostile Bids Regime in Europe, 2004–2023

Luca Enriques and Matteo Gatti

11.1 INTRODUCTION

The EU Directive on Takeover Bids (hereafter, the Takeover Directive or the Directive)[1] lays out rules governing corporate control transactions and takeover bids (or tender offers) targeting EU-listed issuers. Adopted in 2004 after a tortured process,[2] the Directive contained the stated goals of 'establish[ing] minimum guidelines for the conduct of takeover bids and ensur[ing] an adequate level of protection for holders of securities throughout the Community'.[3] One of the main goals of the harmonization effort was to facilitate takeovers as efficient drivers of value creation.[4] It is well-known that even the Directive as finally adopted moved very timidly in that direction. Our chapter argues that further economic, political, legal and governance developments moved the needle further away from the goal of enabling the market for corporate control to allocate control rights in firms across the EU. In particular,

For useful feedback we would like to thank participants in the ECLE Workshop 'Twenty Years of the Takeover Directive', Stockholm, 12–13 October 2023, and especially Paul Davies, Guido Ferrarini and Edmund Schuster.

1 Directive 2004/25/EC of the European Parliament and of the Council of 21 April 2004 on takeover bids [2004] OJ L142/12. The Takeover Directive lays out rules governing corporate control transactions and tender offers for EU-listed issuers. See generally C. Clerc et al., 'A Legal and Economic Assessment of European Takeover Regulation', (2012) (based on the study undertaken for the European Commission, Marccus Partners and the Centre for European Policy Studies (CEPS), 'The Takeover Bids Directive Assessment Report' (2012)).

2 For a history of the long process that led to the adoption of the Directive, see generally B. Clarke and R. Skog, 'The Genesis of the Takeover Directive', in this volume (Chapter 1).

3 Takeover Directive, Recital 25.

4 P. Davies and A. Pietrancosta, 'Defensive Measures', in this volume (Chapter 10, citing Commission Staff Working Document, 'Report on the Implementation of the Directive on Takeover Bids', SEC (2007) 268 (21 February 2007) and noting how, in the mind of EU policymakers '[a] free market in corporate control would promote both the creation of the single European market and the competitiveness of European companies in the wider global markets').

multiple pieces of legislation at both the EU and Member State levels have (further) stifled the market for corporate control, and especially hostile bids.

The chapter is structured as follows. Section 11.2 briefly describes the ostensibly pro-market climate in which the Directive came to be. Section 11.3 illustrates how the past 20 years experienced a series of changes, if not shocks, in markets, corporate governance and the geopolitical and macroeconomic landscapes. Such changes contributed to abandoning openness to contestability of control (or any figment thereof) and made European companies ever more takeover-proof. A series of legislative measures at the EU or national level, which Section 11.4 describes, was the legal counterpart to those changes. Section 11.5 evaluates this new corporatist governance ecosystem and identifies companies' insiders, namely executives and significant shareholders, and national politicians as its main beneficiaries.

11.2 THE THEN: FOSTERING A PAN-EUROPEAN MARKET FOR CORPORATE CONTROL

One of the main objectives of EU takeover legislation was the promotion of a unified market for corporate control across the continent, with a keen focus on ensuring a level playing field. To that end, policymakers initially considered facilitating takeovers, including hostile ones, as a key component.[5] Relatedly, contestability of corporate control was viewed as key to the Union's market integration and competitiveness.[6]

Indeed, the European Commission espoused the British model of takeover regulation, based on the core principle of board neutrality.[7] This approach emphasized the importance for shareholders to be the ultimate decision-makers on whether a takeover should succeed without facing undue interference from target company boards. However, this vision started to crumble early on.

Notably, in 2001, an earlier proposal of the takeover directive, which in its attempt to establish a harmonized takeover market in the vein of the UK's City Code on Takeovers and Mergers imposed the board neutrality rule to all companies subject to the directive, famously failed to be approved by the European Parliament (in what was its first ever rejection of a directive).[8] The opposition to such a proposal was led by German lawmakers and that was no coincidence. Not only was Rhenish capitalism traditionally at odds with hostile takeovers,[9] but Germany had just 'lost' to

5 Clerc et al., n 1, at 202.

6 See n 4 and accompanying text.

7 See e.g. M. Gatti, 'Optionality Arrangements and Reciprocity in the European Takeover Directive' (2005) 6 *European Business Organization Law Review* 553, 561.

8 See Clarke and Skog, 'The Genesis of the Takeover Directive' in this volume (Chapter 1, at title 1.6).

9 J. Mukwiri, 'The End of History for the Board Neutrality Rule in the EU' (2020) 21 *European Business Organization Law Review* 253, 259.

British mobile giant Vodafone one of its 'national champions', telecommunications conglomerate Mannesmann, in what to this day is still the all-time largest mergers & acquisition (M&A) transaction globally.[10]

Following the 2001 debacle, the European Commission quickly set up a committee of experts chaired by Jaap Winter to seek common ground. One of the main findings was that due to different rules and principles of national company laws, companies in certain jurisdictions had a competitive advantage in defending against hostile bidders. The Winter Report recommended adoption of a rule that would override certain pre-bid defences if the takeover offer received a minimum percentage of shares (the so-called breakthrough rule). This rule wasn't enough to bridge the existing gap and broker a deal. To get there, Member States acknowledged they agreed to disagree and that they could not pass anything ambitious: retaining their prerogatives over takeover policies was paramount for a sufficient number of them. The turning point came with the so-called Lisbon compromise, which, among other things, made two of the core provisions of the Directive proposal, namely the board neutrality and the breakthrough rules, optional for Member States.[11] The compromise gave Member States the flexibility to keep establishing their principles and rules on takeover defences.[12] This compromise left what was considered a crucial portion of takeover law effectively at the discretion of individual Member States. Importantly, while the Directive focused on takeover regulation, it became evident that state company laws continued to play a significant role in shaping the corporate landscape, with a number of governance rules untouched upon by the Directive playing a significant role in determining companies' contestability of control.[13]

[10] See M. Gatti, 'Upsetting Deals and Reform Loop: Can Companies and M&A Law in Europe Adapt to the Market for Corporate Control?' (2019) 25 *Columbia Journal of European Law* 1, 5.

[11] The board neutrality rule requires directors of the target to obtain a shareholders' authorization before adopting takeover defences. The breakthrough rule eliminates certain pre-bid defences if an offer wins a considerable amount of support. *See generally* K. J. Hopt, 'Takeover Defenses in Europe A Comparative, Theoretical and Policy Analysis' (2014) 20 *Columbia Journal of European Law* 249; P. Davies, E. Philippe Schuster and E. van de Walle de Ghelke, 'The Takeover Directive as a Protectionist Tool?', in U. Bernitz et al. (eds.), *Company Law and Economic Protectionism* (Oxford: Oxford University Press, 2010), 105; Gatti, n 7.

[12] Article 12 of the Directive, which endorses a proposal by the Italian presidency in late 2003 to grant some flexibility to Member States and companies, allows Member States to opt out of the board neutrality rule and/or the breakthrough rule; at the same time, Article 12 requires Member States that have opted out of Articles 9 and/or 11 to allow their companies to opt into such rules. See Takeover Directive, Art. 12, see also Commission of the European Communities, Commission Staff Working Document: Report on the Implementation of the Directive on Takeover Bids, SEC (2007) 268, 3–5 (21 February 2007) (hereinafter Report on the Implementation of the Directive on Takeover Bids).

[13] See, with specific reference to the UK, but with an analysis that can be extended to other jurisdictions, D. Kershaw, 'The Illusion of Importance: Reconsidering the UK's Takeover Defence Prohibition' (2007) 56 *International & Comparative Law Quarterly* 267. See also n 49 and accompanying text.

Once the Directive was implemented, the new regulatory landscape appeared to be characterized by significant variation, with various countries that had made use of the options provided for by the Directive.[14] Of course, looming in the background of these policy choices were the opportunities presented by corporate migration, something the *Centros* case and its progeny, together with legislation on cross-border mergers made a new reality.[15] European freedom of establishment principles allow companies to relocate to countries with more favourable regulatory environments, further highlighting the complexity and fluidity of the European corporate governance landscape.

11.3 DEATH BY A THOUSAND CUTS, PART 1: MARKET, GOVERNANCE AND GEOPOLITICAL CHANGES

In the twenty years following the adoption of the Directive, the law and practice in the European market for corporate control changed profoundly due to market dynamics (Section 11.3.1), developments in corporate governance practices and priorities (Section 11.3.2), and changes in the political and macroeconomic landscape (Section 11.3.3).

11.3.1 *Changes in the Market*

Several high-profile cross-border deals (both hostile and negotiated) generated unease in national socio-economic circles that reinforced pressures towards an even less takeover-friendly legal environment than resulted from the implementation of the Takeover Bids Directive.

This is unsurprising. In fact, headline-making deals predate the Directive and it was one of the earliest cross-border takeover attempts, Carlo De Benedetti's failed tender offer for Société Générale de Belgique, which prompted European policy-makers to look into takeover legislation.[16] Gucci's attempted takeover by French luxury conglomerate LVMH in 1999 signalled the adaptability of Dutch company

[14] Gatti, n 7; Davies, Schuster and van de Walle de Ghelke, n 11.

[15] Case C-212/97, *Centros Ltd v Erhvervs-og Selskabsstyvelsen* [1999] ECR 1459; Case C–208/00, *Überseering BV v Nordic Construction Company Baumanagement GmbH* [2002] ECR 9919; Case C–167/01, *Kamer van Koophandel en Fabrieken voor Amsterdam v Inspire Art Ltd.* [2003] ECR 10155. See also Tenth Council Directive 2005/56/EC of the European Parliament and of the Council of 26 October 2005 on cross-border mergers of limited liability companies [2005] OJ L310/1; Directive (EU) 2017/1132 of the European Parliament and of the Council of 14 June 2017 relating to certain aspects of company law (codification) [2017] OJ L169/46, Artt. 118–133. [2019] OJ L321/1.

[16] M. Ventoruzzo, 'Europe's Thirteenth Directive and U.S. Takeover Regulation: Regulatory Means and Political Economic Ends' (2006) 41 *Texas International Law Journal* 171, 203; for a description of the Société Générale de Belgique takeover attempt, see J. J. Duffy, 'Financial Services Revolution Looms in Old World' (23 May 1988) AM. *Banker (N.Y.)* at 1.

law in protecting a target company.[17] It was then gigantic acquisition of Mannesmann by Vodafone that grabbed everyone's attention at the turn of the century and effectively resulted in German politicians killing the directive proposal in the famous tied vote of July 2001.[18]

After the Directive's adoption, in the frothy-equity-market, low-interest-rate scenario of the pre-financial-crisis 2000s, cross-border activity intensified, with massive and controversial deals creating profound and enduring effects on legal, regulatory and market landscapes. These deals include Mittal-Arcelor, after which France passed the Florange law;[19] GE-Alstom, after which France extended the government's veto power on takeovers affecting French strategic interests in areas such as energy, transport, telecoms and public health;[20] the acquisition of Endesa by ENEL, which displayed the inability of Spanish targets to defend themselves effectively and resulted in Spain implementing the Takeover Directive with harsher conditions for bidders (the reciprocity principle, a loosened board neutrality rule, and a ban on partial tender offers, which in the past had facilitated creeping acquisitions);[21] and the acquisition of Cadbury by Kraft, whose broken promise to maintain occupational levels and keep some factories open prompted new disclosure rules on, as well as enforceability of, so-called post-offer undertakings.[22]

[17] See L. Enriques and M. Gatti, 'Creeping Acquisitions in Europe: Enabling Companies to Be Better Safe than Sorry' (2015) 15 *Journal of Corporate Law Studies* 55.

[18] See n 8 and accompanying text. See also M. Höpner and G. Jackson, 'Revisiting the Mannesmann Takeover: How Markets for Corporate Control Emerge' (2006) 3 *European Management Review* 142, 146.

[19] Gatti, n 10, at 7. For a brief description of the Florange law, see nn 66 and 67 and accompanying text.

[20] Gatti, n 10, at 7–8. Rumours of a potential acquisition of dairy products giant Danone by PepsiCo are said to have prompted the French legislature to implement the Takeover Directive in 2006 with a taxing provision for acquirers: at its discretion, the Autorité des marchés financiers (AMF, the French securities commission), may require a person who is believed to be launching a takeover bid to state if in fact s/he intends to proceed – any such statement must then be honoured for six months. G. Ferrarini and G. P. Miller, 'A Simple Theory of Takeover Regulation in the United States and Europe' (2009) 42 *Cornell International Law Journal* 301, 319–320.

[21] Gatti, n 10, at 8.

[22] P. Davies, K. J. Hopt and W. G. Ringe, 'Control Transactions', in R. Kraakman et al. (eds.), *The Anatomy of Corporate Law: A Comparative and Functional Approach* (Oxford: Oxford University Press, 2017), 205, 209. In the 2011 reform of the City Code, the Panel promulgated additional wide-ranging rules: it severely limited break-up fees and crystallized in a bright-line rule its 'put up or shut up' approach by fixing to a 28-day deadline the time a potential offeror has to announce either a firm intention to make an offer or that it does not intend to make an offer (in which case it will be prohibited for a six-month period from launching an offer on the same target). See The Takeover Panel-Code Committee, 'Review of the 2011 Amendments to the Takeover Code' (2012) (UK) www.thetakeoverpanel.org.uk/wp-content/uploads/2023/02/Panel-Statement-2012-8.pdf; B. Clarke, 'Directors' Duties During an Offer Period – Lessons from the Cadbury Plc Takeover' *UCD Working Papers in Law, Criminology & Socio-Legal Studies Research Paper No. 44/2011*, https://ssrn.com/abstract=1759953; N. Rogerson,

It wasn't just takeovers. In fact, hedge-fund activism, a phenomenon that had been changing US corporate governance profoundly, became prominent in Europe as well. Large issuers in various Member States soon became targets of activist campaigns, including AkzoNobel, ThyssenKrupp, TIM and Pernod Ricard, all targeted by US hedge fund Elliott; Ericsson, Volvo and ABB, targeted by Swedish hedge fund Cevian Capital; Nestlé and CaixaBank, targeted by US hedge fund Third Point Partners; and Repsol, targeted by US investor Carl Icahn.

Activist campaigns question managers' strategies, including, often, the choice whether to sell (or merge) the company, which can affect their tenure.[23] In fact, the market for corporate control and hedge-fund activism are both substitutes for, and complements to, each other. The greater the pressure on executives, the greater managers' urge for insulation via market or political mechanisms.

11.3.2 *Changes in Corporate Governance*

The Takeover Directive was adopted in a period when the shareholder value maximization norm was at its apogee in Europe, leading many academic, policy-making and business circles to view takeovers, and hostile ones in particular, in a positive light. Times have changed. The late 2010s witnessed phenomena such as the advent of ESG investing and engagement,[24] as well as the reappearance of stakeholderism as a serious contender in the corporate purpose debate.[25]

'A Perspective from the Market for Corporate Control of the Post-Cadbury Takeover Reform' (2017) 38 *Business Law Review* 21.

[23] Some in the activist hedge funds literature point to pressure to get M&A exits as one of the most consequential drivers of activism. See Z. Goshen and R. S. Steel, 'Barbarians Inside the Gates: Raiders, Activists, and the Risk of Mistargeting' (2022) 132 *Yale Law Journal* 411, 457 (noting that 'evidence suggests that the positive returns frequently attributed to hedge-fund activism are largely explained by activists' ability to force a takeover' and adding that 'the primary value of hedge-fund activists, if any, is to act as an auctioneer for corporate raiders'.)

[24] Cf. E. Pollman, 'The Making and Meaning of ESG' (2022) *Eur. Corp. Governance Inst. Law Working Paper* No. 659 https://papers.ssrn.com/sol3/papers.cfm?abstract_id=4219857; L. Enriques and G. Strampelli, 'The Dialogue Between Corporations and Institutional Investors: An Introduction', in L. Enriques and G. Strampelli (eds.), *Board-Shareholder Dialogue: Policy Debate, Legal Constraints and Best Practices* (Cambridge: Cambridge University Press, 2024). On the relationship between takeovers and corporate sustainability, see G. Ferrarini and M. Siri, 'Takeovers and Corporate Sustainability', in this volume, Chapter 12.

[25] Compare C. Mayer, *Prosperity: Better Business Makes Greater Good* (Oxford: Oxford University Press, 2018) and L. E. Strine, Jr., 'Restoration: The Role Stakeholder Governance Must Play in Recreating a Fair and Sustainable American Economy: A Reply to Professor Rock' (2021) 76 *Business Lawyer* 397 and A. Kovvali, 'Stark Choices for Corporate Reform' (2023) 123 *Columbia Law Review* 693; with L. A. Bebchuk and R. Tallarita, 'The Illusory Promise of Stakeholder Governance' (2020) 106 *Cornell Law Review* 91 (2020) and M. Gatti and C. Ondersma, 'Can A Broader Corporate Purpose Redress Inequality? The Stakeholder Approach Chimera' (2020) 46 *Journal of Coprorate Law* 1 and G. Ferrarini, 'Corporate Purpose and Sustainability', in D. Busch et al. (eds.), *Sustainable Finance in Europe: Corporate Governance, Financial Stability and Financial Markets* (London: Palgrave Macmillan, 2021).

In the context of takeovers, stakeholderism should justify non-shareholder-based defences, but in practice that would matter in any given jurisdiction only under two circumstances: (i) the company in question must not be subject to board neutrality; and (ii) post-bid anti-takeover defences are effective tools to fend off unsolicited bidders. With the important exception of the Netherlands, company laws of Member States make it hard to adopt devices that can readily defeat a bid.[26] Therefore, one could be tempted to conclude that embracing a stakeholder approach must have had little impact on the contestability of corporate control. However, that would miss the point: stakeholderism performs an expressive function, justifying opposition to takeovers by targets, incumbents more generally and policymakers.[27] Various regulations and governance reforms become more palatable politically if no one is ready to oppose them from a shareholder-value angle because that angle is no longer broadly shared. In sum, as shareholder value maximization has receded as a guiding principle, many arguments to support pro-takeover policies have lost steam.

There is more: even for those who embrace the shareholder value maximization norm, it is debated whether favouring takeovers and contestability of corporate control ultimately benefits shareholders.[28] This view, pioneered by Henry Manne, strongly advocated by Frank Easterbrook and Daniel Fischel, and endorsed by many others,[29] has been subject to renewed criticism in a series of articles by Zohar Goshen and various co-authors.[30] In their framework, disruptive entrepreneurs

[26] Enriques and Gatti, n 17, at 80–86.

[27] *See* infra note [50] and corresponding text.

[28] There are countless empirical studies describing the wealth effects of takeover activity. For summaries of such studies, see M. Martynova and L. Renneboog, 'A Century of Corporate Takeovers: What Have We Learned and Where Do We Stand?' (2008) 32 *Journal of Banking and Finance* 2148; B. Espen Eckbo, 'Corporate Takeovers and Economic Efficiency' (2014) 6 *Annual Review of Financial Economics* 51. Some studies have focused on data from takeover activity in Europe and reached findings that are in line with similar studies on the US market: target shareholders experience gains, while the evidence for shareholders of buyers is mixed. See M. Martynova and L. Renneboog, 'The Performance of the European Market for Corporate Control: Evidence from the Fifth Takeover Wave' (2011) 17 *European Financial Management* 208 (reporting on deal activity in the 1993–2001 period and finding that hostile deals are expected to create more value for shareholders, even though such value is to some extent already incorporated in the stock prices of buyer and target prior to the deal announcement).

[29] H. G. Manne, 'Mergers and the Market for Corporate Control' (1965) 73 *Journal of Political Economy* 110 (1965); F. H. Easterbrook and D. R. Fischel, 'The Proper Role of a Target's Management in Responding to a Tender Offer' (1981) 94 *Harvard Law Review* 1161; L. A. Bebchuk, 'The Case against Board Veto in Corporate Takeovers' (2002) 69 *University of Chicago Law Review* 973.

[30] See Z. Goshen and A. Hamdani, 'Corporate Control and Idiosyncratic Vision' (2016) 125 Yale Law Journal 560; Goshen and Steel, n 23. Earlier critics expressed concerns during the takeover wave of the 1980s. See M. Lipton, 'Takeover Bids in the Target's Boardroom' (1979) 35 *Business Law* 101 ('Rather than forcing directors to consider only the short-term interests of certain shareholders, national policy requires that directors also consider the long-term interests of the shareholders and the company as a business enterprise with all of its constituencies in addition

prefer keeping the company outside of the market for corporate control to better nurture their long-term idiosyncratic vision.[31] That is especially valuable for innovative companies, whose businesses are harder for markets to understand and price correctly,[32] and explains the wide success of dual-class share structures in tech IPOs in the last twenty years, not only in the US, where Google (now Alphabet) was the trailblazer, but also, if perhaps less prominently, in Europe – Spotify and Just Eat being two examples out of many EU companies going public with a dual-class share structure. Note in this respect that European policymakers sought, but failed, to thwart dual-class structures.[33] In fact, the European Commission later embraced an 'if you can't beat them, join them' approach with the 2023 proposal for a directive requiring, however cautiously,[34] that Member States enable SMEs to go public with dual-class shares under certain conditions.[35]

to the short-term and institutional shareholders'); R. J. Haft, 'Business Decisions by the New Board: Behavioral Science and Corporate Law' (1981) 80 *Michigan Law Review* 1, 5. ('There is growing recognition by the corporate establishment in America that its priorities should be reordered to achieve profit maximization in the long-term rather than in the short-term.'); L. Lowenstein, 'Pruning Deadwood in Hostile Takeovers: A Proposal for Legislation' (1983) 83 *Columbia Law Review* 249 (arguing that some takeovers are the product of short-term pressure by investors); P. F. Drucker, 'Corporate Takeovers – What Is to Be Done?' (1986) 82 *The Public Interest* 3, 12–13 (criticizing takeovers as '[t]hey force management into operating short-term'); J. C. Stein, 'Takeover Threats and Managerial Myopia' (1988) 96 *Journal of Political Economy* 61 (same); A. Shleifer and R. W. Vishny, 'Equilibrium Short Horizons of Investors and Firms' (1990) 80 *The American Economic Review* 148 (same).

31 See generally Goshen and Hamdani, n 29 (defending dual-class share structure on this basis) and Goshen and Steel, n 29 (arguing that Delaware law should extend the protection awarded to targets of a takeover also to targets of shareholder activism).

32 See generally Goshen and Hamdani, n 29.

33 First, the breakthrough rule is only optional and Member States, with minor exceptions, did not embrace it. Only Estonia adopted it (see Clerc et al., n 1, at 80), while since 1998 Italy has had a so-called mini-breakthrough rule in place, under which parties to stockholder agreements, such as voting agreements and restrictions to sell, may terminate such agreements without penalty if they tender their shares to a pending takeover bid (see Art. 123, para. 3, Consolidated Decree on Financial Intermediation, as amended by Law Decree No. 148 of 16 October 2017). Second, a subsequent initiative from the Commission was aborted even before reaching the proposal stage. See European Commission, 'Modernising Company Law and Enhancing Corporate Governance in the European Union – A Plan to Move Forward' COM (2003) 284 final, 25 (proposing a study on the effects of establishing a European one share, one vote principle). The study was commissioned from ISS, ECGI and Shearman & Sterling: see Report on the Proportionality Principle in the EU (2007), available at www.ecgi.global/content/one-share-one-vote-2007 (one of us coordinated the legal scholar network that supported Shearman & Sterling in the preparation of the Comparative Legal Study).

34 See ECLE, 'The European Proposal to Open up Multiple-vote Share Structures to Listing Companies: A Simplification in Trompe l'Oeil', Oxford Business Law Blog (5 September 2023), https://blogs.law.ox.ac.uk/oblb/blog-post/2023/09/european-proposal-open-multiple-vote-share-structures-listing-companies (noting that the Proposal requires Member States to include a number of limitations to the issuance of dual-class shares).

35 Proposal for a directive of the European Parliament and of the Council on Multiple-vote Share Structures in Companies that Seek the Admission to Trading of their Shares on an SME Growth Market, COM/2022/761 final, https://eur-lex.europa.eu/legal-content/EN/TXT/?

11.3.3 *Changes in Geopolitical Landscape and Macroeconomic Shocks*

The Directive was proposed and negotiated in relatively quiet times from a geopolitical perspective. European optimism ran high in the 1990s, with Member States working hard to meet the criteria for a single currency. True, the Directive was ultimately adopted not long after the 9/11 terrorist attacks and its optionality and reciprocity features suggest that Member States wanted to remain in charge on policies affecting the control of their largest domestic firms.

Since then, geopolitical turmoil has only worsened. Security concerns increased as terrorist attacks made victims in many European countries. The Schengen Area has been suspended on several occasions[36] and the ideal of a truly open European market began to crumble.[37]

All the while, anti-EU sentiment started to grow in various Member States. Fuelled by economic insecurity and channelling resentment against 'the elites', this movement had its apogee with the Brexit referendum. In the 2010s economic nationalism (sometimes, but not uniquely, fuelled by nativist movements) resurfaced as a crucial determinant of corporate governance.[38]

Macroeconomic shocks, in turn, gave politicians further justification for yielding to policies protecting incumbents. The financial crisis and the COVID pandemic resulted in steep collapses of stock prices worldwide. Companies soon found out they were trading at fractions of what they were trading at before and feared lower valuations could lead to unsolicited takeover attempts. Many protectionist interventions, as the next section details, were passed in the immediate aftermath of the first of these crises,[39] while the second provided the occasion for broadening the scope of regulations limiting foreign direct investment for national security reasons.[40]

* * *

uri=CELEX%3A52022PC0761. See now Directive (EU) 2024/2810 of the European Parliament and of the Council of 23 October 2024 on multiple-vote share structures in companies that seek admission to trading of their shares on a multilateral trading facility [2024] OJ L 2810/1.

36 S. Melchior, P. Hansens, N. Schmidt, A. Trellevik and I. Eliassen, 'Dismantling Schengen – six months at a time', *EUObserver* (9 September 2022), https://euobserver.com/eu-political/156002.

37 European Parliament, 'At a glance (March 2016): The economic impact of suspending Schengen' (2016), www.europarl.europa.eu/RegData/etudes/ATAG/2016/579074/EPRS_ATA(2016)579074_EN.pdf.

38 See generally M. Pargendler, 'The Grip of Nationalism on Corporate Law' (2020) 95 *Indianna Law Journal* 533.

39 See n 47.

40 See Section 11.4.3.

In short, the (relatively) pro-market and pro-EU climate that inspired the Directive, or at least its proposal,[41] proved ephemeral. In the new market-sceptic, nationalistic environment that established itself not long after, several measures directly or indirectly weakening the market for corporate control were enacted.[42] We provide numerous examples thereof in Section 11.4.

11.4 DEATH BY A THOUSAND CUTS, PART 2: CHANGES IN THE LAW

The forces described in Section 11.3 explain why, in the two decades following the adoption of the Takeover Directive, we have witnessed policy changes significantly departing from the original goal of fostering contestability in a pan-European market for corporate control. In Section 11.4.1, we describe changes to the takeover regime itself and to other financial markets regulations in the EU. In Section 11.4.2, we discuss takeover-hostile changes in national company laws and describe the phenomenon of companies migrating to the Netherlands and other jurisdictions' reactions to it. Section 11.4.3 delves into the bolstering of legislation to tighten the requirements for foreign control of strategic assets.

11.4.1 *Changes to Takeover and Financial Markets Laws*

The very nature of the Directive as a framework directive with various options for Member States has given them much freedom on how to implement some of its crucial features. Famously, two cornerstones of the Directive, the board neutrality rule and the breakthrough rule, are optional for individual Member States.[43] While virtually all states opted out of the breakthrough rule,[44] when Member States implemented the Directive only one-third of them opted out of the board neutrality rule, including Germany, the Netherlands and Belgium.[45] Over the years, other Member States joined the group of pro-incumbents countries. France, after offering a poison-pill-mimicking device in 2007 with the so-called Bons Breton (rights to subscribe shares at a discount once the company becomes a takeover bid target),[46]

[41] See n 4 and accompanying text.

[42] Note that we do not empirically claim that the market for corporate control has become less vibrant. The numerous determinants of mergers and acquisitions volumes make it difficult to isolate the effects we document over time. Even an increase in volumes would not contradict our intuition that M&A activity has been negatively affected by the phenomena we document, because it is impossible to determine what volumes would have been without these changes.

[43] See n 12.

[44] Clerc et al., n 1, at 15–16 (reporting that Estonia is the only jurisdiction that implemented the BTR).

[45] Ibid.

[46] See Art. L 233-32 C. com. These devices came short in mimicking a poison pill because they required shareholder approval and were actioned only in the event of a tender offer and not a creeping acquisition. See Enriques and Gatti, n 17, at 80–81, 89.

abandoned the board neutrality rule in 2014.[47] Italy had done so at the height of the financial crisis[48] but then, after less than one year, reinstated it as a mere default.[49] Among large Member States the only jurisdiction that stayed loyal to the board neutrality rule – it invented it, after all – was the UK, which, however, later decided to opt out of the European Union altogether.

While one can debate the extent to which these statutory changes were ultimately consequential, given that to pass effective defensive measures most jurisdictions require shareholder approval as a matter of company law,[50] their *expressive*[51] significance cannot be understated: by departing from the board neutrality rule, Member States signal their unease with a dynamic market for corporate control.

In the meantime, at a time when hedge-fund activists started campaigning in Europe, EU securities laws were amended to close the loopholes that the use of derivatives exposed in ownership transparency regulations. Directive 2013/50/EU amended the Transparency Directive to provide that long positions held via derivatives are to be counted in for the purposes of the ownership thresholds triggering disclosure obligations.[52] This change requires potential hostile bidders as well as activists to disclose their holdings, and hence de facto, if not de jure, make their intentions known to the public, prior to the timing that the use of derivatives permitted in at least some jurisdictions, like Germany, that failed to consider hidden ownership techniques for the purposes of holdings disclosures.[53] Earlier disclosure of takeover- or activist campaign-sensitive information, in turn, inevitably leads to a jump in share prices that makes further purchases more expensive for bidders and activists.[54] While the amendment was fully justified within the logic of ownership

[47] See n 63 and 64 and accompanying text.

[48] Article 13, § 1, Decreto Legge 29 Novembre 2008, n. 185.

[49] Article 1, § 3.a), Decreto Legislativo 25 Settembre 2009, n. 146.

[50] C. Gerner-Beuerle D. Kershaw and M. Solinas, 'Is the Board Neutrality Rule Trivial? Amnesia about Corporate Law in European Takeover Regulation' (2011) 22 *European Business Law Review* 559; M. Gatti, 'The Power to Decide on Takeovers: Directors or Shareholders, What Difference Does It Make?' (2014) 20 *Fordham Journal of Corporate and Financial Law* 73.

[51] See R. H. McAdams, 'A Focal Point Theory of Expressive Law' (2000) 86 *Virginia Law Review* 1649, 1650–1651 and fn 2 (arguing that 'law influences behavior independent of the sanctions it threatens to impose[; it] ... works by what it says in addition to what it does'.).

[52] Directive 2004/109/EC of the European Parliament and of the Council on the harmonization of transparency requirements in relation to information about issuers whose securities are admitted to trading on a regulated market and amending Directive 2001/34/EC of 15 December 2004, as amended by Directive 2013/50/EU of the European Parliament and of the Council of 22 October 2013 [2004] OJ L390/38, art 13.

[53] D. A. Zetzsche, 'Hidden Ownership in Europe: BAFin's Decision in Schaeffler v. Continental' (2009) 10 *European Business Organization Law Review* 115, 126. On hidden ownership, see generally H. T. C. Hu and B. Black, 'The New Vote Buying: Empty Voting and Hidden (Morphable) Ownership' (2005) 79 *Southern California Law Review* 811.

[54] See e.g. W. J. Carney, 'Toward a More Perfect Market for Corporate Control' (1984) 9 *Delaware Journal of Corporate Law* 593, 601.

disclosure rules, at the margin it had a negative effect on the market for corporate control and corporate influence.

Some Member States, in turn, engaged in 'goldplating' by requiring holders of significant stakes to declare their intentions vis-à-vis the company.[55] The impact of such rules on the market for corporate control should be weaker than that of the corresponding US rules, whose bite hinges upon the high risk of securities litigation they give rise to. That risk is much lower in Europe, given how comparably rare securities litigation is there. At the same time, the risk of administrative sanctions on the part of securities markets regulators is real.[56]

The Market Abuse Regulation (MAR)[57] of 2014 contributed to the stifling of the market for corporate control by significantly increasing the risk of violating insider trading bans for a prospective bidder building a toehold. The rules are extremely unclear as to whether a bidder in the process of deciding whether to launch a takeover bid and a fortiori having decided to do so makes illegitimate use of the information relating to the prospective bid, if the bidder buys the target shares to build a toehold. Article 9(4) provides that, for the purposes of insider trading bans,

> it shall not be deemed from the mere fact that a person is in possession of inside information that that person has used that information and has thus engaged in insider dealing, where such person has obtained that inside information in the conduct of a public takeover or merger with a company and uses that inside information solely for the purpose of proceeding with that merger or public takeover, provided that at the point of approval of the merger or acceptance of the offer by the shareholders of that company, any inside information has been made public or has otherwise ceased to constitute inside information.

And then it adds, puzzlingly, that the quoted provision 'shall not apply to stakebuilding'. While Article 9(5) would appear to help the prospective bidder by clarifying that 'the mere fact that a person uses its own knowledge that it has decided to acquire or dispose of financial instruments in the acquisition or disposal of those financial instruments shall not of itself constitute use of inside

55 See Art. L 233-7 C. com., as introduced by Ord. n° 2009-105 du 30 janvier 2009 (France) (disclosure of intentions due only if ownership stake is above 10 per cent); Art. 120 Consolidated Decree on Financial Intermediation, as amended by Decreto Legge 6 Ottobre 2017 n. 148 (Italy) (same).

56 For instance, the French AMF levied a €20m fine, later reduced to €18m by the Appeals Court, against hedge-fund manager Elliott for irregularities in the ownership disclosure statements, including on its intentions. See SAN-2020-04 – Décision de la Commission des sanctions du 17 avril 2020 les sociétés Elliott Advisors UK Limited et Elliott Capital Advisors L.P., www.amf-france.org/fr/sanctions-transactions/decisions-de-la-commission-des-sanctions/decision-de-la-commission-des-sanctions-du-17-avril-2020-legard-des-societes-elliott-advisors-uk.

57 Regulation (EU) No 596/2014 of the European Parliament and of the Council of 16 April 2014 on market abuse (market abuse regulation) and repealing Directive 2003/6/EC of the European Parliament and of the Council and Commission Directives 2003/124/EC, 2003/125/EC and 2004/72/EC [2014] OJ L173/1.

information', both the Belgian financial market regulator and the Italian highest court have excluded that this provision permits the prospective bidder's trading, if it has 'knowledge of the decision to launch a takeover bid, and thus of the fact that in principle a premium will be paid over the market price'.[58] In addition, Article 9 (6) muddies the waters even further by stating that, no matter what the same Article says in its first five paragraphs, 'an infringement of the prohibition of insider dealing set out in Article 14 may still be deemed to have occurred if the competent authority establishes that there was an illegitimate reason for the orders to trade, transactions or behaviours concerned'.[59]

To be sure, that MAR prohibits prospective bidders' purchases of target shares may well not be the correct interpretation of the relevant (and highly obscure[60]) MAR provisions. However, the emphasis in MAR's preamble (24) on market egalitarianism as the rationale for insider trading rules, and, perhaps even more significantly, the use therein of language reminiscent of the European Court of Justice's opinions on insider trading cases,[61] expose such trades to a significant risk of prosecution for insider trading.[62] Given how important pre-announcement stake-building is for an active market for corporate control,[63] this uncertainty may well have an impact on the vibrancy of the EU market for corporate control.

A similar conclusion might even be reached as to whether a hedge fund in the process of starting an activist campaign against a target may purchase shares in the target to make a gain out of it.[64] Eventually, as we have seen, activist campaigns are launched in Europe, which means hedge-fund managers are undeterred by any such broad interpretation of MAR provisions. And yet one cannot lightly dismiss the prospect of prosecutions against activists for market abuse. What is sure is that EU law prohibits trading by members of a wolf pack other than the hedge fund that will run the campaign.[65] If wolf packs are as instrumental to the success of activist

58 Financial Services Market Authority (Belgium), FAQ6, www.fsma.be/en/faq/6-may-offeror-still-buy-securities-offeree-company-during-preparation-takeover-bid-order; see similarly Cass., 15 Aprile 2021, n. 31507 (Italy).

59 See also MAR's Preamble (31).

60 See A. Pietrancosta, 'Brief Remarks on the Necessary Clarification of Market Abuse Prohibitions in Times of Shareholder Activism' (2019) *Revue Trimestrielle de Droit Financier* 3, 6.

61 See Case C-384/02 *Grøngaard and Bang* [2005] ECR I-9939, para 33; Case C-45/08 *Spector Photo Group and Van Raemdonck* [2009] ECR I-12073, para 61.

62 See S. Lombardo, 'Some Reflections on the Self-insider and the Market Abuse Regulation – The Self-insider as a Monopoly-Square Insider' (2021) 18 *European Company and Financial Law Review* 2, 21–22 (concluding that there is uncertainty as to whether, more generally, 'self-insiders' can be held liable for market abuse).

63 See e.g. F. H. Easterbrook and D. R. Fischel, 'Auctions and Sunk Costs in Tender Offers' (1982) 35 *Stanford Law Review* 1, 15–17.

64 See Pietrancosta, n 56, at 9–13 (discussing the point).

65 See ibid. (conceding that this case is different and reporting that this is the UK regulator's explicit position).

campaigns as some US legal scholars depict them,[66] this is, again, something that may well affect the intensity of hedge-fund activism in Europe.

11.4.2 *Changes in Company Laws and Corporate Governance Practices*

National company laws have experienced important changes since 2004, many of which were direct consequences of controversial acquisitions (rumoured, attempted or completed).[67] France overtly changed course and took an anti-takeover stance when it passed the so-called Loi Florange. To make good on a promise made in 2013 by President François Hollande to a vocal group of workers laid off as a result of the post-acquisition shutdown of a steel mill, the Florange plant of ArcelorMittal,[68] the French Parliament passed a law (aptly named the Florange law) that, among other things, introduced loyalty shares (also known as tenure-voting shares) as a default rule.[69]

Around the same time, the largest Italian manufacturing company, Fiat, and a leading trucks company, CNH, both controlled by the Agnelli family and managed by the same CEO, decided to reincorporate in the Netherlands, each on the

66 See generally J. C. Coffee, Jr. and D. Palia, 'The Wolf at the Door: The Impact of Hedge Fund Activism on Corporate Governance' (2016) 41 *Journal of Corporate Law* 545, 549 and 562–568 (describing wolf packs and their influence).

67 In this chapter we omit to speculate on the plausibly negative effect on mergers and acquisitions of the cross-cutting phenomenon of re-regulation that followed from the less pro-market stance of regulators and public opinion after the Great Financial Crisis. Intuitively, regulation increases barriers to entry and ongoing costs for businesses, especially for smaller players. As a consequence, regulation implies higher rents for shareholders, which in turn may increase private benefits of control (the intuition being that there can be no private benefits of control if there are no rents to appropriate, while the higher the rents, the higher the private benefits of control may be, other things being equal). Higher private benefits of control, especially in the presence of a mandatory bid rule, may make acquisitions more costly. In addition, a more complex regulatory regime (as an outcome of greater regulatory intensity) may, other things being equal, discourage acquisitions by foreign players (who may have a harder time than locals in dealing with the local regulators) or potential financial acquirers with no expertise in the relevant regulated industry, especially in cases where the regulations subject changes of control to authorization by the government or an administrative authority.

68 Hollande had to deal with the fallout of a hostile deal that had occurred seven years earlier during the presidency of Sarkozy. ArcelorMittal's employees were furious with French politicians for failing to sanction the series of unfulfilled commitments to employees by Mittal, a foreign company that had taken over Arcelor (a company incorporated in Luxembourg but headquartered in France) in early 2006. G. Reilhac, 'Hollande Returns to Face "Betrayed" Florange Steel Unions' (26 September 2013) *Reuters*, www.reuters.com/article/us-france-hollande/hollande-returns-to-face-betrayed-florange-steel-unions-idUSBRE98P0JH20130926; S. Davidoff Solomon, 'France Answers Hostile Bids with the Two-Vote Share' (19 May 2015) *NY Times*, www.nytimes.com/2015/05/20/business/dealbook/france-answers-hostile-bids-with-the-two-vote-share.html.

69 See Loi n° 2014–384 du 29 mars 2014, J.O. du 27 mar. 2014, p. 6227 (France) (the law also abandoned the board neutrality approach and imposed hurdles for hostile bidders, such as a minimum tender condition, and strengthened consultation rights with the workforce). See Pargendler, n 37, at 543.

occasion of a merger transaction involving two previously acquired US companies.[70] The choice of the Netherlands for the two companies had much to do with an opinion issued only a few years earlier by a Dutch court, judging loyalty dividends as not contravening the principles of equality and fairness.[71] Despite the absence of Dutch companies with loyalty shares and the Dutch laws' silence on the same, Fiat's lawyers must have reasoned that, similarly, their issuance would be legal under Dutch corporate law. The reincorporation in the Netherlands combined with the issuance of loyalty shares allowed the Agnellis to retain control of the two companies after their merger with the US subsidiaries.[72] Since then, another eight Italian firms have followed suit and similarly chosen Dutch corporate law to consolidate the control of the founding family via tenure voting.[73]

That was despite the Italian government's attempt, in the summer of 2014, and hence even before the Fiat and CNH mergers were executed, to stop the migration of Italian firms to the Netherlands by introducing legislation that would allow companies to issue loyalty shares.[74] Leaving aside the fact that there might be other corporate law features that may have made the Netherlands attractive to Italian listed firms, Italy's loyalty shares were not as attractive as those one could obtain in the Netherlands: first, the former could give no more than one additional vote per share (while, in the complete silence of Dutch law, no limit exists in the Netherlands); second, unlike under the Fiat model, loyalty shares do not operate retrospectively – that is, they must be held for two years once the charter amendment introducing tenure voting is adopted for the loyalty vote to be granted. Still, tenure-voting shares proved popular among non-migrating Italian firms, with sixty-nine listed firms that had tenure voting in their charters at the end of 2021.[75]

Corporate migration in the direction of the Netherlands has not been an exclusively Italian phenomenon. Belcredi, Faverzani and Signori report that thirteen companies out of the universe of EU-listed companies with a capitalization higher than €1bn had reincorporated in the Netherlands from EU Member States other

70 M. Ventoruzzo, 'The Disappearing Taboo of Multiple Voting Shares: Regulatory Responses to the Migration of Chrysler-Fiat' (2015) 114 *Zeitschrift für Vergleichende Rechtswissenschaft* 192, 203–204.

71 HR 14 december 2007, *NJ* 2008, 105, ECLI:NL:HR:2007:BB3523 (Loyaliteitsdividend DSM).

72 See the SEC filing Merger of Fiat S.p.A. with and into Fiat Investments N.V. to be renamed Fiat Chrysler Automobiles N.V., at 218, www.sec.gov/Archives/edgar/data/1605484/000119312514265448/d704286d424b3.htm#toc.

73 See Giovanni Petroboni, 'La struttura finanziaria e di governance delle NV di origine italiana' in Id. (ed), Amsterdam Drive (Giuffrè Francis Lefebvre 2025) 20.

74 See Decreto Legge 24 Giugno 2014, n. 91 (Italy), as approved by Parliament by Art. 20.1(aa), Legge 11 Giugno 2014, n. 116 (Italy). Until January 2015, companies could approve charter amendments to introduce loyalty shares with a majority of the outstanding shares rather than with at least two thirds of the shares present at the relevant meeting: Art. 20.1-*bis* Legge 11 Giugno 2014, n. 116 (Italy).

75 See CONSOB, Report on Corporate Governance of Italian Listed Companies (2022) 15.

than Italy between 2000 and 2021.[76] Only some of them similarly introduced dual-class share structures, but all of them made use of at least one charter provision strengthening, if not insulating, boards vis-à-vis shareholders.[77] Hence, their preference for the Netherlands was also to ascribe to its corporate law's tradition of insulating companies from the risk of hostile takeovers.[78]

The Netherlands also played a role in the (ultimately unsuccessful) defence of two prominent Paris-listed target companies, Luxembourgish Arcelor in 2006 and French Suez in 2020. Under the attack of, respectively, Mittal Steel and Veolia, the two companies set up a Dutch foundation, controlled by their boards, which were given shares in two subsidiaries, whose sale the hostile bidders had planned in order to avoid problems with antitrust authorities. The foundations' consent would be necessary to sell those subsidiaries, making it much harder for the bidders to proceed with their acquisition.[79]

Italy's reform of 2014 not only allowed already listed companies as well as companies at the IPO stage to adopt tenure voting, but it also abandoned a ban on multiple-voting shares that had dated back to 1942. More precisely, it enabled non-listed companies to issue special classes of shares with up to three votes each and clarified that such companies could retain a dual-class share structure when going public. After Italy, other European countries relaxed their bans on voting enhancement mechanisms. The UK revised its Listing Rules to allow companies with dual-class shares to list on the LSE's Premium segment, albeit with several provisos that make the reform unattractive to companies large enough to consider a cross-listing. Belgium introduced tenure-voting shares and multiple-voting shares similarly to Italy, that is, with the latter only available to newly listed companies,[80] while Spain only allowed for tenure-voting shares.[81]

[76] M. Belcredi, L. Faverzani and A. Signori, 'Così non fan tutte: An analysis of Italian companies moving abroad' 19, Working Paper, June 2023, https://centridiricerca.unicatt.it/fin-gov-Cos%C3%AC%20non%20fan%20tutte%20final%20June%202023%20clean.pdf.

[77] Ibid. at 20–21.

[78] On Dutch governance's tradition of managerialism, see e.g. A. Mignoli, 'Idee e Problemi nell'Evoluzione della "Company" Inglese' (1960) 5 *Rivista Della Società* 633, 640–643 (tracking back Dutch managerialism to the Dutch East India Company); A. de Jong, J. Jonker, A. A. Röell and G. Westerhuis, 'Reinventing Institutions: Trust Offices and the Dutch Financial System, 1690s–2000s' (2020) 11–24 https://ssrn.com/abstract=3719550 (documenting the use of the *administratie-kantoren* and now of *stichtingen* as takeover defence tools). Gucci's successfully defeating the acquisition attempt by LVMH, which we mentioned in the text accompanying 17, served as a powerful example of the flexibility that Dutch law offered to target companies.

[79] See D. Martin, 'L'incessibilité ou la cession d'actifs d'une société cible d'une offre publique est-elle possible et dans quelles conditions?' (2021) *Revue de Droit Bancaire et Financier*, Issue 5, Dossier 21, 1–2.

[80] S. Declercq, J. Delvoie, T. Monnens and T. Vos, 'Loyalty Voting Rights in Belgium: Nothing More than a Control-Enhancing Mechanism?' (2023) 20 *European Company and Financial Law Review* 27.

[81] Art. 3 §20, L 5/2021 (BOE 2021, 88), inserting a new Art. 527 ter in the Law on Capital Companies (BOE 2010, 161).

To wit, as we anticipated in our previous work,[82] restrictions to the availability of post-bid defences (not necessarily because of the board neutrality rule, but because inflexible company laws have historically not allowed US-style poison pills in most jurisdictions),[83] pushed companies to be even more takeover-proof by using the impenetrable barrier of dual-class structures.

Finally, national corporate governance codes have nudged companies in the direction of not using executive compensation packages to align the interests of managers with those of shareholders in the event of a takeover bid, a key element of US corporate governance.[84] The German Corporate Governance Code puts a cap of twice the annual remuneration for severance payments[85] and even rules out '[c]hange of control clauses that commit to benefits in the case of early termination of a Management Board member's contract due to a change of control'.[86] Similarly, a recommendation in the Dutch Corporate Governance Code appears to recommend that companies do not allow for the acceleration of stock options or stock grants in the event of a change of control.[87] The French and Italian Corporate Governance Codes contain the same or similar recommendations.[88]

11.4.3 *A Flurry of Foreign Direct Investment Controls Legislation*

The European Commission has been shaping the landscape for foreign direct investment (FDI). The EU Screening Regulation[89] primarily seeks to harmonize

[82] See Enriques and Gatti, n 15, at 94 ('Oddly enough, a company may opt out of the market for corporate control discipline altogether via deviations from one share, one vote (which are in fact quite frequent in the EU), while it cannot do so partially via a poison pill, combined or not with a staggered board.'). One may in fact argue that the resurgence of dual-class share structures in the US became more appealing after institutional investors waged a successful war against staggered boards, which are arguably a milder device (staggered boards are devices for potentially contestable companies, while dual-class companies are structures for controlling shareholders to keep the company outside of the market for corporate control).

[83] See ibid. at 83–84 (describing some of the most cited obstacles to poison pills in Europe). See also Gatti, n 37, at 125–128 (explaining that these limitations stem from national company laws and not takeover regimes).

[84] See M. Kahan and E. B. Rock, 'How I learned to stop worrying and love the pill: Adaptive responses to takeover law' (2002) 69 *University of Chicago Law Review* 871, 896–899.

[85] German Corporate Governance Code, (2022) 20, Recommendation G13, www.dcgk.de/en/home.html.

[86] German Corporate Governance Code, n 84, at 20, Recommendation G14.

[87] § 3.1.2, No. vi) and vii), Dutch Corporate Governance Code (2022) 40, www.mccg.nl/english ('Shares should be held for at least five years after they are awarded; [. . .] share options cannot be exercised during the first three years after they are awarded').

[88] See French Corporate Governance Code (2022), Recommendation 26.5.1, www.ecgi.global/node/10195; Italian Corporate Governance Code (2020) 15, Article 5, Recommendation 27, available at www.borsaitaliana.it/comitato-corporate-governance/codice/codice.en.htm.

[89] Regulation (EU) 2019/452 of the European Parliament and of the Council of 19 March 2019 establishing a framework for the screening of foreign direct investments into the Union [2019] OJ L79I/1.

and coordinate various FDI review mechanisms in Member States. While under such a framework the Commission may issue non-binding opinions on national FDI reviews, Member States still retain the ultimate authority.

Thus far Member States and their authorities have implemented the Screening Regulation in different ways. Some require notification of all transactions involving non-EU investors, particularly in technology, manufacturing and retail.[90] Variations exist among Member States regarding mandatory or voluntary filings, thresholds and the definition of critical sectors.[91] The origin of investors plays a crucial role in risk assessments, with some countries having become more cautious about investments from specific nations, particularly China[92] and Russia.[93]

Importantly, in early 2024 the European Commission proposed a significant overhaul of the existing regime to be adopted in a revised screening regulation:[94] this proposal includes several significant changes, such as mandatory FDI screening for all Member States and expanding the scope to include EU-based investors controlled by non-EU entities.[95] The regulation aims to harmonize procedural rules, reinforce cooperation between enforcement authorities (including requiring Member States to consider comments from other Member States and the European Commission), and apply to 'greenfield investments' if they are reportable at the Member State level.[96] The new regulation addresses regulatory divergence and lack of cooperation among Member States, and mandates that all EU Member States screen investments in specified critical sectors.[97]

While blocking deals altogether on national security grounds is still relatively rare, FDI screening is growing in importance given its expansion to ever more sectors and transactions[98] and investors will have to go over multi-jurisdictional assessments to navigate parallel notification processes.[99]

90 T. Heinrich, T. Kuhn, O. Berg and T. Wienke, 'Foreign direct investment reviews 2023: Europe' (20 March 2023) *White & Case Insight*, www.whitecase.com/insight-our-thinking/foreign-direct-investment-reviews-2023-europe.

91 Ibid.

92 M. von Bieberstein and L. Nigl, 'The evaluation of the German FDI Regime – Cornerstones of potential revisions revealed' (6 September 2023) *Cleary Gottlieb*, www.clearytradewatch.com/2023/09/the-evaluation-of-the-german-fdi-regime-cornerstones-of-potential-revisions-revealed/.

93 Heinrich, Kuhn, Berg and Wienke, n 88.

94 European Commission, 'Proposal for a Regulation of the European Parliament and of the Council on the screening of foreign investments in the Union and repealing Regulation (EU) 2019/452 of the European Parliament and of the Council' COM (2024) 23 final.

95 See Cleary Gottlieb, 'Proposed New EU FDI Screening Regulation – 10 Things to Know', Cleary Gottlieb Alert Memorandum, 12 March 2024, www.clearygottlieb.com/-/media/files/alert-memos-2024/proposed-new-eu-fdi-screening-regulation-10-things-to-know.pdf.

96 Ibid.

97 These include dual-use items, military technology, advanced semiconductors, artificial intelligence and energy technologies. Ibid.

98 von Bieberstein and Nigl, n 90 (discussing proposals to expand controls in Germany); Cleary Gottlieb, Cleary Gottleib FDI Newsletter, August–October 2023, https://client.clearygottlieb.com/84/2734/november-2023/global-fdi-newsletter—august-october-2023(1).asp?sid = d5ce453e-a217-4d2c-baff-c600e948e00c (describing expanded powers in Italy).

99 Heinrich, Kuhn, Berg and Wienke, n 88.

Overall, while FDI reviews are inevitable in a world of intensifying geopolitical tensions, this type of measure (and the current variations among Member States) can hamper a genuinely free and open takeover market in Europe.

11.5 FOR WHOM HAS THE MOAT BEEN DUG?

Section 11.4 reports many multifaceted protections that over the years incumbent boards and controlling shareholders or influential blockholders (collectively, insiders) of European companies have accumulated to keep unwanted acquirers or investors at bay. The result is greater insulation and stability for insiders, which has become possible with the support of national (and to some extent EU) politics. Over the last twenty years a pact between insiders and politicians has kept shareholders out in the cold and fostered a legal, policy and governance environment averse to the efficient functioning of the market for corporate control.[100]

The rent-seeking nature of this environment is for everyone to see. On the one hand, the new ecosystem protects insiders: they can worry less about hostile bids. While these protections may have an upside if they help bolster the idiosyncratic vision of disruptive firms' founders, the increased agency costs for European businesses might become significant. After all, compared to their US peers, European companies tend to be older, and hence less likely to be founder-led, and operate in more mature sectors. Arguably, companies in these sectors benefit from the spur of the market for corporate control even more intensely than other companies to avoid innovation-dilemma dynamics and incumbents' tendency to remain inert in the face of a changing market environment.

At the same time, the new ecosystem preserves and increases the clout of national politics: national government leaders and politicians have gotten themselves a seat at the table and now get to exchange favours with executives (both national and foreign). European politicians have eagerly reclaimed their role as the ultimate arbiters in control contests – a role that leaders from the previous generation had apparently relinquished in favour of a more market-oriented perspective, whether by wholehearted embrace or reluctant acceptance.

In assessing the implications of this new, corporatist and protectionist ecosystem, an essential question is whether investors are worse off.

Ultimately, this question boils down to whether M&A activity, and hostile deals in particular, are beneficial to shareholders. Despite a multitude of studies, which tend

[100] For the observation that the greater the presence of foreign investors, the stronger the political pressure towards investor unfriendly regulation, see Pargendler, n 37, at 537. As she suggests, it is plausible that voters support measures that keep firms under national owners for the same emotional reasons they support their national sports team. See Parglender, n 37, at 538 ('At a basic level, domestic control can be a symbol of national power and pride that epitomizes nationalism irrespective of its effects on the economic well-being of citizens. Citizens may prefer domestic control for the same reason that they cheer for their national sports team').

to answer the question in the positive as far as target shareholders are concerned but are more ambiguous when they account for bidder shareholders as well, it is hard to come to a firm conclusion.[101]

Note that hindering hostile deals has implications on friendly deals as well. This is for two reasons. First, friendly deals are more expensive at the margin if investment screening regulations apply. Second, friendly deals are often the result of an unsolicited approach by a prospective buyer: the threat of a hostile bid pressures the target company to sit at the negotiating table and is helpful to secure its acceptance on behalf of the shareholders. The less credible the threat of a hostile bid, the safer it is for the target to just say no.[102] As a result, the M&A market overall will weaken, making it harder for companies to undergo the restructurings that may be necessary for their survival at a time when technology is disrupting most industries.[103]

The hostile environment to hostile bids affects the debate on dual-class shares as well. If the chances of a shareholder value-creating hostile takeover are low under the current governance, market and legal framework, the expected harm to investors of having a dual-class controlling shareholder must also be low. It may actually be better to have dual class shares than a controlling shareholder with 30/50 per cent of the shares who is unwilling to make acquisitions in order to retain control. At the same time, if hostile takeovers are highly unlikely, why would controlling shareholders fear losing control and go for dual-class share structures? Are there other reasons why controlling shareholders may prefer dual-class shares?

Another question is whether workers and citizens in Member States benefit from a more interventionist political economy that makes deals (especially foreign ones) more difficult to complete. In M&A lawmaking, the alliance between incumbents and labour to thwart acquirers is as well-known as it is tight.[104] While such an alliance has proven to work for incumbents,[105] the record is not as good for the

[101] See n 27 and accompanying text.

[102] Cf. G. W. Schwert, 'Hostility in Takeovers: In the Eyes of the Beholder?' (2000) 55 *Journal of Finance* 2599, 2600 (noting that deals can change from hostile to friendly and vice versa); Gatti, n 48, at 98 (noting that 'the absence of board vetoes increases M&A activity by forcing directors to consider acquisition proposals, which they would otherwise reject outright if they could veto the acquisition upfront').

[103] Cf. R. J. Gilson, 'The Political Ecology of Takeovers: Thoughts on Harmonizing the European Corporate Governance Environment' (1992) 61 *Fordham Law Review* 161.

[104] R. Romano, 'The Future of Hostile Takeovers: Legislation and Public Opinion' (1988) 57 *University of Cincinnati Law Review* 457, 458–465; M. J. Roe, 'Takeover Politics' in M. M. Blair (ed.), *The Deal Decade: What Takeovers and Leveraged Buyouts Mean for Corporate Governance* (Washington, DC: Brookings Institution, 1993) 321, 340–347; Pargendler, n 37, at 535 (describing 'the powerful domestic alliance between elite and labor interests in retaining local corporate control and the popular appeal of nationalist sentiment').

[105] Crucially, national politicians are lobbied intensely and often successfully by incumbent insiders who are threatened by takeover and seek to hamper the market for corporate control. Cf. Ferrarini and Miller, n 20, at 303 (theorizing that targets, as opposed to bidders, 'are likely to expend significant resources lobbying for local rules that increase the costs of unwanted takeover bids'). For the EU, see Hopt, n 11, at 270 (citing Volkswagen lobbying then-

workers, at least judging from empirical evidence from the US.[106] In theory, fewer hostile takeovers, no matter how small the baseline originally was, could mean fewer lay-offs at the firm level. However, lay-offs could still occur because of internal restructurings or even friendly deals, which can be expected to decrease less than hostile ones. Besides, rather than relying on directors to protect employees against hostile bidders (as is the case, at least ostensibly, under US-style constituency statutes[107]), lay-offs in European jurisdictions are typically regulated via employment law. Moreover, it is hardly settled that foreign ownership is more detrimental than domestic controllers for employees, consumers and other stakeholders in the jurisdiction where the firm operates.[108] True, the overall framework we provide is only partially driven by repulsion against foreign buyers, yet this protectionist component has always been prominent in the policy debate[109] and regularly makes good headlines.[110]

Something else has been going on beyond employee protection: significant incumbent shareholders felt weak. In fact, despite the overall low number of hostile takeovers, anecdotal evidence suggests that, once launched, acquisition attempts are hard to fend off in Europe, which over the years resulted in some existing de facto

Chancellor Schröder and the Wallenberg family lobbying other Member States). For the US, see Roe, n 102, at 340–347 (lobbying efforts by corporations resulted in the enactment of various anti-takeover laws throughout the United States, with Delaware adopting a mild approach to avoid the risk of federal intervention).

106 See generally L. A. Bebchuk, K. Kastiel and R. Tallarita, 'For Whom Corporate Leaders Bargain' (2021) 94 *Southern California Law Review* 1467 (showing that directors of firms incorporated in states with constituency statutes did not extract better terms for workers).

107 See ibid. at 1515–1518 (providing evidence that 'in almost all cases, despite the presence of risks to employment, corporate leaders did not negotiate for any limitations on the freedom of private equity buyers to lay off employees and thereby reduce employment levels').

108 See Pargendler, n 37, at 575–579 (evaluating arguments in favour and against and finding mixed evidence).

109 See generally Davies, Schuster and van de Walle de Ghelke, n 11, at 155 (arguing that the Takeover Directive implementation choices were 'influenced by economic nationalism and a desire by Member States to preserve corporate headquarters and employing entities within their own territories.'); Clarke, n 22, at 10 (mentioning that in the aftermath of the Cadbury takeover, there was some debate on the need to introduce protectionist measures to shield British companies from foreign acquisitions); D. Kershaw, Principles of Takeover Regulation (OUP 2016) 362-368 (criticizing the desirability of a stronger governmental role to shield firms in strategic sectors); Hopt, n 11, at 276–278 (mentioning the protectionist trend that followed the Takeover Directive: 'it cannot be overlooked that protectionism of the country's own economy and legal system is considerable and widespread.'); Davis, Hopt and Ringe, n 22, at 239 (citing a 'potential backlash against a perceived sale of strategic firms into foreign hands' as a chief driving factor of the political choices of a given jurisdiction when it comes to M&A legislation).

110 M. Stothard, 'Battle for Spanish Toll Road Operator Abertis Intensifies' (17 December 2017) *Financial Times*, https://perma.cc/S8RC-VBD6 (mentioning France and the Netherlands as two nations uneasy with sell-side cross-border deals). In the most extreme cases, targets even get nationalized. See G. Topham, 'France Nationalises Strategic Shipyard to Thwart Italian Ownership' (27 July 2017) *Guardian*, https://perma.cc/25YB-FMB2. F. Dohmen, D. Hawranek and J. Tietz, 'Vulnerable to Attack: German Companies Fear Wave of Hostile Takeovers' (26 October 2010) *Spiegel Online*, https://perma.cc/VG4A-MCTJ.

controllers losing control.[111] Not only did this make calls to rein in takeovers easier to answer but also resulted in new rules that strengthened de facto controlling shareholders rather than boards, as the former were quick to use devices such as tenure voting to their advantage.

11.6 CONCLUSION

This chapter chronicles the many lethal cuts that concurred to make hostile takeovers more difficult. At the turn of the century, EU institutions were busy seeking to pass harmonized takeover rules that could promote a vibrant market for corporate control. According to the credo at the time, not only did takeovers help foster competitiveness and dynamism for EU firms and improve their governance, but they were also instrumental for the very goal of building a pan-European market. However, several factors, such as controversial deals, broader changes in corporate governance, and massive macroeconomic shocks pushed markets and policies in the opposite direction. While the Takeover Directive itself, a compromise among Member States, failed to create a level playing field, the twenty years following its adoption witnessed a multifaceted sequence of policies and market developments that resulted in the progressive atrophy of the market for corporate control.

Of course, this is not to say hostile bids in Europe have disappeared altogether or will disappear anytime soon. There will always be some. Arguably, though, they will be fewer under the current setting than one could have expected when the Directive was passed. Reasonable minds may differ on the overall effects of hampering a dynamic market for corporate control. What is beyond doubt is that corporate insiders, be they managers or de facto controlling shareholders, and politicians have, respectively, an easier life and a stronger grip on the private sector. It is unfortunate that, historically, this public–private convergence has meant rents for a few insiders and less dynamism for European firms.

[111] See generally Enriques and Gatti, 17 (making this argument for creeping acquisitions); Gatti, 10, at 33–36 (extending the argument to all hostile deals).

12

Takeovers and Corporate Sustainability

Guido Ferrarini and Michele Siri

12.1 CHAPTER'S AIMS

In this chapter, we analyse the relationship between takeover bids and corporate sustainability through an analysis of three significant cases that occurred in different jurisdictions and are paradigmatic of the main issues in this area. Specifically, we ask how boards (should) treat sustainability issues under company law, including the national rules implementing the EU Takeover Directive (TOD), either before or after the launch of a takeover bid, especially if the bid is hostile. Our chapter connects with that by Luca Enriques and Matteo Gatti,[1] who show that in the past twenty years economic, political, and legal developments have hindered the Directive's goal of enhancing the European market for corporate control by reducing the number and impact of hostile bids. The rise of stakeholderism is one of the causes of the lower corporate control contestability, together with other economic and geopolitical causes, as well as changes in financial markets, corporate governance, and law. Resistance to hostile takeovers motivated by ESG considerations was no doubt unlikely at the time of the Directive's adoption, when takeover bids mainly targeted shareholder value enhancement and the protection of stakeholders' interests mainly concerned creditors and employees.

After briefly introducing the economic and legal literature on the topic (Section 12.2), we submit three case studies in which a hostile bid was either rejected by the target's board for reasons including sustainability concerns or accepted by the same for reasons mainly regarding shareholder value (Sections 12.3–12.5). We then discuss, from a comparative and functional perspective, whether and to what extent resistance to a hostile bid by the target's board could be based on sustainability grounds (Section 12.6). We further examine whether and to what extent defensive measures could be justified by sustainability concerns of the target's board, and conclude our chapter (Section 12.7).

[1] See Chapter 11 in this volume.

12.2 MAIN LITERATURE

In answering this chapter's questions, we follow a path developed in our prior papers on corporate sustainability, focusing on the trade-offs between share value and social value and their possible solutions.[2] As often argued today, corporate profits are not and should not be the sole purpose of corporations.[3] Corporate purpose should go beyond profits, covering other important values such as those reflected by environmental, social, and governance sustainability (ESG).[4] In modern corporations, numerous trade-offs arise between shareholder value and social value,[5] while boards and managers promote both types of value under the 'shared value' theory and similar approaches.[6] Takeovers require corporations to look at these trade-offs from a relatively new perspective, which compares the social value generated by target companies through their sustainability actions with the economic gains deriving to shareholders from a bid price which incorporates a premium over the market price of shares.

As argued by economists, corporations enhance social welfare by producing benefits both to shareholders and stakeholders.[7] Caring for stakeholders is in the corporate interest, as widely argued under the enlightened shareholder value approach.[8] The concept of 'instrumental stakeholderism' precisely refers to the cases in which furthering stakeholders' interests is also in the interest of the corporation,[9] while the notion of 'pure stakeholderism' refers to the cases in which the interests of stakeholders are pursued *per se*, with no specific economic benefits directly deriving to the firm.[10] The application of similar concepts to takeovers is relatively new in

[2] G. Ferrarini, 'Firm Value versus Social Value: Dealing with the Trade-offs', (2023), ECGI Law Working Paper No. 686/2023, published as a chapter in K. Alexander, M. Gargantini and M. Siri (eds.), *Cambridge Handbook of EU Sustainable Finance*, (Cambridge: Cambridge University Press, 2025), p. 51–79; G. Ferrarini, M. Siri and S. Zhu, 'The EU's Proposed Reform of Directors' Duties and the Missing Link to Soft Law' (2024), 25 *European Business Organization Law Review* 359.

[3] C. Mayer, *Prosperity: Better Business Makes the Greater Good*, (Oxford: Oxford University Press, 2018); A. Edmans, *Grow the Pie: How Great Companies Deliver Both Purpose and Profit*, (Cambridge: Cambridge University Press, 2020).

[4] R. Henderson, *Reimagining Capitalism: How Business Can Save the World*, (London: Penguin Business, 2020).

[5] Ferrarini, (n 2).

[6] M. E. Porter and M. R. Kramer, 'Creating Shared Value. How to reinvent capitalism – and unleash a wave of innovation and growth' (2011), 89 *Harvard Business Review* 62.

[7] M. C. Jensen, 'Value Maximization, Stakeholder Theory, and the Corporate Objective Function' (2002), 12 *Business Ethics Quarterly* 235, 256; (2010), 22 *Journal of Applied Corporate Finance* 32.

[8] Ibid.

[9] L. A. Bebchuk and R. Tallarita, 'The Illusory Promise of Stakeholder Governance' (2020), 106 *Cornell Law Review* 91.

[10] It could consist of welfare actions which are implemented by the firm to the benefit of employees and their families in an area which is underserved in terms of education and sports facilities. Similar actions could indirectly benefit the firm by making it easier to attract

Europe, but dates back to the experience of 'constituency statutes' in the US.[11] As argued by L. Bebchuk, K. Kastiel, and R. Tallarita, constituency statutes 'embrace an approach similar to that advocated by modern stakeholderists',[12] authorizing corporate leaders to give weight to the interests of stakeholders such as workers and local communities when considering a sale of their companies. Bebchuk et al. investigate empirically whether constituency statutes delivered protections for stakeholders in practice, with special reference to corporate leaders selling their companies to private equity buyers. They find that corporate leaders negotiated and obtained substantial benefits for their shareholders and for themselves. However, despite the clear risks to stakeholders that private equity acquisitions commonly create, target companies generally did not bargain for any protections to stakeholders from such risks. The authors conclude that, in the large sample of analysed transactions, constituency statutes have failed to deliver their purported benefits,[13] confirming the view held by the same authors that corporate stakeholderism is mainly for show and should not be taken seriously.[14]

From another perspective, the theoretical literature on the economics of takeovers highlights that successful firms obtain the trust of their main stakeholders who rely on managers' promises even when not formalized in explicit contracts.[15] The breach of such promises may destroy the trust of employees, suppliers, and other stakeholders. Takeovers, especially when hostile to the incumbent managers, may bring about similar breaches, if the new managers renege on the promises made by the previous ones.[16] Similar arguments are worth reconsidering in the light of today's discussion on stakeholder governance and sustainability. The *ex ante* importance of contractual relationships with stakeholders can have a bearing on the efficacy of takeovers. The

employees and to retain them but could also respond to moral and/or reputational motivations of corporate leaders.

[11] See L. A. Bebchuk, K. Kastiel and R. Tallarita, 'For Whom Corporate Leaders Bargain' (2021), 94 *Southern California Law Review* 1467 who underline that, from the mid 1980s to the early 1990s, many US states adopted statutes that strengthened the power of directors to fend off hostile bids: 'These anti-takeover laws included statutes explicitly permitting the use of "poison pills" against unwanted suitors, statutes preventing freeze-out mergers for a certain period after the acquisition of a significant stake in the company, and statutes requiring bidders to pay a "fair price" in the second part of a two-tier merger' (at 1485). The three authors focus on a specific type of anti-takeover legislation that authorized directors to consider the interests of employees and other stakeholders when assessing an acquisition offer.

[12] Ibid. 1471.

[13] Ibid., 1472.

[14] Bebchuk and Tallarita (n 9).

[15] See D. Greene, O. Kini, M. Shen and J. Shenoy, 'Corporate Takeovers and Non-Financial Stakeholders' (2021, rev. 2025), *Oxford Research Encyclopedia of Economics and Finance* 2, 7, 27.

[16] See A. Schleifer and L. H. Summers, 'Breach of Trust in Hostile Takeovers', in A. J. Auerbach (ed.), *Corporate Takeovers: Causes and Consequences* (Chicago: University of Chicago Press, 1988), p. 41–42; and J. C. Coffee Jr., 'The Uncertain Case for Takeover Reform: An Essay on Stockholders', Stakeholders and Bust Ups' (1988), *Wisconsin Law Review* 435, 447 et seq.

ability to alter contractual relationships *ex post* can affect the propensity to a takeover and impact stakeholders. Stakeholders will be more vested in post-takeover success if they can trust the acquiring firm not to take actions that are detrimental to them. The 'big picture' that emerges from the literature is that 'non-financial stakeholder considerations affect takeover decisions and post-takeover outcomes. Moreover, takeovers also have an impact on non-financial stakeholders.'[17] All this seems to justify the study of stakeholder issues in takeovers also from a legal perspective, exploring the impact of takeover regulation on stakeholderism and the congruence of takeover rules with corporate purpose as defined in recent scholarship.

12.3 CASE STUDY A: ATTEMPTED TAKEOVER OF UNILEVER BY KRAFT

When a takeover is launched, especially when it is hostile to the target's management, conflicts of interest may arise between shareholders, managers, and stakeholders. Shareholders (and managers) aim to maximize the price of their shares in the target. Stakeholders are rather interested either in a failure of the bid or in the negotiation of protections for the case of successful acquisition by the bidder. Employees may fear to lose their jobs because of a corporate restructuring and ask for guarantees of job security. Suppliers may fear a change of ownership in the target for they could lose a client for which they have made important specific investments. To highlight similar conflicts of interest, we refer to three well-known cases that are particularly significant from the perspective of the target board's behaviour and duties. We examine in this section the attempted takeover of Unilever by Kraft Heinz in the UK; we consider, in Section 12.4, the successful takeover of Twitter by Elon Musk in the US; and in Section 12.5 we analyse the failed takeover of AkzoNobel in the Netherlands and the relevant litigation.

The attempted takeover of Unilever by Kraft Heinz for $143 billion took place in February 2017.[18] The target company was already engaged in environmental and social sustainability, while the bidder, the Kraft Heinz Company (KHC), had never been a good performer in this area.[19] When the news of a potential deal became public, the target feared that its corporate culture could be contaminated by the

[17] See Schleifer and Summers (n 16), p. 41–42; Coffee Jr. (n 16), p. 447 et seq.

[18] For a comprehensive and interesting case study, see W. W. George and A. Migdal, 'Battle for the Soul of Capitalism: Unilever and the Kraft Heinz Takeover Bid (A)' (2017, rev. 2024), Harvard Business School Case 317–127.

[19] See 'M. Vandevelde and S. Daneshkhu, 'Culture clash is biggest obstacle to Unilever takeover' (17 February 2017), *Financial Times* 40, recalling that 'when Paul Polman became chief executive of Unilever, the consumer goods company which on Friday rejected a $143bn takeover approach from Kraft Heinz, he told investors to steer clear unless they were prepared to sacrifice short-term profit for "sustainable" ideals'. Therefore, the attempted takeover of Unilever 'could become a battle of wills, pitting the evangelistic Mr. Polman against the hard-headed private equity investors who two years ago swore to strip $1.5bn of costs out of the iconic ketchup maker'.

bidder's dominant focus on shareholder value and its relative neglect of ESG factors.[20] Therefore, Unilever's managers soon made clear that they would resist a takeover, also considering that the economics of the deal, with a proposed premium over the shares' market price of 18 per cent, did not appear as satisfactory to them.[21] Also many of Unilever's top shareholders said that the bid drastically undervalued the company's assets,[22] even though the bidder seemed to be ready to raise the offer price. However, the bid would have increased the leverage of the target to a level which could have been difficult to sustain in the future, given the huge amount of debt that Kraft wanted to raise.[23] Moreover, the name of the bidder was 'toxic' in the UK given some instances of the bidder's behaviour in a previous acquisition concerning Cadbury.[24] In addition, the UK government immediately manifested its opposition to the potential deal which would have sent a wrong signal to the public just after Brexit.[25]

12.4 CASE STUDY B: SUCCESSFUL TAKEOVER OF TWITTER BY MUSK

The successful takeover of Twitter by Elon Musk took place in 2022.[26] In this case, the target's board and top executives were allegedly ready to pass over the social implications of the bid because its financial conditions were attractive to them. This point has been raised by Bebchuk, Kastiel, and Toniolo in a stimulating paper where they suggest that 'Twitter's corporate leaders elected to push under the bus the interests of company employees, as well as the mission statements and core values to which Twitter had pledged allegiance for years.'[27] In the authors' opinion, corporate leaders selling their company should not be expected to look after the interests of stakeholders. Moreover, Twitter's takeover would support the agency critique of stakeholder governance, stressing that corporate leaders have incentives not to serve stakeholders beyond what would serve shareholder value and that corporate mission and purpose statements are mostly for show.

Two categories of stakeholders were allegedly pushed under the bus by corporate leaders. Firstly, Twitter's employees, whose interests Twitter had long promised to look after. Corporate leaders did not even try to allocate a share of the large gains

[20] The relevant aspects are well described in the HBS case study cited at n 19.

[21] See A. Massoudi, J. Fontanella-Khan and B. Elder, 'Unilever rejects $143bn Kraft Heinz takeover bid' (17 February 2017), *Financial Times* 154.

[22] Ibid.

[23] For other reasons, see S. Daneshkhu and L. Barber, 'Paul Polman: How I fended off a hostile takeover bid' (3 December 2017), *Financial Times* 31.

[24] See the video description by R. Armstrong and J. Guthrie, 'Why Kraft Heinz dropped Unilever bid' (20 February 2017), *Financial Times*.

[25] Ibid.

[26] See W. Isaacson, *Elon Musk*, (New York: Simon & Schuster, 2023), p. 441 et seq., for an account of the bid and relevant events.

[27] L. A. Bebchuk, K. Kastiel and A. Toniolo, 'How Twitter Pushed Stakeholders Under the Bus' (2023), 28 *Stanford Journal of Law, Business, and Finance* 307.

from the deal to them: 'Twitter's leaders did not even seek soft pledges or information regarding Musk's plans for the post-deal treatment of employees. Instead, Twitter leaders chose to disregard risks to employees despite the clear presence of such risks at the time that the deal was negotiated.'[28] Secondly, the company's clients were pushed under the bus. Many of them relied on Twitter's business model which allowed for the control of integrity within the network and the protection of human rights, putting some limits to the freedom of expression. Yet, 'Twitter's corporate leaders ... pushed the mission statements and core values to which Twitter had pledged allegiance for years under the bus. In negotiating the terms of the transaction, Twitter's corporate leaders did not bargain for any constraints on post-deal abandonment of these commitments.'[29]

Bebchuk, Kastiel, and Toniolo want to show, in line with their previous papers, that the board and managers of Twitter simply pursued their own and shareholders' enrichment without taking care of stakeholders. However, assuming that the transaction was socially desirable for the efficiencies generated by the bidder's proposed actions, the thesis advanced by the authors would not necessarily be proven. Indeed, if Musk's plans were a good solution to the crisis of Twitter, the directors and managers of the latter would have acted in the interest of the company, also considering that Musk was the only bidder. If we assume, to the contrary, that Twitter's stakeholders (especially its employees and a proportion of its clients) were sacrificed without sufficiently good reasons from the perspective of the company and its future performance, then the authors' argument that they were put under the bus would be grounded. In a similar case and under a socially responsible approach, the board should have sought protections for stakeholders in the bid. Otherwise, it should have considered resistance to the bid, if there were sufficient reasons to believe that the company's future would have been better for both shareholders and stakeholders under a different management and different plans.

However, the price offered in the bid was so advantageous to shareholders that it would have been difficult for Twitter's board to justify resistance to Musk's takeover, which was also the only one proposed to the target's shareholders.[30] A few days after announcing the bid, Musk himself had a strong feeling that he had overpaid: 'Advertising spending was down in the summer of 2022, because of uncertainty about the economy; and the stock price of social media was plummeting.'[31]

12.5 CASE STUDY C: FAILED TAKEOVER OF AKZONOBEL BY PPG

Another interesting example to consider is the failed takeover of AkzoNobel by PPG, the main features of which were partially adjudicated by the Amsterdam Court of

[28] Ibid., 318.
[29] Ibid., 309.
[30] Ibid., 314, showing that the premium to shareholders was about 38 per cent.
[31] See Isaacson (n 26), p. 463.

Appeal on 29 May 2017 in the case of Elliott v. AkzoNobel.[32] The dispute arose between Elliott, a well-known US active investor and hedge fund, and AkzoNobel, a multinational company active in decorative paints, performance coatings and specialty chemicals, based in Amsterdam and listed on Euronext. Elliott requested the Enterprise Chamber to order, by way of provisionally enforceable order, an investigation into AkzoNobel's policy and course of affairs with reference to the decision-making of the management board and the supervisory board concerning the interest of PPG to acquire the share capital of AkzoNobel.

PPG is an international group with main activities in performance coatings, industrial coatings and glass, with emphasis on the first two activities.[33] PPG was market leader at the end of 2016, followed by AkzoNobel. In 2017, PPG made a non-binding proposal to acquire the issued ordinary shares in the capital of AkzoNobel through a public offer, 'preferably recommended by both the Board of Management and the Supervisory Board of AkzoNobel'. AkzoNobel notified PPG that the (management and supervisory) Boards had carefully reviewed their proposal, considering the interests of shareholders, employees, customers, and all other stakeholders. The Boards unanimously rejected PPG's proposal, for it was not in the interest of AkzoNobel and its stakeholders, including AkzoNobel's shareholders. The press release specified that the PPG proposal significantly undervalued AkzoNobel from a shareholder perspective and that it was not in the interest of stakeholder groups such as customers, shareholders, and employees.[34]

PPG made a second proposal to AkzoNobel. This revised proposal involved a price improvement. PPG also addressed the topics of 'Commitment to Research and Development', 'Commitment to Employees', 'Commitment to The Netherlands', 'Pensions', 'Governance and Management', 'Brands' and 'Corporate Social Responsibility'. After its second proposal was also rejected, PPG made a third proposal, declaring *inter alia* that PPG was committed to maintaining AkzoNobel's strong ties with the Netherlands; was prepared not to move any of AkzoNobel's production sites in Europe to the United States and to give all AkzoNobel suppliers in the Netherlands and the UK a fair chance to sell to the combined new company. Moreover, PPG recognized the importance of employees for the long-term success of the company, would respect their existing rights, was willing to pledge that no AkzoNobel employee currently working in a Dutch Specialty Chemicals plant would lose his job as a direct consequence of the acquisition, and would meet AkzoNobel's pension obligations. In addition,

[32] Court of Amsterdam (Enterprise Chamber), 29 May 2017, *Elliott International, L.P. v. AkzoNobel* N.V., ECLI:NL:GHAMS:2017:1965. For a commentary, see T. Vos, 'The AkzoNobel Case: An Activist Shareholder's Battle Against the Backdrop of the Shareholder Rights Directive' (2017), 14 *European Company Law Journal* 238.

[33] Court of Amsterdam (Enterprise Chamber), 29 May 2017, *Elliott International, L.P. v. AkzoNobel* N.V., ECLI:NL:GHAMS:2017:1965, sec. 2 on 'the facts' of the case.

[34] Ibid., para. 2.14.

AkzoNobel's (flagship) brands would be maintained and the combined companies' best practices in sustainability and social responsibility would be applied.[35]

There were essentially two issues at stake in this case: how AkzoNobel came to reject PPG's proposals; the extent to which AkzoNobel was accountable to its shareholders. As to the first, the Enterprise Chamber stated that determining the strategy of a company and its affiliated enterprise is, in principle, a matter for the management board of the company, that this is supervised by the supervisory board, and that the general meeting of shareholders can express its views on the matter by exercising the rights granted to it by law and the articles of association. In general, the management board of a company is accountable for its policy to the general meeting of shareholders but, except for deviating from statutory regulations or regulations under the articles of association, it is not obliged to involve the general meeting in its decision-making in advance if it concerns acts for which the management board is authorized.[36]

The determination of AkzoNobel's response to PPG's proposals belonged therefore to the primacy of AkzoNobel's management board, under the supervision of the supervisory board.[37] The management board and the supervisory board should have accounted to the general meeting *ex post* for the position taken in response to PPG's proposals, but shareholders were not entitled to claim any prior say in this regard. None of the parties disputed that the AkzoNobel management board should be guided by the interests of the company and its affiliated enterprise, which interests are primarily determined by promoting the continued success of this enterprise. Furthermore, in discharging their duties, partly on the basis of the provisions of Section 2:8 of the Dutch Civil Code, managing directors should have exercised due care in respect of the interests of all those involved in the company and its business. This duty of care may entail that the directors, when serving the company's interests, ensure that this does not unnecessarily or disproportionately harm the interests of all those involved in the company or its business.

In the Enterprise Chamber's view, there was no general rule of law requiring an offeree company to engage in substantive discussions with a serious potential bidder that made an unsolicited takeover proposal.[38] Whether substantive discussions or negotiations were required depended on the circumstances of the case. AkzoNobel had not taken the strategic decision to leave the stand-alone scenario at the time PPG presented itself. The points to consider, in addition to the proposed offer price, were the strategic intentions of the potential bidder, the content of the proposals other than the price, the extent to which the offeree company could evaluate the proposals without substantive discussions with the potential bidder, and the content

35 Ibid., para. 2.20.
36 Ibid., sec. 3 including 'the grounds for the decision', especially para. 3.8 et seq.
37 Ibid., para. 3.11.
38 Ibid., para. 3.14.

and course of the other interaction between the offeree company and the potential bidder. The circumstance that substantive discussions with PPG may have contributed to AkzoNobel's judgement on PPG's proposals and ability to explain to its shareholders and other stakeholders why it preferred a stand-alone strategy did not in itself establish an obligation to enter negotiations or substantive discussions with PPG.

In short, the fact that an offeree company's decision not to support a bid was inconsistent with the will of (a majority of) the shareholders did not automatically mean that the offeree company could not reasonably have reached that decision. The Enterprise Chamber left open whether the extent to which and the manner in which AkzoNobel accounted to its shareholders for the rejection of PPG's proposals was a valid reason to doubt proper policy or conduct. In conclusion, the Enterprise Chamber did not see sufficient grounds for immediate injunctive relief. Elliott's requests were therefore rejected and, in the aftermath, PPG walked away from the attempt to buy AkzoNobel (1 June 2017).

12.6 A BRIEF COMPARISON

In the three cases just examined, the role of the board was key. In the relevant jurisdictions (the US, the UK and the Netherlands),[39] directors of the target have wide discretion to decide how to respond to a takeover, if they comply with their fiduciary duties. Such duties require directors to act in the interest of the company, which may include the interests of both shareholders and its main stakeholders (employees, suppliers, communities, etc.). In the EU, Article 3(1)(c) of the TOD provides that 'the board of an offeree company must act in the interests of the company as a whole [. . .]'.[40] As explained by B. Clarke and R. Skog in Chapter 1 of this book,

> after lengthy debates as to the extent to which a broader stakeholder approach should be included in the Directive as opposed to a shareholder primacy approach, the reference to acting in the 'interests of the company' in Principle (c) was agreed. It was understood that this would allow Member States to adopt either a broad or narrow interpretation of the term depending on their chosen national approach.[41]

More generally, a brief comparative analysis shows that European and US laws do not necessarily consider shareholder value as the sole corporate purpose, despite the

[39] For the US, see G. Ferrarini and G. P. Miller, 'A Simple Theory of Takeover Regulation in the United States and Europe' (2009), 42 *Cornell International Law Journal* 301; for the UK, see D. Kershaw, *Principles of Takeover Regulation* (Oxford: Oxford University Press, 2016), p. 88–101; for the Netherlands, see R. G.J. Novak, 'Corporate Boards in the Netherlands', in P. Davies et al. (eds.), *Corporate Boards in Law and Practice. A Comparative Analysis in Europe* (Oxford: Oxford University Press, 2013), p. 435 et seq.

[40] See Chapter 1 by Clarke and Skog.

[41] Ibid.

emphasis put on this concept in financial practice.[42] Noteworthy examples are the 'constituency' jurisdictions in the US and German law, which are more oriented to the enterprise than to the corporation and are to some extent focused on stakeholders, as shown in particular by the codetermination regime applicable in Germany to large corporations.[43] True, other corporate laws in Europe and the US define corporate profit as the main purpose of the company and the shareholders' interest as the main interest to pursue in the management of companies.[44] However, stakeholders are taken care of on governance grounds even in countries that do not follow the pluralist model of corporate governance but a shareholder primacy model. Stakeholders' protection in these countries mainly depends on either contracts or regulation (such as environmental and labour laws), but also on corporate governance to the extent that stakeholders' interests are considered at board and management levels. Under this approach, the task of the board of directors and top management is to reconcile the interests of shareholders with those of stakeholders in view of maximizing the enterprise value over the long term.[45]

In a similar vein, the theory of enlightened shareholder value suggests that shareholder wealth should be maximized in the medium to long term, which requires the interests of stakeholders to be met as a condition for maximizing the value of the firm.[46] Section 172 of the UK Companies Act reflects this theory.[47] Moreover, a shareholder value approach has been widely followed by corporate governance codes applicable to listed companies in all major jurisdictions, including Germany where corporate law is stakeholder-oriented, but shareholder value concepts have been imported as a consequence of capital markets development.[48] In fact, the emphasis on shareholder value is stronger when a company is listed and its shares are traded on the capital markets, given that investors expect a return on their investment which can derive both from dividends and capital gains.[49]

42 G. Ferrarini, 'Corporate Purpose and Sustainability Due Diligence', in D. Busch, G. Ferrarini, and S. Gruenewald (eds.), *Sustainable Finance in Europe. Corporate Governance, Financial Stability and Financial Markets*, (Cham: Palgrave, 2024), p. 121, 127 et seq.

43 See K. Hopt, 'Labour Representation on Corporate Boards: Impacts and Problems for Corporate Governance and Economic Integration in Europe' in R. Buxbaum et al. (eds.), *European Economic and Business Law. Legal and Economic Analyses on Integration and Harmonization*, (Berlin/New York: De Gruyter, 1996), p. 269.

44 See Ferrarini, (n 42), p. 137 et seq.

45 See M. Becht, P. Bolton and A. Roell, 'Corporate Governance and Control', ECGI Finance Working Paper N°. 02/2002, upd. August 2005, 1, arguing that corporate governance is concerned with the resolution of collective action problems among dispersed investors and the reconciliation of conflicts of interest between various corporate claimholders.

46 See Jensen (n 7) (2002), 12 *Business Ethics Quarterly*, p. 345 et seq.; (2010), 14 *Journal of Applied Corporate Finance*, p. 38 et seq.

47 See V. Harper Ho, 'Enlightened Shareholder Value: Corporate Governance beyond the Shareholder-Stakeholder Divide' (2010), 36 *Journal of Corporation Law* 59.

48 See Ferrarini (n 42), p. 128 et seq.

49 See P. Davies, 'Shareholder Value, Company Law, and Securities Markets Law', in K. Hopt and E. Wymeersch (eds.), *Capital Markets and Company Law* (Oxford: Oxford University Press, 2003), p. 261 et seq.

No doubt, it is difficult to state *ex ante* how the trade-offs examined with respect to the first two cases (Unilever and Twitter) should have been solved in general, as they depended on the circumstances of each case. Should the board of Unilever have entered negotiations with Kraft Heinz trying to ameliorate the economic terms of the offer (as the offeror seemed willing to do) and passing over the fact that the two companies' cultures were distant, especially from a sustainability perspective? Unilever's management apparently felt that cultural clashes between the two corporate groups would have made their integration difficult and that the US-style shareholder value culture of the bidder would have in the end prevailed. Moreover, Unilever's corporate leaders believed that the price of the prospective takeover did not sufficiently reflect the value of their company. In addition, the Conservative government of Theresa May did not want the UK to lose an industrial conglomerate like Unilever just after Brexit, fearing that this would appear as a failure of the government's industrial policy. The investors, on their side, were either attracted by the economic terms of the offer or by the prospect of a more efficient management of the combined Kraft Heinz/Unilever Group but were never put to a choice.

In the case of Elliott v. Unilever, the Dutch Enterprise Chamber held that no obligation of the target to negotiate existed towards the potential bidder. The legal relationship between the offeree company and potential bidder was governed by reasonableness and fairness to the extent that the board of the offeree company was obliged, under the circumstances, to respect the legitimate interests of potential ('serious') bidders and to refrain from taking any action that might frustrate potential bids and that might disproportionately harm the interests of the bidders in question, but that did not give the person making an unsolicited takeover proposal a right to negotiate with the target company.[50] An obligation to have substantive discussions or negotiations could only arise from the fulfilment of the duties to which directors and supervisory directors of the target company are bound towards the company. In the circumstances of the case, AkzoNobel's management board and supervisory board deliberated intensively and with considerable frequency on PPG's proposals, with input from reputable external financial and legal advisers.

The issues raised in the decision-making, eventually grouped by AkzoNobel under the headings of Value, Timing, Certainty and Stakeholder considerations, indicated that AkzoNobel seriously and substantively analysed PPG's proposals. There was no basis for an opinion that AkzoNobel would not have seriously considered PPG's proposals or the interests of shareholders or other stakeholders. The (correctness of the) considerations made by the management board and the supervisory board are, as such, not subject to assessment by the Enterprise Chamber. When assessing proposals by a potential bidder, the board of an offeree company should also focus on – in the terms of the Dutch Corporate Governance Code – the long-term value creation of the company and its affiliated business and, to this end,

[50] See n 33 and corresponding text.

weigh up the relevant interests of the stakeholders. It is conceivable that the offeree company might decide not to support a proposal by a potential bidder, even if a majority of the offeree company's shareholders would want to accept a corresponding offer. It is equally conceivable that the offeree company might decide not to support a proposal of a potential bidder when it is likely that a stand-alone scenario would generate less shareholder value (in the long term) than the takeover proposal (in the short term).

In the case of the bid for Twitter by Elon Musk, the target's board faced a similarly difficult choice, but the premium offered by the bidder over the stock market price of the company was substantial and hard to reject. It was also clear that the efficiency gains that Musk was targeting would have been pursued through a drastic reduction in Twitter's headcount. However, a complete turnaround of Twitter's policies concerning hateful conduct, civic integrity, ESG, and human rights was also foreseeable given the public statements in that direction repeatedly made by Musk. Should the board of Twitter have taken responsibility for these issues and negotiated protections for the target's employees and clients?

On social responsibility grounds, keeping the implicit promises made by Twitter to its employees and customers could have been the right course of action for the company to follow. This would have reinforced the trust of the main stakeholders in the company and could have resulted in better financial performance over the long term. However, Elon Musk's planned restructuring of Twitter was based on a sharp headcount reduction and a commitment to unrestrained freedom of speech in corporate policies. Moreover, he was the only bidder and this *de facto* restricted the discretion of Twitter's board. As in the case of the Kraft/Unilever failed takeover, the board had to choose between maximizing the stock price for shareholders through a successful acquisition or abandoning the transaction from the outset. This was also made possible by the poison pill which had been previously adopted by the board.

12.7 SHAREHOLDER VALUE CREATION AND THE MARKET FOR CORPORATE CONTROL: CONCLUDING REMARKS

The main question raised by sustainability with respect to corporate takeovers is whether and to what extent ESG concerns should lead to a restraint on shareholder value creation through an efficient takeover market. If hostile takeovers could fail whenever the target's directors believe that their company's sustainability would be negatively affected by a successful bid, the whole market for corporate control would be disrupted. A compromise must therefore be struck on policy grounds between keeping an unrestricted corporate control market and allowing firms to maximize shareholders' total welfare, including corporate sustainability. In other words, the theoretical model of responsible capitalism requires a takeover regime which, in addition to preserving the takeover market as an efficient means to replace the management of underperforming companies and/or allow shareholders to cash in the true value of their companies, takes the interest of stakeholders into account.

In any case, the trade-offs between an efficient market for corporate control and the social benefits of sustainability should reflect the more general ones between corporate profits and social value. As already argued, firms maximize their long-term value by protecting stakeholders and promoting ESG. Moreover, the board of the target should compare the price offered by the bidder for the target shares with their long-term value, which derives from promoting both the interests of shareholders and those of the main stakeholders.

Similar actions are taken by the board of the target either before a bid is launched, as in the cases of Unilever and AkzoNobel, or after an offer has been made, as in the case of Twitter. When facing a hostile bid, the board of the target also considers whether defensive measures should be taken to protect the interests of shareholders and/or stakeholders. If the board decides in favour of defensive measures, their adoption would further depend on the legal regime applicable to post-bid defences in the jurisdiction at issue, which may require such measures to be taken subject to authorization by the shareholder meeting as foreseen by Article 9 of the TOD.

In addition, the board of the target should consider whether special protections are needed for stakeholders like employees and customers if the bid goes through, as already seen in the failed takeover of AkzoNobel or suggested by commentators on the Twitter takeover by Elon Musk. Board deliberations should compare the interests of the target's shareholders with those of the company's main stakeholders, trying to determine to what extent the former could be sacrificed without disrupting the corporate control market. Moreover, the board should compare the price offered in the bid with the target's estimated value, considering the strategic plans pursued by the corporation also from a sustainability perspective. No doubt, there could be cases in which the target's prospective value – which is based on the company's strategies, including those concerning sustainability – appears to be higher than the price offered by the bidder and therefore suggests resistance to the bid.

All these and similar aspects of takeovers should be commented upon by the target's board under Article 9(5) TOD, which provides that the board

> shall draw up and make public a document setting out its opinion of the bid and the reasons on which it is based, including its views on the effects of implementation of the bid on all the company's interests and specifically employment, and on the offeror's strategic plans for the offeree company and their likely repercussions on employment and the locations of the company's places of business as set out in the offer document in accordance with Article 6(3)(i).

Yet, this provision focuses on one category only of stakeholders, the employees, while other stakeholders should be considered today, such as local communities, suppliers, and customers, as well as climate, environmental, and social issues in general. The Directive should be modified in this respect and require a broader scope of disclosure of all ESG issues.

To avoid some of the problems highlighted above concerning corporate sustainability or to reduce their impact, the corporate leaders of target companies could make takeover bids more difficult or impossible through pre-bid takeover defences. Multiple-voting shares, for example, protect the target from unwanted takeovers, including those by a bidder threatening to worsen the target's approach to sustainability. However, similar defences would prevent any kind of takeover, even one from a bidder promising to improve the target's approach to climate change or to protect employees by granting job security to them. The holders of multiple-voting shares would in fact enjoy full discretion as to whether a takeover could take place or not, even if clearly beneficial to the remaining shareholders and to the main stakeholders of the target.[51]

[51] On the impact of multiple-voting shares on the ability of founders à la Zuckerberg to impose anti-ESG behaviour on their companies, which institutional investors could then contrast through their shareholdings, see V. Battocletti, L. Enriques and A. Romano, 'Dual Class Shares in the Age of Common Ownership' (2022) ECGI Law Working Paper No. 628/2022.

PART IV

New Developments

13

The Alternative to Takeover Offers in the UK

Using Schemes of Arrangement to Effect a Change of Control

Jennifer Payne

13.1 INTRODUCTION

In the UK, it is very common to use a scheme of arrangement as an alternative to a takeover offer to effect a change of control. Indeed, schemes of arrangement are generally the structure of choice for recommended bids. In the year ended March 2025, for example, of fifty-seven firm offers eight were structured as a contractual offer and forty-nine as a scheme of arrangement at the time of the firm offer announcement – that is, schemes of arrangement accounted for 86 per cent of offers.[1]

This chapter will examine the use of schemes of arrangement as an alternative to takeover offers in the UK. In Section 13.2 the mechanism for using a scheme of arrangement is examined. In Section 13.3 the reasons why a bidder might choose to structure a change of control by way of a scheme of arrangement rather than a more traditional offer are discussed. In Section 13.4 the use of these two mechanisms for effecting a change of control are compared, including the level of minority protection that exists in both procedures. Section 13.5 addresses the question whether the use of a scheme of arrangement rather than a traditional offer gives rise to any concerns. It is suggested that there are no reasons to be sceptical about the use of schemes of arrangement to effect a change of control in the UK.

13.2 THE USE OF SCHEMES OF ARRANGEMENT TO EFFECT A CHANGE OF CONTROL

Schemes of arrangement have existed in the UK since the nineteenth century.[2] The current provisions are found in Part 26 of the Companies Act 2006. Section 895(1) defines a scheme of arrangement as 'a compromise or arrangement between a

[1] Takeover Panel, Annual Report and Accounts for the year ended 31 March 2025, 15.

[2] The origins of the scheme of arrangement lie in the UK Companies Act 1862, s 136. For discussion see J. Payne, *Schemes of Arrangements: Theory, Structure and Operation* 2nd ed. (Cambridge University Press, 2021), ch. 1.2.

company and its creditors, or any class of them, or its members, or any class of them'. A scheme of arrangement is therefore a statutory mechanism for the implementation of a wide range of corporate transactions. The statutory provisions in the Companies Act 2006 do not prescribe the subject matter of a scheme and, in theory, a scheme could be a compromise or arrangement between a company and its creditors or members about anything that they can properly agree amongst themselves. As a result, companies can use schemes for a wide variety of internal reorganisations of debt and/or equity capital, as long as the necessary approvals have been obtained. They can be – and are – used for a variety of purposes other than effecting a change of control, but this is now one of the common uses of this mechanism.

Broadly, where the scheme is being used to effect a takeover, it will first involve an arrangement[3] being proposed between the company and its members, that proposal generally coming from the board. An application will then be made to court for an order that meetings of members be summoned.[4] Members will then meet in classes to consider and approve the scheme, the approval level being a majority in number representing 75 per cent in value of the members, or class thereof.[5] A company is free to decide with whom it proposes any particular compromise or arrangement. It is therefore possible for a company to exclude certain members/creditors from the scheme and indeed it is common for any shares held by the bidder to be excluded. Only those included in the scheme of arrangement need to meet and vote on it. An application must then be made to court to sanction the scheme of arrangement.[6] The order sanctioning it takes effect once a copy is delivered to the Registrar of Companies.[7] Thereafter, the court will set aside a scheme of arrangement only on very limited grounds, such as where the consent to it was obtained by fraud.

A change of control effected by way of a scheme of arrangement takes place by way of a transfer scheme, the effect of which is that all of the shares of the target not already owned by the bidder are transferred to the bidder.[8] The only material steps taken by the target company are, typically, the registration of the bidder as shareholder in place of existing shareholders, and the issue of new share certificates to the bidder. A scheme is a statutory mechanism whereby the members can agree to

3 UK Companies Act 2006, s. 895. The courts have interpreted the term 'arrangement' broadly and the view has been taken that a change of control should be regarded as involving an arrangement for this purpose even though generally the company's only role in a scheme of arrangement which is being used to effect a change of control is to register the shares of the new owner: see e.g. *Re Savoy Hotel Ltd* [1981] Ch 351; *Re Jelf Group plc* [2015] EWHC 3857 (Ch).

4 UK Companies Act 2006, s. 896.

5 Ibid., s. 899(1).

6 Ibid.

7 Ibid., s. 899(4).

8 Until 2015 a takeover effected by a scheme of arrangement could occur in one of two ways: by a cancellation scheme or a transfer scheme. A change in the law in 2015 means that only transfer schemes can now be used to effect a change of control: The Companies Act 2006 (Amendment of Part 17) Regulations 2015 (SI 472/2015).

the proposal put forward by the target board, namely that the target shares be transferred to the bidder on the proposed terms. Accordingly, the bidder deals not with the target shareholders, but with the target company. If the scheme is approved by the requisite majorities in the relevant meetings, and the court sanctions the scheme and the order is delivered to the Registrar, then all of the members are bound to transfer their shares in accordance with the terms of the scheme, even if they voted against it.

This is of course very different from the process involved in a takeover offer whereby the bidder deals first and foremost not with the target company but with the target shareholders. The bidder makes an offer to the target shareholders to buy their shares. The relationship is fundamentally one of contract between the bidder and the target shareholders, and the bidder prima facie has no relationship with the target company, although, of course, overlaying this contractual relationship is a significant layer of regulation. Within the UK there is a detailed regulatory regime for takeovers, including Part 28 of the Companies Act 2006 and the Takeover Code, overseen by the Takeover Panel.[9]

Crucially, however, while the processes are distinct, it is clear that where schemes are used to effect takeovers of companies within the jurisdiction of the Takeover Panel,[10] the Takeover Code will apply. The Takeover Code states unequivocally that its provisions 'apply to an offer effected by means of a scheme of arrangement in the same way as they apply to an offer effected by means of a contractual offer' except as set out in Appendix 7 of the Code.[11] Many of the provisions within the Code apply to schemes of arrangement in just the same way as a takeover offer. For example, a scheme effecting a takeover is announced in the same way as an offer, in accordance with Rule 2.7 of the Takeover Code. Similarly, the disclosures required by the Takeover Code apply equally where the change of control is effected by way of a scheme of arrangement.[12] However, there are some important differences too; for instance, it is made clear that the mandatory offer regime does not apply to schemes of arrangement.[13]

One of the important questions to consider is why a change of control may be effected by way of a scheme of arrangement rather than a takeover offer. There are a number of advantages and disadvantages to a scheme of arrangement, as compared to a traditional offer, that might incentivise the parties to choose one rather than the

[9] UK Companies Act 2006, ss. 942–954. For a discussion of the development of takeover regulation in the UK see J. Armour and D.A. Skeel Jr, 'Who writes the rules of hostile takeovers, and why? – The peculiar divergence of US and UK takeover regulation' (2007) *Georgetown Law Journal* 1727.

[10] See Takeover Code, Introduction, s. 3(a).

[11] Takeover Code, App. 7, s. 1. The importance of synchronising the approach towards takeovers by way of schemes with those by way of offers was confirmed in *Re Expro International Group plc* [2008] EWHC 1543 (Ch).

[12] Takeover Code, r. 24.

[13] Ibid., App 7, s. 2. For further discussion see Section 13.3.

other as the mechanism to effect the change of control on a particular set of facts. The most significant ones are given here.[14]

13.2.1 *Ability to Acquire 100 per cent Control of the Target*

A successful scheme of arrangement will always involve the bidder acquiring 100 per cent control of the target: once the scheme of arrangement has been approved by the court, and the order delivered to the Registrar, the bidder has certainty that it can acquire 100 per cent control of the target. By contrast, in a takeover offer, the bidder's offer must be conditional on acceptances being secured by the bidder sufficient to give it (together with securities already held) more than 50 per cent of the voting rights in the target.[15] The bidder can choose to make the offer conditional on a level of acceptances greater than the 50 per cent threshold, but need not do so. A takeover offer can therefore involve the bidder acquiring less than 100 per cent of the target. Only when the acceptance level reaches 90 per cent can the bidder make use of a squeeze-out right to acquire compulsorily the remaining 10 per cent of the shares.[16] Where the acquisition of 100 per cent of the shares is key, some takeover offers will set the minimum level of acceptances at 90 per cent, so that the bidder can then make use of the squeeze-out rules. However, this requires acceptance by the holders of 90 per cent of the shares to which the offer relates, rather than the lower level required for a scheme (a majority in number representing 75 per cent in value of the members, or class thereof).[17] This difference in approval thresholds is a significant advantage for schemes, from the bidder's point of view. However, it has also given rise to a certain level of controversy regarding the use of schemes to effect takeovers, which is discussed further in Section 13.4.1.[18]

[14] Some others do exist – for example, there may be some advantage to using a scheme of arrangement where the transaction involves financial assistance; see UK Companies Act 2006, s 681(2)(e) and *Re Uniq plc* [2011] EWHC 749 (Ch). There may also be an advantage to a scheme of arrangement if US shareholders are involved as using a scheme of arrangement may enable bidders to avoid registering consideration securities under the US Securities Act of 1933 by excluding the US shareholders from the offer. For further discussion see Payne, *Schemes of Arrangement*, ch. 3.2.2.

[15] Takeover Code, r. 10.

[16] UK Companies Act 2006, s. 979(2)(a). A corresponding right to sell out exists for minority shareholders at this point: ss. 983–985.

[17] The fact that the scheme approval level relates only to those present and voting (in person or by proxy) can reduce this percentage further. If only 50% of the votes are cast at the meeting, for example, then a vote in favour by 40% of shareholders (i.e. 80% of those attending and voting) will suffice. If the turnout at the meeting is very low this might be a factor for the court to take into account when determining whether to sanction the scheme at the sanctioning hearing. For discussion see e.g. *Re Vernalis plc* [2018] EWHC 3898 (Ch); *Re Stellar Diamonds plc* [2018] EWHC 1152 (Ch).

[18] The flipside of this, however, is that although it is easier for the bidder to reach the 75% threshold needed to gain 100% control in a scheme, than to reach the 90% level that would be needed in an offer to ensure the same result, it is also easier for a dissenting shareholder to

Accordingly, if it is important for the bidder to acquire 100 per cent control of the target company, then a scheme of arrangement will often be more attractive. There may be a number of reasons why the bidder wants to secure 100 per cent ownership of the target company. For example, if it wants to use the target company's assets as security for loans made to the bidder to finance the bid, it will be important for the bidder to acquire all of the target's shares. This is particularly common in private equity transactions. Alternatively, the bidder may plan to re-register the target as a private company, perhaps to avoid the prohibition on the provision of financial assistance that applies to public companies,[19] or to allow the target to benefit from the less onerous administrative requirements applicable to private companies under the Companies Act 2006. The acquisition of 100 per cent of the shares will avoid giving the minority scope to object to this re-registration.[20] Another reason why the bidder may want 100 per cent control of the target is to avoid sharing the planned gains with any remaining minority. This might be because the bidder is intending to extract cash from the target by way of dividend payments, or because it intends to amalgamate its business with that of the target, thereby creating synergies and cost savings.

13.2.2 *Speed*

The timetable for a takeover offer is more fluid than that for a scheme of arrangement. Because of the need to fit in two court hearings and members' meetings to vote on the scheme, the timetable for a scheme is usually seven to eight weeks from posting. By contrast, the minimum time period from posting to declaring an offer unconditional is twenty-one days,[21] and the maximum is sixty-one days.[22] It may be faster to use a takeover offer than a scheme of arrangement, especially where the offer is straightforward, no competing offer emerges and the bidder only needs to obtain, say, 50 per cent ownership of the target. However, in other circumstances a scheme of arrangement will be quicker, in particular where the bidder wants to acquire 100 per cent control of the target. Under a scheme of arrangement the bidder knows that seven to eight weeks after posting it will have control, if the scheme is successful. Under a takeover offer, the bidder has no such certainty. Furthermore, if the bidder has to rely on the use of the squeeze-out process to acquire the rump 10 per cent shareholders, this process can add a substantial delay.

block a bid that is effected by means of a scheme of arrangement, than to block one effected through an offer.

19 UK Companies Act 2006, s. 678.

20 Ibid., ss. 97–98: s. 98 allows the holders of not less than 5 per cent of the nominal value of a company's issued share capital, or not fewer than fifty members, to apply to court to object to the re-registration.

21 Takeover Code, r. 31.2.

22 Ibid., r. 31.1.

13.2.3 *Lost and Untraceable Shareholders*

In situations where there are lost and untraceable shareholders, it may be beneficial to proceed by way of a scheme. This is because such shareholders cannot be taken into account when calculating the acceptance level for a takeover offer, unless permission is sought from the court. By contrast, in a scheme of arrangement these shareholders will not be relevant when determining whether the 75 per cent acceptance level has been reached. This is because in a scheme of arrangement only 75 per cent of those present and voting (whether in person or by proxy) need to vote in favour.[23]

In addition, in a scheme of arrangement, once the shareholder approval thresholds are met, the court has sanctioned the scheme and the order has been delivered to the Registrar, there is no need for the company to try to trace any untraceable shareholders: they are bound by the scheme. By way of contrast, in a takeover offer these untraceable shareholders can only be dealt with as part of the squeeze-out regime, once the 90 per cent threshold has been reached.[24]

13.2.4 *Who Has Control of the Process*

An important consequence of the structural differences between schemes of arrangement and takeover offers is that in a scheme of arrangement the process is controlled by the target rather than the bidder. It is the target and its directors that are responsible for the scheme of arrangement and producing the scheme documents and it is the target company shareholders that must approve it.

This has two important consequences. First, a scheme of arrangement will generally only be completed if it is recommended by the target directors. As a technical matter, it is possible for a hostile bidder to use its position as a shareholder in the target to launch a scheme, after consultation with the Takeover Panel.[25] However, there are practical difficulties in implementing a hostile scheme of arrangement, so that there seems to be no case where such a scheme has been successful in practice to date.[26] Accordingly, if the bid is to be hostile, a bidder is likely to opt for a takeover offer instead.

Second, it is harder for a bidder to change the terms of the bid during the change of control process – for example, to respond to a competing bid that has arisen.

[23] UK Companies Act 2006, s. 899(1).
[24] Ibid., s. 986(9).
[25] Takeover Code, App. 7, s. 13.
[26] The courts have determined that they will only order member meetings to be held to consider a hostile scheme of arrangement if it is possible that the company's approval (via the board or members in general meeting) will be obtained. See e.g. *Re Savoy Hotel Ltd* [1981] Ch 351. There is also a practical challenge in that there will often be a lack of information in the hands of the hostile shareholder launching the scheme, making it challenging for them to satisfy the disclosure requirements for the scheme.

By contrast, this is relatively easy in a takeover offer, since it is the bidder who is in control. It is potentially more difficult for the bidder to change the terms of a scheme of arrangement – for example, by increasing the amount that it is willing to pay – and it may be necessary to restart the scheme timetable. There is a risk that the target company will simply adjourn the shareholders' meeting(s) if a competing bid is submitted. Since the target, and not the bidder, has control of the scheme process, the bidder cannot prevent this. Alternatively, if the competing bid arises after the shareholders' meetings have been held, further meetings may have to be convened and held.[27] Therefore, if a competing bid is possible, or likely, it may be that a takeover offer will be more suitable.[28]

13.2.5 *Procedural Complexity*

In two ways, the scheme of arrangement process is more procedurally complex than a takeover offer in the UK. First, in a takeover offer there will generally be no court involvement. Indeed, this is regarded as one of the strengths of the UK takeover regime, as compared, say, with the system of takeover regulation in the US.[29] In the UK, the takeover is governed by the rules set out in the Takeover Code, and to the extent that rulings are required during the course of the bid these are made by the Takeover Panel. Although the Panel's decisions are subject to judicial review, the courts have established narrow limits within which any judicial review of a Takeover Panel decision will operate.[30] Crucially, in the UK, the courts have been content to carry out a retrospective review of the Takeover Panel's decisions. Importantly, the courts have not interfered in the course of an existing bid.[31]

[27] However, the courts may be prepared to allow an increase in price, without starting the court process again, provided that the terms other than the price stay the same and shareholders have sufficient time to consider any new information they are receiving before the meeting takes place. This is only likely to apply where the change is more favourable to shareholders. Any revision to a scheme with fewer than fourteen days' notice before the date of the meeting(s) to approve the scheme, or indeed any revision after the date of the meeting, will require the consent of the Takeover Panel: Takeover Code, App. 7, s. 7.

[28] However, concerns relating to the bidder's lack of control over the scheme process and timetable may be mitigated in two important ways. First, if the bidder is concerned that a scheme might be adjourned by the target for a significant period of time, the Takeover Panel will allow conditions to be inserted within the scheme causing the bid to lapse if the scheme is not effective by a certain long-stop date: Takeover Code, App. 7, s. 3(b) and see e.g. *Re Inmarsat plc* [2019] EWHC 3470 (Ch). Second, if a competing bid does arise it is possible to switch to an offer (see Takeover Code, App. 7, s. 8).

[29] See e.g. Armour and Skeel, 'Who writes the rules for hostile takeovers, and why?', n 9.

[30] *R* v. *Panel on Takeovers and Mergers ex p Datafin* [1987] QB 815.

[31] Ibid.; *R* v. *Panel of Takeovers and Mergers ex p Guinness plc* [1990] 1 QB 146; *R* v. *Panel of Takeovers and Mergers ex p Fayed* [1992] BCC 524. See also *Panel* v. *King* [2018] CSIH 30 in which the court continued to apply the deferential approach that is in evidence in *R* v. *Panel on Takeovers and Mergers ex p Datafin* [1987] QB 815.

On this basis there is very little to be gained by a party making use of litigation in the course of a takeover.[32]

By contrast, in a scheme of arrangement there are two compulsory court hearings. This has implications both in terms of cost and for the timetable and the flexibility of the process. As the member meetings in a scheme of arrangement cannot be convened without an order of the court, and the date of the meeting is set by an order of the court, any adjournment will need a further application to the court. The fact that court approval is required before a scheme of arrangement can go ahead might make a bidder nervous, as it potentially provides a forum for disgruntled minority shareholders to object to the change of control. A scheme of arrangement might also add an element of completion risk that does not exist in relation to takeover offers. The sanctioning stage is not a rubber-stamping exercise and the courts do, albeit rarely, exercise their discretion to refuse a scheme of arrangement even where it has been approved by the members/creditors.

Another issue that makes schemes of arrangement potentially more cumbersome than takeover offers is the need to separate the members into classes in order for them to consider and approve the scheme. If the target gets the division of the members into classes wrong, this can be a reason for the court to refuse to sanction the scheme of arrangement at the sanctioning hearing. The starting point is that a class is confined 'to those persons whose rights are not so dissimilar as to make it impossible for them to consult together with a view to their common interest'.[33] In practice this involves an analysis of (i) the rights which are to be released or varied under the scheme and (ii) the new rights (if any) which the scheme gives, by way of compromise or arrangement, to those whose rights are to be released or varied.[34]

The courts seek to strike a balance: those with genuinely different rights require the protection of a separate meeting, but if too many artificial distinctions are drawn, then the scheme will be at the mercy of a veto by any one of the separate meetings. While this test and the courts approach is relatively easily stated, applying it can become difficult in practice.[35]

13.2.6 *Structural Flexibility*

Although schemes of arrangement are procedurally less flexible than traditional offers, they are structurally more flexible. For example, it may be that rather than the bidder company taking over the target, both bidder and target are acquired by a newco, using two schemes of arrangement that are inter-conditional. This may be

[32] Of course, the court can have a role in both squeeze-out and sell-out (see Companies Act 2006, s. 986), but since this occurs only once the bidder has obtained 90 per cent, in practice this does not provide an opportunity for the court involvement to frustrate the bid.

[33] *Sovereign Life Assurance Co* v. *Dodd* [1892] 2 QB 573.

[34] *Re Hawk Insurance Co Ltd* [2001] EWCA Civ 241 at [30].

[35] Payne, *Schemes of Arrangement*, ch. 3.5, n 2.

done to increase the perception that the transaction is a merger of equals rather than a takeover of one company by another. As any arrangement between a company and its members can be effected by way of a scheme, a takeover by way of a scheme of arrangement also affords the companies involved an opportunity to effect a reorganisation at the same time. It is therefore relatively common to see, as part of a takeover scheme, some reorganisation of the resulting group companies.

There are both advantages and disadvantages to progressing with a change of control by way of a scheme of arrangement rather than a takeover offer, and schemes will not be suitable in all cases. They may be slower and more costly than a takeover offer in some circumstances and can give rise to complex issues, such as the need to consider whether separate class meetings are required, that do not arise in a takeover offer. A hostile bidder will often find it easier to proceed by way of a takeover offer than a scheme of arrangement, and a bidder that anticipates competing bids may also prefer to utilise a takeover offer. However, the lower voting threshold in schemes of arrangement makes it easier for a bidder to obtain 100 per cent control of the target, and there are other benefits that schemes of arrangement can offer, such as their structural flexibility. These issues help to explain why schemes of arrangement are now the mechanism of choice for recommended bids.

13.3 A COMPARISON OF MINORITY PROTECTION IN SCHEMES OF ARRANGEMENT AND OFFERS

Schemes of arrangement allow the minority shareholders to be bound by the majority so that, in a takeover scheme, even if they dissent they will be bound to sell their shares to the bidder in accordance with the terms of the scheme. This raises obvious issues of potential minority abuse. However, when the minority protections put in place in a scheme of arrangement are compared with those in place in a takeover offer, it is clear that they are substantially different. The reasons for this differential treatment need to be examined.

13.3.1 *Minority Protection in a Scheme of Arrangement*

There are, broadly, two protections put in place for minority shareholders in a scheme of arrangement. The first is the fact that shareholders meet in classes to consider whether to vote in favour of the scheme. The company needs to obtain the approval of all classes of members or creditors, or classes thereof, that are affected by the scheme. Only if each class meeting approves will the court be able to sanction the scheme – in other words, the cramdown of a whole dissenting class is not possible. The courts can therefore protect minorities by ensuring that they have all the information they need to determine whether to attend, and how to vote at the meetings, and by ensuring that correctly constituted class meetings are held.

In theory, the fact that different class meetings are held means that shareholders should vote alongside others with similar concerns and interests, and this should make it more likely that the minority voice will be heard. However, the level of protection will depend in large part on the determination of how many class meetings are held. The more class meetings there are, the more minority shareholders will have veto rights in relation to the proposed scheme. There has been a shift in recent years away from overzealous distinctions that give minorities strong veto rights. Although it is still important to divide shareholders and creditors into different classes, many distinctions between members and creditors (especially those that may more properly be characterised as different interests rather than different rights) will instead be taken into consideration by the court at the sanctioning stage.

The second form of protection for minorities, then, is the scrutiny of the court at the sanctioning hearing. The court has wide discretion at this stage to refuse to sanction a scheme if minority oppression is present. The court will pay particular attention to whether the statutory requirements are met (e.g. that the votes are passed by the requisite majorities) and the judge will also apply a fairness test. In particular, the court may wish to examine whether different interests held by the majority shareholders in a class meeting influenced their voting behaviour to such an extent that it cannot be said that the majority vote fairly represented the views of the class as a whole. For example, a class might include all those shareholders with the same rights (the same right to vote, to receive a dividend, etc.) but if some of those shareholders are the bidder's or its subsidiaries they may be expected to have a different interest in the outcome of the scheme of arrangement from the other shareholders in the class. It may be appropriate for the court to discount or disregard some or all of the votes of those with different interests to see whether the scheme would still have been approved if those persons had been excluded from the vote. If the scheme would not have been approved, the court might consider it appropriate to refuse to sanction the scheme.

13.3.2 *Minority Protection in an Offer*

The aims of UK takeover regulation are two-fold: first, to regulate the relationship between the target directors and the target shareholders, and resolve this potential conflict in favour of the shareholders; and second, to regulate the relationship between the bidder and the target shareholders. Focusing on the latter, UK takeover regulation has put in place a raft of measures designed to ensure shareholder protection.

At the centre of these measures is the concept of shareholder equality enshrined in General Principle 1 of the Takeover Code.[36] As a result, rules are in place regarding the need for the same offer to be made to all shareholders of the same

[36] UK Companies Act 2006, Sch. 1C.

class,[37] and where a target company has more than one class of equity share capital, a 'comparable' offer to be made for each class, whether it carries voting rights or not.[38] If the offer is subsequently increased by the bidder then even those who accepted the original offer are entitled to the new, higher price.[39] However, the Takeover Code requires not only equality of treatment of shareholders within the bid, but also equality between offerees and sellers outside the bid.[40] The Code seeks to prevent the bidder from doing favourable deals with a few selected shareholders, either before the offer period,[41] or during the offer period.[42] In addition, there are rules in place to ensure that the target shareholders have adequate information upon which to make a decision,[43] and rules that ensure that they have enough time within which to reach a decision.[44] The squeeze-out and sell-out rules also have built-in protection for the minority.[45]

Last, but not least, there is the mandatory bid rule that states that once a person, together with anyone with whom they are acting in concert, acquires 30 per cent of the shares carrying voting rights, or holds between 30 and 50 per cent and acquires additional shares carrying voting rights, then a mandatory bid is required.[46] That person must extend offers to the holders of any class of equity share capital (voting or non-voting) and also to the holders of any other class of transferable securities carrying voting rights. The offer must be a cash offer, or with a cash alternative, and must be at the highest price paid by the offeror or a member of its concert party within the twelve months prior to the commencement of the offer.[47]

13.3.3 *A Comparison of These Minority Protection Provisions*

Comparing the levels of minority protection in these two mechanisms reveals that the minority protection available in a scheme of arrangement appears to be quite distinct from that available in a takeover offer. The reasons for this can be

37 Takeover Code, GP 1.

38 Ibid., r. 14. The Takeover Code has in place rules designed to prevent the bidder offering disguised enhanced deals to only some of the shareholders: r. 16.

39 Ibid., r. 32.3.

40 For discussion see P. L. Davies, 'The notion of equality in European takeover regulation', in J. Payne (ed.), *Takeovers in English and German Law* (Oxford: Hart Publishing, 2002).

41 Takeover Code, r. 6.1.

42 Ibid., r. 6.2.

43 Ibid., rr. 23, 24, 25.

44 The offer must be kept open for acceptance by the shareholders for at least twenty-one days (Takeover Code, r. 31.2). Any revised offer must be kept open for a further period of fourteen days (r. 32.1) and any shareholders who accepted the original offer are entitled to the revised consideration (r. 32.3).

45 UK Companies Act 2006, Part 28 Ch 3.

46 Takeover Code, r. 9.1.

47 Ibid., r. 9.5.

understood once the different reasons for the existence of minority protection in a scheme and in an offer are appreciated.

The strongest argument justifying the minority protection provisions in a takeover offer is that based on the need to ensure that shareholders' decisions should be made in a manner that is distorted as little as possible by any actions of the bidder. In the absence of specific takeover regulation, bidders could offer different deals to different shareholders, or make offers with very short periods for acceptance. Bidders would have the opportunity to 'divide and conquer', skewing the offer in order to acquire the company at the lowest possible price. The collective action problems faced by the target shareholders potentially increase the bargaining strength of the bidder at the expense of the target shareholders.[48] If the decision on the outcome of the bid is given primarily to the shareholders rather than the target board, as it is in the UK, it is crucial that the shareholders' decision-making is as undistorted as possible. A result of the pressure to tender might be that the bidder will succeed in gaining control over a target even if the value-maximising course of action for the target shareholders would be to reject the bid. The undistorted choice argument is therefore an allocative efficiency argument.

An alternative argument is that shareholders should be entitled to a right of exit (at the bid price) when a change of control occurs following a takeover; otherwise, the minority might become 'trapped' in the target company under the control of the bidder and therefore the minority shareholder needs to be provided with the opportunity to exit, and furthermore to exit at the bid price. However, in a takeover situation, a minority shareholder in a publicly listed company is not trapped in any meaningful sense since the opportunity to sell the shares in the market always exists. A minority shareholder might argue that the market price for the shares in those circumstances does not reflect a fair price, since the actions of the new controller have depressed the market value of the shares, but shareholders in a publicly traded company know, or ought to, that the value of their shares may go down as well as up. The only exception to this might be where the bidder makes use of a successful bid to take the company private, which would then result in minority shareholders holding shares for which there is no ready market.

By way of contrast, in a scheme of arrangement, because the decision is taken by the company by the shareholders collectively (in one or more class meetings) rather than individually, there is no opportunity for the bidder to divide and conquer. There are no individual contracts for the sale and purchase of shares being entered into between the bidder and individual shareholders. There is no collective action problem akin to that which faces the dispersed shareholders in the majority of UK publicly traded companies confronted with a takeover offer. The concerns regarding distorted choice

48 L. Bebchuk, 'The pressure to tender: an analysis and a proposed remedy' (1987) 12 *Delaware Journal of Corporate Law* 911; L. Bebchuk, 'Towards an undistorted choice and equal treatment in corporate takeovers' (1985) 98 *Harvard Law Review* 1693.

therefore do not arise in the context of a scheme. Furthermore, there is no need to worry about the minority shareholders needing a right of exit. All shareholders are bound by a successful scheme to transfer their shares to the bidder. The bidder acquires 100 per cent of the shares and there is therefore no possibility of any shareholders being left behind who might wish to exit the target company after the bid.

In the scheme of arrangement, the focus of concern regarding minority oppression is on the process of deciding whether to accept the scheme. Since a successful scheme binds all shareholders, the effect is that even dissenting shareholders will be required to sell their shares to the bidder for the price agreed as part of the scheme. This can be regarded as triggering the need for some kind of a protective response. However, in line with the approach adopted in other areas of UK company law, the response adopted in this regard is relatively *laissez faire*. In general, UK law has taken the view that shares can be expropriated as long as a fair price is paid for them. A good example of this are the squeeze-out rules, which generally do allow shareholders' shares to be purchased, as long as the price is fair and, broadly, the bid price will be regarded as a good indication of fairness.[49]

In fact, the potential for oppression in a scheme is most akin to that facing the rump shareholders in a takeover offer who are required by the squeeze-out rules to sell their shares to the bidder. In both scenarios, the minority shareholders are being required to sell their shares at a price that is imposed upon them. In squeeze-outs the minority can apply to court for an order that there should be no acquisition, or that the offer price be amended. It is for the petitioner to establish that the squeeze-out is unfair. Generally, the fact that 90 per cent of the shareholders have accepted the offer will be taken as evidence that the offer is fair, unless the petitioner can demonstrate unfairness despite this 90 per cent acceptance level – for example, where the 90 per cent acceptors are not independent of the bidder.[50] These instances are rare, however. Usually, the court will not intervene to prevent the squeeze-out occurring on the final terms of the offer. This seems appropriate. A shareholder has no intrinsic right to retain its shares, and expropriation should be allowed if the price is fair. In general, the fact that the remainder of the shareholders have accepted the price will be a good indication of fairness. Only in exceptional circumstances, where this is not the case, should the court interfere.

The protections in place in a scheme of arrangement perform a fundamentally different function from most of the rules put in place in a takeover offer. The concern that is raised in a scheme, namely the possibility of expropriation at an unfair price, is dealt with appropriately by the courts in this regard. This conclusion also feeds into the discussion in the next section. It is sometimes suggested that

[49] *Allen* v. *Gold Reefs of West Africa Ltd* [1900] 1 Ch 656; *Citco Banking Corp NV* v. *Pusser's Ltd* [2007] UKPC 13 (PC).

[50] *Re Bugle Press Ltd* [1961] Ch 270; *Re Chez Nico (Restaurants) Ltd* [1992] BCLC 192; *Fiske Nominees Ltd* v. *Dwyka Diamond Ltd* [2002] EWHC 770 (Ch).

bidders should not be allowed to make use of schemes to effect takeovers (since this allows them to bypass the rigorous regulatory regime in place in relation to takeover offers) or, at least, if a scheme is used in this regard additional regulatory requirements should be put in place to ensure that bidders do not gain an unscrupulous advantage by bypassing takeover regulation in this way. The discussion in this section suggests that the lower minority protections available in a scheme should not be seen as undermining the substantial minority protection provisions put in place in an offer.

13.4 SHOULD TAKEOVERS BE ALLOWED BY WAY OF A SCHEME OF ARRANGEMENT IN THE UK?

Concerns are sometimes raised about the use of schemes of arrangement to effect a change of control and it is notable that some jurisdictions that have imported the scheme of arrangement from the UK have added some additional elements into the process when a scheme is used as an alternative to a takeover offer, in order to address perceived concerns.[51]

There are three concerns that can arise in this context, namely:

(1) that the approval threshold for a bidder to obtain 100 per cent ownership of a company via a scheme of arrangement is lower than that required for a takeover offer;
(2) that schemes of arrangement may be used to bypass the detailed requirements of the takeover regime; and
(3) that schemes of arrangement do not maximise shareholder value for the target shareholders.

These concerns are addressed in turn. The question arises whether the current English approach to this issue – namely, neutrality as to whether a change of control occurs by way of a scheme of arrangement or of a takeover – is correct. Should this issue be regulated in order to reduce the frequency of takeover schemes in some way, whether that is by making schemes in this context harder to achieve (perhaps by raising the approval threshold for such schemes), or by requiring such transactions to proceed by way of a traditional takeover offer, unless the parties can show a good reason why not? It is suggested that none of these concerns justifies a change to the current English practice regarding schemes of arrangement to effect a change of control.

13.4.1 *Approval Thresholds*

The first concern relates to the approval threshold required for schemes of arrangement, in particular that the minority can effectively be bound by a lower percentage

[51] See e.g. section 411(17) of the Australian Corporations Act 2001; sections 236A–236B into New Zealand Companies Act 1993, discussed in Payne, *Schemes of Arrangement*, ch. 3.7, n 2.

of the members in a scheme (75 per cent of the shares and a majority in number of them) than in a takeover offer (where the minority could not be forced to sell their shares unless 90 per cent of the other shareholders had already accepted the offer). It has been suggested that approving a scheme of arrangement in such circumstances should require a very high standard of proof.[52] In Hong Kong, there is a different, higher, approval threshold for schemes of arrangement involving a change of control – namely, a requirement that, in addition to 75 per cent by value voting in favour, less than 10 per cent of the total voting rights attached to the 'disinterested shares' in the company may vote against it,[53] if the approval threshold is to be reached. The question arises whether the English scheme needs to modify the approval threshold for schemes that effect a change-of-control transaction, in order to recognise a perceived disparity between the approval threshold that currently exists for schemes and that which exists for traditional takeover offers.

Two points can be made in this regard. The first point is a practical one. Although the approval level for schemes of arrangement appears to be lower than that for takeover offers, in practice the effect might be less dramatic than it seems. This is for a number of reasons. First, in a scheme of arrangement the members vote in classes and every class must approve a scheme before a court can consider whether to sanction it; so, if a dissenting minority of a class of members opposes it, the scheme of arrangement cannot go ahead. Second, the operation of the court's fairness discretion means that the votes of the bidder and its subsidiaries will not be counted in determining whether the appropriate majorities have been met. Third, in a scheme of arrangement it is only the votes of those that attend and vote (in person or by proxy) that count for these purposes and, given shareholder apathy in many listed companies, this may mean that relatively few shareholders actually attend and vote at the meeting. The typical levels of those attending and voting at class meetings is low. These last two points are particularly important. Disinterested minorities holding relatively few votes, who turn up and vote at a meeting, might be in a position to block a scheme. So, for example, even with only one class meeting, and assuming that all shareholders attend and vote at the meeting, if the bidder and its subsidiaries hold 60 per cent of the shares in the target company, 10 per cent of the shareholders (i.e. 25 per cent of the 'disinterested' shares) would be able to block the scheme. If only half of the disinterested shareholders attend and vote, then 10 per cent of the disinterested shareholders could block a scheme in which the bidder and its associates hold just 20 per cent of the voting shares in the target. Schemes of arrangement might therefore put more power in the hands of a dissenting minority than appears from the approval threshold stated in the legislation, and accordingly the disparity between this threshold and that in takeover offers might not be as significant as is sometimes claimed.

[52] See e.g. *Re Hellenic and General Trust Ltd* [1976] 1 WLR 123.

[53] Hong Kong New Companies Ordinance, Cap. 32 s. 674(2).

The second point relates to the more philosophical question of whether this disparity in approval levels is something that the court ought to take into account. The English courts have considered on a number of occasions whether the approval threshold for schemes of arrangement should be raised to bring it into line with the position regarding takeovers, and have always rejected this approach.[54] The approach of the English courts is that whether a company proceeds by way of a scheme of arrangement or a takeover offer is a matter of choice for that company.[55] The courts have rejected the argument that where a scheme is used as an alternative to an offer the court should insist on a 90 per cent approval of the scheme by shareholders.[56] On this view, the lower threshold in a scheme is countered by the court oversight of the scheme of arrangement process.

This seems correct. There are different approval thresholds in place for schemes and offers, but those different levels are justifiable. Schemes of arrangement have a number of protective safeguards that an offer does not, the two most significant being the requirement for the members to consider and approve the scheme in classes (which increases the minority protection), and the involvement of the court in both approving the meetings of members and/or creditors, and then in sanctioning the scheme. The role of the court at the sanctioning hearing operates as a particularly important protective device. Minorities are able to air their views at the sanctioning hearing, and the exercise of the court's fairness discretion can operate as a significant safeguard. The court's role in taking account of these issues and determining whether to sanction the scheme is an important counterbalance to the lower approval threshold in place for schemes, which justifies the different approval levels required for these different change-of-control mechanisms.

13.4.2 *The Use of Schemes to Bypass the Takeover Regime*

A second criticism sometimes raised in relation to schemes of arrangement is that they allow bidders to effect a takeover without having to comply with the detailed disclosure and other requirements of the takeover regime. This concern seems to explain the introduction of section 411(17) of the Australian Corporations Act 2001, for example, which provides that a court will have the jurisdiction to approve a scheme of arrangement only where either (i) it is satisfied that the scheme has not been proposed to avoid the operation of the takeover legislation or (ii) a statement is received from the Australian Securities and Investment Commission indicating that it has no objection to the arrangement.

54 *Re National Bank Ltd* [1966] 1 WLR 819 at 829–830.

55 *Re BTR plc* [1999] 2 BCLC 675, *Re BTR plc (Leave to appeal)* [2000] 1 BCLC 740; *Re TDG plc* [2008] EWHC 2334 (Ch).

56 *Re National Bank Ltd* [1966] 1 WLR 819; *Re TDG plc* [2008] EWHC 2334 (Ch); *Re Realm Therapeutics plc* [2019] EWHC 2080 (Ch) at [63].

However, as discussed, schemes of arrangement used to effect the change of control of a company subject to the Takeover Code in the UK must comply with that regime in the same way as a more traditional offer. Many of the obligations under the Takeover Code – for example, disclosure requirements – apply identically to offers and schemes. Where differences do exist, there are good reasons for their existence, mostly based on the structure and operation of a scheme as compared to an offer. Many of the rules in the Takeover Code that provide for equality between target shareholders in an offer are not necessary in a scheme, because there is no opportunity for the bidder to 'divide and conquer' in the same way, and there is no possibility of minority shareholders being left in the target company following a successful scheme. The protections that are put in place for minority shareholders in schemes of arrangement are adequate and appropriate for the dangers that face those shareholders. For English schemes, both the courts and the Takeover Panel play a significant role in overseeing the use of schemes to effect change-of-control transactions, and ensuring that minority protection is upheld.

The position in Australia appears to provide the strongest counterpoint to the English position. The scheme of arrangement provisions in Australia are otherwise very similar to those in the English scheme.[57] However, the operation of section 411 (17) in practice means that the existence of this provision should not lead us to doubt the current English practice. The approach of the courts,[58] as well as of the Australian regulator, ASIC,[59] and of the Australian Takeovers Panel,[60] appears to be that, despite the existence of section 411(17), schemes of arrangement and takeover offers should be treated as genuine alternatives in effecting a change of control. Nevertheless, difficulties still remain and the precise operation of section 411 (17) remains a source of lingering uncertainty and adds an element of completion risk to any schemes of arrangement in Australia. As a result, there have been strong arguments made for the repeal of section 411(17) by the Corporations and Markets Advisory Committee (CAMAC), among others.[61] In light of this, it should be clear that adopting a provision akin to section 411(17) for English schemes is neither necessary nor desirable.

57 The same three-stage process is required for schemes in Australia as that set out in Section 13.2 for English schemes: a scheme is proposed on behalf of the company; an application is made to court for meetings to be held (Australian Corporations Act 2001, s. 411(1)); the members and/or creditors meet in classes to consider and approve the scheme (s. 411(4)(a)); a second court hearing is required to sanction the scheme (s. 411(4)(b)); and, if sanctioned, the order of the court becomes effective once lodged with the Australian Securities and Investment Commission (ASIC) (s. 411(10)) (rather than the Registrar of Companies, under the English provisions).

58 *Re ACM Gold Ltd (1992)* 7 *ACSR* 231; *Re Capilano Honey* (2018) 132 ACSR 332.

59 ASIC has provided guidance as to the circumstances in which it will issue a 'no-objection' letter: ASIC Regulatory Guide 60, 'Schemes of arrangement', September 2011, at [60.17].

60 *Re St Barbara Mines Ltd and Taipan Resources NL* (2000) 18 ACLC 913 at 917; Takeovers Panel, GuidanceNote 15, 'Trust scheme mergers', second issue, 6 May 2011 at [8].

61 CAMAC, *Members' schemes of arrangement, Report*, December 2009, 95–108, available at www.camac.gov.au.

13.4.3 *Maximising Value for Target Shareholders*

A further concern that is sometimes raised regarding the use of schemes of arrangement is that they do not facilitate auctions for control, and therefore do not maximise shareholder value for the target shareholders. However, if a scheme is announced, there is nothing to prevent a subsequent bidder launching a rival takeover offer, or a rival scheme of arrangement. Indeed, it is not uncommon to see competing bids being introduced after a scheme of arrangement is announced. There have also been occasions on which rival offers for a target have been made by way of schemes of arrangement.

The fact that generally bidders will not seek to purchase large stakes in the target company prior to a scheme of arrangement (because these shares will not be counted towards the approval threshold) means that the way is left more open for competing bids to arise, as compared to the scenario in a takeover offer, where the bidder will generally have locked up a large stake in the target company in advance. If a rival bidder wishes to proceed by way of a takeover offer there will be a larger pool of shares available for it to purchase as a springboard into its offer. If the rival bidder wishes to proceed by way of a scheme of arrangement then there is no requirement for it to purchase a large stake in the target before it can do so. Either way, it may be argued that commencing a change of control by way of a scheme of arrangement does not stifle the market for corporate control in any way, and may even facilitate it in some circumstances. It is also possible for the court at the sanctioning hearing to take account of changes of circumstances between dates of meetings and sanctioning hearing which could have an effect on price.[62]

Finally, there is also no evidence that companies are sold at a lower premium under a scheme than under a takeover bid.[63] All in all, there seems little support for the view that schemes have a dampening effect on the market for corporate control, or the proposition that they do not maximise shareholder value for the target shareholders, when compared to traditional offers.

13.5 CONCLUSION

Schemes of arrangement are now a very common mechanism for recommended bids to take place in the UK. This chapter has explored the reasons for the use of schemes of arrangement in this context and explored some of the questions and issues that can sometimes arise in this context. Crucially, the Takeover Code in the UK governs changes of control of relevant companies by way of a scheme of

[62] *Re Cobham plc* [2020] EWHC 320 (Ch).

[63] See, for example, (in the context of Australian deals) T. Damian and A. Rich, *Schemes, Takeovers and Himalayan Peaks: The Use of Schemes of Arrangement to Effect Change of Control Transactions* (3rd ed., The Ross Parsons Centre of Commercial, Corporate and Taxation Law, University of Sydney, 2013) at 712–713.

arrangement as an alternative to a traditional takeover offer. While the minority protection available to shareholders in a scheme and in an offer are distinct (and the protections available to minorities in a scheme are lower than those in an offer), these differences are understandable entirely explicable when the purpose and function of these different mechanisms is considered. Where the parties decide to use a scheme rather than an offer there is no reason to be concerned or sceptical about the use of a scheme, nor for insisting on additional safeguards being put in place beyond those that the law currently provides. In particular, supervision by the English courts and, where appropriate, the Takeover Panel, operates to provide sufficient safeguards and protections for dissenting and minority shareholders and other parties concerned about the impact of the transaction on their rights.

14

Change of Control by Merger of Corporations

Susanne Kalss

14.1 PURPOSES OF TAKEOVER LAW AND COMPANY LAW

The aim of takeover law is to ensure equal treatment of all shareholders when control of a listed company is acquired for the first time or when control of a listed company changes, so that the new controlling shareholder must make an offer to the other shareholders to buy their shares at a legally prescribed price. The other shareholders therefore have the *right to withdraw*. The key term under takeover law is therefore *control*; derived from this are the acquisition of control and the change of control.

Takeover law lies at the interface between capital market law and company law. It is intended to ensure the principle of *equal treatment* under capital market law and the safeguarding of a price determined by information in favour of all shareholders and holders of equity securities. The aim of company law is to organise influence and economic benefit within the shareholders and to provide the controlled shareholders with an exit option when control is gained.[1] Takeover law is fundamentally neutral in its application; it does not make its application or legal consequences dependent on whether the transfer of shares is a purchase transaction, an exchange transaction or any other synallagmatic or other transaction under the law of obligations.

The provision refers to the *acquisition of control* and not to a purchase or any other specific transaction. The application of takeover law is also independent of whether control is acquired by way of singular or universal succession. It is irrelevant what type of material transfer agreement is applied. This is obvious because the connecting factor is the acquisition of control and not the way or the legal technique for the acquisition of control. Takeover law therefore covers both exchange and

[1] H. Fleischer, 'Entwicklungslinien des deutschen und europäischen Übernahmerechts', in N. Paschos and H. Fleischer (eds.), *Handbuch Übernahmerecht nach dem WpÜG* (Munich: C.H. Beck, 2017), § 1 mn. 10 et seq.

purchase agreements, contributions or other measures that lead to a change of control. The legal technique is just as irrelevant as the consideration.

In the case of a transaction involving a change of control, shareholders have the right to withdraw from the company in return for cash compensation as part of a mandatory offer. The cash alternative is mandatory under Austrian law. However, merger law does not provide for a cash alternative; instead, the rule is a non-cash settlement, which is granted even without an express declaration by the recipient.[2]

In this chapter, the problems will be discussed primarily from the perspective of German and Austrian law and, to some extent, Swiss law, simply because merger and division transactions are frequently carried out in these countries and therefore provide illustrative material for the questions at hand.

14.2 THREE CORE AREAS OF MERGER AND DIVISION REGULATION

Broadly speaking, merger and division law pursues three regulatory objectives, namely:

- legally secure implementation
- protection of shareholders
- protection of creditors.

(a) The legal and technical implementation of the merger requires the contractually precise mapping of the entire process and the inclusion of all assets in the transfer as well as the proper implementation with the involvement of the competent authorities and courts. The legal implementation of a division is much more complicated, as only part of the assets are transferred and therefore the assets must be divided and individualised.[3]

(b) The interests of the shareholders are massively affected, especially as assets are merged or divided and the shareholders become members of other companies. The value of the respective shareholding and the extent of influence is affected and must therefore be protected. It is thus a matter of safeguarding the existing influence and protecting the value of the shareholding. The law provides various instruments for this purpose – namely, appropriate and externally reviewed information at an early stage of the process, participation in decision-making and judicial review of the entire process and the intrinsic value of the

[2] S. Kalss, *Verschmelzung – Spaltung – Umwandlung* (Vienna: Manz, 2021), 3 ed., § 219 AktG mn. 10; M. Winner, 'Übernahmeangebot bei Verschmelzung? Die Entscheidung Hypo Vereinsbank/Bank Austria der österreichischen Übernahmekommission', in S. Kalss, H. Fleischer and H.-U. Vogt, *Bahnbrechende Entscheidungen – Gesellschafts- und Kapitalmark trechtsgeschichten* (Tübingen: Mohr Siebeck, 2016), p. 45, 47.

[3] Kalss, *Verschmelzung*, before §§ 1–16 SpaltG mn. 16.

consideration. In certain situations, shareholder protection is safeguarded by additional instruments such as individual consent (in the case of the loss of individual special rights) or the right to withdraw.

(c) The interests of the creditors are also massively affected, especially as the creditors have no right of consent and cannot prevent the measure. In the case of a merger, creditors of the transferring company will receive a different creditor, and in the case of a division, they might receive another creditor. The liability fund to cover their claims changes significantly, as at least two different sets of assets are merged or a previous set of assets is divided. The law responds with certain capitalisation and security requirements as well as additional liability of the companies.

(d) However, merger and division law does not address the fact that control over a company is newly acquired as a result of the merger or division. It does not provide for a special right of approval, a right of withdrawal or any other protective measure.

14.3 ACQUISITION OF CONTROL THROUGH MERGERS AND DIVISIONS

A takeover can be carried out through the acquisition of shares. However, the takeover can also be completed through a merger or division. Several variants are available:

(a) The company to be acquired – that is, the target company – can act as a listed acquiring company and the controlling shareholder of the transferring company also takes control of the acquiring company.

(b) The company to be transferred is listed on the stock exchange and is transferred to another listed or unlisted company. The shareholders of the transferred and defunct company now find themselves in a minority position compared to a new controlling shareholder in the acquiring company.[4]

(c) Control can also be obtained one level higher – that is, at the level of the shareholders of the listed company – through a merger or division at the level of the associated companies. In this case, the listed company is only the subsidiary or otherwise held company.[5]

(d) Finally, it is possible that a merger or division may result in the transferring company losing its stock exchange listing as a result of the transfer of its assets, and thus also the protection of takeover law and the overall ease of trading of the shares due to the loss of a regulated marketplace (*delisting*).

4 Winner, 'Übernahmeangebot bei Verschmelzung?', p. 45, 47.

5 Ibid., p. 45, 57.

14.4 SPECIAL FEATURES OF MERGERS AND DIVISIONS

According to Article 88 of the Company Law Directive, a merger is a corporate law measure characterised by the transfer of the entire business of one company to another without liquidation in return for the granting of shares in the acquiring company to the shareholders of the transferring company.

A division is the transfer of parts of the assets of a corporation by way of partial universal succession to one or more other newly formed or existing companies in return for the granting of shares in the acquiring company to the shareholders of the transferring company. The transferring company can therefore either transfer only part of its assets and remain in existence after the division ('spin-off') or divide its entire assets among several legal entities and cease to exist upon registration of the division without liquidation ('split-up').[6] The main difference between a merger and a division is that, in the case of a division, the transferring company does not necessarily have to cease to exist and therefore a residual company can remain, which also increases the variety of possible structures. In any case, it is necessary to clearly allocate the assets in order to find the entrepreneurial substrate again.[7]

What are the special features of mergers and divisions? Firstly, a merger or division is not a purchase transaction, but an exchange transaction.[8] Secondly, the special feature of this exchange transaction is that the contractual partner and debtor of the performance is the transferring company. The recipient of the consideration, on the other hand, is not the transferring company, but its shareholders. This shifts the level of the provider and the recipient.[9] This will later be of decisive importance for the treatment under takeover law.

Thirdly, no agreement between three parties is required, only a consensus between the two parties.[10] The fact that the assets are transferred by way of universal succession and that the material transfer is effected by entry in the commercial or company register is, however, not of paramount importance for the treatment under takeover law. Takeover law deals with the transfer of shares and assets by way of both individual and universal succession.

Fourthly: of greater importance, however, is the second defining element of the merger – namely, the demise of the transferring company, so that this legal entity is no longer available as an element of attribution.[11] Therefore, the consideration must be allocated to the shareholders. This is also reflected in the aforementioned aspect

6 Kalss, *Verschmelzung*, § 1 SpaltG mn. 5.

7 Ibid., 8; J. Lieder, '§ 123 UmwG', in W. Bayer and J. Vetter (eds.), *Lutter – Umwandlungsgesetz Kommentar* (Cologne: Verlag Dr. Otto Schmidt, 2024), 7th ed., § 123 UmwG mn. 9 et seq.; D. A. Verse, '§ 123 UmwG', in M. Habersack and H. Wicke (eds.), *Umwandlungsgesetz – Kommentar* (Munich: C. H. Beck, 2023), 3rd ed., § 123 UmwG mn. 28.

8 Kalss, *Verschmelzung*, § 219 AktG mn. 8.

9 Ibid.

10 Ibid., 7.

11 Ibid.

of the recipients of the consideration. The consideration for the transfer of the company are shares in the acquiring company and these shares do not go to the transferring company as the contractual partner of the merger agreement, but rather directly to its shareholders.[12] The company itself is dissolved as part of the merger. The crucial point is therefore that this measure, the transfer of assets and the granting of shares, does not create a parent–subsidiary relationship. The transferor does not receive any shares in the recipient of the entrepreneurial assets; rather, the level shifts.

In the event of a division, the transferring company also transfers assets and is thus disenriched. It is not the company but its shareholders who receive the shares in return. Again, there is an exchange transaction at two different levels – namely, at the company and the shareholder level.[13] This shifted exchange process is a form of permissible return of capital contributions.[14] The difference from a merger is that the transferring company can continue to exist with fewer assets.

Fifthly, the consideration for the merger is shares in the acquiring company. The shares are granted to the shareholders regardless of whether they actually want them or not. The merger is characterised by the non-cash consideration. In any case, an individual shareholder receives the shares in the acquiring company as a non-cash consideration, even if they would rather have money instead.[15] Only a supplementary cash payment is possible in accordance with the provisions of the Company Law Directive. A consideration in the form of other assets is also not permitted without the consent of the shareholders concerned.[16]

As in the case of a merger, shares must also be granted in the case of a division. Compensation only in return for cash, profit participation capital or other surrogate capital is not permitted. Only an additional cash payment of up to 10 per cent of the shares granted is permitted.[17]

Sixth: in the case of a merger or division, it is not the individual shareholder who decides, but the shareholders as a whole. A qualified majority decides whether the measure is to be implemented.

Seventh: the consideration for the merger or division must be appropriate. The specific determination is left to company valuers. The law does not provide for specific regulations on appropriateness. No minimum time interval or a specific reference date for a price comparison is specified. The review of appropriateness is

[12] Ibid., 6.

[13] Ibid., § 1 SpaltG mn.10.

[14] G. Eckert, 'Einlagenrückgewähr bei Umgründungen', in S. Kalss and U. Torggler (eds.), *Einlagenrückgewähr* (Vienna: Manz, 2014) p. 73; E. Napokoj, 'Die Spaltung – die legalisierte Einlagenrückgewähr', in S. Kirchmayr-Schliesselbeger et al. (eds.), *Umgründungen – Festschrift für Hanns Hügel* (Vienna: LexisNexis ARD ORAC, 2016) p. 271, 272.

[15] Kalss, *Verschmelzung*, § 219 AktG mn. 8 et seq.

[16] Ibid., 10.

[17] Ibid., § 1 SpaltG mn. 9.

only carried out by an auditor chosen by the company itself, not by an independent supervising authority.

Eighth: an additional special feature of a division may be that a change of control is implemented at the acquiring company or at the transferring company through the non-equal allocation of shares – namely, in the case of a non-proportional division. A non-proportional division is characterised by the fact that the shareholders of the transferring company do not hold the same proportion of shares in the acquiring company as they did in the transferring company.[18] This can lead to double shifts in the shareholding structure.

Ninth: the legality and appropriateness of the consideration can only be reviewed on the basis of an individual initiation of proceedings by a shareholder. This consideration is not reviewed ex officio. In many cases, the review of the consideration in the context of the implementation of the measure is expressly excluded by law. Examples of this are Section 225b of the Austrian Stock Corporation Act (*Aktiengesetz*). Only the legality of the entire merger procedure is reviewed as part of the registration procedure by the commercial register court.

Tenthly, merger law and division law – at national level and partly at European level – provide for a right of withdrawal for individual dissenting shareholders for special forms of mergers and divisions – namely, in the case of a change of legal form, of a cross-border merger or division and in the case of a non-proportional division. Examples for this are Section 29 of the German Transformation of Companies Act (*Umwandlungsgesetz*), Section 234b of the Austrian Stock Corporation Act, Sections 9 and 11 of the Austrian Division Act (*Spaltungsgesetz*) and Articles 126a (1) to (3) of the Company Law Directive. Similarly, Section 313 of the German Transformation of Companies Act and Sections 40 and 60 in conjunction with Section 16 of the Austrian Cross-Border Transformation of Companies Act (EU-*Umgründungsgesetz*) recognise the right of exit in the event of a cross-border merger or division. The circumstances that trigger the right of exit are the change of legal form or the transfer of the business assets of the company that is ceasing to exist to another EU Member State.[19] The change of control in the course of the merger or division, on the other hand, does not trigger a right of objection or right of exit under merger or division law.[20]

14.5 THE LEGISLATOR'S APPROACH

At European level, neither the Takeover Directive, nor the Merger or Division Directive, nor the Mobility Directive addresses the circumstance of the acquisition

[18] H.-J. Priester and J. Lieder, '§ 128 UmwG', in W. Bayer and J. Vetter (eds.), *Lutter – Umwandlungsgesetz Kommentar* (Cologne: Verlag Dr. Otto Schmidt, 2024), 7th ed., § 128 UmwG mn. 9 et seq.; Kalss, *Verschmelzung*, § 1 SpaltG mn. 19.

[19] V. Obradovic, '§ 40 EU-UmgrG', in T. Talos and M. Winner (eds.), *EU-Umgründungsgesetz* (Vienna: Verlag Österreich, 2024), § 40 EU-UmgrG mn. 4 et seq.

[20] Kalss, *Verschmelzung*, § 9 SpaltG mn. 8.

of control or change of control through a merger or division. The Austrian legislator, who enacted the Austrian Takeover Act before the adoption of the Takeover Directive, but clearly orientated himself on the Directive, also refrained from regulating this circumstance and was content to point out that the takeover of shares was an alternative to mergers and divisions.[21] The German legislator – despite being aware of a very well-known case (see Section 14.6) and despite being aware of the clash of different areas of regulation, the lack of an appropriate regulation at European level and the existence of national room for manoeuvre – refrained from a clear provision and from ordering the application of certain regulations, but simply acknowledged the problem and left the finding of solutions to science and practice.[22] The German legislator expressly emphasised that experience should first be gained before a regulation is created.[23]

14.6 THE LEADING CASE FROM AUSTRIA

The merger of the German bank Bayrische Hypo Vereinsbank AG with the Austrian Bank Austria AG (HVB/Bank Austria), which was to be assessed under Austrian law, provided the decisive sensitisation for the question of the application of takeover law to mergers and divisions. A multi-stage transaction was carried out in the year 2000.[24] The decision was the first in the German-speaking area and probably in the entire EU following the entry into force of the Takeover Directive, which dealt with the legal question of how the interaction between merger and takeover law is or at least should be legally organised.

14.7 THE CENTRAL TRANSACTION: A MULTI-STAGE MERGER OF SEVERAL CREDIT INSTITUTIONS

In 2000, the German Bayrische Hypo Vereinsbank (HVB) acquired the Austrian Bank Austria AG. Economically, the largest Austrian bank was to come under the control of a German credit institution. The transaction was officially taken up and investigated by the Austrian Takeover Commission. The Austrian Bank Austria had two major shareholders – namely, the so-called Anteilsverwaltung-Zentralsparkasse (AVZ), which held 23 per cent of the voting rights, and the German West LB AG, which held more than 10 per cent of the voting rights. For historical reasons, AVZ

[21] Explanatory remarks on the government bill for the Takeover Act, no. 1276 Supplements to the Stenographic Protocols of the National Council, 20th Legislative Period, p. 18.

[22] Explanatory memorandum to the government draft of the German Securities and Takeover Act, Bundestags-Drucksache 14/77034, p. 31.

[23] H. Fleischer, 'Übernahmerecht und benachbarte Rechtsmaterien', in N. Paschos and H. Fleischer (eds.), *Handbuch Übernahmerecht nach dem WpÜG* (Munich: C.H. Beck, 2017), § 2 mn. 42.

[24] In detail, Winner, 'Übernahmeangebot bei Verschmelzung?', p. 45 et seq.

was granted special rights – for example, special approval rights for amendments to the articles of association or other significant corporate measures.

In addition to several listed subsidiaries, Bank Austria also held the shares in another credit institution in the form of a stock corporation, namely Sparkasse Stockerau AG. The transaction was completed in several stages.

In a first step, the entire business operations of Bank Austria AG, including all shareholdings, were transferred to its wholly owned subsidiary Sparkasse Stockerau AG by way of a division (spin-off for absorption by a wholly owned subsidiary). In accordance with the law, no shares had to be granted for this. As a result of this step, Bank Austria, which was still listed on the stock exchange, became a holding company and its business operations were reorganised in the unlisted Sparkasse Stockerau AG. Sparkasse Stockerau AG was then renamed Bank Austria neu AG.

In a second step, Bank Austria contributed its shares in Sparkasse Stockerau/Bank Austria neu AG to HVB. The contribution was made in the form of a contribution in kind within the framework of existing authorised capital pursuant to Sections 202 et seq. of the German Stock Corporation Act. The entire assets of Bank Austria AG were thus transferred in accordance with Section 237 of the Austrian Stock Corporation Act. This required a resolution by the Annual General Meeting.

In a third step, Bank Austria AG was merged into its now granddaughter, Bank Austria neu AG. However, the capital of Bank Austria neu AG was not increased, but the shares in HVB held by Bank Austria AG were used directly to compensate the shareholders of Bank Austria AG. The listed Bank Austria AG thus ceased to exist as a result of the merger.

Under company law, it was noteworthy that it was not shares in the acquiring Bank Austria AG that were granted, but shares in HVB, which was placed between the grandparent company and the sub-subsidiary.[25] This special structure of the three-tier group of companies thus constituted a cross-border merger, even though the granting of shares did not directly fulfil the mechanism of granting shares in the acquiring company as consideration for the transfer of assets provided for in Article 89 of the Company Law Directive.

As a result, the former shareholders of Bank Austria had now become shareholders of HVB, as they were granted shares in this company. The shareholders of Bank Austria AG were now faced with the shareholders of the listed HVB. The latter held 79% of the shares. AVZ, which previously held around 23% of the voting rights in

[25] D. Weber-Rey and B. G. Schütz, 'Zum Verhältnis von Übernahmerecht und Umwandlungsrecht' (2001) *Die Aktiengesellschaft* 325; J. Vetter, 'Pflichtangebot nach Kontrollerwerb im Wege der Verschmelzung oder Spaltung' (2002) *Wertpapier-Mitteilungen* 1999, 2001; H. Grabbe and T. Fett, 'Pflichtangebot im Zuge von Verschmelzungen? Zugleich ein Beitrag zur Schnittstelle von Kapitalmarkt und Gesellschaftsrecht' (2003) *Neue Zeitschrift für Gesellschaftsrecht* 755, 756 ff.; H.-D. Assmann, 'Unternehmenszusammenschlüsse und Kapitalmarktrecht' (2008) *Zeitschrift für das gesamte Handelsrecht und Wirtschaftsrecht* 635, 660 ff.

Bank Austria AG, still held 6.8% of the voting rights, while West LB AG, which had held more than 10% of the voting rights in Bank Austria AG, now only held 1.7%. Finally, Bank Austria AG's free float shrank to 11.5%.

The issue was taken up by the Austrian Takeover Commission. It ruled on three questions:[26]

- Is a merger as a transaction involving the granting of shares in the acquiring company (subsidiary of the acquiring company) a takeover bid?
- Does the merger trigger a duty to make an offer in favour of the existing shareholders of Bank Austria AG?
- Does the transaction trigger the duty to make an offer for the minority shareholders of the listed subsidiaries?

The second of the three questions was of crucial importance.

a) Is a transaction involving the granting of shares in the acquiring company (subsidiary of the acquiring company) a takeover bid?

The first important question is whether a merger can constitute a takeover bid. As already explained, it is not each individual shareholder who decides on a merger, but the shareholders as a whole with a qualified majority. The dissenting or non-consenting shareholder also receives non-cash compensation – that is, shares – in return.

However, can this absence of an individual decision in relation to the shareholders as a whole mean that the takeover law is completely ignored? The question is important because a simple exchange offer is permissible in the case of a merger, whereas under Austrian national law the takeover offer must include a cash component. The Takeover Directive and the Austrian Takeover Act prescribe strict statutory regulations for the consideration. If the shares are acquired, they can be sold in any case, so this is not so important for a liquid share.[27]

The standard for determining the consideration is different. In the case of mergers, it is a question of determining the appropriate exchange ratio. In principle, this involves fundamental values based on a company valuation.[28] In the case of a takeover, the market price and ensuring equal treatment become decisive parameters for determining the price for the consideration. The requirement of equal treatment under takeover law goes much further than equal treatment through a merger, which occurs through the mandatory inclusion of all shareholders. Equal treatment in takeover law also covers pre-acquisitions and parallel transactions. In company law, a change in the exchange ratio is not necessarily required

[26] Austrian Takeover Commission, 12 September 2000 – 2000/1/4-171, 10.
[27] Winner, 'Übernahmeangebot bei Verschmelzung?', p. 45, 53.
[28] Ibid.

in the case of a prior acquisition from a single shareholder.[29] Finally, legal protection and official monitoring are completely different. In the case of a merger, the commercial register court does not review the appropriateness of the exchange ratio. This is only done at the request of a shareholder of one of the companies involved in the merger.[30] In takeover law, an accompanying control is already carried out ex ante and the Takeover Commission takes up its control activities ex officio. The Austrian Takeover Commission stated that a merger as such does not constitute an offer. The decisive consideration of the Takeover Commission was that no individual decision on the offer was possible.[31] The Takeover Commission also emphasised that, although the protection concepts for the merger and the takeover offer are different, the protection system does not diverge to such an extent that an analogous application of the takeover law regulations to the merger would be necessary.

The decision of the Takeover Commission was thus in line with a part of the doctrine according to which takeover law is not applicable to a merger because it is subject to independent regulations anyway.[32]

In Germany, some scholars also see no need to apply mandatory takeover bids to transactions under transformation law.[33] However, the majority of scholars consider a fundamental coexistence of transformation and takeover law to be necessary.[34] The decisive argument is that the protective objectives and mechanisms of takeover law and merger law are not congruent.[35] It can therefore be assumed that merger and takeover law coexist.[36] The Takeover Commission expressly left open whether

[29] Austrian Takeover Commission, 12 September 2000 – 2000/1/4-171, 13; Winner, 'Übernahmeangebot bei Verschmelzung?', p. 45, 54.

[30] Kalss, *Verschmelzung*, § 225c AktG mn. 3 et seq.

[31] Austrian Takeover Commission, 12 September 2000 – 2000/1/4-171, 11.

[32] Ch. *Nowotny*, 'Zur Auslegung des Übernahmegesetzes' (2000) *Österreichisches Recht der Wirtschaft* 330; further, P. Huber and Löber, *Übernahmegesetz – Kommentar* (Vienna: LexisNexis ARD ORAC), 1 ed., § 22 mn. 92 et seq.; dissenting, S. Kalss and M. Winner, 'Umgründungs- und Übernahmerecht. Versuch einer Synthese' (2000) *Österreichiches Bankarchiv* 51. See also P. Doralt, 'Übernahme, Verschmelzung, Konzern und der City Code' (2000) Der Gesellschafter 197.

[33] Weber-Rey and Schütz, 'Zum Verhältnis von Übernahmerecht und Umwandlungsrecht', 328 et seq.; Vetter, 'Pflichtangebot nach Kontrollerwerb im Wege der Verschmelzung oder Spaltung', 2001 et seq.

[34] H. Krause and T. Pötzsch, '§ 35 WpÜG', in H.-D. Assmann, T. Pötzsch and U. H. Schneider (eds.), *WpÜG Kommentar* (Cologne: Verlag Dr. Otto Schmidt, 2024), § 35 WpÜG mn. 136 et seq.; U. Noack and D. Zetzsche, '§ 35 WpÜG', in E. Schwark and D. Zimmer (eds.), Kapitalmarktrechts-Kommentar (Munich: C. H. Beck, 2020), 5th ed., § 35 WpÜG mn. 20 et. seq.; Fleischer, 'Übernahmerecht und benachbarte Rechtsmaterien', § 2 mn. 45; C. Rothenfußer, 'Kontrollerlangung und S timmrechtszurechnung ', in N. Paschos and H. Fleischer (eds.), *Handbuch Übernahmerecht nach dem WpÜG* (Munich: C.H. Beck, 2017), § 11 mn. 119 et seq.

[35] Noack and Zetzsche, '§ 35 WpÜG', § 35 WpÜG mn. 20; Fleischer, 'Übernahmerecht und benachbarte Rechtsmaterien', § 2 mn. 46.

[36] Further G. Durstberger, 'Discussion report on Martin Winner's presentation', in S. Kalss, H. Fleischer and H.-U. Vogt, *Bahnbrechende Entscheidungen – Gesellschafts- und Kapitalmark trechtsgeschichten* (Tübingen: Mohr Siebeck, 2016), p. 64, on Swiss practice.

individual provisions of the Takeover Act, such as the prohibition of parallel transactions for mergers, must also be applied to a merger by analogy.[37]

In Switzerland, however, the question of whether the merger as such should be categorised as a takeover bid has not yet been decided.[38] Teleological considerations, in particular, speak in favour of coexistence, because merger law and takeover law do not offer equivalent protective instruments. Despite being partially aware of the problem, neither Austrian law nor German law has taken up and clearly regulated this issue, but both have deliberately left it to be clarified by academics and practitioners. This is quite remarkable for this central question. In any case, it would be welcome from a legal policy perspective to clarify that certain takeover law provisions, in particular on parallel acquisitions and price determination, should be applied to mergers and, in parallel, to divisions in order to realise not only the principle of equal treatment under merger law, but also the principle of equal treatment under capital market law and takeover law. This also ensures that the legal technique does not lead to a breach of value and a lack of protection to the detriment of the shareholders of one of the companies involved.

b) Does the transaction trigger the duty to make an offer for the existing shareholders of Bank Austria AG – that is, in favour of the shareholders of the company that transferred the corporate assets?

This is the decisive question for the clarification of the relationship between takeover law and merger law. The Takeover Commission affirmed an obligation to make an offer in favour of the existing shareholders of Bank Austria AG as a result of the merger.[39]

The decisive argument is that, according to the wording of the law, which speaks of acquisition, the legal technique by which control is achieved is not decisive. This means that, in the case of the merger of a company into a listed company, a mandatory offer must always be made if a new shareholder controls the listed company as a result of the merger, thus acquiring a new controlling shareholding in the listed company.[40] However, the Takeover Commission also affirmed the application of takeover law as a result of a merger in the event that the listed company ceases to exist and therefore, according to the wording of the law, no change of control can take place in this company.

According to the purpose of the Takeover Act, however, a mandatory offer must also be made to the community of shareholders of the transferring company who are now newly exposed to a controlling shareholder, analogous to the acquisition of

37 Austrian Takeover Commission, 12 September 2000 – 2000/1/4-171, 14.

38 Durstberger, 'Discussion report', p. 64.

39 Austrian Takeover Commission, 12 September 2000 – 2000/1/4-171, 16; Kalss and Winner, 'Umgründungs- und Übernahmerecht. Versuch einer Synthese' 56.

40 Kalss and Winner, 'Umgründungs- und Übernahmerecht. Versuch einer Synthese' 57; Winner, 'Übernahmeangebot bei Verschmelzung?', p. 45, 56.

control of a continuing acquiring company. Are the shareholders exposed to a controlling shareholder or a controlling shareholder group for the first time after the transaction? If this is the case, takeover law must also be applied as a result of the merger, regardless of the direction of the merger. In this case, the mandatory offer is not to be made to all shareholders, but only to those shareholders who are exposed to a controlling shareholder for the first time.

The Austrian Takeover Commission has therefore taken a very far-reaching view on this issue and, according to that Commission, the decisive question is whether control previously existed and whether this has changed for the respective group of shareholders. It must therefore be examined whether the shareholder groups are now each faced with a new controlling shareholder. In the opinion of the Takeover Commission, the affected shareholders of a listed company must therefore, in the event of a change of control in the course of a merger, be offered not only an appropriate exchange ratio but also the opportunity to withdraw from the company in return for a cash consideration. The direction of the merger is irrelevant to this question.[41] It is clear from this that takeover law is not only intended to ensure equal treatment of shareholders, but also offers protection from being involuntarily integrated into a group for listed companies and recognises this additional right of withdrawal in the event of a change of control.

The Takeover Commission recognised this not only in the original proceedings[42], but also in further proceedings. The Austrian Takeover Commission consistently adhered to this legal opinion and also required the submission of an offer to the shareholders in the case of a merger of an Austrian company into a French company, where as a result a shareholder of the French company was the new controlling shareholder.[43] In another decision, the Takeover Commission determined that an upstream merger of a subsidiary into its parent company triggers a mandatory offer.[44]

Under German law, the change of control is, according to the prevailing literature, only recognised if a shareholder receives more than 30 per cent of the shares in the acquiring company as a result of the merger and thus acquires control as usual.[45] However, the case where only the former shareholders of the transferring company are now faced with a new controlling shareholder in the acquiring company is

[41] Kalss and Winner, 'Umgründungs- und Übernahmerecht. Versuch einer Synthese' 60; Winner, 'Übernahmeangebot bei Verschmelzung?', p. 45, 57.

[42] Austrian Takeover Commission, 12 September 2000 – 2000/1/4-171, 20 et seq.

[43] Winner, 'Übernahmeangebot bei Verschmelzung?', p. 45, 61.

[44] Austrian Takeover Commission, 8 May 2013 – 2013/2/1-146, 146; C. Diregger, 'Zusammenspiel von Übernahmerecht und Verschmelzungsrecht bei Sachverhalten mit internationalem Bezug – ein Grenzfall', in F. Schuhmacher et al. (eds.), *Festschrift für Josef Aicher* (Vienna: Verlag Österreich, 2012), p. 37.

[45] Rothenfußer, 'Kontrollerlangung', § 11 mn. 124; M. Schlitt, '§ 35 WpÜG', in W. Goette and M. Habersack (eds.), *Münchener Kommentar zum Aktiengesetz* (Munich: C.H. Beck, 2021), 5th ed., § 35 WpÜG mn. 133 et seq.

rejected. The reason given is simply the lack of regulation of such a partial offer and the fact that an incorrect application would not be in line with the prohibition of analogy in administrative criminal law. However, the lack of protection in these arrangements is clearly recognised, but at the same time only understood as a legal policy problem.[46]

In any case, it is advisable from a legal policy perspective – even at the European level – to establish a clear regulation on the applicability or non-applicability of takeover law as the result of a merger on both the shareholders of the acquiring company and the shareholders of the transferring company. The applicability of the supplementary provisions of takeover law should be stipulated in the law – that is, in addition to the offering of shares as non-cash consideration, a cash alternative should also be provided for. Furthermore, the application of the provisions on pricing under takeover law, including the consideration of prior acquisitions and parallel transactions, should be stipulated.

c) Does a merger trigger the duty to make an offer for the minority shareholders of a listed subsidiary of a company involved in the merger?

If the merger can already lead to a change of control on the part of the shareholders of both the acquiring and the transferring company, it is only logical that a merger affecting the parent or ultimate parent company can also lead to a change of control in listed subsidiaries.[47] If there is a change of control in a listed subsidiary, a mandatory offer to the non-controlling shareholders of the subsidiary has to be made.

14.8 DELISTING OFFER

A special form of takeover law regulation applies to mergers between a listed company and a non-listed company. There is no regulation for this at the European level. However, there – permissibly – are national regulations. For example, in addition to a general voluntary delisting pursuant to Section 38 of the Austrian Stock Exchange Act (*Börsegesetz*),[48] Austrian law provides for special regulations for so-called cold delistings, which is the merger or division of a listed company into a non-listed company. In the event of such a transaction, a mandatory takeover offer with special requirements pursuant to Section 26a of the Austrian Takeover Act must be made, regardless of whether the transaction involves a change of control or not. The reason for this is that the company leaves the "protective radar" of takeover law and loses easy tradability of its shares. In addition to the resolution by the Annual General Meeting

[46] Rothenfußer, 'Kontrollerlangung', § 11 mn. 125 et seq.

[47] Austrian Takeover Commission, 12 September 2000 – 2000/1/4-171, 20 f.

[48] See P. Fidler, '§ 38 BörseG', in S. Kalss, M. Oppitz, U. Torggler and M. Winner (eds.), *Börsegesetz 2018 – Marktmissbrauchsverordnung Kommentar* (Vienna: Linde, 2018), §38 mn. 1 et seq.

and the associated publicity, the core of the provision is the necessity of a takeover bid and control by the Takeover Commission as well as the material price fixing.[49] At the European level, a clear regulation is also recommended for the termination of the listing and the loss of the protection of takeover law; in any case, the obligation to make an offer should be required.

14.9 SUMMARY

The Takeover Directive does not address the special features of reorganisations by way of merger or division, nor does the Company Law Directive with its provisions on mergers or divisions address the first-time acquisition of control or change of control in one of the companies involved in the transaction.

Neither does the Takeover Directive absorb merger and division transactions nor does the Company Law Directive conclusively regulate such change of control transactions. Contrary to early opinions in the literature, the two areas of law exist side by side and must therefore be harmonised.

Even if not all elements of a public offer are present in a merger or division, it is appropriate to apply supplementary takeover law provisions to a merger or division in order to avoid circumvention solely on the basis of legal technique, in particular to determine the value of the consideration in order to ensure an appropriate exchange ratio.

In particular, pre-acquisitions and parallel acquisitions within a certain period prior to a merger or division should be included in the price determination.

Any existing share price must also be taken into account when determining the exchange ratio.

In any case, takeover law regulations must be applied if the shareholders of the acquiring company are faced with a new controlling shareholder for the first time. This must apply to all companies involved, not only to the acquiring company, but also to the transferring company.

The company law regulations should therefore be supplemented by measures under takeover law; in particular, an additional right of withdrawal due to a change of control should be recognised. The few cases known from practice in Austria, Germany and Switzerland should therefore be recognised and used as a basis for a clarifying regulation.

In addition, a public offer should also be made mandatory in the event of a delisting in order to provide adequate protection for the loss of takeover rights and tradability. Here, too, there are already models at national level.

49 Kalss, *Verschmelzung*, § 225 mn. 72 et seq., § 12 SpaltG mn. 62 et seq.

15

The Changing Ownership Landscape

Anna Christie

15.1 INTRODUCTION

The Takeover Directive placed considerable power and trust in the hands of target shareholders to decide a takeover bid, in the form of the board neutrality rule.[1] However, the identity of these shareholders, and the ownership landscape of European companies more broadly, has fundamentally changed in the twenty years that have passed since the adoption of the Takeover Directive. The growth of institutional investors and asset managers has impacted companies across the globe, including in Europe. The shift from active fund management to passive index funds also changes the incentives of shareholders considerably. Hedge fund activism was virtually unheard of in Europe when the Takeover Directive was adopted in 2004, but there are now cases of M&A activism across the various Member States. Foreign investment in European companies also affects takeover bids, with such investors potentially acting as facilitators in cross-border mergers and acquisitions.

Overall, the willingness of shareholders to tender their shares to a hostile bidder can differ quite dramatically depending on the type of shareholder and the size of their shareholding. The major changes to the shareholder base in European companies can have a significant impact on the likelihood of success of a takeover bid and therefore whether there is an effective European market for corporate control as the Takeover Directive originally envisaged.

During various high-profile and controversial takeovers, such as Kraft's hostile bid for Cadbury in the UK in 2009, the composition of the shareholder base has become a focal point for public debate. In that particular case, the former Chairman of Cadbury, Roger Carr, insisted that 'the seeds of destruction for this company lay in its [shareholder] register'.[2] Namely, it was the dramatic shift in the composition of

[1] Article 9 of Directive 2004/25/EC of the European Parliament and of the Council of 21 April 2004 on Takeover Bids (the 'Takeover Directive').

[2] Jenny Wiggins, 'The inside story of the Cadbury takeover', 12 March 2010, www.ft.com/content/1e5450d2-2be5-11df-8033-00144feabdc0.

the shareholder register, from long-term institutional investors to short-term merger arbitrageurs, that sealed Cadbury's fate and ultimately enabled Kraft to succeed in its hostile bid. In the aftermath of the bid, this led to pressure to disenfranchise such 'short-term' shareholders from determining the outcome of takeovers.

Certain shareholder protections enshrined in the Takeover Directive can also improve the ability of shareholders, particularly activist hedge funds, to successfully oppose takeovers, usually with the intention of driving up the bid price or soliciting a more attractive offer. The interplay between (foreign) institutional investors and activist hedge funds can also potentially alter the market for corporate control in ways that were not envisaged when the Takeover Directive was adopted.

This chapter is structured as follows. Section 15.2 discusses the first fundamental change to the ownership landscape in Europe – the growth of institutional investors. There is a particular focus on the rise of asset managers and the shift from active to passive asset management, in the form of index funds. The impact of the concentration of asset managers as the largest shareholders in many European companies is considered. Fundamentally, the role of these institutional investors, asset managers and index funds in takeover bids in Europe is assessed, although there is a general lack of disclosure from such funds regarding the specific actions they take. In theory, index funds should not sell their shares during the offer period, as this goes against the principle of indexation. Whether such fund managers alternatively exercise voice (rather than exit) in the form of M&A stewardship is also unclear. Overall, it seems that the growth of institutional investment would facilitate the European market for corporate control, but the shift to index funds may have the opposite effect. Additionally, asset managers do not generally appear to take an active role in M&A stewardship when takeover bids are either contemplated or ongoing. Section 15.3 examines hedge fund activism, and specifically the various forms of M&A hedge fund activism that take place in European companies. Three major forms of M&A activism are discussed – the activist hedge fund pushing for a takeover, opposing a takeover and launching a takeover bid itself. It is considered how squeeze-out rules in the Takeover Directive may facilitate activist opposition to a takeover to practise 'bumpitrage', where the bid is opposed to agitate for a superior takeover offer. The more recent phenomenon of activist merger arbitrage is also analysed, where there can be major shifts in the shareholder base of a company during the course of a takeover bid. The sale of shares from long-term shareholders to short-term merger arbitrageurs during the bid process has been particularly controversial, leading to national proposals to disenfranchise such shareholders. Finally, the interaction between institutional investor ownership and hedge fund activism is briefly discussed. Section 15.4 considers the impact of increased levels of foreign investment in European companies, and how foreign investors may serve to facilitate a European market for corporate control, as originally envisaged by the Takeover Directive. It discusses the rise of foreign ownership in European countries and how bidders and also hedge fund activists are more likely to target firms with high levels of foreign institutional ownership. Section 15.5 considers the role that cash-settled derivatives played as a takeover instrument, enabling potential acquirers to build hidden ownership stakes in listed companies. It concludes by discussing national and European reforms to ensure derivatives and other similar financial instruments must be included in disclosure obligations. Finally, Section 15.6 considers private capital and the growth of alternative sources of financing for companies. The reduction in the number of listed companies in Europe is highlighted, as well as the increased prevalence of private equity deals. The attitude of institutional investors and asset managers to such private equity deals is also discussed. Section 15.7 concludes.

15.2 INSTITUTIONAL INVESTORS, ASSET MANAGERS AND INDEX FUNDS

15.2.1 *The Growth of Institutional Investors in Europe*

During the twenty years that have passed since the adoption of the Takeover Directive, the proportion of shares of European companies that are held by institutional investors has grown considerably. Prior to the adoption of the Takeover Directive, studies reported that Continental Europe featured large blockholdings, with the median largest voting block for listed industrial companies being close to 50 per cent in various Member States, such as Austria, Belgium, Germany, Italy and the Netherlands.[3] Although institutional ownership can vary considerably across Member States, the clear overall trend is increased levels of institutional investor ownership, even in jurisdictions which traditionally featured large controlling shareholders. It has been reported by the OECD that institutional investor ownership still exhibits large cross-country differences, with countries such as the UK having more than 60 per cent institutional investor ownership, whereas large European economies such as France, Germany, Italy and Spain range between 20 and 30 per cent of shares held by institutional investors.[4]

Within each jurisdiction, the level of institutional investor holdings can also vary considerably among different types of companies. Often the most economically

[3] Marco Becht and Ailsa Röell, 'Blockholdings in Europe: An International Comparison' (1999) 43 *European Economic Review* 1049, 1052, noting that the median large voting block in Austria was 52 per cent, in Belgium 50.6 per cent (45.1 per cent in the BEL20), in Germany 45.1 per cent (52.1 per cent in the DAX30), in Italy 54.53 per cent and in the Netherlands 9.9 per cent. France and Spain were reported to have smaller blockholdings, at 20 per cent and 34.2 per cent, respectively. The UK was an outlier with the median largest voting block comprising only 9.9 per cent.

[4] OECD, 'Institutional Shareholding, Common Ownership and Productivity: A Cross-Country Analysis', Economics Department Working Papers no. 1769, 4 August 2023, https://one.oecd.org/document/ECO/WKP(2023)23/en/pdf, 8, citing Alejandra Medina, Adriana De La Cruz and Yun Tang, 'Corporate ownership and concentration', OECD Corporate Governance Working Paper, 2022, based on OECD-ORBIS Corporate Finance dataset, Refinitiv.

significant companies which are constituents of major indices have higher levels of institutional investor ownership. For example, in Germany, institutional investors now hold 58.2 per cent of shares of DAX 40 constituents.[5] In large European companies more generally, data collected by Luca Enriques and Giovanni Strampelli illustrated that leading institutional investors are among the largest shareholders in most constituents of the Euro Stoxx 50 index.[6] Increasing ownership concentration has been demonstrated, with the top institutional shareholder (as at April 2022) owning on average 6.54 per cent of equity, the top three institutional shareholders owning 14.09 per cent, and the top five institutional shareholders 18.5 per cent.[7]

15.2.2 *The Rise of Asset Managers and Passive Index Funds*

In addition to the growth of institutional investors, in the years following the 2008 financial crisis, there has been a dramatic shift from active to passive asset management, with capital gravitating towards index mutual funds and exchange traded funds.[8] Although the active fund industry remains relatively fragmented, the passive index fund industry is extremely concentrated.[9] In terms of stewardship and investor engagement, this aggregation of shareholdings among the largest asset managers who offer passive index funds at the lowest cost can potentially be seen as a positive development, as the concentration of power can to some extent overcome the collective action problems that have plagued retail investors.[10] In terms of takeover bids, it is an open question what impact

5 'Who owns the German DAX? The Ownership Structure of the German DAX in 2022', a joint study of S&P Global Market Intelligence and DIRK – Deutscher Investor Relations Verband, Tenth Edition, 2023, www.dirk.org/wp-content/uploads/2023/06/DAX-Studie-Wem-gehoert-die-Deutschland-AG-10.0.pdf, 8.

6 It was noted by the authors that the Euro Stoxx 50 Index comprises 50 blue-chip stocks from eight Eurozone countries (Belgium, Finland, France, Germany, Ireland, Italy, the Netherlands and Spain) so is the most representative index of large European listed companies. *See* Luca Enriques and Giovanni Strampelli, 'The Dialogue Between Corporations and Institutional Investors: An Introduction' ECGI Working Paper No 725/2023, January 2024, http://ssrn.com/abstract_id=4519073, at 5; Luca Enriques and Giovanni Strampelli, The 'Dialogue Between Corporations and Institutional Investors: An Introduction', in Luca Enriques and Giovanni Strampelli (eds.), *Board-Shareholder Dialogue: Policy Debate, Legal Constraints and Best Practices* (Cambridge University Press, 2024).

7 Enriques and Strampelli (n 6).

8 *See* Lucian Bebchuk and Scott Hirst, 'Index Funds and the Future of Corporate Governance: Theory, Evidence, and Policy' (2019) 119 *Columbia Law Review* 2029, 2033; Jill Fisch, Assaf Hamdani and Steven Davidoff Solomon, 'The New Titans of Wall Street: A Theoretical Framework for Passive Investors' (2019) 168 *University of Pennsylvania Law Review* 17, 19.

9 John C. Coates, 'The Future of Corporate Governance Part I: The Problem of Twelve', Harvard Public Law Working Paper No. 19-07, 2018, 2, https://ssrn.com/abstract=3247337.

10 See generally Bernard S. Black, 'Agents Watching Agents: The Promise of Institutional Investor Voice' (1992) 39 *UCLA Law Review* 811 for a discussion on the promise and limitations of major institutional investors.

such asset managers have on the bid process and thus on the European market for corporate control.

In the United States, the 'Big Three' asset managers – BlackRock, Vanguard and State Street – are now the largest investors in the vast majority of economically significant companies. This is increasingly also the case in many European jurisdictions,[11] where the transition from active to passive investing can similarly be seen (albeit not to the same extent as the United States). By 2020, around 26 per cent of assets under management in the United Kingdom, and up to 20 per cent of assets under management in Europe were held in passive index funds.[12] As at the end of 2023, Morningstar data shows that 26.7 per cent of assets under management in Europe were attributable to passive strategies. This figure has more than doubled from ten years ago, when the equivalent figure was 12.3 per cent of assets under management.[13] Other European regulation, such as MiFID II, is also likely to contribute to the growth of passive investing in Europe.

It tends to be the largest companies that are most impacted by this shift to passive index investing. In the US, the Big Three control more than 20 per cent of the shares of the average S&P 500 company.[14] In Europe, data collected by Luca Enriques and Giovanni Strampelli showed that, as at the end of April 2022, the percentage of shares held by the Big Three asset managers in Stoxx 50 companies amounted to 8.31 per cent.[15] In large German companies index funds hold 24 per cent of institutional holdings in DAX 40 constituents, which amounts to around 14 per cent of DAX 40 shares overall.[16]

15.2.3 *The Role of Institutional Investors and Index Funds in Takeover Bids*

Institutional investors, especially large asset managers, are the pivotal voters in proxy contests in the United States.[17] In the same vein, given that the board neutrality rule in Article 9 of the Takeover Directive places the decision on takeovers in the hands of target company shareholders, institutional investors (given their prevalence) are likely to also be the pivotal voters in many if not most European takeovers.

[11] Anna Christie, 'The Agency Costs of Sustainable Capitalism' (2021) 55 *UC Davis Law Review* 875, 879.

[12] Ibid., at 888, citing Steve Johnson, 'Passive Funds' Share of European Investment Market Jumps to 20%', *Financial Times*, 7 December 2020, www.ft.com/content/0b5325da-585f-41ad-8267-0741e9693a7a.

[13] Valerio Baselli, 'Are ETFs Taking Over Europe Too?', *Morningstar*, 19 February 2024, www.morningstar.co.uk/uk/news/246333/are-etfs-taking-over-europe-too.aspx.

[14] Lucian Bebchuk and Scott Hirst, 'The Specter of the Giant Three' (2019) 99 *Boston University Law Review* 721 at 724.

[15] Enriques and Strampelli (n 6), at 5.

[16] 'Who owns the German DAX?' (n 5), at 11.

[17] See generally Christie (n 11).

Therefore, it will ultimately be for institutional investors, and in particular large asset managers, to determine whether or not takeover bids will succeed.[18]

The role that asset managers of passive index funds play in takeover bids is less clear. The rationale underpinning the role that such asset managers can play in governance is premised upon the assumption that they must use voice to influence as they cannot exit the stock.[19] Theoretically, if a takeover bid is made for a target company that is part of a stock market index, passive index funds cannot sell their shares during the bid process, in contrast to the fund managers of active funds. This is because selling their shares during the offer process would amount to an active decision on the part of the fund to exit the stock, and thus lose track of the index. This goes against the fundamental principle of indexation and passive investing. Therefore, if we assume that fund managers of passive index funds adhere to these principles, we would not expect passive index funds to tender their shares until the very final stage of the bid process, if at all. If this is actually the case in practice, we might expect the rise of passive investing to have a negative impact on the likelihood of successful takeovers of listed companies – especially large cap companies that are constituents of major indices. Therefore, while the rise of (active) institutional investor ownership might make European companies more attractive takeover targets, the rise of indexation could potentially have the opposite effect and impede an active European market for corporate control.

Such a result has indeed been documented in an empirical study from Germany, which analysed the impact of index fund and ETF ownership on the success of takeover bids.[20] Based on a sample of 323 takeover offers of publicly listed German companies between 2006 and 2018, the authors documented a significant negative impact of index fund and ETF ownership on takeover success. It was shown that the fraction of outstanding shares tendered decreased with the increase in the stake of index funds and ETFs. It was therefore suggested that indexation weakened the German market for corporate control. A real-life example presented by the authors was the takeover offer by private equity firms Bain Capital and Cinven for STADA Arzeimittel AG, a pharmaceutical company listed on the German stock exchange in Frankfurt. Because STADA was part of the German MDAX index at the time of the bid, index funds held 7.6 per cent of the shares. In the German press, the high levels of index fund ownership of the company, combined with increased ownership by hedge funds, was identified as a reason why the bidders had difficulty reaching the requisite ownership threshold to succeed in their bid.[21] Nevertheless, the takeover

[18] On the role of merger arbitrageurs, see Section 15.3.3.

[19] See generally, Albert O. Hirschman, *Exit, Voice, and Loyalty: Responses to Decline in Firms, Organizations and States* (Harvard University Press, 1970).

[20] Ludwig Dobmeier, Renata Lavrova and Bernhard Schwetzler, 'Index fund and ETF ownership and the German market for corporate control', Working Paper 3 September 2019, https://papers.ssrn.com/sol3/papers.cfm?abstract_id=3443622.

[21] Ibid., at 3.

bid ultimately succeeded when the bidder reduced the threshold for the bid to succeed and increased the takeover premium. Despite the conclusion that index fund ownership weakened the German market for corporate control, the paper also analysed the propensity of index funds and ETFs to tender their shares during the bid period. Here, the authors found a 25 per cent decrease in the average ownership stake of these funds during the acceptance period. Therefore, it is clear that at least *some* index funds sell their shares during the offer period. As a result, it is unclear (in the absence of additional empirical studies) how often, and under what specific conditions, index funds sell their shares during the process of a takeover bid.

It has been acknowledged by law firms involved in such takeovers that index funds do sometimes sell their shares during the offer period, even though at first glance it may seem that they cannot sell their shares. Overall, the behaviour of the asset managers of such funds will depend on how strictly a fund applies its mandate. According to law firm Herbert Smith Freehills, 'A fund which seeks to apply its mandate strictly will not accept at all and will wait to be compulsorily acquired. However, some funds are willing to consider selling on market or into a bid to maximise benefits for their investors once it is clear that the bid is going to be successful.'[22] Similarly, Kirkland and Ellis have noted that 'The policies and practices of index and quantitative funds with respect to participation in tender offers vary widely. Many such funds will not tender into an offer where the market price is above the offer price.'[23] Overall, apart from these anecdotal observations on the part of law firms, there is very little published information on the actual behaviour of index funds in takeover offer situations, either as a general matter or in terms of specific disclosures made by individual asset managers or funds themselves.

15.2.4 *M&A: A Black Hole in Stewardship?*

Although it is not obvious whether large asset managers, especially those managing passive index funds, are selling their shares during offer periods, or tendering their shares at the conclusion of the bid, large asset managers are particularly known for their investor stewardship and corporate engagement. As noted earlier, the concentration of power in the hands of global asset managers is likely beneficial for investor stewardship, as it potentially overcomes the collective action problems that plague retail investors. However, stewardship around portfolio companies' M&A activity appears to be virtually non-existent.

[22] Robert Nicholson, Herbert Smith Freehills, 'Jack Bogle's legacy and the evolution of index funds in control transactions', 31 May 2019, www.herbertsmithfreehills.com/insights/2019-05/jack-bogles-legacy-and-the-evolution-of-index-funds-in-control-transactions.

[23] David Fox, Kirkland & Ellis LLP, 'Some Tender Offer Quirks', Harvard Law School Forum on Corporate Governance, 2 November 2009, https://corpgov.law.harvard.edu/2009/11/02/some-tender-offer-quirks/.

In 2022, the Pensions and Investment Research Consultants (PIRC) in the United Kingdom called for a review of investor stewardship of M&A activity, arguing that investor stewardship in relation to mergers and acquisitions is a 'black hole' in the UK's governance framework and that the UK Stewardship Code should extend to M&A.[24] They recommended that new guidance on M&A-related disclosures should be incorporated into the next iteration of the UK's Stewardship Code, arguing that 'changes in ownership and control represent one of the most fundamental transformations that companies go through. It ought to be an area of heightened stewardship activity. Instead, we see a black hole in stewardship.'[25] This observation is not limited to the UK; it could apply universally across Europe.

15.2.4.1 M&A in Stewardship Codes

Mergers and acquisitions do not feature in Stewardship Codes across Europe. A search of leading text on Stewardship Codes around the world resulted in virtually no results for investor stewardship on takeovers or M&A.[26] Indeed, most Stewardship Codes do not mention mergers and acquisitions at all. When takeovers are mentioned, the references tend to be quite brief. For example, the Dutch Stewardship Code does reference mergers and acquisitions, but only briefly in Principle 2, noting that 'Asset owners and asset managers monitor their Dutch listed investee companies on material issues, including, but not limited to [...] corporate actions such as mergers and acquisitions. Material issues are those matters that are likely to significantly affect the company's ability to create long-term value.'[27] It is clear, therefore, that engaging with companies on takeover bids or mergers and acquisitions more generally has not been a key focus for any Stewardship Codes across Europe. Therefore, the observation by PIRC that it represents a 'black hole in stewardship' seems to be justified.

15.2.4.2 M&A in Voting Bulletins and Stewardship Reports

Consistent with the lack of references to mergers and acquisitions in Stewardship Codes across Europe, there are also very few references to takeovers in asset manager voting bulletins and investor stewardship reports detailing corporate engagement. Despite the fact that investor stewardship departments of large asset managers produce ever greater reporting on responsible investment and stewardship,

24 Pensions & Investment Research Consultants Ltd, 'New PIRC report on Democratic Deficit in Stewardship', September 2022, www.pirc.co.uk/wp-content/uploads/2022/09/PIRC-analysis-of-takeovers-turnout-and-use-of-derivatives-September-2022.pdf.

25 Ibid.

26 See generally Dionysia Katelouzou and Dan W. Puchniak, *Global Shareholder Stewardship* (Cambridge University Press, 2022).

27 Dutch Stewardship Code, available at www.eumedion.nl/en/public/knowledgenetwork/best-practices/2018-07-dutch-stewardship-code-final-version.pdf.

discussion on their approach to changes in the control of companies is extremely limited. For example, when searching publications from BlackRock Investment Stewardship, such as stewardship reports, voting spotlights and vote bulletins, there is scant reference to changes of control. Most of the references to takeovers in Europe relate to the use of anti-takeover defences in certain countries.[28] In terms of actual transactions, there is virtually nothing in the various stewardship reports or vote bulletins regarding mergers and acquisitions. This finding is not limited to BlackRock. The position is similar for other large US and European asset managers. To use an example of a European asset manager, Legal & General Investment Management (LGIM) break down their corporate engagement into 'E', 'S' and 'G', and M&A forms only 2 per cent of its governance 'G' engagement.[29]

Despite the lack of disclosures on individual transactions, BlackRock does have some general information on takeovers in its Global Principles on Investment Stewardship, as follows:

> In assessing mergers, asset sales, or other special transactions, BlackRock's primary consideration is the long-term economic interests of our clients as shareholders. Boards proposing a transaction need to clearly explain the economic and strategic rationale behind it. We will review a proposed transaction to determine the degree to which it can enhance long-term shareholder value. We find long-term investors like our clients typically benefit when proposed transactions have the unanimous support of the board and have been negotiated at arm's length. We may seek reassurance from the board that the financial interests of executives and/or board members in a given transaction have not adversely affected their ability to place shareholders' interests before their own.
>
> As a matter of sound governance practice, shareholders should have a right to dispose of company shares in the open market without unnecessary restriction ... In our view, shareholders are broadly capable of making decisions in their own best interests. We encourage any so-called 'shareholder rights plans' proposed by a board to be subject to shareholder approval upon introduction and periodically thereafter.[30]

However, it is not clear how these Global Principles translate into BlackRock's engagement with portfolio companies, as very few disclosures are made. There are occasional exceptions; for example, in 2020 BlackRock issued a voting bulletin regarding its vote against the discharge of the Board and President of Finnish utility firm, Fortum Oyj, for undertaking an acquisition that increased its exposure to coal-fired power.[31] However, there are countervailing pressures on asset managers such as

[28] See Section 15.2.4.3.
[29] Legal and General Investment Management, Investment Stewardship, www.lgim.com/uk/en/responsible-investing/investment-stewardship/.
[30] BlackRock Investment Stewardship Global Principles, January 2024, www.blackrock.com/corporate/literature/fact-sheet/blk-responsible-investment-engprinciples-global.pdf, 9–10.
[31] BlackRock Investment Stewardship Group, Voting Bulletin: Fortum Oyj, 23 April 2020, www.blackrock.com/corporate/literature/press-release/blk-vote-bulletin-fortum-apr-2020.pdf, 2.

BlackRock from 'anti-ESG' parties. For example, in a letter to BlackRock from the attorneys general of nineteen US states, specific reference was made to BlackRock voting to penalise the board of Fortum for investing in coal.[32] Nevertheless, statements are not made by BlackRock regarding its voting rationale on M&A that does not involve ESG issues either. M&A does not therefore seem to be the focus of investor stewardship, at least in terms of what is publicly reported in the media and in stewardship reports and voting bulletins.

Although it is not always obvious how (or if) large asset managers are influencing takeovers from an investor stewardship perspective, on occasion they have written to boards during takeover attempts. For example, during the proposed acquisition of the UK pharmaceutical company AstraZeneca by its US rival Pfizer in 2014, both BlackRock and LGIM wrote to the AstraZeneca board, expressing views about the potential takeover. BlackRock (which owned 8 per cent of AstraZeneca and 6.8 per cent of Pfizer) backed AstraZeneca's rejection of Pfizer's bid but urged the board to re-engage in talks with Pfizer to seek a higher price.[33] Other institutional investors, such as Aberdeen Asset Management and Fidelity, similarly supported the board's rejection of the bid.[34] On the other hand, other institutional investors, such as LGIM, urged the company's board to reverse its rejection of the deal.[35] This is a rare occasion where the large asset managers' positions on a potential takeover bid have been made public during the bid itself. In most instances, their positions have not been disclosed. Even on the rare occasions where asset managers have expressed a public opinion, there is a lack of disclosure regarding what factors sway their votes one way or another. It would be helpful if asset managers disclosed their voting rationale on takeovers in their voting bulletins, in the same manner in which they disclose their voting rationale for shareholder proposals.

15.2.4.3 Anti-takeover Defences

One area where institutional investors have long been vocal is anti-takeover defences. Indeed, institutional investors can largely be credited with dismantling defensive measures in many companies in the US. Similarly in Europe, large asset managers such as BlackRock make their opposition to takeover defences extremely

[32] Letter to Larry Fink of BlackRock from the attorneys general of Arizona, Arkansas, Alabama, Georgia, Idaho, Indiana, Kansas, Kentucky, Louisiana, Mississippi, Missouri, Montana, Nebraska, Ohio, Oklahoma, South Carolina, Texas, Utah, West Virginia, www.texasattorney general.gov/sites/default/files/images/executive-management/BlackRock%20Letter.pdf at 5.

[33] Hester Plumridge, 'AstraZeneca Shareholder Backs Board Rejection of Pfizer Bid', *The Wall Street Journal*, 22 May 2014, www.wsj.com/articles/astrazeneca-shareholder-blackrock-sides-with-board-on-rejecting-pfizer-bid-1400791061.

[34] Ibid.

[35] Hester Plumridge, 'Legal & General Urges AstraZeneca to Engage with Pfizer', *The Wall Street Journal*, 21 May 2014, www.wsj.com/articles/SB10001424052702303749904579575543066 735038.

clear. For example, in BlackRock's proxy voting guidelines for Europe, they highlight European Member States that permit forms of takeover defence, such as Belgium, France, Luxembourg, Switzerland and the Netherlands, and stress that they will vote against any company proposals that can be used as a takeover defence.[36] Therefore, even in Member States that may have chosen to take advantage of the opt-out nature of the board neutrality rule in Article 9 of the Takeover Directive, there may be considerable pressure from large institutional investors (together with activist hedge funds, if necessary) at companies where takeover defences are implemented.

15.3 HEDGE FUND ACTIVISM

The other major change in the shareholder landscape during the past twenty years since the adoption of the Takeover Directive is the emergence and growth of hedge fund activism. In the United States, activist hedge funds began making an impact on corporate governance in the early 2000s and had become a dominant force by the mid 2000s.[37] The growth of hedge fund activism in Europe occurred later than in the US, and compared with the US, Europe still has modest levels of hedge fund activism. However, the number of hedge fund activist campaigns in Europe has increased steadily in the years since the Takeover Directive was adopted. According to data by Lazard, there were twenty-eight activist campaigns across Europe in 2013, which had grown to fifty-seven in 2018.[38] By 2023, activism in Europe represented 28 per cent of all activism campaigns globally.[39] This rise in hedge fund activism has been attributed to the European shareholder base becoming more receptive to activist campaigns.[40]

Various studies have documented activist hedge fund interventions outside the US, including in Europe. For example, a study by Dionysia Katelouzou analysed activist campaigns in twenty-five countries between 2000 and 2010.[41] During this time period, UK companies were by far the most prevalent targets of activist campaigns in Europe, followed by Germany, France, the Netherlands, Italy and

36 BlackRock Investment Stewardship, 'Proxy voting guidelines for European, Middle Eastern, and African securities', January 2024, www.blackrock.com/corporate/literature/fact-sheet/blk-responsible-investment-guidelines-emea.pdf, 12 (generally), 28 (Belgium), 29 (France), 31 (Luxembourg), 33 (Switzerland) and 34 (the Netherlands).

37 Stuart L. Gillan and Laura T. Starks, 'The Evolution of Shareholder Activism in the United States' (2007) 19(1) *Journal of Applied Corporate Finance* 55, 68.

38 David Keohane and Harriet Agnew, 'Activist investors lay down challenge to corporate France', 29 November 2019, www.ft.com/content/02eedd92-11d3-11ea-a225-db2f231cfeae.

39 Cooley M&A, 'Cooley's 2023 Activism Year in Review: Wolf Packs at the Gate', 30 January 2024, https://cooleyma.com/2024/01/30/cooleys-2023-activism-year-in-review-wolfpacks-at-the-gate/.

40 Ibid.

41 Dionysia Katelouzou, 'Worldwide Hedge Fund Activism: Dimensions and Legal Determinants' (2015) 17(3) *University of Pennsylvania Journal of Business Law* 789.

Switzerland.[42] In another study of global hedge fund activism from 2000 to 2010 authored by Marco Becht, Julian Franks, Jeremy Grant and Hannes Wagner, activism was shown to be unevenly distributed across European jurisdictions. The UK had the most activist interventions by far (165 campaigns), followed by Germany (53 campaigns), Italy (42 campaigns), France (27 campaigns), the Netherlands (22 campaigns), Switzerland (19 campaigns) and Sweden (15 campaigns).[43] Although the institutional holdings of the targeted European companies (24 per cent) were much less on average than the institutional holdings of companies targeted in the US (77 per cent), the authors found that the level of institutional holdings were larger at targeted firms than in the population of companies overall in each respective jurisdiction.[44] Therefore, it would be reasonable to conclude that the increasing levels of institutional investment across Europe since the adoption of the Takeover Directive could further pave the way for increased levels of hedge fund activism.

15.3.1 *M&A Hedge Fund Activism*

M&A activism is one of the most common strategies for activist hedge funds. Indeed, there is an argument that the abnormal positive returns of activist hedge funds are largely explained by the ability of activists to force target firms into a takeover.[45] Unlike institutional investors, activist hedge funds are proactive rather than reactive, so they take a much more active role in M&A transactions compared with more traditional institutional investors and asset managers. While M&A is not often referenced by institutional investors or large asset managers, M&A is very firmly on the agenda of activist hedge funds.

In terms of M&A activist demands in Europe, according to Activist Insight data there were thirty-six M&A campaigns in Europe in 2015, which had risen to sixty-two M&A campaigns in 2021.[46] Most hedge fund activism M&A demands are in the UK, where such campaigns have risen steadily in the past two decades. In 2013, there were six M&A activist campaigns in the UK, and this had risen to twenty-seven M&A activist campaigns by 2019.[47] Other European jurisdictions have also seen increased levels of M&A activism, although the total number of campaigns is still modest. In France, there were two campaigns in 2013, and five campaigns in 2019.[48]

[42] Ibid., at 833.
[43] Marco Becht, Julian Franks, Jeremy Grant and Hannes F. Wagner, 'Returns to Hedge Fund Activism: An International Study' (2017) 30(9) *Review of Financial Studies* 2933, 2938 and 2939.
[44] Ibid.
[45] See generally Robin Greenwood and Michael Schor, 'Investor Activism and Takeovers' (2009) 92(3) *Journal of Financial Economics* 362.
[46] Insightia, 'Shareholder Activism in Europe 2022',www.insightia.com/europe2022/, 21.
[47] Insightia, 'Shareholder Activism in Europe 2021', www.activistinsight.com/research/Insightia_Europe2021.pdf, 7.
[48] Ibid., at 15.

In Germany, there were five campaigns in 2013, and eight campaigns in 2019.[49] Elliott Management – one of the earliest US activist funds to have operations in Europe – set up its London office in 1995. A significant portion of Elliott's European activism focuses on M&A, following its London office's initial merger arbitrage focus.[50]

M&A hedge fund activism takes three main forms. Firstly, activist hedge funds contribute to the market for corporate control most commonly by identifying potential takeover targets to be acquired by a third-party bidder and pushing for a takeover bid to be made.[51] Secondly, activist hedge funds may oppose takeovers (often with the motivation of increasing the price of the bid). Finally, and more rarely, activist hedge funds may go so far as to make takeover bids themselves, or in conjunction with other parties such as private equity funds.[52]

15.3.1.1 Pushing for a Takeover

The most common form of M&A hedge fund activism is when the activists push for a company to be acquired by a third-party bidder. There are various examples of this form of M&A activism in Europe. An early example from France is the British activist hedge fund TCI putting pressure on the Euronext exchange in 2006 to merge with its rivals Deutsche Börse or the New York Stock Exchange. At the time, 76 per cent of the voting rights in Euronext were controlled by international institutional investors, which was viewed as pivotal in facilitating Euronext's merger with the NYSE in 2007.[53] A more recent example from 2020 is Sweden's Alfa Laval making a tender offer for Finland's Neles. The takeover bid was announced with the support of Cevian Capital, a Swedish investment firm which is the largest activist in Europe. Cevian Capital was Neles' second largest shareholder with a 10.9 per cent stake. Often, in cases where hedge fund activists push for takeovers, other shareholders (sometimes other activist hedge funds) might oppose the deal. In this particular case, Neles' largest shareholder Valmet (which had a 14.9 per cent holding) opposed the takeover, stating, 'This is not in

49 Ibid., at 23.

50 Ronald Orol, 'How Elliott Management's Paul Singer Took Activist Investing Global', *The Street*, 1 June 2018, www.thestreet.com/investing/stocks/how-elliott-management-paul-singer-took-activism-global-14603404.

51 Anna L. Christie, 'The New Hedge Fund Activism: Activist Directors and the Market for Corporate Quasi-Control' (2019) 19(1) *Journal of Corporate Law Studies*, 1, 5.

52 *See* Nicole M. Boyson, Nickolay Gantchev and Anil Shivdasani, 'Activism Mergers' (2017) 126 *Journal of Financial Economics* 54, 64, noting that in their sample of 467 'activism mergers', the hedge fund that initiates the campaign is also the bidder in 76 (16 per cent) of cases. Activist bidders include well-known activist hedge funds, such as Carl Icahn, Elliott Associates and ValueAct.

53 Becht, Franks, Grant and Wagner (n 43), at 2944.

the interest of Neles or Neles' shareholders', adding that the company saw Neles as a 'long-term investment'.[54]

When an activist hedge fund supports a third-party bidder, the activist fund can potentially serve a useful role by credibly signalling whether a takeover bid is adequate, as the activist's incentives are most often aligned with those of the target shareholders. This can help to overcome limitations faced by other target firm shareholders in assessing the merits of an offer.[55]

15.3.1.2 Opposing a Takeover

In the United States, it is much more common for activist hedge funds to push for takeovers by third parties as opposed to opposing takeover bids by third parties.[56] However, in Europe there have been some high-profile instances of activist hedge funds opposing takeovers, often with the intention of pushing up the takeover bid price.

Perhaps the best-known case of activist hedge funds blocking a takeover in Europe is the campaign led by the British activist hedge fund, The Children's Investment Fund (TCI) in 2005 to block the takeover of the London Stock Exchange by Deutsche Börse. TCI believed the German exchange's stock would suffer if it acquired the London Stock Exchange. Together with multiple other activist funds, TCI ultimately succeeded in their campaign to block the takeover. The success of the campaign has been attributed to Deutsche Börse becoming a widely held company and the fact that 93 per cent of its investors were institutions, particularly foreign investors.[57]

Some provisions of the Takeover Directive can give activist hedge funds leverage to block takeovers. Article 15 of the Takeover Directive provides that Member States must introduce the possibility of a squeeze-out procedure after a takeover bid. Member States could opt to set a threshold between 90 and 95 per cent of the capital carrying voting rights. This procedure allows bidders to force minority shareholders to transfer their shares to them if they reach a certain threshold of shares. The rationale behind squeeze-out rights in the Takeover Bids Directive was to encourage takeovers while also protecting minority shareholders and affording

[54] Johannes Hellstrom and Tarmo Virki, 'Alfa Laval makes $2 billion bid for Finland's Neles, biggest owner sceptical', *Reuters*, 13 July 2020, www.reuters.com/article/business/alfa-laval-makes-2-billion-bid-for-finland-s-neles-biggest-owner-sceptical-idUSKCN24E1BB/.

[55] Alon Brav, Wei Jiang and Rongchen Li, 'Governance by Persuasion: Hedge Fund Activism and Market-Based Shareholder Influence', ECGI Finance Working Paper No 797/2021, January 2022, available at http://ssrn.com/abstract_id = 39955116, 53, citing Adrian Aycan Corum and Doron Levit, 'Corporate Control Activism' (2019) 133(1) *Journal of Financial Economics* 1.

[56] Anna Christie, 'Activist Directors: The Evolution of Hedge Fund Activism in the S&P 500' (2025) 57(2) *Connecticut Law Review* 523.

[57] Becht, Franks, Grant and Wagner (n 43), at 2944. For a discussion on foreign investors, see Section 15.4.

them equal treatment. The squeeze-out allows bidders to finalise a takeover while at the same time protecting minority shareholders by forcing a bidder to make a full takeover bid at an equitable price for all the remaining voting securities of the company. A by-product of improving minority shareholder rights and protections in the Takeover Bids Directive was that these provisions can give activist hedge funds leverage to block takeovers. Squeeze-out provisions usually mean that a shareholder controlling 10 per cent or more of the shares can block an acquisition. Activists can therefore potentially force the price of the bid higher with a blocking stake.

An example of a case where an activist hedge fund explicitly utilised a blocking stake was the hedge fund Alta Fox Capital cooperating with shareholders owning over 10 per cent to put forward a blocking stake. Alta Fox Capital opposed the 40 SEK per share tender offer by the British company Entain for the Swedish gaming company Enlabs, arguing it was worth at least 55 SEK per share. The hedge fund only had a 3.3 per cent stake itself, but grouped together with other shareholders to block the takeover. Alta Fox noted in an open letter signed by nearly 11 per cent of Enlab's shareholders: 'Alta Fox confidently believes we have the support to block a squeeze-out of minority shareholders, legal counsel to ensure their fair treatment under Swedish Law, and the determination to obtain a fair price that is reflective of Enlab's growth prospects.'[58] This resulted in an increased bid of 53 SEK per share (a 32 per cent increase from its initial offer), which Enlab's shareholders then accepted. This case illustrates how shareholders can use the squeeze-out rights in the Takeover Directive to block takeovers or drive up the offer price of a takeover bid.

High squeeze-out thresholds, such as 90 or 95 per cent, help US activist funds to engage in a practice known as 'bumpitrage'[59] in Europe. Activist hedge funds such as Elliott Management brought 'bumpitrage' to Europe, where activist funds build up a sufficient stake – either alone or with the support of other investors – to enable them to oppose takeover bids in order to agitate for a rise in the bid price.[60] Germany and France are known as popular jurisdictions for bumpitrage.[61] For example, Elliott opposed a friendly takeover of the French software company Altran, using bumpitrage to attempt to force its rival French bidder, Capgemini,

58 Morningstar, 'Entain's "Inadequate" Enlabs Bid Faces Opposition From Hedge Fund', *Morningstar*, 19 January 2021, www.morningstar.co.uk/uk/news/AN_1611039614810004800/entains-inadequate-enlabs-bid-faces-opposition-from-hedge-fund.aspx.

59 For a discussion of 'activist risk arbitrage' in the US, see generally Wei Jiang, Tao Li and Danqing Mei, 'Influencing Control: Jawboning in Risk Arbitrage' (2018) 73(6) *Journal of Finance* 2635.

60 Kate Burgess, 'Elliott looks to play "bumpitrage" over Poundland deal', *Financial Times*, 7 August 2016, www.ft.com/content/5c6cb3d0-5976-11e6-8d05-4eaa66292c32.

61 Activist Insight, 'Activist Investing in Europe 2018', www.skadden.com/-/media/files/publications/2018/11/activistinvestingineurope2018.pdf, 22; Insightia, 'Shareholder Activism in Europe 2021' www.activistinsight.com/research/Insightia_Europe2021.pdf, 14.

to increase its bid.[62] US activist funds have even practised bumpitrage where UK bids are structured as a scheme of arrangement, meaning that the activists would need the support of at least 25 per cent of shareholders to block the transaction. For example, Elliott bought a 17.5 per cent stake in the UK's Poundland in order to push up the price of a takeover bid from South African retailer Steinhoff.[63] Elliott later increased its stake to 22.7 per cent,[64] then to almost 25 per cent.[65] As a result, Steinhoff increased its offer price, which resulted in 98 per cent of votes (with 79 per cent of shareholders voting) in favour of the deal. Elliott also voted in favour.[66]

15.3.1.3 Activist Hedge Funds Launching Takeover Bids

It has often been said that activist hedge funds differ from corporate raiders because they 'tend to accumulate strict minority equity stakes and do not seek direct control'.[67] Whereas corporate raiders clearly operate in the market for corporate control, activist hedge funds created a 'market for corporate influence'.[68]

However, in some instances, in both the US and Europe, activist hedge funds launch takeover bids themselves. It has been suggested that there could be three reasons why activist hedge funds may become bidders for firms themselves. Firstly, activist hedge funds may simply be attempting to put firms into play in order for a higher offer to be made by a third-party bidder. Secondly, activist bidders could be attempting to signal that the target company is undervalued. Thirdly, the activist could genuinely seek to take over the firm in order to make operational changes and profit from increases in value.[69]

One recent example of an activist hedge fund attempting a hostile takeover itself is Inclusive Capital Partners (an ESG spin-off from ValueAct Capital Partners) making a hostile bid for the UK housebuilder Countryside, a FTSE 250 company, in 2022. Inclusive Capital Partners noted that 'we believe Countryside is meeting a

62 Sudip Kar-Gupta, Gwenaelle Barzic and Alexander Smith, 'Activist Elliott ends opposition to CapGemini's Altran bid', *Reuters*, 18 March 2020, www.reuters.com/article/altran-tech-ma-capgemini-elliott/update-1-activist-elliott-ends-opposition-to-capgeminis-altran-bid-idUSL8N2BB1YM/.

63 Ibid.

64 Tiisetso Motsoeneng, 'Activist investor Elliott ups stake in Steinhoff target Poundland', *Reuters*, 31 August 2016, www.reuters.com/article/business/activist-investor-elliott-ups-stake-in-steinhoff-target-poundland-idUSKCN11625O/.

65 Graham Ruddick, 'Poundland shareholders approve £610m takeover by Steinhoff', *The Guardian*, 7 September 2016, www.theguardian.com/business/2016/sep/07/poundland-shareholders-approve-takeover-by-steinhoff.

66 Ibid.

67 Alon Brav, Wei Jiang and Rongchen Li, 'Governance by Persuasion: Hedge Fund Activism and Market-Based Shareholder Influence, ECGI Finance Working Paper No 797/2021, January 2022, available at http://ssrn.com/abstract_id=39955116.

68 Brian R. Cheffins and John Armour, 'The Past, Present, and Future of Shareholder Activism by Hedge Funds' (2011) 37 *Journal of Corporation Law* 51.

69 Boyson, Gantchev and Shivdasani (n 52), at 67.

critical societal need and, as a holder of approximately 9% of the issued share capital of Countryside, In-Cap believes Countryside is best positioned to serve this role and to succeed as a private company under ownership of investors with a long-term investment approach'.[70] Inclusive Capital Partners was the second largest shareholder in Countryside, with a 9.2 per cent stake.[71] The hostile takeover by the activist hedge fund led to significant shareholder pressure to sell the company. The company then announced the following month that it was seeking a buyer, and it was ultimately acquired by Vistry Group.[72] Another factor that helped to facilitate the acquisition was Countryside's shareholder base which was made up of largely foreign (primarily US) shareholders, including another activist fund, Browning West, which held a 15.3 per cent stake.[73]

15.3.2 *Merger Arbitrageurs*

Risk arbitrageurs have long played a role in the market for corporate control.[74] Traditionally, however, risk arbitrageurs have simply taken more passive long positions in the target shares (and/or short positions in the bidder shares), in the hope that the takeover bid will succeed.[75] There is a spectrum of activist risk arbitrage. At one end of the spectrum, risk arbitrage funds can invest passively in takeover targets following bid announcements in the hope that the deal will ultimately succeed, and the share price will increase further.[76] At the other end of the spectrum, risk arbitrageurs take (varying degrees of) activist positions in relation to pushing for or opposing the takeover bid itself. Activist risk arbitrage is an even newer form of shareholder activism. Activist merger arbitrageurs have been described as 'virtually non-existent prior to 2000'.[77]

This investment strategy has been described positively as an important corporate governance mechanism in the United States, as activists often target takeover bids with low premiums and deals that are susceptible to managerial conflicts of interest (such as going-private transactions, transactions where management have an affiliation with the acquirers, or transactions where the CEO will receive an outsized

70 Henry Saker-Clark, 'Inclusive Capital eyes £1.5bn takeover move for housebuilder Countryside', Independent, 30 May 2022, www.independent.co.uk/business/inclusive-capital-eyes-ps1-5bn-takeover-move-for-housebuilder-countryside-b2090146.html.

71 George Hammond, 'US investor launches £1.5bn bid for Countryside', *Financial Times*, 30 May 2022, www.ft.com/content/953f1564-c79c-43c7-9fab-c46e14f97827.

72 George Hammond, 'Housebuilder Vistry agrees £1.25bn deal to buy rival Countryside', *Financial Times*, 5 September 2022, www.ft.com/content/70e4cd68-aeb4-40ba-ac8c-5892f330e978

73 See Section 15.4 on foreign investment.

74 Francesca Cornelli and David D. Li, 'Risk Arbitrage in Takeovers' (2002) 15(3) *Review of Financial Studies* 837.

75 Ibid.

76 Jiang, Li and Mei (n 59) at 2640.

77 Ibid., at 2636.

payment or 'golden parachute').[78] The activism of merger arbitrageurs can then result in a fairer deal for target shareholders, through an increased deal premium, or a more desirable acquisition from a different bidder.

Due to the recent nature of this form of activism, it is only in the years since the adoption of the Takeover Directive that activist hedge funds in Europe have combined risk arbitrage with active intervention in the takeover bid itself. Although there are positive aspects of merger arbitrage, as detailed above, it has largely negative connotations in Europe. The popularity of this activist strategy has meant that the nature of the shareholder base can shift considerably during an offer period, from 'long-term' institutional investors to 'short-term' merger arbitrageurs.

15.3.2.1 Changing Shareholder Base during Takeover Bids

The transfer of shares from long-term institutional holders to short-term merger arbitrageurs during the course of a takeover bid has become a particularly controversial issue across European jurisdictions. In the UK, this was a major point of contention in both of the country's most highly publicised and controversial hostile takeovers – Kraft's acquisition of Cadbury in 2009 and Melrose's acquisition of GKN in 2018.

When the US company Kraft ultimately succeeded in acquiring the UK company Cadbury, it was claimed that hedge funds and other short-term investors owned close to one-third of Cadbury's shares, compared to only five per cent before Kraft had gone public with its hostile bid a few months earlier.[79] Therefore, there was a substantial change in the composition of the shareholder base during the offer period. When this happens, the new shareholders, primarily hedge funds, are only concerned about the offer price and how quickly a deal could be completed.[80] The pressure from such shareholders on the Cadbury board resulted in the board ultimately recommending an increased bid from Kraft[81] and 72 per cent of Cadbury shareholders voted in favour of the improved deal.[82] In contrast to the merger arbitrageurs, some of Cadbury's largest and longest-term shareholders opposed the takeover. For example, LGIM, Cadbury's second largest shareholder, issued a statement expressing its disappointment that management had ultimately recommended the offer for an 'iconic and unique British company', stating that the

[78] Ibid., at 2635–2636 and 2638.

[79] Wiggins, 'The inside story of the Cadbury takeover' (n 2).

[80] Scott Moeller, 'Case study, Kraft's takeover of Cadbury', *Financial Times*, 9 January 2012, www.ft.com/content/1cb06d30-332f-11e1-a51e-00144feabdc0.

[81] Dan Roberts, 'Cadbury board agrees £12bn sale to Kraft', *The Guardian*, 19 January 2010, www.theguardian.com/business/2010/jan/19/cadbury-board-agrees-kraft-sale.

[82] David Jones and Brad Dorfman, 'Cadbury shareholders approve Kraft takeover', *Reuters*, 2 February 2010, www.reuters.com/article/world/cadbury-shareholders-approve-kraft-takeover-idUSTRE61124D/.

final price did not 'fully reflect the long-term value of the company'.[83] In the aftermath of the transaction, the House of Commons Business, Innovation and Skills Committee expressed concern that 'the takeover of Cadbury by Kraft was ultimately decided by institutional investors motivated by short-term profits rather than those investors who had the company's long-term interests at heart'.[84] The controversy led to a public consultation by the UK's Takeover Panel to consider reforms to takeover regulation and a government review (discussed in Section 15.3.2.2).

The influence of 'short-term' shareholders, such as hedge fund merger arbitrageurs, was again raised in 2018 during the UK's next most high-profile hostile takeover since Kraft's acquisition of Cadbury. Here, the hostile bidder, Melrose, acquired the company GKN. Again, hedge funds, mostly merger arbitrage funds, were estimated to control 20–25 per cent of GKN's shares, either directly or through derivative contracts.[85] The activist hedge fund Elliott Management, which had a 3.8 per cent shareholding, was particularly vocal in its support of the hostile bid. However, long-term investors, such as Aviva Investors, also publicly supported the hostile bidder, Melrose. Moreover, the support of LGIM, a long-term passive investor with a 2.6 per cent shareholding, also helped the hostile bid to succeed.[86] BlackRock was the largest shareholder in both the target, GKN, and the bidder, Melrose. However, whether BlackRock voted in favour of the takeover bid or not has never been reported. Given that long-term shareholders as well as short-term merger arbitrageurs supported this acquisition, it can be seen that the picture is not as clear-cut as the critics present it. Indeed, for short-term merger arbitrageurs to own shares in the target at all requires longer-term shareholders to make a decision to sell their shares during the offer period.

15.3.2.2 UK Proposals to Disenfranchise Short-Term Shareholders

The broader goals underpinning the Takeover Directive included encouraging cross-border takeover bids to create an active European market for corporate control. These goals assumed to some extent that takeovers are generally positive. However, national Member States have often taken a different view on takeovers affecting their own jurisdictions, especially when these involve a foreign bidder. There are also genuine concerns that opportunistic short-term shareholders who become involved

[83] Wiggins (n 2).

[84] House of Commons Business, Innovation and Skills Committee, 'Mergers, acquisitions and takeovers: The takeover of Cadbury by Kraft. Ninth Report of Session 2009–10', https://publications.parliament.uk/pa/cm200910/cmselect/cmbis/234/234.pdf, at 3.

[85] Nils Pratley, 'It's futile to rage at hedge funds over GKN – short-termism runs deeper', *The Guardian*, 27 March 2018, www.theguardian.com/business/nils-pratley-on-finance/2018/mar/26/hedge-funds-gkn-takeovers.

[86] Peggy Hollinger, Michael Pooler and Jim Pickard, 'Melrose victorious in hostile bid for GKN', *Financial Times*, 29 March 2018, www.ft.com/content/c6afe24c-3356-11e8-b5bf-23cb17fd1498.

during the course of a takeover bid may put the long-term value creation of important national companies or industries at risk. As has been discussed above, the changing ownership landscape can facilitate takeovers and potentially make launching a hostile bid easier. In the years that followed the adoption of the Takeover Directive, these concerns have led to various proposals to protect national interests. One such proposal in the UK was to 'disenfranchise' short-term shareholders who acquire shares during the offer period.

Following the controversy surrounding the Kraft/Cadbury takeover in the UK, whereby hedge funds and other short-term shareholders amassed around 30 per cent of the shares during the course of the hostile takeover bid, the Takeover Panel held a public consultation on aspects of takeover bids, including whether certain shareholders should be 'disenfranchised' during an offer period.[87] A key principle of both the UK's Takeover Code and the Takeover Directive is equality of treatment of shareholders, whereby 'All holders of the securities of an offeree company of the same class must be afforded equivalent treatment.'[88] Therefore, as noted by the Takeover Panel in its consultation, 'The Code does not currently make any distinction between persons who are already shareholders in the offeree company at a time when an offer period commences and persons who come to acquire shares in the offeree company during the course of the offer period.'[89] The main argument in favour of the 'disenfranchisement' of certain classes of shareholders is that it would ensure

> the outcome of takeover bids is determined by the core shareholder base, not by short term speculative investors who may acquire shares in order to facilitate the takeover. It is argued that ensuring that only those who are registered shareholders at the start of the offer period are eligible to 'vote' on the takeover proposal would allow long term shareholders to accept the offer based on the long term interests of the company, without being 'squeezed out' by speculators.[90]

However, the Takeover Panel also acknowledged that there were various legal, and in particular practical, impediments to disenfranchising shareholders in this manner. The Takeover Panel therefore brought in various changes post Cadbury/Kraft, but not to the fundamental principle that all shareholders should have an equal vote on whether a takeover bid is accepted.[91] Following the Takeover Panel's

[87] The Takeover Panel, 'Consultation Paper Issued by the Code Committee of the Panel: Review of Certain Aspects of the Regulation of Takeover Bids', PCP 2010/2, 1 June 2010, www.thetakeoverpanel.org.uk/wp-content/uploads/2008/11/PCP201002.pdf, section 3.

[88] Takeover Code, General Principle 1; Article 3(1)(a) Takeover Directive.

[89] The Takeover Panel (n 87), at 20 (section 3.3).

[90] Ibid, at 21 (section 3.5)

[91] The Takeover Panel Code Committee, 'Review of Certain Aspects of the Regulation of Takeover Bids' 2010/22, 21 October 2010, www.thetakeoverpanel.org.uk/wp-content/uploads/2023/02/Panel-Statement-2010-22.pdf. See also John Armour, Jack B. Jacobs and Curtis J. Milhaupt, 'The Evolution of Hostile Takeover Regimes in Developed and Emerging Markets: An Analytical Framework' (2011) 52(1) *Harvard International Law Journal* 219, 239.

review, the UK government commissioned a review into UK equity markets and long-term decision-making, chaired by Professor John Kay. The final report, the Kay Review of UK Equity Markets and Long-Term Decision Making, was published on 23 July 2012.[92] The report included a recommendation that the government study the feasibility of a policy to restrict the role of short-term shareholders during a takeover bid. While the UK government supported the objective of ensuring that the interests of those seeking short-term returns from a merger or acquisition do not override the long-term interests of the companies involved, the government analysis identified significant practical obstacles to such disenfranchisement in practice.[93] The ultimate conclusion was that disenfranchising short-term shareholders would be practically difficult to introduce and largely ineffective in achieving the intended objective.[94]

15.3.2.3 Loyalty Shares in Europe

Other European jurisdictions have developed 'disenfranchisement' rules that can theoretically weaken the voting power of short-term shareholders so as to reduce their impact on takeover bids.[95] Loyalty shares – aimed at rewarding long-term shareholders and combatting short-termism – are possible in various Member States, including France, the Netherlands, Italy and Belgium.

Loyalty shares can be implemented under Dutch law, and in practice such schemes are being utilised by companies. However, in the absence of a statutory basis for loyalty shares in the Netherlands, such voting structures must comply with the principle of equal treatment of shareholders.[96] Therefore, there will have to be a clear basis for the loyalty shares, whereby there is a reasonable and objective justification for unequal treatment of shareholders.[97] The recent case of

92 The Kay Review of UK Equity Markets and Long-Term Decision Making, Final Report, July 2012, https://assets.publishing.service.gov.uk/media/5a7cccdbed915d6b29fa8bea/bis-12-917-kay-review-of-equity-markets-final-report.pdf.

93 UK Parliament, 'The Kay Review of UK Equity Markets and Long-term Decision Making – Business, Innovation and Skills Committee', Annex B: Summary of analysis of the policy proposal to disenfranchise short-term shareholders during a takeover bid, https://publications.parliament.uk/pa/cm201314/cmselect/cmbis/762/76206.htm.

94 Department for Business Innovation & Skills, 'Practical and legal issues related to limiting the rights of short-term shareholders during takeover bids: Note of BIS roundtable', October 2014, https://assets.publishing.service.gov.uk/media/5a749dcced915d0e8e399a5c/bis-14-1159-note-of-bis-roundtable-issues-related-to-limiting-the-rights-of-short-term-shareholders-during-takeover-bids.pdf, 2.

95 The European Commission's Action Plan on '*Modernising Company Law and Enhancing Corporate Governance in the European Union*' in 2012 had suggested the introduction of loyalty shares, aimed at encouraging long-term investment and combatting short-termism.

96 F.C. M. In de Braekt, 'Limitations to the Development of Loyalty Shares in the Netherlands?' (2023) 20(2) *European Company Law Journal*, 40, 43.

97 Ibid., citing Supreme court 31 December 1993, *NJ* 1994/436 with annotation J. M. M. Maeijer (*Verenigde Bootlieden*).

Mediaset[98] in the Netherlands, where the Court of Appeal considered that the loyalty scheme violated the equality principle, does, however, raise the question under what circumstances loyalty schemes should be permissible in the Netherlands.

Italian firms have been able to adopt loyalty shares since 2014. Such shares have historically allowed a double-voting right if the shares are held continuously for a two-year period. Around 20 per cent of Italian listed firms have adopted loyalty shares, with family-controlled firms being the most likely to do so.[99] Loyalty shares have recently been enhanced in Italy, with new measures effective from 27 March 2024 which increase the number of votes allocable in respect of such shares. The by-laws of listed companies can now permit holders of loyalty shares to receive up to ten votes per loyalty share, which is a significant increase on the previous limit of two votes per loyalty share.[100] In Italy, loyalty shares are negatively associated with the probability of a company receiving a takeover bid.[101]

France has an established tradition of loyalty shares, and it is now the default position for French companies. One share, one vote was originally the default rule in France, with shareholders able to opt out by giving double-voting rights to long-term shareholders, usually after holding the shares for two years.[102] In 2014, the new French *Loi Florange* altered the default position for IPO companies. Listed companies that wanted to keep one share, one vote also had just over two years to opt out of tenure voting.[103]

Finally, in Belgium, listed companies were allowed to adopt loyalty voting rights from 2019.[104] These reforms gave double-voting rights to shareholders who have held their shares for more than two years. The rights are almost exclusively used by controlling shareholders (or at least by large insiders).[105]

Institutional investors tend to be opposed to loyalty shares, in line with their opposition to takeover defences more broadly. In both Italy and France, institutional

98 Amsterdam Court of Appeal, 1 September 2020, *JOR 2020/279*, with annotation A. F. J. A. Leijten (*Mediaset*).

99 Emanuele Bajo, Massimiliano Barbi, Marco Bigelli and Ettore Croci, 'Bolstering family control: Evidence from loyalty shares' (2020) 65 *Journal of Corporate Finance* 1.

100 Ibid.

101 Ettore Croci, 'Controlling-Enhancing Mechanisms: Loyalty Shares and Multiple-Voting Shares in Italy', Working Paper ECGI Roundtable on Loyalty Shares, June 2018, www.ecgi.global/sites/default/files/6._controlling-enhancing_mechanisms-_loyalty_shares_and_multiple-voting_shares_in_italy.pdf.

102 Marco Becht, Yuliya Kamisarenka and Anete Pajuste, 'Loyalty Shares with Tenure Voting: Does the Default Rule Matter? Evidence from the *Loi Florange* Experiment', (2020) 63(3) *Journal of Law and Economics* 473.

103 Ibid.

104 Steven Declercq, Jeroen Delvoie, Theo Monnens and Tom Vos, 'Loyalty Voting Rights in Belgium: Nothing More than a Control-Enhancing Mechanism?' (2023) *European Company and Financial Law Review* 27.

105 Ibid.

investors have voted against the introduction of loyalty shares, as a deviation from the one share, one vote principle.[106] For example, in 2015, more than 100 investors, including major institutional investors such as Fidelity, LGIM, Aviva and Schroders, published an open letter calling on the Italian prime minister to strike down a legal provision creating multiple-voting rights at Italian listed companies, a move that they viewed as making Italy hostile to foreign investment.[107]

15.3.3 *Institutional Investor Ownership and Hedge Fund Activism*

Hedge fund activist targets in the US exhibit significantly higher institutional ownership than firms that are not targeted.[108] Global studies have similarly shown that institutional investor ownership is strongly correlated with the level of activist hedge fund campaigns within particular European countries.[109] This is particularly the case if the activist hedge fund is US-based.[110] Therefore, the changes to the ownership landscape in terms of the growth of institutional investor ownership documented in Section 15.2 likely also facilitates the growth of hedge fund activism.

Shareholder dissent on the part of activist hedge funds can also catalyse recommendations by proxy advisors. Proxy advisors can serve as important voting intermediaries between activist hedge funds and institutional investors. In terms of takeovers, a study has shown that the proxy advisor Institutional Shareholder Services (ISS) 'virtually never issues a recommendation against a deal unless there is a public dissention by shareholders'.[111] Institutional investors may then be influenced by ISS in terms of their voting behaviour. The study then showed that a negative recommendation from ISS is associated with a 21 per cent decrease in the probability of deal completion.[112]

15.4 FOREIGN INVESTMENT

A key objective of the Takeover Directive was to create an active cross-border European market for corporate control. However, this goal was met with significant protectionism on the part of many Member States. While the protectionism of various Member States may have hindered this goal to some extent, the changing ownership landscape since the adoption of the Takeover Directive may actually

[106] Becht, Kamisarenka and Pajuste (n 102); Bajo, Barbi, Bigelli and Croci (n 99), at 3.
[107] Rachel Sanderson, 'Italy makes U-turn on loyalty shares', *Financial Times*, 5 February 2015, www.ft.com/content/9473eaca-ad2c-11e4-bfcf-00144feab7de.
[108] Alon Brav, Wei Jiang, Frank Partnoy and Randall Thomas, 'Hedge Fund Activism, Corporate Governance, and Firm Performance', (2008) 63(4) *The Journal of Finance* 1729, 1730.
[109] Becht, Franks, Grant and Wagner (n 43), at 2946.
[110] Ibid.
[111] Jiang, Li and Mei (n 59) at 2637.
[112] Ibid.

further that goal, or at least put conditions in place that would help an active European market for corporate control to develop.

One major feature of the changing ownership landscape that may facilitate the European market for corporate control is the growth of foreign investment across Europe. The presence of foreign institutional investors can be especially pivotal when acquisitions are cross-border. Studies have shown that foreign institutional ownership is positively associated with the intensity of cross-border M&A activity worldwide.[113] Indeed, the success of some major European cross-border transactions has been attributed to the level of international ownership of the target company. One such example is the British mobile operator Vodafone's hostile bid for the German company Mannesmann (in 1999, prior to the adoption of the Takeover Directive). Here, the success of Vodafone's offer, and the vulnerability of Mannesmann to a hostile bid, has been attributed to Mannesmann's extremely international and dispersed ownership structure. This ownership structure was unusual at the time for a German company, but it is more common now. The Vodafone/Mannesmann transaction predated the developments discussed in Section 15.2, where asset managers had large holdings in European companies. Rather, most of the asset managers that held shares in Mannesmann held relatively small stakes in the company. Importantly, more than 60 per cent of Mannesmann's shares were held by foreign institutions, including 40 per cent held by investors in the US and the UK.[114] Another example of a company's foreign shareholder base facilitating a cross-border acquisition is the recent takeover of Countryside in the UK, discussed in Section 15.3.1.3. In that case, major pressure in favour of a takeover came from the foreign shareholder base. The largest five shareholders in the housebuilder, holding 39 per cent of the shares, were all US-based. US funds are more amenable to activism and to takeovers so if the proportion of foreign shareholders, and in particular US shareholders, increases at European companies, potential pressure to sell the company from the shareholder base is also more likely.

How common is foreign ownership of European companies? By the end of 2022, the proportion of UK shares held by overseas investors reached a record high of 57.7 per cent of the stock market.[115] The highest proportion of foreign investors in the UK market were US investors.[116] In Germany, a recent study reported that, between 2006 and 2021, foreign institutional ownership (as a proportion of overall institutional ownership) of German companies grew from 61 per cent in 2006 to 83 per cent in

113 Miguel Ferreira, Massimo Massa and Pedro Matos, 'Shareholders at the Gate? Institutional Investors and Cross-Border Mergers and Acquisitions' (2010) 23(2) *Review of Financial Studies* 601.

114 Martin Höpner and Gregory Jackson, 'Revisiting the Mannesmann takeover: How markets for corporate control emerge' (2006) 3(3) *European Management Review* 142, 147.

115 Office of National Statistics, 'Ownership of UK quoted shares; 2022', 4 December 2023, www.ons.gov.uk/economy/investmentspensionsandtrusts/bulletins/ownershipofukquotedshares/2022.

116 Ibid.

2021 (among all German companies) and from 64 per cent in 2006 to 83 per cent in 2021 among DAX companies.[117] In 2022, domestic ownership of the German DAX fell to 11.9 per cent, with US investor ownership rising to 43.3 per cent.[118] This changing ownership landscape could pave the way for more hostile bids, more hedge fund activism and more institutional investor engagement.

It has been shown that US hedge fund activists seek out targets with high levels of institutional ownership and, when engaging in activism outside of the US, foreign and in particular US institutions play a key role in such activism.[119] Indeed, domestic institutional investors have historically been less willing to support US or UK activist funds, especially if they are pursuing aggressive or hostile strategies.[120] Therefore, activists are more likely to launch campaigns at targets with a high proportion of foreign institutional investors. As a result, foreign institutions can act as facilitators in an international or European market for corporate control. On occasion, foreign shareholders can also push for activism or cross-border M&A based on a dislike of a certain jurisdiction's corporate governance. For example, in 2016, UK activist hedge fund TCI called for reforms at Volkswagen following the diesel emissions test-cheating scandal, citing that 'at VW we see an extreme form of the weaknesses of the German management model'.[121]

15.5 DERIVATIVES

Since 2003, when the first major case of an activist investor using cash-settled derivatives as a powerful takeover instrument was reported,[122] the use of derivatives became widespread in Europe.[123] Therefore, with the adoption of both the Takeover Directive and the original Transparency Directive in 2004,[124] the use of cash-settled derivatives increased substantially. Such derivatives could be used to build hidden stakes in a listed company in order to acquire or exercise influence over such a

[117] Marc Steffen Rapp, Andrew Reek, Michelle Schlosser and Justus von Appen, 'Recent Developments in Ownership Structures of German Listed Firms: From Cross-ownership to Common Ownership', https://ssrn.com/abstract=4507626, 9.

[118] 'Who owns the German DAX?' (n 5), at 9.

[119] Becht, Franks, Grant and Wagner (n 43), at 2936.

[120] Ibid.

[121] Maria Sheahan and Maiya Keidan, 'Hedge fund TCI backs Deutsche Boerse–LSE merger – Der Spiegel', *Reuters*, 27 May 2016, www.reuters.com/article/business/hedge-fund-tci-backs-deutsche-boerse-lse-merger-der-spiegel-idUSKCN0YI1Z4/.

[122] *Ithaca (Custodians) Ltd v. Perry Corp.* [2004] 2 N.Z.L.R. 182 (CA).

[123] Pierre Henri Conac, 'Cash-Settled Derivatives as a Takeover Instrument and the Reform of the EU Transparency Directive', in Hanne S. Birkmose, Mette Neville and Karsten Engsig Sørensen (eds.), *The European Financial Market in Transition* (Kluwer Law International, 2011), p. 50.

[124] 2004/109/EC of the European Parliament and of the Council of 15 December 2004 on the Harmonisation of Transparency Requirements in Relation to Information About Issuers Whose Securities Are Admitted to Trading on a Regulated Market.

company. Cash-settled derivatives were used for this purpose in various hostile bids in Europe. One example is LVMH's announcement on 27 October 2010 that it owned 17.1 per cent of Hermès' shares, despite disclosure rules requiring notification of stakes of 5 per cent.[125] In fact, LVMH only owned 4.9 per cent of Hermès outright, with the remaining stake being acquired through cash-settled equity swaps with three French banks.[126] Another striking example of the use of cash-settled derivatives was Porsche building up an almost 75 per cent stake in Volkswagen in 2008, in part through undisclosed derivatives.[127]

In the mid 2000s, many companies in Switzerland, Germany and France were targeted by hostile bidders or investors who attempted to gain control by building stakes through cash-settled derivatives.[128] As a result of these practices, some Member States, including the UK, Germany, the Netherlands, France and Switzerland, amended domestic legislation to ensure that disclosure obligations included disclosure of derivatives. The Transparency Directive was ultimately also amended in 2013 to ensure that such financial instruments would be included in disclosure obligations across the Member States.[129] As a result of these amendments, it has become much more difficult in the past decade for activists or hostile bidders to quietly build up stakes in their European targets without disclosing this to the market, thus closing what one commentator described as 'the biggest current loophole in European financial regulation'.[130]

15.6 PRIVATE CAPITAL

A final change in the ownership landscape of European companies over the past two decades is the increasing number of deals being driven by private capital and the growth in alternative sources of financing for companies. Private equity has grown from a $500–600 billion industry in the early 2000s to being worth more than $7.5 trillion in 2022.[131] These developments have resulted in a number of European

[125] 'Hidden predators: Most countries no longer let firms build up unseen stakes', *The Economist*, 6 July 2013, www.economist.com/finance-and-economics/2013/07/06/hidden-predators.

[126] Ibid.

[127] Ibid. *See also* Conac (n 123) at 54.

[128] Conac (n 123) at 52.

[129] Transparency Directive Amending Directive (2013/50/EU).

[130] Conac (n 123) at 50 and 53–55, citing examples such as Victory Industriebeteiligung AG and Viktor Vekselberg disclosing a 42 per cent stake in the Swiss company Unaxis in 2005; Schaeffler acquiring 36 per cent of shares in the German listed company Continental in 2008 to launch a hostile takeover; and Wendel building a 17.6 per cent stake in French company Saint-Gobain in 2007.

[131] Schroders, 'How should investors respond to the stock market's dwindling status?', *Schroders*, 24 July 2023, www.schroders.com/en-us/us/individual/insights/how-should-investors-respond-to-the-stock-market-s-dwindling-status-/, citing McKinsey Global Private Markets Review 'A routinely exceptional year', *McKinsey & Company*, February 2017, www.mckinsey.com/~/media/mckinsey/industries/private%20equity%20and%20principal%20investors/our%20insights/a%

companies being taken private, and (alongside other contributing factors) to a reduction in the number of listed companies across European jurisdictions. It was reported in 2024 that the London stock market had shrunk by 25 per cent in the past decade alone.[132] Similar trends have been witnessed across Europe. For example, in Germany, there has been a drop of more than 40 per cent of public companies since 2007.[133]

In the US, activist hedge funds have teamed up with private equity funds for activism or takeovers. The line has therefore blurred somewhat between shareholder activism and private equity transactions. This practice does not seem to be commonplace in Europe.

Although institutional investors have not been particularly involved in takeovers generally through their stewardship roles, they have been vocal about some private equity transactions. For example, when the UK supermarket Morrisons was involved in a private equity bidding war in 2021, LGIM and other institutional investors publicly expressed their opinions on the proposed transaction. LGIM noted:

> As responsible stewards of our clients' capital, it is important that the company isn't taken over for the wrong reasons. If an acquirer makes strong returns this should come from making the company a better business. It should not come from buying its property portfolio too cheaply, levering the company up with debt, and potentially reducing the tax paid to the exchequer.[134]

However, other asset managers disagreed; for example, Aberdeen (a passive shareholder in Morrisons) supported the transaction, stating that it represents 'good value'.[135] The result was a 25 per cent increase in the bid price, with Morrisons being bought by the American private equity firm Clayton Dubillier & Rice in October 2021, who paid a 61 per cent premium to the price of Morrisons' shares before the bidding war.[136]

2 and McKinsey Global Private Markets Review 2023, 'Private markets turn down the volume', *McKinsey & Company*, March 2023, www.mckinsey.com/~/media/mckinsey/industries/private%20equity%20and%20principal%20investors/our%20insights/mckinseys%20private%20markets%20annual%20review/2023/mckinsey-global-private-markets-review-2023.pdf.

132 Joe Easton, 'Number of London-Listed Companies Shrank 25% Over a Decade', *Bloomberg UK*, 29 January 2024, www.bloomberg.com/news/articles/2024-01-29/london-s-stock-market-has-shrunk-25-in-the-past-decade?embedded-checkout=true.

133 Emma Charlton, 'The global supply of equities is shrinking – here's what you need to know', *World Economic Forum, Forum Agenda*, 24 April 2024, www.weforum.org/agenda/2024/04/equities-stock-market-health-investing/.

134 Ellie Duncan, 'LGIM issues warning about Morrisons takeover as US firms circle supermarket – reports', *Investment Week*, 6 July 2021, www.investmentweek.co.uk/news/4033983/lgim-issues-warning-about-morrisons-takeover-us-firms-circle-supermarket-reports.

135 Carolyn Cohn, Dhara Ranasinghe and Alexander Smith, 'Fortress-led bid for Britain's Morrisons is "good value" – abrdn CEO', *Reuters*, 5 July 2021, www.reuters.com/world/uk/fortress-offer-morrisons-is-good-value-investor-abrdn-ceo-2021-07-05/.

136 Jonathan Eley, 'CD&R triumphs in £10bn Morrisons battle', *Financial Times*, 2 October 2021, www.ft.com/content/4d990b0f-2728-4126-adee-d4111aae7a45.

15.7 CONCLUSION

The effectiveness of the goals of the Takeover Directive are impacted not only by the legal provisions themselves, and the choices made by individual Member States in implementing the Directive, but also by changing market conditions. The changing ownership landscape in Europe during the twenty years that have passed since the adoption of the Takeover Directive has the potential to significantly impact the prevalence, and success or failure, of takeover bids and, ultimately, how active the European market for corporate control is. This chapter has focused on several major changes to the shareholder landscape, including the growth of institutional investors and asset managers, the shift to passive index investing, the emergence of M&A hedge fund activism in Europe, and the controversies associated with the influence of merger arbitrageurs on takeovers. Increasing levels of foreign investment and the growth of private equity were also discussed. Each of these individual developments can affect takeovers and the market for corporate control in a positive or negative manner. Companies with high levels of institutional investment, especially foreign investment, are more likely to become a takeover target. Asset managers might theoretically be expected to engage in stewardship around M&A deals, but the evidence reveals very little M&A engagement. The position with respect to whether passive index funds sell or tender shares during a takeover bid is opaque. It seems that some such funds do sell their shares, despite this contradicting a strict indexation strategy, while others may observe a stricter indexation mandate. Therefore, in some respects institutional investment and asset managers may encourage takeovers, and in other respects they may impede the European market for corporate control. The growing influence of merger arbitrageurs in high-profile takeovers of companies of national importance to various Member States has also called into question some of the shareholder-friendly provisions of the Takeover Directive.

16

Multiple-Voting Rights and Takeovers

Erik Lidman and Andrés Recalde Castells

16.1 MULTIPLE-VOTING SHARES AND TAKEOVERS

16.1.1 *Introduction*

The use of multiple-vote share (MVS) structures has been described as '[o]ne of the most contentious and long-standing debates in corporate governance',[1] and for many decades, the use of multiple-voting shares has been a corporate governance taboo in listed companies.[2] In recent years, however, there has been an upswing in the use of MVS structures globally, as well as related structures such as loyalty shares, and the permissibility of MVS listings has become an increasingly important matter of competitiveness for capital markets around the world. Most recently, a directive with the purpose of promoting the use of MVS structures has been adopted in the EU, requiring Member States to ensure that companies that seek the admission to trading of their shares on an SME growth market have the possibility to adopt such structures.[3] In the context of takeovers, this development gives policymakers in the Member States reason to consider how to regulate takeover bids when the target company has an MVS structure, and the questions arising are new and challenging. The Takeover Directive[4] gives very little guidance, there is no EU case law on the topic, and little has been written or said about the questions arising in a bid on an

[1] See A. Winden and A. Baker, 'Dual-Class Index Exclusion' (2019) 13 *Virginia Law & Business Review*, 101 et seq.

[2] Although this has not always been the case; see Section 16.1.2.

[3] See Directive (EU) 2024/2810 of the European Parliament and of the Council of 23 October 2024 on multiple-vote share structures in companies that seek admission to trading of their shares on a multilateral trading facility. On a former draft of the Directive see also ECLE, *The European proposal to open up multiple-vote share structures to listing companies: A simplification in trompe l'oeil*, available at: https://blogs.law.ox.ac.uk/oblb/blog-post/2023/09/european-proposal-open-multiple-vote-share-structures-listing-companies.

[4] Parliament and Council Directive 2004/25/EC On takeover bids, herein the Takeover Directive.

MVS firm. Obviously, there are very few normative solutions, and each regulator must consider how to address the issues arising in their national context.

In this chapter, we aim to highlight the questions that takeover regulators will have to consider regarding bids on MVS firms and firms with loyalty share structures, and how one may reason regarding solutions in light of the general principles of takeover regulation laid down in the Takeover Directive. We draw on experiences from our native countries, where MVS structures are prevalent in Sweden, and loyalty shares have been introduced in Spain by some listed companies since they were permitted in 2021.

The structure of the chapter is as follows. In Section 16.2, we first give a background to the current development and political economy, with a particular focus on the development in the EU, to underline why these issues matter. In Section 16.3, we discuss the empirical evidence on the effects of MVS structures, which we believe takeover regulators have reason to consider. In Section 16.4, we present legal questions that arise in a bid on an MVS firm, including the pricing of multiple-vote shares (MV shares) in the context of a bid (Section 16.4.2); the possibility of offering different forms of compensation for subordinated voting right (SV) and MV shares (Section 16.4.3); whether it is possible, through a partial bid, to acquire only the MV shares in a company (Section 16.4.4); and the effects of vote changes in a firm with MV shares or loyalty shares on the duty to launch a mandatory bid (Section 16.4.5).

16.1.2 *Terminology Regarding Multiple-Voting Shares*

MVS structures come in many shapes and forms that, from a regulatory perspective, differ quite a bit from each other. Before we go any further, we need to say something of what we refer to here as MVS structures and loyalty shares.

Multiple-voting shares represent a straightforward form of control-enhancement mechanism that generally builds on dividing shares into two classes with regard to voting rights. One of the classes has a lower or *subordinate* voting value (commonly one vote), which we refer to here as *SV shares*. The other class carries multiple votes. We refer to these as *MV shares*. The purpose of MVS structures is generally to permit a shareholder (or shareholders) to hold a controlling stake in a company without having to make the proportionate economic investment required for the size of the stake, should all shares have the same voting power. According to the OECD, about half of the forty-nine jurisdictions covered in the OECD Corporate Governance Factbook allow companies to utilize such structures in national company law.[5] In some jurisdictions, the MVS structures may have a limited lifespan, where a convergence of the share classes will occur automatically after a certain

[5] See OECD Corporate Governance Factbook 2023, OECD Publishing, p. 74 ff.

time period, such as five years (a time-based sunset clause), or if the MV shares are transferred (a transfer-based sunset clause).[6]

One 'variant' of the MV structure that has been introduced in several countries, including Belgium, Italy, France and Spain, are so-called *loyalty shares*, which grant extra voting rights to shareholders after a certain holding period.[7] This preferential voting right can by definition not be transferred, when the shareholder sells his/her shares. Therefore, 'loyalty shares' do not raise the same takeover issues as regular MVS structures, though, as we shall see, they raise other ones.[8]

In this chapter, we refer to the first type of structure as MVS structures, and to the second type of structure as simply *loyalty shares* or *loyalty share structures*.

16.2 CURRENT DEVELOPMENTS

16.2.1 *Recent Trends in MVS Structures in Non-EU Jurisdictions*

MVS structures are nothing new, but in many markets, this has been a heavily contested subject. Looking to the US, while MVS companies were not uncommon at the beginning of the twentieth century, the New York Stock Exchange (NYSE) stopped listing MVS shares in the 1940s, following a couple of decades of criticism of such structures by investors,[9] and the structures were not allowed again until many decades later.[10] The pattern was pretty much the same in the UK, where MVS structures were neither uncommon nor particularly criticized in the first half of the twentieth century (rather, the introduction of MVS structures was often associated with positive price effects).[11] In the 1950s, however, the climate around MVS

6 See for instance J. Fisch and S. Solomon, 'The problem of sunsets' (2019) 99 *Boston University Law Review*, 1057 et seq., and L. Bebchuk and K. Kastiel, 'The untenable case for perpetual dual-class stock' (2017) 10384 *Virginia Law Review*, 585 et seq. In our definition of MVS structures, we do not include shares with 'specified weighted voting rights' that the LSE now allow listing of on the premium segment. These shares are not transferable, and in addition, designed to block takeover bids. See for an in-depth analysis B. Reddy, *Founders without Limits* (Cambridge University Press, 2021).

7 For instance, the shareholders will be granted two votes (instead of one) when they have held the shares for an uninterrupted period of two years, and if the shares were registered in the correspondent company's loyalty shares register.

8 Though some questions nevertheless arise, see Section 16.4.5.

9 See R. W. Jennings, 'The Role of the States in Corporate Regulation and Investor Protection' (1958) 23 *Law and Contemporary Problems*, 193 et seq., and Robbins, 'An Evaluation of the New York Stock Exchange Listing Policy on Voting', (1978) New York Stock Exchange Study, 183.

10 See J. Howell, 'The Survival of the U.S. Dual Class Share Structure' (2017) 44 *Journal of Corporate Finance*, 440 et seq., and B. Reddy, 'More than Meets the Eye: Reassessing the Empirical Evidence on US Dual-Class Stock' (2020) 23 *University of Pennsylvania Journal of Business Law*, 963 et seq.

11 See J. Ang and W. Megginson, 'Restricted voting shares, ownership structure, and the market value of dual-class firms' (1989) 12 *The Journal of Financial Research*, 301 et seq.

structures started to change, particularly from institutional investors who developed a 'marked distaste' for multiple-voting shares.[12] While the London Stock Exchange (LSE) did not ban the MVS listings outright like the NYSE, the practice was, following the debate during the 1950s and 1960s, discouraged to the point of extinction, and the tradition has long been not to allow MVS companies on the premium segment.[13]

For the past ten years, however, MVS structures have seen a significant rise in popularity. In Singapore, allowing dual-class listings was first considered in 2012, following the proposed listing of Manchester United on the Singapore Stock Exchange (SGX).[14] At the time, SGX upheld the 'one share, one vote' principle, with reference to the risk of the abuse of power by MV shareholders. However, in 2016, the prohibition against the use of MV shares was removed from the Singapore Companies Act, and the discussion concerning MVS listings on SGX reignited. The SGX referred the question to an independent committee which in August 2016 recommended permitting MVS listings.[15] After a public consultation, the SGX announced on 20 January 2018 that it would allow primary MVS listings,[16] and the first MVS-IPO followed in June 2018.[17] The SGX's change in its listing regulation was almost immediately followed by a similar revision of the Hong Kong Stock Exchange's (HKEX) listing rules the same year. After the story of how Alibaba chose the NYSE for its 25 billion USD IPO in 2014 after the HKEX refused to accept its MVS structure, HKEX started to reconsider its thirty-year-long prohibition on MVS listings.[18] In August 2014, HKEX launched a public consultation on the allowing of MVS structures, and from the responses concluded that there was ample support to continue to explore acceptable structures for a draft proposal of a regulation allowing the listing of companies with dual-class shares. But after the Securities and Futures Commission of Hong Kong opposed the draft proposal, HKEX put the plans on ice. However, Hong Kong made a second attempt towards changing the regulation

[12] See further F. Braggion and M. Gianetti, 'Changing corporate governance norms: Evidence from dual class shares in the UK' (2019) 37 *Journal of Financial Intermediation*, 15 et seq.

[13] See www.ft.com/content/e18a6138–2b49–11e3-a1b7–00144feab7de. Of course, this also makes the recommendation in the Hill Review controversial, especially to institutional investors, who have heavily criticized the recommendation in light of Deliveroo's spectacularly unsuccessful MVS-IPO; see www.ft.com/content/72de7a53-e7af-4c6b-af0f-cfd1f8fcbdf5.

[14] See, for instance: reuters.com/article/us-singapore-us-ipo-manchester-united-if/exclusive-manchester-united-drops-asia-ipo-for-u-s-idUSBRE85C0MO20120613/, learn.asialawnetwork.com/2018/02/05/taking-stock-dual-class-shares-discussions-singapore/, and knowledge.freshfields.com/m/Global/r/1644/singapore_exchange_s_listing_advisory_committee_opens_door.

[15] The SGX Listings Advisory Committee also recommended that MVS structures should only be allowed for new listings, that the reasons for each particular MVS listing should be subject to assessment, and that the voting ratio between SV and MV shares should not be allowed to exceed 1:10.

[16] See www.straitstimes.com/business/companies-markets/sgx-introducing-dual-class-shares.

[17] See www.reuters.com/article/sgx-regulation/singapore-details-rules-for-offering-dual-class-shares-follows-hong-kong-idUKL4N1TS3E3.

[18] See www.ft.com/content/6f0e9914-fa96–11e7-a492–2c9be7f3120a.

in 2017. This time the attempt was not met with the same opposition, and HKEX has also allowed MVS listings since 2018 (in response, Alibaba founder Jack Ma announced that Alibaba would 'seriously consider' an HKEX listing, which followed in 2022).[19] Thus, the Singapore and Hong Kong exchanges joined the likes of NYSE, Nasdaq New York, the Toronto Stock Exchange (TSX), and many of the European exchanges, such as Euronext, to allow MVS listings. Even in London – the European bastion of the 'one share, one vote' principle – things have changed. Following the Hill Review, the Listing Rules for the LSE premium segment were revised in December 2021, now allowing firms with 'specified weighted voting rights' to list on the segment, aiming to increase the listing activity in London.[20]

This development is also evident in listing trends. The use of MVS structures has had an upswing during the last decade on markets that have allowed MVS listings for a long time, with the US being the prime example. With Google's dual-class IPO opening the floodgates in 2004, companies such as Facebook, LinkedIn, Groupon, Snap, Zynga and Fitbit have joined old US companies with MVS structures, such as Ford and The New York Times.[21] And the rise in MVS-IPOs has not stopped. While in 2016 around 10 per cent of companies that went public in the US were MVS companies, the figure was 20 per cent for the companies that listed in the US in 2017 and 2019.[22]

16.2.2 *The Development in the EU*

The EU has long had a sceptical view of MVS structures, and the European Commission has historically made several attempts towards adopting the 'one share, one vote' principle as a mandatory principle in EU company law. The first attempt was made in the 1970s, in the proposal for the fifth company law directive, in which Article 33 stated that '[t]he shareholder's right to vote shall be proportionate to the fraction of capital subscribed which the share represents'.[23] The entire proposed directive, which mostly aimed at harmonizing the corporate governance model

[19] See www.reuters.com/article/us-alibaba-hongkong-listing/alibaba-will-seriously-consider-hong-kong-listing-says-founder-ma-idUSKBN1EY062. It can also be noted that SGX, after the Hong Kong decision, decided to lower the bar for proposed MVS listings by allowing such listings for companies with an expected market capitalization of S$300 million (lowered from S$500 million).

[20] For a discussion on this change, see E. Lidman and R. Skog, 'London allowing dual class premium listings' (2021) 22 *Journal of Corporate Law Studies*, 83 et seq. Note also the distinction between 'specified weighted voting rights' and multiple-vote shares, where the former are subject to stronger limitations.

[21] See www.ft.com/content/25348bd8-9dd9-11e7-9a86-4d5a475ba4c5.

[22] See Committee of Capital Markets Regulation, the rise of dual class shares, and implications: www.capmktsreg.org/wp-content/uploads/2020/04/The-Rise-of-Dual-Class-Shares-04.08.20-1.pdf and www.bloomberg.com/news/articles/2018-02-15/alphabet-to-snap-s-dual-class-shares-chided-by-sec-official.

[23] See the draft for a fifth company law directive, COM/1972/887/FINAL.

within the EU, was eventually abandoned, and with that the early 'one share, one vote' effort.[24] Later attempts were also made, however, in conjunction with the development of the Takeover Directive, more specifically in relation to the breakthrough rule (Article 11).[25] The most significant and latest push toward a 'one share, one vote' principle was the one spearheaded by Commissioner Charlie McCreevy up until 2006, which generated a heavy debate, with calls for evidence on *why* a 'one share, one vote' principle was necessary in EU law. Studies were then commissioned from ISS, Shearman & Sterling, and the European Corporate Governance Institute, which led to an abrupt end of McCreevy's ambitions in the area,[26] since the studies delivered in no way supported the 'one share, one vote' principle in any regulatory intervention.[27] This ended any effort to introduce a 'one share, one vote' mandatory principle in EU company law.

Recently, and aligning with the trends seen in Asia, the US and the UK, we have instead seen a development in the opposite direction. To promote listings of new companies on the EU markets, a directive was proposed allowing the use of MVS structures as a part of the Capital Markets Union (CMU) work on improving access to market-based sources of financing within the EU. The directive was adopted in the spring of 2024 after intense negotiations, and Member States will, after the directive has entered into force, be required to ensure that companies that seek the admission to trading of their shares on an SME growth market have the possibility of adopting MVS structures.[28] It is also notable that several Member States that have previously been steadfast proponents of the 'one share, one vote' principle have opted to allow MVS structures (such as Germany,[29] Italy (*azioni a*

[24] See J. Dine, 'Implications for the United Kingdom of the EC Fifth Directive' (1989) 38 *International & Comparative Law Quarterly*, 547 et seq., and J. Temple, 'The Fifth Directive on the harmonization of company law' (1975) 12 *Common Market Law Review*, 345 et seq. However, the idea surfaced from time to time; see, for instance, COM (2003) 284 final, Modernising Company Law and Enhancing Corporate Governance in the European Union – a Plan to Move Forward.

[25] See for instance B. Clift, 'The Second Time as Farce? The EU Takeover Directive, the Clash of Capitalisms and the Hamstrung Harmonization of European (and French) Corporate Governance' (2008) 47 *Journal of Common Market Studies*, 55 et seq.

[26] This development started in 2020, when the High Level Forum on the Capital Markets Union included among its recommendations to allow MVS structures as a measure to improve the public market ecosystem; see Final Report of the High Level Forum on the Capital Markets Union: A New Vision for Europe's Capital Markets, June 2020.

[27] See *Proportionality between ownership and control in EU listed companies: External study commissioned by the European Commission*, carried out by ISS, Shearman & Sterling and the ECGI, available at: https://ec.europa.eu/docsroom/documents/14881/attachments/2/translations/en/renditions/pdf.

[28] See Directive (EU) 2024/2810 of the European Parliament and of the Council of 23 October 2024 on multiple-vote share structures in companies that seek admission to trading of their shares on a multilateral trading facility.

[29] A legal amendment came into force in December 2023 (Gesetz zur Finanzierung von zukunftssichernden Investitionen Zukunftsfinanzierungsgesetz – ZuFinG), opening the way

voto plurimo)[30] and France[31]), and in addition, several Member States have also elected to introduce loyalty share structures, including Belgium, France, Italy and Spain.

Thus, it looks like MVS structures are here to stay in the EU. Meanwhile, all Member States will from now on be required to consider the theme of this chapter – how to regulate the impact of MVS on takeovers.

16.3 THE EMPIRICAL EVIDENCE ON MVS STRUCTURES

The MVS debate is at least in part an ideological one, where assumptions and sometimes also emotions run high, and where it seems very hard for those of different views to find common ground. While the topic of this volume is, indeed, takeovers, we believe it necessary to also address this debate.[32] Our starting point in this chapter is that it should be up to the shareholders to decide on divergences, such as by introduction in the articles of association of different share classes, unless there are at least fairly solid reasons for limiting this freedom through mandatory legal intervention. The regulatory starting point is that shareholders should be free to utilize any share and capital structure, unless it is shown with some certainty that a particular structure might be harmful to shareholders. And investors must be free not to invest in companies that are not structured to their liking.

Three principal arguments have been made as to why MVS structures might be harmful, and hence why such structures should not be allowed or at least why MVS companies should not be allowed to list their shares. The first is that MVS structures reduce company value. The second is that MVS structures may lead to increased

to a more liberal model, providing the possibility for listed companies to adopt multiple-voting structures. This is a relevant change. Although it was traditionally possible to set voting caps in German public limited companies, this was ruled out for listed companies in a legal amendment in 1998 to Article 134 of the German Aktiengesetz. Admitting multiple-voting shares, the shift towards a more liberal model is now clearer (K. Schmolke, 'Dual-class shares on the rise. Some remarks on the (re)introduction of multiple-voting rights in German stock corporation law', available at: https://blogs.law.ox.ac.uk/oblb/blog-post/2023/02/dual-class-shares-rise-some-remarks-reintroduction-multiple-voting-rights).

30 R-D Legislativo 21.2024 (Legge capitali); v. The report of *Assonime*, 'Legge 5 marzo 2024,n. 21: interventi a sostegno della competitività del mercato dei capitali', Circolare 6/2024, p. 91 et seq.

31 A first step was made by the *Loi Florange* 2014. But new amendments have been made to open it up. (See A. Pietrancosta, 'Propositions françaises et européennes pour ouvrir le vote multiple aux sociétés entrant en bourse', *Bulletin Joly Sociétés*, núm. 1, 2023, pp. 63 et seq.; K. Hopt and S. Kalls, 'Multiple-voting shares in Europe: A comparative law and economic analysis', *ECGI* Working Paper no. 786/2024. P. Oudin and O. Gossner, 'Multiple Voting Rights are Arriving in France' https://blogs.law.ox.ac.uk/oblb/blog-post/2024/06/multiple-voting-rights-are-arriving-france.

32 Loyalty share structures for some reason seem less contested, and we do not address the debate here. For an overview of the discussion on loyalty shares, see C. Mosca, 'Experiments on the Wedge between Tenured Voting and Takeover Law' (2019) 8 *Michigan Business & Entrepreneurial Law Review*, 276 et seq.

tunnelling of company assets to controlling shareholders or managers (increased agency costs). The third, of particular relevance in this context, is that MVS structures are argued to pose a hindrance to liquidity and to the possibility of takeovers being launched, undermining the market for corporate control. We shall briefly comment on each of these arguments.

16.3.1 *Argument 1: MVS Structures Reduce Company Value*

The first argument, that MVS structures reduce company value, has been put forth by almost all critics of MVS structures. The reasoning behind the argument is often that holders of MV shares are not incentivized to maximize the company's potential, due to the free-rider problem. The argument has been studied empirically at length.[33] In several studies, empiricists have found evidence of MVS structures damaging company value over time, that MVSfirms trade at lower valuations, and that MVS companies offer lower returns:[34]

> G. Jarrell/A. Poulsen, 'Dual-class recapitalizations as antitakeover mechanisms' (1988) 20 *Journal of Financial Economics*, 129 et seq.; E. Maynes, 'Reallocation of voting rights and shareholders' wealth' (1992) 25 *Canadian Journal of Economics*, 538 et seq.; S. Taylor/G. Whittred, 'Security design and the allocation of voting rights: Evidence from the Australian IPO market' (1998) 4 *Journal of Corporate Finance*, 107 et seq. (not on MVS firm value per se, but in their sample, MVS firms have lower market-to-book ratios); S. Claessens/S. Djankov/L. Lang, 'Disentangling the incentive and entrenchment effects of large shareholdings' (2002) 57 *Journal of Finance*, 2741 et seq.; K. Lins, 'Equity ownership and firm value in emerging markets' (2003) 38 *Journal of Financial and Quantitative Analysis*, 159 et seq.; A. Pajuste, 'Determinants and Consequences of the Unification of Dual-Class Shares', ECB Working Paper 2005 no. 465 (showing increase in market-to-book ratios for MVS company share class unifications); S. Smart/R. Thirumalai/C. Zutter, 'What is in a vote? The short- and long-run impact of dual-class equity on IPO firm values' (2008) 45 *Journal of Accounting and Economics*, 94 et seq. (showing no difference in MVS company returns, though a valuation discount); M. Bennedsen/K. Nielsen, 'The Principle of Proportional Ownership, Investor

[33] Including, for instance, studies of value effects of dual-class recapitalizations or unifications, on the relation between market capitalization and asset value in MVS firms compared to single-class firms (most commonly through Tobin's Q), on differences in stock returns between MVS companies and matched single-class companies, on relative operating performance, and on the effects of acquisitions.

[34] The studies referenced were collected by using the search terms 'dual-class shares', 'dual class shares', 'differential voting rights' and 'multiple voting rights' in Scopus, ScienceDirect, Google Scholar and JSTOR, and we have included studies using data from the UK, the US, Canada, Western Europe, Israel, Brazil and Australia. We also identified further studies through references in papers we found and cross-referenced with other similar literature reviews. We have commented on the results of the studies where they are not easily categorized here.

Protection and Firm Value in Western Europe', ECGI – Finance Working Paper No. 134/2006; B. Villalonga/R. Amit, 'How do family ownership, control and management affect firm value?' (2006) 80 *Journal of Financial Economics*, 385 et seq.; I. Dittman/N. Ulbricht, 'Timing and wealth effects of German dual class stock unifications' (2008) 14 *European Financial Management*, 163 et seq.; M. King/E. Santor, 'Family values: Ownership structure, performance and capital structure of Canadian firms' (2008) 32 *Journal of Banking & Finance*, 2423 et seq.; R. Masulis/C. Wang/F. Xie, 'Agency problems at dual-class companies' (2009) 64 *Journal of Finance*, 1697 et seq.; B. Smith/B. Amoako-Adu/M. Kalimipalli, 'Concentrated control and corporate value: A comparative analysis of single and dual class structures in Canada' (2009) 19 *Applied Financial Economics*, 955 et seq.; M. Bennedsen/K. Nielsen, 'Incentive and entrenchment effects in European ownership' (2010) 34 *Journal of Banking & Finance*, 2212 et seq.; P. Gompers/J. Ishii/A. Metrick, 'Extreme governance: An analysis of dual-class firms in the United States' (2010) 23 *The Review of Financial Studies*, 1051 et seq.; S. Ikäheimo/V. Puttonen/T. Ratilainen, 'External corporate governance and performance: evidence from the Nordic countries' (2011) 17 *European Journal of Finance*, 427 et seq. (showing negative impact on evaluation of MVS companies); B. Amoako-Adu/V. Baulkaran/B. Smith, 'Dual class discount, and the channels of extraction of private benefits' (2013) 16 *Advances in Financial Economics*, 165 et seq.; V. Baulkaran, 'Management entrenchment and the valuation discount of dual class firms' (2014) 54 *Quarterly Review of Economics and Finance*, 70 et seq.; B. Lauterbach/A. Pajuste, 'The long-term valuation effects of voluntary dual class share unifications' (2015) 31 *Journal of Corporate Finance*, 171 et seq.; R. Anderson/E. Ottolenghi/D. Reeb, 'The dual class premium: A family affair', Fox School of Business Research paper no. 2017–021 (finding that MVS companies without family owners exhibit Tobin's Q values that are higher than those of their single-class peers, though the opposite is the case when MV shares are held by family owners); and de L. Andrade/A. Bressan/R. Iquiapaza, 'Dual class shares, board of directors' effectiveness and firm's market value: An empirical study' (2017) 21 *Journal of Management & Governance*, 1053 et seq.

However, one can find just as many empirical studies showing exactly the opposite – that MVS structures have positive effects on company value or that they have no effect:

V. Jog/A. Riding, 'Price effects of dual-class shares' (1986) 42 *Financial Analysis Journal*, 58 et seq.; M. Partch, 'The creation of a class of limited voting stock and shareholder wealth' (1987) 18 *Journal of Financial Economics*, 313 et seq. (concluding that 'there is no evidence that current shareholders are harmed by the creation of limited voting common stock'); J. Ang/W. Megginson, 'Restricted voting shares, ownership structure, and the market value of dual-class firms' (1989) 12 *The Journal of Financial Research*, 301 et seq.; M. Cornett/M. Vetsuypens, 'Voting rights and shareholder wealth: The issuance of limited voting common stock' (1989) 10 *Managerial and Decision Economics*, 175 et seq. (finding that the 'data do not lend support to the hypothesis that the concentration of voting power with incumbent management is detrimental to shareholder interests'); K. Lehn/J. Netter/A. Poulsen, 'Consolidating corporate control: dual-class recapitalizations versus leveraged buyouts' (1990) 27 *Journal of Financial Economics*, 557 et seq.; S. Foerster/D. Porter, 'Dual class shares: Are there returns differences?' (1993) 20 *Journal of Business Finance & Accounting*, 893 et seq.; W. Mikkelson & Partch, 'The consequences of unbundling managers' voting rights and equity claims' (1994) 1 *Journal of Corporate Finance*, 175 et seq.; E. Böhmer/G. Sanger/S.Varshney, 'The effect of consolidated control on firm performance: The case of dual-class IPOs', in Lewis (ed.), *Empirical Issues in Raising Equity Capital* (Elsevier, 1995); L. Kryzanowski/ H. Zhang, 'Introduction of dual-class shares: Further evidence on Canadian pro-rata distributions' (1995) *International Review of Financial Analysis* 467 et seq.; R. Kunz, 'Simplification of equity capital structure and market value' (2002) 16 *Financial Markets and Portfolio Management*, 30 et seq.; S. Smart/C. Zutter, 'Control as a motivation for underpricing: A comparison of dual and single-class IPOs' (2003) 69 *Journal of Financial Economics*, 85 et seq.; S. Bauguess, 'Recontracting Ownership and Control: The Effects of Differential Voting Rights after Dual Class Recapitalization', PhD thesis at Arizona State University; A. Pajuste, 'Determinants and Consequences of the Unification of Dual-Class Shares', ECB Working Paper 2005, no. 465 (showing no change in operating performance after share class unification in MVS firms); W. Ben-Amar/P. André, 'Separation of ownership from control and acquiring firm performance: The case of family ownership in Canada' (2006) 33 *Journal of Business Finance & Accounting*, 517 et seq. (studying the effects of acquisitions); V. Dimitriov/P. Jain, 'Recapitalization of one class of common stock into dual-class: Growth and long-run stock returns' (2006) 12 *Journal of Corporate Finance*, 342 et seq.; S. Smart/R. Thirumalai/C. Zutter, 'What is in a vote? The short- and long-run impact of dual-class equity on IPO firm values' (2008) 45 *Journal of Accounting and Economics*, 94 et seq. (showing a valuation discount but on the other hand no difference in MVS company returns, and concluding that 'there is at best only scant evidence suggesting that duals exhibit abnormally low operating performance'); R. Anderson/ A. Duru/D. Reeb, 'Founders, heirs, and corporate opacity in the United States' (2009) 92 *Journal of Financial Economics*, 205 et seq. (finding that MVS structures 'appear to be associated with better firm performance' 'in transparent founder or heir firms'); O. Arugaslan/D. Cook/R. Kieschnick, 'On the decision to go public with dual class stock' (2010) 16 *Journal of Corporate Finance*, 170 et seq.; C. Hoi/A. Robin, 'Agency conflicts, controlling owner proximity, and firm value: An analysis of dual-class firms in the United States' (2010) 18 *Corporate Governance: An International Review*, 124 et seq.; T. Chemmanur/I. Paeglis/K. Simonyan, 'Management quality and antitakeover provisions' (2011) 54 *Journal of Law & Economics*, 651 et seq.; S. Ikäheimo/V. Puttonen/T. Ratilainen, 'External corporate governance and performance: Evidence from the Nordic countries' (2011) 17 *European Journal of Finance*, 427 et seq. (showing no effect of MVS structures on stock returns, but positive effect on operating performance); B. Lauterbach/Y. Yafeh, 'Long term changes in voting power and control structure following the unification of dual class shares' (2011) 17 *Journal of Corporate Finance*, 215 et seq.;

S. Bauguess/M. Slovin/M. Sushka, 'Large shareholder diversification, corporate risk taking, and the benefits of changing to differential voting rights' (2012) 36 *Journal of Banking & Finance*, 1244 et seq.; B. Jordan/M. Liu/Q. Wu, 'Corporate payout policy in dual class firms' (2013) 26 *Journal of Corporate Finance*, 1 et seq.; S. Nüesch, 'Dual-class shares, external financing needs, and firm performance' (2016) 20 *Journal of Management and Governance*, 525 et seq.; R. Anderson, E. Ottolenghi & D. Reeb, 'The dual class premium: A family affair', Fox School of Business Research paper no. 2017–021 (finding that MVS companies without family owners exhibit Tobin's Q values that are higher than their single-class peers, though the opposite is the case when MV shares are held by family owners); G. Morey, 'Multi-class stock and firm value', CII publication, May 2017; M. Cremers/B. Lauterbach/A. Pajuste, 'The Life-Cycle of Dual Class Firms', ECGI Working Paper N° 550/2018 (showing higher valuation for MVS firms early in the life cycle); D. Melas, 'Putting the Spotlight on Spotify: Why Have Stocks with Unequal Voting Rights Outperformed?' MSCI: GLOBAL INVESTING, 3 April 2018; H. Kim/R. Michaely, 'Sticking around Too Long? Dynamics of the Benefits of Dual-Class Voting', ECGI Finance Working Paper No. 590/2019; and B. Anh/J. FischP. Patatoukas/S. Solomon, 'Synthetic Governance', ECGI Finance Working Paper no. 693/2020.

As far as we are aware, all overviews that have been carried out, including the rigorous research project carried out by ECGI on behalf of the European Commission, have shown that there is no conclusive evidence on the effects of MVS structures on company value in either direction.[35] From a theoretical and scientific point of view, the argument, that MVS structures in general damage company value, must therefore, at this point, be viewed as unsupported. Available data *does* show that MVS structures in some cases seem to have a negative effect on company value, but also that in other cases, MVS structures have the opposite, positive, effect on company value. A call for prohibiting MVS structures based on the best available understanding of the effects of MVS structures on company value cannot therefore be made.

[35] See the study 'Proportionality between ownership and control in EU listed companies: External study commissioned by the European Commission', carried out by ISS, Shearman & Sterling and the ECGI, and R. B. Adams and D. Ferreira, 'One Share-One Vote – The Empirical Evidence' (2008) 12 *Review of Finance*, 51 et seq. See, also, mostly since then, Fisch and Solomon, 'The problem of sunsets', 1057 et seq.; Reddy, 'More than Meets the Eye: Reassessing the Empirical Evidence on US Dual-Class Stock', 956 et seq. (concluding 'that although dual-class firms are generally valued less than similar one-share, one-vote firms, they perform as well as, and, in many cases, outperform, such firms from the perspective of operating performance and stock returns'); T. Hossain and L. Kryzanowski, 'A review of the literature on dual-class firms' (2019) 45 *Managerial Finance*, 1199 et seq. (concluding that 'The literature arrives at no consensus on the benefits/drawbacks of' MVS structures); J. Shen, 'The anatomy of dual class share structures: A comparative perspective' (2016) 46 *Hong Kong Law Journal*, 477 et seq.; A. Pacces, 'Featuring Control Power' (2007) RILE (p. 757–759); and A. Rydqvist, 'Dual-class shares: A review' (1992) 8 *Oxford Review of Economic Policy*, 45 et seq.

16.3.2 *Argument 2: MVS Structures Lead to Increased Agency Costs*

The second argument often made in the MVS debate is that MVS structures lead to increased shirking and tunnelling of company assets to controlling shareholders, or in other words, that MVS structures exacerbate principal-agent risks for investors since they skew the alignment of ownership and voting rights.[36] One could, of course, argue that since MVS structures do not seem to have a negative effect on company value when comparing the populations of companies with and without MVS structures, this seems implausible, since decreased company value should be the consequence of increased agency costs.

Still, the argument does not hinge on the market reaction to tunnelling, only that it occurs with higher frequency in MVS companies than in others. Such occurrences are, of course, hard to measure directly, since tunnelling is by definition a covert activity. However, economists have used control premiums paid for control blocks as well as MVS as a proxy measure, the logic being that premiums paid for controlling shares as compared to the price paid for non-controlling shares are viewed as a sign of the private benefits of control that can be siphoned.[37] If MVS structures lead to increased tunnelling of company assets, one would expect that control premiums would be higher in markets where MVS structures are prevalent, since a bidder would be willing to pay more for shares that would allow them to extract additional value from the company. Tatiana Nenova's study, 'The value of corporate voting rights and control: A cross-country analysis', shows high control

[36] See, for instance: H. DeAngelo and E. Rice, 'Anti-Takeover charter amendments and stockholder wealth' (1983) 11 *Journal of Financial Economics*, 329 et seq.; G. Jarrell and A. Poulsen, 'Dual-class recapitalizations as antitakeover mechanisms' (1988) 20 *Journal of Financial Economics*, 129 et seq.; R. S. Ruback, 'Coercive dual-class exchange offers' (1988) 20 *Journal of Financial Economics*, 153 et seq.; M. Kang, H. Lee, M. Lee and J. Park, 'The Association between related-party transactions and control-ownership wedge: Evidence from Korea' (2014) 29 *Pacific-Basin Finance Journal*, 272 et seq.; L. Bebchuk, R. Kraakman and G. Triantis, 'Stock Pyramids, Cross-Ownership and Dual Class Equity: The Mechanisms and Agency Costs of Separating Control From Cash-Flow Rights', in R. Morck (ed.), Concentrated Corporate Ownership (Chicago University Press, 2000), p. 445 et seq.; and R. Masulis, C. Wang and F. Xie, 'Agency problems at dual-class companies' (2009) 64 *Journal of Finance*, 1697 et seq.

[37] Though other measurements, such as discounts (Tobin's Q), financial performance, return on firm investments, and level of CEO pay, are also used, cf. H. Cronqvist and M. Nilsson, 'Agency Costs of Controlling Minority Shareholders' (2003) 38 *Journal of Financial and Quantitative Analysis*, 695 et seq.; Masulis, Wang and Xie, 'Agency problems at dual-class companies', 1697 et seq.; L. Andrade, A. Bressan and R. Iquiapaza, 'Dual class shares, board of directors' effectiveness and firm's market value: an empirical study' (2017) 21 *Journal of Management & Governance*, 1053 et seq.; K. Cieślak, 'Agency conflicts, executive compensation regulations and CEO pay-performance sensitivity: evidence from Sweden' (2018) 22 *Journal of Management and Governance*, 535 et seq.; and S. Bauguess, 'Recontracting Ownership and Control: The Effects of Differential Voting Rights after Dual Class Recapitalization' (2004) PhD thesis at Arizona State University, in particular p. 88–110 (finding 'no evidence to support the hypothesis that these [sample] firms adopt a dual class share structure [. . .] to expropriate wealth from minority shareholders').

premiums in some countries where MVS structures are prevalent, including Brazil and Mexico. However, the study also shows that the control premium for MVS is very low in the Scandinavian countries, including Sweden, where MVS listings are common, and the same goes for Canada – also a market with plenty of MVS listings.[38]

Considering the argument being made – that MVS structures lead to increased risk of tunnelling of company assets to controlling shareholders – the argument does not seem to be supported by what can be measured. While there are examples of markets where MVS structures are prevalent and where agency costs seem heightened, causality between MVS structures and the latter is not shown.[39] Furthermore, studies comparing stock returns of MVS companies as compared to single-class companies fairly consistently show *higher* returns in MVS firms, which can hardly be reconciled with disproportionate agency costs,[40] and the same goes for studies on MVS-company profitability.[41] To conclude, the causality seems to be between the general strength of minority protection in company law as well as in takeover law, as the countries with high control premiums are also judged to have weak protection of minority shareholders.[42]

38 T. Nenova, 'The value of corporate voting rights and control: A cross-country analysis' (2003) 68 *Journal of Financial Economics*, 325 et seq.

39 Indeed, while there are studies supporting the argument (see above), there are, again, plenty of studies showing the opposite: W. Ben-Amar and P. André, 'Separation of ownership from control and acquiring firm performance: The case of family ownership in Canada' (2006) 33 *Journal of Business Finance and Accounting*, 517 et seq.; X. Cheng, H. Mpundu and H. Wan, 'Investment efficiency: Dual-class vs. single-class firms' (2020) 45 *Global Finance Journal*, 100477; B. Jordan, M. Liu and Q. Wu, 'Corporate payout policy in dual class firms' (2013) 26 *Journal of Corporate Finance*, 1 et seq.; and S. Banerjee and R. Masulis, 'Ownership, Investment and Governance: The Costs and Benefits of Dual Class Shares', (2013) ECGI – Finance Working Paper No. 352, finding that 'dual-class shares can be a solution to agency conflicts rather than a result of agency conflicts'.

40 We have not found any studies on the stock returns of MVS firms showing abnormal negative returns, but several showing the opposite (Reddy, 'More than Meets the Eye: Reassessing the Empirical Evidence on US Dual-Class Stock', 956 et seq. for a discussion on the US studies on MVS share returns).

41 For a summary of eleven studies on profitability in US MVS companies, seeibid., concluding that they 'either showed that dual-class firms outperform matched OSOV [one share, one vote] firms by at least one performance measure [...] or showed no difference in operating performance between dual-class and OSOV firms'.

42 See Nenova, 'The value of corporate voting rights and control', at 345. See also C. Doidge, 'U.S. cross-listings and the private benefits of control: Evidence from dual-class firms' (2004) 72 *Journal of Financial Economics*, 519 et seq. (concluding that differences in voting premiums decreases when minority shareholder protection improves); B. Amoako-Adu, V. Baulkaran and B. Smith, 'Dual class discount, and the channels of extraction of private benefits' (2013) 16 *Advances in Financial Economics*, 165 et seq. (finding 'that the discount in the value of dual class shares in relation to the value of closely controlled single class company shares is directly related to the channels through which controlling shareholder-managers can extract private benefits'); and A. da Silva and A. Subrahmanyam, 'Dual-class premium, corporate governance, and the mandatory bid rule: Evidence from the Brazilian stock market' (2007) 13 *Journal of Corporate Finance*, 1 et seq. (finding that 'the MVS-premium is inversely related to an index

16.3.3 *Argument 3: MVS Structures Undermine the Market for Corporate Control*

The third argument often made against MVS structures, and of particular relevance in this volume, is that MVS structures undermine the market for corporate control and constitute an anti-takeover defence measure.[43] Another way of putting it is that MVS structures lead to managerial or controlling shareholder entrenchment.[44] Such arguments are often targeted at specific individuals, such as Mark Zuckerberg or Larry Page, or as a critique against family ownership.[45]

The law and economics framework of the market for corporate control in essence states that when a listed company is poorly managed, and the underperformance is identified by the market, the company will be the target of a takeover offer, in which the shares will be acquired by someone better suited to oversee the company and change the management accordingly.[46] The claim is that MVS structures will hamper this disciplinary market function, since holding MV shares will protect a controlling shareholder from the risk of a 'hostile' takeover bid.

While we do not argue against the possibility that, in individual cases, this might indeed be true and a problem, this cannot be enough to take a stance against permitting MVS structures from a policy perspective. The question is whether MVS structures in general hinder the proper workings of the market for corporate control. And here, the evidence seems quite clear. If MVS structures were an obstacle to takeovers, one would expect such stock to be significantly less common among takeover targets than among listed companies in general. Available data does not support this. In a study carried out in Sweden, with one of the most active takeover markets in the world that also have a high percentage of MVS companies, the conclusion was that, among the 245 Swedish listed companies that were subject to takeovers during the 13-year measuring period, 64 per cent of the acquired companies (157) were MVS companies, compared to 69 per cent of all listed

designed to capture the firm's corporate governance practices. The results suggest that expropriations of minority shareholders are more likely at firms with poor corporate governance provisions and weak takeover rules relating to mandatory bids').

43 See Davies and Pietrancosta's contribution in this volume (Chapter 10).

44 See, most prominently, S. Grossman and O. Hart, 'One share-one vote and the market for corporate control' (1988) 20 *Journal of Financial Economics*, 175 et seq.; Ruback, 'Coercive dual-class exchange offers', 153 et seq.; M. Burkart, D. Gromb and F. Panunzi, 'Why higher takeover premia protect minority shareholders' (1998) 106 *Journal of Political Economy*, 172 et seq.; M. Harris and A. Raviv, 'Corporate Governance: Voting rights and majority rules' (1988) 20 *Journal of Financial Economics*, 203 et seq.; and Bebchuk, Kraakman and Triantis, 'Stock Pyramids, Cross-Ownership and Dual Class Equity', 445 et seq.

45 See for instance, Shari Redstone in the *Financial Times* View, 15 May 2018, 'A dysfunctional family reunion at CBS/Viacom'.

46 See foremost H. Manne, 'Mergers and the Market for Corporate Control' (1965) 73 *Journal of Political Economy*, 110 et seq.

companies during the same period being MVS companies.[47] Similar results have been found in several studies.[48] Though other studies have shown the opposite,[49] the conclusion is again that available data does not offer more support for the argument that MVS structures have negative effects on takeover frequency or the market for corporate control than for the opposite.[50]

To summarize, neither the arguments made against MVS structures nor those in favour of prohibiting them are supported by the empirical evidence. With this, we do not, however, mean to say that there are no drawbacks with MVS structures. Though MVS structures might be useful for some companies in some regards, as Thomas Sowell eloquently phrased it, 'There are no solutions, only trade-offs.'[51] The question is not whether MVS structures are a solution to any particular problem, or whether MVS structures come with governance problems, but whether these

[47] See R. Skog, 'The European Union's Proposed Takeover Directive, the "Breakthrough" Rule and the Swedish System of Dual Class Common Stock' (2004) 15 *European Business Law Review*, 294 et seq.

[48] See, for instance: R. Comment and G. Schwert, 'Poison or placebo? Evidence on the deterrence and wealth effects of modern anti-takeover measures' (1995) 39 *Journal of Financial Economics*, 3 et seq.; L. Fields, 'Control considerations of newly public firms: The implementation of antitakeover provisions and dual class shares before the IPO', Working paper (1999), Penn State University; B. Amoako-Adu and B. Smith, 'Dual class firms: Capitalization, ownership structure and recapitalization back into single class' (2001) 25 *Journal of Banking & Finance*, 1083 et seq.; O. Arugaslan, D. Cook and R. Kieschnick, 'On the decision to go public with dual class stock' (2010) 16 *Journal of Corporate Finance*, 170 et seq.; S. Bauguess, M. Slovin and M. Sushka, 'Large shareholder diversification, corporate risk taking, and the benefits of changing to differential voting rights' (2012) 36 *Journal of Banking & Finance*, 1244 et seq. (even finding that MVS companies are taken over more often, and with higher premiums, than single-class firms); and Bauguess, 'Recontracting Ownership and Control: The Effects of Differential Voting Rights after Dual Class Recapitalization' (finding 'no evidence to support the hypothesis that' MVS structures are adopted 'as an anti-takeover device', and that, to the contrary, 'firms that conduct dual class recapitalizations are acquired at a greater rate and receive higher takeover premiums than benchmark firms with a single class share structure').

[49] See W. Mikkelson and M. Partch, 'The consequences of unbundling managers' voting rights and equity claims' (1994) 1 *Journal of Corporate Finance*, 175 et seq.; S. Smart and C. Zutter, 'Control as a motivation for underpricing: a comparison of dual and single-class IPOs' (2003) 69 *Journal of Financial Economics*, 85 et seq.; M. Holmen and E. Nivorozhkin, 'The impact of dual class shares on takeover risk and the market for corporate control' (2007) 17 *Applied Financial Economics*, 785 et seq.; V. Baulkaran, 'Management entrenchment and the valuation discount of dual class firms' (2014) 54 *Quarterly Review of Economics and Finance*, 70 et seq.; B. Jordan, S. Kim and M. Liu, 'Growth opportunities, short-term market pressure, and dual-class share structure' (2016) 4 *Journal of Corporate Finance*, 304 et seq.; and M. Cremers, B. Lauterbach and A. Pajuste, 'The Life-Cycle of Dual Class Firms', ECGI Working Paper N° 550/2018.

[50] See also Reddy, concluding that 'the empirical evidence is inconclusive as to whether takeovers of dual-class firms are in fact less prevalent than OSOV [one share, one vote] firms' (B. Reddy, 'More than Meets the Eye: Reassessing the Empirical Evidence on US Dual-Class Stock' (2020) University of Cambridge Faculty of Law Research Paper No. 20, at p. 29); Adams and Ferreira, 'One Share-One Vote – The Empirical Evidence', 60.

[51] T. Sowell, *The Vision of the Anointed* (Basic Books, 1996), p. 113.

problems are so severe that MVS companies should not even be allowed to list their shares on stock markets. And regarding this matter, we claim that there are not only no compelling reasons to stop MVS listings, but, in fact, no clear empirically supported reasons at all.

All governance structures have drawbacks. Yet, there is no general demand to prohibit listings of companies with staggered board structures,[52] poison pills,[53] voting caps, or other management insulating mechanisms, or companies with other control-enhancement mechanisms in place – for instance, corporate pyramids. The drawbacks of MVS structures are not unique to this particular form of control-enhancement mechanism. They are even present in companies without MVS structures or any other control-enhancement mechanism, and therefore it does not make any sense to ban MVS structures in particular – the situation is, as we have shown, far more complex than that.[54] Regulators will instead have to consider how MVS structures should be regulated in the different situations where they merit specific regulation. In the next section, we will consider such situations in a takeover context.

16.4 REGULATORY ISSUES IN TAKEOVER BIDS ON MVS FIRMS

16.4.1 *Introduction and Teleological Interpretation of the Mandatory Bid Rule*

MVS structures have thus become more common in many markets, and this trend can be expected to continue. And as we have shown, there is no reason for regulators to impede this development. However, thought must be given to how to handle some of the particular governance issues arising due to the presence of MVS structures. And as we have already touched upon, there is no *one way* to do this. There are no one-size-fits-all solutions for corporate governance issues, and a good solution will *always* take into consideration and even be dependent on national legal and market conditions.[55] This too applies to the regulation of takeovers, as other

[52] Which have been shown to have negative effect on company value in some studies (see, for instance: L. Bebchuck and A. Cohen, 'The costs of entrenched boards' (2005) 78 *Journal of Financial Economics*, 409 et seq.; O. Faleye, 'Classified boards, firm value and managerial entrenchment' (2007) 83 *Journal of Financial Economics*, 501 et seq.; and A. Cohen and C. Wang, 'How do staggered boards affect shareholder value? Evidence from a natural experiment' (2013) 110 *Journal of Financial Economics*, 627 et seq.), but not in all (for instance, M. Cremers, L. Litov and S. Sepe, 'Staggered boards and long-term firm value, revisited' (2017) 126 *Journal of Financial Economics*, 422 et seq.).

[53] Also shown to have negative effects on company values in some studies, while positive in others (see Adams and Ferreira, 'One Share-One Vote – The Empirical Evidence', 69–70).

[54] Though not the topic of this chapter, we have discussed how to handle the specific governance risks tied to MVS structures in other papers; see, for instance, Lidman and Skog, 'London allowing dual class premium listings', 83 et seq.

[55] See, for instance, OECD, 'Flexibility and proportionality in corporate governance' (OECD Publishing, 2018).

chapters in this volume have shown.[56] And needless to say, the Takeover Directive does not provide any detailed answers on how to address issues arising in bids on MVS firms.[57]

In this section, we will therefore not argue for any particular way to regulate bids on companies with MVS structures. Instead, our goal here is to draw on experiences regarding what questions may (and in many cases will) arise in such bids, and ways for regulators to approach them, considering the general principles of takeover regulation laid down in the Takeover Directive and its purpose.[58] Before we move on to the issues at hand, something should be said about this purpose.

Regulation of takeovers in Europe, from the early days of regulation in the 1960s London Code to the Takeover Directive, has in principle had one overarching purpose: to protect minority shareholders in listed companies in the event of a change of control.[59] Today, this protection is laid down in detail and in many different ways in the Member States and the UK. At the core of the regulation is the principle of equivalent treatment of shareholders, which (among other ways) manifests in the sharing of the control premium, and which is laid down in Article 3(1)(a) of the Takeover Directive.[60] In order to ensure that this protection is not circumvented and to add an exit opportunity for minority shareholders in a change of

56 See, for instance, the contribution by Clarke and Skog in this volume (Chapter 1).

57 It is also worth mentioning that there is no other general principle of equal treatment in EU law that can supplement the discussion; see, for instance, C101/08 (paragraph 37) and F. M. Mucciarelli, 'Equal Treatment of Shareholders in European Union Law' (2010) 7 *European Company and Financial Law Review*, 158 et seq.

58 Not to say that the Directive cannot provide normative guidance for the Member States, given the prevalence of the teleological method in EU law; see, for instance: A. Llorens, *The European Court of Justice, More than a Teleological Court* (Cambridge University Press, 2017), p. 373–398; M. Lasser, *Judicial Deliberations: A Comparative Analysis of Judicial Transparency and Legitimacy*, (Oxford University Press, 2004), p. 231; and T. Schilling, 'Beyond Multilingualism: On Different Approaches to the Handling of Diverging Language Versions of a Community Law' (2010) 16 *European Law Journal*, 47 et seq.; and Paunio, *Legal Certainty in Multilingual EU Law* (Ashgate, 2013), in particular p. 193–194. See also EPRS Briefing PE 599.364 (2017), p. 6 ('This is explained by numerous factors, in particular the open-ended and policy-oriented rules of the EU Treaties, as well as by EU legal multilingualism. Under the latter principle, all EU law is equally authentic in all language versions. Hence, the Court cannot rely on the wording of a single version, as a national court can, in order to give an interpretation of the legal provision under consideration. Therefore, in order to decode the meaning of a legal rule, the Court analyses it especially in the light of its purpose 'teleological interpretation' as well as its context "systemic interpretation"') and EPRS Briefing PE 595.914 p. 7–8.

59 See, for instance, reasons (1), (2) and (9) in the Takeover Directive. See also A. Johnston, *The City Take-Over Code* (Oxford University Press, 1980), p. 16 ff. and 27 ff.; R. Roberts, 'Regulatory Responses to the Rise of the Market for Corporate Control in Britain in the 1950s' (1992) 34 *Business History*, 183 et seq.; A: Johnston, 'Takeover Regulation: Historical and Theoretical Perspectives on the City Code' (2007) 66 *The Cambridge Law Journal*, 442 et seq.; and J. Armour and D. Skeel, 'Who Writes the Rules for Hostile Takeovers, and Why? The Peculiar Divergence of US and UK Takeover Regulation' (2007) 95 *Georgetown Law Journal*, 1756 et seq.

60 The Article states that 'all holders of the securities of an offeree company of the same class must be afforded equivalent treatment' in a takeover bid.

control event, a mandatory bid rule complements the principle of equivalent treatment in Article 5.[61] This is the *telos* of the Directive that must be kept in mind in the following discussion.

16.4.2 *Pricing MV Shares*

A fundamental question that arises when deciding how takeover regulation should be applied or construed in a bid on an MVS firm is how the requirement for equivalent treatment should be applied in relation to the offer price, and the sharing of the control premium, since the bidder will generally be willing to pay a premium for the MV shares. Should such a difference in the premium paid then be allowed?

The Takeover Directive does not offer us much guidance. General Principle (a) only states that all shareholders in the offeree of the *same class* must be afforded *equivalent treatment*. The principle does not therefore extend to shareholders of different share classes such as MV and SV shares, *nor* does it per the phrasing require the exact same treatment *within* a share class. Arguments can be made both for and against allowing a premium for the MV shares.

Looking to the general purpose of takeover regulation, one can argue that a premium for MV shares in no fundamental way differs from the control premium offered for a majority block of shares, inferring control of the company. MV and SV shares have the same economic rights,[62] and a premium for the MV shares would be nothing more than a control premium. They should therefore be treated in the same way as control premiums when there is only one share class in the target company, based on the idea embodied in Article 5.4 of the Takeover Directive that a control premium belongs to all shareholders.[63]

On the other hand, there is no getting around the fact that MV and SV shares are different instruments, and that General Principle (a) of the Directive by its phrasing obviously does not require equivalent treatment between different instruments. As we will get back to (see Table 16.1), MV shares in any company tend to trade at a

61 In London, the mandatory bid rule was introduced four years after the City Code, in 1972, in order to ensure that all shareholders of the target company have the same exit options in the event of a change of control, as well as an equal share in the control premium paid by the acquirer for control of the company. See Johnston, *The City Take-Over Code*, p. 75, and Panel Statement 1972/2. In Takeover Panel PCP 2009/2, the panel observes that a 'general offer at the highest price' is required 'so that all shareholders have the opportunity to share the premium', paragraph 2.4. The same observation is made in the Panel's Annual Report from 1991, where it is stated that 'the principle of equal treatment for shareholders requires that all shareholders should have the opportunity to obtain the price per share paid for that control'. Regarding the connection between equal treatment and the mandatory bid rule, see also D. Kershaw, *Principles of Takeover Regulation* (Oxford University Press, 2016), p. 251–252.

62 This is of course not necessarily the case but must be a starting point for the analysis.

63 See R. Skog, 'No Rule, Just Exemptions? Mandatory Bids in Sweden and in the EU' (2014) 11 *European Company and Financial Law Review*, 393 et seq., and Winner, 'Does the European Union have a mandatory bid rule', in *Festschrift in Honour of Rolf Skog* (Norstedts Juridik, 2021), p. 1179 et seq.

premium over the SV shares in the market.[64] The MV shareholders may also have paid a premium for the MV shares when the shares were first issued in the primary market.[65] Put simply, control has an objective economic value that, in our view, cannot logically be discarded in a bid situation by saying that the bidder must pay *exactly* the same price for MV and SV shares with reference to the principle of equivalent treatment.[66] This also aligns with how the notion of equal treatment of shareholders in EU law in general has been viewed as 'not, according to the prevailing opinion [...] as an obligation [...] to treat shareholders in the same way, but is understood to mean that *unequal treatment needs sufficiently objective justification*'.[67]

However, the question then becomes where to draw the line, so that a premium to the MV shareholders does not become arbitrary nor simply a control premium that is not shared with the SV shareholders without being justified by the difference between the share classes. Is it reasonable that the bidder can pay a premium of 10,000 per cent for the MV shares over the SV shares? Surely, this would be exactly the type of unequal treatment that takeover regulation aims to curb, and we believe it uncontroversial to say that such considerations should not be accepted by regulators or supervisory authorities. But would a premium of 50 per cent be tolerable? 25 per cent? 15? Or 5?

There is obviously no single right answer to this question, and perhaps any somewhat reasonable limit decided by the regulator is adequate to protect the minority and allow foreseeability and correct pricing of MV and SV shares in the market when a bid is expected. The focus in drawing this line should be to find a general rule that is to be applied in the market, rather than requiring that the premium should be proved to be 'equitable' in the individual bid, to ensure foreseeability and proper pricing of the different share classes in the market, as well as facilitating a quick bid process.[68] And here, guidance can be found in the empirical data on how MV shares are generally priced in the market, of which there are quite a few empirical studies:

64 Regardless of whether there is a bid hanging over the company or not.

65 One could argue that they even *should* have paid a premium for their shares compared to the price for the SV shares, if the company has a purpose to generate profit, which would require the board to charge as high a price as possible in an issuance for any given instrument, cf. R. Skog, 'The Importance of Profit in Company Law' (2015) 12 *European Company and Financial Law Review*, 563 et seq.

66 Cf. C. Lam and P. Raimbourg, 'Les actions à droits de vote multiples' (2023) 3 *Revue Trimestrielle de Droit Financier*, 51 et seq.

67 See Opinion of Advocate General Case C 338/06 para 61, with references.

68 It would otherwise be quite easy to imagine that the decided premium would be contested in court by minority shareholders or activist funds, leading to lawsuits following each and every bid on MVS firms. In addition, pricing of control in an individual case is always highly complex and uncertain; see, for instance: R. Beatty, 'Corporate Control and the Corporate Asset Theory' (1966) 27 *Montana Law Review*, 153 et seq.; K. Rydqvist, *The Pricing of Shares with Different Voting Power and the Theory of Oceanic Games* (Stockholm School of Economics, 1987); P. Bolton and E. von Thadden, 'Blocks, Liquidity, and Corporate Control' (1998) 53 *Journal of Finance*, 1 et seq., and R. Albuquerque and E. Schroth, 'The Value of Control and the Costs of Liquidity' (2015) 70 *Journal of Finance*, 1405 et seq.

TABLE 16.1 *Studies regarding MV share pricing*

Study	MV premium	Market
Chung & Kim (1999)[69]	9.6%	South Korea
Cox & Roden (2002)[70]	7.7%	US
Hauser & Lauterbach (2004)[71]	10%	Israel
Hoffmann-Burchardi (1999)[72]	26%	Germany
Gardiol, Gibson-Asner & Tuchschmid (1997)[73]	5–40%[74]	Switzerland
Horner (1998)[75]	>10%[76]	Switzerland
Lease, McConnell & Mikkelsson (1983)[77]	5.4%	US
Levy (1983)[78]	45.5%	Israel
Megginson (1990)[79]	13.3%	UK
Muus (1998)[80]	51.4%	France
Muus & Tyrell (1999)[81]	29%	Germany

(*continued*)

69 K. Chung and J. Kim, 'Corporate ownership and the value of a vote in an emerging market' (1999) 5 *Journal of Corporate Finance*, 35 et seq.

70 S. Cox and D. Roden, 'The source of value of voting rights and related dividend promises' (2002) 8 *Journal of Corporate Finance*, 337 et seq.

71 S. Hauser and B. Lauterbach, 'The value of voting rights to majority shareholders: Evidence from dual-class stock unifications' (2004) 17 *The Review of Financial Studies*, 1167 et seq.

72 U. Hoffmann-Burchardi, 'Corporate governance rules and the value of control: A study of German dual-class shares' (1999) Financial Markets Group Discussion Paper 315, London School of Economics.

73 L. Gardiol, R. Gibson-Asner and N. Tuchschmid, 'Are liquidity and corporate control priced by shareholders? Empirical evidence from Swiss dual class shares' (1997) 3 *Journal of Corporate Finance*, 299 et seq.

74 The study does not compile an average price difference between bearer shares and registered shares for the measurement period (see graph on p. 303) and the data reported in the study does not allow such a conversion, but an average for the time period can be roughly estimated at around 20 per cent.

75 M. R. Horner, 'The value of the corporate voting right: evidence from Switzerland' (1989) 12 *Journal of Banking and Finance*, 69 et seq.

76 The study does not conclude that the price difference between bearer shares and registered shares differs in terms of voting rights within a 1:10 ratio, but the author notes that '[t]he majority of the observed discounts is greater than 10 per cent, implying that the voting right of even a bearer share is of considerable value'; see ibid.

77 R. Lease, J. McConnell and W. Mikkelson, 'The market value of control in publicly-traded corporations' (1983) 11 *Journal of Financial Economics*, 440 et seq.

78 H. Levy, 'Economic evaluation of voting power of common stock' (1983) 38 *Journal of Finance*, 79 et seq.

79 W. Megginson, 'Restricted voting stock, acquisition premiums, and the market value of corporate control' (1990) 25 *Financial Review*, 175 et seq.

80 C. Muus, 'Non-Voting Shares in France: An Empirical Analysis of the Voting Premium' (1988) Working Paper No. 22, University of Frankfurt.

81 C. Muus and M. Tyrell, 'An empirical analysis of the voting premium in Germany' (1999) Working Paper, Johan Wolfgang Goethe-Universität, Frankfurt am Main.

TABLE 16.1 (*continued*)

Study	MV premium	Market
Neumann (2003)[82]	12.2%	Denmark
Rydqvist (1996)[83]	12%	Sweden
Smith & Amoako-Adu (1995)[84]	10.4%	Canada
Robinson & White (1990)[85]	23.3%	Canada
Zingales (1994)[86]	80%	Italy
Zingales (1995)[87]	10.5%	US
Ødegaard (2007)[88]	10%	Norway

Obviously, all MV shares are not created the same (or in the same way). The voting ratio between MV and SV shares differs from jurisdiction to jurisdiction (and company to company), and they function differently in different markets. But the studies we have found fairly consistently show that, in developed markets, transferable MV shares with the same economic rights as SV shares trade at a premium of around 10 per cent, regardless of voting ratio. To us, it would therefore seem to strike a reasonable balance that regulation allow a bidder to offer a 10 per cent premium for MV shares over SV shares. Incidentally, in jurisdictions that have regulated MV premiums in bids (as far as we are aware, Canada, Sweden and Switzerland), this level has also been the one applied.[89]

Finally, the line of reasoning here applies in the situation where the extra votes carried by the MV shares are transferable. In situations where the votes are not transferable, such as when there is a transfer-based sunset for the MV shares in the target company, the situation changes. In these cases, we see no reason why the

82 R. Neuman, 'Price Differentials between Dual-Class Stocks: Voting Premium or Liquidity Discounts?' (2003) 9 *European Financial Management*, 315 et seq.

83 K. Rydqvist, 'Takeover bids and the relative prices of shares that differ in their voting rights' (1996) 20 *Journal of Banking and Finance*, 1407 et seq.

84 B. Smith and B. Amoako-Adu, 'Relative prices of dual class shares' (1995) 30 *Journal of Financial and Quantitative Analysis*, 223 et seq.

85 C. Robinson and A. White, *The Value of a Vote in the Market for Corporate Control* (Mimeo, 1990).

86 L. Zingales, 'The Value of the Voting Right: A Study of the Milan Stock Exchange Experience' (1994) 7 *The Review of Financial Studies*, 125 et seq.

87 L. Zingales, 'What determines the value of corporate votes?' (1995) 110 *Quarterly Journal of Economics*, 1047 et seq.

88 B. Ødegaard, 'Price Differences Between Equity Classes. Corporate Control, Foreign Ownership or Liquidity?' (2007) 31 *Journal of Banking and Finance*, 3621 et seq.

89 See regarding Canada, MI 62-104 Take-over Bids and Issuer Bids och 62-203 Take-over Bids and Issuer Bids, div. 2 art. 5.2–3; regarding Sweden, Lidman and Skog, 'London allowing dual class premium listings', 83 et seq.; and regarding Switzerland, Swiss Takeover Board Decisions 623/01, 623/02, 623/03 of 2016 regarding Kiwi Holding IV SarlKuoni Travel Holding Ltd. Note that the Swiss and Swedish rules regarding premiums were introduced after the empirical studies referenced above were conducted.

bidder should be allowed to offer a higher consideration for the MV shares, since the transferable economic value of the votes is the same as that of the SV shares.

16.4.3 *Different Forms of Consideration for Different Share Classes*

A question relating to the one in the previous section is whether the bidder can offer different forms of consideration for MV and SV shares (assuming that the value of the different forms of consideration is equal or that any difference in value is within acceptable parameters, as discussed in the previous section). The starting point here must be, in accordance with the Takeover Directive, that all different forms of consideration should be available to all shareholders in the target company, regardless of share class, unless the difference in share classes allows for *equivalent* treatment without offering the different considerations to all shareholders.[90]

In relation to a bid on an MVS firm, at least one such situation can be imagined: when both the offeror (the BidCo) and the offeree company has an MVS structure, and the consideration in the bid consists of shares in the BidCo.[91] Can the MV shareholders of the target company then be offered MV shares in the BidCo, and the SV shareholders in the target be offered BidCo SV shares? Here, we see no reason why the different forms of consideration for the different share classes should not be allowed. If the value of the consideration is the same for both share classes,[92] the situation is in our view more straightforward than if a slight premium is offered for the MV shares, since the shareholders in the offeree company will be in the same position after the bid as they were before.

More complicated scenarios can arise, however, where a more restrictive view should be taken. It would, for example, hardly align with the principle of equivalent treatment to allow that the consideration for one share class in the offeree company consist of cash, while the consideration for the other share class consists of shares in the BidCo.[93]

16.4.4 *Partial Bids on a Single-Share Class*

A third takeover question arising when the target company has an MVS structure is whether the bidder should be allowed to make a bid for only one class of shares – that is, a partial bid.

Partial bids are in themselves nothing untoward. In a partial bid on a company with only one share class, the terms of the offer would be that the bidder offers to purchase

[90] See Article 5.5 paragraph 3 of the Takeover Directive.

[91] This is at least not uncommon in Sweden; see, for instance, Swedish Securities Council statement 2017:22.

[92] Note that such a consideration might not mean that the exchange ratio is 1:1 for both MV and SV shares, nor the same for the different share classes.

[93] Cf. Articles 5.5 and 15.5 in the Takeover Directive.

a maximum of, say, 29 per cent of the shares in the target company through the bid, and that in the event of oversubscription, the bidder would purchase shares at a pro rata basis from the shareholders that wish to tender their shares.[94]

However, such a partial bid is only possible if the bid does not result in the acquirer passing the mandatory bid threshold.[95] The scenario that we are considering here is different from a 'regular' partial bid in that the offeror is making a bid for only the MV shares or a part of them, with a limitation to not acquire so many votes in the target company that the bidder would cross the mandatory bid threshold. In the event of the bidder exceeding the number of votes of a mandatory takeover threshold, the takeover bid should be launched for all the shares.

A partial bid as outlined here is, as far as we can see, no different from an acquisition of a block of shares directly from one or a group of shareholders. There is therefore no reason for a bidder not to be allowed to make a partial offer limited to only one share class, as long as the bid does not cross the mandatory bid threshold and treats all shareholders within the share class for which the bid is made equivalently.[96]

16.4.5 *Vote Changes Triggering the Mandatory Bid?*

MVS structures may also give rise to a number of situations where the mandatory bid rule must be considered, both with regard to 'regular' MVS structures and loyalty shares. At least four scenarios can be imagined, where changes in the number of votes allocated to shareholders may trigger the mandatory bid rule:

(1) Introduction of an MVS structure midstream, where a shareholder goes from holding regular shares to MV shares, and as a result he/she crosses the mandatory bid threshold.
(2) A shareholder crosses the mandatory bid threshold due to another shareholder converting his or her shares from MV to SV shares, thereby decreasing his or her total number of votes in the company.
(3) A shareholder holds loyalty shares long enough to get the extra votes, and thereby crosses the mandatory bid threshold.
(4) A shareholder crosses the mandatory bid threshold due to another shareholder selling loyalty shares, decreasing the total number of shares in the company and thereby increasing the first shareholder's relative share (similar to scenario 2).[97]

[94] If the offer is for 29 per cent of the shares in the target company, and shareholders of 50 per cent of the shares in the target company accept the bid, the bidder would then acquire 58 per cent of the shares of each tendering shareholder.
[95] See Article 5 in the Takeover Directive.
[96] This is also the regulation in Sweden; see Swedish Securities Council statement 2017:22.
[97] A variant thereof would be if Y holds MV shares with a transfer-based sunset and sells their shares.

In these scenarios, it should be considered whether crossing the mandatory bid threshold as a consequence of the change of the voting rights or the activation (or deactivation) of loyalty shares shall be deemed to trigger the rule, or whether, on the contrary, it should be included among the exceptions to the duty to launch a takeover bid.[98] We shall consider each of these scenarios below.

16.4.5.1 Scenario 1: Introduction of an MVS Structure Midstream

In the first scenario, a shareholder (X) goes from holding regular shares in the company to MV shares through a change of the articles of association, and through this change, X crosses the mandatory bid threshold. Is X then required to make a mandatory bid?

According to the mandatory bid rule in Article 5 of the Takeover Directive, a person is required to make a bid on all of the shares in the company if the person 'as a result of his/her own *acquisition*' passes the mandatory bid threshold. Whether X is obliged to make a mandatory bid therefore depends on whether one views the conversion of X's SV shares into MV shares as an *acquisition*. While one would perhaps not necessarily view X's attainment of the MV shares by process of conversion as an acquisition of shares in a strict sense, it is not apparent to us that the attainment of the MV shares should not be viewed as an acquisition of voting rights either. Looking at the purpose of the Takeover Directive and the mandatory bid rule in particular, it is clear that X has *gained control* of the company (as quantitatively defined by Article 5 in the Takeover Directive) through an active action, presumably by voting for the change of the articles of association leading to the conversion of X's shares.[99] The purpose behind the mandatory bid rule thus applies in the situation, and it would seem reasonable to require that X make a mandatory bid.[100] The reasoning in the scenario might also consider the process of the conversion of the shares. If the conversion has been decided on by the general meeting with a supermajority by the shareholders fully informed that the outcome of the decision would be that X would pass the mandatory bid threshold, parallels may perhaps be drawn with the whitewash procedure used, for instance, in the UK by the Takeover Panel when granting dispensation to the mandatory bid rule.[101]

[98] Either by not considering it a trigger event at all, or by granting a waiver. It should of course also be noted that the Takeover Directive is, in the now relevant parts, a *de minimis* directive.

[99] It seems unrealistic that X would not be an active party in the conversion of his/her shares, but if that was nevertheless the case, the conclusion would likely change; see further below.

[100] The price possibly calculated based on the average market value over a particular period; see Article 5.4 paragraph 2 in the Takeover Directive.

[101] See Rule 9 in the UK Takeover Code, under which the Takeover Panel will normally waive the obligation to make a mandatory bid if there is an independent vote at a shareholders' meeting, and Note 1(a), 'Notes on Dispensation' to Rule 9 in the UK Takeover Code, and Appendix 1, Whitewash Guidance Note, paragraphs 2 and 4. See also the contribution by Skog

16.4.5.2 Scenarios 2 and 4: Passing of the Mandatory Bid Threshold Due to Actions by Another Decreasing the Total Number of Votes in the Company

In scenarios 2 and 4, shareholder X passes the mandatory bid threshold due to actions taken by another shareholder Y leading to a decrease in the total number of votes in the company, and to X's share of the votes in the company increasing. This can occur in a firm with a 'regular' MVS structure where the MV shares are convertible to SV shares and shareholder Y chooses to convert his or her shares, leading to X's share of the votes increasing over the mandatory bid threshold (scenario 2)[102] or when a sunset clause is triggered in an MVS firm. It can also occur in a company with loyalty shares where a shareholder Y has held his or her shares long enough to gain the extra loyalty votes and then sells them, thereby reducing the total number of his or her votes in the company and causing X to cross the mandatory bid threshold (scenario 4).

In both scenarios 2 and 4, X has crossed the mandatory bid threshold. However, the mandatory bid threshold has not been crossed by X through his or her own actions, but through the actions of another shareholder Y, and thus not through an *acquisition* as stated in Article 5 in the Takeover Directive,[103] meaning that the mandatory bid rule is not directly applicable. A teleological interpretation of the mandatory bid rule would not motivate an application of the rule in scenarios 2 and 4 either, again since there has been no acquisition of control of the company, and since there is no control premium to be shared. Parallels can be drawn with other situations where a shareholder passes the mandatory bid threshold as a result of another's action, such as when the company repurchases or redeems shares, where a mandatory bid would, in many jurisdictions, not be required.[104] Additionally, enforcing the mandatory bid rule when the threshold is crossed due to actions by another shareholder than the one crossing the threshold in the scenarios under discussion would also create considerable uncertainty for the company subject to

and Sjöman in this volume (Chapter 7), which discusses the merits and use of whitewash procedures in derogations from the mandatory bid rule in general. It can be noted that some jurisdictions also include among the triggers for a mandatory bid other events, such as an agreement entered into by several shareholders who, even if they do not individually exceed the control threshold, they do so jointly and act in concert. Accordingly, in some jurisdictions the mandatory bid sometimes includes the mere agreement of several shareholders to act in concert (see the contribution by García de Enterría and Gargantini in this volume (Chapter 8)).

102 It is not uncommon for the MV shares to be convertible to SV shares to facilitate exit for MV shareholders in situations where the MV shares are not listed or illiquid.

103 Regarding the prerequisite 'acquisition', see the previous section.

104 See for instance Rule 37.1 in the UK Takeover Code, and accompanying Note 1. The same applies in Sweden. Related situations to consider are when the company conducts buybacks, or if a voting cap is removed from the articles of association, leading to a shareholder whose voting rights were restricted and who was not obliged to make a takeover bid, suddenly exceeds the control threshold.

the bid, for the shareholder being required to make the bid, and for the market, since it may be quite unpredictable when actions by another shareholder (or the aggregated consequences of actions by a number of uncoordinated shareholders) will result in a mandatory bid being triggered.[105]

An alternative solution applies in other jurisdictions, including Spain or Germany. This is provided when the shareholder passes the threshold due to corporate transactions (mergers, capital decrease) or actions by another shareholder. She or he is given a period of time in which either to launch the bid or sell his or her shares to fall below the threshold.[106]

In a company with loyalty shares, the situation could be particularly problematic, since the total number of votes could shift frequently in the company, potentially resulting in a shareholder 'skipping rope' with the mandatory bid threshold. We would therefore argue that the mandatory bid rule should not be enforced in scenario 2 or 4.[107]

16.4.5.3 Scenario 3: Passing the Mandatory Bid Threshold due to Holding Loyalty Shares for a Sufficient Period

The third scenario, when a shareholder X holds loyalty shares long enough to get the extra loyalty votes and thereby crosses the mandatory bid threshold, is the opposite of scenario 4 discussed above. In this scenario, X has passed the mandatory bid threshold through X's own actions, and one could argue that X has 'acquired' the additional votes leading to the crossing of the mandatory bid threshold by holding the loyalty shares for a sufficient time. Therefore, the mandatory bid rule should apply.[108] But enforcing the mandatory bid in scenario 3 is not without issues either. Control through extra loyalty voting rights grants less stable control than if X had acquired a 'regular' control block of shares, since the control can be shifted by another shareholder also receiving loyalty shares (either leading to just diluting X below the mandatory bid threshold, or a dilution in combination with another shareholder passing the threshold). In addition, X's control through holding extra loyalty voting rights does not block another shareholder from acquiring control of the company, either by making a takeover offer or by successively building a control

[105] Cf. J. García de Enterría, 'Acciones de lealtad: efectos en junta, OPAs y participaciones Significativa', *La Ley Mercantil*, N° 79, April 2021, 1–23.

[106] These practical issues may be alleviated by giving the shareholder a period (i.e. three months) to launch the bid, or alternatively to sell or otherwise reduce the excess of voting rights to be exempt from the duty to make the mandatory bid, cf. the contribution by Skog and Sjöman in this volume (Chapter 7), referring to the cases of Ireland, Germany (§ 37 WpÜG), France, Italy or Spain (Art. 7 RD 1066/2007).

[107] This is the chosen solution in Sweden, see Securities Council Statements 2000:09 and 2000:14. For a similar conclusion, see also Mosca, 'Experiments on the Wedge between Tenured Voting and Takeover Law', 276–277.

[108] See what we have discussed regarding 'acquisition' and control transactions in Section 16.4.5.1.

block. In this sense, control through holding mature loyalty shares is not the same type of control that the mandatory bid rule was originally designed for, and perhaps unsurprisingly, Member States have elected for different solutions, where France and Spain enforce the mandatory bid rule in scenario 3, along with Italy (though in the latter case with a higher threshold than if control has been acquired in the 'regular' sense).[109] Other Member States, including Belgium, do not enforce the mandatory bid rule when the threshold has been crossed due to the shareholder receiving the extra loyalty votes.[110]

In our view, there are arguments to be made in both directions, and neither solution seems inherently more appropriate than the other. Rather, both solutions give rise to different difficulties, highlighting that the mandatory bid rule is not particularly suitable for handling control changes due to shareholders receiving (or losing) loyalty votes. If a Member State elects not to apply the mandatory bid rule in scenario 3, the question becomes when a mandatory bid will be required. When shareholder X has acquired enough shares and votes to pass the mandatory bid threshold without consideration of the extra loyalty shares? Or when shareholder X has acquired one additional share after passing the threshold? If the mandatory bid rule is applied in the scenario, one would instead have to consider the situation where shareholder X crosses the mandatory bid threshold due to holding the loyalty votes for long enough and being forced to make a bid, and two weeks later, shareholder Y also passes the mandatory bid threshold due to holding the loyalty votes for long enough, lowering X back to under the threshold. Should both X and Y be required to make a bid in this situation? Or only the shareholder passing the mandatory bid threshold first, or only the one with the most votes? Again, there is also the risk that a shareholder will be 'skipping rope' with the mandatory bid threshold, creating uncertainty in the market as well as in the target company. In the end, the most important thing for the market is perhaps to have a clear and predictable regime that the market can easily relate to.[111]

16.5 CONCLUDING REMARKS

As we have shown in this chapter, while it is often argued otherwise, there is nothing inherently good or bad in MVS structures. It is a governance tool that may be 'good' in certain companies while 'bad' in others, and in the end, it ought to be up to the shareholders and the market to decide on the appropriate capital and voting

[109] See C. Mosca, 'Should Shareholders Be Rewarded for Loyalty: European Experiments on the Wedge between Tenured Voting and Takeover Law' (2019) 8, *Michigan Business & Entrepreneurial Law Review*, 245 et seq.

[110] See J. García de Enterría, 'Spanish Loyalty Shares: Effects on the General Shareholders' Meeting, on Takeover Bids and on Significant Holdings' (2022) Ibero-American Institute for Law and Finance Working Paper 1.

[111] Cf. Section 16.4.2.

TABLE 16.2 *Summary of analysis in Section 16.4*

Situation/issue	Our suggested solution
Should premiums be allowed for MV shares?	Yes, but with restrictions, see Section 16.4.2.
Should different forms of consideration be allowed for different share classes?	Yes, but with restrictions, see Section 16.4.3.
Should partial bids be allowed on a single share class?	Yes (with due regard to the mandatory bid threshold), see Section 16.4.4.
Should a shareholder converting his/her shares from SV to MV shares, thereby crossing the mandatory bid threshold, be required to make a mandatory bid?	Yes, but there might be grounds for dispensation/exemptions (at least for a period to permit the selling of the shares), see Section 16.4.5.1.
Should a shareholder that crosses the mandatory bid threshold due to a reduction of the total number of shares in the company caused by the action of another shareholder be required to make a mandatory bid?	No, see Section 16.4.5, but there might be grounds for permitting the selling of the shares for a period to profit from the exemption.
Should a shareholder that crosses the mandatory bid threshold due to holding loyalty shares long enough to get the extra loyalty votes be required to make a mandatory bid?	Both applying and not applying the mandatory bid rule in this scenario has its merits and drawbacks, see Section 16.4.5.3.

structure in each firm. Regardless of this, however, MVS structures, as well as 'variants' such as loyalty shares, do give rise to certain issues that regulators need to handle in one form or another, and current developments outlined in Section 16.2 indicate that these issues are not solely theoretical. The aim of this chapter has been to present these issues, as well as possible solutions to them, to provide regulators and supervisory authorities with a roadmap when considering bids on MVS firms. In Table 16.2, we summarize the issues, and while the Takeover Directive offers no guidance, our own suggested solutions.

17

Reform of the Takeover Directive

Harmonisation or Member State Autonomy?

Jesper Lau Hansen and Therese Strand

17.1 INTRODUCTION

It is well known that the Directive on Takeover Bids[1] had a troubled start and was almost not adopted at all.[2] Only by making some of its more contentious provisions optional was it possible to muster the necessary support. To paraphrase the Duke of Wellington after a different battle in Belgium: it was a damn close-run thing.

This system of 'opt-out and opt-in', whereby Member States could opt out of the regulation mandated by a particular provision of the Directive but would have to accept that their national companies had the choice to opt in and accept the regulation was a novelty at the time. It was readily accepted by the Member States, as they knew well that few if any of their national companies would choose to opt into something that the Member State itself found too alien to its own system and consequently the solution was really just and only an opt-out system with the opt-in added to mitigate the fact that it is questionable, to say the least, whether something that can be optional fulfils the treaty-bound requirements of subsidiarity and proportionality enshrined in Article 5, Sections 3–4, of the Treaty on European Union (TEU). Fortunately for the Directive, its compliance with Art. 5 TEU was never brought before the Court of Justice of the EU (CJEU), and since then the idea of making controversial provisions optional in EU legislative acts to enable their adoption has been frequently utilised and is by now widely seen as unobjectionable, even though the optionality prevents the harmonisation that is the very raison d'être of EU legislation. Apparently, pretending to provide harmonisation even if no harmonisation is provided is preferred by the EU legislators to accepting that harmonisation is not politically feasible at the moment and waiting until the need for harmonisation manifests itself.

1 Parliament and Council Directive 2004/25/EC On Takeover Bids, 2004 O.J. (L142).

2 See B. J. Clarke and R. Skog, 'The Genesis of the Takeover Directive', ECGI Law Working Paper N° 770/2024, May 2024; and E. Berglöf and M. Burkart, 'European Takeover Regulation' (2003) *Economic Policy* 171, on the troubled adoption of the Directive.

In a world as fast-changing as ours, where new legislative acts and amendments to existing legislation are constantly produced, which is especially true of the EU, contemplating the 20th anniversary of the Directive must give reason to pause and observe that it has not changed since its adoption. Since takeovers are an important and recurrent theme in most Member States, the reason for the Directive's immunity to change cannot be that it has been forgotten and ignored. A possible explanation is more likely binary: either the Directive was like Aphrodite emerging from the foam of European politicking as a perfect creation in every way or it is a Pandora's box that nobody wants to open. Judging from the occasions when the Commission has performed a check-up on the Directive only to leave it unreformed, the odds are with the latter explanation.[3] The Directive is, alas, considered untouchable, even though it is generally accepted that it did not provide the harmonisation originally intended.

In this chapter it is argued that this sorry state of affairs is not a necessary outcome but has been caused by regulatory overreach. Unfortunately, this has been a recurring feature also in later proposals for directives to the extent that it could perhaps even be considered an unfortunate characteristic of European legislative work in the corporate area. Too much was bundled together in the proposal for a directive to enable agreement on harmonisation. Reform of the Directive is possible, as is achieving actual harmonisation, but only in some of the parts covered by the present Directive and to achieve this the other unruly parts should be left out of any future reform.

This contribution is thus not a traditional legal analysis of how to construe the various provisions of the Directive; rather, it is a political analysis of public choice based not on economics, as is customary within public choice theory, but on an analysis of the characteristics of the relevant areas of law covered by the Directive. It argues that some areas of law lend themselves to harmonisation more easily than others and that it is preferable to strive for actual harmonisation in some areas, and to delete provisions that are not easily harmonised and for that reason are likely to jettison the political support necessary to harmonise the parts that could and should be harmonised.

As its starting point, the argumentation begins with some basic observations to test when an area of law is easy to harmonise in EU law and when it is not. Obviously, this is a crude distinction as an area of law is seldom so clearly delineated, but its relevance to lawmaking is borne out by the problems experienced at the adoption of the Directive, and which, by the way, continue to complicate new legislative

[3] Commission Staff Working Document, 'Report on the Implementation on Takeover Bids' SEC(2007) 268 (21 February 2007); Report from the European Commission to the European Parliament, the Council, the European Economic and Social Committee and the Committee of the Regions on the application of Directive 2004/25/EC on takeover bids COM(2012)347; the Takeover Bids Directive assessment report (external study by Marccus Partners) on behalf of the Commission (2013).

initiatives, and so it is sensible to take these characteristics into account in future lawmaking efforts.[4]

That basic test is then applied to the various parts of the present Directive to indicate what should be the subject of a reformed and more focused Directive that can provide actual harmonisation within the European Union and as such provide an important building block of the Capital Markets Union, or, as the political ambition is to be known, the Savings and Investments Union, as suggested in the Letta Report.[5] The argument will not extend to a detailed description of what this harmonisation should be; for this the reader is advised to read the other contributions to this project of analysing the Directive on its 20th anniversary.

17.2 THE PURPOSE OF HARMONISATION IN EU LAW

Contrary to the individual Member States, where legislation is available usually within wide constitutional limits to accommodate the ordinary democratic discourse of its subjects and cater for the wishes of any given political majority, EU legislation is strictly conditioned on Article 5 of the Treaty on European Union, which dictates that EU secondary law can only be adopted where based on provisions in the primary law of the Treaties (the principle of conferral), and where such competence is provided by primary law, it can only be exercised as secondary legislation in accordance with the principles of subsidiarity and proportionality. In other words, the EU legislators are consigned to playing second fiddle to the national parliaments of the Member States. It is not enough that there is a political majority in favour of a piece of legislation among the EU legislators, the intended legislation must objectively fulfil the strict requirements of Art. 5 TEU.

The importance of Art. 5 TEU is underlined by the fact that, once EU legislation is adopted, the Member States lose their sovereign right to legislate in that respect,[6] which of course is a serious restriction on their national democracy, not to be taken lightly. For this reason, the observance of Art. 5 TEU is supported by various

[4] For more recent examples of the complications experienced when trying to harmonise areas of law better left alone, see the Study on directors' duties and sustainable corporate governance (external study by EY Italy) on behalf of the Commission (2020) which was later abandoned while certain elements were transferred to the Parliament and Council Proposal for a Directive (EU) 2019/1937 on Corporate Sustainability Due Diligence and amending Directive, 2022 COM/2022/71 final ('Corporate Sustainability Due Diligence Directive' (CSDDD)) only to derail that proposal's adoption until they were deleted as well.

[5] E. Letta, 'Much More Than a Market. Speed, securitiy, solidarity, empowering the Single Market to deliver a sustainable future and prosperity for all EU Citizens', April 2024, www.consilium.europa.eu/media/ny3j24sm/much-more-than-a-market-report-by-enrico-letta.pdf.

[6] The primacy of EEC/EU law to national law, whereby Member States may not set aside European law by national legislation, was adopted early; see the judgment of the Court of 5 February 1963, Case 26/62, *van Gend & Loos vs Netherlands Inland Revenue Administration* [1963], ECLI:EU:C:1963:1.

procedural safeguards.[7] Notable among these is the impact assessment required by the rules on good lawmaking to be made and published by the Commission along with any new legislative proposal to document that the strict conditions of Art. 5 TEU are fulfilled in every case.

Harmonisation in EU law is not an end in itself, but a means to bring about greater unity among the different European nations, especially to facilitate cross-border activities by their nationals. In this way, harmonisation serves as the alternative to the different legal systems of its constituent Member States that is the default position – that is, harmonisation is a measure by which to remove such differences and provide a single regulatory outcome. As is apparent from Art. 5 of TEU, the EU is not obliged or envisaged to provide full harmonisation on all matters of law; rather, harmonisation must be justified piece by piece while leaving all other existing differences to the Member States' discretion. As the CJEU has stated clearly in its case law, a mere difference among the laws of the individual Member States does not in and of itself constitute a restriction contrary to EU law, but only if it interferes with a right provided by EU primary or secondary law in which case it may even be justified by the Member State as necessary and proportionate.[8] The Member States have a wide discretion to establish their own legal order within their borders as long as they do not treat nationals of other Member States worse than their own nationals or in a way that restricts the rights they are provided with by EU law. Conversely, a Member State cannot expect other Member States to apply or even accommodate its choice of legislation, not even by arguing for a 'level playing field' within the EU. As long as the Member States respect existing primary and secondary EU law, they are free to experiment with national legislation of their own making of which they can expect acceptance from other Member States but not their submission.[9]

7 Article 263 of the Treaty of the Functioning of the European Union (TFEU) holds that privileged applicants, such as Member States' parliaments, have the right to take action before the Court of Justice of the European Union to challenge the legality of the Union's legal acts. See, for example, Judgment of the Court (Second Chamber) of 18 June 2015, Case C-508/13, *Republic of Estonia v. European Parliament and Council of the European Union* [2015] ECLI: EU:C:2015:403, action for annulment of certain provisions of Directive 2013/34/EU under Article 263 TFEU, based on alleged infringement of the principles of proportionality and subsidiarity.

8 See, for example, Case C-212/97, *Centros Ltd v Erhvervs- og Selskabsstyrelsen* [1999] ECLI:EU: C:1999:126, prm. 27, where the mere difference in national law among Member States did not in itself represent 'abuse' contrary to EU law, a point reiterated in the subsequent cases on mutual recognition of foreign companies.

9 The argument of a level playing field is increasingly invoked to justify EU legislation in areas where some Member States have adopted national legislation that burden their companies, burdens they then try to extend to other Member States by way of EU legislation. As a case in point, see the adoption of the Corporate Sustainability Due Diligence Directive (CSDDD), originally the Parliament and Council Proposal for a Directive (EU) 2019/1937 on Corporate Sustainability Due Diligence and amending Directive, 2022 COM/2022/71 final. In this way and by the helping hand of the European Commission, some Member States, usually the larger ones, get to legislate extraterritorially.

If harmonisation by EU legislation is to be justified as required by Art. 5 TEU, it should in each and every case provide a single mandatory provision that is applicable across the EU – that is, a one-size-fits-all solution to provide a single predetermined outcome of a beneficial character. That kind of harmonisation will make it clear and transparent to all subjects within the EU what is required and available, which in turn will help cross-border activities to improve the overall economic welfare of all Member States.

On the other hand, if it is not possible to devise such a single Union-wide solution, perhaps because several different and equally good solutions are available without it being possible with any sufficient empirical support to determine which is superior, then it is likely an area unsuited for harmonisation that should be left open for experimentation and competition among Member States. After all, the well-known beneficial effects of competition per se are enshrined in the founding Treaties, which also acknowledge the stifling effect of coordination on innovation.

It is not a convincing argument that harmonisation should be preferred anyway simply because we should strive to remove all hindrance to cross-border activities in law. The multitude of languages and endless differences in cultures and mores among the Member States will always present obstacles to cross-border activities within the EU that one must accept and expect to encounter. Since there will always be differences that may offer obstacles to any 'seamless' interaction across borders, harmonisation should only be pursued where it truly provides a single optimal solution that is evidently better than the national differences that it replaces.

Based on this understanding of Art. 5 TEU and its narrow scope of harmonisation in EU law, the various legal areas covered by the Directive on Takeover Bids should be examined.

17.3 ADMINISTRATIVE LAW

17.3.1 *In General*

Administrative law concerns the organisation and procedures of public authorities – that is, how their competences are delineated and how they should operate.

In respect of takeover bids, this is an area of law where harmonisation is suitable. The Directive is premised on the fact that investments are made across borders within the EU and may involve several jurisdictions, and consequently it is necessary to establish which Member State is competent to fulfil the tasks of supervision and enforcement that the Directive entails when a takeover bid plays out across different Member States to avoid the confusion of several national competent authorities' involvement.

The need to establish a clear delineation of powers *among* the Member States does not necessarily extend to the arrangements made *within* an individual Member State. It can be left to the Member State's discretion whether the competences assigned to it should be carried out by one or more bodies and whether these bodies should be organised as public authorities or private bodies as long as the relevant tasks can be fulfilled adequately, and judicial review is available. Member States may want to assign different tasks to different bodies; supervision and enforcement are often separated and, where enforcement relates to criminal matters, they must be.[10]

Whereas the assignment of competences to national bodies is for each Member State to decide, the Directive should address first and foremost the criteria for determining which Member State is competent to handle a takeover bid and secondly, but no less importantly, describe the tasks of supervision and enforcement that are necessary in cases of takeover bids involving issuers, bidders and investors in multiple jurisdictions. To lay down uniform rules on this would in and of itself justify having a Directive of this kind, as that kind of pan-European coordination cannot take place without harmonisation in EU law.

17.3.2 *The Provisions of the Directive*

Article 4 on supervisory authority and applicable law is an excellent example of how a directive may delineate competences between the authorities of the various Member States to avoid confusion and uncertainty. Section 2 points out in a clear and transparent way which Member State is competent to deal with supervision according to the Directive. Section 3 on confidentiality is perhaps unnecessary as it is likely to be observed in national law already but is natural to maintain in the context of describing the powers of national competent authorities. In Section 4, cooperation among Member States is authorised, which prevents lacuna from arising due to the delineation of competences in Section 2. Section 5 describes very broadly the powers to be vested with the national competent authority, thus allowing considerable flexibility for the Member States to avail themselves of measures in national law. It is also noteworthy that Section 5 does not extend to detailing how the national authorities in respect of supervision or judicial review should be organised, which is better left to the Member States, observing the relevant requirements of national constitutional law and fundamental human rights.

Article 10 obliges publicly traded (listed) companies to make public certain information about themselves which may be of relevance to a potential bidder. This information is usually made public by the company by filing the information with the public authorities in the Member State of its main seat and as such may be seen as administrative in nature even when mandated by that Member State's company law legislation. Many of the items listed in Article 10 are already subject to publicity by way of the Company Law Directive,[11] mainly because they are

[10] Case C-546/18, *FN and Others v Übernahmekommission* [2021] ECLI:EU:C:2021:711.

[11] Parliament and Council Directive (EU) 2017/1132 relating to certain aspects of company law (codification), 2017 O.J. (L169).

addressed in the articles (bylaws) of the company. This appears to be the case for Points a, b, c, d, f, h and i. Since such information is available throughout the EU due to the Business Registers Interconnection System (BRIS), there is no need to duplicate these provisions and they may be deleted, at least where they are already provided by BRIS to ensure a one-stop disclosure process by listed companies.

In respect of the other information required by Article 10 to be made public – for example, Point g (shareholders' agreements, not likely in listed companies); Point j (contracts with change-of-control provisions); and Point k (redundancy compensation for management) – it is questionable whether the benefit of this kind of publication to a potential bidder exceeds the costs of the publication every single year by every listed company. Probably not, especially as a public bid is normally accompanied by an in-depth due diligence exercise that would reveal these matters anyhow to any bidder that cares about these things.

17.4 SECURITIES TRADING ON PUBLIC TRADING VENUES

17.4.1 *In General*

The regulation of trading venues for securities such as the shares in limited liability companies that are the object of takeover bids is harmonised by MiFID2 and MiFIR.[12] This regulation concerns not only the organisation and design of the main trading venues – formerly known as stock exchanges, now called regulated markets – but also details the requirements of admission to trading.[13]

[12] Parliament and Council Directive 2014/65/EU on markets in financial instruments and amending Directive 2002/92/EC and Directive 2011/61/EU, 2014 O.J. (L173) (MiFID2), and Parliament and Council Regulation (EU) No 600/2014 on markets in financial instruments and amending Regulation, 2014 O.J. (L173) (MiFIR), respectively, both with later amendments. Trading in other assets than traditional financial instruments is governed by other legislative acts; notably, trading in derivatives is subject to Parliament and Council Regulation (EU) No 648/2012 on OTC derivatives, central counterparties and trade repositories, 2012 O.J. (L201) (EMIR), and trading in cryptoassets is regulated by Parliament and Council Regulation (EU) 2023/1114 on markets in cryptoassets, and amending Regulations (EU) No 1093/2010 and (EU) No 1095/2010 and Directives 2013/36/EU and (EU) 2019/1937, 2023 O.J. (L150) (MiCA).

[13] The notion of 'admitted to trading' has effectively replaced the older conception of 'official stock exchange listing' as signifying a company subject to EU securities regulation, including the Directive on Takeover Bids, although the latter concept is still mentioned in Parliament and Council Directive 2001/34/EC on the admission of securities to official stock exchange listing and on information to be published on those securities, 2001 O.J. (L184). The recently adopted Directive (EU) 2024/2811 of the European Parliament and of the Council of 23 October 2024 amending Directive 2014/65/EU, to make public capital markets in the Union more attractive for companies and to facilitate access to capital for small and medium-sized enterprises and repealing Parliament and Council Directive 2001/34/EC on the admission of securities to official stock exchange listing and on information to be published on those securities, 2001 O.J. (L184) ('Listing Act Directive') recognises the interchangeable use of both regimes among Member States and by its repeal of the 2001 Directive removes the concept from EU law, while allowing Member States to keep it in national law.

Furthermore, the conduct on these public trading venues is harmonised by EU securities trading law, notably the Market Abuse Regulation (MAR)[14] but also the Transparency Directive.[15]

Harmonisation of securities trading on public trading venues makes eminent sense.[16] The parties engaged in a securities transaction have but the briefest contact – often simply the exchange of rudimentary buy or sell orders according to the trading facility applied by the trading venue. The parties of an on-exchange transaction have not the opportunity, or the time, to negotiate the conditions of their transaction or consider the understanding or intention of the other party. Their contact is brief and fleeting and is consequently entirely based on the rudimentary conditions and information laid down and made applicable by the regulation of the trading venue, either in the private rules of the operator's own design or mandated by applicable legislation. Since this legislation is aimed at 'anonymous' trading based on rudimentary information that is highly likely to be uniform across different jurisdictions, it is suitable for harmonisation in EU law.

The aspects of a public takeover bid that involves on-exchange trading should be harmonised by EU law. This would cover such elements as the takeover bid itself, what information the offer document must contain and how it is made public; the time the offer must stay open, by a minimum to ensure sufficient time for the shareholders of the target company to assess the bid, and by a maximum to avoid the paralysing effect on the target company of having been put 'into play'; and, finally, how the bid is concluded, the outcome communicated, and any exchange of shares and payment made.

17.4.2 *The Provisions of the Directive*

Article 3 of the Directive states the 'General Principles' applicable to takeover bids, whether voluntary or mandatory. These principles are truly general in the sense that – almost – all of them can be seen as uncontroversial and applicable to the special case of securities trading on public trading venues that is the public offer, and indeed they reflect the principles that were already promoted in the 1977 Recommendation (77/534/EEC) concerning a European code of conduct

[14] Parliament and Council Regulation (EU) No 596/2014 on market abuse (market abuse regulation) and repealing Directive 2003/6/EC of the European Parliament and of the Council and Commission Directives 2003/124/EC, 2003/125/EC and 2004/72/EC, 2014 O.J. (L173) (MAR).

[15] Parliament and Council Directive 2004/109/EC on the harmonisation of transparency requirements in relation to information about issuers whose securities are admitted to trading on a regulated market and amending Directive 2001/34/EC, 2004 O.J. (L390) (Transparency Directive), as amended by Parliament and Council Directive 2013/50/EU, 2013 O.J. (L294).

[16] On the charateristics of securities trading and its inherent difference from company law, see J. Lau Hansen, Reflections on the Difference Between Company Law and Capital Markets Law, pp. 21–31 in R. Veil, Regulating EU Capital Markets Union, Volume II, Market Conduct and Corporate Disclosure in a European Code, Oxford University Press, 2025.

relating to transactions in transferable securities that foreshadowed the Commission's harmonisation efforts in respect of capital markets law.[17]

Most of the general principles are uncontroversial and thus apt for harmonisation. This includes the first part of Point a (equal treatment of the target company's shareholders by the bidder); Point b (sufficient time and information to enable the target company's shareholders to reach a properly informed decision on the bid – that is, a minimum time frame for the bid's duration); Point c (the obligation of the target company's management to act in the interests of the company as a whole); Point e (offeror's obligation to ensure fulfilment of the bid's conditions); and Point f (a maximum duration of the bid so as not to hinder the target company's operations).

Point d (no false markets) is today effectively replaced by the ban on market manipulation in Arts. 12 and 15 MAR and should be deleted as unnecessary.

Whereas most of the general principles in Article 3 are apt for harmonisation, this is not quite the case for a few of them.

The second part of Point a on the need to protect the minority in case of a transfer of control concerns company law more than securities trading, because the need to protect minority shareholders against abuse of control is a persistent need not tied to the random event of a takeover bid, and consequently all Member States can be expected to have the necessary measures to protect against such abuse according to their own national corporate governance structure. To the extent that the general principle concerns protection against an abuse of control brought about by a public takeover bid, it is unnecessary in a Directive covering the ex ante process of making a public bid because this concerns the post-bid affairs of the target company and will be covered by the national company law of the Member States.

Equally, the second part of Point c requires that the target company's management 'must not deny' the shareholders the opportunity to decide on the merits of the bid. This provision may interfere with the discretion of the management's duty to act in the interest of the whole company, as per the first part of Point c, depending on the corporate governance system of the individual Member States. Some Member States, notably Germany, oblige the management to place a greater interest on the whole company and all its stakeholders, whereas other Member States, notably the Nordic ones, prioritise the interest of the shareholders viewed as a group. This wide range of different views among Member States makes the provision difficult to construe and open to misunderstandings making its deletion preferable.

Central to the Directive is its Article 6 on the offer document that conveys the public bid and its conditions to the target company's shareholders and the public.

[17] 1977 Recommendation (77/534/EEC) concerning a European code of conduct relating to transactions in transferable securities, L 212, 20.8.1977, p. 37–43.

Section 1 of Article 6 contains disclosure obligations on the bidder in respect of the intended bid and, once the bid has been made public, on the target company as well in respect of their employees. The disclosure obligation on the bidder, and its requirement that disclosure should be made once the decision to make a bid has been taken, is necessary to expedite the bid and avoid abuse of this price-sensitive information before publication. It is thus related to the continuous disclosure obligation according to Art. 17 MAR, which is already harmonised as useful for the operation of public trading venues, but the bidder may not be a listed company itself and thus not subject to disclosure, which necessitates the inclusion of a disclosure obligation in the Directive. Although useful and necessary, the disclosure obligation in Section 1 should not be construed too onerously. The bidder should have discretion to decide when the bid is ready to be made, especially since the bidder is liable for being able to fulfil its bid once made (see Art. 3, Point e). Furthermore, it could perhaps be argued that the latter disclosure obligation concerning the employees of the bidder and the target company is unnecessary as the bid is by then public and thus known to all, and most companies would voluntarily consult their employees anyhow or be required to do so according to national law on business relations.

Section 3 of Article 6 details the issues that must be addressed in the offer document, which is done as minimum harmonisation, thus allowing Member States to make further requirements and, what is probably more usual, to allow the bidder to add additional information that the bidder deems necessary. This is an area apt for minimum harmonisation, especially because the list of information to be provided does not specify the material content of this information which is left to the bidder to decide. Effectively, Article 6 serves as a to-do list for the bidder to check and thereby ensures that the target company's shareholders are served with the necessary information equally throughout the EU.

The same can be said for Article 7 on the time allowed for acceptance. The need for the recipients of the offer document to acquaint themselves with its information necessitates a minimum acceptance period, and considerations to the target company dictate a maximum period to limit the inconvenience of being a company 'in play'.

Article 13 simply states certain measures that each Member State must take to make the bidding process transparent and clear. Considering that other provisions of the Directive go too far in detailing the way national law should operate after harmonisation, it is strange that these matters (lapsing of bids; revision of bids; competing bids, disclosure of the result; and conditionality of a bid) are left open and not sought to be harmonised although that would help to create transparency of cross-border bids. Where these measures simply concern the public bid as a transaction concerning the acquisition of shares in a public traded company, a more detailed harmonisation would be beneficial.

17.5 COMPANY LAW: COMMUNICATION BETWEEN A COMPANY AND ITS STAKEHOLDERS

17.5.1 *In General*

Takeover bids concern the shares of limited liability companies, which obviously involves aspects of company law. One such aspect of company law is the relationship between a company and its various stakeholders. Of these stakeholders, shareholders are afforded special consideration in company law because they provide the initial funding enabling the establishment of the company, and, just as the shareholders made the company come alive, they may end its existence by liquidating it, in which case they are residual claimants entitled to any proceeds.

The position of shareholders is different from that of partners in a partnership. First, shareholders derive their standing in the company by virtue of their shares, not in their personal capacity. If a shareholder holds two shares and another shareholder holds only one, then the former will have twice the rights than the latter even when their shares are equal.

Due to their limited liability, shareholders occupy a restrained position in the company, removed as they are from directly accessing the company's funds. The notion of limited liability for shareholders cuts both ways: the shareholders are isolated from the financial affairs of the company and vice versa. Depending on the corporate governance system of the individual Member State, shareholders may have considerable influence on the governance of the company or hardly any, but it is a common feature that the shareholders are removed from the capital of the company as it primarily serves its creditors, whereas shareholders remain residual claimants. The restrained, almost remote, position of the shareholders has the effect that any transaction of shares among shareholders made on the so-called secondary market has no immediate effect on the company, its finances or business in general.[18]

The remote position of shareholders as 'external' to the listed company's daily affairs makes it necessary for the company to communicate externally whenever it engages its shareholders. This kind of external communication – for example, communications on corporate events such as summons to the annual general meeting, or news about emissions or dividends – will be directed at investors who may be nationals or residents of different Member States. In this way, the regulation

[18] The management of a listed company may nonetheless take an interest in the transactions on the secondary markets partly because the prices obtained inform it of its possibilities of obtaining new financing from new emissions, partly to the extent that its applicable jurisdiction provides shareholders with governance rights.

of communication between a company and its shareholders is suitable for harmonisation, and indeed such harmonisation of a listed company's communication with its shareholders has been enacted by the SRD2.[19]

To the extent that the Directive on Takeover Bids contains similar provisions on the communication between the target company and its shareholders, they are suitable for harmonisation and should continue to form part of the Directive.

Furthermore, company law does not cater only to shareholders. The very concept of limited liability for the shareholders necessitates that company law also safeguard the interests of creditors. However, as transactions on the secondary market, such as takeover bids, do not affect the financial position of the company, there is no need to address the concerns of creditors in a directive on takeover bids.[20]

Another group of stakeholders often considered by company law is that of employees, who may be entitled to consultation or at least information about major developments of importance to their employment with the company. Again, where such communication takes place in the context of a takeover bid, it is suitable for harmonisation to ensure equal treatment of employees that may be employed in different Member States by the target company, irrespective of the home state of that company.

17.5.2 *The Provisions of the Directive*

The Directive does not address the communication between shareholders and their company. It does, of course, address the communication of the bid from the bidder to the target company's shareholders (see Art. 6), and it has provisions in Article 10 on information that should be made public, which are of an administrative law nature. The absence of provisions concerning the communication between a company and its shareholders is justified, because these matters are already regulated to the necessary extent by Arts. 3 et seq. of the SRD2.[21]

Article 14 on information for and consultation of employees' representatives refers to the existing directives concerning employees and as such has no independent meaning, which makes its possible deletion less relevant.

19 Parliament and Council Directive (EU) 2017/828 amending Directive 2007/36/EC as regards the encouragement of long-term shareholder engagement, 2017 O.J. (L132).

20 Company law displays a strange asymmetry between funding by shares (equity) and by loans/bonds, where the former is closely regulated, and the latter is left to management. A change of control may affect the finances of the company if one or more of its financial contracts has provisions that are triggered by the change.

21 Parliament and Council Directive (EU) 2017/828 amending Directive 2007/36/EC as regards the encouragement of long-term shareholder engagement, 2017 O.J. (L132).

17.6 COMPANY LAW: INTERNAL DECISION-MAKING

17.6.1 *In General*

Contrary to securities trading on public trading venues, where the interaction between the involved parties is swift, fleeting and based on predetermined rudimentary information, the law concerning the internal operations of a company concerns the continuous cooperation of the shareholders and is for that reason open, allowing them to negotiate and design the conditions and framework of their cooperation. This difference explains why company law has maintained a close similarity to contract law, which indeed was a relevant area of law before the advent of limited liability companies resulted in specific legislation deemed to constitute company law as a separate field of law. Company law, when it concerns internal organisation and procedures, is mostly based on default provisions, allowing a considerable degree of flexibility for the involved parties to negotiate and determine the relevant framework of their cooperation. Mandatory provisions on the internal affairs of a company are usually restricted to decisions where those affected by the decision are not able to fend for themselves. The typical example in limited liability companies is the interests of creditors, who are dependent on the prudent management of the company to satisfy their claims against the company but without direct involvement in the decision-making process.[22]

Another reason for the statutory acceptance of party autonomy and the ensuing flexibility in company law is not solely based on the fact that the parties involved in a company have the time and opportunity to arrange for themselves, but also on the realisation that the legislator is not able to predetermine the best outcome of managerial decisions because such decisions have to take into account ever-changing and unforeseeable circumstances. This is why companies exist in the first place.[23] If it is possible to accurately and fully describe how a particular business operation should be executed, it is easier to simply order an independent party to perform the operation and pay for it. The company exists in this context to allow a hierarchical organisation that enables the continuous issuance of orders to persons, be they managers or employees, to perform the operations deemed necessary by those empowered to run the business, taking into account the present and ever-changing circumstances that make predetermined decisions impossible. Those who are the executive decision-makers of the company's governance empowered to act on behalf of the company are usually termed *the management* and it depends on the characteristics of the individual governance system of each Member State to what extent the management can operate under its own discretion or is subject to

[22] This is not to deny that major creditors may be able to influence the decision-making process, and once insolvency law takes effect, creditors may supplant shareholders completely.

[23] The seminal contribution to this view of the company is R. Coase, 'The Nature of the Firm' (1937) *Economica*, 386.

following the wishes of the shareholders, but the presence of decision-makers with a power to make continuous discretionary and hence unforeseeable orders to the employees on how to conduct its business is a given in any company.

Consequently, a directive on takeover bids, or indeed any other piece of legislation in national or EU law, should not try and dictate how a privately owned company should be run – for example, when a takeover bid should be made, how much should be offered, or how the shareholders and the management of the target company should respond. These are all subjects better left to the directly involved private parties to decide ad hoc.

However, as mentioned above, company law is not alien to mandatory provisions trying to protect the interests of those deemed unable to fend for themselves, known as creditor and minority protection. Provisions of this type are indeed well known in the company law legislation of all Member States. Here, the problem for harmonisation is the lack of clarity of identifying a single outcome that is superior to the rest, as minority protection depends on the governance system applicable in the individual Member States and, in this area, there are considerable differences without any one model standing out as superior.[24]

The mere fact that these differences exist and have persisted for a very long time, despite the competitive pressure within and among Member States and the mutual learning process that the clear visibility of these differences allows, suggests that there is no single optimal solution on how to design a corporate governance system or to protect the minority. This should counsel against harmonising the systems of corporate governance and the provisions of minority protection that form an inherent part of such systems.[25]

One of the things that greatly complicated the legislative process of adopting the Directive on Takeover Bids was the anxiety felt by Member States that their national companies were uniquely vulnerable to takeovers by foreign bidders.[26] Although basic logic dictates that not *all* Member States can be *more* vulnerable than the rest, it is perhaps more reasonable to accept that this anxiety is deeply felt and respect it by

[24] Indeed, if any corporate governance model was superior, competitive pressure would long since have produced harmonisation on its own.

[25] Creditor protection has, nonetheless, been harmonised by what was the second Company Law Directive and now part of the Company Law Directive; see n 11. This is also unfortunate, because the protection afforded is based on what was originally the German concept of *Kapitalschutz* (capital maintenance), which is only one and not obviously the best way of protecting creditors. The growth in the use of private limited companies and the invention of new forms of private companies in the various Member States are testament to a desire to avoid the capital regime for public companies of the AG type embodied in the Company Law Directive Annex I and a warning against creating a one-size-fits-all harmonisation when indeed there is more than one size available.

[26] The interplay of national protectionism and takeover regulation is dealt with in U. Bernitz and W. G. Ringe (eds.), *Company Law and Economic Protectionism* (Oxford University Press, 2010).

limiting harmonisation to transactions carried out on public trading venues and preserving the design of the national corporate governance system, including the distribution of powers, duty of care and protection of minorities, for the national law of the Member States.

17.6.2 The Provisions of the Directive

The Directive contains four provisions that concern the design of the corporate governance system of the individual Member States: Article 5 on the mandatory bid rule, Article 9 on the non-frustration rule, Article 11 on the breakthrough rule, and Articles 15 and 16 on the squeeze-out/sell-out rule. The first three are highly controversial, two of them so much so that the Directive had to make them optional, whereas the last one should be controversial but is not.

Article 5 was not viewed as controversial on its adoption. There may be many reasons for this. It is generally seen as a protection of the minority, which to some extent excuses its undeniable effect as an anti-takeover device. It is, however, questionable as a protective device, because, as mentioned in Section 17.3, it can hardly be seen as a protection against the abuse of control, because it is triggered by the mere *change* of control and not its subsequent abuse, and protection against such abuse is usually already available in national company law. It could be described as a protection from a change of the business usually conducted by the target company which may follow a change of control, but again it is not triggered by any actual change of business, nor are minority shareholders usually protected against such a change of business where the change is decided by current management. Finally, a mandatory bid rule is not a fundamental principle of EU company law;[27] in fact, it was not even part of the national law of some Member States until its inclusion in the Directive. It does, however, have its merits. As an anti-takeover measure, it protects incumbent management and is probably seen as beneficial by Member States less convinced of the merits of takeovers as a blunt tool for industrial restructuring and when combined with the arbitrary highest-price-paid principle in Section 4 of Article 5, it provides a windfall much appreciated by institutional investors. Its origin in UK law, where the early attempts to prevent anti-takeover measures being taken by incumbent management, such as those carried out in the Savoy Hotel affair, ironically ended with self-regulation by the City Panel on Takeovers and Mergers that would allow it a few years later in the form of the mandatory bid rule,[28] is well known, but it should

[27] Cf. Case C-101/08, *Audiolux SA e.a v Groupe Bruxelles Lambert SA (GBL) and Others and Bertelsmann AG and Others*, [2009] ECLI:EU:C:2009:626.

[28] On the Savoy affair, see A. Johnston, 'Takeover Regulation: Historical and Theoretical Perspectives on the City Code' (2007) *Cambridge Law Journal* 422, 428.

not be overlooked that the idea of a mandatory bid rule to provide the minority shareholders with an equitable exit in a company that has a controlling shareholder also fitted existing German law on company groups.[29] Thus, the rule was already included in the 1977 Recommendation[30] and was carried by the Directive unopposed. It is only with the advent of stronger shareholder engagement, in the US by activist funds to challenge hitherto unaccountable directors and in the EU by activist shareholders bent on sustainability, that the possible drawbacks of the mandatory bid rule and its wider hold on 'parties acting in concert' to challenge incumbent management have become recognised outside the Nordic countries, where active ownership by shareholders has always been the norm.

While the mandatory bid rule was unopposed at the time by the major Member States, this could certainly not be said of the two other rules on anti-frustration and breakthrough, respectively. This is plain from the protracted negotiations that marred the Directive.

To recap the prolonged negotiations: first, Germany was threatened by provisions in the proposal that would prevent management from obstructing a takeover (the non-frustration rule), which rule would be contrary to the management's mandatory duty under German company law if the independent management (Vorstand) deems the takeover to be detrimental. Then, Germany argued that their lack of multiple-voting right (MVR) shares at the time made German companies more vulnerable to takeovers than Member States who allowed them.[31] This lament paved the way for a provision that would annul the extra voting rights of MVR shares once the bid had been accepted by a certain majority of the shareholders (the breakthrough rule).[32] This was fine with the UK, whose manager-centric system disliked MVR shares anyway, but it alarmed the Nordic and other Member States, where MVR shares are customary. The outcome was to make both rules optional by way of what became Article 12. The optionality has, of course, not provided any

[29] See J. L. Hansen, 'The Mandatory Bid Rule: Still Unnecessary, Unjustifiable and Inefficient After All These Years', in R. J. Gilson, M. Isaksson, E. Lidman, J. Munck and E. Sjöman (eds.), *Festschrift in honour of Rolf Skog* (Norstedts Juridik, 2021), p. 509.

[30] See n 17.

[31] This was back in the days when MVR shares were regarded as 'dangerous' and possibly also unfair. How sentiments have changed. MVR shares are becoming customary even in jurisdictions where they were once frowned upon, and stock exchanges globally accept them to stay competitive. In the EU, Germany recently reintroduced them into its national law, and the Commission's proposal to make them mandatory for SMEs seeking admission on an SME Growth Market, COM/2022/761 final, has been adopted as Directive (EU) 2024/2810 of the European Parliament and of the Council of 23 October 2024 on multiple-vote share structures in companies that seek admission to trading of their shares on a multilateral trading facility, though not without some confusion as to the merits of such harmonisation, see J. L. Hansen, 'Multiple Voting Rights in Shares – Old Misconceptions and New Challenges', (2023) Nordic & European Company Law Working Paper No. 23-06.

[32] The rule was inspired by French company law. Again, sentiments have changed, and the rule has been removed in French law.

harmonisation, but has mainly served to preserve the existing differences in national corporate governance.

Considering that no harmonisation was obtained by the Directive in this area, a decision to delete these optional provisions in a reformed Directive would not affect harmonisation but would just preserve the status quo of leaving this with the law of each Member State.

The worry that Member States may prevent takeovers of their national companies from purely protectionist reasons has to some considerable extent been countered by the case law of the CJEU in the so-called golden share cases.[33] This application of primary EU law shows that secondary EU law such as the Directive was unnecessary. It has become apparent that takeovers which are not welcomed by the target company's management and for that reason are termed 'hostile takeovers' are viewed less favourably and are becoming less frequent.[34] Instead, we can expect an increase in the use of mergers, or schemes of arrangement, as a tool for takeovers as they are less onerously regulated in EU law by way of the Company Law Directive,[35] their popularity probably spurred by being less threatening to incumbent management. However, it is not clear that this reluctant approach to takeovers could be overcome by harmonisation through an instrument of secondary EU law such as a directive; rather, this appears to be a job for primary EU law as enforced by the European Commission and the CJEU. Nor is it obvious that there is sufficient empirical justification for harmonisation that aims to further takeovers. Takeovers are not always efficient, the prospect of 'synergies' often evaporating post-bid and showing itself to be a delusion of grandeur suffered by the management of the bidder.[36]

[33] Case C-367/98, *Commission of the European Communities v. Portuguese Republic* [2002] ECLI:EU:C:2002:326; Case C-483/99, *Commission of the European Communities v. French Republic* [2002] ECLI:EU:C:2002:327. See also Bernitz and Ringe (n 25).

[34] See L. Enriques and M. Gatti, 'Death by a Thousand Cuts: The Hostile Bids Regime in Europe, 2004–2023' (2024) European Corporate Governance Institute – Law Working Paper No. 755/2024.

[35] See n 11.

[36] Seminal literature on the market for corporate control posits that takeovers contribute to mitigate agency problems by reallocating assets and replacing management in underperforming firms. See e.g. H. G. Manne, 'Mergers and the Market for Corporate Control' (1965) *Journal of Political Economy* 110; F. H. Easterbrook and D. R. Fischel, *The Economic Structure of Corporate Law* (Harvard University Press, 1991); S. Bhagat, M. Dong, D. Hirshleifer and R. Noah, 'Do Tender Offers Create Value? New Methods and Evidence' (2005) *Journal of Financial Economics* 3. However, other contributions have questioned the effectiveness of corporate takeovers as they may be driven by irrationality, objectives to transfer wealth or provide gains only to target firms but not to the bidders. See e.g. A. Shleifer and R. W. Vishny, 'Stock Market Driven Acquisitions' (2003) *Journal of Financial Economics* 295; S. B. Moeller, F. P.Schlingemann and R. M. Stulz, 'Firm Size and the Gains from Acquisitions' (2004) *Journal of Financial Economics* 201; M. Burkart and F. Panunzi, 'Takeovers' (2006) ECGI Finance Working Paper No. 118/2006. The tendency to overpay for a coveted prize is colloquially known in behavioural finance as 'the winner's curse'.

The fact that the present Directive contains no minority protection of the shareholders unfortunately trapped in a company bent on making a ruinous takeover bid should suggest that we can also do without the other provisions in the Directive to protect the minority of the target company.

Consequently, the non-frustration rule in Article 9 and the breakthrough rule in Article 11 that are made optional by Article 12 should all be deleted in a reformed Directive. It would be logical also to delete Article 5 on the mandatory bid rule, and it might help the timid to consider that any deletion would probably be inconsequential anyway as the rule is favoured by the strong self-interests of so many influential parties that they will probably guarantee the rule's continuation in the national laws of the Member States even without its inclusion in a reformed Directive.

The same could be said of Article 15 on the right of a squeeze-out and the corresponding Article 16 on the right of a sell-out; however, judging from legal literature, these tandem rights appear to be generally accepted and are seldom, if ever, criticised. However, they are, when viewed objectively, rather odd provisions; especially the squeeze-out right is dangerously close to expropriation of private property rights contrary to Article 17 of the EU Charter on Fundamental Rights and outside the competence of the EU due to Article 345 of the Treaty on the Functioning of the EU.[37] What makes the tandem squeeze/sell rights less controversial is probably the fact that the squeeze-out right serves the understandable wish of a new controlling shareholder having obtained more than 90 per cent control of the target company to squeeze out the remaining minority which would enable it to run the target company without concern to the minority. It probably also helps that, like the mandatory bid rule, it resembles a measure of German company law that enables a controlling shareholder in the form of a parent company to absorb a subsidiary by ousting its minority shareholders and paying a 'fair' price.[38]

If logic prevails, contrary to all expectations, and a reformed Directive is relieved of its provisions on the internal affairs of listed companies, then Articles 15 and 16 should go as well, even if they are uncontroversial and by now probably well integrated into the national laws of the Member States. Removing a provision from the reformed Directive does not in itself entail the provision's banishment from the national laws of the Member States, it only provides the Member States with greater self-determination in this respect and enables them to continuously reconsider their value.

[37] The fact that a squeeze-out requires the payment of a fair price to the minority shareholders is not a distinction from expropriation but a similarity.

[38] Cf. Aktiengesetz § 320 (*Eingliederung durch Mehrheitsbeschluß*); control has to be at least 95%.

17.7 SANCTIONS AND DAMAGES

The Directive instructs Member States to have 'sanctions' available for violations of the Directive's provisions. This is a customary provision in secondary EU legislation although it does not expand on the obligations already placed on the Member States since it builds on the case law of the CJEU that requires Member States to treat EU law on a par with national law also in respect of sanctions, due to the principle of loyalty in Art. 4 TEU.[39]

The move towards an EU criminal law system has been gradual, even glacial at times. We now see harmonisation of criminal law in some areas – for example, in CS-MAD[40] detailing the criminal sanctions for various offences of market abuse contained in MAR. It is noteworthy that CS-MAD does not prescribe criminal sanctions for all the offences of MAR, because Art. 30 MAR attempts a parallel system of administrative sanctions. The wisdom of operating a parallel system based on a distinction between administrative and criminal sanctions is questionable considering that the 1950 European Convention on Human Rights applies its own and rather far-reaching understanding of what constitutes a 'criminal' offence as per its Article 6. Some Member States, like Denmark, consider the criminal system the only appropriate system by which to 'punish' offenders.[41] What is more noteworthy, though, is the fact that CS-MAD is one of the only two directives used as EU legislation in respect of market abuse, where all the other legal acts are directly applicable regulations.[42] This use of a directive is probably because the Member States, notwithstanding their approach to administrative or criminal sanctioning, are reluctant to harmonise their system of sanctioning as this is closely knit into their fabric of culture and tradition. The reason that harmonisation was done after all, if only by a directive, in the area of market abuse is probably because in this area public sanctioning is the most likely reaction to violations. The great discrepancies in sanctioning among the Member States under the previous Market Abuse

39 Case 68/88, *Commission of the European Communities v Hellenic Republic* [1989] ECLI:EU:C:1989:339.

40 Parliament and Council Directive 2014/57/EU on criminal sanctions for market abuse, 2014 O.J. (L173) (Market Abuse Directive).

41 See the dignified remark in the Swedish Green Paper on the implementation of MAD: 'To motivate the introduction of a system of administrative sanctions that the level of necessary proof could be lowered and more people could be "punished" is incompatible with basic principles of legal certainty', cf. SOU 2004-69, 'Marknadsmissbruk', (own translation from Swedish), p. 69.

42 The only other directive concerning market abuse is found on level 2 where it concerns whistleblowing, which again is closely associated with criminal law; see Commission Implementing Directive (EU) 2015/2392 of 17 December 2015 on Regulation (EU) No 596/2014 of the European Parliament and of the Council as regards reporting to competent authorities of actual or potential infringements of that Regulation, 2015 O.J. (L332).

Directive (MAD)[43] uncovered in the preparation of MAR, in what are effectively identical offences, were rightly considered unacceptable. However, public takeover bids seldom result in public sanctions and thus there is no equal need to set aside the Member States' justifiable reluctance to harmonise public sanctions in this area. Consequently, the open, and basically superfluous, provision in Article 17 should remain unchanged and not supplemented with a harmonised system of sanctioning.

Whereas the Directive is open and vague on sanctioning, it does not mention civil liability at all. This is probably for the best. The concerns that apply to public sanctioning, whether criminal or disguised as administrative, apply even more to civil liability. Civil liability is very different from public sanctioning, because its purpose is not to punish offenders but to provide restitution in each separate case depending on the circumstances. The automatic reaction to a violation that a public sanction represents is absent from civil liability where damages depend not only on a wrongful or illegal act but also on the fulfilment of a string of other conditions, such as causation, foreseeability, proof of loss, and so on. Civil liability, furthermore, is closely connected with the basic principles of civil law more generally and this is an area where harmonisation has been considered for a very long time, but mostly and wisely rejected. Inspiration can be taken from Article 11 of the Prospectus Regulation,[44] which does contain a provision on civil liability, probably because prospectus liability is more common than in takeovers, but which provision is nevertheless kept as open and deferent to national law, as is Article 17 of the Directive in respect of public sanctioning. In its recent report and after examining civil liability for prospectuses, ESMA concluded that there was no immediate need for reform,[45] which is probably equally true for civil liability in respect of takeovers.

17.8 CONCLUSION

The Directive on Takeover Bids had a troubled history, and its final adoption arose more from a stubborn reluctance to admit defeat than from a desire to provide a harmonisation of public takeover bids, and indeed the Directive has failed to provide harmonisation in many of the areas it covers. This unfortunate legacy has prevented subsequent reforms of the Directive. However, considering that the Directive is now among the dinosaurs of EU legislation, especially within the area of financial law and securities trading that it occupies while also covering that of company law, it is

[43] Parliament and Council Directive 2014/57/EU on criminal sanctions for market abuse, 2014 O.J. (L173).

[44] Parliament and Council Regulation (EU) 2017/1129 on the prospectus to be published when securities are offered to the public or admitted to trading on a regulated market, and repealing Directive 2003/71/EC, 2017 O.J. (L168).

[45] ESMA, Final Report, Technical advice concerning civil prospectus liability, ESMA32-117195963-1413, 12 June 2025. The report was commissioned by the European Commission vide Article 48(2a) of the Prospectus Regulation (n 44).

not impossible to contemplate a reform. If such a reform is undertaken, admittedly a major 'if', this chapter argues that a reformed Directive should concentrate on the areas of law that are suitable for harmonisation and refrain from wasting political capital and precious time on harmonising areas of law better left to the Member States as envisaged in Article 5 of the TEU on the principles of subsidiarity and proportionality as necessary prerequisites for EU lawmaking. The chapter then tries to provide an analysis of which areas are suitable for harmonisation and which are not and to apply that analysis to the individual provisions of the present Directive. A reformed Directive *can* bring genuine and efficient harmonisation if, and only if, it is rid of the provisions unsuitable for harmonisation.

Index